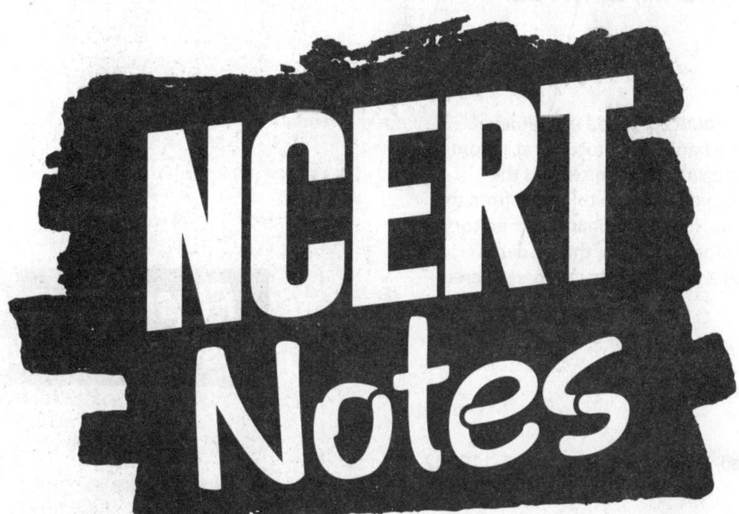

India & World Geography

Class 6-12 (Old + New)

Authors
Vipul Kumar Tripathi
Aqsa Jamil

Series Editor
Santosh Dutt Pandey

ARIHANT PUBLICATIONS (INDIA) LIMITED

卐 **Administrative & Production Offices**

Regd. Office

'Ramchhaya' 4577/15, Agarwal Road, Darya Ganj, New Delhi -110002
Tele: 011- 47630600, 43518550

卐 **Head Office**

Kalindi, TP Nagar, Meerut (UP) - 250002
Tel: 0121-7156203, 7156204

卐 **Sales & Support Offices**

Agra, Ahmedabad, Bengaluru, Bareilly, Chennai, Delhi, Guwahati, Hyderabad, Jaipur, Jhansi, Kolkata, Lucknow, Nagpur & Pune.

卐 **PRICE** ₹365.00

卐 PO No. : TXT-59-T070953-5-26

Published by Arihant Publications (India) Ltd.

For further information about the books published by Arihant, log on to www.arihantbooks.com or e-mail at info@arihantbooks.com

Follow us on    

Two Words

NCERT are the Foundation in the Journey of IAS...

Civil Services Examinations are the most prestigious and coveted examinations in India. Being the toughest exam, it automatically consists of a vast and a detailed syllabus. Aspirants often find it difficult to cover the entire syllabus and lack a right direction for a proper and a systematic study for the exam.

The most important aspect of this preparation journey are the **NCERT books**. Every year approximately **35-40 questions** directly come from NCERT books.

NCERT books also play a key role in understanding the **Basic Concepts**; so that aspirants can easily form the basic foundation of the entire syllabus. But due to the demand for many NCERT books which are required for study, it becomes exhausting to cover each and every NCERT book.

NCERT NOTES SERIES presented by Arihant Publications covers complete text from Class 6th to 12th NCERT books in a comprehensive manner.

Features of Revised Edition

- Extra and relevant facts from exam point of view are covered from Tamil Nadu Board Books.
- Most important facts from NIOS books also compiled to enrich the content.
- Theory in each chapter is facilited with charts, tables, etc. to make the preparation easy and convenient.
- Exam focused last minute revision topics are also covered in the appendix.

The book is adorned with questions prepared by a team of experts along with a vital role played by the Project Management team with members: Mona Yadav (Project Manager), Sumit Verma (Project Coordinator), Seema Saini (Proof Reading TL), Pradeep Chaudhary, (DTP TL), Bilal Hashmi, Rakesh Rawat and Ankit Tyagi (Cover and Inner designer).

We hope this book will help the aspirants to achieve their goals of clearing UPSC as well as State PCS exams. Your valuable suggestions have always inspired us to strive for useful, authentic and more trustworthy publications. So your inputs and suggestions are welcomed for subsequent editions.

We wish you all the very best for your preparation and journey!!

Authors

CONTENTS

WORLD GEOGRAPHY

Chapter 1. Geography as a Discipline 1-3
- Geography 1
- Branches of Geography 2

Chapter 2. The Universe 4-9
- Universe 4
- Our Solar System 6

Chapter 3. The Earth 10-17
- Origin of the Earth 10
- Evolution of the Earth 11
- Latitude and Longitude 13
- Motions of the Earth 15

Chapter 4. Geomorphology 18-44
- Interior of the Earth 18
- Earthquake 20
- Volcanoes 22
- Rocks 25
- Major Theories for the Evolution of Landforms 27
- Movements of the Indian Plate 30
- Geomorphic Processes 31
- Earth Movements 31
- Landforms 36
- Mountains 42
- Plains 43
- Islands 44

Chapter 5. Climatology 45-68
- Atmosphere 45
- Insolation and Temperature 48
- Heat Budget of the Earth 50
- Wind 54
- Jet Streams 58
- Cyclone 58
- Thunderstorms and Tornadoes 59
- Water in the Atmosphere 60
- Humidity 60
- Evaporation 60
- Condensation 61
- Clouds 62
- Precipitation 63
- Air Masses 64
- Fronts 64
- Koeppen's Scheme of Classification of Climate 65

Chapter 6. Oceanography 69-89
- Water and Its Distribution 69
- Oceans and Seas 69
- Oceans of the World 71
- Oceanic Circulation and Ocean Currents 72
- Salinity of the Ocean 75
- Ocean Density 76
- Ocean Temperature 76
- Ocean Tides 79
- Ocean Deposits 80
- Coral Reefs 82
- Marine Resources 83
- Maritime Zone 85
- Lakes 87
- Wetlands 88

Chapter 7. Soil and Natural Vegetation 90-96
- Soil 90
- Natural Vegetation 94

Chapter 8. Agriculture and Animal Husbandry 97-106
- Hunting and Gathering 97
- Agriculture 97
- Major Crops of the World 100
- Animal Husbandry 105

Chapter 9. Mineral Resources 107-112
- Minerals 107
- Types of Minerals 108
- Conservation of Minerals 112

Chapter 10. Energy Resources **113-118**
- Classification of Energy Resources 113
- Conventional Sources 113
- Non- Conventional Sources of Energy 116
- Nuclear or Atomic Energy 117

Chapter 11. Industries **119-130**
- Manufacturing 119
- Classification of Manufacturing Industries 121
- Industrial System 122
- Industrial Regions 122
- Iron and Steel Industry 124

Chapter 12. Transport and Communication **131-138**
- Transport 131
- Communication 137

Chapter 13. Population and Settlement **139-152**
- World Population 139
- Trends in Population Growth 142
- Demographic Transition 143
- Human Development 145
- Settlement 147
- Human Race 150

Chapter 14. Continents **153-175**
- Asia 153
- Africa 158
- Australia 161
- North America 163
- South America 167
- Europe 170
- Antarctica 173

Chapter 15. Map Studies **176-179**
- Map 176
- History of Map Making 176
- Types of Maps 177
- Uses of Maps 178
- Essentials of Map Making 178

INDIAN GEOGRAPHY

Chapter 16. Location and Structure of India **180-183**
- Geographical Location 180
- India and Its Neighbourhood 181
- India and the World 183

Chapter 17. Geological History and Physiography of India **184-194**
- Geological History of India 184
- Geological Aspects of India 184
- Physical Divisions of India 186

Chapter 18. Drainage System of India **195-203**
- Types of Drainage Pattern 195
- Classification of Drainage Systems of India 196
- Drainage System of India 197
- Lakes 202

Chapter 19. Climate in India **204-213**
- Climate and Weather 204
- Climate of India 204
- Indian Monsoon 207
- Nature of Indian Monsoon 207
- Seasons 211

Chapter 20. Natural Vegetation and Soil in India **214-229**
- Natural Vegetation 214
- Types and Distribution of Forest 219
- Forest Conservation 219
- Community and Conservation 221
- Soil 221

Chapter 21. Natural Resources of India **230-241**
- Natural Resources 230
- Land Resource in India 231
- Water Resource 235

Chapter 22. Indian Agriculture and Irrigation **242-259**
- Agriculture 242
- Major Crops Grown in India 244
- Animal Husbandry/Cattle Rearing/Livestock Farming 254
- Irrigation 255

Chapter 23. Energy and Mineral Resources in India **260-270**
- Mineral Resources 260
- Energy Resources 264
- Conservation of Resources 270

Chapter 24. Transport and Communication in India 271-284
- Transport 271
- Land Transport 271
  1. Road Transport in India 271
  2. Indian Railways 274
  3. Ports and Waterways 277
  4. Pipelines 280
  5. Airways 281
- Communication 283

Chapter 25. Industries in India 285-299
- Major Industries 287
- Industrial Regions in India 296

Chapter 26. Population and Human Settlement 300-312
- Human Settlement 300
- Population 304
- Demographic Composition 306
- Migration 309
- Tribes of India 310

ENVIRONMENT AND ECOLOGY

Chapter 27. Environment 313-315
- Types of Environment 313
- Parts of Environment 313
- Human Impact on Environment 315
- Impact of Environment on Human 315

Chapter 28. Ecology, Ecosystem and Biome 316-327
- Ecology 316
- Ecosystem 317
- Trophic Level 322
- Food Chain 322
- Food Web 323
- Ecological Niche 323
- Biogeochemical Cycles 323
- Bioindicators 324
- Ecological Succession 324
- Biomes 326
- Inter-species Interactions 327

Chapter 29. Biodiversity 328-334
- Meaning of Biodiversity 328
- Geographical Biodiversity 330
- Biodiversity Hotspots 332
- Biodiversity Conservation 333

Chapter 30. Biosphere Reserves, National Parks and Wildlife Sanctuaries 335-340
- National Park 335
- Wildlife Sanctuary 335
- Biosphere Reserves 335
- Wildlife Conservation Projects 337
- Ramsar Convention for Wetland Conservation 339

Chapter 31. Climate Change, Greenhouse Effect and Ozone Depletion 341-347
- Climate Change 341
- Global Warming 342
- Greenhouse Effect 346
- Ozone Layer Depletion 346
- Acid Rain 347

Chapter 32. Environmental Issues 348-353
- Environmental Pollution 348
- Types of Pollution 348
- Soil Erosion and Desertification 352
- Strategies to Control Environmental Pollution 353
- International Efforts to Control Environment Pollution 353

Chapter 33. Sustainable Development 354-357
- Meaning of Sustainable Development 354
- Objectives of Sustainable Development 354
- Sustainable Development Goals 356

Chapter 34. Disaster Management 358-365
- Disaster 358
- Natural Disasters in India 358
- Man-Made Disasters 364
- Disaster Management in India 364
- Government Initiatives for Disaster Management 364

- **APPENDIX** 366-378

01

World Geography

Geography as a Discipline

[SOURCES]

Class-XI New NCERT Chap 1 (Geography as a Discipline),
Class-XI Old NCERT Chap 1 (Geography as a Discipline),
Class-XII New NCERT Chap 1 (Human Geography : Nature and Scope),
Tamil Nadu Board (Class XI), NIOS

Geography

- Geography is the description of the Earth. The term geography was first coined by a Greek scholar **Eratosthenes** in 276-194 BC.
- The word has been derived from Greek language, *geo* (Earth) and *graphos* (description), which together mean **description of the Earth**.
- The geographical phenomena, both the physical and human, are not static but highly dynamic.
- They change over time as a result of the interactive processes between ever changing Earth and untiring and ever-active human beings.
- Thus, geography, is concerned with the study of nature and human interactions as an integrated whole, 'human' is an integral part of 'nature' and 'nature' has the imprints of 'human'. 'Nature' has influenced different aspects of human life.
- Its imprints can be noticed on food, clothing, shelter and occupation.
- Human beings have come to terms with nature through **adaptation** and **modification**.

Definitions of Geography

- According to **Richard Hartshorne**, "Geography is concerned with the description and explanation of the areal differentiation of the Earth's surface."
- According to **Alfred Hettner**, "Geography studies the differences of phenomena usually related in different parts of the Earth's surface".

Geography as an Integrating Discipline

- Geography is a discipline of synthesis. It attempts spatial synthesis and history attempts temporal synthesis. Its approach is holistic in nature. It recognises the fact that the world is a system of interdependencies.
- Geography attempts to comprehend the associations of phenomena as related in sections of reality.
- Every discipline, concerned with scientific knowledge is linked with geography as many of their elements vary over space. Geography helps in understanding the reality in totality in its spatial perspective.
- Thus, geography not only takes note of the differences in the phenomena from place to place but integrates them holistically, which may be different at other places.

Geography as Relation to Human and Environment

In early 20th century, geography developed as a mutual relationship between human and environment. There are two different ideologies related to this, which are as follows:

(i) **Possibilism** According to this, humans can transform their environment accordingly. This ideology was supported by **Vedal de La Blache**. This ideology says that nature provides opportunities and humans make use of these and slowly nature gets humanised and starts bearing the imprints of human endeavour.

(ii) **Environmental Determinism** According to this, every human activity is decided by environment. This ideology was supported by **Friedrich Ratzel** and **Ellsworth Huntington**.

Concept of Human Environment

There are three concepts of human environment

(i) **Concept of Determinism** Determinism is based on the notion that the physical environment has a massive and controlling impact on human being. Humans have no option but to follow the dictates of nature.

(ii) **Concept of Possibilism** Possibilism came as a reaction to environmental determinism. This approach attempts to explain the man-environment relationship in a different way, taking man as an active agent.

(iii) **Concept of Neo-Determinism** (Geographer, **Griffith Taylor**) introduced the concept in 1920s which reflects a middle path between the two ideas of environmental determinism and possibilism. He termed it as neo-determinism or 'stop and go determinism'.

Branches of Geography

Geography is an interdisciplinary subject of study. The study of every subject is done according to some approach. The major approaches to study Geography have been as follows :

Systematic Approach

- The systematic geography approach is the same as that of general geography. This approach was introduced by a German Geographer, **Alexander Von Humboldt** (1769-1859).
- In systematic approach, a phenomenon is studied world over as a whole and then the identification of typologies or spatial patterns is done.
- For example, if one is interested in studying natural vegetation, the study will be done at the world level as a first step.

Branches of Geography on the Basis of Systematic Approach

Branches of Geography
(Based on Systematic Approach)

Physical
Principles/Philosophy
Methods and Techniques
Human

Geographical Thought
Human Ecology (Land and Human Interaction)
Quantitative Techniques
Cartography
Field Survey Methods
Geo Informatics
GIS
GPS
LIS

Interface Biogeography

Geomorphology
Climatology
Hydrology
Soil Geography
Social/ Cultural
Historical
Population and Settlements
Political
Economic

Ecology
Plant Geography
Environmental Geography
Zoo Geography
Rural
Urban

Agriculture
Industrial
Trade and Transport
Infrastructure
Services
Tourism

Physical Geography

- **Geomorphology** It is devoted to the study of landforms, their evolution and related processes.
- **Climatology** It encompasses the study of structure of atmosphere, elements of weather, climate, its types and regions.
- **Hydrology** It studies the realm of water i.e., oceans, lakes, rivers and other water bodies and its effect on different life forms including human life and their activities.
- **Soil Geography** The geography of soil is concerned with the study of distribution and variability of soils on terrestrial landscapes ranging from local to global scales, soil formation, etc.

Human Geography

- **Social/Cultural Geography**
It encompasses the study of society and its spatial dynamics as well as the cultural elements contributed by the society.
- **Historical Geography** It studies the historical processes through which the space gets organised. Every region has undergone some historical experiences before attaining the present day status. The geographical features also experience temporal changes and these form the concerns of historical geography.
- **Population and Settlement Geography** (Rural and Urban) It studies population growth, distribution, density, sex ratio, migration and occupational structure, etc. Settlement geography studies the characteristics of rural and urban settlements.
- **Economic Geography** It studies economic activities of the people including agriculture, industry, tourism, trade and transport, infrastructure and services, etc.
- **Political Geography** It studies political boundaries, space relations between neighbouring political units, delimitation of constituencies, election scenario and develops theoretical framework to understand the political behaviour of the population.
- Political geography studies the spatial distribution of political processes and how these processes are impacted by one's geographical location.

Biogeography

- **Ecology / Ecosystem** It deals with the scientific study of the habitats characteristics of species.
- **Plant Geography** It studies the spatial pattern of natural vegetation in their habitats.
- **Environmental Geography** It deals with the spatial aspects of interaction between humans and the natural world and its impact of human presence on the environment such as land degradation, pollution, etc. It also raises concerns for conservation which has resulted in the introduction of this new branch in geography.
- **Zoo Geography** It studies the spatial patterns and geographic characteristics of animals and their habitats.

Regional Approach

- In the regional approach, the world is divided into regions at different hierarchical levels and then all the geographical phenomena in a particular region are studied. These regions may be natural, political or designated region.
- This approach was introduced by German Geographer **Alrnander Von Humbolat** and also by another German Geographer **Karl Ritter** Karl Ritter.

Branches of Geography on the Basis of Regional Approach

Branches of Geography
(Based on Regional Approach)

- Regional Studies/ Area Studies
  - Macro Regional Studies
  - Meso Regional Studies
  - Micro Regional Studies
- Regional Development
- Regional Analysis
- Regional Planning
  - Country/Rural Planning
  - Town/Urban Planning

- **Regional Studies / Area Studies** It comprising macro, meso and micro regional studies.
- **Regional Development** It is about geography of welfare and its evolution.
- **Regional Planning** It comprising country/rural and town/urban planning.
- **Regional Analysis** There are two aspects, which are common to every discipline. These are as follows
  (i) **Philosophy**
    (a) Geographical Thought
    (b) Land and Human Interaction / Human Ecology
  (ii) **Methods and Techniques**
    (a) Cartography Including Computer Cartography
    (b) Quantitative Techniques / Statistical Techniques
    (c) Field Survey Methods
    (d) Geo - Informatics Comprising Techniques, such as Remote sensing, GIS, GPS, etc

The above classification gives a comprehensive format of the branches of geography.

Physical Geography and Its Importance

The study of physical geography is emerging as a discipline of evaluating and managing natural resources. Physical geography comprises the study of lithosphere, atmosphere, hydrosphere and biosphere.

- **Lithosphere** It is the solid crust or the hard top layer of the Earth. It is an irregular surface with various landforms such as mountains, plateaus, plains, valleys, etc. These landforms provide the base on which human activities are located.
- **Hydrosphere** It refers to the domain of water. It comprises various sources of water and different types of water bodies like river, lakes, seas, oceans, etc.
- **Atmosphere** It is the thin layer of air that surrounds the Earth. The gravitational force of the Earth holds the atmosphere around it.
- **Biosphere** Plant and animal kingdom together make biosphere or the living world. It is a narrow zone of the Earth where land, water and air interact with each other to support life.

Extra Facts From Tamil Nadu Board and NIOS

- Economic geography is concerned with the study of resources endowment and patterns of utilisation.
- The sy tematic approach to the 'Study of Geography, is also known as 'nomothetic approach'.
- The re ional approach to the study of Geography is also known as 'ideographlical approach'.
- Human geography is the synthetic study of the relation hip between human societies and the Earth's surface.
- Meteorology provides basic information on the compositio , structure and changes in the atmosphere.

Development of Geography

- **Ancient Period** The scholars of this time understood the physical facts of the Earth through map making and astronomical measurments. Homer, Herodotus, thales, Aristotle and Eratosthenes where prominent among the early Greek scholars.
- **Early Modern Period** This period lasted from the middle of the 15th century to the beginning of the 18th century.
- Christopher columbus, vasco dalgama, Mangalan and Thomas Cook were the major explorers of this period.
- Varenius, Kant, Humboldt and Ritter were the major geographers of this period.
- **Modern Period** The period of the second half of the 19th century is considered to be the period of modern geography.
- **New Era** American and European geographers like Hawthorne mode more contributions during this period Hartshorne defined geography as a science which studies regional differences.

The Universe

[SOURCES]

Class-VI New NCERT Chap 1 (The Earth in the Solar System),
Class-VI Old NCERT Chap 1 (The Earth in our Solar System),
Class-XI New NCERT Chap 2 (The Origin and Evolution of the Earth),
Tamil Nadu Board (Class XI), NIOS

Universe

- The vast and infinite space having millions of galaxies is called **universe.**
- **Star** is a celestial body having its own heat and light. **Galaxy** is a family or system of millions of stars.
- The nearest star to the Earth after the Sun is the star Proxima Centauri. It is a companion star to the binary star system. Alpha Centauri is 4.2 light years away from Earth. The study of universe is called **Cosmology**.

Origin of the Universe

There are following theories related to the origin of the universe :

Big Bang Theory

- The most popular argument regarding the origin of the universe is the Big Bang Theory. It is also called **expanding universe hypothesis.**
- In 1920, **Edwin Hubble** provided evidence that the universe is expanding. As time passes, galaxies move further and further apart. This theory was proposed by **Georges Edouard Lemaitre** in 1960-1970.
- Scientists believe that only the space between the galaxies is increasing, the galaxies themselves are not expanding.

Stages in the Development of the Universe

- The Big Bang Theory considers the following stages in the development of the universe :
  - In the beginning, all matter forming the universe existed in one place in the form of a 'tiny ball' (**singular atom**) with a small volume, infinite temperature and infinite density.
  - At the Big Bang, the 'tiny ball' exploded violently and it led to a huge expansion.
- It is now generally accepted that the event of Big Bang took place 13.7 billion years before the present.
- The expansion continues even to the present day.
- As it grew, some energy was converted into matter.
- There was particularly rapid expansion within fractions of a second after the bang.
- Thereafter, the expansion has slowed down. Within first three minutes from the Big Bang event, the first atom began to form.
- Within 3,00,000 years from the Big Bang, temperature dropped to 4,500 K (Kelvin) and gave rise to atomic matter. The universe became transparent.

Steady-State Theory

- This was an alternative to the **Big Bang Theory**. The most influential papers on Steady-State theory were published by **Hermann Bondi, Thomas Gold** and **Fred Hoyle** in 1948.
- It considered the universe to be roughly the same at any point of time.
- However, with greater evidence becoming available about the expanding universe, scientific community at present favours argument of expanding universe.

Pulsating Universe Theory

- It is a variation of the Big Bang Theory, in which the universe goes through successive periods of expansion and contraction.
- Thus, according to this theory, the universe pulsates endlessly between the Big Bang and the 'Big Squeeze'.
- This theory was proposed by **Allan Sandage**.

Celestial Bodies

- The Sun, the Moon and all those objects shining in the night sky are called celestial bodies. These are also called **heavenly bodies**.
- The one who study the celestial bodies and their movements is known as an **Astronomer**. The Earth on which we live is also a celestial body.
- There are mainly two types of celestial bodies
  - Some celestial bodies have their own heat and light and are called **stars**. They are actually very big and hot bodies made of gases.
  - Some celestial bodies do not have their own heat and light. They only reflect the light, which they receive from a star like the Sun. These are called **planets**.
- The word **planet** means **wanderer**.
- Our Earth is also a planet, which receives its light and heat from the Sun.

Galaxies

- Galaxy is a system of stars held together by mutual gravitation and is isolated from similar systems in the vast region of space.
- It also contains a large number of gas clouds, some of which are quite huge. In these gas clouds new stars are born. A galaxy has billions of stars very close to one another.
- Dimensions of Galaxies may be 80,000 to 1,50,000 light years.

Types of Galaxies

Galaxies are of three types :

(i) **Elliptical Galaxies** These are like flattened balls of old stars and contain very little gas. It also includes the most massive galaxies containing a trillion stars.

(ii) **Spiral Galaxies** These have a flattened shape. They have a projection in the centre composed of old stars surrounded by a disk of young stars and all arranged in spiral arms.

(iii) **Irregular Galaxies** These have no particular shape. There are billions of galaxies in the universe, the centre of the galaxy releases a huge amount of heat, radiation, radio waves and X-rays.

Major Galaxies

Major galaxies are as follows :

- **The Milky Way** Our solar system is a part of the Milky Way. It is known as Milky Way because it appears as a milky band of light in the sky. Our Milky Way is a large barred spiral galaxy.
- **Andromeda Galaxy** It is also known as Messier 31. It is a barred spiral galaxy approximately 2.5 million light years from the Earth and the nearest large galaxy to the Milky way.

Galaxy and the Star Formation

- The distribution of matter and energy was not even in the early universe.
- These initial density differences gave rise to differences in gravitational forces and it caused the matters to get drawn together.
- These formed the basis for development of galaxies.
- Galaxies spread over vast distances that are measured in thousands of light years.
- A light year is a measure of distance.
- The distance, the light will travel in one year is taken to be one light year. This equals to $\mathbf{9.461 \times 10^{12}}$ **km**.
- The mean distance between the Sun and the Earth in terms of light years is **8.311 minutes**. This implies that it takes 8.311 minutes for the light to reach the Earth from the Sun.
- A galaxy starts to form by accumulation of hydrogen gas in the form of a very large cloud called **nebula**.
- Eventually, growing nebula develops localised **clumps of gas**. These clumps continue to grow into even denser gaseous bodies, giving rise to formation of stars. The formation of stars is believed to have taken place some 5-6 billion years ago.

Stars

- Stars are huge bodies of glowing gases which have heat and light of their own. The distances of stars are expressed in terms of **light years** (one light year is the distance travelled by light in 1 year at the speed of light which is about 3,00,000 km/s).
- The colour of a star is determined by its surface temperature. Stars which have low temperature appear red, those with higher temperature appear yellow and those with very high temperature are blue.
- With high speed, the stars appear to move from East to West. This is because the Earth rotates from West to East about an imaginary axis that passes through its centre.
- The Earth completes one rotation in 24 hours. Therefore, a star travels at an angle of about one degree in 4 minutes.

Life Cycle of Stars

- The age of the stars ranges from millions to billions of years. Stars are like gigantic nuclear furnace.
- The nuclear reactions inside the star convert the hydrogen into helium by the process of fusion and this nuclear reaction gives stars their energy. Stars begin their lives as clouds of dust and gases and are called **nebula**.
- The gravity of a passing star and the shockwave from a nearby **Supernova** (explosion of a star) may cause the nebula to contract. Matter in the gas cloud will begin to coalesce into a dense region called **Proto Star**. As the **Proto Star** continues to condense, it heats up. Eventually, it reaches a critical mass and nuclear fusion begins. Thus, begins the main phase of the star. It will spend most of its life in this stable phase.
- The life span of stars depend upon their size. Massive stars burn their fuel much faster than smaller stars. Eventually, stars' fuel will begin to run out. Then they will expand to form the **red giant**.
- This phase lasts until the star exhausts its remaining fuel. At this point, the pressure of the nuclear reaction is not strong enough to equalise the force of gravity and the star collapses.

Constellations

- Constellations are various patterns formed by different groups of stars in the night sky.
- **Ursa Major** or **Big Bear** is one such constellation.
- One of the most easily recognisable constellation is the **Saptarishi** (sapta - seven, rishi stages). It is a group of seven stars that forms a part of Ursa Major Constellation.

Pole Star

- Since, the Pole Star indicates the North direction, it is also called the **North Star**. It always remains in the same position in the sky.
- We can locate the position of the Pole Star with the help of the Saptarishi.

Chandrashekhar Limit

The size of a white dwarf star is comparable to that of a planet. The mass of such stars is always less than about 1.44 times the mass of the Sun. This result was proved by **S. Chandrashekhar**. The maximum mass is, therefore, called the **Chandrashekhar limiting mass**.

Our Solar System

- 'Sol' is the personification of Sun and God in ancient Roman Mythology. 'Solar' means 'related to the Sun'. The family of the Sun is, therefore, called the **solar system.**
- Our solar system consists of the **Sun** (the star), **8 planets, 293 moons**, millions of smaller bodies like asteroids, meteoroids and comets and huge quantity of dust-grains and gases.
- Our solar system is a part of Milky Way galaxy. It is also known as *Akash Ganga*.

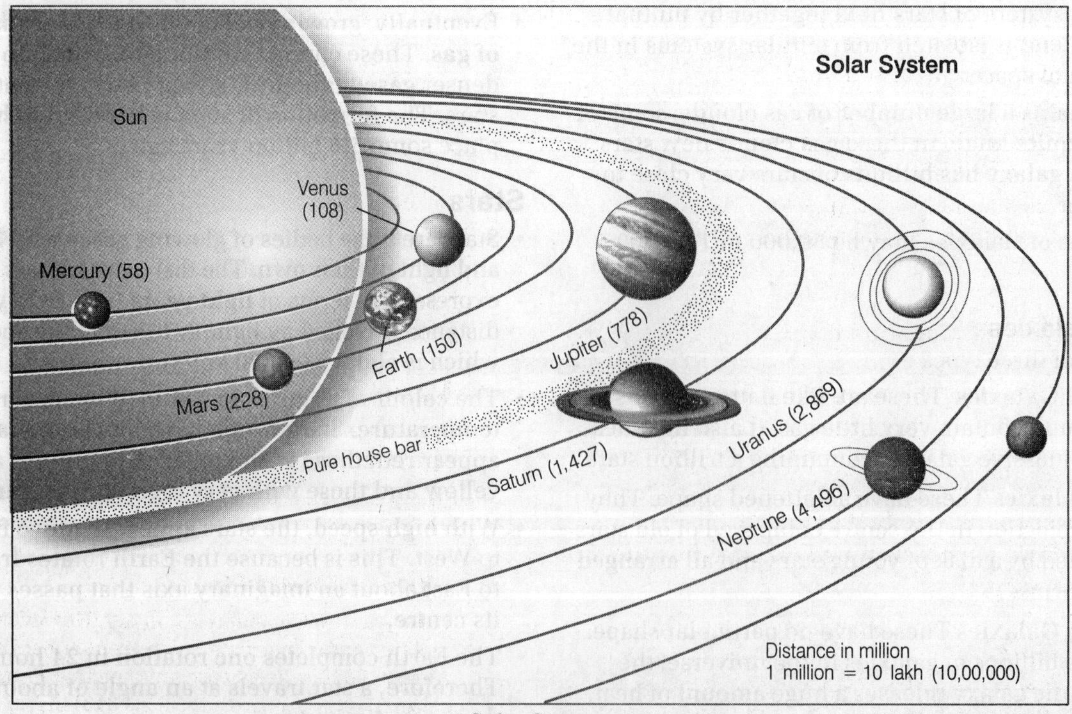

Solar System

The Sun

- The Sun is in the centre of the solar system.
- It is made up of extremely hot gases.
- The Sun is the ultimate source of all energy i.e heat and light for the entire solar system.
- The Sun is about 150 million kilometres away from the Earth.

Planets

- There are **eight planets** in our solar system.
- In order of their distance from the Sun, they are Mercury, Venus, Earth, Mars, Jupiter, Saturn, Uranus and Neptune.
- All the eight planets of the solar system move around the Sun in fixed paths. These paths are elongated. They are called **orbits.**
- All of them move in the same direction in their revolution.
- The planets also rotate on their own axis.
- Except **Venus** and **Uranus,** all other planets rotate in the same direction in which they revolve.
- As the distance of the planet from the Sun increases, the time taken by it to complete one revolution also increase.
- Since, **Mercury** is nearest to the Sun, it takes only about 88 days to complete one round along its orbit.
- Our **Earth** revolves once in about 365 days and six hours. The amount of heat received by a planet is controlled by the distance of that planet from the Sun.
- In other words, the closer planet is to the Sun, the higher its temperature. As Mercury is nearest to the Sun, it receives a great amount of heat from it.
- Out of the eight planets, Mercury, Venus, Earth and Mars are called as the **Inner planets** as they lie between the Sun and the belt of asteroids.
- The other four planets i.e Jupiter, Saturn, Uranus and Neptune are called the **Outer planets.**

Mercury

- This planet has no water and no gases like CO_2, H_2, N_2 and O_2 on it.
- It is devoid of protective blanket like ozone.

Venus

- It is considered as 'Earth's-twin' because its size and shape are very similar to that of the Earth.
- Venus is known as the **Evening Star** and **Morning Star**.
- It is the **hottest planet**.

Earth

- The Earth is slightly flattened at the poles. That is why, its shape is described as a **Geoid**. Geoid means an Earth-like shape.
- From the outer space, the Earth appears blue because its two-third surface is covered by water. It is therefore, called a **Blue Planet.**
- The Earth is a unique planet in the solar system because conditions favourable to support life are probably found only on the Earth. The Earth is neither too hot nor too cold.
- It has water and air, which are very essential for our survival. The air has life supporting gases like oxygen.

Mars

- It is the fourth planet from the Sun.
- It is also called **'Red Planet'** because of its reddish appearance as seen from the Earth (due to presence of iron oxide).
- It has thin atmosphere comprising of nitrogen and argon.
- It is the site of **Olympus Mons**, the highest known mountain in the solar system.

Jupiter

- It is the fifth planet from the Sun.
- It is the largest of all planets.
- It is also known as 'winter planet' as its average temperature is very low.
- It lacks well-defined solid surface.

Saturn

- Saturn has bright concentric rings, which are made up of ice and ice-covered dust particles, which revolve around it.
- It is the second largest planet and 95 times massive than the Earth.

Uranus

- It is about four times the size of the Earth. It is also called as **God of Heavens.**
- This planet appears greenish in colour because of methane gas present in its atmosphere.

Neptune

- Neptune is very similar to Uranus and can be considered as its twin.
- It is surrounded by methane rings of sub-zero temperature.

Pluto : A Dwarf Planet

Pluto was also considered a planet. However, in a meeting of the International Astronomical Union, (in August, 2006) a decision was taken that Pluto like other celestial objects (Ceres, 2003 UB 313) discovered in recent past may be called 'Dwarf Planet'.

Terrestrial Planets vs Jovian Planets

Terrestrial Planets	Jovian Planets
Terrestrial means Earth-like	Jovian means Jupiter-like
Mercury, Venus, Earth and Mars are called Terrestrial planets	Jupiter, Saturn, Uranus and Neptune are called jovian planets
They are made up of rock and metals	They have thick atmosphere, mostly of helium and hydrogen
They have relatively high densities	Most of them are much larger than the Terrestrial planets
These planets were formed in the close vicinity of the parent star where it was too warm for gases to condense to solid particles	Jovian planets were formed at quite a distant location
The solar wind was most intense near the Sun so, it blew off lots of gas and dust from the Terrestrial planets	The solar winds were not all that intense to cause similar removal of gases from the Jovian planets

Planets of the Solar System

Planet	Revolution	Rotation	No. of Moons
Mercury	88 days	58.65	0
Venus	243.02 days	243.02 days	0
Earth	365 days	24 hrs	1
Mars	687 days	24.6 hrs	2
Jupiter	12 years	9.8 hrs	95
Saturn	29 years	10.3 hrs	146
Uranus	84 years	17.9 hrs	28
Neptune	165 years	19.1 hrs	16

Formation of Planets

The following are considered to be the stages in the development of planets :

- The stars are localised clumps of gas within a nebula. The gravitational force within the clumps leads to the formation of a core to the gas cloud and a huge rotating disc of gas and dust develops around the gas core.
- In the next stage, the gas cloud starts getting condensed and the matter around the core develops into small-rounded objects.
- These small-rounded objects by the process of collision develop into planetesimals.
- Larger bodies start forming by collision and gravitational attraction causes the material to stick together.
- In the final stage, these large number of small planetesimals accrete to form a fewer large bodies in the form of planets.

Satellites

- The word 'satellite' means a 'smaller companion to anything'.
- A satellite is a celestial body that moves around the planets in the same way as the planets move around the Sun.
- They also follow them in their revolution around the Sun.
- For instance, the **Moon** is a satellite of the Earth, which moves around the Earth and around the Sun along with the Earth.
- Except **Mercury** and **Venus**, all the other planets have one or more than one satellites.
- Like planets, the satellites too have no light of their own. They just reflect the light received from the Sun.

Man-made Satellite

- A man-made satellite is an artificial body.
- It is designed by scientists to gather information about the universe or for the purpose of communication.
- It is carried by a rocket and placed in the orbit around the Earth.
- Some of the Indian satellites in space are **INSAT**, **IRS**, **EDUSAT**, etc.

The Moon - The Earth's Companion

- The Moon is the **only natural satellite** of the Earth.
- Its diameter is only one-fourth of that of the Earth.
- It appears so big because it is nearer to our planet than other celestial bodies.
- It is about 3,84,000 km away from us.
- The light reflected by the Moon reaches us in just one and a quarter seconds.
- The Moon revolves around the Earth in about 27 days and 8 hours.
- It takes exactly the same time for it to complete one rotation about its axis.
- As such we always see only one side of the Moon while the other side always remains away from us.
- The Moon does not have conditions favourable for life. There is no air or water on the Moon.
- It is very hot during the day and very cold during the night.
- There is no soil on the surface of the Moon. The surface of the Moon is very uneven.
- It has mountains, plains and depressions on its surface. These cast shadows on the Moon's surface.
- **Neil Armstrong** was the first man to step on the surface of the Moon on 20th July, 1969.
- We can see the full Moon only once in about a month's time. It is full Moon Night or *Poornima*.
- A fortnight later, we cannot see it at all. It is a New Moon Night or *Amavasya*. On this day, we can see the night sky at its best and provided it as a clear night.

Theories Related to the Formation of Moon

There are following three theories related to the formation of the Moon :

(i) **Fusion Theory** According to this theory, the Earth was spinning very rapidly and inside 2900 km its surface, an extent of a part was broken away due to fusion. This broken part led to the formation of the Moon.

(ii) **Capture Theory** According to this theory, a small planet while moving in an elliptical orbit came very close to the Earth, got capture and put to a circular orbit around the Earth.

(iii) **Theory of Co-existence and Growth** According to this theory, the Earth and Moon are formed together by the accretion of gravitating debris and dust.

Formation of the Moon

- There have been many attempts to explain how the Moon was formed. Three explanations were suggested in this regard.
- In 1838, **Sir George Darwin** suggested that initially, the Earth and the Moon formed a single rapidly rotating body.
- The whole mass become a dumb-bell shaped body and eventually it broke.
- It was suggested that the material forming the Moon was separated from what we have at present the depression occupied by the Pacific ocean.
- However, the present scientists do not accept either of the above explanations.
- It is now generally believed that the formation of Moon, as a satellite of the Earth, is an outcome of 'giant impact' or what is described as '**the Big Splat**'.
- A body of the size of one to three times that of Mars collided into the Earth sometime shortly after the Earth was formed.
- It blasted a large part of the Earth into space.
- This portion of blasted material then continued to orbit the Earth and eventually formed into the present Moon about 4.44 billion years ago.

Other Celestial Objects of the Solar System

- **Asteroids** They are a group of small bodies in between the orbits of Mars and Jupiter, which revolve around the Sun. They are believed to be the pieces of a planet, which probably exploded after its birth.
- **Meteoroids** The small pieces of rocks which move around the Sun are called **meteoroids**. Sometimes these meteoroids come near the Earth and tend to drop upon it. During this process, due to friction with the air they get heated up and burn. It causes a flash of light. Sometimes, a meteor without being completely burnt, falls on the Earth and creates a hollow.
- **Comets** A comet is an icy and smaller celestial body which revolves around the Sun in highly elliptical orbit. However, their period of revolution around the Sun is usually very long. They become visible from the Earth only when they come close to the Sun.

  A comet appears generally as a bright head with a long tail. The length of the tail grows in size as it approaches the Sun. The tail disappears again when the comet moves away from the Sun. The tail of a comet is always directed away from the Sun.

  Many comets are known to appear periodically. One such comet is **Halley's Comet** which appears after nearly every **76 years**. It was last seen in 1986. The study of comet tail has shown the existence of molecules of carbon, nitrogen and hydrogen.
- **Kuiper Belt** It is region of the solar system beyond the orbit of Neptune. It is believed to contain many asteroids, comets & other smaller bodies made of ice.

Black Hole

- It is a region of space time where gravity is so strong that nothing (no particles or even electromagnetic radiation such as light) can escape from it.
- The theory of general relativity predicts that a sufficiently compact mass can deform space time to form a black hole.

Pulsar

- It is rotating neutron star observed to have pulses of radiation at very regular intervals that typically range from milliseconds to seconds. A pulsar is formed when a massive star collapses exhausts its supply of fuel.

Extra Facts From Tamil Nadu Board and NIOS

- In 1927, **Abbe Georges Lemaitre** a Belgian astronomer was the first to propose, a theory on the origin of the universe.
- Sirius is the second brightest star after Sun, which is viewed from Earth. Solar system can have more than one star. These are called 'Binary Star Systems'.
- The Milky Way has four main spiral arms i.e., the Norma, Cygnus, Sagittarius, Scutum Centaurus and Perseus.
- Saturn is the only planet in our solar system whose average density is less than water.
- Neptune was the first planet located through mathematical calculations.
- Mars has two satellites- **Phobos and Deimos**.
- Ganymede, the satellite of Jupiter, is the largest natural satellite in the solar system. Venus and Uranus are only two planets that rotate from East to West.
- Jupiter and Saturn have the highest number of satellites in the solar system.
- Uranus is named after the ancient Greek, 'God of sky'.
- Beyond the fringes of the Kuiper Belt lies the Oort cloud. This giant spherical shell surrounds our solar system.
- The satellites move around a planet from West to East.

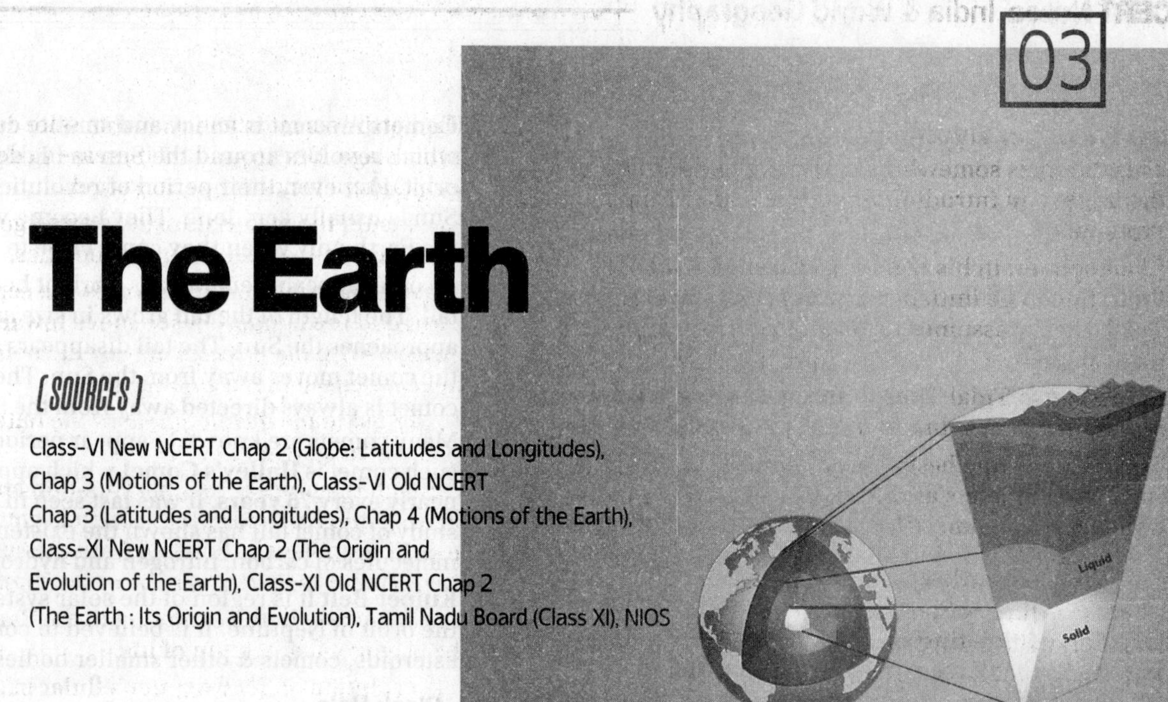

03

The Earth

(SOURCES)

Class-VI New NCERT Chap 2 (Globe: Latitudes and Longitudes), Chap 3 (Motions of the Earth), Class-VI Old NCERT Chap 3 (Latitudes and Longitudes), Chap 4 (Motions of the Earth), Class-XI New NCERT Chap 2 (The Origin and Evolution of the Earth), Class-XI Old NCERT Chap 2 (The Earth : Its Origin and Evolution), Tamil Nadu Board (Class XI), NIOS

Earth is not a sphere. It is slightly flattened at the North and the South poles and bulge in the middle. It moves around its axis, from West to East, which is an imaginary line.

Origin of the Earth

A large number of hypothesis were put forth by different philosophers and scientists regarding the origin of the Earth. Some of the important hypothesis are as follows :

Monistic Concept (One Star Hypothesis)

According to this hypothesis, the solar system originated from one star due to the gradual evolutionary process. The hypothesis of **Kant** and **Laplace** comes under this category.

Gaseous Hypothesis

- One of the earlier and popular argument was given by German philosopher **Immanuel Kant** in 1755.
- His argument is known as **Gaseous Hypothesis.**
- According to this hypothesis, a system of a few concentric rings separated from a hot and moving nebula due to centrifugal force.
- By the process of condensation of these rings, the planets of the solar system including the Earth were formed.

Nebular Hypothesis

- It was first put forward by **Immanuel Kant** and later revised by **Laplace** in 1796.
- The hypothesis considered that the planets were formed out of a cloud of material associated with a youthful Sun, which was slowly rotating.
- In 1950, **Otto Schmidt** and **Carl, Weizascar** revised the 'Nebular Hypothesis.
- They considered that the Sun was surrounded by **Solar Nebula** containing mostly the hydrogen and helium along with what check to be termed as dust.
- The friction and collision of particles led to formation of a disc-shaped cloud and the planets were formed through the process of accretion.

Dualistic Concept

- According to dualistic concept (Binary Hypothesis), the solar system originated from two stars. The hypothesis of **James Jeans**, **Chamberlain** and **Moulton**, **Weitzacker's** and **Russell** comes under this category.

Planetesimal Hypothesis

- The Planetesimal Hypothesis of **Chamberlain** (1905) belongs to the dualistic concepts of the origin of the Earth.
- According to Chamberlain, initially there were two heavenly bodies (stars) in the universe i.e., Proto-Sun and its Companion Star or Intruding Star.
- This theory states that when the intruding star came very close to the Proto-Sun, infinite numbers of small particles were detached from the outer surface of Proto-Sun due to massive gravitational pull exerted by the giant intruding star.
- The matter which is dust, gases, rock fragments eventually accrete forming planets and other celestial bodies that revolve around the Proto-Sun.

Tidal Theory or Hypothesis

- This theory is somewhat similar to **Chamberlain's** theory that an intruding star ejects matter from the Proto-Sun.
- Chamberlain, in his theory, had assumed the Proto-Sun to be initially as a cold body whereas, the Tidal Theory assumes the Proto-Sun to be hot and incandescent.
- According to Tidal Theory, the matter ejected are not randomly thrown dust, gases or planetesimal.
- This theory is the best interpretation in explaining the sizes of the planets as they have arranged themselves away from the Sun.

Binary Star Hypothesis

- There is a Binary Star System (two stars coupled together and rotating around a fixed centre of mass).
- This theory is convenient to explain, why the composition of planets is different from the Sun.

Supernova Hypothesis

- According to Hoyle, initially there were two stars in the universe i.e. **Primitive** Sun and **Companion** Star.
- The companion star was giant and later on became supernova due to nuclear reaction.
- Over time, all of the hydrogen nuclei of companion star were consumed in the process of nuclear reaction and it collapsed and violently exploded.
- The violent explosion of companion star resulted in the spread of enormous mass of dust which started revolving around the primitive Sun in the form of a circular disc.
- Thus, the planets of our solar system were formed due to condensation of the matter of the disc.

Interstellar Hypothesis

- According to this theory, the initial universe comprised of stars and randomly distributed matter filling up the space in between.
- According to **Schmidt**, this dark matter started to revolve around the primitive rotating Sun and gradually the dark matter stars accreting and condensing and thus, forming the solar system.

Evolution of the Earth

- The Earth has a layered structure. Initially, Earth was a barren, rocky and hot object with a thin atmosphere of hydrogen and helium.
- This is far from the present day picture of the Earth.
- From the surface to deeper depths, the Earth's interior has different zones and each of these contains materials with different characteristics.
- The Earth was mostly in a volatile state during its initial stage. Due to gradual increase in density, the temperature inside it has increased.
- As a result, the material inside started getting separated on the basis of their densities.
- Heavier materials to sink towards the centre of the Earth and the lighter ones to move towards the surface. With the passage of time, it cooled, solidified and condensed into a smaller size.
- It later led to the development of the outer surface in the form of a **crust**.
- Through the process of differentiation and partial melting, the Earth forming materials got separated into different layers. Starting from the surface to the centre, there are layers like the **crust, mantle** and **core**.
- The last phase in the evolution of the Earth relates to the origin and evolution of life.
- The evolution of life from unicellular bacteria to the modern man can be easily defined by the help of **Geological Time Scale.**
- The Earth is the only planet where some special environmental conditions are responsible for the existence and continuation of life.
- These include the right distance from the Sun, so it has the right temperature range, the presence of water, soil, minerals, suitable atmosphere and a blanket of ozone.

Evolution of Earth's Lithosphere

The main stages in the development of Earth's lithosphere are given as under :

- In its **primordial stages**, Earth was in volatile state.
- With increase in density, the temperature inside the Earth also increased. It resulted into separation of material according to their densities.
- The heavier materials like iron sank towards Earth's centre whereas lighter ones moved towards Earth's surface.
- As time passed, material cooled down further, solidified and condensed into smaller size. The outer surface of the Earth took the form of crust.
- The Earth's interior divided into different layers *viz.* **Crust, Mantle** and **Core.**

Evolution of Earth's Atmosphere

In the process of evolution, the Earth's atmosphere has gone through three different stages :

- **Stage-I** The early atmosphere of the Earth was primarily composed of hydrogen and helium.
  It was stripped off from the Earth by solar winds.
  It happened with all terrestrial planets.

- **Stage-II** As the Earth cooled down, many gases were released from inside. It contained water vapour, nitrogen, carbon dioxide, methane, ammonia and small amount of oxygen. This process through which the gasses were outpoured from the interior is called degassing.
- **Stage-III** As Earth cooled down further, the water vapour began to condense and heavy rainfall started. It dissolved carbon dioxide into rainwater. Therefore, atmosphere lost much of its carbon dioxide.

  As photosynthesis began on the Earth, further absorption of CO_2 occurred and oxygen was released and filled in the atmosphere. That's how, the present compositions of atmosphere came into being.

Evolution of Earth's Hydrosphere

- The earlier rainwater containing carbon dioxide filled the large basins and depressions on the Earth's surface. These water filled basins are known as Oceans.
- The oceans were formed within 500 million years from the formation of the Earth.

Evolution of Life on the Earth

- Around 3.8 million years ago from present, the first sign of life emerged as a result of chemical reactions. It generated complex organic molecules and assembled them. This assemblage had the capacity to duplicate themselves.
- The photosynthesis was started around 3 million years ago from present. The first life began in form of **unicellular blue algae.**

Geological Time Scale

Eons	Era	Period	Epoch	Age/Years Before Present	Life/Major Events
		Quaternary	Holocene	0-10,000, 10,000-2 million	Modern Man
			Pleistocene		Homo Sapiens
	Cenozoic (from 65 million years to the present times)	Tertiary	Pliocene	2-5 million	Early Human Ancestor
			Miocene	5-24 million	Ape Flowering Plants and Trees
			Oligocene	24-37 million	Anthropoid Ape
			Eocene	37-58 million	Rabbits and Hare
			Palaeocene	57-65 million	Small Mammals
					Rats-Mice
	Mesozoic 65-245 million Mammals	Cretaceous	—	65-144 million	Extinction of Dinosaurs
		Jurassic		144-208 million	Age of Dinosaurs
		Triassic		208-245 million	Frogs and Turtles
	Palaeozoic 245-570 million	Permian	—	245-286 million	Reptile Dominate Replace
		Carboniferous		286-360 million	Amphibians
		Devonian		360-408 million	First Reptiles
		Silurian		408-438 million	Vertebrates Coal Beds
		Ordovician		438-505 million	Amphibians
		Cambrian		505-570 million	First Trace of Life on Land Plants
					First Fish
					No Terrestrial Life
					Marine Invertebrate
Proterozoic	Pre-Cambrian 570 million - 4,800 million	—	—	570-2,500 million	Soft-bodies Arthropods
Archean				2,500-3,800 million	Blue-green Algae
Hadean				3,800-4,800 million	Unicellular Bacteria
					Oceans and Continents form - Ocean and Atmosphere are rich in Carbon dioxide
Origin of Stars	5,000-13,700 million	—	—	5,000 million	Origin of the Sun
Supernova				12,000 million	Origin of the Universe
Big Bang				13,700 million	

Latitude and Longitude

Both latitudes and longitudes define the relative position of a point in terms of angular distances from centre of the Earth from North to South and East to West.

Latitude

- Latitude is a measure of the angular distance of a given point from the Equator. It is measured in degrees from the Equator towards either pole.
- One degree (°) is divided into **sixty** equal parts and each unit is called a **minute** ('). A minute is further divided into sixty equal parts and each unit is called a **second** (").

Equator

- The Equator is an imaginary circular line that divides the Earth into two equal halves.
- The Northern half of the Earth is known as the **Northern Hemisphere** and the Southern half is known as the **Southern Hemisphere**.
- The Equator represents the **zero degree latitude**. Since, the distance from the Equator to either of the poles is one-fourth of a circle round the Earth, it will measure 1/4th of 360°, i.e 90°.
- Thus, 90° **North latitude** marks the North Pole and 90° South latitude marks the South Pole.
- As such, all parallels North of the Equator are called **North latitudes** and all parallels South of the Equator are called **South latitudes**.
- The value of each latitude is, therefore, followed by either the word North or South. Generally, this is indicated by the letter 'N' or 'S'.
- As we move away from the Equator, the size of the parallels of latitude decreases. The Equator is the largest possible circle which can be drawn around the Earth.

Important Parallels of Latitudes

All parallel circles drawn in East-West direction from the Equator upto the poles are called parallels of latitudes.

Besides the Equator (0°), the North Pole (90°N) and the South Pole (90°S), there are following four important parallels of latitudes :

- **Tropic of Cancer** It is an important parallel of latitude in the Northern Hemisphere. It is at an angular distance of $23\frac{1}{2}°$ (23° 30′ N) from the Equator.
- **Tropic of Capricorn** It is at a distance of $23\frac{1}{2}°$ (23°30′ S) South of the Equator.
- **Arctic Circle** It lies at a distance of $66\frac{1}{2}°$ (66° 30′ N) North of the Equator.
- **Antarctic Circle** It lies at a distance of $66\frac{1}{2}°$ (66° 30′ S) South of the Equator.

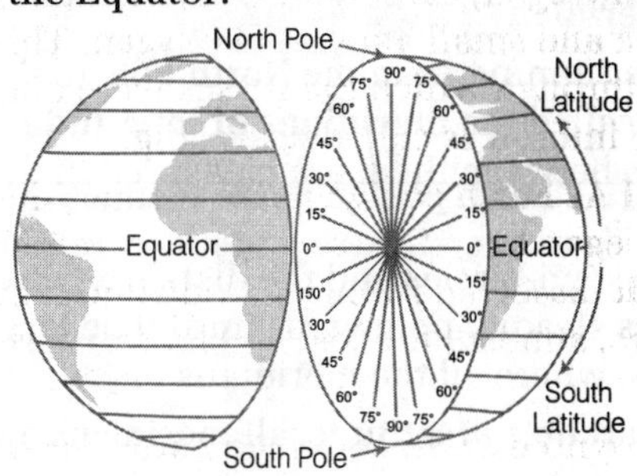

Latitudes on the Earth

Heat Zones of the Earth

Torrid and Temperate zones are the heat zones of the Earth.

Torrid Zone

- The extent of this zone is ($23\frac{1}{2}°$N - $23\frac{1}{2}°$ S).

  The mid-day Sun is exactly overhead atleast once in a year on all latitudes in between the Tropic of Cancer and the Tropic of Capricorn.
- Therefore, this area receives the maximum heat and is called the **Torrid Zone.**

Temperate Zone

- The extent of this zone is ($23\frac{1}{2}°$ N - $66\frac{1}{2}°$ N and $23\frac{1}{2}°$S - $66\frac{1}{2}°$ S). The mid-day Sun never shines overhead on any latitude beyond the **Tropic of Cancer** and the **Tropic of Capricorn.**
- The angle of the Sun's rays goes on decreasing towards the poles.
- The areas bounded by the Tropic of Cancer and the Arctic Circle in the Northern Hemisphere and the Tropic of Capricorn and the Antarctic Circle in the Southern Hemisphere, have moderate temperatures.
- Therefore, these are called **Temperate zones.**

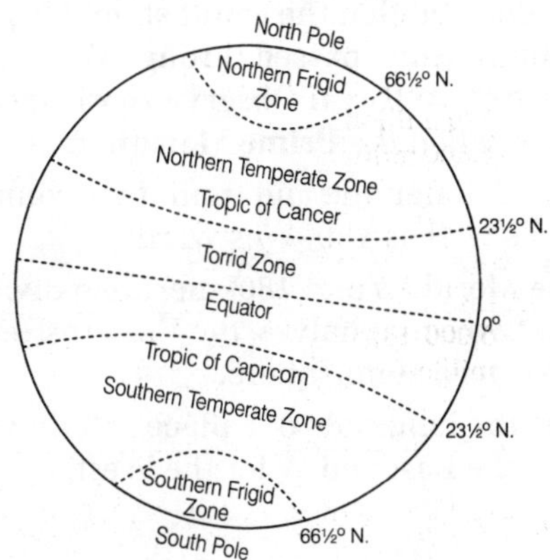

Heat Zones of the Earth

Longitude

- Longitude is an angular distance of a place from the Prime Meridian.
- The lines running from the North Pole to the South Pole are called the **meridians of longitude** and the distances between them are measured in **degrees of longitude**.
- They are semi-circles and the distance between them decreases steadily polewards until it becomes zero at the poles, where all the meridians meet.
- Unlike parallels of latitude, all meridians are of equal length.

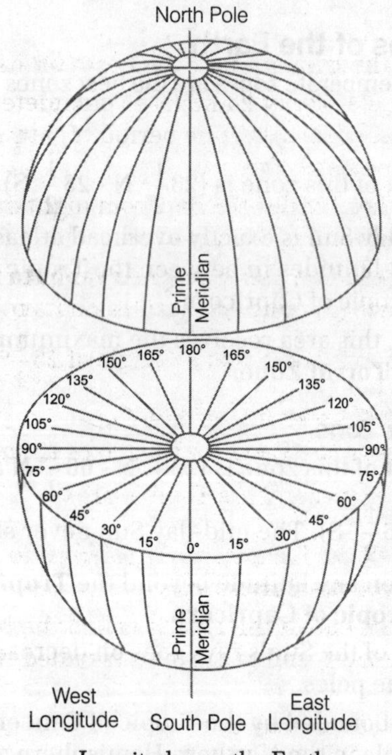

Longitudes on the Earth

Prime Meridian

- It was difficult to number the meridians. Hence, all countries decided that the count should begin from the meridian, which passed through Greenwich, where the **British Royal Observatory** is located. This meridian is called the **Prime Meridian**.
- Its value is 0° longitude and from it we count 180° Eastward as well as 180° Westward.
- The Prime Meridian and 180° meridian divide the Earth into two equal halves, the Eastern-Hemisphere and the Western-Hemisphere.
- Therefore, the longitude of a place is followed by the letter E for the East and W for the West.
- **It is however, interesting to note that 180° East and 180° West Meridians are on the same line.**

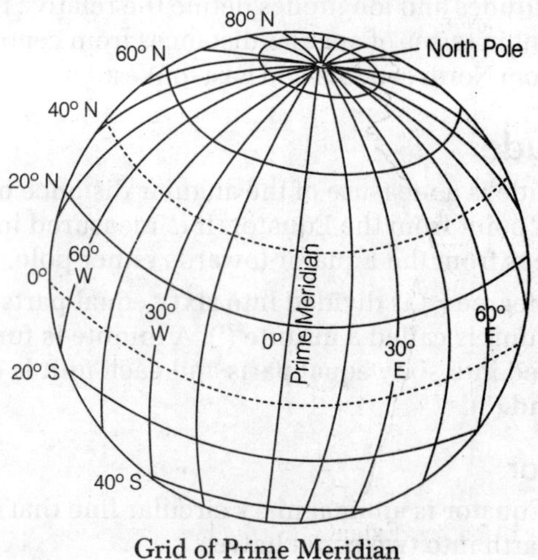

Grid of Prime Meridian

Longitude and Time

- **Local time is the time reckoned by the noon-Sun at a given place.**
- **In other words, local time can be considered by the shadow East by the Sun, which is the shortest at noon and longest at sunrise and sunset.**
- **When the Prime Meridian of Greenwich has the Sun at the highest point in the sky, all the places along this meridian will have mid-day or noon.**
- **As the Earth rotates from West to East, those places East of Greenwich will be ahead of Greenwich time and those to the West will be behind it.**
- **The rate of difference can be calculated as follows :**
  - **The Earth rotates 360° in about 24 hours, which means 15° an hour or 1° in four minutes.**
  - **Thus, when it is 12 noon at Greenwich, the time at 15° East of Greenwich will be $15 \times 4 = 60$ minutes, i.e, 1 hour ahead of Greenwich time, which means 1 pm.**
  - **But at 15° West of Greenwich, the time will be behind Greenwich time by one hour, i.e, it will be 11:00 am.**
  - **Similarly, at 180°, it will be mid-night when it is 12 noon Greenwich.**
  - **At any place a watch can be adjusted to reach 12 'O' clock when the Sun is at the highest point in the sky, i.e., when it is mid-day.**
  - **The time shown by such a watch will give the local time for that place.**

- All the places on a given meridian of longitude have the same local time.

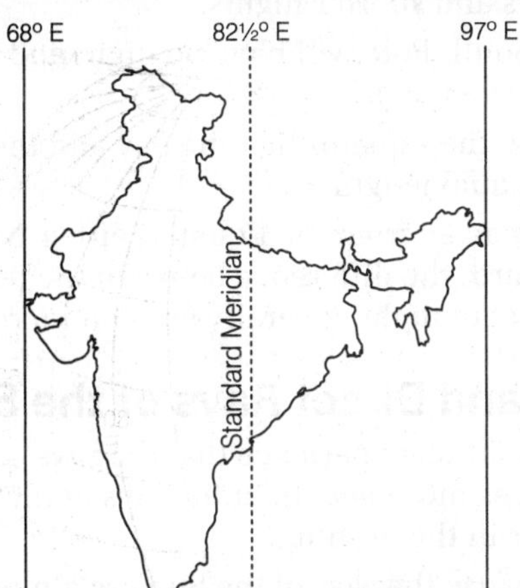

India : Extent and Standard Meridian

Standard Time

- Standard time is the local time of the Standard Meridian of a country.
- In India, the longitude of $82\frac{1}{2}$°E (82° 30′ E) is treated as the Standard Meridian.
- The local time at this meridian is taken as the standard time for the whole country. It is known as the Indian Standard Time (IST).
- India is located **East of Greenwich at 82° 30′ E** is 5 hours and 30 minutes ahead of Greenwich Mean Time (GMT).
- Some countries have a great longitudinal extent and so they have adopted more than one standard time. For example, in Russia, there are as many as eleven standard times.
- The Earth has been divided into twenty-four time zones of one hour each. Each zone covers 15° longitude.

International Date Line

- International Date Line (IDL) marks the place where each day officially begins. At the International Date Line, the West side of the line is always one day ahead of the East side, no matter what time of day it is when the line is crossed.
- The International Date Line has no astronomical or physical meaning. It is an imaginary line drawn at the 180° longitude, avoiding the continuous land parts.
- It is bent at **75° North latitude** towards East to avoid division of Siberia and to separate Siberia and Alaska. Again, it is bent over the bering strait towards West. To maintain the continuity of land in the Island of Fiji and New Zealand, the **International Date Line** (IDL) bends towards East in the Southern Pacific ocean.
- There is a difference of 24 hours in East and West therefore, one day is either gained or lost while crossing this line.
- In the year 2011, **Samoa islands** and **Tokelau** (South Pacific islands) as 29th December ended, then fast forwarded by 31st December, missing out on 30th December entirely. It is because of shifting towards West side of IDL for better trading with its neighbours, Australia and New Zealand.

Motions of the Earth

Rotation and Revolution are the two motions of the Earth.

Rotation

- Rotation is the movement of the Earth on its axis.
- The Earth takes about 24 hours to complete one rotation around its axis. The period of rotation is known as the **Earth day**.
- The circle that divides the day from night on the globe is called the circle of illumination.
- The Ancient Indian astronomer **Aryabhata** had stated that 'the Earth is round and rotates on its own axis'.
- The Earth's axis is tilted at an angle of $23\frac{1}{2}$° from a perpendicular to the orbital plane.
- In other words, the Earth's axis makes an angle of $66\frac{1}{2}$° with the plane of the Earth's orbit.
- This tilting of the Earth's axis is referred to as the **inclination of the Earth's axis.**
- The Northern end of this axis is called the **North Pole** and the Southern end of this anis is called the **South Pole**.

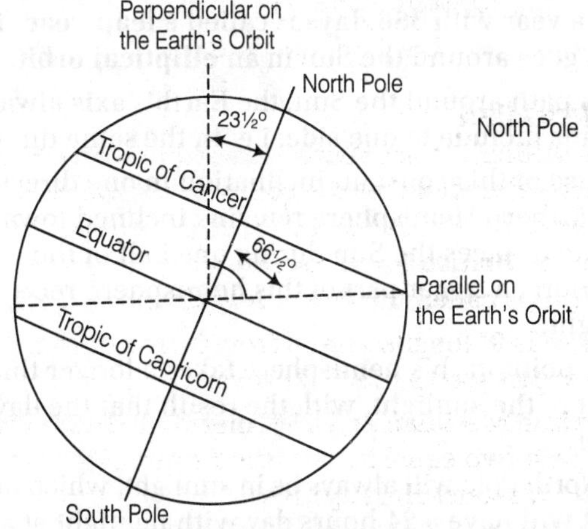

Tilt of the Earth Axis

- The Earth receives its light and heat from the Sun.
- When the Earth rotates on its axis, one half of it, facing the Sun is lit. The other half remains in darkness.

- Thus, each part of the Earth's surface comes into the sunlight for a certain period and then turns away from it in 24 hours.
- The lighted part of the Earth has day and the other half in darkness has night.
- If the Earth stops rotating the portion of the Earth facing the Sun would always a experience day, thus bringing continuous warmth to the region. The other half would remain in darkness and be freezing cold all the time.
- Thus, it is because of the rotation of the Earth that day and night follow each other in regular succession in all parts of the Earth.

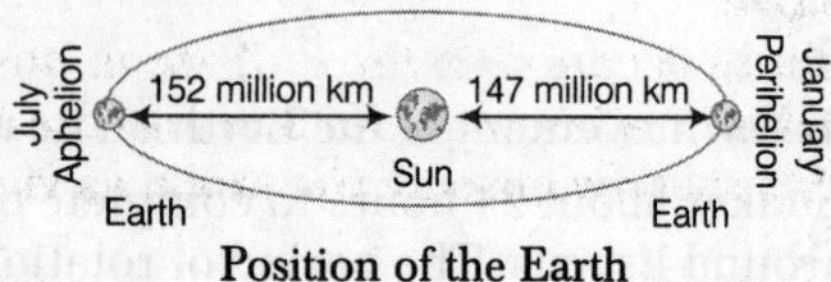

Position of the Earth

Revolution

- The movement of the Earth around the Sun in a fixed path or orbit is called **Revolution.**
- While rotating on its axis, the Earth also moves around the Sun at a speed of about 1,00,000 km per hour.
- The Earth completes one revolution in about 365 days and 6 hours.
- For the sake of our convenience, we consider a year as consisting of only 365 days and ignore 6 hours.
- 6 hours saved every year are added to make one day (24 hours) over a span of four years.
- This surplus day is added to the month of February.
- Thus, every fourth year, February is of 29 days instead of 28 days.
- Such a year with **366 days** is called a **leap year**. The Earth goes around the Sun in an **elliptical orbit**.
- On its path around the Sun, the Earth's axis always remains include to one side. i.e. in the same direction.
- Because of this constant inclination in one direction, the Northern Hemisphere remains inclined towards the Sun or faces the Sun during one half of the year. Therefore, a larger part of this hemisphere receives sunlight.
- Every point in this hemisphere takes a longer time to go out of the sunlight, with the result that the days are longer.
- The North Pole will always be in sunlight, which means that it will have a 24 hours day with no night at all.
- In contrast, the Southern Hemisphere is away from the Sun. Therefore, it has shorter days and longer night. The South Pole will have a 24 hours night with no day at all.
- During the other half of the year, the Southern Hemisphere is inclined towards the Sun. Hence, it has longer days and shorter nights.
- Now, the South Pole will have no night and the North Pole will have no day.
- It is only on the Equator that the day and the night are always of equal length.
- On moving away from the Equator, either Northward or Southward, the difference between the length of day and that of night generally goes on increasing.

Slanting and Direct Rays of the Sun

- It is our common experience that the rays of the Sun at noon gives more heat than the rays of the Sun in the morning or in the evening.
- This is because the rays of the Sun are almost vertical at noon and slanting in the morning and in the evening.
- Vertical rays of the Sun fall over a small area, giving it a greater amount of heat.
- Slanting rays, on the other hand, spread over a wide area and give less heat.

Summer Solstice

- On **21st June**, the Northern Hemisphere is tilted towards the Sun.
- The rays of the Sun fall directly on the **Tropic of Cancer**. As a result, these areas receive more heat.
- The areas near the poles receive less heat as the rays of the Sun are slanting.
- The longest day and the shortest night at these places occur on 21st June.
- The North Pole is inclined towards the Sun and the places beyond the Arctic Circle experience continuous daylight for about six months.
- Since, a large portion of the Northern Hemisphere is getting light from the Sun, it is summer in the regions North of the Equator.
- At this time in the Southern Hemisphere, all these conditions are reversed. i.e.,
  - It is winter season there.
  - The nights are longer than the days.
- This position of the Earth is called the **Summer Solstice.**

Winter Solstice

- On **22nd December**, the **Tropic of Capricorn** receives direct rays of the Sun as the South Pole tilts towards it.
- As the Sun's rays fall vertically at the Tropic of Capricorn ($23\frac{1}{2}°$ S), a larger portion of the Southern Hemisphere gets light.

- Therefore, it is summer in the Southern Hemisphere with longer days and shorter nights.
- The reverse happens in the Northern Hemisphere.
- This position of the Earth is called the **Winter Solstice**.

Equinox

- On 21st March and 23rd September, direct rays of the Sun fall on the Equator.
- At this position, neither of the poles is tilted towards the Sun; so, the whole Earth experiences equal days and equal nights. This is called an **Equinox**.
- On 23rd September, it is Autumn season in the Northern Hemisphere and Spring season in the Southern Hemisphere.
- On 21st March, the opposite happens and it is Spring in the Northern Hemisphere and Autumn in the Southern Hemisphere.
- Thus, there are days and nights and changes in the seasons because of the rotation and revolution of the Earth respectively.

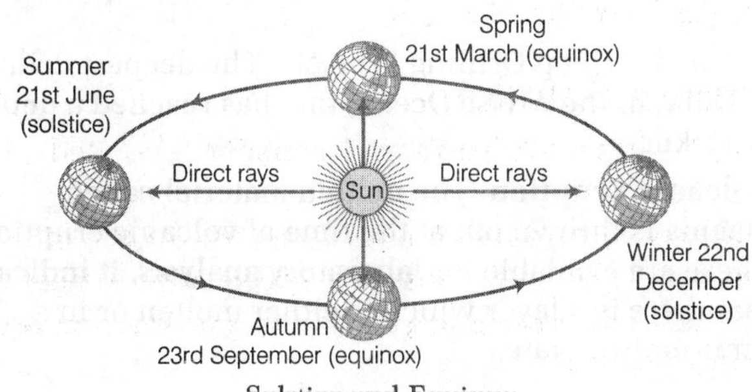

Solstice and Equinox

Eclipse

- An eclipse is a complete or partial obscuration of light from a celestial body as it passes through the shadow of another celestial body.
- Moon's orbital plane inclined 5° to the orbital plane of the Earth, so eclipses do not occur every Full Moon or New Moon positions.
- **Syzygy** is the position of alignment when the Earth comes in between Sun and Moon on a straight line; in such position a lunar eclipse occurs. The conjunction is the position when Sun and Moon lie on one side of the Earth and then solar eclipse occurs.
- The portion of the Sun or Moon covered by the vertical shadow of any celestial body like Earth or Moon is called **Umbra** and it is deep dark whereas the faint shadow region is called **Penumbra**.
- During a total eclipse, as the Moon's shadow is short enough to cover the whole of the Sun, then the outer region of the Sun still glows and looks bright as a ring as observed from the Earth. Such a phenomena is called **diamond ring**.

Solar Eclipse

- Solar eclipse occurs near the New Moon position, when the Moon is between the Sun and Earth, thus, obscuring a part of whole of the Sun as viewed from the Earth.

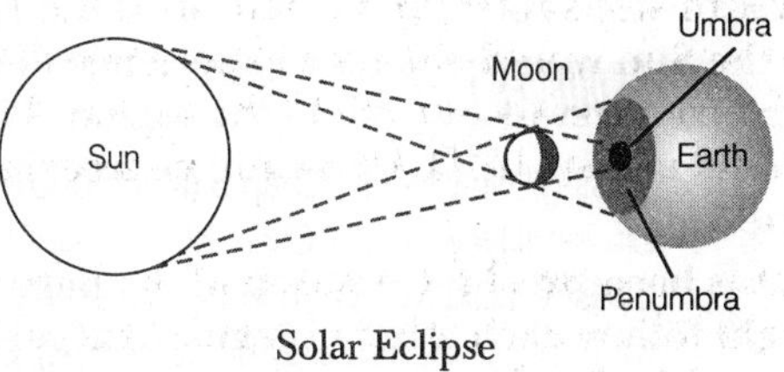

Solar Eclipse

Lunar Eclipse

- Lunar eclipse occurs near the Full Moon position, when the Earth is between the Sun and the Moon and Earth's shadow obscure the Moon as viewed from the Earth.
- Unlike a solar eclipse, which can only be viewed from a certain relatively small area of the world, a lunar eclipse may be viewed from anywhere on the night side of the Earth.

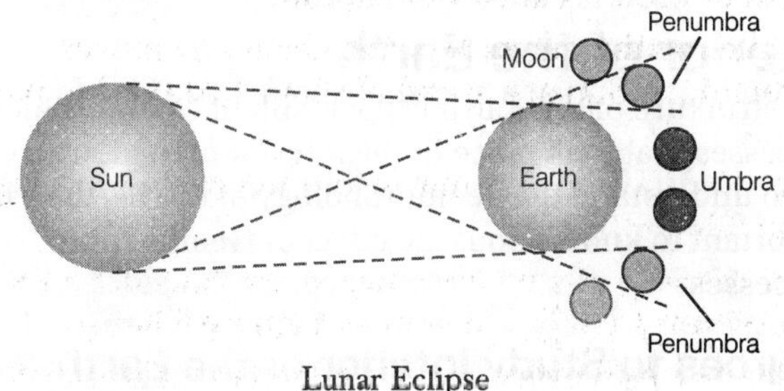

Lunar Eclipse

Extra Facts From Tamil Nadu Board and NIOS

- Theoretical astronomer, Lyttleton propounded the accretion theory of the Earth's formation.
- Rotation causes a flattening of Earth at the two poles and bulging at the Equator. Hence, there is a difference in diameter at the poles and Equator.
- A time zone is a region on the Earth, where uniform standard time should be maintained for transport, commercial and social purposes.
- Earth rotates in an Eastward direction (anticlockwise direction) opposite to the apparent movement of the Sun.
- The velocity of the Earth's rotation varies depending on the distance of a given place from the Equator.
- A partial lunar eclipse can be observed when only a part of the Moon's visible surface is obscured by the Earth's umbra.
- A penumbral lunar eclipse happens when the Moon travels through the faint penumbral portion of the Earth's shadow.
- A total lunar eclipse occurs when the Earth's umbra obscures the entire Moon's surface.

04

Geomorphology

[SOURCES]

Class-VI New NCERT Chap 5 (Major Domains of the Earth), Class-VII New NCERT Chap 2 (Inside Our Earth), Chap 3 our (Changing Earth), Class-VIII Old NCERT Chap 2 (Inside the Earth), Class-IX Old NCERT Chap 1 (Our Environment : Part and Processes), Chap 2 (Landforms of the Earth), Class-XI New NCERT Chap 3 (Interior of the Earth), Class-XI New NCERT Chap 6 (Landforms and their Evolution), Chap 4 (Distribution of Continents and Oceans, Chap 5 Minerals and Rocks), Chap 5 (Geomorphic Processes), Class-XI Old NCERT Chap 5 (Earth Movements, Volcanoes and Earthquake), Class-XI Old NCERT Chap 3 (Interior of the Earth), Chap 4 (Materials of Earths, Crust), Chap 6 (Landforms and Their is Significance), Tamil Nadu Board (Class XI), NIOS

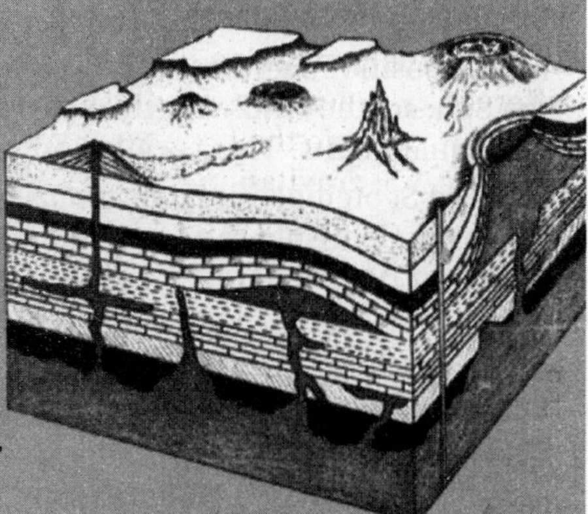

Interior of the Earth

The structure of the Earth is the result of Geomorphic processes that took place in the interior of the Earth. So, to understand the geomorphology of the Earth, it is important to know about the effect of **Geomorphic Processes.**

Sources to Study Interior of the Earth

- The factual sources concerning the interior of the Earth are not readily available.
- Therefore, the study of the interior of the Earth is based on **direct** and **indirect sources.**

Direct Sources

The important direct sources that give information about the interior of the Earth are underground mining, deep drilling projects, volcanic eruption, etc.

- **Underground Mines** A large part of the Earth's surface is composed of rocks derived from within the Earth's body. The most important direct source about the interior of the Earth is the solid Earth material in surface rock or the rocks we get from mining areas. e.g., certain Gold mines in South Africa are as deep as 3-4 km. Since, the temperature increases with the depth, it is not possible to go beyond more depth.
- **Deep Drilling Project** There are a number of projects to penetrate deeper depths to explore the conditions in the crustal portions. It provides a large volume of information through the analysis of materials collected at different depths. 'Deep Ocean Drilling Project' and 'Integrated Ocean Drilling Project' are the two major Deep Drilling Projects. The deepest drill is at **Kola**, in the Arctic Ocean, that has reached a depth of 12 km.
- **Volcanic Eruption** The molten material called magma is thrown out at the time of volcanic eruption. These are available for laboratory analysis. It indicates that there is a layer which is either molten or in a semi-molten state.

Indirect Sources

Analysis of properties of matter indirectly provides information about the interior of Earth. The important sources that provide details about the interior of the Earth are information from the meteors, density, gravitation, magnetic field and seismic activity.

- **Meteors** The material and the structure observed in the meteors are similar to that of the Earth. Hence, meteors are an important source of information about the interior of the Earth.
- **Density** The density and temperature of the material increases with depth. The average density of Earth was calculated as 55 g/cm^3 by using the spherical shape, mean radius and mass of the Earth.

  The density of the Earth is higher at core than all other parts of the Earth. With the help of rate of change of density and temperature and the total thickness of the Earth, it is possible to estimate the values of temperature, pressure and the density of materials at different depths.
- **Pressure** Even though the density increases with pressure, there is a critical limit beyond which its density cannot be increased. The high density in the

core is the result of the presence of heavy metallic material of high density there.

- **Temperature** Heat flows outwards from the interior of the Earth in the form of thermal convective currents. The temperature increases by 1°C for every 32 m of depth. This rate of change of temperature is not uniform while going down the surface of the Earth. Relatively higher temperatures are found in tectonically active regions.
- **Gravity** The gravitational force (g) is different at different latitudes on the surface. Since, the distance from the centre to the Equator is greater than that from the poles, the gravitational force is greater near the poles and less at the Equator. The gravity values also differ according to the mass of material. The reading of the gravity at different places differs from the expected values. Such a difference is called a gravity anomaly. Gravity anomalies give us information about the distribution of mass of the material in the crust of the Earth.
- **Magnetic Surveys** Magnetic surveys provide information about the distribution of magnetic materials in the crustal portion. This provides information about the distribution of materials in this part.
- **Seismic Activity** Seismic waves are generated during earthquakes. There are various types of earthquake waves. The nature of these earthquake waves and their travel speeds reveal the internal layered structure of the Earth.

Structure of the Earth's Interior

- The structure of the Earth's interior is layered. It is broadly classified into three layers such as:

1. Crust 2. Mantle 3. Core

Diagrammatic Representation of Earth Interior

Crust

- Crust is the brittle outermost solid part of the Earth.
- Crust is mainly divided in two parts, such as **continental crust** and **oceanic crust.**
- The continental crust is thicker than the oceanic crust.
- It means thickness of oceanic crust is 5 km whereas that of the continental is around 30 km.
- It only possesses less than 1% of the total volume of the Earth.

Continental Crust

- The continental crust is thicker in the areas of major mountain systems. It is about 70 km thick in the Himalayan region.
- It is composed of SiAl, i.e., **silicon** (Si) and **aluminium** (Al).
- SiAl is a light coloured rock, thus it called **Felsic**.
- Continental crust is lighter than oceanic crust.

Oceanic Crust

- It is denser and thinner than continental crust.
- It is composed of SiMa, i.e., **silicon** (Si) and **magnesium** (Ma). These are dark coloured mafic Crocks.

Lithosphere

- The crust and the uppermost part of the mantle together forms lithosphere.
- It is **100 km** thick. It is the outermost mechanical layer, which behaves as a brittle, rigid solid.
- The lithosphere is broken into a number of plates known as the **Lithospheric plates**.

Mantle

- The mantle is the portion of the interior beyond the crust. It is also known as **Pyrosphere**.
- The thickness of the mantle is about the depth of **2,900 km** from **Moho's discontinuity**.
- It is the bulkiest layer and forms 83% of Earth's volume.
- This layer is rich in magnesium, calcium and iron.
- The lower mantle extends beyond the asthenosphere. It is in solid state.

Asthenosphere

- Asthenosphere is the upper portion of the mantle.
- The word *'astheno'* means 'weak'.
- Asthenosphere is in a plastic state and is the main source of magma. It is considered to be extending up to 400 km.

Core

- The core mantle boundary is located at a depth of 2,900 km. It lies between 2900-6400 km depth.
- It is also known as the **Barysphere**. It is about 16% of Earth's volume.
- The core is mainly divided into two, i.e.,
  1. Liquid Outer Core
  2. Solid Inner Core
- The core is made up of very heavy material mostly composed of **Nickel** (Ni) and **Iron** (Fe).
- It is sometimes referred to as the **NiFe** layer.
- The presence of a metallic core gives magnetic fields to the Earth.
- The heat that keeps the outer core from solidifying is produced by the breakdown of radioactive elements in the inner core.
- This layer has maximum gravitational pull among all three.

Discontinuity

- The change in the speed of **P-waves** at different depths suggests the occurrence of discontinuity.
- Important discontinuities are:
  - **Conrad Discontinuity** It separates SiAl from SiMa.
  - **Mohorovicic Discontinuity** It separates crust from mantle.
  - **Repetti discontinuity** It is found between upper and lower mantle.
  - **Gutenberg-Weichert Discontinuity** It is located between mantle and core.
  - **Lehmann Discontinuity** It separates liquid outer core from solid inner core.

Earthquake

- An earthquake is shaking of the Earth. It is a natural event caused due to the release of energy, which generates waves that travel in all directions.
- This release of energy occurs along a fault. A fault is a sharp break in the crustal rocks.
- Rocks tend to move in opposite directions along a fault.
- As a result of this fault, the blocks get deformed and eventually, they slide past one another abruptly. This causes a release of energy.
- These energy waves (Seismic waves) travel in all directions.
- The study of **Seismic waves** also help to understand about the interior of the Earth.

Hypocentre and Epicentre

- The point where the energy is released is called the **Focus** or the **Hypocentre** of an Earthquake.
- The energy waves released from the focus travels in all directions to reach the surface of the Earth.
- The point on the surface directly above or nearest to the focus is called **Epicentre**. It is the first one to experience the waves.

Earthquake Waves

- All-natural Earthquakes take place in the lithosphere. An instrument called **Seismograph** records the waves reaching the surface.
- A curve of earthquake waves recorded on the seismograph, shows three distinct sections, each representing different types of wave patterns.
- The velocity of waves changes according to the density of material through, which they travel. As the density increases, the velocity of seismic waves increases.
- When seismic waves pass through materials with different densities, their direction will change as a result of their **Reflection** or **Refraction**.
- Reflection causes waves to rebound whereas refraction makes waves move in different directions.
- These variations in the direction of waves are studied with the help of their record on seismographs.
- Earthquake waves are basically of two types. They are **Body waves** and **Surface waves**.

Body Waves

- Body waves are generated due to the release of energy at the focus and move in all directions travelling through the body of the Earth.
- There are two types of body waves. They are called **P-waves** and **S-waves**.

P-Waves

- These are also called **Primary waves**. They are short waves of high frequency.
- P-waves move faster than S-waves. It is the first wave to arrive at the surface.
- The P-waves are **longitudinal** similar to sound waves so it can travel through gaseous, liquid and solid materials.
- P-waves have their highest velocity in solid. But their velocity decreases when they passes through liquid or gas.
- P-waves vibrate parallel to the direction of the wave. When P-waves pass through a material, they exert pressure on the material in the direction of the propagation.

- As a result, they creates density differences in the material leading to stretching and squeezing of the material.

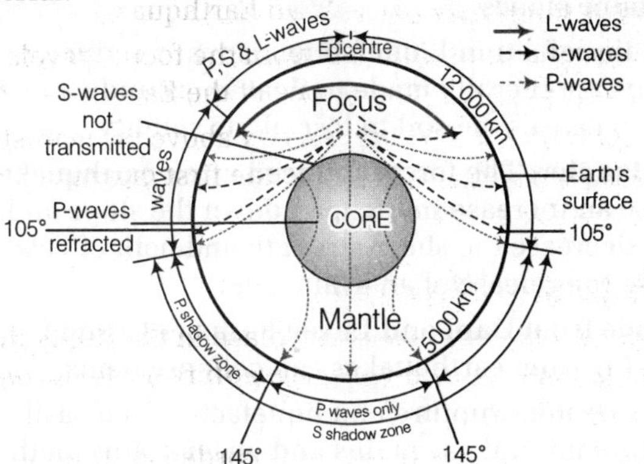

Types of Seismic Waves and Shadow Zones

S-Waves

- S-waves are transverse waves which are also called **Secondary waves**. S-waves are that they can travel only through solid materials.
- This characteristic of the S-waves helped scientists to understand the structure of the interior of the Earth.
- The direction of vibrations of S-waves is perpendicular to the wave direction in the vertical plane. Hence, they create troughs and crests in the material through which they pass.
- They arrive at the surface after the P-waves.

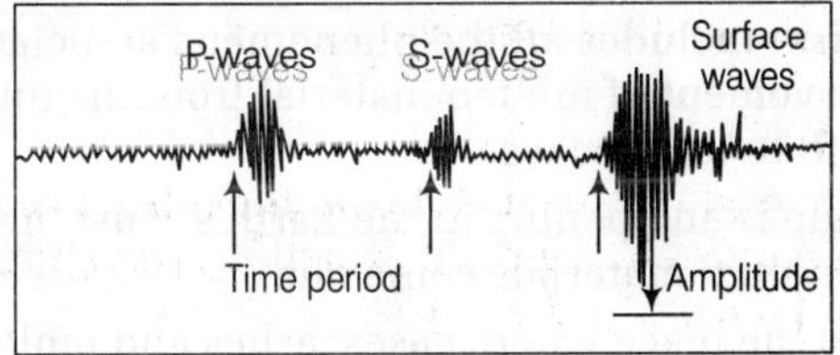

Earthquake Graph

Surface Waves

- The body waves interact with the surface rocks and generate a new set of waves that move along the surface, hence called **Surface waves.**
- The surface waves are the last to report on **Seismographs**.
- These waves vibrate perpendicular to the direction of propagation.
- They cause displacement of rocks and hence, the collapse of structures occurs. Surface waves are considered to be the most damaging waves.
- There are two types of surface waves. They are **Love wave** or **L-wave** and **Rayleigh wave** or **R-wave.**
- These are of long wavelength and low frequency. They travel slower than body waves.

Shadow Zone

- There exist some specific areas where the earthquake waves are not reported. Such a zone is called the **Shadow Zone.**
- The **Seismographs** located at any distance within 105° from the epicentre, recorded the arrival of both P and S-waves.
- The seismographs located beyond 145° from epicentre, record the arrival of P-waves, but not that of S-waves.
- A zone between 105° and 145° from epicentre was identified as the shadow zone for both P and S waves.
- The entire zone beyond 105° does not receive S-waves. It is known as the **Shadow zone of S-wave.**
- The shadow zone of the S-wave is much larger than that of the P-waves.
- The shadow zone of P-waves appears as a band around the Earth between 105° and 145° away from the epicentre.

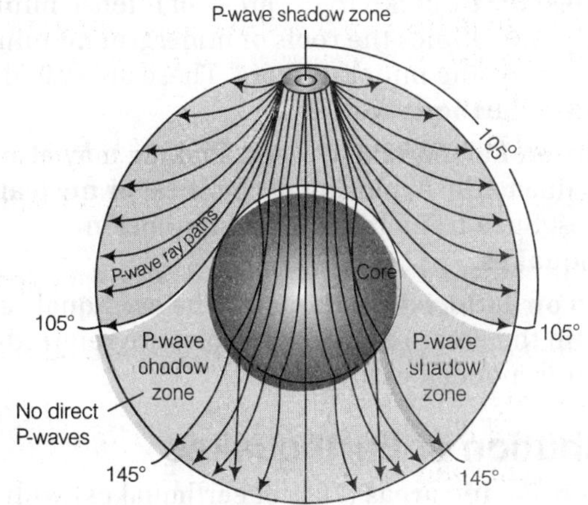

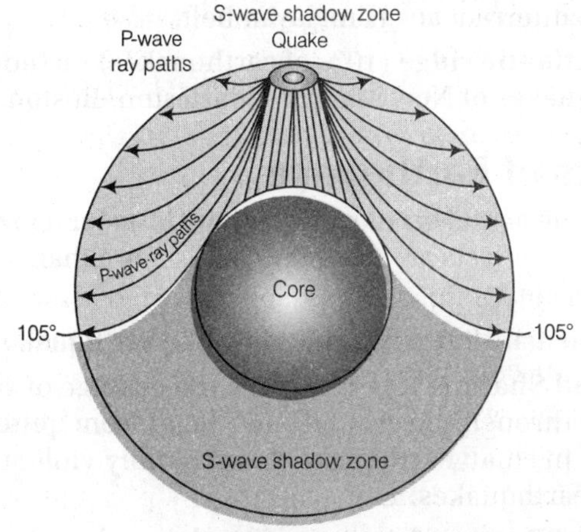

Shadow Zone

Magnitude and Intensity of Earthquake

- The magnitude of the earthquake refers to the energy released during the earthquake.
- The magnitude scale is known as the **Richter scale.** The magnitude is expressed in numbers, **0-10.**
- The intensity scale categorise the intensity or severity of ground shaking at a given location.
- The intensity scale is named after **Mercalli**, an Italian seismologist. The range of intensity scale is from **1-12.**

Types of Earthquake

- **Tectonic Earthquake** The most common ones are the tectonic earthquakes. These are generated due to sliding of rocks along a fault plane.
- **Volcanic Earthquake** It is a special class of tectonic earthquakes however, these are confined to areas of active volcanos.
- **Collapse Earthquake** In the areas of intense mining activity, sometimes the roofs of underground mines collapse causing minor tremors. These are called **Collapse Earthquakes.**
- **Explosion Earthquake** Ground shaking may also occur due to the explosion of chemical or nuclear devices. Such tremors are called Explosion **Earthquakes.**
- **Reservoir Induced Earthquake** The earthquakes that occur in the areas of large reservoirs are referred to as reservoir induced earthquakes.

Distribution of Earthquakes

- **Circum-Pacific areas** (70% of earthquakes) with most frequent occurrence along the Pacific ring of fire.
- **Mid-Continental belt** (20% of earthquakes) includes the Mediterranean- Himalayan belt.
- **Mid-Atlantic ridge** (10% of earthquakes) includes the earthquakes of New Madrid, Charleston, Boston, etc.

Effects of Earthquake

Though the actual earthquake activity lasts for a few seconds, its effects are devastating it is more than 5 on the Richter scale.

The immediate hazardous effects of the earthquake are

- **Ground Shaking** It is a result of the passage of seismic waves through the ground and ranges from quite gentle in small earthquakes to incredibly violent in large earthquakes.
- **Ground Rupture** It occurs when the earthquake movement along a fault actually breaks the Earth's surface.
- **Land and Mudslides** They are caused by earthquakes both by direct rupture and by sustained shaking of unstable slopes.
- **Soil liquefaction** Liquefaction is when sediment grains are literally made to float in groundwater, which causes the soil to lose all its solidity.
- **Avalanches** The forces induced by an earthquake can cause an increase in the load down the slope and can also decrease the shear strength and both effects can cause the release of an avalanche.
- **Floods from Dam and Levee Failures** Ground shaking from earthquakes can collapse dams.
- **Fires** Ground rupture and liquefaction can easily rupture natural gas mains and water mains, both contributing to the ignition of fires and hindering the efforts to control them.

– Ground displacement – Structural collapse
– Falling objects – Tsunami

Tsunami

- Tsunamis are waves generated by the tremors and not an earthquake in itself.
- The effect of tsunami would occur only if the epicentre of the tremor is below oceanic waters and the magnitude is sufficiently high.

Volcanoes

- Volcanism includes all the phenomena associated with movement of molten material from the interior of the Earth to the surface.
- A volcano is an opening in the Earth's crust through which molten materials come out.
- It is also the place where gases, ashes and molten rock material escape to the ground.
- The mantle contains a weaker zone called the **Asthenosphere**. From the asthenosphere, molten rock material comes out to the surface.
- The material in the upper mantle portion is called **Magma**. Once it starts moving towards the crust or it reaches the surface, it is referred to as **Lava.**
- The material that reaches the ground includes lava flows, pyroclastic debris, volcanic bombs, ash and dust and gases such as nitrogen compounds, sulphur compounds and minor amounts of chlorine, hydrogen and argon.
- **Bullet Crater** of a volcano is a cylindrical opening through which magma or lava comes out to the surface of the Earth.
- The main causes of volcanic eruption are **Plate-tectonics,** weak layer of the crust, high temperature of core and evolution of gases near sea floor.

Parts of Volcano

- **Magma Chamber** It is a large underground pool of molten rock under pressure sitting underneath the Earth's crust. Generally, magma chambers are located close to the Earth's surface, usually between 1 km to 10 km deep.
- **Volcanic Vent** It is the weak point in the Earth's crust where hot magma has been able to rise from the magma chamber and reach the surface.
- **Volcanic Cone** It is made of layers of igneous rocks formed from previous eruptions. Each lava flow add a new layer to the volcanic cone.
- **Volcanic Crater** It is depression or hollow from which eruptions expel magmatic material (lava, gas, steam, ash, etc).

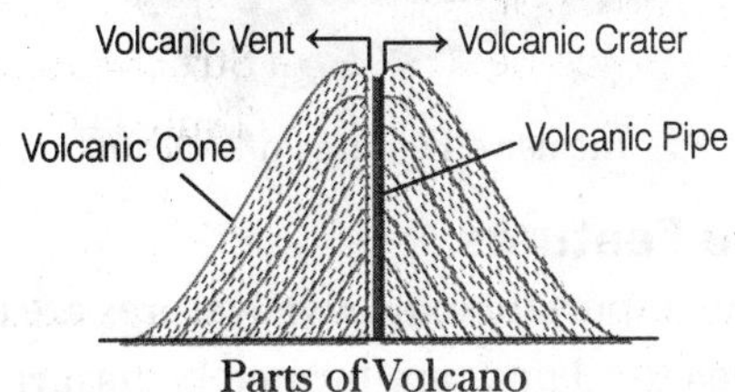

Parts of Volcano

Types of Volcano on the Basis of Eruption

- **Hawaiian Type** In this type of volcano, extremely fluid lava comes out on the surface of the Earth. It is mostly basaltic and spreads over large areas.
- **Strombolian Type** Strombolian type is the most typical volcano which are less explosive. There are several small explosive activities, where lava is more viscous.
  It has the power to explode the crust. e.g., Stromboli volcano, Lipari island (North Sicily), Mauna Loa volcano (Hawaiian island).
- **Volcanian Type** In this type, lava is very viscous and the eruptions take place at longer intervals. Large quantities of pyroclastic materials are erupted from them. e.g., volcanoes in Lipari island group of Mediterranean sea.
- **Vesuvian Type or Plinian Type** In this type, long intervals take place between two eruptions. These are extremely violent and their lava is highly viscous. e.g., volcano that once existed near Naples in Italy.
- **Pelean Type** In this type, lava is viscous and highly destructive and fast-moving mass gets erupted. e.g., Mount Pelee on Martinique island in the West Indies.
- **Fissure Eruption** or **Quiet Eruption** Large quantity of lava quietly flows up from fissures and spreads out over the surrounding areas. Successive flow of lava results in the growth of Lava plateau. e.g., Deccan plateau.

Types of Volcano on the Basis of Activity

- **Active Volcano** A volcano is called an active volcano if the materials mentioned are being released or have been released in the recent past. These volcanoes constantly eject volcanic lava, gas and ashes. e.g., Cotopaxi, Mt. Erebus, Mt. Etna, Strombolian, etc. Due to its recent activity and nearby population, Mount Etna has been designated a Decade Volcano by the United Nations.
- **Dormant Volcano** These are volcanoes, which were active in past, but for several years have not shown any activity. They can erupt very violently and cause huge damage. e.g., Mt. Krakatoa, Vesuvius (Italy), Fujiyama (Japan), etc.
- **Extinct Volcano** A volcano which erupted in the distant geological past and there is no longer any active volcanicity. They show no indications of future eruptions. e.g., Popa (Myanmar), Mt. Demvand and Koh-Sultan (Iran).

Types of Volcano on the Basis of Nature of Eruption

- **Shield Volcanoes** Barring the basalt flows, the shield volcanoes are the largest of all the volcanoes on the Earth. The Hawaiian volcanoes are the most famous examples.
- Since, the volcanoes are mostly made up of very fluid basalt, this is the reason, these volcanoes are not steep. They are characterised by low-explosivity. When water gets into the vent, they become explosive.
  The upcoming lava moves in the form of a fountain and throws out the cone at the top of the vent and develops into a cinder cone.
- **Composite Volcanoes** Composite volcanoes are characterised by the eruptions of cooler and more viscous lavas than basalt. These volcanoes often result in explosive eruptions.
  This material accumulates in the vicinity of the vent openings leading to formation of layers and this makes the mounts appear as composite volcanoes.
- **Caldera** These are the most explosive of Earth's volcanoes. When they erupt, they tend to collapse on themselves rather than building any tall structure.
  The collapsed depressions are called **Calderas**. Their magma chamber supplying the lava is not only huge but is also in close vicinity.
- **Flood Basalt Provinces** These volcanoes outpour highly fluid lava that flows for long distances. There can be a series of flows with some flows attaining thickness of more than 50 m.
  The Deccan Traps from India, are a much larger flood basalt province. It is believed that initially the trap formations covered a much larger area than the present.

- **Mid-Ocean Ridge Volcanoes** These volcanoes occur in the oceanic areas. There is a system of mid-ocean ridges more than 70,000 km long that stretches through all the ocean basins. The central portion of this ridge experiences frequent eruptions.

Topographic Features of Volcanoes

- Magma is of two types i.e., **Basaltic** and **Granitic**. Basaltic magma is fluid while granitic magma is viscous.
- Once magma comes to the surface of the Earth, it is lighter than the adjoining rocks, moves upward towards the surface and gives rise to certain topographic features.
- The cooling of Magma may take place either on reaching the surface or also while the lava is still in the crustal portion.
- Depending on the location of the cooling of the lava, igneous rocks are classified as Volcanic rocks and Plutonic rocks.
- When rocks are formed by cooling at the surface, it is known as **Volcanic rocks**. When cooling is in the crust, it is known as **Plutonic rocks**.

Intrusive Features

When the volcanic features are formed beneath the surface, they are called Intrusive features. Some of the important intrusive features are as follows :

- **Batholiths** These are the cooled portion of magma chambers. A large body of magmatic material that cools in the deeper depth of the crust develops in the form of large domes. These are granitic bodies.
- **Lacoliths** These are large dome-shaped intrusive bodies with a level base and connected by a pipe-like conduit from below. It resembles the surface volcanic domes of composite volcano, only these are located at deeper depths.
- **Lapolith** As and when the lava moves upwards, a portion of the same may tend to move in a horizontal direction wherever, it finds a weak plane. It may get rested in different forms. In case it develops into a saucer shape, concave to the sky body, it is called lapolith.
- **Phacoliths** A wavy mass of intrusive rocks, at times, is found at the base of synclines or at the top of anticline in folded igneous country. Such wavy materials have a definite conduit to source beneath in the form of magma chambers. These are called the phacoliths.
- **Sills** The near horizontal bodies of the intrusive igneous rocks are called sill or sheet, depending on the thickness of the material. The thinner ones are called sheets while the thick horizontal deposits are called sills.
- **Dykes** When the lava makes its way through cracks and the fissures developed in the land, it solidifies almost perpendicular to the ground. It gets cooled in the same position to develop a wall-like structure. Such structures are called dykes.

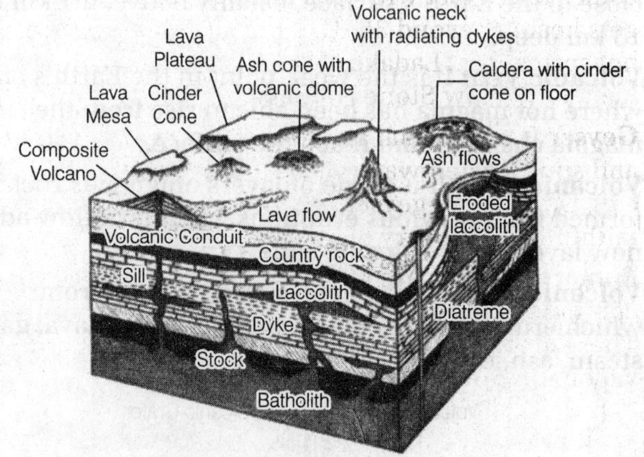

Intrusive Features of Volcano

Extrusive Features

Some of the important extrusive features are as follows :

- **Flood Basalts** These are formed by fissure eruption. Due to the less viscous basaltic lava it erupts with no explosive activity. e.g., Deccan trap.
- **Shield Volcanoes** These are huge domes of basalt. It is formed as a result of continued outpouring of great quantities of highly fluid basaltic lava. e.g., Mt. Mauna Kea and Mauna Loa on Hawaii.
- **Ash or Cinder Cone** These are usually of low height and are formed of volcanic dust, ashes and pyroclastic matter. They are formed when the eruption is of central type with a predominance of pyroclastic materials. e.g., Paricutin, Mexico.
- **Shield Type** These volcanoes vary in size from less than 20 m across. Shield volcanoes are formed from low viscosity, runny lava. When lava spreads far from the source and forms a volcano with gentle slopes. Mauna Kea and Mauna Loa are shield volcanoes.
- **Composite or Strata Cone** It is the highest of all volcanic cones. These are formed due to accumulation of different layers of various volcanic materials and hence, called as strato-cones. These are built up by alternate layers of lava and fragmental flows. e.g., Pinatubo of Philippines, Fuji in Japan.
- **Parasitic Cone** Several branches of pipes come out from the main centre pipe of the volcano. Lava and other volcanic material will come out from these minor pipes and get deposited around these newly formed vents. The smaller cones formed on major cones are termed as a parasitic cone.
- **Crater** The depression formed at the mouth of a volcanic vent is known as crater or volcanic mouth. It is usually funnel shaped.

- **Caldera** It is the enlarged form of a crater. These are either formed by the subsidence of a crater or by the violent and explosive eruption of volcanoes.
- **Hot springs** These are formed when groundwater comes in contact with the magma. When ground water gets heated beyond 36° C, it comes to the surface as a hot spring. e.g., Ladakh, Manali, volcanic regions of Iceland, Yellow Stone National Park.
- **Geyser** It is a special type of hot spring. It ejects steam and superheated water at regular intervals e.g., Old faithful geyser in the USA, which erupts faithfully after every 66 minutes.
- **Fumaroles** They are characterised by full-scale continuous jet-like emission of hot water from a vent. These are the vent through which gases and water vapour are emitted.

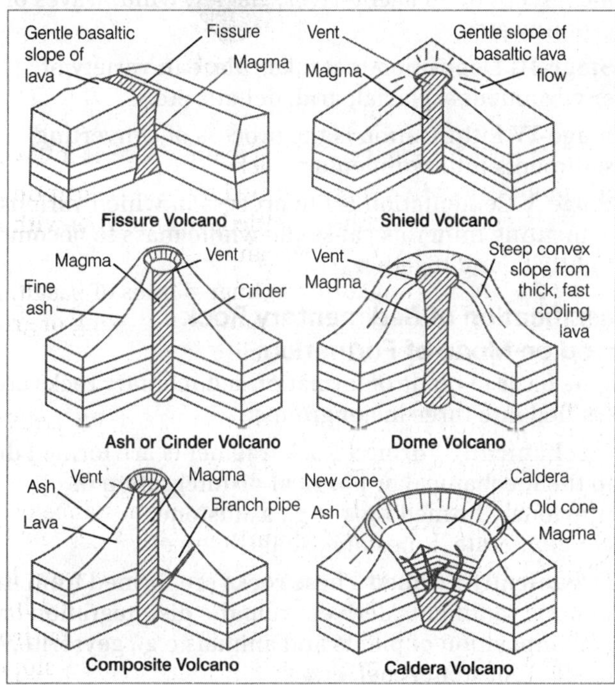

Extrusive Features of Volcano

Distribution of Volcanic Belts

Distribution of volcanic belts is uneven in the world. There are following three prominent volcanic belts :

Circum-Pacific Belt

- Circum-Pacific region popularly termed as the **'Pacific Ring of Fire'**.
- It has the greatest concentration of active volcanoes. Volcanic belt and earthquake belt closely overlap along the 'Pacific Ring of Fire'.
- It extends across the Kamchatka Peninsula, Kuril islands, the islands of Japan, Philippines, New Guinea, New Zealand and the Solomon islands.
- It also passes through Antarctica and the Western coast of North and South America.

Mid-Continental Belt

- This belt is formed as a result of convergence between the Eurasian Plate and the Northward-moving African Plate.
- It includes volcanoes of the Alpine mountain chain, the Mediterranean sea and the fault zone of Eastern Africa of Stromboli, Vesuvius, Etna, Kilimanjaro, etc.

Mid-Atlantic Belt

- These are located on divergent plate boundaries. The Mid-Atlantic Ridge is a volcanic mountain range that rises from the Atlantic abyssal plain, extending from the Arctic to the Antarctic.
- In this belt, the volcanoes are fissure eruption type, e.g., Iceland, Canary islands, Cape Verde, Azores, etc.

Rocks

- The Earth's crust is composed of rocks. A rock is an aggregate of one or more minerals.
- **Petrology** is the science of rocks. A petrologist studies rocks in all their aspects *viz.*, mineral composition, texture, structure, origin, occurrence, alteration and relationship with other rocks.

Types of Rocks

- On the basis of mode of formation, rocks are grouped under three families. They are:

  (i) Igneous Rocks (ii) Sedimentary Rocks
  (iii) Metamorphic Rocks

Igneous Rock

- Igneous rocks form out of magma and lava from the interior of the Earth. They are known as **Primary rocks**.
- The igneous rocks are formed when magma cools and solidifies. The process of cooling and solidification can happen inside the Earth's crust on the surface of the earth.
- Granite, gabbro, pegmatite, basalt, volcanic breccia and tuff are some of the examples of igneous rocks.

Classification of Igneous Rock Based on Texture

- Texture depends upon size and arrangement of grains or other physical conditions of the materials. Igneous rocks are classified based on texture as coarse grained, fine grained and intermediate grained.
  - **Coarse Grained** If molten material is cooled slowly at great depths, mineral grains may be very large.
  - **Fine Grained** Sudden cooling (at the surface) results in small and smooth grains.

- Intermediate Grained Intermediate conditions of cooling would result in intermediate sizes of grains making up igneous rocks.

- Some igneous rocks have been produced through two stage of cooling. The large crystals formed by slow cooling called phenocryst are found embedded in a matrix of very small crystals called **porphyry** formed by rapid cooling.

Classification of Igneous Rock Based on Occurrence

On the basis of mode of occurrence igneous rocks are classified into three types:

- **Plutonic or Intrusive Rocks** These are formed due to the cooling of magma very deep inside the Earth. These are coarse grained rocks since, they are formed due to slow cooling. e.g., granite.
- **Hypabyssal Rocks** Intruded rocks occurring at shallow depths. The magma solidifies in different forms depending upon the hollow place such as batholith, laccolith, phacolith, lopolith, sill, dyke etc.
- **Volcanic Rocks** These are formed due to the cooling and solidification of hot and molten lavas at the Earth surface. Because of the rapid cooling it is made up of fine grained crystals.
- **Pyroclastic Rocks** These are accumulated material of explosive volcanic activity. e.g., lava clot, ash and dust.

Classification of Igneous Rock Based on Chemical Composition

On the basis of mineralogical and chemical composition igneous rocks are classified as:

- **Felsic or Silica Rocks** Acidic in nature with over 65 to 85% of silica content. e.g., granite and granodiorite.
- **Acid Igneous Rocks** They are hard and relatively resistant to erosion. These are light coloured and light weighted rock.
- **Mafic or Basic Rocks** Basic in nature with 45 to 60% of silica content. e.g., gabro, basalt, dolerite.
  These igneous rocks are dominated by ferro-magnesium minerals. These rocks are heavy and dark coloured.
- **Ultrabasic or Ultramafic Rocks** These rocks contain less than 45% silica content. Peridotite is the typical example of this group of rock.

Sedimentary Rocks

- The word 'sedimentary' is derived from the Latin word *sedimentum*, which means 'settling'.
- Rocks of the earth's surface are exposed to denudational agents and are broken up into various sizes of fragments. Such fragments are transported by different exogenous agencies and deposited.
- These deposits through compaction turn into rocks. This process is called **lithification.**
- In many sedimentary rocks, the layers of deposits retain their characteristics even after lithification. Hence, we see a number of layers of varying thickness in sedimentary rocks like sandstone, shale etc.
- Sedimentary rocks are found over about 95% area of the crust, but they contribute only 5% in the formation of the crust.
- Fossils are generally found in sedimentary rocks.

Stages in the Formation of Sedimentary Rocks

- **Stage-I** Weathering of any rock whether igneous, sedimentary or metamorphic.
- **Stage-II** Transportation either involves mass movement or an agent–river, glacier, wind, waves or groundwater.
- **Stage-III** Deposition that takes place in variety of environments– glacial, arid, deltaic, etc.
- **Stage-IV** Lithification is the process of converting sediments into sedimentary rocks.
- **Stage-V** Cementation is the process in which various cementing minerals cause the whole mass to become tightly bound together.

Classification of Sedimentary Rock Based on Mode of Formation

On the basis of mode of formation sedimentary rocks are classified into three major groups:

- **Mechanically Formed** Rock fragments are formed due to the mechanical or physical disintegration of previously formed rock. e.g., sandstone, conglomerate, limestone, shale, loess etc.
- **Organically Formed** These rocks are formed from the organic sediments derived from the disintegration or decomposition of plants and animals e.g., geyserite, chalk, limestone, coal, etc.
- **Chemically Formed** Chemically derived sediment are formed when chemically active water comes in contact with country rocks. e.g., chert, limestone, halite, potash, etc.

Metamorphic Rocks

- The word 'metamorphic' means 'change of form'.
- Metamorphic rocks form under the action of pressure, volume and temperature changes.
- **Metamorphism** is a process by which already consolidated rocks undergo recrystallisation and reorganisation of materials within original rocks. Metamorphism occurs when rocks are forced down to lower levels by tectonic processes.

- Metamorphic rocks are also formed when molten magma rising through the crust comes in contact with the crustal rocks or the underlying rocks are subjected to great amounts of pressure by overlying rocks.
- Gneissoid, granite, syenite, slate, schist, marble, quartzite etc., are some examples of metamorphic rocks.
- Metamorphic rocks formed through the igneous rocks are called **meta-igneous** or **ortho-metamorphic rocks**. Gneiss from granite, amphibolite from basalt, schist from basalt.
- Metamorphic rocks formed by the further metamorphosis of metamorphic rocks are phyllite from slate, schist from phyllite, serpentine from gabbro.

Metamorphism is of following two types:

Dynamic Metamorphism

- Mechanical disruption and reorganisation of the original minerals within rocks due to breaking and crushing without any appreciable chemical changes is called **dynamic metamorphism**.

Thermal Metamorphism

- The materials of rocks chemically alter and recrystallise due to thermal metamorphism.

  There are two types of thermal metamorphism :

  - **Contact Metamorphism** In the process of contact metamorphism, the rocks come in contact with hot intruding magma and lava and the rock materials recrystallise under high temperatures. Quite often new materials form out of magma or lava are added to the rocks.
  - **Regional Metamorphism** In regional metamorphism, rocks undergo recrystallisation due to deformation caused by tectonic shearing together with temperature or pressure or both. In the process of metamorphism, in some rocks grains or minerals get arranged in layers or lines.

Foliation

- A parallel arrangement of minerals or grains in metamorphic rocks is called **foliation or lineation.**
- Minerals or materials of different groups are arranged into alternating thin to thick layers appearing in light and dark shades. Such a structure in metamorphic rocks is called banding and rocks displaying banding are called **banded rocks.**
- Types of metamorphic rocks depend upon original rocks that were subjected to metamorphism.
- Metamorphic rocks are classified into two major groups such as:
  1. Foliated rocks 2. Non-foliated rocks

Rock Cycle

- Rock cycle is a continuous process through which old rocks are transformed into new ones.
- **Igneous rocks** are primary rocks and other rocks form from these primary rocks. Igneous rocks can be changed into **metamorphic rocks.**
- The fragments derived out of igneous and metamorphic rocks form into sedimentary rocks.
- **Sedimentary rocks** themselves can turn into fragments and the fragments can be a source for formation of sedimentary rocks.
- The crustal rocks such as igneous, metamorphic and sedimentary once formed may be carried down into the mantle through subduction process.
- The same melt down due to increase in temperature in the interior and turn into molten magma i.e., the original source for igneous rocks.

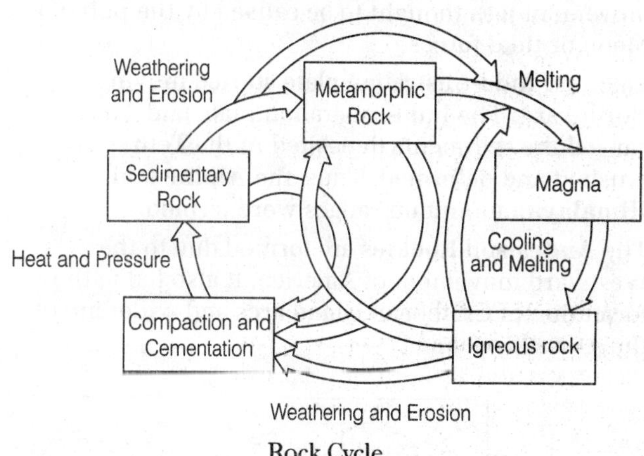

Rock Cycle

Major Theories for the Evolution of Landforms

Many theories have been given for the explanation of evolution of landforms on the surface of the Earth.

- Most important theories for the evolution of landforms are :
  - Continental Drift Theory
  - Sea Floor Spreading Theory
  - Plate Tectonics Theory

Continental Drift Theory

- In 1912, **Alfred Wegener** in a book 'The Origin of Continents and Oceans' put forward the idea of lateral movement of continents or continental drift.
- In this theory, he claimed that the changes in the appearance of the Earth were largely due to the shifting of continents.

- There was only one supercontinent called Pangaea about 250 million years ago. It was surrounded by the super-ocean named **Panthalassa**.
- About 200 million years ago, the Pangaea began to break up into two. They are:
  - **Laurasia** that started floating Northward.
  - **Gondwanaland** that started floating Southward.
- Laurasia and Gondwanaland was intervened by a narrow and shallow water body known as **Tethys sea**.
- Laurasia consisted of present North America and Greenland and Eurasia (without India and Arabia).
- Gondwanaland contained Africa with Arabia attached with South America, Australia, Antarctica and India. The South Pole was located near Durban, near Natal in South Africa.
- Wegner states that the Northward movement was caused by gravitational forces, i.e. because of intense gravitational pull of the poles. Whereas, the Westward movement was thought to be caused by the pull of the Moon or tidal forces.
- Later on, Indo-Australian plate started moving Northward. The Indo-Australian plate and Africa caused the sediments deposited in the Tethys to be crushed and deformed. Thus, the **Alpine** and **Himalayan** mountain ranges were formed.
- The **Andes** and **Rockies** are formed due to the Westward movement of America. It also led to the formation of Caribbean island arcs and widening of the Atlantic ocean.

Evidence of Continental Drift Theory

The evidences in support of the theory are :

- **Jigsaw Fit of continents** It refers to the similarities between the coastlines of South America and Africa, suggest that these were once joined together.
- **Structural similarities** The continuity of tectonic trends of the block of these countries across their present boundaries.
- The distribution of the fossil plants in Argentina, South Africa, India, Western Australia and Antarctica.

Rocks of Same Age across the Oceans

The belt of ancient rocks of 2,000 million years from Brazil coast matches with those from Western Africa. The earliest marine deposits along the coastline of South America and Africa are of the Jurassic Age.

- **Tillite** It is the sedimentary rock formed out of deposits of glaciers. The glacial tillite provides unambiguous evidence of palaeoclimates and also of drifting of continents.
- **Placer Deposits** The occurrence of rich placer deposits of gold in the Ghana coast and the absolute absence of source rock in the region is an amazing fact.
- **Distribution of Fossils** When identical species of plants and animals adapted to living on land or in fresh water are found on either side of the marine barriers, a problem arises regarding accounting for such distribution.

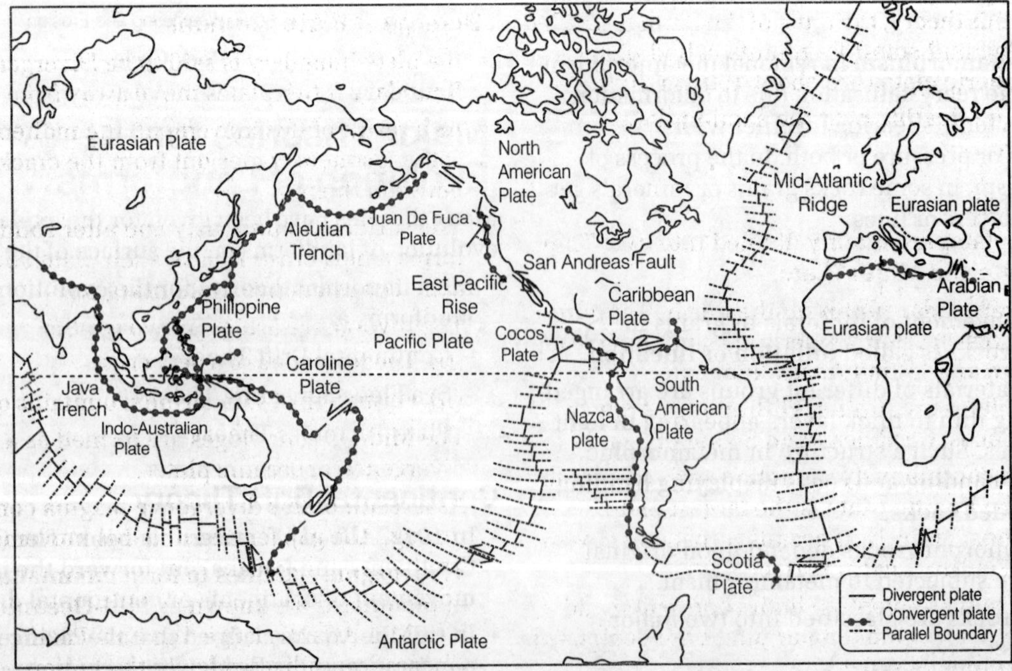

Evidence of Continental Drift Theory

Criticism of Continental Drift Theory

- The responsible forces for the whole process of the continental drift were not sufficient enough.
- But still the evidence provided by the Continental Drift Theory provided a platform for future work.

Sea Floor Spreading Theory

- The Sea Floor Spreading hypothesis was proposed by the geophysicist **Harry H Hess.**
- The theory was based on a concept that the age of the rocks of the seafloor is not the same.
- The youngest rocks are found in the central parts of the oceans while older rocks are found towards the margins of the oceans.
- The new crust is formed from the central part of the ocean and spreads towards the margins of the ocean, pushing the older rocks towards the margins. This concept is known as **Sea Floor Spreading**.

Plate Tectonics Theory

- The Plate Tectonics Theory deals with the whole mechanism of evolution, nature of motion of plates and resultant reaction.
- Plate Tectonics Theory explains the large-scale motions of Earth's lithosphere.
- Though, this theory was proposed by **Harry Hess** in 1962, the term plate was first coined by **JT Wilson** in 1965.
- Later the theory was explained scientifically by **WJ Morgan, Dan McKenzie, Robert I Parker** and **Arthur Holmes.**
- According to this theory, the crust of the Earth is divided into several big and small fragments called plates. These lithospheric plates are about 100 km thick.
- These plates are floating over the semi-molten asthenosphere.

Types of Plates

- Lithospheric plates are mainly divided into two. They are **Major Plate** and **Minor Plate.**
- There are **seven major plates** on the Earth. They are Eurasian, Antarctican, North American, South American, Pacific, African and Indian Australian plate.
- Other minor plates are, China, Philippines, Arabian, Iran, Nazca, Cocos, Caribbean and Scotia plates.
- The plates are continuously in motion with respect to each other. The **Pacific plate** is the largest plate, composed almost entirely of oceanic crust and covers about 1/5th of entire Earth's surface.
- Almost all large plates contain both continental and oceanic crusts. None of the major plates are composed entirely of continental crust.

Cause of Plate Movement

- The lithospheric plates are situated above the asthenosphere which is in a **semi plastic** state.
- Due to the high temperature at the Earth's interior magma in the asthenosphere undergoes continuous convection.
- This convection currents in the asthenosphere causes the movement of lithospheric plates.
- The plates move at a speed of 2 cm to 12 cm a year. The speed of this movement has not always been uniform.

Plate Boundaries

- Plate boundaries are generally of three types namely:

1. Constructive Margins or Divergent Plate Boundary
2. Destructive Margin or Convergent Plate Boundary
3. Conservative Margin or Parallel Boundary or Transform Fault Boundary

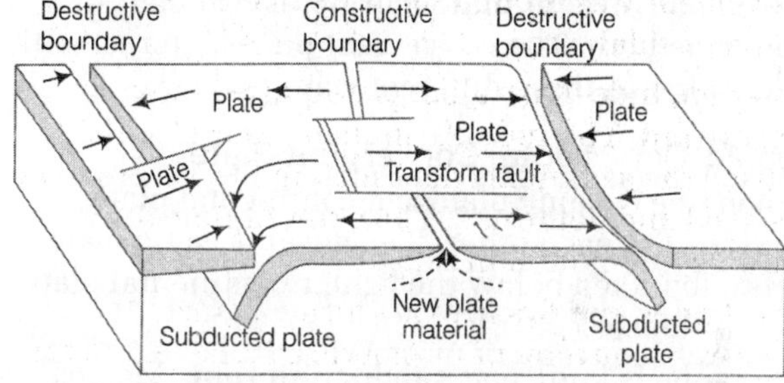

Types of Plate Boundaries

Constructive Plate Margin or Divergent Plate Boundary

- If a plate boundary is said to be Divergent Plate Boundary if two plates move away from each other.
- As a result of this movement, the molten lava from the asthenosphere comes out from the crack that develops between them.
- The surface continuously and after solidification forms a new crust. Hence, such plate boundaries are called **constructive plate margins.**
- The divergence brings in two results:
  (i) The formation of a new crust
  (ii) Formation of submarine mountains or ridges
- The Mid-Oceanic ridges are formed as a result of the divergence of oceanic plates.
- As a result of this divergence magma comes out through the gap formed due this movement.
- This magma solidifies to form mountains. These types of mountains are known as **Mid-Oceanic ridges.** e.g., Mid-Atlantic ridge, the East-Pacific ridge and the Chagos-Laccadives ridge in the Indian ocean.

- Such plate margins passing through the continents result in the formation of **rift valleys.** For example, the rift, which broke Arabia away from Africa and grafted it on to Asia, changed the appearance of both continents and opened up new seas-the Red sea and the Gulf of Aden.
- In these areas, earthquakes and volcanoes are frequent, even though of moderate to low intensity.

Destructive Plate Margin or Convergent Plate Boundary

- When two plates move towards each other, it is known as **Destructive Plate Margin.**
- As two plates collide with each other, the denser one is subducted below the lighter one. The region where the subduction takes place is called **Benioff zone** or **Subduction zone**. This plate margin is also known as **consuming plate margin.**
- The subducting plate is lost in the mantle. It is also called **convergent plate margin** as two plates converge here. The convergent plates interact with each other in three different ways :

Oceanic-Continental Convergent Plate

- When one oceanic plate and continental plate collide with each other, the denser oceanic plate gets subducted below the lighter continental plate as it is denser.
- This zone is known as **subduction zone**. Magma created in this zones comes out breaking the weak part of the crust and results in the formation of volcanoes.
- Trenches are seen associated with these types of margin. For example, the Western side of the American plate, where the Pacific plate is subducted below the American plate.
- It is the zone of active volcanoes.

Oceanic-Oceanic Convergent Plate

- When the margins of one oceanic plate collide with another, one plate descends under the adjacent plate and melt down to form the part of the mantle. This may lead to the formation of **Oceanic trenches.**
- Convergence of the **Pacific** and the **Philippines plates** explains the formation of island, festoons and chain of volcanoes in that region. e.g., Philippines and Indonesian islands.

Continent-Continent Convergent Plate

- Due to the collision of the plate margins where continents occur on both sides of the plate margin **fold mountains** are formed.
- The **Himalayan ranges** were formed this way. The collision of the Indian plate with the Eurasian plate has formed the Himalayas.

Conservative Margin or Parallel Boundary

- In some regions where two lithospheric plates slide past one another in opposite directions, noticeable changes may not occur. But these may cause fissures on the Earth's crust. These are called **zones of faulting.**
- **San Andreas Fault Zone** of California is an example for this. Shear margins are zones of frequent earthquakes of varied intensity. It marks the meeting place of two parallel plates, one carrying North America and the other carrying the Pacific ocean.

Movement of the Indian Plate

- The Indian plate includes Peninsular India and the Australian continental portions. The subduction zone along the Himalayas forms the Northern plate boundary in the form of continent-continent convergence.
- In the East, it extends through **Rakinyoma** mountains of Myanmar towards the island are along the **Java trench.** The Eastern margin is a spreading site lying to the East of Australia in the form of an Oceanic ridge in South-West Pacific.
- The Western margin follows **Kirthar** mountain of Pakistan. It further extends along the **Makrana** coast and joins the spreading site from the Red sea rift South-Eastward along the Chagos Archipelago.
- India was a large island situated off the Australian coast, in a vast ocean. The **Tethys sea** separated it from the Asian continent till about 225 million years ago.

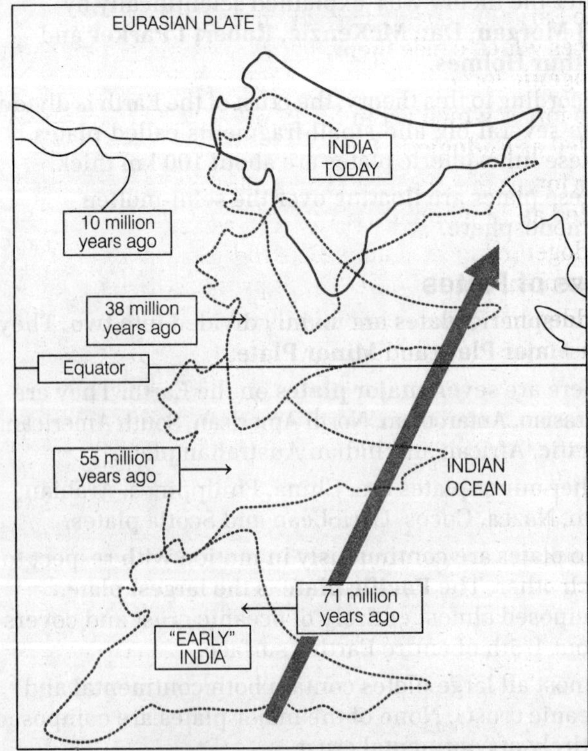

Movement of the Indian Plate

Geomorphic Processes

- The endogenic and exogenic forces causing physical stresses and chemical actions on Earth materials and bringing about changes in the configuration of the surface of the Earth are known as Geomorphic processes.
- **Diastrophism** and **volcanism** are endogenic geomorphic processes, whereas **weathering**, **mass** movement, **erosion** and **deposition** are exogenic geomorphic processes.
- Any exogenic element of nature (like water, ice, wind, etc.,) capable of acquiring and transporting Earth material can be called a **Geomorphic agent**. When these elements of nature become mobile due to gradients, they remove the material and transport them over slopes and deposit them at lower level.
- Gravity besides being a directional force activating all downslope movements of matter also causes stresses on the Earth's materials. Indirect gravitational stresses activate wave and tide induced currents and winds.
- Without gravity and gradients there would be no mobility and hence, no erosion, transportation and deposition are possible.

Earth Movements

- The lithosphere is broken into a number of plates known as the **Lithospheric plates.**
- The movements of these plates cause changes on the surface of the Earth.
- The Earth movements are divided on the basis of the forces which cause them. They are **Endogenic force and Exogenic force.**
- The forces which act in the interior of the Earth are called as **Endogenic forces.**
- The forces that work on the surface of the Earth are called as **Exogenic forces.**
- Endogenic forces sometimes produce sudden movements and at other times produce slow movements.
- Sudden movements like earthquakes and volcanoes cause mass destruction over the surface of the Earth.

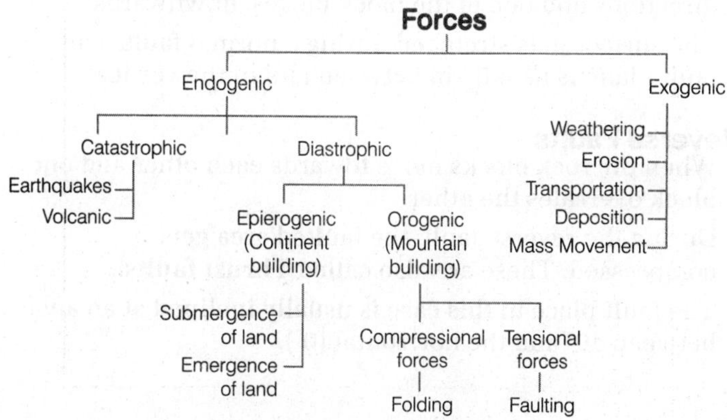

Endogenic Movements

- The endogenic movements are the types of Earth movements resulting from the works of endogenetic forces.
- Endogenetic forces give rise to land upliftment, subsidence folding, fracturing and volcanic eruptions.
- Endogenetic movements are classified into two major categories :

1. Catastrophic Movement

- Catastrophic movements are sudden movements caused by the action of sudden endogenetic forces which are originating from deep within the Earth.
- They cause sudden and rapid events at and below Earth's surface. These sudden events are termed as **destructive movements.** e.g., volcanic eruptions and earthquakes.

2. Diastrophic Movement

- The diastrophic movements are vertical and horizontal movements, which lead to production of primary landforms such as mountains, plateau, plains, lakes, big faults, etc.
- As these diastrophic forces operate very slowly and their effects become observable after thousands and millions of years. These forces are also termed as **Constructive movements.**
- The diastrophic processes are classified as **epeirogenic** and **orogenic.**

(i) Epeirogenic Movement

- Epeirogeny refers to regional uplift without marked deformation.
- **Epeirogeny** is a vertical movement mainly caused by radial forces, the forces that operate at right angles to the Earth's surface.
- Vertical movement is either uplift or subsidence. Upwarping and downwarping are the two results of the vertical movement.

(ii) Orogenic Movement

- Orogeny is the mountain-building that causes deformation in the crust and the Earth's surface.
- Orogenic movements are far more localised and occur in episodes, widely spaced in geologic time and are world-wide in extent.
- **Orogeny** is a horizontal Earth movement. Orogeny is tangential in that the movement is parallel to the Earth's surface.
- Both compression and tension, pushing in and pulling out, lead to horizontal movements.
- Folding, faulting and continental drift constitute horizontal movements.

Folding

- The bending of rock Strata due to compressional forces acting tangentially or horizontally towards a common point or plane from opposite direction is known as **Folding.**
- It results in the crumbling of strata into folds.
- Folds occur in a series of troughs and crests alternating with each other.
- The upfolds are termed **Anticline** and the downfolds are termed the **Syncline.**
- On the crest of the anticline, along the axis from where the limbs dip away, is a zone of tension and therefore, of weakness.
- The rivers flowing here breach the anticline and gradually erode the material and deepen the valley where the anticline is fully eroded the ridge is replaced by a valley. This is termed as **anticlinal valley**.
- It is an example of what is commonly known as **inversion** or **relief** or **topography**. So are the synclinal ridges.
- The sides of both these features correspond to very steep, scarp slopes. Synclines correspond to valleys.
- Between two anticlinal valleys the synclinal portion stands higher than the valleys. This is termed a **Synclinal ridge**.

Types of Folding

The different types of folding are as follows:

- **Monocline** It formed as a results when horizontally laid beds clip and then flatten out producing simple flexure.
- **Symmetrical Fold** A fold is said to symmetrical, if both the limbs are equal and inclined at the same angle.
- **Asymmetrical Fold** These types of folds are generated when one limb in a fold structure is steeper than the other.
- **Overturned Fold** When one limb occupies the normal position, while the other bends more than 90°. It is said to be an overturned fold.
- **Isoclinal Fold** Isoclinal fold are formed as a results of continued lateral compression upon an overturned fold. Here, both the limbs dip at equal angles in the same direction.
- **Recumbent Fold** These are fold lying down. These are formed as a result of continuation of pressure. The axial plane and both limbs of a fold lie roughly and horizontally.
- **Nappe** This is a result when the pressure exerted upon a recumbent fold is sufficiently great to cause it to be torn from its roots and to be thrust forward.

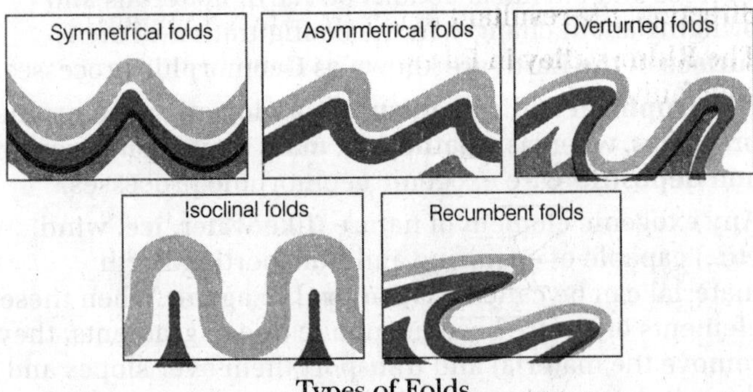

Types of Folds

Faulting

- Faults are formed when tensional forces play a significant role in it.
- Excessive stresses and strains produce **Fracturing** and are usually accompanied by **Dislocation.** This rapid movement results in the creation of horsts and rift valley or graben.
- **Horsts** and **grabens** are found in association with one another. The plane along which the rocks are displaced is called the **Fault plane.**
- When the rocks are compressed from two opposite directions, the rock blocks move forward or backward instead of upward or downward. The part above the fault plane is known as the hanging block and the one below it is termed the **foot block.**
- The surface of the hanging block on the fault plane is the hanging wall and that of the foot block on the fault plane is the footwall.
- Displacement is of two types, the vertical displacement termed throw and horizontal displacement termed as **heave.**
- The different types of faults are as follows:

Normal Faults

- When the rock blocks are displaced in opposite directions and one of the block moves downwards.
- The surface gets stretched during a normal fault. The fault plane is usually in between and in the vertical.

Reverse Faults

- When the rock blocks move towards each other and one block overrides the other.
- During the reverse fault, the faulted area gets compressed. These are also called **Thrust faults.**
- The fault place in this case is usually inclined at an angle between 40° and the horizontal (0°).

Step Faults

- When a series of faults occur in any area in such a way that the slopes of all the fault planes are in the same direction, the resultant faults are called **Step faults.**
- The **Rhine valley** in Europe is situated in such step faults.

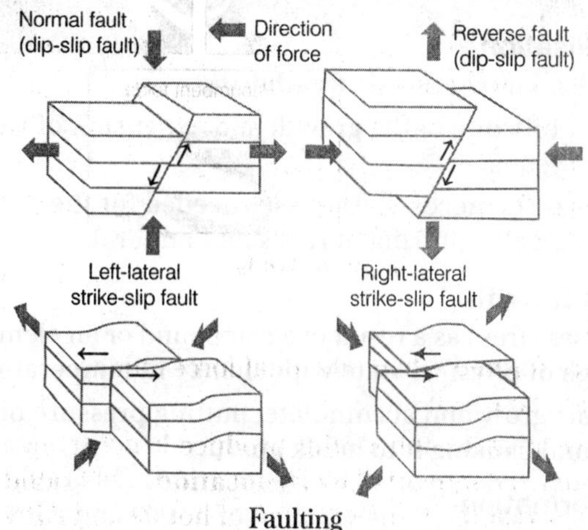

Faulting

Exogenic Movements

- The exogenic movements derive their energy from the atmosphere determined by the ultimate energy from the Sun and also the gradients created by tectonic factors.
- **Gravitational force** acts upon all Earth materials and tends to produce movement of matter in down slope direction. Stress is produced in a solid by pushing or pulling. This induces deformation.
- **Shear stresses** are forces acting along the faces of Earth materials that break rocks and other Earth materials and result in angular displacement or slippage.
- Earth materials are also subjected to **molecular stresses** caused by temperature changes, crystallisation and melting.
- Chemical processes lead to loosening of bonds between grains, dissolving of soluble minerals or cementing materials.
- The basic reason that leads to weathering, mass movements and erosion is development of stresses in the body of the earth's materials.

Denudation

- **Denudation** is a general term that covers all the exogenic geomorphic processes. The word **'denude'** means **'to strip off or to uncover'**.
- Weathering, mass wasting/movements, erosion and transportation are included in denudation.
- The denudational processes are weathering, mass movement, erosion, transportation and deposition.
- The exogenic geomorphic processes vary from one climatic region to other.
- Precipitation and temperature also exert influence indirectly on **Exogenic geomorphic processes.**

Gradation

- Gradation is the process by which the original irregularities of the Earth's surface are removed and a level surface is created.
- Gradation is accomplished by the twin process of **degradation** and **aggradation.**
- Degradation constitutes those processes by which material from a high relief feature is removed by exogenous or external processes and geomorphic agents. Degradation removes material from the high relief features thus reduce their elevation.
- Degradation comprises of three processes such as weathering, erosion and mass wasting.

Weathering

- Weathering is defined as mechanical disintegration and chemical decomposition of rocks through the actions of various elements of weather and climate.
- As very little or no motion of materials takes place in weathering, it is an ***in-situ*** or **on-site process.**
- Factors affecting weathering are rock, climatic, topographic and vegetative factors.
- Not only weathering processes but also the depth of the weathering differ from climate to climate.
- There are three types of weathering:
  (i) Chemical weathering
  (ii) Physical or mechanical weathering
  (iii) Biological weathering

Chemical Weathering

- A type of weathering processes *viz*; solution, carbonation, hydration, oxidation and reduction act on the rocks. They act to decompose, dissolve or reduce them to a fine state through chemical reactions by oxygen, surface and/or soil water and other acids.
- Water and air along with heat must be present to speed up all chemical reactions. Over and above the carbon dioxide present in the air, decomposition of plants and animals increases the quantity of carbon dioxide underground.

Solution

- Sometimes the nitrogen and carbon dioxide in the atmosphere dissolve in the rain water.
- When the rain falls on the rocks chemical action takes place between the minerals in the rocks and the rain water. As a result of this, there can be disintegration of the rocks.

- Solution is the most potent in limestone regions where rainwater attacks and carried away the dissolved calcium carbonate.
- Joints and cracks in the rock are quickly widened and whole systems of caves and passages are formed.

Oxidation

- When rocks with iron content come in contact with air, it is changed to iron oxide that crumbles easily and far more easily erodes than the original iron.
- It is thus removed, loosening the overall structure of the rocks and weakening them.

Hydrolysis

- Hydrolysis is the reaction between mineral ions and the ions of water.
- Since, the common silicate and alumino-silicate minerals have electrically charged crystal surfaces, hydrolysis is especially effective .

Reduction

- Reduction is caused by the addition of one or more electrons producing a more stable compound.
- It is simply the reverse of oxidation.

Hydration

- Hydration occurs when the chemical bonds of the mineral are changed as it interacts with water.
- Hydration also led to the decomposition reactions by expanding the crystal lattice offering more surface area for reaction.

Carbonation

- Carbonation is the mixing of water with carbon dioxide to make carbonic acid. The main factor affecting carbonation is climate.
- Climatic conditions control the rate of weathering that takes place by regulating the catalysts of moisture and temperature.

Physical Weathering

- Physical or mechanical weathering processes depend on some applied forces.
- The applied forces are:
  - (i) Gravitational forces such as overburden pressure, load and shearing stress.
  - (ii) Expansion forces due to temperature changes, crystal growth or animal activity.
  - (iii) Water pressures controlled by wetting and drying cycles.
- Physical weathering processes are caused by thermal expansion and pressure release. It causes damage to the rocks by repetition of contraction and expansion.

Abrasion

- It occurs due to the interaction of two rock surfaces causing mechanical wearing or grinding of their surfaces.
- Collision between rock surfaces results in erosion, which is followed by the transport of material by wind, water or ice.

Crystallisation

- It is also known as **salt weathering**.
- It is mainly due to the growth and expansion of various salts crystals.
- It causes the necessary stresses needed for the mechanical rupturing of rocks and minerals.

Crystal Growth

- It causes stress as a result of a compound or an element's change of physical state with change in temperature.
- crystals grow and accumulate, putting pressure on the rock and causing it to break apart.

Transformation

- During the day, the heat of the Sun causes the snow to melt and water fills the cracks in the rocks. At night, when the temperature drops to below freezing point, the water in these cracks freezes and becomes ice.
- The volume of ice is more than that of water. Thus, when the water freezes in the cracks, it exerts pressure on the lateral sides of the rock which eventually causes the rocks to break.

Insolation

- During the day, rocks expand due to the heat of the Sun. The different minerals in the rocks expand in different magnitudes.
- On these rocks, if suddenly rain falls or at night the temperature drops, the expanded areas contract.
- This type of changes in terms of expansion and contraction cause the rocks to disintegrate in due course.

Slaking

- The action of dissolved sodium sulphate can disintegrate rock in only twenty cycles of wetting and drying.
- Pressure release of rock can cause mechanical weathering due to unloading.

Biological Weathering

- Biological weathering is the removal of minerals and ions and physical changes due to growth or movement of organisms.
- **Burrowing and wedging** by organisms like earthworms, termites, rodents etc., help in exposing the new surfaces to chemical attack and assists in the penetration of moisture and air.

- Human beings by disturbing vegetation, ploughing and cultivating soils, also help in mixing and creating new contacts between air, water and minerals in the Earth materials.
- Decaying plant and animal matter help in the production of humus, carbonic and other acids, which enhance decay and solubility of some elements.
- Plant roots exert a tremendous pressure on the Earth materials mechanically breaking them apart.

Exfoliation

- Exfoliation is a result but not a process.
- Exfoliation is the flaking off of more or less curved sheets of shells from over rocks or bedrock results in smooth and rounded surfaces.
- Exfoliation can occur due to expansion and contraction induced by temperature changes. **Exfoliation domes** and **tors** result due to unloading and thermal expansion respectively.

Erosion

- Erosion is the process of removal of rock **debris** from one place to another.
- When massive rocks break into smaller fragments through weathering and any other process, erosional geomorphic agents remove and transport it to other places according to the dynamics of each of the agents.
- The process of **abrasion** by rock debris carried by these geomorphic agents aids greatly in erosion.
- The landscape is worn down by the erosion, relief degrades. Weathering, mass-wasting and erosion are degradational processes.
- Erosion is largely responsible for continuous changes on the Earth's surface.
- The denudational processes like erosion and transportation are controlled by kinetic energy.
- The erosion and transportation of the Earth materials is brought about by wind, running water, glaciers are controlled by climatic conditions.
- The work of the other two agents of erosion-waves and groundwater is not controlled by climate.

Deposition

- The erosional agents lose their velocity and hence, energy on gentler slopes and the materials carried by them start to settle themselves.
- The coarser materials get deposited first and finer ones later. By the process of deposition, depressions get filled up.
- The same erosional agents viz., running water, glaciers, wind, waves and groundwater act as aggradational or depositional agents also.

Mass Movement

- Mass movement is transferring the mass of rock debris down the slopes under the direct influence of gravity.
- The movements of mass may range from slow to rapid, affecting shallow to deep columns of materials and include **creep**, **flow**, **slide** and **fall**.
- Gravity exerts force on all matter, both bedrock and the products of weathering. Mass movements are very active over weathered slopes rather than over unweathered materials.
- Mass movements are aided by gravity and no **geomorphic agent** like running water, glaciers, wind, waves and currents participate in the process of mass movements.
- The mass movements do not come under erosion though the materials shifts from one place to another.
- Materials over the **slopes** have their own resistance to disturbing forces.
- Weak unconsolidated materials, thinly bedded rocks, faults, steeply dipping beds, vertical cliffs or steep slopes, abundant precipitation and torrential rains and scarcity of vegetation etc., favour mass movements.
- The activities that precede mass movements are:
  - Removal of support from below to materials above through natural or artificial means.
  - Increase in gradient and height of slopes.
  - Overloading through addition of materials naturally or by artificial filling overloading due to heavy rainfall, saturation and lubrication of slope materials.
  - Removal of material or load from over the original slope surfaces.
  - Occurrence of earthquakes, explosions or machinery.
  - Excessive natural seepage.
  - Heavy drawdown of water from lakes, reservoirs and rivers leading to slow outflow of water from under the slopes or river banks.
  - Indiscriminate removal of natural vegetation.
- The three forms of movements are **heave**, **flow** and **slide**.

Landslides

- These are relatively rapid and perceptible movements. The materials involved in landslides are relatively dry.
- Depending upon the type of movement of materials, following types are identified :
  - **Slump** It is the slipping of one or several units of rock debris with a backward rotation with respect to the slope over which the movement takes place.

- **Debris Slide** rapid rolling or sliding of Earth debris without backward rotation of mass is known as debris slide.
- **Debris Fall** It is nearly a free fall of Earth debris from a vertical or overhanging face.
- **Rockslide** Sliding of individual rock masses down bedding, joint or fault surfaces is rockslide. Over steep slopes, rock sliding is very fast and destructive. Slides occur as planar failures along discontinuities like bedding planes that dip steeply.
- **Rock Fall** It is free falling of rock blocks over any steep slope keeping itself away from the slope. Rock falls occur from the superficial layers of the rock face, an occurrence that distinguishes it from rockslide which affects materials up to a substantial depth.

Landforms

- The erosion and deposition cause changes on the surface of the Earth.
- Small to medium tracts or parcels of the Earth's surface are called **landforms**. Several related landforms together make up landscapes.
- Each landform has its own physical shape, size, materials and is a result of the action of certain geomorphic processes and agents.
- Landforms once formed may change in their shape, size and nature slowly or fast due to continued action of geomorphic processes and agents.
- Landforms are classified on the basis of the process of their origin.

Fluvial Landforms

- Fluvial landforms are carved out or build up by the running water.
- There are two components of running water :
  1. **Sheet Flow** Overland flow on land surface as a sheet.
  2. **Linear Flow** Overland flow as streams and rivers.
- Depending upon irregularities of the land surface, the overland flow may concentrate into narrow to wide paths.
- Because of the sheer friction of the column of flowing water, materials are removed from the land surface in the direction of flow.
- Gradually small and narrow rills will form. These rills will gradually develop into long and wide gullies; the gullies will further deepen, widen, lengthen and unite.
- Gradually, the valley sides are reduced to lower and lower slopes.
- The divides between drainage basins are likewise lowered until, they are almost completely flattened leaving finally, a lowland of faint relief with some low resistant remnants called **monadnocks**.
- This type of plain forming as a result of stream erosion is called a **Peneplain**.
- The different stages of landscape developing by the action of running water are:

Youth

- In the early stages, down-cutting dominates.
- Streams are with poor integration and flow over original slopes showing shallow V-shaped valleys.
- Streams divide are broad and flat, with marshes, swamp and lakes.
- Meanders developed during this stage may eventually entrench themselves into the uplands.
- Waterfalls and rapids may exist where local hard rock bodies are exposed.

Mature

- In the middle stages, streams cut their beds slower and lateral erosion of valley sides becomes severe.
- Gradually, the valley sides are reduced to lower and lower slopes.
- During this stage, valleys are still V-shaped but deep; trunk streams are broad enough to have wider floodplains within which streams may flow in meanders confined within the valley.
- The flat and broad inter-stream areas, swamps and marshes of youth disappear and the stream divides turn sharp. Waterfalls and rapids disappear.

Old

- Smaller tributaries during old age are few with gentle gradients. Streams meander freely over vast floodplains showing natural levees, oxbow lakes, etc. Divides are broad and flat with lakes, swamps and marshes.
- Most of the landscape is at or slightly above sea level.

Erosional Landforms of River

Some of erosional landforms of river are as follows :

Valleys

- Valleys start as small and narrow rills; the rills will gradually develop into long and wide gullies; the gullies will further deepen, widen and lengthen to give rise to valleys.
- Depending upon dimensions and shape, many types of valleys like V-shaped valley, gorge, canyon, etc., can be recognised.

V-Shaped Valleys

- Deepening on rivers occurs through intense erosion resulting from an increase in the velocity of water flow.
- The valleys take a distinct shape as a result of the intensity of erosion along the river bed. Such valleys are called **V-shaped valleys**.

Gorge

- A gorge is a deep valley with very steep to straight sides. Gorges form in hard rocks.

Canyon

- It is characterised by steep steplike side slopes and may be as deep as a gorge. A gorge is almost equal in width at its top as well as its bottom.
- In contrast, a canyon is wider at its top than at its bottom. Canyons commonly form in horizontal bedded sedimentary rocks.

Waterfalls

- Waterfalls are generally formed at the upper course of rivers as a result of erosion.
- Soft rocks are easily eroded in the valleys, where soft and hard rocks are found intermingled. This results in the formation of waterfalls.

Potholes

- More or less circular depressions formed over the rocky beds of hill-streams are called **potholes**. It is formed because of stream erosion aided by the abrasion of rock fragments.
- When pebbles and boulders get collected in these depressions, it gets rotated by flowing water and consequently the depressions grow in dimensions.
- A series of such depressions eventually join and the stream valley gets deepened.

Plunge Pools

- At the foot of waterfalls large potholes of quite deep and wide are formed because of the sheer impact of water and rotation of boulders.
- Such large and deep holes at the base of waterfalls are called **plunge pools**.

Incised or Entrenched Meanders

- Due to active lateral erosion, streams flowing over gentle slopes, develop sinuous or meandering courses. It is common to find meandering courses over.
- Floodplains and delta plains where stream gradients are very gentle.
- But very deep and wide meanders can also be found cut in hard rocks. Such meanders are called incised or entrenched meanders.

River Terraces

- River terraces are surfaces marking old valley floor or floodplain levels.
- River terraces are basically products of erosion as they result due to vertical erosion by the stream into its own depositional floodplain.
- There can be a number of such terraces at different heights indicating former river bed levels.
- The river terraces may occur at the same elevation on either side of the rivers in which case they are called **Paired terraces**.

Depositional Landforms of River

Some of depositional landforms of river are as follows :

Alluvial Fans

- Alluvial fans are formed when streams flowing from higher levels break into foot slope plains of low gradient.
- The very coarse load carried by streams flowing over mountain slopes becomes too heavy for the streams to be carried over gentler gradients.
- It gets dumped and spread as a broad low to high cone shaped deposit called **Alluvial fan**.
- Alluvial fans in humid areas show normally low cones with gentle slope from head to toe and they appear as high cones with steep slope in arid and semi-arid climates.

Deltas

- The load carried by the rivers is dumped and spread into the sea. If this load is not carried away far into the sea or distributed along the coast, it spreads and accumulates as a low cone called **Delta**.
- The deposits making up deltas are very well sorted with clear stratification. The coarsest materials settle out first and the finer fractions like silts and clays are carried out into the sea.
- As the delta grows, the river distributaries continue to increase in length and delta continues to build up into the sea. On the basis of the shape, following are various types of Deltas :
  1. **Arcuate Delta** A bowed or curved delta with the convex margin facing the body of water. It is also known as fan-shaped delta. Example, River Nile delta in Egypt and Ganga delta in India.
  2. **Estuarine Delta** It is formed at the mouth of submerged rivers depositing down the sides of the estuary. Example, Seine river of France.
  3. **Birds Foot Delta** They are formed due to deposition of finer materials by river water. Deposited alluvial material divides the river into smaller distributaries. Such delta is also called as finger delta. Example, Mississippi river delta, the USA.
  4. **Lacustrine Delta** It is formed when a river flows into a lake. Example, Lough Laune river delta, Ireland.
  5. **Truncated Delta** Sea waves and ocean currents modify and even destroy deltas deposited by the river through their erosional work. Thus, eroded and dissected deltas are called truncated deltas.

6. **Abandoned Delta** When the river shifts its mouth, the delta already made is left abandoned. Such a delta is called abandoned delta. Example, yellow river delta, China and the Western part of Ganga delta made by Hoogly river, India.
7. **Cuspate Delta** It is a tooth shaped delta formed when a single distributary flow through and deposits its boad in either side.

Floodplains

- Floodplain is a major landform of river deposition. Normally, fine sized materials like sand, silt and clay are carried by relatively slow-moving waters in gentler channels usually found in the plains.
- They get deposited over the bed and when the waters spill over the banks during flooding above the bed. A river bed made of river deposits is the active floodplain.
- The floodplain above the bank is an inactive floodplain. Inactive floodplain above the banks basically contains two types of deposits such as flood deposits and channel deposits.
- The floodplains in a delta are called **delta plains.**

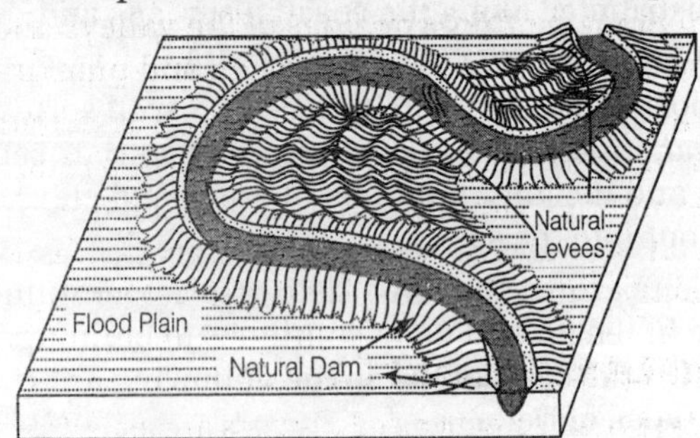

Flood Plains and Natural Levees

Natural Levees

- Natural levees are found along the banks of large rivers.
- They are low, linear and parallel ridges of coarse deposits along the banks of rivers, quite often cut into individual mounds.

Point Bars

- Point bars also known as **meander bars.**
- They are found on the concave side of meanders of large rivers. They are almost uniform in profile and in width and contain mixed sizes of sediments.

Meanders

- The river flowing through comparatively gentle slopes takes deviation when the sediments or rock forms create obstruction to the flow.
- The sinuous curves formed along the river course are called **meanders.**
- Meander is not a landform but is only a type of channel pattern. The factors affecting the formation of meander are:
  (i) Propensity of water flowing over very gentle gradients to work laterally on the banks.
  (ii) Unconsolidated nature of alluvial deposits making up the banks with many irregularities which can be used by water exerting pressure laterally.
  (iii) Coriolis force acting on the fluid water deflecting it like it deflects the wind.

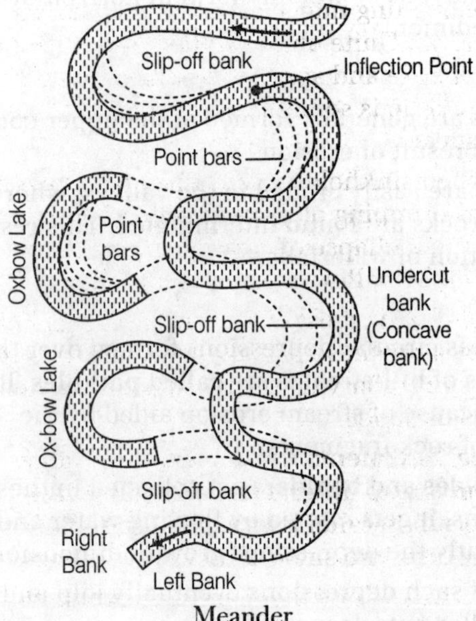

Meander

- When the gradient of the channel becomes extremely low, water flows leisurely and starts working laterally.
- Slight irregularities along the banks slowly get transformed into a small curvature in the banks; the curvature deepens due to deposition on the inside of the curve and erosion along the bank on the outside.
- If there is no deposition and no erosion or undercutting, the tendency to meander is reduced.
- The concave bank is known as **cut-off bank,** which shows up as a steep scarp and the convex bank present a long, gentle profile. As meanders grow into deep loops, the same may get cut-off due to erosion at the inflection points and are left as Oxbow lakes.

Groundwater

- In rocks like limestones or dolomites rich in calcium carbonate, the surface water as well as groundwater through the chemical process of solution and precipitation deposition develop varieties of landforms.
- These two processes of **solution** and precipitation are active in **limestone** or dolomite.
- Limestone or dolomitic region showing typical landforms produced by the action of groundwater through the processes of solution and deposition is called **Karst topography.**

Erosional Landforms of Groundwater

- **Swallow Holes** Small to medium sized round to sub-rounded shallow depression called **swallow holes** form on the surface of limestone through solution.
- **Sinkholes** A sinkhole is an opening more or less circular at the top and funnel-shaped towards the bottom.
- **Doline** If the bottom of a sinkhole forms the roof of a void or cave underground, it might collapse leaving a large hole opening into a cave or a void called collapse sinks. Quite often, sinkholes are covered up with soil mantle and appear as shallow water pools. The term doline is sometimes used to refer to the collapse sinks.
- **Uvalas** When sinkholes and dolines join together because of slumping of materials along their margins or due to roof collapse of caves, long, narrow to wide trenches called valley sinks or uvalas form.
- **Lapies** Gradually, most of the surface of the limestone is eaten away by these pits and trenches, leaving it extremely irregular with a maze of points, grooves and ridges or lapies.
- **Limestone Pavements** Especially, these ridges or lapies form due to differential solution activity along parallel to sub-parallel joints. The lapies field may eventually turn into smooth limestone pavements.
- **Caves** In areas, where there are alternating beds of rocks with limestone or dolomite in between or in areas where limestone are dense, massive and occurring as thick beds, cave formation is prominent. Water percolates down either through the materials or through cracks and joints and moves horizontally along bedding planes. The limestone dissolved and long and narrow to wide gaps called caves were formed.
- **Tunnels** Caves normally have an opening through which cave streams are discharged. Caves having openings at both the ends are called tunnels.

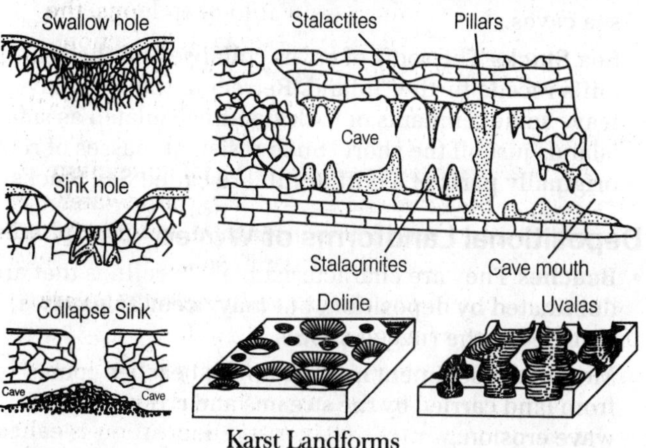

Karst Landforms

Depositional Landforms of Groundwater

- **Stalactites** It is an icicle-shaped formation that hangs from the ceiling of a cave having different diameters. Normally, they are broad at their bases and taper towards the free ends showing up in a variety of forms.
- **Stalagmites** They rise up from the floor of the caves. In fact, stalagmites form due to dripping water from the surface or through the thin pipe of the stalactite, immediately below it.

  Stalagmites may take the shape of a column, a disc, with either a smooth, rounded bulging end or a miniature crater like depression.
- **Pillars** The stalagmite and stalactites eventually fuse to give rise to columns and pillars of different diameters.

Glaciers

- Masses of ice moving as sheets over the land or as linear flows down the slopes of mountains in broad trough-like valleys are called glaciers. Glaciers move basically because of the **force of gravity**.
- Erosion by glaciers is tremendous because of friction caused by sheer weight of the ice.
- The material plucked from the land by glaciers get dragged along the floors or sides of the valleys and cause great damage through abrasion and plucking.
- As glaciers continue to move, debris gets removed and divides get lowered. Eventually, the slope is reduced to such an extent that glaciers will stop moving leaving only a mass of low hills and vast outwash plains along with other depositional features.

Erosional Landforms of Glaciers

Some of erosional landforms of glaciers are as follows :

Cirque

- The cirques quite often are found at the heads of glacial valleys. The accumulated ice cuts these cirques while moving down the mountain tops.
- They are deep, long and wide troughs or basins with very steep concave to vertically drop high walls at its head as well as sides.
- A lake of water can be seen quite often within the cirques after the glacier disappears. Such lakes are called cirque or tarn lakes.

Horns and Serrated Ridges

- If three or more radiating glaciers cut headward until their cirques meet, high, sharp pointed and steep sided peaks called **horns form**.
- The divides between cirque side walls or headwalls get narrow because of progressive erosion. They turn into serrated or saw-toothed ridges sometimes referred to as aretes with very sharp crests and a zig-zag outline.

Glacial Valleys/Troughs

- Glaciated valleys are trough-like and U-shaped with broad floors and relatively smooth and steep sides.
- The valleys may contain littered debris or debris shaped as moraines with swampy appearance. There may be lakes gouged out of rocky floor or formed by debris within the valleys.
- There can be hanging valleys at an elevation on one or both sides of the main glacial valley.
- **Fjords** are very deep glacial troughs filled with sea water and making up shorelines.

Depositional Landforms of Glaciers

- The unassorted coarse and fine debris dropped by the melting glaciers is called **glacial till**.
- Most of the rock fragments in the till are angular to sub-angular in form. The glacio-fluvial deposits are called outwash deposits. Unlike till deposits, the outwash deposits are roughly stratified and assorted.

Moraines

They are long ridges of deposits of glacial till. These are :

- **Terminal Moraines** They are long ridges of debris deposited at the end of the glaciers.
- **Lateral Moraines** These form along the sides parallel to the glacial valleys. The lateral moraines may join a terminal moraine forming a horse-shoe shaped ridge.
- **Ground Moraines** Many valley glaciers retreating rapidly leave an irregular sheet of till over their valley floors. Such deposits varying greatly in thickness and in surface topography are called Ground moraines.
- **Medial Moraines** The moraine in the centre of the glacial valley flanked by lateral moraines is called Medial moraine. They are imperfectly formed as compared to lateral moraines.

Eskers

- When glaciers melt in summer, the water accumulate beneath the glacier and flow like streams in a channel beneath the ice. Such streams flow over the ground with ice forming its banks.
- Very coarse materials like boulders and blocks along with some minor fractions of rock debris carried into this stream settle in the valley of ice beneath the glacier and after the ice melts can be found as a sinuous ridge called Esker.

Outwash Plains

- The plains at the foot of the glacial mountains or beyond the limits of continental ice sheets are covered with **glacio-fluvial deposits**. These deposits are in the form of broad flat alluvial fans, which may join to form outwash plains of gravel, silt, sand and clay.

Drumlins

- Drumlins are smooth oval shaped ridge-like features composed mainly of glacial till with some masses of gravel and sand.
- The long axes of drumlins are parallel to the direction of ice movement.
- The end of the drumlins facing the glacier called the **stoss.** It is blunter and steeper than the other end called Tail.
- The drumlins form due to dumping of rock debris beneath heavily loaded ice through fissures in the glacier.

Waves and Currents

- The coastal landforms depend upon:
  (i) The configuration of land and sea floor.
  (ii) Whether the coast is advancing (emerging) seaward or retreating (submerging) landward.
- Two types of coasts are considered to explain the concept of evolution of coastal landforms. They are:
  (i) High, rocky coasts (submerged coasts).
  (ii) Low, smooth and gently sloping sedimentary coasts (emerged coasts).

Erosional Landforms of Waves

- **Cliffs** Wave-cut cliffs and terraces are two forms usually found where erosion is the dominant shore process. Almost all sea cliffs are steep and may range from a few meter to more than 30 m.
- **Wavecut Terrace** At the foot of such cliffs there may be a flat or gently sloping platform covered by rock debris derived from the sea cliff behind. Such platforms occurring at elevations above the average height of waves is called a Wavecut terrace.
- **Sea Caves** The lashing of waves against the base of the cliff and the rock debris that gets smashed against the cliff along with lashing waves create hollows and these hollows get widened and deepened to form sea caves.
- **Sea Stacks** The roofs of caves collapse and the sea cliffs recede further inland. Retreat of the cliff may leave some remnants of rock standing isolated as small islands just off the shore. Such resistant masses of rock, originally parts of a cliff or hill are called Sea Stacks.

Depositional Landforms of Waves

- **Beaches** They are characteristic of shorelines that are dominated by deposition, but may occur as patches along even the rugged shores.

  Most of the sediment making up the beaches comes from land carried by the streams and rivers or from wave erosion.

- **Bar** A ridge of sand and shingle formed in the sea in the off-shore zone lying approximately parallel to the coast is called an **off-shore bar.**
- **Barrier bar** An off-shore bar which is exposed due to further addition of sand is termed a barrier bar. The off-shore bars and barriers commonly form across the mouth of a river or at the entrance of a bay.
- **Spits** Sometimes such barrier bars get keyed up to one end of the bay when they are called spits. Spits may also develop attached to headlands/hills.
- **Lagoon** The barriers, bars and spits at the mouth of the bay gradually extend leaving only a small opening of the bay into the sea and the bay will eventually develop into a lagoon. The lagoons get filled up gradually by sediment coming from the land or from the beach itself and a broad and wide coastal plain may develop replacing a lagoon.

Winds

- Wind is the two dominant agent in hot deserts. The heated floors of the desert heat up the air directly above them.
- It result in upward movements in the hot lighter air with turbulence and any obstructions in its path sets up eddies, whirlwinds, updrafts and downdrafts.
- The wind action creates a number of interesting erosional and depositional features in the deserts.

Erosional Landforms of Wind

- **Pediments** These are gently inclined rocky floors close to the mountains at their foot with or without a thin cover of debris. Such rocky floors form through the erosion of the mountain front through a combination of lateral erosion by streams and sheet flooding.

  Once, pediments are formed with a steep wash slope followed by a cliff or free face above it, the steep wash slope and free face retreat backwards. This method of erosion is termed as parallel retreat of slopes through back wasting.
- **Pediplains** The high relief in desert areas is reduced to low featureless plains called pediplains.
- **Inselberg** Through parallel retreat of slopes, the pediments extend backwards at the expense of the mountain front and gradually, the mountain gets reduced leaving an inselberg which is a remnant of the mountain.
- **Playas** They are shallow lakes where water is retained only for short duration due to evaporation are called playas. Often the playas contain good deposition of salts. The playa plain covered up by salts is called **Alkali flats.**
- **Deflation Hollows** Weathered mantle from over the rocks or bare soil, gets blown out by persistent movement of wind currents in one direction. This process may create shallow depressions called deflation hollows.
- **Caves** The rock faces suffer impact and abrasion of wind-borne sand and first shallow depressions called blowouts are created and some of the blowouts become deeper and wider fit to be called caves.
- **Mushroom** Many rock-outcrops in the deserts are easily worn out quickly leaving some remnants of resistant rocks polished beautifully in the shape of mushroom with a slender stalk and a broad and rounded pear-shaped cap above.

  Sometimes, the top surface is broad like a table top and quite often, the remnants stand out like pedestals.

Depositional Landforms of Wind

Depositional landforms of wind are as follows :

- **Sand Dunes** A sand dune is a mound of sand formed by the wind usually along the beach or in a desert. Sand dunes are hills of sand built up and shaped by the wind.
- **Barchans** They are crescent shaped dunes with the points or wings directed away from wind direction i.e., downwind.

  They form where the wind direction is constant and moderate and where the original surface over, which sand is moving is almost uniform.
- **Parabolic Dunes** They are formed when sandy surfaces are partially covered with vegetation. That means parabolic dunes are reversed barchans with wind direction being the same.
- **Seif Dune** Seif is similar to barchan with only one wing or point. This happens when there is shift in wind conditions. The lone wings of seifs can grow very long and high.
- **Longitudinal Dunes** These dunes are formed when supply of sand is poor and wind direction is constant. They appear as long ridges of considerable length but low in height.

- **Transverse Dunes** They are aligned perpendicular to wind direction. These dunes form when the wind direction is constant and the source of sand is an elongated feature at right angles to the wind direction.

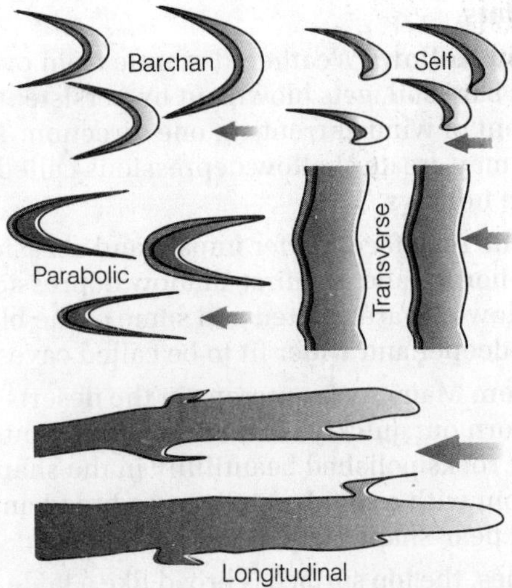

Various types of sand dunes arraws indicate wind direction

Mountains

Those landforms which have a height of 900 m or more above sea level are called Mountains.
They are divided into four on the basis of their origin.
They are:

1. Fold Mountains
2. Block Mountains
3. Residual Mountains
4. Volcanic Mountains

Fold Mountains

- Fold mountains are higher when compared to other mountains. Due to the collision of the plate margins where continents occur on both sides of the plate margin, fold mountains are formed.
- Fold mountains are formed, when a thickly bedded sedimentary layer is subjected to horizontal compressional forces for millions of years.
- The sediments get bent into up and down-folds. This leads to the formation of **anticlines and synclines.**
- These mountains are characterised by a more developed system of anticlines and synclines wherein folds are arranged in a wave-like pattern.

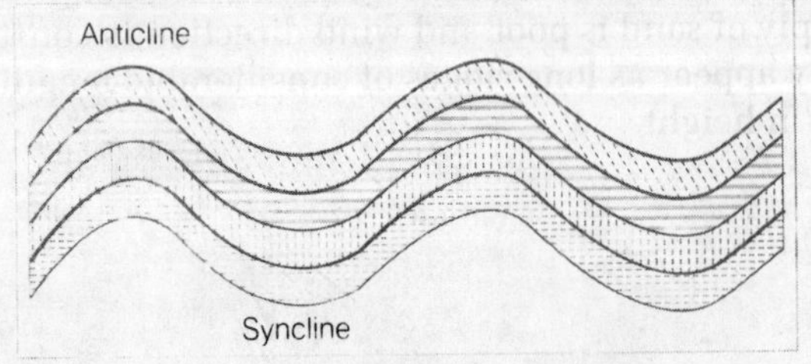

Fold Mountains

Types of Fold Mountains

Types of fold mountains based on the period of their evolution fold mountains are:

- **Young Fold Mountains** The Himalayas, Alps, Rockies, Andes, Atlas and Southern Alps. The highest peak in the world is Mt. Everest, it is part of the Himalayan mountains, one of the youngest fold mountains of the world.
- **Mature Fold Mountains** The Pennines, Appalachians and Cape range of South Africa were formed during the carboniferous age.
- **Old Fold Mountain** The high mountain of Scotland and Norway, Sayan and Stanovai mountains of Russia and Aravalli and Mahadeo mountain of India.

Block Mountains

- The block mountains are formed as a result of uplift of landforms due to faulting.
- The block mountain or horst represents the upstanding part of the ground between two faults or on either side of a Rift valley or graben.
- These mountains have flat tops and steep sides. e.g., Black Forest in Germany, Vosges in France.

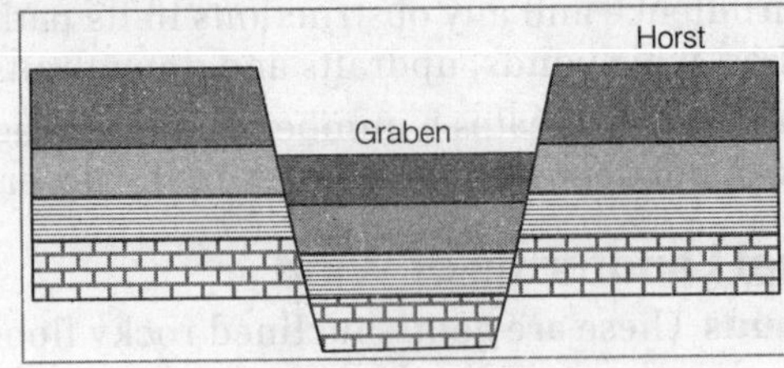

Block Mountains

Major Mountain Ranges

Ranges	Locations	Length (in km) (Approx)
Andes	South America	7,200
Rockies	North America	4,800
Great Dividing Range	East Australia	3,500
Himalayas	India, Pakistan, Nepal	2,400
Atlas	North-West Africa	1,930
Western Ghats	Western India	1,610
Caucasus	Europe	1,200
Alaska	USA	1,130
Alps	Europe	1,050

Residual Mountains

- Due to the different weathering processes of prolonged duration, the rocks that are not very resistant get disintegrated and only those resistant parts remain.

- These mountains are called residual mountains. e.g., the Aravalli ranges and Nilgiris in India.

Volcanic Mountains

- The continuous deposition of lava over Earth's surface leads to formation of conical peaks.
- It is called **volcanic peak**. e.g., Mount Mauna Kea, Hawaii in Pacific ocean.

Plateaus

- Comparatively flat areas, but higher than the plains and water bodies surround it are called Plateaus. When compared to other areas, these places look like tables.
- Steep slopes and flat tops are the characteristic features of this land.
- They can be divided into three on the basis of the location where they are situated:
  - **Intermontane Plateaus** Plateaus that are completely surrounded or partially surrounded by mountains. e.g., Tibetan plateau.
  - **Piedmont Plateaus** Plateaus that are found at the foot of a range of mountains. e.g., Colorado plateau.
  - **Continental Plateaus** When compared to the surrounding plains, some plateaus are found to be higher. e.g., East African plateau.
  - **Dome Shaped Plateau** These are formed when the landmass is uplifted in such a manner that the middle portion is raised and rounded. e.g., Chhota Nagpur plateau in India.
  - **Volcanic Plateau** Formed due to accumulation of a thick layer of basaltic lavas. Fissure eruption of volcanoes is the main cause for the formation of these plateaus. e.g., Deccan Lava plateau.

Famous Plateaus of the World

Plateaus	Situation
Tibetan Plateau	Between Himalayas and Kunlun Mountains
Deccan Plateau	Peninsular India
Arabian Plateau	South-West Asia
Plateau of Brazil	Central-Eastern South America
Plateau of Columbia	North-West North America
Plateau of Bolivia	Andes Mountains
Great Basin Plateau	South of Columbia Plateau, USA
Colorado Plateau	South of Great Basin Plateau, USA

Plains

- Places that are not so rugged and are not much higher than sea level are called Plains.
- Based on their formation, they have been divided into three types such as **structural plains**, **erosional plains** and **depositional plains**.

Structural Plains

- Due to endogenic forces, an area can be raised or lowered. These actions are called **uplift** and **subsidence** respectively.
- These actions cause plains to be formed. They are called Structural Plains.

Erosional Plains

- Some areas on the Earth's surface which originally were rugged are leveled due to friction or plantation. This is possible due to the action of several agents.
- The plains that are formed thus are called Erosional Plains. Various erosional plains are:
  - **Riverine Erosion Plains** These are in the form of peneplains which are characterised by residual hills known as **Monadnocks**.
  - **Glaciated Plains** It forms ice-scoured plain, e.g. ice scoured plains of North-Western Europe and North America.
  - **Wind Eroded Plains** In arid and semi-arid regions, wind deflation blows desert materials away, lowering the level of land and forming extensive plains. e.g., the Reg of North Africa.

Depositional Plains

Running water, winds, glaciers, sea waves and other external agents carry rock materials from the hills to depressions on the surface of the Earth or to the water bodies.

In course of time these deposits lead to the formation of plains called the Depositional plain.

Various depositional plains are:

- **Riverine Alluvial Plains** These plains are formed by the deposition of sediments brought down by rivers. It includes piedmont alluvial plains, flood plains and delta plains.
- **Glacial Plains** These plains are formed by the deposition of unsorted sands and gravels brought down by glaciers. Glacial plains are divided into three types on the basis of composition and structure; Till plains, Morainic plains and Outwash plains.

- **Loess Plains** These plains are formed due to the deposition of sand and clay brought by the winds. These plains lack in layers but are highly porous. The soil of these plains is very fertile e.g., the Great plain of Northern China.
- **Lacustrine Plains** These are the plains formed by lakes filled up by the sediments brought down by the rivers. The valley of Kashmir is an example of this type.

Islands

- An island is any piece of land that is surrounded by water on all sides.
- A grouping of geographically or geologically related islands is called an **archipelago**.

Types of Islands

The various types of islands are named according to the way they were formed. They are as explained below:

- **Continental Islands** It is simply an island that rests on the continental shelf. Because of this, these islands are always quite close to a continent. Also, the water level around a continental island is very shallow, typically less than 600 feet.
- **Newfoundland** and **Labrador** provinces of Canada are actually Continental Islands. Great Britain is the largest continental island in Europe.
- **Volcanic Islands** They are formed when volcanoes deep in the ocean rise above the water's surface, e.g., St. Helena in the Atlantic ocean.
- **Coral Islands** A coral island is an island that forms a ring and partially or totally encloses a shallow body of water or lagoon. Lakshadweep island in the Indian ocean is the best example of coral islands.
- **Alluvial Islands** They are formed by the outward flow of water depositing silt and gravel at the mouth of a river. New Moore island at the mouth of Ganga river in West Bengal is known as alluvial island.
- **Barrier islands** which are formed by waves depositing sand on the shallow ocean bottom as they crash on the shoreline.
- **Tectonic Islands** They are formed by the result of tectonic activity. By the tectonic movement and associated volcanism, long island arcs (archipelagoes) are formed. Indonesia, Philippines, Japan groups of islands are the best example of it.

Extra Facts From
Tamil Nadu Board and NIOS

- Russia drilled Kola Superdeep borehole between 1970 and 1994. The deepest part of it, named SG-3 (Star Gate), extends 12.3 km into the Earth.
- The term lithosphere was introduced by **Joseph Barrel,** an American Geologist.
- The density of the crust is less than 2.7 g/cm^3.The density of the mantle is 3.9 g/cm^3. The density of core is 13.0 g/cm^3 and its temperature is about 5500°C to 6000°C.
- Narrow oceans represent young divergent boundaries and wide oceans are indications of old ocean basins. Ocean ridges are the boundaries between plates of the lithosphere.
- A subduction zone is a boundary, where one plate sinks under the other plate. It was first identified by **Kiyoo Wadati and Benioff**. The area in the subduction zone where most earthquakes occur is known as the **Benioff zone**.
- The lithosphere is neither destroyed nor created by the transform plate boundary.
- The plate movements are caused by the convection cells. Convection cell is the circulation of the molten materials caused by the heat derived from the core. When the molten materials (magma) circulate in different directions, they push or pull the plates in different directions.
- The greatest volcanic explosion known to humans is perhaps **Mt. Krakatau** in August, 1883. The explosion could be heard in Australia, almost 4,000 km away. Cotopaxi in Ecuador is the world's highest active volcano.
- Circum-Pacific region, popularly termed the **Pacific Ring of Fire**, has the greatest concentration of active volcanoes.
- There are no volcanoes in the Himalayan region of India. However, Barren island, lying 135 km North-East of Port Blair became active in 1991 and 1995.
- Granite is less dense and is lighter in colour than basalt rocks.
- The Karnataka plateau is spotted with dome hills of granite rocks. Most of these, now exfoliated, are examples of **Laccoliths**. The accumulation of rock debris at the base of a steep slope is called **Talus**.
- A mudflow originating on a volcanic slope is called a **Lahar.**
- Angel falls, in Venezuela, is Earth's highest waterfall (979 m).
- An interlocking spur, also known as an overlapping spur, is a projecting ridge that extends alternately from the opposite sides of a V-shaped valley. A river with a winding course flows down the interlocking spur.
- Zeugen is a landscape of alternate horizontal ridges and furrows made by the action of wind abrasion. It may be as high as 30 m height.
- Palaeomagnetism is the study of the direction of pole through ages. Magnetically susceptible minerals like **haematite, pyrrhotite, magnetite,** etc., get aligned with the magnetic pole of the Earth and recorded in the solidification of magma during that time.
- **Attrition** This is the wear and tear of the transported materials themselves when they roll and collide with one another. In the process, the coarser boulders are broken down into smaller pieces. The angular edges are smoothened and rounded to form pebbles.

Climatology

(SOURCES)

Class-VII New NCERT Chap 4 (Air), Class-VII Old NCERT Chap 1 (The Atmosphere and its Temperature), Chap 3 (Water in the Air), Chap 2 (Local Weather and the Sky), Class-IX Old NCERT Chap 4 (The Air Around Us), Class-XI New NCERT Chap 8 (Solar Radiation, Heat Balance and Temperature), Chap 7 (Composition and Structure of Atmosphere), Chap 9 (Atmospheric Circulation and Weather Systems), Chap 11 (World Climate and Climate Change), Class-XI Old NCERT Chap 10 (Composition and Structure of Atmosphere), Chap 11 (Insolation and Temperature), Chap 12 (Atmospheric Pressure, Winds and Air Masses), Chap 13 (Moisture in the Atmosphere), Chap 14 (Classification of Climates), Tamil Nadu Board (Class XI), NIOS

Atmosphere

- Atmosphere is the envelope of air consisting of gases, water vapour and dust particles that surrounds Earth.
- Air is essential to the survival of all organisms. Atmosphere contains life-giving gases like oxygen for humans and animals and carbon dioxide for plants.
- The air is colourless and odourless and can be felt only when it blows as wind.
- The number of molecules present in a unit volume determines the density of air.
- 99% of the total mass of the atmosphere is confined to the height of 32 km from the Earth's surface. Therefore, the density of the atmosphere is high near the surface.

Composition of Atmosphere

- The atmosphere is composed of gases, water vapour and dust particles.
- 99% of gases are confined up to the height of 30 km. 90% of the dust particles and water vapour are found only within the height of 10 km.

Gases in the Atmosphere

- Air is a mixture of different gases in varying proportions.
- The two important gases in the atmosphere are **Nitrogen** and **Oxygen**.
- Nitrogen is composed of 78% of the total gases in the atmosphere while oxygen comprises 21%.
- The remaining 1% includes argon, carbon dioxide, ozone, water vapour and many other gases.
- The most important constituents for Earth's atmosphere are water vapour, dust, carbon dioxide and ozone.

Percentage of Gases in Atmosphere

	Gases	Formula	Percentage
Heavy Gases	Nitrogen	N_2	78.08%
	Oxygen	O_2	20.95%
	Argon	Ar	0.93%
	Carbon dioxide	CO_2	0.036%
Light Gases	Neon	Ne	0.002%
	Helium	He	0.0005%
	Krypton	Kr	0.001%
	Zenon	Xe	0.00009%
	Hydrogen	H_2	0.00005%

Nitrogen

- Nitrogen is the most plentiful gas in the air.
- Nitrogen is essential for the survival of plants. But plants cannot take nitrogen directly from the air.
- It is bacteria, that live in the soil and roots of some plants, take nitrogen from the air and change its form so that plants can use it.

Oxygen

- Oxygen is the second most abundant gas in the air.
- Humans and animals take oxygen from the air as they breathe. Green plants produce oxygen during photosynthesis. In this way oxygen content in the air remains constant.

Carbon dioxide

- Green plants use carbon dioxide to make their own food and release oxygen. Humans or animals release carbon dioxide while respiration. Carbon dioxide is transparent to the incoming solar radiation but opaque to the outgoing terrestrial radiation.
- It absorbs a part of terrestrial radiation and reflects back some part of it towards the Earth's surface. Carbon dioxide is largely responsible for the **greenhouse effect**.
- While the volume of other gases is constant, the volume of carbon dioxide has been rising in the past few decades. It is mainly because of the burning of fossil fuels. This results in the increase of temperature of the air.

Ozone

- Ozone is found between 10 and 50 km above the Earth's surface. It acts as a filter that absorbs the ultraviolet rays radiating from the Sun and prevents them from reaching the surface of the Earth.
- The nitrous oxide released by the jet planes, **Choloroflurocarbon** and Hydrocholoflurocarbon released by air conditioners, refrigerators, etc., are harmful to the Ozone layer.

Inert gases

- Of the inert gases, the most important is **argon**. By volume, it forms about 0.93% of the atmosphere.
- Other inert gases include **Neon**, **Helium**, **Krypton** and **Xenon**. All of these have no significance in the weather processes of the Earth.

Water Vapour

- Water vapour is a variable gas in the atmosphere. The amount of water vapour is about 4% of the air by volume in the warm and wet tropics.
- But, it may be less than 1% of the air in the dry and cold areas of desert and polar regions. The amount of water vapour decreases with altitude. Water vapour absorbs parts of the insolation and is the immediate cause of condensation and precipitation.

Dust Particles

- The small solid particles in the atmosphere are originated from different sources such as sea salts, fine soil, smoke-soot, ash, pollen, dust and disintegrated particles of meteors.
- These particles play an important role in the heating of the atmosphere by scattering and diffusing insolation. Dust and salt particles act as hygroscopic nuclei around which water vapour condenses to produce clouds.
- Dust particles are generally concentrated in the lower layers of the atmosphere.
- The higher concentration of dust particles is found in sub-tropical and temperate regions due to dry winds than in equatorial and polar regions.

Structure of the Atmosphere

- The structure of the atmosphere is highly complex. The atmosphere consists of different layers with varying densities and temperatures.
- The temperature changes irregularly with height. Density is highest near the surface of the Earth and decreases with increasing altitude.
- The column of the atmosphere is divided into five different layers depending upon the temperature condition. They are
  1. Troposphere 2. Stratosphere 3. Mesosphere
  4. Thermosphere 5. Exosphere

Troposphere

- The troposphere is the **lowermost layer** of the atmosphere which immediately overlies the Earth's surface. The air we breathe exists here.
- Its average height is 13 km and extends roughly to a height of 8 km near the poles and about 18 km at the Equator.
- This layer contains dust particles and water vapour. Almost all the weather phenomena like rainfall, fog and hailstorm occur in this layer.
- The troposphere is the important layer since it is the locale of all the vital atmospheric processes which create the climatic and weather conditions on the Earth's surface.
- The troposphere is the densest part of the atmosphere.
- The thickness of the troposphere is greatest at the Equator because heat is transported to great heights by strong convection currents.
- The troposphere at any latitude is thicker in summer than in winter.
- The temperature in this layer decreases at the rate of 1°C for every 165 m of height. This is called **Normal Lapse Rate**. This is the most important layer for all biological activity.
- In the lower part of the troposphere, the lapse rate along the vertical is very steep.

- Innumerable vertical currents moving throughout the year cause the troposphere to remain unstable.
- This instability leads to upward movement, condensation, formation of clouds and precipitation.

Tropopause

- The transition separating the troposphere from the stratosphere is termed as tropopause. Its thickness is 1 km to 1.5 km. In its lower strata, jet streams blow.
- The air temperature at the tropopause is about-80°C over the Equator and about-45°C over the poles.
- Here, temperature remains constant, that's why it is called as tropopause.

Stratosphere

- The stratosphere is found above the tropopause and extends upto a height of 50 km.
- One important feature of the stratosphere is that it contains the ozone layer.
- The lower portion of the stratosphere has a maximum concentration of ozone is called **Ozonosphere**.
- It is found in between the height of 15 km to 35 km above sea level.
- This layer absorbs ultraviolet radiation and shields life on the Earth from intense, harmful forms of energy. Therefore, temperature rises in this layer.
- This layer is free from atmospheric disturbance, making conditions **most ideal for flying aeroplanes.**
- This layer is almost free from clouds and associated weather phenomena.
- The transition separating the stratosphere from the mesosphere is termed as stratopause.

Mesosphere

- This is the third layer of the atmosphere.
- The mesosphere lies above the stratosphere, which extends up to a height of 80 km.
- **Meteorites** burn up in this layer on entering from space.
- In this layer, the temperature starts decreasing with the increase in altitude and reaches up to -100°C at the height of 80 km. The upper limit of the mesosphere is known as **mesopause**.
- In summers, **Noctilucent clouds** appear in this layer above the polar areas.

Thermosphere

- In the thermosphere, the temperature rises very rapidly with increasing height.
- The ionosphere is a part of this layer.

Ionosphere

- The ionosphere is located between 80km and 400 km above the mesopause.
- Since, the layer contains electrically charged particles called ions, it is known as the ionosphere.
- **Radio waves** transmitted from the Earth are reflected back to the Earth by this layer.
- The temperature here starts increasing with height. It can be further divided into following layers :
  - **D Layer** (between the height of 60 km to 90 km) It reflects the signals of low-frequency radio waves but absorbs the signals of medium and high frequency. This layer disappears with the sunset.
  - **E Layer** (between the height of 99 km to 130 km) It is also known as the Kennelly-Heaviside layer. This layer reflects the medium and high-frequency radio waves back to Earth. Phenomena like **Aurora Borealis** and **Aurora Australis** occur in this layer.
  - **F layer** (at the height of 250 km) It reflects back high-frequency radiowaves. It is also known as Appleton layer.
  - **G-Layer** It is the outermost layer of the ionosphere. In this layer, all the radiowaves get refracted.

Exosphere

- The uppermost layer of the atmosphere above the thermosphere is known as the exosphere. It extends beyond 640 km.
- The charged particles are concentrated in two bands at about 3000 km and 16000 km above the surface.

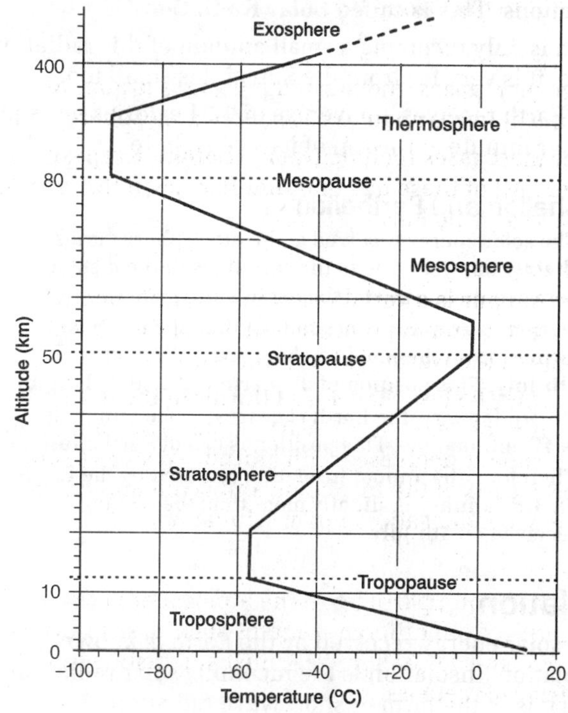

Structure of Atmosphere

- These particles are the result of traping of the cosmic particle by Earth's magnetic field and is called the **Van Allen radiation belt.**
- The particles seen in the layer are extremely rarefied and it gradually merges with outer space.

Zones of Atmosphere

The Earth's atmosphere can be classified into Homosphere and Heterosphere.

- **Homosphere** The homosphere is a zone of the atmosphere where the constituent gases are mixed. On an average, the composition of atmosphere is homogeneous throughout. The homosphere is the portion of the Earth's atmosphere, upto an altitude of about 50 miles above sea level.

  In this part, there is continuous mixing and hence, the composition of the atmosphere is relatively constant.
- **Heterosphere** The heterosphere lies above the homosphere and is a zone of poor mixing, where the average composition varies depending on the location within it. The heterosphere is characterised by variation in the composition and the mean molecular weight of constituent gases. This region starts at 50 to 60 miles (80-100 km) above the Earth. Therefore, it coincides with the ionosphere and the thermosphere.

Insolation and Temperature

- The Sun is the ultimate source of heat on our Earth. The Sun is constantly radiating light and heat in all directions. This is called **Solar Radiation**.
- Earth is only receiving a small amount of this radiation since, it is very far from the Sun and is small too.
- The Earth receives an average of 1.94 calories per sq. cm per minute at the top of its atmosphere.

Aphelion and Perihelion

- The solar energy received at the atmosphere varies slightly in a year due to the variations in the distance between the Earth and the Sun.
- During its revolution around the Sun, the Earth is farthest from the Sun i.e., about 152 million kms on **4th July**. This position of the Earth is called **Aphelion**.
- On 3rd January, the Earth is nearest to the Sun which is 47 million kms. This position is called **Perihelion**.
- Therefore, the annual insolation received by the Earth on **3rd January** is slightly more than the amount received on 4th July.

Insolation

- The solar energy received by the Earth is known as Insolation. Insolation is the incoming solar radiation which is in the form of short wave radiation.
- As the insolation enters the atmosphere
  - a part is reflected
  - another part is absorbed
  - the remaining reaches the Earth's surface.
- The insolation received by the Earth is only 1/2000 millionth part of the total energy radiated from the Sun's surface.
- Reflection of insolation takes place by clouds, snowfields, oceans and other water bodies.
- About 35% of the insolation is lost by reflection.
- The Ozone layer in the stratosphere has absorbed the harmful ozone gas. The other gases in the atmosphere and dust particles together absorb only 14%.
- This insolation that passes through the atmosphere does not heat the air. But, the Earth's surface is heated by this Insolation.
- When the surface gets heated, the air in contact with the surface may also get heated i.e., the atmosphere of the Earth is heated from below.
- That is why the temperature in the lower atmosphere is lower than that of the higher atmosphere.
- The maximum insolation is received at the Equator. There is a gradual reduction in a regular manner towards the poles, at the poles, the amount received is the minimum and is 1/40th of that received at the Equator.
- During the **Spring Equinox** and **Autumn Equinox**, the duration of Sunlight is equal at all the parallels.
- At Solstices, mid-day rays of the Sun fall vertically on the **Tropic of Cancer** in June and on the **Tropic of Capricorn** in December.
- The incoming solar radiation passes through the atmosphere before striking the Earth's surface. Water vapour, ozone and other gases in the troposphere absorb much of the near-infrared radiation.
- The scattering of the visible spectrum by the very small-suspended particles adds colour to the sky. The red colour of the rising and the setting Sun and the blue colour of the sky are the results of the scattering of light within the atmosphere.

Factors Affecting Insolation

The factors influencing the amount of insolation received by different parts of the Earth are as follows

Rotation of the Earth on its Axis

- The Earth's axis makes an angle of 66½ with the plane of its orbit around the Sun.
- This inclination of the Earth's axis has a greater influence on the amount of insolation received at different latitudes.

Angle of Inclination of the Sun's Rays

- The angle of the Sun's rays is nearly perpendicular at Noon. So, the rays get concentrated over a small area and give more heat.
- When the **angle of incidence** is high, the area affected is small and insolation is concentrated on a smaller area, hence the heat received per unit area is large and heated to a higher degree.
- The angle of incidence of the sunrays is oblique during morning and evening. Therefore, they spread over a large area and hence the heating effect is less.
- The **high angle of incidence** means that the length of the path of the insolation rays through the atmosphere is shortest and it loses only a small amount of its heat through absorption, scattering and reflection.
- When the angle of incidence is smaller, the area affected is larger and the heat per unit of area is much less.
- At the same time, the longer path through the atmosphere results in a larger amount of loss of heat.
- The Sun's rays are more direct in summer than in winter. The angle of the sunrays also varies with latitude. The angle of the sunrays is vertical at the lower latitudes and as we go towards the poles, the sunrays are more oblique.

Duration of the Day

- During summer, days are longer and nights are shorter. During winter, nights are longer and days are shorter.
- The amount of insolation is higher during summer than in winter.

Transparency of the Atmosphere

- The atmosphere is largely transparent to shortwave solar radiation.
- Within the troposphere, water vapour, ozone and other gases absorb much of the near-infrared radiation.
- Very small-suspended particles in the troposphere scatter visible spectrum both to space and towards the Earth surface.
- This process adds colour to the sky. The **red colour** of the rising or setting sun and the **blue colour** of the sky are the results of the scattering of light within the atmosphere.

Spatial Distribution of Insolation

- The insolation received at the surface varies from about 320 watt/m^2 in the tropics to about 70 watt/m^2 in the poles.
- Maximum insolation is received over the subtropical deserts. The Equator receives comparatively less insolation than the tropics.
- At the same latitude, the insolation is more over the continent than over the oceans.
- In winter, the middle and higher latitudes receive less radiation than in summer.

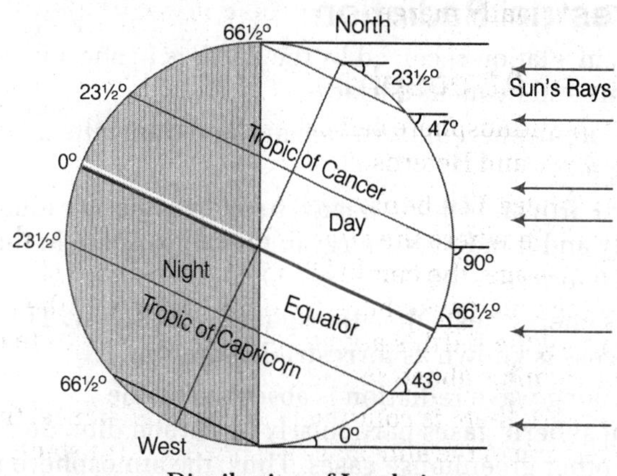

Distribution of Insolation

Process to Transfer Heat

- The heating of the atmosphere takes place through mainly three processes, i.e., **Conduction, Convection** and **Advection.**

Conduction

- Conduction is the flow of energy from the warmer to cooler body when two bodies of unequal temperature are in contact with one another.
- The transfer of heat continues until both the bodies attain the same temperature or the contact is broken.
- The Earth is getting heated by the insolation. The air in contact with the land gets heated slowly.
- The upper layers in contact with the lower layers also get heated. This process of heating of the atmosphere is called **conduction.**
- Conduction is important in heating the lower layers of the atmosphere.

Convection

- The air in contact with the Earth is heated and rises vertically on heating in the form of currents.
- This also helps in further transmitting the heat of the atmosphere. This process of vertical heating of the atmosphere is known as **convection.**
- The convective transfer of energy is confined only to the troposphere.

Advection

- The transfer of heat through the horizontal movement of air is called **advection.**
- The horizontal movement of the air is relatively more important than vertical movement. In middle latitudes, the most diurnal variation in daily weather is caused by advection alone.

- In tropical regions particularly in Northern India during the summer season, local winds called **'Loo'** is the outcome of the advection process.

Terrestrial Radiation

- The insolation received by the Earth is in short wave forms and heats its surface.
- The atmosphere in turn radiates and transmits heat to space.
- The Earth after being heated itself becomes a radiating body and it radiates energy to the atmosphere in long wave form.
- This energy heats the atmosphere from below. This process is known as **terrestrial radiation.**
- The long wave radiation is absorbed by the atmospheric gases particularly by carbon dioxide and the other greenhouse gases. Thus, the atmosphere is heated by this terrestrial radiation.

Heat Budget of the Earth

- The Earth as a whole does not accumulate or lose heat. It maintains its temperature.
- The amount of heat received in the form of short wave radiation insolation is equal to the amount lost by the Earth through the short wave terrestrial radiation.
- Consider that the insolation received at the top of the atmosphere is 100%.
- Roughly 35 units are reflected space even before reaching the Earth's surface. Of these, 27 units are reflected from the top of the clouds, 6 units are from the top of the atmosphere and 2 units are from the snow and ice-covered areas of the Earth.
- The reflected amount of radiation is called the **Albedo of the Earth.**
- The remaining 65 units reach the Earth surface. 14 units within the atmosphere and 51 units by the Earth's surface.
- The Earth radiates back 51 units in the form of terrestrial radiation.
- Of these, 17 units are radiated to space directly and the remaining 34 units are absorbed by the atmosphere. Of these 34 units, 6 units are absorbed directly by the atmosphere, 9 units through convection and turbulence and 19 units through **latent heat of condensation.**
- Totally 48 units absorbed by the atmosphere, 14 units from insolation and 34 units from terrestrial radiation. These 48 units are also radiated back into space.
- Thus, the total radiation returning from the Earth and the atmosphere respectively is 65 units, which balance the total of 65 units received from the Sun.
- This is termed the heat budget or **heat balance of the Earth.**
- This explains why the Earth neither warms up nor cools down despite the huge transfer of heat that takes place.
- The Earth's surface absorbs and radiates back the same amount of heat.
- Therefore, there is no net gain or loss by the Earth and the atmosphere.

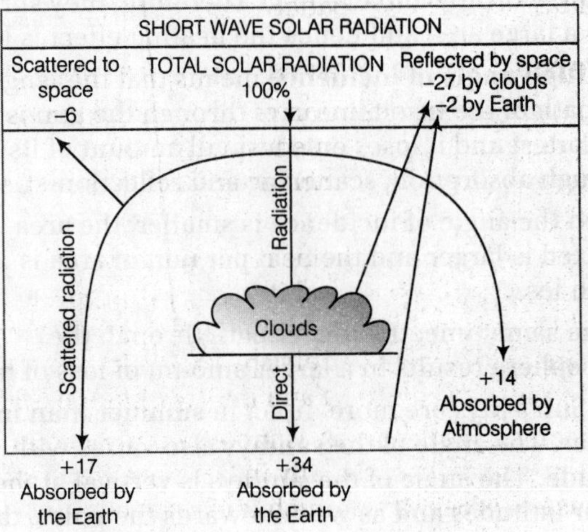

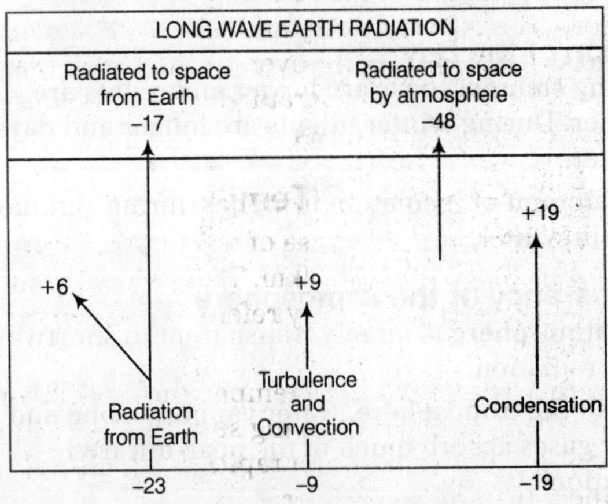

Heat Budget of the Earth

Variation in the Net Heat Budget

- When some parts of the Earth have a surplus radiation balance while the other part has a deficit.
- There is a surplus of net radiation balance between 40° North and South and the regions near the poles have a deficit.
- The surplus heat energy from the tropics is redistributed towards the **poles.**
- As a result, the tropics do not get progressively heated up due to the accumulation of excess heat or the high latitudes get permanently frozen due to excess deficit.

Temperature of Air

- The temperature is the degree of hotness or coldness. The standard unit of measuring temperature is (0°C).
- The interaction of insolation with the atmosphere and the Earth's surface creates heat. This heat is measured in terms of temperature.

Distribution of Temperature

The temperature distribution can be studied as horizontal, vertical and spatial distribution.

Horizontal Distribution of Temperature

- The horizontal distribution of temperature on the Earth surface is represented with the help of isotherms. These isotherms are generally **parallel to latitudes.**
- The gap between isotherms represents the **temperature gradient** and it is steep increase of closely spaced isotherms and indicate meteorological turbulence, whereas widely spaced isotherms shows **gentle thermal gradient** and indicate fair weather.
- The isothermal deviation is more pronounced in January than July, especially in Northern Hemisphere because of presence of much land surface.
- There is a definite Northward movement of all isotherms between January and July. This movement of the isotherms is greater over the land than the oceans. The highest temperature for both January and July are over the continents.

Vertical Distribution of Temperature

- The average rate of decrease of temperature upward in the atmosphere is 6.5°C/km. This vertical gradient of temperature is commonly referred to as **normal lapse rate.**
- The vertical distribution of temperature is influenced by the nature of the underlying surface. For example, temperature decreases most rapidly with altitude over continental areas in summer.

Spatial or Zonal Distribution

- The distribution of temperature over the Earth's surface is closely linked with the amount of insolation received by it. In general, temperature decreases from the equator to the poles.

  There are three heat zones. They are as follows

Torrid Zone

- The zone between 23° 30′ North and 23° 30′ South latitudes is known as the Torrid Zone or **Tropical Zone.**
- As the axis of the Earth is inclined at 23° 30′ from the vertical plane, all places that lies between the Tropic of Cancer and the Tropic of Capricorn receives vertical Sun's rays.
- The Sun's rays are almost vertical in this zone throughout the year. Hence, this zone receives maximum insolation and is very hot.
- This zone receives maximum insolation as the angle of incidence of the Sun's rays between 43° and 90° at the Tropic of Cancer and Tropic of Capricorn.
- The Angle of Incidence and the duration of sunshine are greater in summer than winter in the Tropical zone.
- As the latitude increases, the angle of incidence of Sun decreases though the duration of sunshine may be longer in summer.

Temperate Zone

- The region is between the Tropic of Cancer (23° 30′ N) and Arctic Circle (66° 30′ N) and the Tropic of Capricorn (23° 30′ S) and Antarctic Circle (66° 30′ S).
- They are neither too hot nor too cold. They are called Temperate zones. In these zones, the Sun's rays are never vertical during the year.

Frigid Zone

- The zones between 66° 30′ North latitude and North pole and 66° 30′ South latitude and South pole are termed as Frigid zones.
- The South latitude and the South pole receive minimum insolation. Therefore, they are very cold.
- In these zones, the duration of sunlight may be more than 20 hours during summer, but the temperature is quite low even in summer.

Daily/Monthly/Yearly Average Temperature Difference

- Average Daily Temperature = $\dfrac{\text{Maximum Daily Temperature} - \text{Minimum Daily Temperature}}{2}$
- Daily Temperature Difference = Maximum Temperature of Day – Minimum Temperature of Day
- Average Monthly Temperature = $\dfrac{\text{Total Average Daily Temperature of a Month}}{\text{Number of Days in a Month}}$
- Average Yearly Temperature = $\dfrac{\text{Average Monthly Temperature of a Year}}{12}$
- Average Yearly Temperature Difference = Maximum Average Monthly Temperature – Minimum Average Monthly Temperature

Factors Controlling Temperature Distribution

The temperature of the air at any place is influenced by the following factors such as

Latitude

- The insolation varies according to the latitude, hence the temperature also varies accordingly.
- The amount of insolation is higher in the Equator than that at a higher altitude.

Altitude

- The atmosphere is indirectly heated by terrestrial radiation from below.
- Therefore, places near the sea-level record higher temperatures than the places situated at higher elevations.
- So, the temperature generally decreases with increasing height. The temperature is decreasing at a rate of 6.5°C per every 1,000 m. This is termed as the **normal lapse rate**.

Distance from the Sea

- The location of a place with respect to the sea influences the temperature.
- Compared to land, the sea gets heated slowly and loses heat slowly. Land heats up and cools down quickly.
- Therefore, the variation in temperature over the sea is less compared to land.
- The places situated near the sea comes under the moderating influence of the sea and land breezes which moderate the temperature.

Air Mass and Ocean Currents

- The passage of air masses also affects the temperature.
- The places which come under the influence of warm air masses experience higher temperatures.
- The places which come under the influence of cold air masses experience low temperatures.
- The places located on the coast where the warm ocean currents flow record higher temperatures than the places located on the coast where the cold currents flow.

Annual Ranges of Temperature

- The annual range of temperature is defined as the difference between the average temperature of the warmest and the coldest month.
- Large annual ranges occur in the **Northern Hemisphere**, on the continents in middle and higher latitudes. The smaller ranges occur in the **Southern Hemisphere**, near the equator and over large water bodies.

Diurnal and Seasonal Cycle

- The daily cycle of temperature shows a gradual increase from sunrise to about **3:00 pm** when the maximum temperature is recorded.
- Temperature decreases in the evening and night and reaches a minimum before sunrise.
- The difference between maximum temperature in a day and minimum during the night is known as the **diurnal range of temperature**.
- The diurnal range of temperature is greater at places in the interior of continents than those along the coast.
- The seasonal difference in temperature is primarily due to the difference in the angle of the Sun rays and duration of Sunlight.
- Generally, In the Northern Hemisphere, the maximum temperature is recorded in July though the maximum insolation is received around **21st June**.
- Similarly, the minimum temperature is generally recorded in January about a month after the period of minimum insolation on **22nd December**.
- The annual range of temperature is lowest in the equatorial region as the amount of insolation received does not show much variation between summer and winter.
- The annual range of temperature is greater in the interior of the continent in middle latitude.

Inversion of Temperature

- The **normal lapse rate** is the decrease in temperature with an increase in elevation.
- Sometimes, the situation is reversed and the normal lapse rate is inverted. It is called **Inversion of temperature**. Inversion is usually of short duration but quite common nonetheless.
- **Surface inversion** promotes stability in the lower layers of the atmosphere. This inversion commonly lasts for a few hours until the Sun comes up and begins to warm the Earth.
- There are six favourable conditions producing surface inversion as follows
  1. long nights
  2. clear skies or high clouds
  3. relatively dry air
  4. slight air movement
  5. snow-covered surface
  6. flattish surfaces with a few topographic depressions

Air Drainage

- The inversion takes place in hills and mountains due to air drainage.
- Cold air at the hills and mountains, produced during the night, flows under the influence of gravity.

- Being heavy and dense, the cold air acts almost like water and moves down the slope to pile up deeply in pockets and valley bottoms with warm air above. This is called air drainage.
- It protects plants from frost damages.

  - Plank's law states that hotter a body the more energy it will radiate and shorter the wavelength of that radiation.
  - Specific heat is the energy needed to raise the temperature of 1 gm of substance by 1° C celsius.

Isotherms

- The isotherms are lines joining places having an equal temperature.
- The horizontal distribution of temperature is shown by **isothermal maps**. In drawing an isotherm, the temperature is reduced to sea level to eliminate the effects of altitude.
- Three general characteristic features of isotherms are
  - Isotherms trend East-West direction.
  - Isotherms take a sudden bend at the land-water edge because of land-water contrasts.
  - The spacing of isotherms indicates the latitudinal thermal gradient.

Temperature Anomaly

- The difference between the mean temperature of any place and the mean temperature of its parallel is defined as the temperature anomaly or **thermal anomaly**.
- It expresses the **deviation from the normal**. This deviation is caused by the land and water contrasts, ocean currents and prevailing winds.
- **Isanomal** is line joining the places of equal thermal anomalies. The distribution of anomalies is studied on the maps showing isanomal.
- The largest anomalies occur in the Northern Hemisphere and the smallest in the Southern Hemisphere.

Atmospheric Pressure

- The weight of a column of air contained in a unit area from the mean sea level to the top of the atmosphere is called the atmospheric pressure.
- Air expands when heated and gets compressed when cooled. This results in variations in the atmospheric pressure. Atmospheric pressure also determines when the air will rise or sink.
- The wind redistributes the heat and moisture across the planet, thereby, maintaining a constant temperature for the planet as a whole.
- In simple words, it is defined as the pressure exerted by the weight of air on the Earth's surface.
- The atmospheric pressure is expressed in units of a **millibar**. At sea level, the average atmospheric pressure is 1,013.2 **millibar.**
- Air pressure is measured with the help of a mercury barometer or the aneroid barometer.
- Due to gravity, the air at the surface is denser and hence, has higher pressure. The air pressure is highest at sea level and decreases with height.
- As the temperature increases, the molecules in the air start moving vigorously. Therefore, the air expands and its density decreases. Pressure decreases with an increase in temperature.
- As a result, the air becomes lighter and moves upward. Therefore, cold air is dense and heavy. It moves downwards while hot air rises up. Pressure increases with a decrease in temperature.

Vertical Variation of Pressure

- In the lower atmosphere, the pressure decreases rapidly with height.
- The atmospheric pressure decreases at a rate of about **1 millibar** for each 10 m increase in elevation. It does not always decrease at the same rate. The lower layers of atmosphere have high density and high pressure.
- The **vertical pressure gradient** force is much larger than that of the **horizontal pressure gradient.**
- The pressure gradient is defined as the decrease in pressure per unit distance in the direction in which the pressure decreases most rapidly.

Horizontal Distribution of Pressure

- As the Earth's land and water surfaces warm-up and cool down, the air near them also does the same. The air starts moving from places of high pressure to places of low pressure.
- The horizontal movement of air near the Earth's surface is known as wind. The horizontal distribution of pressure is studied by drawing isobars at constant levels.
- **Isobars** are lines connecting places having equal pressure. In order to eliminate the effect of altitude on pressure, it is measured at any station after being reduced to sea level for purposes of comparison.
- The **low-pressure system** is enclosed by one or more isobars with the lowest pressure in the centre. A **high-pressure system** is also enclosed by one or more isobars with the highest pressure in the centre.

Standard Temperature and Pressure at a Given Height

Level	Pressure (in millibar)	Temperature (in cm)
Sea level	1,013.25	15.2
1 km	898.76	8.7
5 km	540.48	-17.3
10 km	265.00	-49.7

World Distribution of Sea Level Pressure

- The main feature of the distribution of pressure is its **zonal** or **belted character**.
- Each zone or belt comprises several cells of high or low pressure.
- The cells can be either circular or elongated. The zonal or belted character is strikingly developed in the Southern Hemisphere, which has a more homogeneous, water-covered surface.
- Low pressure is experienced near the Equator and the area is known as **Equatorial low**.
- Along 30° N and 30° S are found the high-pressure areas known as the **subtropical highs**.
- Further pole wards along 60° N and 60° S, the low-pressure belts are termed as the **subpolar lows**.
- Near the poles the pressure is high and it is known as **the polar high**.
- These pressure belts are not permanent. They oscillate with the apparent movement of the Sun.
- In the Northern Hemisphere in winter, they move Southwards and in the summer Northwards.

Global Pressure Belts

- Atmospheric pressure on the Earth's surface is not uniform. It varies from place to place. It is influenced by the temperature of the air at a given place. But on a global scale, there are a few permanent pressure belts. They are
  1. Equatorial Low-Pressure Belt
  2. Subtropical High-Pressure Belt
  3. Subpolar Low-Pressure Belt
  4. Polar High-Pressure Belt

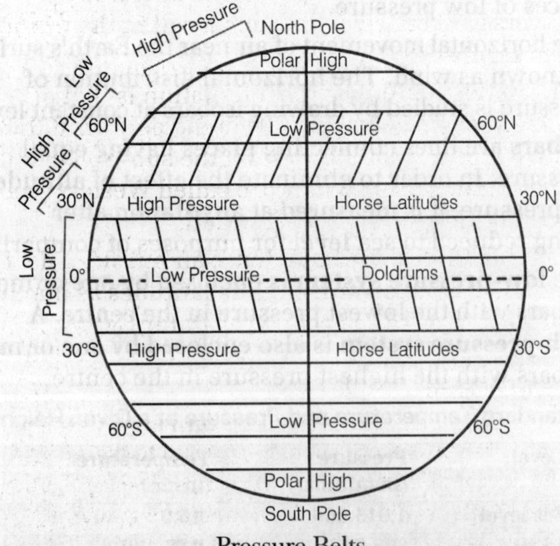

Pressure Belts

Equatorial Low-Pressure Belt

- The temperature is high throughout the year near the Equator. As a result, the lower layers of the atmosphere get heated.
- Air expands and rises continuously in this region. As a result, a low-pressure belt is created in this region. It is known as the Equatorial Low-Pressure Belt.
- Since winds are weak here the zone is also known as **Doldrums**.

Subtropical High-Pressure Belt

- The rising air at the Equator cools down after reaching the upper parts of the atmosphere.
- This air spreads out towards the poles and starts sinking near 30°N and 30°S latitudes and piles up there.
- Thus, high-pressure belts are produced in these regions. They are known as the Subtropical high-pressure belt or **Horse latitudes.**
- The subsiding air is relatively dry because its moisture has already been released near the Equator. The world's tropical deserts are located in this belt.
- As soon as the subsiding air reaches the Earth's surface, it splits into two branches. One start flowing towards the Pole and the other towards the Equator.

Subpolar Low-Pressure Belt

- In both the hemispheres, the air moving from the two high-pressure belts i.e., polar and the subtropical high-pressure belts, meet each other near 60° latitude.
- Converging air starts rising and a low-pressure belt is created named sub-polar low-pressure belt.
- Sub-polar low-pressure belts are developed near **60°N** and **60°S latitudes.**

Polar High-Pressure Belt

- The air is very cold throughout the year in the North and South poles.
- Therefore, the air is dense and heavy. As a result, it keeps on piling up. This produces a high-pressure belt around the two poles. It is known as **Polar High-Pressure Belt.**

Wind

- Winds are generated as a result of the horizontal differences in pressure.
- The horizontal differences in the air density led to the horizontal differences in the air pressure. This generates the winds.
- The winds blow from the high-pressure to the low-pressure areas.

Forces Affecting the Velocity and Direction of Wind

The factors affecting the velocity and direction of wind are

Pressure Gradient Force

- The difference in atmospheric pressure produces a force. The rate of change of pressure with respect to distance is the pressure gradient.
- The pressure gradient is strong where the isobars are close to each other and is weak where the isobars are apart. If the pressure gradient is strong, the velocity of wind is higher.

Frictional Force

- It affects the speed of the wind. It is greatest at the surface and its influence generally extends upto an elevation of 1-3 km.
- Over the sea surface, the friction is minimal. The velocity of the wind decreases with the increase in frictional force.

Coriolis Force

- The rotation of the Earth about its axis creates Coriolis force that affects the direction of the wind.
- This Coriolis force deflects the wind to the right direction in the Northern Hemisphere and to the left in the Southern Hemisphere.
- The deflection is more when the wind velocity is high.
- The Coriolis force changes wind direction but not its speed.
- The Coriolis force is directly proportional to the angle of latitude. It is maximum at the poles and is absent at the Equator.
- The Coriolis force acts perpendicular to the pressure gradient force.
- The pressure gradient force is perpendicular to an isobar. The higher is the pressure gradient force, the more is the velocity of the wind and the larger is the deflection in the direction of the wind.

Pressure and Wind

- The winds in the upper atmosphere are free from the frictional effect of the surface and are controlled mainly by the pressure gradient and the Coriolis force.
- When isobars are straight and when there is no friction, the pressure gradient force is balanced by the Coriolis force and the resultant wind blows parallel to the isobar.
- This wind is known as the **geostrophic wind**.
- The direction of the geostrophic wind is towards the right in the Northern Hemisphere and towards the left in the Southern Hemisphere.
- The wind circulation around a low is called **cyclonic circulation**. The wind circulation around a high is called **anti-cyclonic circulation.**
- The direction of winds around such systems changes according to their location in different hemispheres.

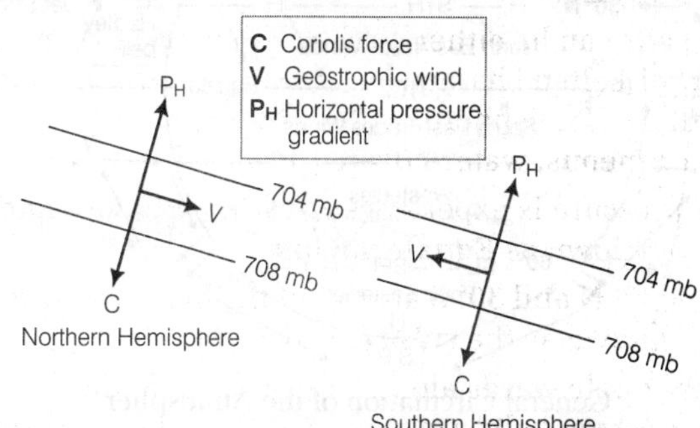

Pressure and Wind

Planetary Winds

- Winds blowing constantly throughout the year in a particular direction are called **Planetary winds.**
- There are three main planetary winds that blow constantly from high to low-pressure belts of the world throughout the year. They are the **Trade winds**, the **Westerlies** and the Polar winds.

General Circulation of the Atmosphere

- The pattern of the movement of the planetary winds is called the general circulation of the atmosphere.
- Down below near the land surface, the air flows towards the Equator as the Easterlies. The Easterlies from either side of the Equator converge in the **Inter-Tropical Convergence Zone** (ITCZ).
- Such circulations from the surface upwards and vice-versa are called cells. Such a cell in the tropics is called **Hadley Cell.**
- In the middle latitudes, the circulation is that of sinking cold air that comes from the poles and the rising warm air that blows from the sub-tropical high. At the surface, these winds are called Westerlies and the cell is known as the **Ferrel Cell.**
- At polar latitudes, the cold dense air subsides near the poles and blows towards middle latitudes as the **Polar Easterlies**. This cell is called the **Polar Cell.**

Ferrel's Law

- According to this law, the winds turn towards their right in the Northern Hemisphere and to their left in the Southern Hemisphere.
- The winds are deflected from their true gradient course as a result of the Coriolis force, which is generated by the rotation of the Earth.

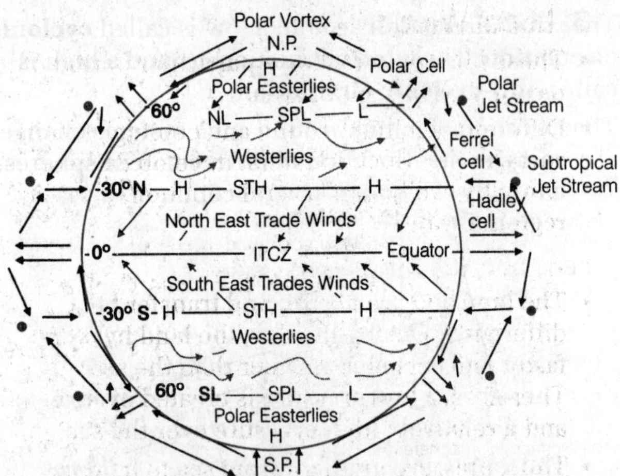

General Circulation of the Atmosphere

El-Nino and La-Nina

- The El-Nino and La-Nina are oceanic phenomena driven by atmospheric circulation. They are ocean atmosphere coupled phenomena.
- The warm water of the Central Pacific Ocean slowly drifts towards the South American coast and replaces the cool Peruvian current. Such an appearance of warm water off the coast of Peru is known as the **El-Nino.**
- In Spanish, the word El-Nino means the 'Child Christ' since, it appears around Christmas.

El-Nino Condition

- The ITCZ's normal seasonal migration is from 10°N latitude in August to 3°N in February.
- But, during **El-Nino Southern Oscillation** (ENSO) events, it may move South of the Equator in Eastern Pacific.
- This shift causes the weakening of the trade winds. The warm surface waters remain off the South and Central American coast for an entire year or longer.
- Upwelling continues to be suppressed and reduced by the overriding warm ocean current and the failure of the trade winds to blow it away. This effect is called as **El-Nino.**

Southern Oscillation

- The El-Nino event is closely associated with the pressure changes in the Central Pacific and Australia. This change in pressure condition over the Pacific is known as the Southern Oscillation.
- Southern Oscillation refers to shifting the surface air pressure between the **Tropical Eastern Pacific and Eastern Indian Oceans.**

ENSO

- The combined phenomenon of El-Nino Southern Oscillation and is known as ENSO.
- In the years, when the ENSO is strong, large-scale variations in weather occur over the world.

Effects of El-Nino

- The arid West coast of South America receives heavy rainfall, drought occurs in Australia and sometimes in India and floods in China.
- Warm water inhibits the growth of microscopic algae as the supply of nutrient from deep water is blocked.
- This has a devastating effect on marine life and fish die in large numbers.
- The consequent release of CO_2 from the decomposition of fish, darkens the water and makes it toxic.

La-Nina Condition

- The El-Nino is generally followed by the La-Nina. It leads to the intensification of the high pressure conditions as found with the **Humboldt current**.
- The effect is the same as that of Humboldt current but in a highly intensified manner.
- La-Nina has reversed effect of El-Nino.
- It causes high precipitations in India, Australia and enhanced drought conditions in Chile, Peru and Ecuador.

Types of Wind

Winds can be broadly divided into three types :

1. Permanent Winds

- The Trade winds, Westerlies and Easterlies are the Permanent winds.
- These blow constantly throughout the year in a particular direction between high pressure belt to low pressure belts.

Trade Winds

- Winds blowing from the sub-tropical high pressure belts towards the equatorial low pressure belt are called Trade winds.
- The word 'trade' has been derived from a Latin word, 'tread', which means constant direction.
- The monsoons are also part of the planetary wind system but of a different nature.
- These trade winds blow from the North-East direction in the Northern Hemisphere and from the South-East in the Southern Hemisphere.
- The trade winds from both hemispheres converge at the **Inter Tropical Convergence Zone** (ITCZ). Trade winds have contrasting properties in different parts.
- In their areas of origin, they are descending and stable. Hence, the poleward areas are dry.
- As the trade wind approaches the Equator, they become more humid and warmer and their instability produces copious rainfall.

Westerlies

- The Westerlies are the winds blowing from the sub-tropical high-pressure belts towards the sub-polar low-pressure belts. They blow from the South-West in the Northern Hemisphere and from the North-West in the Southern Hemisphere.
- The poleward boundary of the Westerlies is highly fluctuating and there are many seasonal and short fluctuations. Westerlies carry much West to East moving temperate cyclones with them. **Roaring forties, Furious fifties** and **Shrieking sixties** are popular terms used by navigators.

Polar Easterlies

- The Polar Easterlies or Polar winds blow from the polar high pressure to the sub-polar low-pressure areas. In the Northern Hemisphere, their direction is from the North-East.
- In the Southern Hemisphere, they blow from the South-East.

2. Seasonal Winds

- These winds change their direction in different seasons.
- The pattern of wind circulation is modified in different seasons due to the shifting of regions of maximum heating, pressure and wind belts.
- The most pronounced effect of such a shift is noticed in the monsoons, especially over South-East Asia.

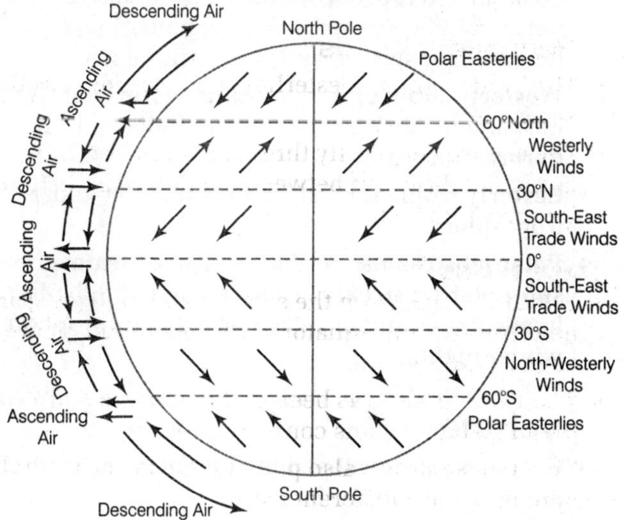

Direction of the Prevailing Wind and the Impact of Pressure Belt

Monsoon Winds

- The surface winds which change their directions with changing seasons in Indian ocean are called monsoon winds.
- These winds blow from sea to land in summer and from land to sea in winter. This is because of differential heating of land and water.
- These winds originate in the belt of trade winds lying between the Tropic of Cancer and the Tropic of Capricorn. These winds are common in South and South-East Asia.

3. Local Winds

- These blow only during a particular period of the day or year in a small area.
- Differences in the heating and cooling of Earth surfaces and the cycles that develop daily or annually can create several common, local or regional winds.

Land and Sea Breezes

- The land and sea absorb and transfer heat differently. During the day, the land heats up faster and becomes warmer than the sea. Therefore, a low pressure is created over the land and a relatively high pressure over the sea.
- Thus, pressure gradient from sea to land is created and the wind blows from the sea to the land as the **sea breeze**. In the night, the reversal of conduction takes place.
- The land loses heat faster and is cooler than the sea. The pressure gradient is from the land to the sea and hence, **land breeze blow.**

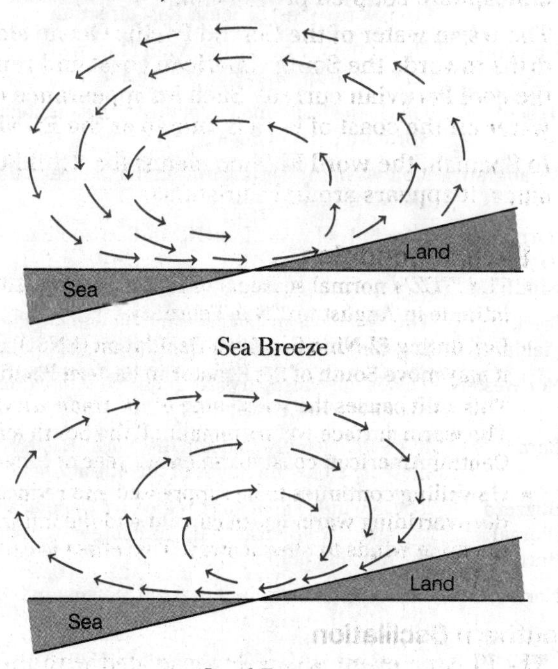

Land and Sea Breezes

Mountain and Valley Winds

- In mountainous regions, during the day the slopes get heated up and as a result the air moves upslope and to fill the resulting gap.
- The flow of air from the valley blows up the valley is known as the **valley breeze.**
- During the night, the slopes get cooled and the dense air descends into the valley as the mountain wind.

Katabatic Wind

- The cool air of the high plateaus and ice fields draining into the valley is called Katabatic wind.
- Another type of warm wind occurs on the leeward side of the mountain ranges. The moisture in these winds, while crossing the mountain ranges condense and precipitate.
- When it descends down the leeward side of the slope, the dry air gets warmed up by an adiabatic process. This dry air may melt the snow in a short time.

Major Local Winds

Local Wind	Description
Foehn (Fohn)	It is a strong, dusty, dry and warm wind which develops towards Northern side of the Alps mountain.
Chinook (Snow Eater)	This is the hot and dry wind blowing along the Eastern slope of the Rockies mountains.
Sirocco (Blood rain)	It blows in North direction from the Sahara desert and after crossing over the Mediterranean sea it reaches Italy, Spain, etc.
Mistral	This is the cold local wind blowing in Spain and France from North-West to South-East direction.
Simoom	This is the warm and dry wind blowing in the Arabian desert, Kurdistan region of Iran and Iraq.
Haboob	This is the fast wind full of dust and sand, blowing in the Northern parts of Sudan.
Karaburan	It blows in the Tarim basin in the Central Asia towards the North-East.
Harmattan (Doctor wind)	It's winds blowing from North-East and East to the West in the Sahara desert.
Brick Fielder	This is the warm and dry wind blowing in the Victoria province of Australia.
Nor'wester	This is the warm, dry and gusty wind blowing in Northern New Zealand.
Bora	It is an extremely cold and dry North-Easterly wind blowing along the shores of the Adriatic sea.
Blizzard (Purgal Burran)	These winds affect polar regions of Canada and USA. On the arrival of Blizzards, the air temperature drops below the freezing point.
Norte	This is the North-Eastern wind blowing in the Central America in winter.
Pampero	These are the cold polar winds blowing very fast in the Pampas region of South America.
Levanter	It is a strong Easterly cold wind in Southern Spain.
Papagayo	These are the fast blowing North-Easterly cold and dry winds that blow in the coastal region of Mexico.
Puna	This is the cold local wind in the Andes region.
Loo	It is a very hot and dry wind which blow from West to East in the plains of Northern India and Pakistan in May and June (usually in the afternoons). Its temperature ranges between 45° to 50° and often causes sunstroke to people exposed to it.
Cold Waves	These waves blow in Ganga plain from West to East in the month of December and January.

Jet Streams

- Jet streams have been termed as the high-altitude river of air. These are high velocity winds blowing at high altitudes.
- These are tubular-shaped meandering flow of the wind moving from West to East located at altitudes of 5 to 12 km. They are more pronounced in the Southern Hemisphere.
- The jet stream winds have velocities of 300 to 500 km per hour.
- The greatest velocities generally occur over the Eastern parts of the **continents** and the Western sides of the **ocean basins**.
- The lowest velocities occur in the longitudinal or West-East sectors near the surface sub-tropical high-pressure cells.
- Velocities change seasonally and the winter velocities are double than the summer velocities.
- The highest speeds in the winter occur along the Asian Coast, over South-Eastern USA and in the region between North Africa and the Indian ocean.

Types of Jet Streams

- **Polar front jet streams** are found where tropical and polar air interact between 40° and 60° latitude. The polar front jet stream is very irregular in its longitudinal section and is discontinuous.
- **Westerly sub-tropical jet streams** run from West to East and is more persistent over India and Africa during summer.
- **Easterly tropical jet streams** run in the upper troposphere.
- **Polar jet streams** are also known as **stratospheric sub-polar jet stream**. These are found in both hemispheres and develop above the troposphere in winter nights.

Cyclone

- Cyclones are developed in areas of air mass conflict and well-developed front.
- Cyclones are areas of low pressure. A centre of low pressure is surrounded by closed, concentric isobars, which indicate the movement of the winds towards the centre from all the **quadrant** and **cardinal direction**.
- They move in anti-clockwise direction in the Northern Hemisphere and clockwise direction in Southern Hemisphere due to **Coriolis effect.**
- Cyclones are classified into two types, such as:
  1. Temperate Cyclone
  2. Tropical Cyclone

1. Temperate Cyclones

- Temperate cyclones are concentrated in the middle latitude between 35° and 65°. The origin and influence of these cyclones is in the temperate zones due to which they are known as **temperate cyclone.**
- The systems developing in the mid and high latitudes, beyond the tropics are called the **middle latitude** or **extra-tropical cyclones.**
- Temperate cyclones are generally extensive. They have a vertical thickness ranging from 9 to 11 km and diameter of 1000 km.
- They are more active in winter in the Northern Hemisphere, but due to prominence of water in the Southern Hemisphere, they are active throughout the year.
- The extra-tropical cyclone affects a much larger area as compared to the tropical cyclone.
- The extra-tropical cyclones move from West to East but tropical cyclones move from East to West.

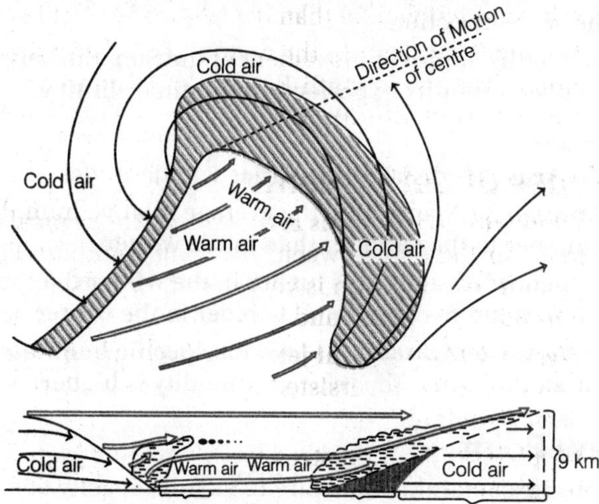

Extra Tropical Cyclones

2. Tropical Cyclones

- Tropical cyclones are violent storms that originate over oceans in tropical areas and move over to the coastal areas bringing about large-scale destruction caused by violent winds, very heavy rainfall and storm surges. They are known as:
  - **Cyclones** in the Indian Ocean
  - **Hurricanes** in the Atlantic Ocean
  - **Typhoons** in the Western Pacific Ocean and the South China Sea
  - **Willy-Willies** in Western Australia.
- Tropical cyclones originate and intensify over warm tropical oceans. With a continuous supply of moisture from the sea, the storm is further strengthened.
- On reaching the land, the moisture supply is cut off and the storm dissipates. The place where a tropical cyclone crosses the coast is called the **landfall of the cyclone.**
- The wind reaches maximum velocity in this region, reaching as high as 250 km per hour.

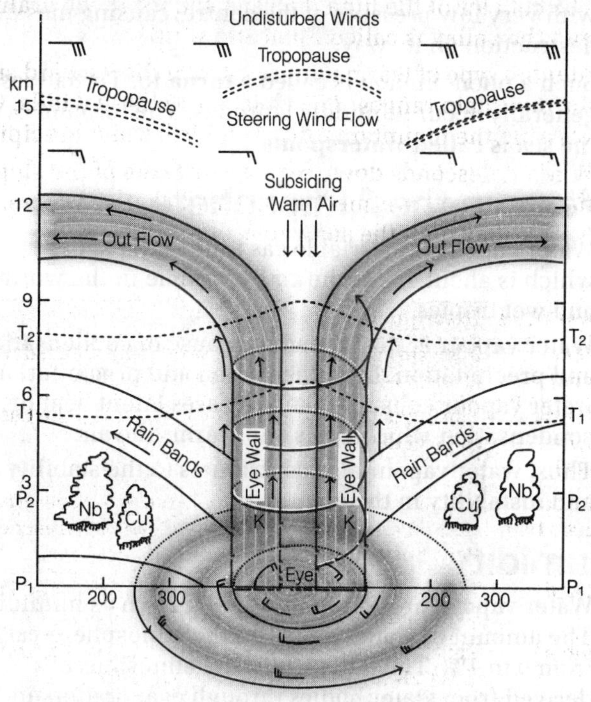

Vertical Section of the Tropical Cyclones (After Rama Sastry)

Eye of the Cyclone

- A mature tropical cyclone is characterised by the strong spirally circulating wind around the centre, called the eye.
- The diameter of the circulating system can vary between 150 and 250 km. The eye is a region of calm with subsiding air.
- Around the eye is the eye wall, where there is a strong spiraling ascent of air to greater height reaching the tropopause.

Thunderstorms and Tornadoes

- Thunderstorms and tornadoes are the other severe local storms of short duration, occurring over a small area but are violent.
- **Thunderstorms** are caused by intense convection on moist hot days. It is a well-grown cumulonimbus cloud producing thunder and lightning.
- When the clouds extend to heights where sub-zero temperature prevails, hails are formed and they come down as hailstorms. If there is insufficient moisture, a thunderstorm can generate **dust storms.**
- A thunderstorm is characterised by intense updraft of rising warm air, which causes the clouds to grow bigger and rise to greater height. This causes **precipitation.**

- From severe thunderstorms sometimes spiraling wind descends like a trunk of an elephant with great force, with very low pressure at the centre, causing massive destruction on its way.
- Such a phenomenon is called a **tornado**. Tornadoes generally occur in middle latitudes. The tornado over the sea is called **waterspouts.**

Water in the Atmosphere

- Water vapour is a variable gas in the atmosphere which is about 4% of the air by volume in the warm and wet tropics.
- Water vapour is the immediate cause of condensation and precipitation. In condensation and precipitation, water vapour consumes and releases latent heat of condensation which cools and warms the air.
- Thus, water vapour also contributes to the stability and instability in the air.

Humidity

- Water vapour present in the air is known as humidity. The amount of water vapour in the atmosphere varies from 0 to 4%. The moisture in the atmosphere is derived from water bodies through evaporation and from plants through transpiration.
- There is a continuous exchange of water between the atmosphere, the oceans and the continents through the processes of evaporation, transpiration, condensation and precipitation.

Forms of Humidity

The different forms of humidity are :

Vapour Pressure

- Vapour pressure refers to that part of the whole atmospheric pressure that is due to water vapour.
- It is expressed in **millibars** or **inches** or **millimetres of mercury**.

Specific Humidity

- Specific humidity is the ratio of the weight of water vapour (gm) to the weight of air (kg) expressed as grams per kilogram of air. It represents the actual amount of moisture present in the air.

Absolute Humidity

- The actual amount of water vapour present in the atmosphere is known as absolute humidity. The absolute humidity differs from place to place.
- It is the weight of water vapour **per unit volume of air**. It is expressed in terms of **grams per cubic metre**.
- The ability of the air to hold water vapour depends entirely on its temperature.

Relative Humidity

- The percentage of moisture present in the atmosphere as compared to its full capacity at a given temperature is known as relative humidity.
- With the change of air temperature, the capacity to retain moisture increases or decreases and the relative humidity is also affected. It is greater over the oceans and least over the continents.

Distribution of Relative Humidity

The distribution of relative humidity is zonal and seasonal.

Zonal

- The relative humidity is highest at the Equator and decreases towards the poles.
- It is minimum in sub-tropical anti-cyclones.
- It increases from 30°N and 30°S. But towards the poles, it decreases with the decrease in temperature in the same direction.
- Due to the apparent movement of the Sun, the belts of relative humidity experience latitudinal shifting.

Seasonal

- The seasonal distribution varies with latitudes.
- Between 30°N and 30°S, the average relative humidity is higher in the summer than in the winter.
- In higher latitudes, it is higher in the winter than in the summer because land is colder in the winter here.
- Thus, the temperature is low, the specific humidity is the same, hence, the relative humidity is higher.

Dew Point

- The air containing moisture to its full capacity at a given temperature is said to be saturated.
- It means that the air at the given temperature is incapable of holding any additional amount of moisture at that stage.
- The temperature at which saturation occurs in a given sample of air is known as the dew point.

Evaporation

- Evaporation is a process by which water is transformed from liquid to a gaseous state.
- The main cause for evaporation is heat. The **latent heat of vapourisation** is referred to as the temperature at which the water starts evaporating.
- It takes approximately 600 calories of energy to convert one gram of water to water vapour.
- An increase in temperature also increases water absorption and retention capacity of the given parcel of air.

- The low moisture content implies that the air has the potential of absorbing and retaining moisture.
- The movement of air replaces the saturated layer with the unsaturated layer. Hence, the greater the movement of air, the greater is the evaporation.

Factors Controlling Evaporation

Three factors that control the rate of evaporation are :

- **Humidity** When and where aridity is high, air has a potentiality of absorbing and retaining a larger amount of moisture. In air with higher humidity, this potentiality is reduced hence, evaporation is slow and small in amount.
- **Temperature** Warm water also experiences quicker evaporation than cold. The lower layer of cold air is heated from below, becomes unstable, develops turbulence and promotes evaporation.
- **Movement of air** The movement of air replaces the moisture filled layer by a drier layer which has a larger capacity of absorbing moisture.

Condensation

- The transformation of water vapour into water is called condensation. It is caused by the loss of heat.
- When moist air is cooled, its capacity to hold water vapour ceases. Then, the excess water vapour condenses into liquid form.
- If it directly condenses into solid form, it is known as sublimation. In free air, condensation results from cooling around very small particles termed as **hygroscopic condensation nuclei**.
- Particles of dust, smoke and salt from the ocean are particularly good nuclei because they absorb water.
- Condensation also takes place when the moist air comes in contact with colder objects and when the temperature is close to the dew point.
- Condensation, therefore, depends upon the amount of cooling and the relative humidity of the air.
- The factors influencing condensation are; volume of air, temperature, pressure and humidity.
- Condensation takes place:
  - when the temperature of the air is reduced to dew point with its volume remaining constant.
  - when both the volume and the temperature are reduced.
  - when moisture is added to the air through evaporation.
- The decrease in air temperature is the most favourable condition for condensation.
- Condensation can take place when the dew point is :
  - **Lower than 32°F** White frost, snow and some clouds.
  - **Higher than the freezing point** Dew, fog and clouds.
- Condensation takes place when the dew point is lower than the freezing point as well as higher than the freezing point.

Forms of Condensation

Forms of condensation can be classified on the basis of temperature and location. Different forms of condensation are as follows :

Dew

- The moisture is deposited in the form of water droplets on cooler surfaces of solid objects such as stones, grass blades and plant leaves; it is known as dew.
- The ideal conditions for the formation of the dew are clear sky, calm air, high relative humidity and cold and long nights.
- For the formation of dew, the dew point should be **above the freezing point**.

Frost

- Frost forms on cold surfaces when condensation takes place **below freezing point** (0°C). i.e., the dew point is at or below the freezing point.
- The excess moisture is deposited in the form of minute ice crystals instead of water droplets.
- The ideal conditions for the formation of white frost are the same as those for the formation of dew, except that the air temperature must be at or below the freezing point.

Fog

- When the temperature of an air mass containing a large quantity of water vapour falls, sudden condensation takes place on fine dust particles.
- So, the fog is a cloud with its base at or very near to the ground. Because of the fog and mist, the visibility becomes poor to zero.
- In such conditions, fog is mixed with smoke and is described as smog.
- Fogs are prevalent where warm currents of air comes in contact with cold currents.
- Fogs are mini clouds in which condensation takes place around nuclei provided by the dust, smoke, and the salt particles.
- Three types of fog have been identified as follows :
  - **Radiation Fog** It is the commonest type of fog. It is formed when air is under a cloud cover with rain falling through it the day before the fog occurs. Pools of air, cooled to an excessive degree, collected in depressions or valleys also form radiation fog.
  - **Advection Fog** It is formed through the transportation of warm, moist air over cold surfaces. This type occurs frequently along the sea-coasts and shores of large inland bodies of water. It is common on the lands in the winter and on the oceans in the summer.

- **Frontal Fog** It is formed along the front separating cold and warm air masses. Frontal fog is common in the cool temperate latitudinal belt where fronts are frequent.

Mist

- Mist is also a kind of fog in which the visibility is more than 1 km but less than 2 km.
- The mist contains more moisture than the fog. In mist, each nuclei contains a thicker layer of moisture.
- Mists are frequent over mountains as the rising warm air up the slopes meets a cold surface.

Clouds

- Cloud is a mass of minute water droplets or tiny crystals of ice formed by the condensation of the water vapour in free air at considerable elevations.
- As the clouds are formed at some height over the surface of the Earth, they take various shapes.

Types of Clouds

According to their height, expanse, density and transparency or opaqueness clouds are grouped under four types :

- **Cirrus** Cirrus clouds are formed at high altitudes (8,000-12,000 m). They are thin and detached clouds having a feathery appearance. They are always white in colour.
- **Cumulus** Cumulus clouds look like cotton wool. They are generally formed at a height of 4,000-7,000 m. They exist in patches and can be seen scattered here and there. They have a flat base.
- **Stratus** These are layered clouds covering large portions of the sky. These clouds are generally formed either due to loss of heat or the mixing of air masses with different temperatures.
- **Nimbus** Nimbus clouds are black or dark grey. They form at middle levels or very near to the surface of the Earth. These are extremely dense and opaque to the rays of the Sun. Sometimes, the clouds are so low that they seem to touch the ground. Nimbus clouds are shapeless masses of thick vapour.

Other Types of Clouds

A combination of these four basic types can give rise to the following types of clouds:

- **High clouds** Cirrus, cirrostratus, cirrocumulus
- **Middle clouds** Altostratus and altocumulus
- **Low clouds** Stratocumulus and nimbostratus
- **Clouds with extensive vertical development** Cumulus and cumulonimbus

High Clouds (6-12 km)

- **Cirrus Clouds** The high altitude detached clouds having fibrous or silky appearance are called cirrus clouds. These clouds are indicative of dry weather. These clouds can be seen when cyclones arrive.
- **Cirrocumulus Clouds** These are coloured clouds having patches of small white flakes or small round particles. These are arranged in distinct groups or wave-like form called mackerel sky. They generally appear as ripples similar to sand ripples in the desert.
- **Cirrostratus Clouds** These are white almost transparent sheet which causes the Sun and Moon to have halo. They are so transparent that the Sun and Moon are visible through them.

Middle Clouds (2-6 km)

- **Altostratus Clouds** They are thin sheets of grey or blue colour clouds having fibrous or uniform appearance. They do not form halo around the Sun and Moon. They cover the sky partly or totally or appear as smoothly distributed over the entire sky.
- **Altocumulus Clouds** They are characterised by wavy layers of globular (round) form. High globular groups of altocumulus are sometimes called as sheep clouds or wool pack clouds. They are fitted closely together in geometrical patterns.

Low Clouds (2 km)

- **Stratocumulus Clouds** They are of grey or whitish colour. They are generally associated with fair or clear weather, but occasional rain or snow is not ruled out.
- **Stratus Clouds** They are dense, lowlying fog-like clouds of dark grey colour but are sometimes close to the ground surface. They are composed of several uniform layers.
- **Nimbostratus Clouds** They create darkness because Sunlight is not seen due to their high thickness. They are low clouds of dark colour, very close to the ground surface. They are associated with rain, snow and sleet but are not accompanied by lightning, thunder or hailstorm.

Clouds with Extensive Vertical Development

- **Cumulus Clouds** They are very dense, widespread, dome-shaped and have flat bases. They are white cloud masses and are associated with fair weather but sometimes they become thunder clouds.
- **Cumulonimbus Clouds** They show great vertical development and produce heavy rains, snow or hailstorm accompanied by lightning, thunder and gusty winds. They are thunderstorm clouds.

Precipitation

- The process of continuous condensation in free air helps the condensed particles to grow in size.
- When the resistance of the air fails to hold them against the force of gravity, they fall onto the Earth's surface.
- So, after the condensation of water vapour, the release of moisture is known as precipitation.
- This may take place in liquid or solid form.

Forms of Precipitation

Various forms of precipitation are :

Snowfall

- When the temperature is lower than 0°C, precipitation takes place in the form of fine flakes of snow and is called snowfall.
- Moisture is released in the form of hexagonal crystals. These crystals form flakes of snow.
- The other forms of precipitation are sleet and hail.

Hails

- Hails are limited in occurrence and are sporadic in both time and space.
- Raindrops, which leave the warm air, encounter the cooler air below.
- As a result, they solidify and reach the ground as small pellets of ice not bigger than the raindrops from which they are formed.
- Sometimes, drops of rain after being released by the clouds become solidified into small rounded solid pieces of ice and which reach the surface of the Earth are called **hailstones**.
- These are formed by the rainwater passing through the colder layers. Hailstones have several concentric layers of ice one over the other.

Sleet

- Sleet is frozen raindrops and refrozen melted **snow-water**.
- When a layer of air with the temperature above freezing point overlies a sub freezing layer near the ground, precipitation takes place in the form of sleet.

Rainfall and its Types

- The precipitation in the form of water is called rainfall.
- On the basis of origin, rainfall may be classified into convectional, orographic or relief and cyclonic or frontal.

Convectional Rainfall

- The air on being heated becomes light and rises in convection currents.
- As it rises, it expands and loses heat and condensation takes place and cumulous clouds are formed.
- With thunder and lightning, heavy rainfall takes place but this does not last long. Such rain is common in the summer or the hotter part of the day.
- It is very common in the equatorial regions and interior parts of the continents, particularly in the Northern Hemisphere.

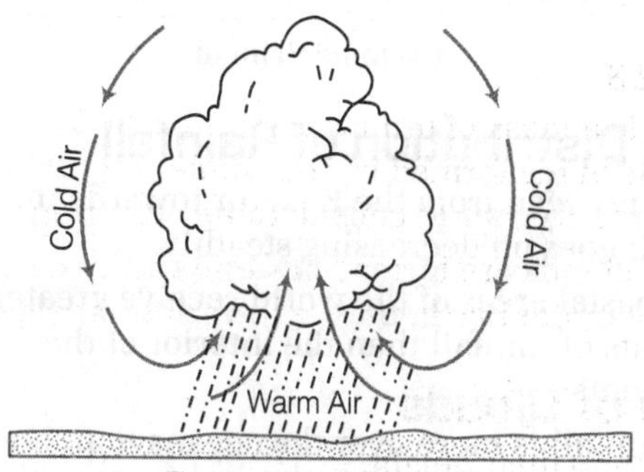

Convectional Rainfall

Orographic Rainfall

- When the saturated air mass comes across a mountain, it rises and expands. As a result, the temperature falls and the moisture is condensed.
- The windward slopes receive greater rainfall.
- After giving rain on the windward side, when these winds reach the other slope, they descend and their temperature rises.
- As the capacity to take in moisture increases, these leeward slopes remain rainless and dry.
- The area situated on the leeward side, which gets less rainfall is known as the **rain-shadow area.**
- It is also known as the **relief rain.**

Orographic Rainfall

Cyclonic Rainfall

- Cyclonic activity causes cyclonic rain that occurs along the fronts of the cyclone.
- It is formed when two masses of air of unlike density, temperature and humidity meet.

- At the warm front, the warm lighter wind increases slightly over the heavier cold air.
- As the warm air rises, it cools and the moisture present in it condenses to form clouds.
- This rainfalls gradually for a few hours to a few days.

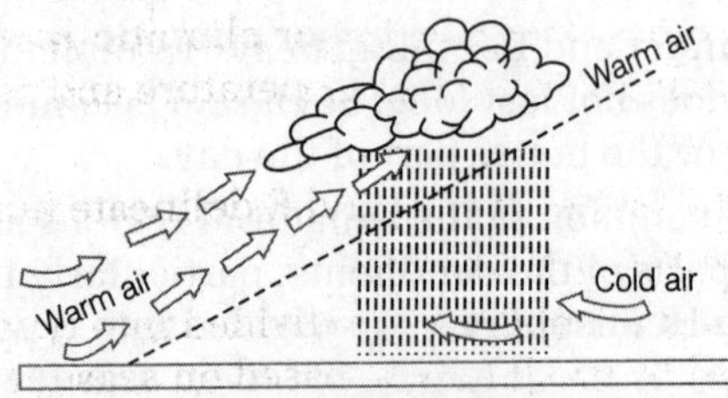

Cyclonic Rainfall

World Distribution of Rainfall

- As we proceed from the Equator towards the poles, rainfall goes on decreasing steadily.
- The coastal areas of the world receive greater amounts of rainfall than the interior of the continents.
- The rainfall is more over the oceans than on the landmasses of the world.
- Between the latitudes 35° and 40° N and S of the Equator, the rain is heavier on the Eastern coasts and goes on decreasing towards the West.
- But, between 45° and 65° N and S of the Equator, due to the Westerlies, the rainfall is first received on the Western margins of the continents and it goes on decreasing towards the East.
- Wherever mountains run parallel to the coast, the rain is greater on the coastal plain, on the windward side and it decreases towards the leeward side.
- Major precipitation regimes of the world are identified as:
  - In the **Equatorial belt**, the windward slopes of the mountains along the Western coasts in the cool temperate zone and the coastal areas of the monsoon land receive heavy rainfall of over 200 cm per annum.
  - **Interior continental areas** receive moderate rainfall varying from 100-200 cm per annum. The coastal areas of the continents receive moderate amounts of rainfall.
  - The **central parts of the tropical land** and the Eastern and interior parts of the temperate lands receive rainfall varying between 50-100 cm per annum.
  - **Areas lying in the rain shadow zone** of the interior of the continents and high latitudes receive very low rainfall-less than 50 cm per annum.

Air Masses

- When the air remains over a homogenous area for a sufficiently longer time, it acquires the characteristics of the area.
- The air with distinctive characteristics in terms of temperature and humidity is called an air mass. It is defined as a large body of air having little horizontal variation in temperature and moisture.
- The homogenous regions can be the vast ocean surface or vast plains. The homogeneous surfaces over which air masses form, are called the **source regions.**
- The air masses are classified according to the source regions. There are five major source regions. These are
  - (i) Warm tropical and sub-tropical oceans
  - (ii) The sub-tropical hot deserts
  - (iii) The relatively cold high latitude oceans
  - (iv) The very cold snow-covered continents in high latitudes
  - (v) Permanently ice-covered continents in the Arctic and Antarctica
- Accordingly, following types of air masses are recognised:
  - (i) Maritime tropical (mT)
  - (ii) Continental tropical (cT)
  - (iii) Maritime polar (mP)
  - (iv) Continental polar (cP)
  - (v) Continental arctic (cA)
- Tropical air masses are warm and polar air masses are cold.

Fronts

- The sloping boundary which separates two opposing air masses having contrasting characteristics in terms of air temperature, density, pressure, humidity and wind direction is called front.
- An extensive transition zone between two converging air masses is called **frontal surface** or **frontal zone.**
- Fronts are most clearly developed in areas where air masses converge, as in mid-latitude frontal depressions. The term front was originally used by **V Bjerknes** and **J Bjerknes** in 1918.

Types of Fronts

Fronts are classified into four principal types on the basis of their different characteristic features :

1. Warm Front

- It is well-defined boundary zone at the front of the warm-sector of a depression, where a mass of warm air is overriding and rising above the overtaking cold air.

- The relatively slow ascent of warm moist air at the front results in cooling and condensation over a wide area and the development of nimbus clouds. The frontal surface is at a very low angle of only **1/2° and 1°**.
- Ahead of the warm front, a broad belt of continuous heavily rains occurs in overcast conditions.

2. Cold Front

- It is the clearly defined boundary between a warm and a cold air mass, where the latter is advancing and undercutting the warm air mass.
- There is an appreciable drop in temperature, extensive cumulonimbus clouds develop, rain falls in heavy showers (sometimes accompanied by thunder) and the wind blows from a Northern or North-Western direction (in the Northern Hemisphere).
- The gradually rising warm air along the gently sloping warm front is cooled adiabatically. It gets saturated and after condensation precipitation occurs over a relatively large area for several hours in the form of moderate to gentle precipitation.

3. Occluded Front

- The overtaking of a warm front by a cold front in an atmospheric depression, which ultimately lifts the warm sector off from the surface of the Earth, is called an **occluded front**. Here, the cold air in the rear of the depression comes up against the cold air against which the warm front is originally formed.
- As the cold front normally travels more quickly than the warm front, it slowly reduces the areas of the warm sector until it merges with the preceding front to complete the occlusion process.
- Therefore, the occlusion is a compound zone with warm and cold front characteristics. The associated weather has characteristics of both warm front and cold front weather.

4. Stationary Front

- This front is formed when two contrasting air masses converge in such a way that they become parallel to each other and there is no ascent of air.

Koeppen's Scheme of Classification of Climate

- The most widely used classification of climate is the empirical climate classification scheme developed by **V. Koeppen.**
- Koeppen identified a close relationship between the distribution of vegetation and climate.
- He used the values of temperature and precipitation and related them to the distribution of vegetation and used these values for classifying the climates.
- It is an empirical classification based on mean annual and mean monthly temperature and precipitation data.
- He uses capital and small letters to designate climatic groups and types.
- Koeppen recognised **five major climatic groups**, four of them are based on temperature and one on precipitation.
- The capital letters A, C, D and E delineate humid climates and B dry climates.
- The climatic groups are sub-divided into types, designated by small letters, based on seasonality of precipitation and temperature characteristics.
- The seasons of dryness are indicated by the small letters: f, m, w and s.
  - f- no dry season
  - m- monsoon climate
  - w- winter dry season
  - s- summer dry season
- The small letters a, b, c and d refer to the degree of severity of temperature.
- The B-dry climates are sub-divided using the capital letters S for steppe or semi-arid and W for deserts.

Group A: Tropical Humid Climates

Tropical humid climate exists between Tropic of Cancer and Tropic of Capricorn. Here, the Sun is overhead throughout the year and the presence of **Intertropical Convergence Zone** (ITCZ) makes the climate hot and humid. Here, the annual range of temperature is very low and annual rainfall is high. The tropical group is divided into following three types :

Tropical Wet Climate (Af)

- Tropical wet climate is found near the Equator and the major areas where the climate is experienced are the Amazon basin in South America, Western equatorial Africa and the islands of East Indies.
- Significant amount of rainfall occurs in every month of the year as thunder showers in the afternoon.
- The temperature is uniformly high and the annual range of temperature is negligible. The maximum temperature on any day is around 30°C while the minimum temperature is around 20°C.
- Tropical evergreen forests with dense canopy cover and large biodiversity are found in this climate.

Tropical Monsoon Climate (Am)

- Tropical monsoon climate (Am) is found over the Indian sub-continent, North-Eastern part of South America and Northern Australia.
- Here, heavy rainfall occurs mostly in summer and winter is dry.

Tropical Wet and Dry Climate (Aw)

- Tropical wet and dry climate occurs North and South of Af type climate regions.
- It borders with dry climate on the Western part of the continent and Cf or Cw on the Eastern part.
- Extensive Aw climate is found to the North and South of the Amazon forest in Brazil and adjoining parts of Bolivia and Paraguay in South America, Sudan and South and Central Africa.
- The wet season is shorter and dry season is longer with drought being more severe. Temperature is high throughout the year and diurnal ranges of temperature are the greatest in the dry season.

Group B : Dry Climates

- Dry climates are characterised by very low rainfall. But the rainfall is inadequate for the growth of plants.
- These climates cover a very large area of the planet extending over large latitudes from 15° - 60° North and South of the Equator.
- At low latitudes, from 15°-30°, they occur in the area of sub-tropical high.
- As a result of subsidence and inversion of temperature rainfall is not produced.
- On the Western margin of the continents, adjoining the cold current, particularly over the West coast of South America, they extend more equatorward and occur on the coast land.
- In middle latitudes, from 35°-60° North and South of Equator, they are confined to the interior of continents where maritime-humid winds do not reach and to areas often surrounded by mountains.
- Dry climates are divided into two such as Steppe or semi-arid climate (*BS*) and desert climate (*BW*).
- They are further sub-divided as:
  - **Sub-tropical steppe** (BSh) and **Sub-tropical desert** (*BWh*) at latitudes from 15°-35°.
  - **Mid-latitude steppe** (*BSk*) and **Mid-latitude Desert** (*BWk*) at latitudes between 35°-60°.
  - **Sub-tropical Steppe** (*BSh*) and **Sub-tropical Desert** (*BWh*) have common precipitation and temperature characteristics.
- They are located in the transition zone between humid and dry climates.
- Sub-tropical steppe receives adequate enough rainfall for the growth of sparse grasslands.
- The variability in the rainfall affects the life in the steppe much more than in the desert, more often causing famine.

Group C : Warm Temperate (Mid-Latitude) Climates

Warm temperate (mid-latitude) climates extend from 30°-50° of latitude mainly on the Eastern and Western margins of continents that have warm summers with mild winters.

They are grouped into four types, such as:

Humid Sub-tropical Climate (*Cwa*)

- Humid sub-tropical climate occurs poleward of Tropic of Cancer and Tropic of Capricorn, mainly in North Indian plains and South China interior plains.
- The climate is similar to Aw climate except that the temperature in winter is warm.

Mediterranean Climate (*Cs*)

- As the name suggests, Mediterranean climate occurs around Mediterranean sea, along the West coast of continents in sub-tropical latitudes between 30°- 40° latitudes. e.g., Central California, Central Chile, along the coast in South-Eastern and South-Western Australia.
- These areas come under the influence of sub-tropical high in summer and Westerly wind in winter. Hence, the climate is characterised by hot, dry summer and mild, rainy winter.
- Monthly average temperature in summer is around 25° C and in winter below 10°C. The annual precipitation ranges between 35-90 cm.

Humid Sub-tropical (*Cfa*) Climate

- Humid sub-tropical climate lies on the Eastern parts of the continent in sub-tropical latitudes.
- In this region, the air masses are generally unstable and cause rainfall throughout the year.
- They occur in Eastern United States of America, Southern and Eastern China, Southern Japan, North-Eastern Argentina, coastal South Africa and Eastern coast of Australia.
- The annual averages of precipitation vary from 75-150 cm. Thunderstorms in summer and frontal precipitation in winter are common.
- Mean monthly temperature in summer is around 27°C, and in winter it varies from 5°-12° C. The daily range of temperature is small.

Marine West Coast Climate (*Cfb*)

- Marine West coast climate is located poleward from the Mediterranean climate on the West coast of the continents.
- The main areas are North-Western Europe, West coast of North America, North of California, Southern Chile, South-Eastern Australia and New Zealand.

- Due to marine influence, the temperature is moderate and in winter, it is warmer than for its latitude. The mean temperature in summer months ranges from 15°-20°C and in winter 4°-10°C.
- The annual and daily ranges of temperature are small. Precipitation occurs throughout the year. Precipitation varies greatly from 50-250 cm.

Group D : Cold Snow Forest Climates

- Cold snow forest climates occur in the large continental area in the Northern Hemisphere between 40°-70° North latitudes in Europe, Asia and North America.
- The **severity of winter** is more pronounced in higher latitudes. Cold snow forest climates are divided into two types:

Cold Climate with Humid Winters (*Df*)

- Cold climate with humid winter occurs poleward of marine West coast climate and mid latitude steppe.
- The winters are cold and snowy. The frost-free season is short. The annual ranges of temperature are large.
- The weather changes are abrupt and short. Poleward, the winters are more severe.

Cold Climate with Dry Winters (*Dw*)

- Cold climate with dry winter occurs mainly over North-Eastern Asia.
- The development of pronounced winter anti-cyclone and its weakening in summer sets in monsoon like reversal of wind in this region.
- Poleward summer temperatures are lower and winter temperatures are extremely low with many locations experiencing below freezing point temperatures for upto seven months in a year.
- Precipitation occurs in summer. The annual precipitation is low from 12-15 cm.

Group E : Polar Climates

Polar climates exist poleward beyond 70° latitude. Polar climates consist of two types:

Tundra Climate (*ET*)

- The tundra climate (ET) is so called after the types of vegetation, like low growing mosses, lichens and flowering plants.
- This is the region of permafrost where the sub soil is **permanently frozen.**
- The short growing season and water logging support only low growing plants. During summer, the tundra regions have very long duration of day light.

Ice Cap Climate (*EF*)

- The ice cap climate (EF) occurs over interior Greenland and Antarctica.
- Even in summer, the temperature is below freezing point.
- This area receives very little precipitation.
- The snow and ice get accumulated and the mounting pressure causes the deformation of the ice sheets and they break.
- They move as icebergs that float in the Arctic and Antarctic waters. Plateau Station, Antarctica, 79°S, characterises this climate.

Group H : Highland Climates

- Highland climates are governed by topography.
- In high mountains, large changes in mean temperature occur over short distances.
- Precipitation types and intensity also vary spatially across highlands.
- There is a vertical zonation of layering of climatic types with elevation in the mountain environment.

Climatic Groups According to Koeppen

Groups	Types	Letter Codes	Characteristics
A-Tropical Humid Climates	Tropical Wet	Af	No dry season
	Tropical Monsoon	Am	Monsoonal, short dry season
	Tropical Wet and Dry	Aw	Winter dry season
B-Dry Climates	Sub-tropical Steppe	BSh	Low-latitude semi-arid or dry
	Sub-tropical Desert	BWh	Low-latitude arid or dry
	Mid-latitude Steppe	BSk	Mid-latitude semi-arid or dry
	Mid-latitude Desert	BWk	Mid-latitude arid or dry
C-Warm Temperate Climates	Humid Sub-tropical	Cfa	No dry season
	Mediterranean	Cs	Dry hot summer
	Marine West coast	Cfb	No dry season, warm and cool summer
D- Cold Snow-forest Climates	Humid Continental Sub-Arctic	Df	No dry season, severe winter
	Sub-Arctic	Dw	Winter dry and very severe
E-Cold climates	Tundra	ET	No true summer
	Polar ice cap	EF	Perennial ice
H-Highland	Highland	H	Highland with snow cover

Extra Facts From Tamil Nadu Board and NIOS

- Meteors falling from the space get burned in mesosphere. It is because when meteors hit the air, the air gets compressed and heated up causing meteors to burn out.
- The temperature increases rapidly upto 1,000°C in thermosphere. It is due to the absorption of very short wave and high energy solar radiation by the atoms of hydrogen and oxygen gases.
- The credit of discovering ionosphere goes to **Hennelly** and **Heaviside**. The gravitational pull is minimal in **exosphere**.
- The average time taken by the solar radiation to reach the Earth's surface is 8 minutes 20 seconds.
- The angle formed by the solar radiation to the ground is called **angle of incidence**. The angle of incidence decreases from Equator towards the poles.
- Water takes 2.5 times of heat energy to heat a unit area compared to land. Thus, the land will have higher temperature than the water in summer and *vice-versa* during the winter.
- Albedo is the amount of solar radiation reflected from the surface. The variation is based on the nature of the Earth's surface. Snow has higher Albedo compared to forest.
- Wind direction is identified by an instrument called wind vane and wind speed is measured by Anemometer.
- The high pressure on the surface always coincide with the low pressure at higher altitude while the low pressure on the surface always coincide with higher pressure on the higher altitude.
- The sub-tropical high and sub-polar low pressure belts are formed due to movement and collision of wind system. So, they are called as 'Dynamically formed pressure belt system'.
- Mawsynram holds the Guinness Record for **the wettest place on Earth**. The average annual rainfall is 11,872 mm, according to the Guinness Book of World Records. The irony is that **the wettest place on Earth** grapples with an acute water shortage after monsoon ends around October. Hence, people also call it world's wettest desert.
- **Nor'easters** Strong winds from the North-East in the Eastern United States, especially New England.
- **Zonda wind** On the Eastern slope of the Andes in Argentina.
- As jet streams encircle the poles they are called as **Circum-polar wind system**.
- **Hygrometer** is used to measure the relative humidity of a region.
- When water droplets of more than 0.5 mm diameter falls from the atmosphere to the ground, it is called as **rainfall**. If the diameter is less than 0.5mm, it is called as **drizzle**.
- A **cloud burst** is a sudden aggressive rainstorm falling in a short period of time limited to a small geographical area.
- Meteorologists say that the rain from a cloud burst is usually of the heavier rain with a fall rate equal to or greater than 100 mm (3.94 inches) per hour. Generally, cloud bursts are associated with thunderstorms.
- The condition at which the eye of the tropical cyclone crosses the land is called **Land fall** of the cyclone.
- An isohyets or isohyetal line is a line joining points of equal rainfall on a map in a given period. A map with isohyets is called an isohyetal map.
- In the polar regions, the heat gain is less than the heat loss. Hence, it is a region of deficit heat. Thus, the insolation creates an imbalance of heat at different latitudes.
- This is being nullified to some extent by winds and ocean currents, which transfer heat from surplus heat regions to deficit heat regions. This is commonly known as **Latitudinal Heat Balance**.
- In Northern Hemisphere, the isotherms on leaving the land usually bend rather sharply towards poles in winter and towards the Equator in the summer.
- This behaviour of the isotherms is due to the differential heating and cooling of landmasses.
- **Verkhoyansk** in Siberia records 66°C the highest annual range of temperature in the world. Its lowest average winter temperature is 50°C. Hence, it is aptly called **cold pole** of the Earth.
- High pressure belts are dry while low pressure belts are humid.
- With the movement of Sun Northwards and Southwards thermal Equator also shifts Northwards and Southwards. Pressure belts also shift Northwards and Southwards with the shift of thermal Equator.
- Relative humidity $= \frac{\text{Vapour pressure in the air}}{\text{Saturation vapour pressure}}$
- About 2% land areas of the world receive precipitation only in winter. These include Mediterranean regions of the world and Coromandel coast of India.

Oceanography

[SOURCES]

Class-VII New NCERT Chap 5 (Water), Class-VII Old NCERT Chap 3 (Ocean Waters and Their Circulation), Class-IX Old NCERT Chap 3 (Realms of Water), Class-XI New NCERT Chap 12 Water (Oceans), Chap 13 (Movements of Ocean Water), Class-XI Old NCERT Chap 15 (The Profile of the Ocean Floor), Class-XI Old NCERT Chap 16 (Ocean Waters and Their Circulation), Class-XI Old NCERT Chap 17 (Marine Life and Deposits), Tamil Nadu Board (Class XI), NIOS

Water and its Distribution

- Water is a cyclic resource. It can be used and re-used. Water also undergoes a cycle from the ocean to land and land to ocean.
- The **Hydrological Cycle** is the circulation of water within the Earths hydrosphere in different forms i.e. the liquid, solid and the gaseous phases. It also refers to the continuous exchange of water between the oceans, atmosphere, land surface and sub-surface and the organisms.
- **Oceanography** is the interdisciplinary study of the global oceans i.e., from shallow coastal areas to the deepest ocean trenches and from the tropics to the polar seas.

Distribution of Water

- The distribution of water on Earth is quite uneven. Many locations have plenty of water while others have very limited quantity. About **71%** of the planetary water is found in the oceans.
- The remaining is held as freshwater in glaciers and ice caps, groundwater sources, lakes, soil moisture, atmosphere, streams and within life. Nearly **59%** of the water that falls on land returns to the atmosphere through evaporation from over the oceans as well as from other places. The remainder runs-off on the surface, infiltrates into the ground or a part of it becomes glacier.
- Renewable water on the Earth is constant while the demand is increasing tremendously. This leads to water crisis in different parts of the world, **spatially** and **temporally**. The pollution of river waters has further aggravated the crisis.

Distribution of Water on the Earth's Surface

Reservoir	Volume (million cubic km)	Percentage of the Total
Oceans	1370	97.25
Ice caps and glaciers	29	2.05
Groundwater	9.5	0.68
Lakes	0.125	0.01
Soil moisture	0.065	0.005
Atmosphere	0.013	0.001
Streams and rivers	0.0017	0.0001
Biosphere	0.0006	0.00004

Oceans and Seas

- Nearly 71% of Earth's surface is covered by seas, among which Pacific ocean comprises 35.4%, Atlantic ocean comprises 18.4%, Indian ocean 14.5%, Arctic ocean 3% and land surface covers about 29%.
- The Northern Hemisphere is called Continental **Hemisphere** as it contains about 40% of continents and 60% ocean, whereas Southern Hemisphere is called **Oceanic Hemisphere** as oceans cover about 81% of the total surface.

Profile of Oceanic Floor

Oceanic surface is heavier and denser than their continental counterpart. An oceanic basin is the land surface under an ocean that includes the topography under the water.

From continent to ocean floor, the relief features can be divided into six major parts on the basis of angle of slope. These are :

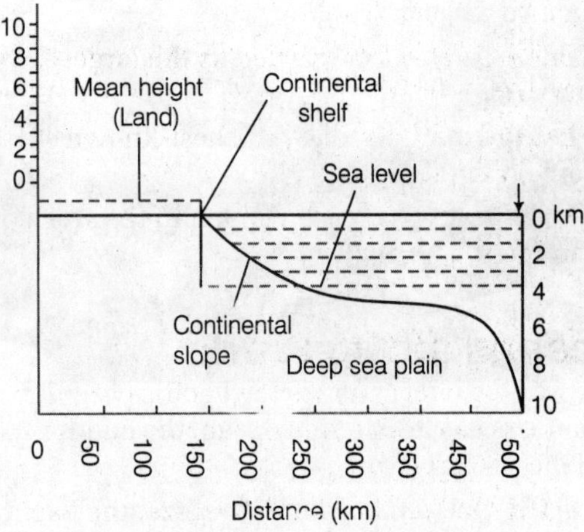

Division of the Ocean Basin Relief

(i) Continental Shelf

- The continental shelf is margin of continent that is submerged under ocean water upto 100 fathoms (600 feet).
- Its overs 8.6% of total ocean basin. Its slope varies from 1° to 3°. It is the shallowest part of the ocean.
- It is determined by the coastal reliefs. Narrow shelf is found where a high mountain runs parallel to coast.
- In Atlantic ocean, it is 2 km to 80 km wide.
- The continental shelf in Pacific ocean varies between 160 km to 1600 km of width. The width of continental shelves largely depends on the mature of reliefs of coastal land.
- On an average continental shelf of Indian ocean in the West is 640 km wide and in the East near Java and Sumatra is as narrow as 160 km and further narrower along the coast of Antarctica.
- The average width of continental shelf is about 80 km.
- The point where a mark increase in slope angle occurs is called as **shelf break**. About 20% of oil and gas production is extracted from them.
- They support productive fishing ground and are good source of marine food (**Dogger bank** and **Grand bank**).
- The submergence and emergence of the continent play an important role in the origin of continental shelf.

(ii) Continental Slope

- Continental slope is formed due to erosion, tectonic movement and aggradations (increase in land elevation).
- Continental slope has a steep slope, beyond continental shelf towards ocean.
- It varies from 2°C to more than 5°C at different places.
- It occupies 8.5% of the total area of ocean basin
- The depth of the slope region various between 200 to 3000 m.
- The scope boundary indicates the end of the continents. Canyons and trenches are observed in this region.

(iii) Continental Rise

- A continental rise is a wide, gentle incline from a deep ocean plain (abyssal plain) to a continental slope.
- The continental rise has an average slope of between 0.5° to 1°.
- A continental rise consists mainly of silts, mud and sand, deposited by turbidity flows and can extend for several hundreds of miles away from continental margins.
- Although it usually has a smooth surface, it is sometimes crosscut by submarine canyons extending seaward of continental slope regions.
- The continental rise is generally absent in regions where deep-sea trenches exist and subduction zones are active.
- Continental rises feature **deep-sea fans**. In appearance they are much like alluvial fans on land found along the fronts of mountain ranges.
- Deep-sea fans are accumulations of sediment deposited by **turbidity currents** (called turbidities) at the foot of the continental slope. Turbidities are underwater landslide deposits.

(iv) Deep Sea Plain or Ocean Basin

Ocean basin is a vast submarine regions which collectively cover nearly three-quarters of Earth's surface. Together they contain the majority of all water on the planet and have an average depth of almost 4 km (about 2.5 miles).

A significant features of the ocean floor include aseismic ridges, abyssal hills and seamounts and guyots.

- **Abyssal Plain** It is an underwater plain on the deep ocean floor, usually found at depths between 4500 and 6000 m. It extends from the continental rise (continental Lithogenous sediments accumulate along continental margins) to the distant deep ocean basin where continental-derived sediment deposition is not significant. Abyssal plains are large horizontal seafloor regions - typically some of the flattest places on the Earth's surface.

Abyssal plains are underlain by oceanic crust that formed and moved away from spreading centres associated with mid-ocean ridges and rises. Because they are so far from land they have very slow sedimentation rates.

Some places less than 1 cm per 1000 years. The dominant geologic process is 'Planktonic rain' which blankets seafloor with organic sediments.

- **Seamount** A seamount is any isolated mountain-sized feature that rises above the seafloor. A seamount may be a large tectonic block that separated from a large continental landmass or may be an ancient or even active submarine volcano.
  A submarine mountain that is partly exposed above the ocean surface is called an **island**. Many seamounts (and islands) are isolated volcanic peaks rising off seafloor. Many are part of mid-oceanic ridges or associated with oceanic hotspots. For instance, the Hawaiian islands are part of the Emperor Seamount Chain. The South Pacific region is a region with numerous seamounts, of which many are islands, atolls or guyots.
- **Atoll** An atoll is a ring-shaped reef, island, or chain of islands formed of coral, typical on a foundation of an extinct volcano in the ocean. The limestone ring forms along the margins of the volcano. Over the time, the volcano either erodes away or sinks below the surface, but the limestone rim continues to grow and expand over time.
- Atoll It may be a part of the sea (Lagoon), or sometimes form enclosing a body of fresh, brackish or highly saline water.
- **Guyots** A guyots is a submarine volcanic mountain (seamount) with a flat top. Most guyots are ancient submarine volcanoes that have been developed by the wave action before sinking into ocean depth. They may lack the fringing limestone reefs associated with atolls.
- It is estimated that more than 10,000 seamounts and gayots exist in the Pacific ocean alone.

(v) Oceanic Deeps or Trenches

- Deep ocean trenches are formed during a process known as **subduction**. In subduction, one tectonic plate (a large portion of the Earth's crust) slides under another.
- These are the deepest parts of the oceans with their bottom for below the average level of the ocean floors.
- The plate that is slipping under the other plate bends and forms an ocean trench. The subduction zones where ocean trenches form become long and deep valleys.
- The Mariana trench off the Guam islands in the Pacific ocean in the deepest, with dept of approx, 11 km.
- As many as 57 deeps have been explored so far out of which 32 are in the Pacific ocean; 19 in the Atlantic ocean and 6 in the Indian ocean.

(vi) Submarine Canyons

- These are a kind of narrow steep-sided valleys. They originate either within continental slopes or on a continental shelf.
- **Congo Canyon** is regarded as the largest river canyon.
- The **Hudson Canyon** is the best-known submarine canyon in the world.
- The largest submarine canyon in the world is **Zhemchug Canyon.**

Oceans of the World

The five major oceans are the Pacific ocean, the Atlantic ocean, the Indian ocean, the Southern ocean and the Arctic ocean :

- **Pacific Ocean** In order of the size, the Pacific ocean is the largest ocean. It is spread over one-third of the Earth. **Mariana Trench**, the deepest part of the Earth, lies in the Pacific ocean. The Pacific ocean is almost circular in shape. Asia, Australia, North and South Americas surround it.
- **Atlantic Ocean** It is the second largest ocean in the world. It is 'S' shaped. It is flanked by the North and South Americas on the Western side, and Europe and Africa on the Eastern side.
  The coastline of Atlantic ocean is highly indented. This irregular and indented coastline provides ideal location for natural harbours and ports. From the point of view of commerce, it is the busiest ocean.
- **Indian Ocean** It is the only ocean named after a country, that is, India. The shape of ocean is almost triangular. In the North, it is bound by Asia, in the West by Africa and in the East by Australia.
- **Southern Ocean** It encircles the continent of Antarctica and extends Northward to 60 degrees South latitude.
- **Arctic Ocean** It is located within the Arctic Circle and surrounds the North Pole. It is connected with the Pacific ocean by a narrow stretch of shallow water known as **bering strait.** It is bound by Northern coasts of North America and Eurasia.

Oceanic Circulation and Ocean Currents

The ocean current is a general movement of a mass of water in a fairly defined direction over great distances.

Type of Currents

There are two types of ocean currents :

- **Warm Currents** These are those which flow from the low latitudes in tropical zones towards the high latitudes in the temperate and sub-polar zones.

  These currents are flow away from the equatorial region and move towards the poles or latitudes which are on the Western side of oceans basins. They bring warm waters in areas of cold water and are mainly observed in the Eastern continents. The prominent example of warm currents is the **North Atlantic** and the **Kuroshio Current.**
- **Cold Currents** These are those which flow from the high latitudes towards the low ones. These currents flow towards the Equator and move towards the Tropics or lower latitudes which are on the Eastern side of ocean basins. They bring cold water into those areas where there is warm water which are mainly observed in the West coasts of the continent.

  The prominent example of cold current is the **Labrador Ocean Current** and the **East Greenland Current** flows.

Factors influencing Nature and Movement of Ocean Current

- **Rotation of the Earth** The Earth rotates from West to the East. The speed of the rotation of the Earth is maximum at the Equator, all moving bodies move in a clockwise direction in the Northern Hemisphere and anti-clockwise in the Southern Hemisphere. This is also known as the **Coriolis Effect**.
- **High pressure** It causes lowering of the sea level and low pressure causes the sea level to rise. Water moves from low pressure to high pressure area. At high pressure, air diverse and in oceanic surface, diverting air lower the sea level. So, the cold current in lower level now come out to surface, called **upwelling** and in low pressure region **down welling** occur.
- **Salinity** Oceans with a higher level of salinity are denser than oceans having lower levels of salinity. Generally, ocean currents are generated from areas of less salinity to areas of high salinity. Since the Mediterranean sea is more saline than the Atlantic ocean, most of the ocean currents flow from the Mediterranean sea to the Atlantic ocean.
- **Precipitation** It dilutes salinity and density, so influence the current in oceans.
- **Temperature** Temperature affects the origin and nature of ocean currents. As the Equator and tropical regions are warm, the oceans lying near the Equator and the tropics are warmer than the oceans lying near the Polar regions.

  Thus, the ocean currents from warm equatorial regions move towards the Polar regions as warm currents. Similarly, the cold currents move from the Polar regions to the Equatorial regions as the cold currents.
- **The Planetary Winds** Winds affect ocean currents. The trade winds blow between the Equator and the Tropics. These winds thus move the equatorial water towards the Pole. *For example*, the South-East trade winds drift the Equatorial Current to the Eastern coast of Australia as the **warm East Australian Current.**
- **Landforms** A landform may influence ocean currents. *For example*, the shape of various landmasses may obstruct the flow of water and influence its movement such as the South Equatorial Current gets deflected towards the Northern Hemisphere.
- **Direction, shape, configuration of coastlines and bottom reliefs** They also influence the ocean current, but never be the cause of current. They only create secondary waves in the ocean.

General Characteristics of Ocean Currents

- The general movement of the currents in the Northern Hemisphere is clockwise and in the Southern Hemisphere, anti-clockwise.
- This is due to the **Coriolis force** which is a deflective force and follows **Ferrel's law**. A notable exception to this trend is seen in the Northern part of the Indian ocean. Here the current movement changes its direction in response to the seasonal change in the direction of monsoon winds.
- On the surface, oceanic current are powerful i.e., more than 5 knots. In depth, their speed decreases (less than 0.5 knot).
- The warm currents move towards the cold seas and cool currents towards the warm seas.
- In the lower latitudes, the warm currents flow on the Eastern shores and cold on the Western shores.
- The situation is reversed in the higher latitudes-the warm currents move along the Western shores and the cold currents move along the Eastern shores.
- Convergence along which the warm and cold currents meet and divergence from which they move out in different directions also control the currents.
- The shape and position of coasts play an important role in guiding the direction of currents.

- The currents flow not only at the surface but also below the sea surface. Such currents are caused by the differences in salinity and temperature.

  For example, heavy surface water of the Mediterranean sea sinks and flows Westward past Gibraltar as a sub-surface current.

Currents of the Pacific Ocean

- **North Equatorial and Kuroshio Current** Under the influence of prevailing trade winds, the North Equatorial current starts from the West coast of Central America. It traverses a distance of 14,500 km moving from East to West before it turns Northward off the Philippines to form the Kuroshio current.

  From the South-East coast of Japan, under the influence of prevailing Westerlies, the current turns Eastwards and moves as the North-Pacific current, reaches the West coast of North America and bifurcates into two.
- **Alaska Current** The Northern branch flows anti-clockwise along the coast of British Columbia and Alaska and is known as the Alaska current. The water of this current is relatively warm as compared to the surrounding waters in this zone.
- **Californian Current** The Southern branch of the current moves as a cold current along the West coast of USA and is known as the Californian current.

  The Californian current joins the North equatorial current to complete the circuit.
- **Oyashio and Okhotsk Current** Also, there are two cold currents in the Northern Pacific. Oyashio flows across the East coast of Kamchatka Peninsula to merge with the warmer waters of Kuroshio. The Okhotsk current flows past Sakhlain islands to merge with the Oyashio current of Hokkaido.
- **South Equatorial and East Australian Current** Following the pattern in the Northern Hemisphere, the South equatorial current flows from East to West and turns Southwards as the East Australian current. It then meets the South Pacific current near Tasmania which flows from West to East.
- **Peru Current** Reaching the South-Western coast of South America, it turns Northward as the Peru current or Humboldt current. It is a cold current, which finally feeds the South equatorial current, thus completing the great circuit.
- **Counter-Equatorial Current** Another current flows parallel to the North and South equatorial currents but in the opposite direction from West to East. This current is known as the counter-equatorial current. The genesis of this current is explained by an upset in the water balance because of accumulation of water in the Western sector due to movement of the two equatorial currents.

  The West to East flowing counter-equatorial currents maintain the water balance.

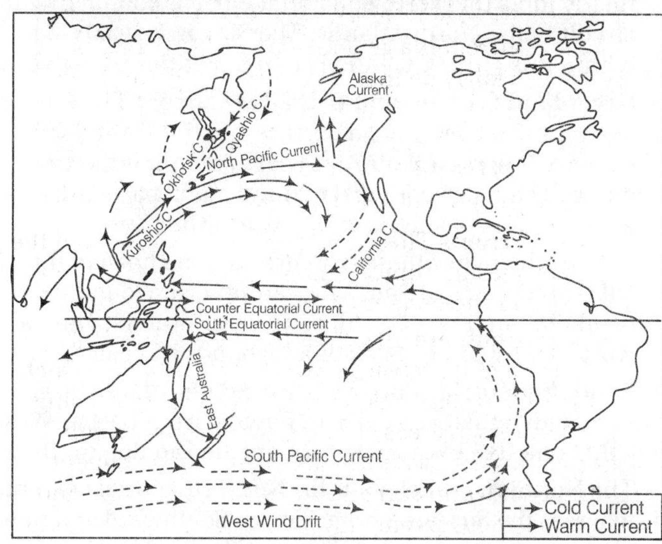

Pacific Ocean Currents

Currents of the Atlantic Ocean

- **South Equatorial Current** As in the Pacific ocean, the two equatorial currents move from East to West in Northern and Southern Hemispheres and a counter-equatorial current flows from West to East. The South equatorial current bifurcates into two branches near **Cape de Sao Roque** (Brazil). Its Northern branch reinforces the North equatorial current.
- **Antilles Current** Part of the combined current enters the Caribbean sea and the Mexican Gulf, while the remainder passes along the Eastern side of the West Indies as the Antilles current.
- **Florida Current** At this stage, there is a rise in water level in the Mexican Gulf, because of large amounts driven by trade winds and because of water brought by the Mississippi river. As a result, a current flows out through the Strait of Florida to be joined by the Antilles current from the South.

  This combined current moves along the shallow continental slope between the **Straits of Florida** and **Cape Halters** as the Gulf Stream beyond that.
- **Gulf Stream** From the Grand Banks, the Gulf Stream flows Eastward across the Atlantic as the North Atlantic Drift. The main motive force for this current is supplied by the prevailing South-Westerly winds.
- **North Atlantic Current** The North Atlantic Current breaks up into two branches on reaching the Eastern part of the ocean. The main current, continuing as the North Atlantic Drift, reaches the British Isle from where it flows along the coast of Norway as the Norwegian current and enters the Arctic ocean.

- **Canary Current** The Southerly branch flows between Spain and Azores as the cold Canary current. This current finally joins the North equatorial current completing the circuit in the North Atlantic. The Sargasso sea, lying within this circuit, is full of large quantities of seaweed.
- **Greenland Current and Labrador Current** The two cold currents–East Greenland current and the Labrador current flow from the Arctic ocean into the Atlantic ocean. The Labrador current flows along part of the East coast of Canada and meets the warm Gulf Stream.

  The confluence of these two currents, one hot and the other cold, produce the famous fogs around Newfoundland. As a result of mixing of cold and warm waters, one of the world's most important fishing grounds is created.
- **South Equatorial Current** In the South Atlantic ocean, the South equatorial current, flowing from East to West, splits into two branches near Cape de Sao Roque (Brazil).

  The Northern branch joins the North equatorial current, whereas the Southern branch turns Southward and flows along the South American coast as the Brazil current.
- **Brazil Current** The Brazil current swings Eastward at about latitude 35°S to join the West Wind Drift flowing from West to East. A branch of the South Atlantic current flows along the West coast of South Africa as the cold Benguela current, which joins the South equatorial current to complete the circuit.
- **Falkland Current** Another cold current, the Falkland current, flows along the South-Eastern coast of South America from South to North.

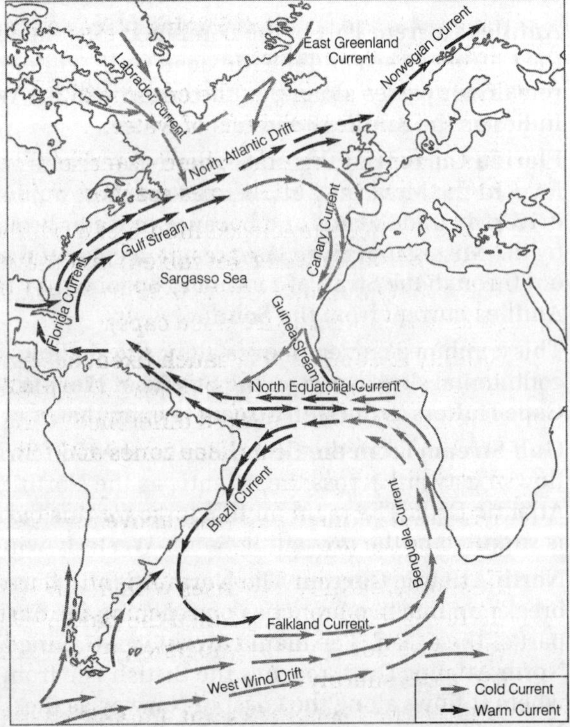

Currents of the Atlantic Ocean

Currents of the Indian Ocean

- Being only half an ocean, completely landlocked in the North, the characteristic current circulation of the Indian ocean is different from that of Atlantic or the Pacific ocean.
- The currents in the Northern portion of the Indian ocean differ entirely from the general pattern of circulation. They change their direction from season to season in response to the seasonal rhythm of the monsoons. The effect of winds is comparatively more pronounced in the Indian Ocean.
- **South Equatorial Current** In the Northern section of the Indian ocean, there is a clear reversal of currents between winter and summer. In winter, the North equatorial current and the South equatorial current flow from East to West.

  A counter-equatorial current flows from West to East, between the two equatorial currents.

  The Southern part of the Indian ocean is less marked by the seasonal changes. The general pattern of circulation is simple and is anti-clockwise like that of the other Southern oceans.

  The South equatorial current, partly led by the corresponding current of the Pacific ocean, flows from East to West and thus, Southward along the coast of Mozambique in Africa.
- **Monsoon Current** The North-East monsoons drive the water along the coast of Bay of Bengal to circulate in an anti-clockwise direction. Similarly, along the coasts of the lands bordering the Arabian Sea, an anti-clockwise circulation of currents develop known as monsoon current.

  In summer, a strong current flow from West to East, which completely obliterates the North equatorial current during this season. It is due to the effects of the strong South-West monsoon and the absence of the North-East trades.

  There is no counter-equatorial current at this time of the year. Thus, the circulation of water in the Northern part of the ocean is clockwise during this season.
- **Mozambique Current** The current flowing through the Mozambique channel is known as the warm Mozambique current. Further Southward, the Mozambique current is joined by another branch of the South equatorial current flowing past Madagascar island.
- **Agulhas Current** After the confluence of these two streams, it is known as the Agulhas current. It still continues to be a warm current, till it merges with the West Wind Drift.

- **West Australian Current** The West Wind Drift, flowing across the ocean in the higher latitudes from West to East, reaches the Southern tip of the West coast of Australia.

  One of the branches of this cold current turns Northwards along the West coast of Australia. This current, known as the West Australian current, flows Northward to feed the South equatorial current.

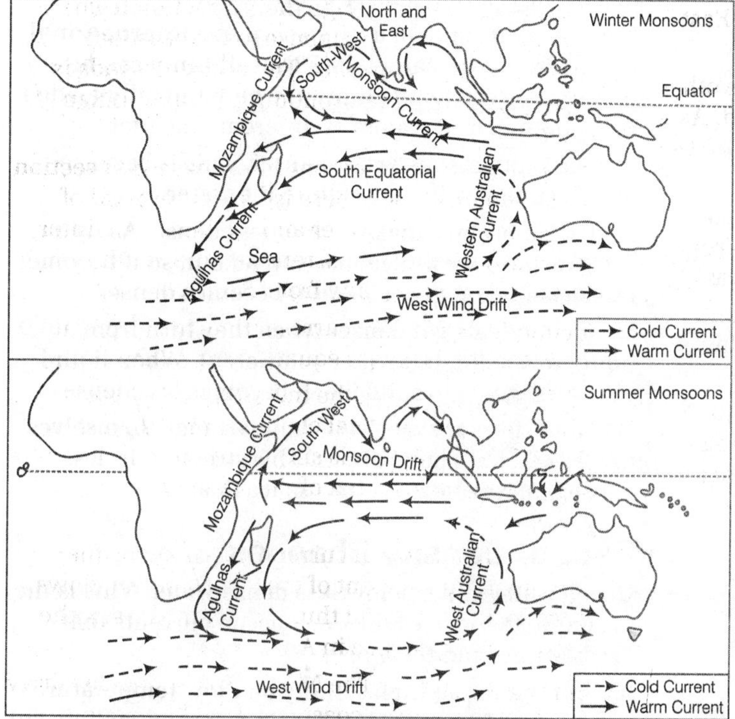

Current of the Indian Ocean

Effects of Ocean Currents

- **Effect on Heat Balance** Currents influence the climatic conditions of the regions in which they flow. The warm equatorial currents raise the temperature of the region in which they flow. Similarly, the cold currents lower the temperature of the places where they flow.

  For example, British Isles would have been extremely cold without the warm North Atlantic Drift. The hot climate of Peru is cooled by the cold Peru current.

- **Effect on Rainfall** The winds blowing over warm currents pick up and carry moisture and bring rainfall like the North Atlantic Drift bring rainfall in some areas located along the Western coasts of Europe.

  On the contrary, cold currents do not bring rainfall and make the region cooler and drier. The Kalahari Desert hardly experiences rainfall due to the cold Benguela current.

  At times the meeting line of a warm and a cold current may result into a violent storm. The hurricanes which occur off the coast of USA follow the line where the Gulf Stream merges with the Labrador current.

- **Stimulation to Fishing** The mixing of warm and cold currents results in the deposition of planktons. Therefore, at such places, fishes can be found in abundance.

- **Effect on Trade and Navigation** Currents help ships to sail if they follow the directions of the currents. Many warm currents keep the ports of Europe ice free even during the winters. This helps in trade and commerce.

  The ships face danger due to the fogs caused by the meeting of the warm currents with the cold currents. This has resulted in the wreckage of many ships in the past as they are not able to view icebergs due to poor visibility.

Salinity of the Ocean

- Salinity means the total content of dissolved salts in sea or ocean.
- Salinity is calculated as the amount of salt dissolved in 1,000 gm (1kg) of seawater.
- It is generally expressed as 'parts per thousand' (ppt)(‰). A salinity of 24.7% has been regarded as the upper limit to fix **Brackish water.**
- It is a significant factor in deciding several characteristics of the chemistry of natural waters and biological processes.
- **Isohalines** are used on maps to show the salinity of different places.
- Isohalines are the lines joining places having an equal degree of salinity.
- The average salinity of the ocean – 35.2‰ or 35% parts of salt in 1000 parts of water.
- In hot and dry regions, where evaporation is high, the salinity sometimes reaches to 70‰.
- In the estuaries (enclosed mouth of a river where fresh and saline water get mixed) and the Arctic, the salinity fluctuates from 0-35‰, seasonally (freshwater coming from ice caps).
- Salinity at depth is very much fixed, because there is no way that water is 'lost' or the salt is 'added.' There is a marked difference in the salinity between the surface zones and the deep zones of the oceans.
- The lower saline water rests above the higher saline dense water.
- Generally, salinity increases with depth and there is a distinct zone called the **halocline** (compare this with thermocline), where salinity increases sharply.
- Other factors being constant, increasing salinity of seawater causes its density to increase.

- High salinity seawater, generally, sinks below the lower salinity water. This leads to **stratification by salinity.**

Quantity of Oceanic Salinity

Oceanic Saline	Salinity (in PPT)	Quantity (in percentage)
Sodium Chloride (NaCl)	27.213	77.8
Magnesium Chloride (MgCl)	3.807	10.9
Magnesium Sulphate ($MgSO_4$)	1.658	4.7
Calcium Sulphate ($CaSO_4$)	1.260	3.6
Potassium Sulphate (KSO_4)	0.863	2.5
Calcium Carbonate ($CaCO_3$)	0.123	0.3
Magnesium Bromide (MgBr)	0.076	0.2
Total	**35**	**100**

Factors Affecting Salinity

- **Depth** With depth, the salinity also varies, but this variation again is subject to latitudinal difference.
- **Current** The decrease is also influenced by cold and warm currents.
- **Latitude** In high latitudes, salinity increases with depth. In the middle latitudes, it increases upto 35 metres and then it decreases. At the Equator, surface salinity is lower.
- **Location of Sea** Salinity changes with depth, but the way it changes depends upon the location of the sea.
- **Evaporation** Salinity at the surface increases by the loss of water to ice or evaporation, or decreased by the input of freshwaters, such as from the rivers.

World's Highest Saline Bodies

- Lake Van (Turkiye) – 33.8‰
- Dead Sea – 33.7‰
- Great Salt Lake – 32.0‰

Ocean Density

- The density of seawater plays a vital role in causing ocean currents and circulating heat because of the fact that dense water sinks below less dense. **Salinity, temperature** and **depth** all affect the density of seawater.
- Density is a measure of how tightly a certain amount of matter is packed into a given volume.
- The more the stuff is packed in, the higher the density. Density can be calculated by dividing an object's mass by its volume. It is commonly measured in grams per millilitre or grams per cubic centimetre.
- For example, basalt is a very dense rock with an average mass of around 3 g/cm^3 but it is still not as dense as elemental iron, with a mass of nearly 8 g/cm^3.
- Seawater is denser than pure water. The higher the salinity, the higher the density.

Variation in Density

- Seawater density varies from place to place because it is affected by salinity and temperature. This means that ships float higher or lower in the water, depending on the density of the ocean.
- Near the waterline of a cargo ship, the **International Load Line** (once called the **Plimsoll Line**) can be found. This shows the limit of where the fully loaded ship should sit in waters of different densities.
- High salinity makes water denser. This is because there is more salt packed into the water.
- High temperature makes water less dense. As water gets warmer, its molecules spread out, so it becomes less dense. As it gets colder, it becomes denser.
- Most chemicals get denser when they turn from a liquid to a solid, but water is different. When liquid water freezes into solid ice, it becomes less dense. When ice forms, water molecules arrange themselves into a rigid but open pattern. This structure is less dense than the liquid water, so ice floats.

Effect of Density Changes

- Dense water sinks below less dense water. This is the principle that drives the deep ocean currents that circulate around the world.
- A combination of high salinity and low temperature near the surface makes seawater dense enough to sink into the deep ocean and flow along the bottom of the basins. Deep water is denser than shallow water. The water molecules are packed together more tightly because of the weight of water above pushing down.

Ocean Temperature

- Ocean Temperature is a measure of the energy due to the motion of molecules in the ocean.
- Satellites enable measurement of **Sea Surface Temperature** (SST) from approximately 10 um below the surface (infrared bands) to 1 mm (microwave bands) depths using radiometres.
- The spatial patterns of SST reveal the structure of the underlying ocean dynamics, such as, ocean fronts, eddies, coastal upwelling and exchanges between the coastal shelf and open ocean.
- SST is a vital component of the climate system as it exerts a major influence on the exchanges of energy, momentum and gases between the ocean and atmosphere.
- The heat and moisture exchanges are a main driver of global weather systems and climate patterns.

- The temperature of the oceanic water is important for marine organisms including plants (*Phytoplankton*) and animals (*Zooplanktons*). The temperature of sea water also affects the climate of coastal lands and plants and animals there in.
- The major source of the temperature of the oceanic water is the Sun. The radiant energy transmitted from the photosphere of the Sun in the form of electromagnetic shortwaves and received at the ocean surface is called **insolation**.
- Besides, some energy, though insignificant, is also received from below the bottom and through the compression of seawater.
- The amount of insolation to be received at the sea surface depends on the angle of sun's rays, length of day, distance of the Earth from the Sun and effects of the atmosphere.
- The mechanism of the heating and cooling of ocean water differs from the said mechanism on land because besides horizontal and vertical movements of water, the evaporation is most active over the oceans.
- There are three layers in the oceans from surface to the bottom in the tropics *viz* :
  - (i) **First Layer** It represents the top-layer of warm oceanic water and is 500m thick with temperature ranging between 20°C and 25°C. This layer is present within the tropics throughout the year but it develops in mid-latitudes only during summer.
  - (ii) **Second Layer** The **thermocline** layer represents vertical zone of oceanic water below the first layer. It is characterised by rapid rate of decrease of temperature with increasing depth.
  - (iii) **Third Layer** It is very cold and extends upto the deep ocean floor. The polar areas have only one layer of cold water from the surface (sea-level) to the deep ocean floor.

Range of Temperature of Oceanic Water

There are following two ranges of temperature of oceanic water :

Daily Range of Temperature

- The difference of maximum and minimum temperature of a day (24 hours) is known as daily range of temperature. The daily range of temperature of surface water of the oceans is almost insignificant as it is around 1°C only.
- On an average, the maximum and minimum temperatures of sea surface water are recorded at 2 pm and 5 am respectively. The daily range of temperature is usually 0.3°C in the low latitudes and 0.2°C to 0.3°C in high latitudes.
- The diurnal range depends on the conditions of sky (cloudy or clear sky), stability or instability of air and stratification of seawater.
- The heating and cooling of ocean water is rapid under clear sky (cloudless) and hence, the diurnal range of temperature becomes a bit higher than under overcast sky and strong air circulation.
- The high density of water below surface water causes very little transfer of heat through conduction and hence the diurnal range of temperature becomes low.

Annual Range of Temperature

- The maximum and minimum annual temperatures of ocean water are recorded in August and February respectively (in the Northern Hemisphere).
- Usually, the average annual range of temperature of ocean water is –12°C (10°F) but there is a lot of regional variation which is due to regional variation in insolation, nature of seas, prevailing winds, location of seas, etc.
- Annual range of temperature is higher in the enclosed seas than in the open sea (Baltic sea records annual range of temperature of 4.4°C or 40°F).
- The size of the oceans and the seas also affects annual range of temperature e.g., bigger the size, lower the annual range and vice versa. The Atlantic Ocean records relatively higher annual range of temperature than the Pacific ocean.

Factors Controlling Ocean Temperature

The factors which affect the distribution of temperature of ocean water are :

- **Latitude** The temperature of surface water decreases from Equator towards the poles because of the slanting rays of the Sun poleward.
- **Unequal distribution of land and water** The ocean in Northern Hemisphere receives more heat due to their contact with large extent of land than oceans in the Southern Hemisphere.
- **Prevailing wind** Direction of the wind affects the distribution of temperature of ocean water. The off shore winds blowing from the land towards ocean or sea raise the temperature of ocean water.

  Winds blowing from snow covered regions in winter lower the surface temperature. In trade wind belt, the off shore winds initiate upwelling of cooler water from beneath and on shore winds pile up warm water to increase the temperature to certain extent.
- **Ocean currents** Warm ocean currents raise the temperature of the oceans where they flow whereas cold currents lower down the temperature.
- **Gulf Stream** (warm current) increases the temperature of the Eastern part of North America and the West coast of Europe.
- Labrador cold current reduces the temperature near North Eastern coast of North America.

- Apart from these, some minor factors like submarine ridges, local weather conditions like storms, cyclones, hurricanes, fog, cloudiness, evaporation and condensation also affect the surface temperature of ocean water.
- The temperature of the sea surface is highest (27° C to 30°C) not near Equator but few degrees North of the Equator. The lowest temperature recorded is –1.9°C near the poles.
- The maximum and minimum annual temperatures of ocean water are recorded in August and February in the Northern Hemisphere and reverse in case of the Southern Hemisphere.

Distribution of Temperature in Oceans

The distribution of temperature can be Ocean Mean temperature, Horizontal Distribution of Temperature and Vertical Distribution of Temperature.

Ocean Mean Temperature

- Ocean Mean Temperature(OMT) is measured up to a depth of 26 degrees' isotherm. It is measured with the help of satellites that orbit the Earth. In the Indian ocean, OMT is analysed by measuring the ocean thermal energy during the period from January to March.
- Scientists from Pune's **Indian Institute of Tropical Meteorology** (IITM) find that **Ocean Mean Temperature** (OMT) has a better ability to predict Indian summer monsoon than the **Sea Surface Temperature** (SST).

Horizontal Distribution of Temperature

- Average temperature of surface water of the oceans is 26.7°C and the temperature gradually decreases from Equator towards the poles.
- The rate of decrease of temperature with increasing latitudes is generally 0.5°C per latitude.
- The average temperature become 22°C at 20°N and S latitudes, 14°C at 40° N and S latitude, 10°C at 60°0 latitude and 0°C near the poles. The oceans in the Northern Hemisphere record relatively higher average temperature than in the Southern Hemisphere.
- Please note that the highest temperature is not recorded at the Equator rather it is a bit North of it.
- The average annual temperature of all the oceans is 17.2°C. The average annual temperatures for the Northern and Southern Hemispheres are 19.4°C and 16.1°C respectively.
- The variation of temperatures in the Northern and Southern Hemispheres is because of unequal distribution of land and water as Northern Hemisphere is made up of more land, while the Southern Hemisphere is made up of more oceans.

Vertical Distribution of Temperature

- The maximum temperature of the oceans is always on the surface because it directly receives the insolation.
- The heat is transmitted to the lower sections of the oceans through the mechanism of conduction.
- Solar rays very effectively penetrate upto 20 m depth and they seldom go beyond 200 m depth.
- Consequently, the temperature decreases from the ocean surface with increasing depth but the rate of decrease of temperature with increasing depth is not uniform everywhere.
- The temperature falls very rapidly upto the depth of 200 m and there after the rate of decrease of temperature is slowed down.

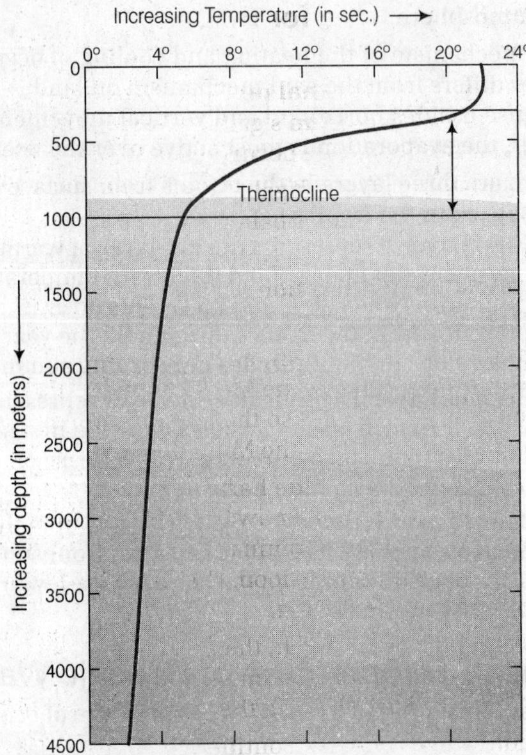

Relationship Between Density, Temperature and Salinity

- Temperature and density are inverse i.e., as temperature increases, density decreases.
- Salinity and density are proportional i.e., as salinity increases, density increases.
- The ocean currents contribute to the salinity variations, salinity temperature and density of water are interrelated. Hence, any change in the temperature or density influences the salinity of water in an area.

Ocean Tides

- The periodical rise and fall of the sea level, once or twice a day, mainly due to the attraction of the Sun and the Moon, is called a **Tide**.
- Movement of water caused by meteorological effects (winds and atmospheric pressure changes) are called **surges**. Surges are not regular like tides.
- Surges are non-regular and non-periodic movement of water caused by meteorological effects e.g., winds and atmospheric pressure changes.
- The study of tides is very complex, spatially and temporally, as it has great variations in frequency, magnitude and height.

Causes Responsible for the Occurrence of Tides

- The **Moon's gravitational pull** to a great extent and to a lesser extent the **Sun's gravitational pull**, are the major causes for the occurrence of tides.
- Another factor is centrifugal force, which is the force that acts to counter balance the gravity.
- The tide-generating force is the difference between the **gravitational attraction** of the Moon and the **centrifugal force**.
- On the surface of the Earth, nearest the Moon, pull or the attractive force of the Moon is greater than the centrifugal force and so there is a net force causing a bulge towards the Moon.
- On the opposite side of the Earth, the attractive force is less, as it is farther away from the Moon, the centrifugal force is dominant. Hence, there is a net force away from the Moon. It creates the second bulge away from the Moon.
- On the surface of the Earth, the horizontal tide generating forces are more important than the vertical forces in generating the **tidal bulges**.
- The tidal bulges on wide continental shelves, have greater height. When tidal bulges hit the mid-oceanic islands they become low.
- The shape of bays and estuaries along a coastline can also magnify the intensity of tides.
- Funnel-shaped bays greatly change tidal magnitudes. When the tide is channeled between islands or into bays and estuaries they are called **tidal currents**.
- Tidal bulges have greater height at wide continental shelves and low mid-oceanic islands.
- At bay or estuaries, intensity of tides also magnified by the shape of the water body. Here, the tide is called **tidal current**.

Types of Tides

Different types of tides are discussed below occur because different positions of the Sun and the Moon with relation to the Earth and based on their frequency of occurrence in 1 day or 24 hours or based on their height

Tides based on frequency are as follows

- **Semi-diurnal tide** The most common tidal pattern, featuring two high tides and two low tides each day. The successive high or low tides are approximately of the same height.
- **Diurnal tide** There is only one high tide and one low during each day. The successive high and low tides are approximately of the same height.
- **Mixed tide** Tides having variations in height are known as mixed tides. These tides generally occur along the West coast of North America and on many islands of the Pacific ocean.

Tides based on the sun, moon and the Earth positions are as follows

Spring Tides

- The phases of the Moon also affect tides. When the Moon is at its Full or New Moon phase, high tides are at their highest, while low tides are lower than usual.
- These tides occur when the Sun, Moon and the Earth are in a straight line. The added gravity of the Sun can make the oceans bulge more than at other times.
- It occur twice a month one on Full Moon period and another during New Moon period.

Neap Tides

- During the Moon's quarter phases, the Sun pulls against the Moon's gravitational pull instead of with it. During these tides, the result is the lowest high tide and the highest low tide.
- In other words, the least extreme difference between high and low tides. This is called a neap tide.

High Tides

- The side of the Earth facing the Moon will have a tidal bulge called the direct tide. Similarly, on the opposite side of the planet, the ocean will also be bulging.
- This is called the **opposite tide,** and it happens because the inertial force of the Earth exceeds the gravitational force of the Moon at this location. Therefore, high tides occur simultaneously on the opposite sides of the Earth.

Low Tides

- Low tides are the receding waters between the high tides. In some places, low tide can be only a few feet, while in others the ocean can recede much farther.
- High and low tides both appear two times each in a day or 24-hour, but since the Moon rises 50 minutes later each day, the tide cycles will differ by the same 50 minutes daily.

Periodic Tides

- Apogean tides and perihelion tides occur when Moon's position is at **apogee** (farthest) or **perigee** (nearest) to the Earth.
- These are monthly tides. During **aphelion** and **perihelion**, tides varies their nature and are called yearly tides. Equinoctial spring tides occurs in every 6 months.

Importance of Tides

- Since, tides are caused by the Earth-Moon-Sun positions which are known accurately, the tides can be predicted well in advance.
- This helps the navigators and fishermen to plan their activities. Tidal flows are of great importance in navigation.
- Tidal heights are very important, especially harbours near rivers and within estuaries having shallow 'bars' at the entrance, which prevent ships and boats from entering into the harbour.
- Tides are also helpful in differences in water density affect vertical mobility of ocean currents.
- Water with high salinity is denser than water with low salinity and in the same way cold water is denser than warm water. Denser water tends to sink, while relatively lighter water tends to rise.
- Cold-water ocean currents occur when the cold water at the poles sinks and slowly moves towards the Equator.
- Warm-water currents travel out from the Equator along the surface, flowing towards the poles to replace the sinking cold water.

Ocean Deposits

- Most important types of ocean deposits are Terrigenous deposit and Pelagic deposits. There are unconsolidated sediments, deposited on the ocean floor. These are ocean deposits. They vary from location to location.
- The study of ocean deposits is important in understanding the rocks exposed on the Earth's surface which were once laid under sea.
- The ocean deposits can broadly be divided into two types—the **Terrigenous deposits** and the **Pelagic deposits**. The Terrigenous deposits are those which are found on the continental shelves and slopes and mainly consist of the rock material derived because of wear and tear. The Pelagic deposits are those which are found over deep sea, plains and the deeps.
- These deposits mainly consist of organic remains of plants and animals. But this distinction between the two types of deposits is not absolute.
- For instance, the Terrigenous deposits may not always consist of the fragmented rock material and may be carried deep into the sea.
- Also, the Pelagic deposits may not always consist of the plant and animal remains and may be extended for upto the continental slope.

Terrigenous Deposits

- Terrigenous deposits are derived from the wear and tear of land, volcanic and organic products. The greater part of the deposits on the continental shelf and slopes is derived from rock material by disintegration and decomposition.
- It is done by the agents of weathering and carried to sea by the agents of erosion, such as running water, wind, etc.
- The process and extent of disintegration depends on the nature of rock material, climate and time taken. The larger particles of the Terrigenous deposits are found near the shore and the finer ones carried deeper.
- The extent to which they are carried outwards depends on the size of rock material and the strength of sea waves and currents.
- On the basis of size of particles, the Terrigenous deposits may be categorised into three classes mud, sand and gravel.
  - **Mud** refers to the finest particles which comprise the minute particles of rock forming minerals, principally quartz. Murray has classified the mud deposits into **blue, green** and **red** types, based on the colour of constituents.
  - **Sand** refers to the coarser particles.
  - **Gravel** has even bigger particles.

Volcanic Products

- In volcanic regions, the deposits of continental shelf and slope consist chiefly of products of volcanism, which are subject to chemical and mechanical weathering and are carried to the ocean by actions of running water and wind.
- The volcanic deposits differ from the ordinary Terrigenous deposits in one respect they are made of pyroclastic volcanic products and lava, rather than quartz.

Organic Products

- Such deposits consist of shells and skeletons of various plants and animals that live and grow on the sea floor and are changed into mud and sand by chemical and mechanical processes.
- They differ from the ordinary Terrigenous deposits in the sense that they consist of calcium carbonate only.

Pelagic Deposits

- Pelagic deposits are the most conspicuous of all deposits covering about 75% of the total sea floor.
- This is because, except for fine volcanic ash, little Terrigenous material is carried into the deeps. The Pelagic deposits consist of both organic and inorganic material.

Organic Material

- This is in the form of a kind of liquid mud called ooze, which contains shells and skeletons of various marine organisms. The **ooze** is said to be calcareous when the shell is made of calcium carbonate.
- The calcareous ooze may be either Pteropod ooze or Globogerina ooze. Most parts of the Indian and Atlantic oceans have **calcareous ooze** as deposits.
- When the shell is made of silica, the ooze is said to be siliceous ooze, which can be either the diatom type or the radiolarian type of ooze. The Southern fringes of the Indian and the Atlantic oceans have the **siliceous** type of ooze.

Inorganic Material

- This is in the form of red clay, which is apparently of a volcanic origin.
- The chief constituents of red clay are silicon and aluminium dioxide, while other constituents include iron, manganese, phosphorus and radium. The red clay is the most widely spread Pelagic deposit and covers 38% of the sea floor.
- The red clay covers more than half of the Pacific floor.

Major Trenches of the World

Trench	Description
Mariana Trench	It is located in the Western Pacific ocean. It is considered to be the deepest part of the Earth's surface. In fact, it is the Challenger Deep in the Mariana Trench that is known as the deepest point. It appears as a crescent-shaped scar, the trench measures around 2,550 km long, 69 km wide on average and has a maximum depth of 10.91 km at the Challenger Deep. At the same time, some other efforts measured the deepest portion at 11.034 km.
Tonga Trench	It is located in the South-West Pacific ocean and at the Kermadec Tonga Subduction Zone's Northern end. It lies around 10.882 km below sea level. The deepest point in the Tonga trench, known as the Horizon Deep, considered to be the second deepest point on Earth after the Challenger Deep and the deepest trench of the Southern Hemisphere.
Puerto Rico Trench (28,900 ft)	It is located between the Caribbean sea and the Atlantic ocean. It marks the deepest point in this region and the eighth deepest point found on the Earth's surface. Lies at a depth of 8.64 km, spotted at Milwaukee Deep and measures a length of over 800 km. This trench has been responsible for many tragic Tsunamis and Earthquake activities in this region.
Peru-Chile Trench (26,460 ft)	It (the Atacama Trench) is located around 160 km off the coast of Peru and Chile in the Eastern Pacific ocean. The Atacama Trench has a maximum depth of 8.06 km below sea level. The deepest point of the trench is known as Richards Deep.
Aleutian Trench	It extends from Alaska to the Kamchatka Peninsula it results from the Pacific plate sliding beneath the North American plate.
Ryukyu Trench	It is located near the Ryukyu island it marks the boundary between the Pacific plate and the Eurasian plate this zone is marked by intense seismic activity.
Japan Trench	It is deep submarine trench located East of the Japanese islands. It is part of the Pacific Ring of Fire in the Northern Pacific ocean. With a maximum depth of 9 km, the Japan Trench stretches from the Kuril islands to the Bonin islands. It is also the extension of the Kuril-Kamchatka Trench and the Izu-Ogasawara Trench to the North and South respectively.
Kuril Trench	It is the deepest part of ocean belonging to the Pacific ocean. This trench lies at a considerable depth of 10.5 km below sea level. Lying close to Kuril island and off the coast of Kamchatka. This trench is responsible for a number of oceans bed volcanic activities in the region. The trench was formed due to the subduction zone that was developed in the late cretaceous, which created the Kuril island and the Kamchatka volcanic arcs.
Philippines Trench	It is the third deepest point in the world, the Galatea Depth. It is 10.54 km below sea level. Also known as Mindanao Trench, this submarine trench is located in the Philippine sea, spreads in a length of 1,320 km and 30 km width in the East of Philippines. Prominent among other trenches in the Philippine Sea, this trench was formed due to a collision between the Eurasian plate and the smaller Philippine plate. The other major trenches in the Philippine sea include Manila Trench East Luzon Trench, Negros Trench, Sulu Trench and Cotabato Trench.
Kermadec Tonga Trench	It is located in North of New Zealand where the Pacific plate meets the Australian-Indian plate. It reaches depths of 2000 km non- linear karmadec Tonga subduction system.
Java (Sunda) Trench	It is located in South of Indonesia between the Australian-Indian and the Eurasian plates. It is the deepest point in the Indian ocean with 3200 km depth.

Major Ridges of the World

Ridge	Description
Aden Ridge	• It is located in Gulf of Aden. • It is divergent boundary between the Somalian and the Arabian tectonic plates.
Cocos Ridge	• It is located in the East Pacific ocean, Ecuador. • It is volcanic hotspot.
Explorer Ridge	• It is located in the West of Vancouver island, British Columbia, Canada. • It is divergent tectonic plate boundary between Vancouver island, British Columbia and Canada.
Gorda Ridge	• It is located at the Northern coast of California and Southern Oregon. • It is tectonic spreading centre broken into three segments the Northern ridge, Central ridge and the Southern ridge.
Juan de Fuca Ridge	• It is located at the off coast of the Pacific North-West region of North America. • It is a mid-ocean spreading centre and divergent plate boundary. • It separates the Pacific plate to the West and the Juan de Fuca plate to the East.
American-Antarctic Ridge	• It is located between the South America and Antarctica. • It is the tectonic spreading centre between the South American plate and the Antarctic plate.
Chile Rise	• It is located in the Peru-Chile Trench. • It is a tectonic divergent plate boundary between the Nazca and Antarctic plates.
East Pacific Rise	• It is located along the floor of the Pacific ocean. • It is a divergent tectonic plate that separates the Pacific plate to the West from (North to South) the North American plate, the Rivera plate, the Cocos plate, the Nazca plate and the Antarctic plate.
East Scotia Ridge	• It is located on the edge of the South Atlantic and Southern ocean.
Nazca Ridge	• It is located in the Southern Pacific ocean.
Pacific- Antarctic Ridge	• It is located on the seafloor of the South Pacific ocean. • It is a divergent tectonic plate that separates the Pacific plate from the Antarctic plate.
Carlsberg Ridge	• It is located in the Northern section of the Central Indian Ridge. • It is a divergent tectonic plate boundary between the African plate and the Indo-Australian plate, traversing the Western regions of the Indian ocean.
South-East Indian Ridge	• It is located in the Southern Indian ocean. • It is a divergent tectonic plate boundary stretching between the Rodrigues Triple Junction in the Indian ocean and the Macquarie Triple Junction in the Pacific ocean, the SEIR forms the plate boundary between the Australian and Antarctic plates.
Central Indian Ridge	• It is located in the Western Indian ocean.It is a North-South-trending mid-ocean ridge.
South-West Indian Ridge	• It is located along the floors of the South-West Indian ocean and South-East Atlantic ocean. • It is a divergent tectonic plate boundary separating the African plate to the North from the Antarctic plate to the South.
Mid-Atlantic Ridge	• It is located along the floor of the Atlantic ocean, and part of the longest mountain range in the world. • It is a divergent plate or constructive plate.

Coral Reefs

- Coral reefs are large underwater structures composed of the skeletons of colonial marine invertebrates called coral.
- The coral species that build reefs are known as hermatypic, or 'hard', corals because they extract calcium carbonate from seawater to create a hard, durable exoskeleton that protects their soft, sac-like bodies.
- Other species of corals that are not involved in reef building are known as **'soft corals'**.
- These types of corals are flexible organisms often resembling plants and trees and include species such as sea fans and sea whips, according to the **Coral Reef Alliance** (CORAL), a non-profit environmental organisation.
- Each individual coral is referred to as a polyp. Coral polyps live on the calcium carbonate exoskeletons of their ancestors, adding their own exoskeleton to the existing coral structure.
- As the centuries pass, the coral reef gradually grows, one tiny exoskeleton at a time, until they become massive features of the marine environment.
- Corals are found all over the world's oceans, from the Aleutian Islands off the coast of Alaska to the warm tropical waters of the Caribbean sea.
- The biggest coral reefs are found in the clear, shallow waters of the tropics and sub-tropics.
- The largest of these coral reef systems, the **Great Barrier Reef** in Australia, is more than 1,500 miles long (2,400 kilometres).

Conditions for Coral Formation

The following favourable conditions are essential for the development and existence of corals :

- **Temperature** Corals are generally found in 30° North and 30° South latitude. They need temperature of 20°C for development. They live in the depth of 45-55 m where sunlight reaches in sufficient quantity.

- **Salinity** Corals develop in clean saline water. Freshwater and highly saline water is not favourable for their development. They also not develop in deltaic regions.
- **Oxygen and Plankton** They need oxygen and plankton to remain alive and growth. That's why corals rapidly develop towards the continental slope.

Areas of Coral Reefs

- Coral reefs are widely regarded as one of the top conservation priorities globally. Such as ecosystem harbours an extraordinary biodiversity, marine ecosystem services and are highly vulnerable to human stressors.
- However, most of this knowledge is derived from studies on nearshore and shallow-water reefs, with coral reef ecosystems remaining virtually unstudied in marine **Areas Beyond National Jurisdiction** (ABNJ), commonly known as the **high seas.**
- The majority of reef-building coral records in ABNJ were in association with geomorphological features that have steep topographies. These habitats, which include escarpments, seamounts, and submarine ridges accounted for >74% of the records in international waters.

Types of Coral Reefs

Coral reefs are classified as follows

Fringing Reefs

- These reefs that grow directly from a shore. They are located very close to land and often form a shallow lagoon between the beach and the main body of the reef.
- A fringing reef runs as a narrow belt (1-2 km wide). This type of reef grows from the deep sea bottom with the seaward side sloping steeply into the deep sea. Coral polyps do not extend outwards because of sudden and large increase in depth.
- The fringing reef is by far the most common of the three major types of coral reefs, with numerous examples in all major regions of coral reef development.
- Fringing reefs can be seen at the **New Hebrides Society islands** off Australia and off the Southern coast of Florida.

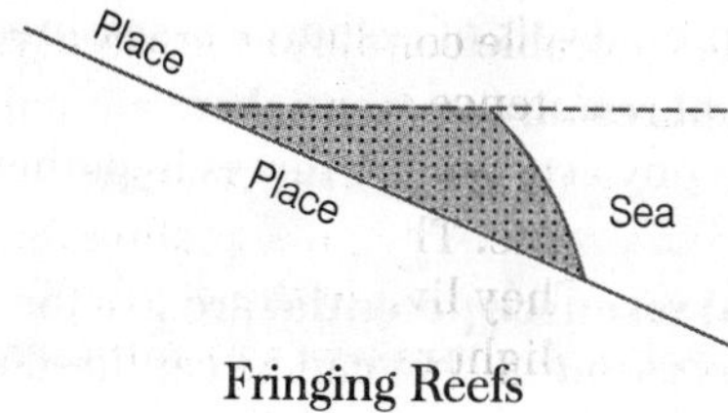

Fringing Reefs

Barrier Reefs

- These are extensive linear reef complexes that parallel a shore and are separated from it by lagoon.
- This is the largest (in size, not distribution) of the three reefs runs for hundreds of kilometres and is several kilometres wide. It extends as a broken, irregular ring around the coast or an island, running almost parallel to it.
- Barrier reefs are far less common than fringing reefs or atolls, although examples can be found in the tropical Atlantic as well as the Pacific.
- The 1200-mile long Great Barrier Reef off the North-Eastern coast off Australia is the world's largest example of this reef type.
- The **Great Barrier Reef** is not actually a single reef as the name implies, but rather a very large complex consisting of many reefs.

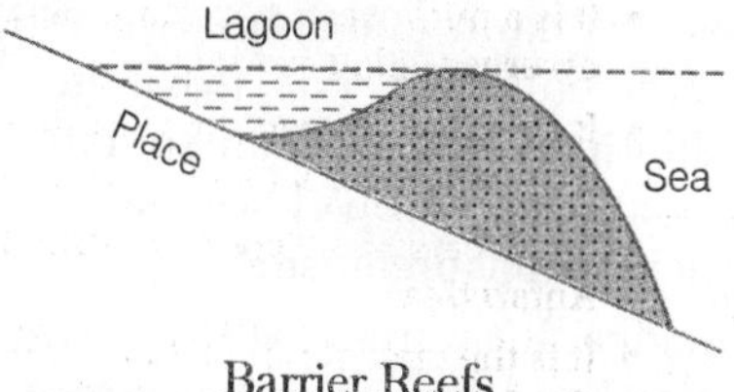

Barrier Reefs

Atoll

- An atoll is a roughly circular (annular) oceanic reef system surrounding a large (and often deep) central lagoon.
- The lagoon has a depth 80-150 m and may be joined with seawater through a number of channels cutting across the reef.
- Atolls are located at great distances from deep sea platforms, where the submarine features may help in formation of atolls, such as a submerged island or a volcanic cone which may reach a level suitable for coral growth.

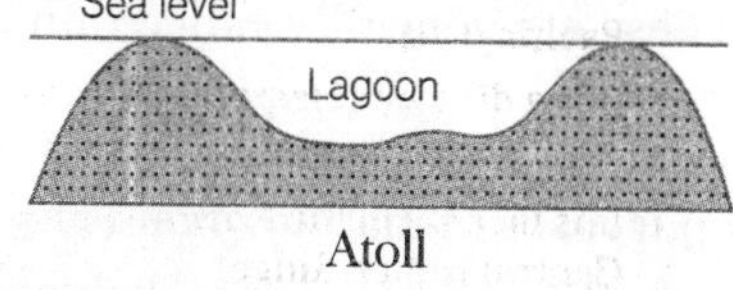

Atoll

Marine Resources

- The ocean is one of Earth's most valuable natural resources.
- It provides food in the form of fish and shellfish-about 200 billion pounds are caught each year.
- Ocean resources provide jobs, goods and services for billions of people around the world and have immense economic importance.

- Their resources includes food, fuel, renewable energy, minerals, sand and gravel and tourism.
- It is mined for minerals (salt, sand, gravel and some manganese, copper, nickel, iron and cobalt can be found in the deep sea) and drilled for crude oil.
- The ocean plays a critical role in removing carbon from the atmosphere and providing oxygen. It regulates Earth's climate.

Classification of Marine Resources

Marine resources can be divided into the following categories.

Marine Biological Resources (MBR)

- The biotic and abiotic resources found in the oceanic water and bottoms are called marine resources. They include marine water, inherent energy in the oceanic water (e.g., wave energy, tidal energy, etc.), biotic life of marine water (plants and animals), marine deposits and abiotic elements (minerals, fossil fuels, etc.), biotic and abiotic matter of ocean bottoms, benthic organisms, etc. Even a drop of oceanic water contains countless microscopic organisms.
- Marine Biological Resources (MBR) are divided into two parts - Food and Non-Food Resources.

(i) Food Resources

- On the basis of uses, marine food resources are divided into two types :
  - (a) Protein rich food resources for the use as food for human being (e.g. fishes).
  - (b) Animal feed mainly for domesticated animals. The contribution of fish in the world annual income from marine resources of all categories stands second.

(ii) Non-Food Resources

- The important marine non-food resources includes corals. They are animals in the groups of marine organisms. These are generally called rainforests of the oceans.
- The coral colonies provide different types of habitats for different purposes of marine organisms.
- Most of sea fish lay eggs in the coral colonies. In fact, corals are the base of marine biological community. The marine biological health depends on the richness of corals.
- Marine organisms (plants and animals) are also divided into three categories on the basis of their habitats :

(a) **Planktons** are floating and drifting micro plants and animals of photic zone. These are divided into phytoplankton (plant planktons) and zooplanktons (animal planktons).

(b) **Nektons** include algae, strong and powerful floating and swimming marine animals mainly fish. These marine animals move in all the zones of the oceanic environments. e.g., Pelagic fish, Demersal fish, etc.

(c) **Benthos** include those plants (non-photosynthetic or non-phototrophs) and animals which live at the bottoms of the seas and oceans e.g., ephibenthic community, benthic organisms, inflora and infauna.

Benthos comprise both the mobile and immobile. Mobile benthos are lobsters, crabs, snails, burrowing calms and worms.

Immobile benthos, plants like seaweeds and edgrass and animals like corals, sponges, barnacles and oysters.

Most are found in shallow waters only some are found in the deep oceans.

Marine Mineral Resources

This can be categorised into two parts

(i) On the Basis of Location

- Minerals of the continental shelf deposits
- Minerals of the continental slope deposits
- Minerals of the deep sea bottom deposits

(ii) On the Basis of Nature

- Metallic minerals
- Fuel minerals (petroleum and natural gas)
- Construction materials (gravels, sands, etc)

Energy Resources

- To understand the full potential for future electricity production that can be harnessed through our nation's water resources, the **Water Power Technologies Office** (WPTO) conducted the following resource assessments :
  - **Waves** energy contained in ocean surface waves.
  - **Tidal streams** energy contained in the flow of water from tides.
  - **Ocean currents** energy contained in the flow of water resulting from large-scale ocean circulation patterns.
  - **River currents** energy contained in rivers that can be harnessed without flow diversion structures such as dams.
  - **Ocean thermal gradients** energy contained in the temperature difference between ocean surface and deeper waters.
- There are three levels of resource assessments :
  - **Theoretical resource potential** are annual average amount of physical energy that is hypothetically available
  - **Technical resource potential** are portion of a theoretical resource that can be captured using a specific technology

- **Practical resource potential** are portion of the technical resource that is available when other constraints (e.g., economic, environmental, and regulatory considerations) are factored in.

Fresh Water Resources

- Fresh water is vital to life and yet it is a finite resource. Of all the water on Earth, just 3% is fresh water. Although critical to natural and human communities, fresh water is threatened by a myriad of forces including overdevelopment, polluted runoff and global warming.
- With this in mind, World Wildlife Fund (WWF) partners with communities, businesses and others to decrease pollution, increase water efficiency and protect natural areas to ensure enough clean water exists to conserve wildlife and provide a healthy future for all.

Maritime Zone

- **United Nations Convention on the Law of the Sea** (UNCLOS) 1982 (Law of the Sea)
- UNCLOS is the only international convention which stipulates a framework for state jurisdiction in maritime spaces. It provides a different legal status to different maritime zones.
- It provides the backbone for off shore governance by coastal states and those navigating the oceans. It not only zones coastal states' off shore areas but also provides specific guidance for states' rights and responsibilities in the five concentric zones.
- **Baseline** It is the low-water line along the coast as officially recognised by the coastal state.
- It divides marine areas into five main zones namely— **Internal Waters, Territorial Sea, Contiguous Zone, Exclusive Economic Zone** (EEZ) and the **High Seas.**

Internal Waters

- Internal waters are waters on the landward side of the baseline from which the breadth of the territorial sea is measured.
- Each coastal state has full sovereignty over its internal waters as like its land territory. Examples of internal waters include bays, ports, inlets, rivers and even lakes that are connected to the sea.
- There is no right of **innocent passage** through internal waters.
- The innocent passage refers to the passing through the waters which are not prejudicial to peace and security. However, the nations have the right to suspend the same.

Territorial Sea

- The territorial sea extends seaward up to **12 Nautical Miles** (NM) from its baselines.
- A nautical mile is based on the circumference of the Earth and is equal to one minute of latitude. It is slightly more than a land measured mile (1 nautical mile = 1.1508 land miles or 1.85 km).
- The coastal states have Sovereignty and Jurisdiction over the territorial sea. These rights extend not only on the surface but also to the seabed, subsoil and even airspace.
- But the coastal state's rights are limited by the innocent passage through the territorial sea.

Contiguous Zone

- The contiguous zone extends seaward up to 24 nm from its baselines.
- It is an intermediary zone between the territorial sea and the high seas.
- The coastal state has the right to both prevent and punish infringement of fiscal, immigration, sanitary, and customs laws within its Territory and Territorial sea.
- Unlike the territorial sea, the contiguous zone only gives jurisdiction to a state on the ocean's surface and floor. It does not provide air and space rights.

Exclusive Economic Zone (EEZ)

- Each coastal State may claim an EEZ beyond and adjacent to its territorial sea that extends seaward up to 200 miles from its baselines.
- Within its EEZ, a coastal state has :
  - Sovereign rights for the purpose of exploring, exploiting, conserving and managing natural resources, whether living or non-living, of the seabed and subsoil.
  - Rights to carry out activities like the production of energy from the water, currents and wind.
- Unlike the territorial sea and the contiguous zone, the EEZ only allows for the above-mentioned resource rights. It does not give a coastal state the right to prohibit or limit freedom of navigation or overflight, subject to very limited exceptions.

High Seas

- The ocean surface and the water column beyond the EEZ are referred to as the high seas.
- It is considered as "The common heritage of all mankind" and is beyond any national jurisdiction.
- States can conduct activities in these areas as long as they are for peaceful purposes, such as transit, marine science and undersea exploration.

Major Straits of the World

Strait	Description
Palk Strait	It connects the Bay of Bengal with the Gulf of Mannar.
Strait of Gibraltar	It connects the Atlantic ocean with the Mediterranean sea and separates Gibraltar and Spain in the North from Morocco in the South.
Duncan Passage	It is a strait separating Rutland to the North and Little Andaman to the South.
Nine Degree Channel	This Channel connects Laccadive islands of Kalapeni, Suheli Par and Maliku Atoll.
Ten Degree Channel	It separates the Andaman islands from the Nicobar islands in the Bay of Bengal.
Strait of Hormuz	It lies between UAE and Oman on the South-West and Iran on the North-East. It connects the Persian Gulf with the Gulf of Oman. It is strategically very important as it controls the oil trade from the Gulf countries.
Strait of Bab-El- Mandab	It connects the Red sea with the Gulf of Aden and separates Asia from Africa.
Malacca Strait	It is a longest strait. It separates Peninsular Malaysia from Sumatra island of Indonesia. It connects the Pacific ocean to the Indian ocean. It provides a shorter route from the Andaman sea to the South China sea and therefore is the busiest waterway of the world.
Sunda Strait	It connects the Java sea to the Indian ocean and separates Java island of Indonesia from its Sumatra island.
Bering Strait	It separates Russia and Alaska and connects the East Siberian Sea in the Arctic ocean with the Bering sea in the Pacific ocean.
Oranto Strait	It connects the Adriatic sea with the Ionian sea and separates Italy from Albania.
Bosphorus Strait	It connects the Black sea with the sea of Marmara. It is the world's narrowest navigable strait.
Dardanelles Strait	It lies between the Asian Turkey and European Turkey and connects the Aegean sea with the sea of Marmara. It is a vital link of transportation between the Black sea and the Mediterranean sea.
La Parouses Strait	It lies between the Sakhalin island and Hokkaido island of Japan and connects the sea of Okhotsk with the sea of Japan.
Strait of Tartary/Tartar	It separates Russian island Sakhalin from Mainland Asia. It connects the sea of Okhotsk in the North to the sea of Japan in the South.
Tsugaru Strait	It lies between Hokkaido and Honshu in Northern Japan and connects the Sea of Japan to the Pacific ocean.
Taiwan Strait or Formosa Strait	It lies between Taiwan (Republic of China) and Mainland China (People's Republic of China). It connects South China Sea with the East China Sea.
Mozambique Strait	It lies in the Indian ocean between Mozambique from Madagascar.
Yucatan Strait	It lies between Mexico and Cuba and connects the Gulf of Mexico with the Caribbean sea.
Florida Strait	It lies between the Florida state of the USA and Cuba.
Hudson Strait	It connects the Hudson Bay (Canada) with the Labrador sea.
Davis Strait	It connects the Baffin Bay with the Atlantic ocean.
Cook Strait	It lies between the North and the South islands of New Zealand and connects the Tasman sea with the South Pacific ocean.
Bass Strait	It separates Tasmania from the Australian mainland.
Torres Strait	It lies in the Pacific ocean, between Cape York Peninsula of Australia and Papua New Guinea
Magellan Strait	It separates Mainland South America from Tierra Del Fuego (an archipelago off the Southern-most tip of the South American Mainland)
Dover Strait	It lies in the narrowest part of the English Channel, connecting it with the North Sea. It separates Britain from Continental Europe.
North Channel	It separates Ireland from Scotland and connects the Irish sea with the Atlantic ocean.

Major River Systems in the World

River	Country	Source	Destination
Amazon	Peru, Ecuador, Brazil	Andes Mountain	Atlantic Ocean
Amur	China, Mongolia, Russia	Lake Khanka	Sea of Okhotsk
Brahmaputra	China, India, Bangladesh	Tibet	Andaman Sea
Chang Jiang	Kunlun Shan	China	East China Sea
Danube	Germany, Austria, Hungary, Slovakia, Croatia, Serbia, Romania, Bulgaria, Moldova	Black Forest Mountain	Black Sea
Dnieper	Russia, Belarus, Ukraine	Valdai Hills (Russia)	Black Sea
Ganga	India	Gangotri	Bay of Bengal
Huang Ho	China	Kunlun Mountain	Gulf of Bohai
Indus	India, China, Pakistan	Mt. Kailas	Arabian Sea
Irrawaddy	Myanmar	Mali River	Andaman Sea
Lena	Russia	Lake Baikal	Laptev Sea
Mississippi	Canada, USA	Lake Itasca	Gulf of Mexico
Mackenzie	Canada	Great Slave Lake	Beaufort Sea
Mekong	China, Thailand, Laos, Vietnam, Cambodia, Myanmar	Lasagongma Spring	South China Sea
Murray	Australia	Australian Alps	Southern Ocean
Madeira	Brazil, Bolivia	Mamore River	Amazon River
Nile	Democratic Republic of Congo, Tanzania, Uganda, Sudan, Egypt	Blue Nile, White Nile	Mediterranean Sea
Niger	Nigeria, Mali, Niger, Benin, Guinea	Guinea Highlands	Gulf of Guinea
Irtysh	China, Russia	Altai Mountain	Ob River
Orinoco	Columbia, Venezuela	Parma Mountains	Atlantic Ocean

Lakes

- A lake (from the Latin word *lacus*) is an inland body of water, not part of the ocean, that is larger and deeper than a pond and is localised at the bottom of a basin.
- In ecology, the environment of a lake is described as **lacustrine**. The study of lakes, ponds, and other inland bodies of water and related ecosystems is called limnology.

Classification of Lakes

- There are two types of lakes based on geography and circulation patterns, *viz*
  - **Polar lakes** The surface temperature of these lake never exceeds 4°C.
  - **Lakes in temperate regions** The surface temperature of these lake varies above and below 4°C. The bottom temperature maintains circulation in all seasons like the surface.
- Classification of lakes based on temperature cycles and stratification
  - **Amictic** Permanently frozen and always below 4°C. There is never any circulation.
  - **Cold monomictic** The water at any depth never rises above 4°C. Circulation occurs independently in summer and the temperature stays at or below 4°C.
  - **Dimictic** In spring the lake also has full circulation. At this time, the water temperature is 4°C. Stays on top of it. Layering occurs in summer and mixed again in autumn. At this time, the lake is cold.
  - **Warm monomictic** The water temperature at any level is never below 4°C. Circulation occurs independently in winter or directly above 4°C in summer.
  - **Oligomictic** Such lakes are located in very warm areas. Water temperature is always above 4°C and permanent stratification is normal. As a result of the flow of air, this stratification is soon broken. Such lakes are found in humid tropical regions.
  - **Polymictic** Mixtures occur continuously but only at low temperatures (just above 4°C). There is no thermal stratification.

Important Lakes and Countries

Lake	Location	Area	Length	Maximum Depth
Caspian Sea	Azerbaijan, Russia, Kazakhstan, Turkmenistan-Iran	394,299 Sq. km	1,199 km	946 m
Superior	US, Canada	82,414 Sq. km	616 km	406 m
Victoria	Tanzania, Uganda	69,485 Sq. km	322 km	82 m
Huron	US, Canada	59,596 Sq. km	397 km	229 m
Michigan	U.S.	58,016 Sq. km	517 km	281 m
Aral	Kazakhstan, Uzbekistan	33,800 Sq. km	428 km	68 m
Tanganyika	Tanzania, Congo	32,893 Sq. km	676 km	1,435 m
Baikal	Russia	31,500 Sq. km	636 km	1,741 m
Great Bear	Canada	31,080 Sq. km	373 km	82 m
Nyasa	Malawi, Mozambique, Tanzania	30,044 Sq. km	579 km	706 m
Great Slave	Canada	28,930 Sq. km	480 km	614 m
Chad	Chad, Niger, Nigeria	25,760 Sq. km	-	7 m
Erie	US, Canada	25,719 Sq. km	388 km	64 m
Winnipeg	Canada	23,553 Sq. km	425 km	62 m
Ontario	US, Canada	19,477 Sq. km	311 km	237 m
Balkhash	Kazakhstan	18,428 Sq. km	605 km	27 m
Ladoga	Russia	18,130 Sq. km	200 km	225 m
Onega	Russia	9,891 Sq. km	248 km	110 m
Titicaca	Bolivia, Peru	8,135 Sq. km	177 km	370 m
Nicaragua	Nicaragua	8,001 Sq. km	177 km	70 m
Athabasca	Canada	7,920 Sq. km	335 km	124 m
Rudolf	Kenya	6,405 Sq. km	248 km	
Reindeer	Canada	6,330 Sq. km	245 km	
Eyre	South Australia	6,216 Sq. km	209 km	
Issyk, Kul	Kyrgyzstan	6,200 Sq. km	182 km	700 m
Great Salt	US	4,662 Sq. km	121 km	5–8 m
Kioga	Uganda	4,403 Sq. km	80 km	9 m

Wetlands

- A wetland is a place where the land is covered by water, either salt, fresh or somewhere in between. Marshes, the edge of a lake or ocean, the delta at the mouth of a river, low-lying areas that frequently flood, all of these are wetlands.
- WWF, governments and other organisations have pursued efforts to conserve and protect wetlands for more than 40 years through the **Ramsar Convention**, the only international treaty devoted to a single ecosystem type.

Types of Wetlands

On the basis of location, wetlands can be classified as follows :

Marshes

- Marshes are wetlands that are always inundated, rather than being submerged under water just during the summer or a couple of months over the year, for instance.
- Marshes can be freshwater or saltwater and amount of water in the marsh can change with the seasons. Marshes wildlife include beavers, alligators, newts, shrimp and turtles.

Swamps

- Swamps differ from marshes in that, typically, they are dominated by woody plants (rather than soft-stemmed plants).
- Some of these trees are often used as timber and to build their homes. This which can affect the ecosystem drastically if too many are taken without being replaced with new saplings. There are two main types of swamps
  (i) Swamp forests and (ii) Shrub swamps.

Bogs

- Bogs are characterised by more acidic waters and spongy peat deposits as well as a covering of sphagnum moss.
- Unlike marshes and swamps, bogs tend to get their wetness from precipitation rather than waterways such as streams or runoffs from rivers.
- These wetlands are fantastic for preventing downstream flooding since, they absorb precipitation as it falls and prevents the swelling of rivers and other waterways.

Fens

- Fens are, like bogs, peat-forming wetlands, although they usually get their wetness from groundwater rather than precipitation, which means that they are slightly less acidic.
- This means that they tend to support a greater array of wildlife, from plants to fish to birds and everything in between.

Major Wetlands

iSimangaliso Wetland Park	It resides on the Zululand coast in South Africa. This park went on to become the first World Heritage Site located in South Africa.
Kakadu Wetlands	It is located in the Northern Territory of Australia, is spread nearly to 20,000 sq km. Kakadu is home to exceptional natural beauty and unique biodiversity.
Pantanal	These are the world's largest freshwater wetland, is a seasonally flooded plain nourished by the tributaries of the Paraguay river in Brazil.
Camargue	The city of Arles, France hosts one of the famous wetlands in the world known as Camargue.
Mekong Delta	Located in South-Western Vietnam, Mekong Delta is the region where the Mekong river merges into the sea through a network of tributaries.
Wasur National Park	It is the part of the largest wetland in Indonesia.
Okavango Delta	These are the Botswana exists, like a dazzling ornament at the heart of the Kalahari desert. A maze of gleaming pools, rambling channels and astonishing islands teeming with unique wildlife consolidates together to describe Okavango Delta. It is a habitat to a variety of animals like Elephant, Hippopotamus, Giraffe, Crocodile, Lion, Cheetah, Rhinoccros and Zebra.
Kerala Backwaters	The spectacular backwaters of Kerala, India consists of a placid stretch of lakes, canals, and lagoons which reside parallel to the coast of the Arabian Sea.
Everglades	Everglades National Park protects an exceptional mural which attracts millions of tourists from all over the world. Everglades is located in South Florida, the USA had 1.5 million acres of wetland.
Sunderbans	It lies in West Bengal, India and stretches to Bangladesh. Sundarbans, being the largest halophytic mangrove forest in the world has an area of approximately 10,000 sq km.

Extra Facts From Tamil Nadu Board and NIOS

- Lake **Baikal** is the deepest freshwater lake in the world and **Caspian Sea** is the largest saltwater lake in the world.
- **Pallikaranai wetland** is a freshwater swamp adjacent to the Bay of Bengal situated in the Southern part of Chennai.
- The Southern ocean is the youngest ocean and was formed 30 million years ago when South America moved away from Antarctica, opening the Drake Passage.
- The Arctic ocean's salinity is the lowest on an average of the five major oceans.
- The configuration of an ocean floor is shown with the help of a 'Hypsometric curve' or 'Hypsographic curve'.
  It is a graph denoting the proportion of a landmass standing above or below the sea level.
- Isaac Newton (1642-1727) was the first person to explain tides scientifically.
- Interval between two high tides or low tides is exactly 12 hours 25 minutes.
- In the Bay of Fundy, between Nova Scotia and New Brunswick of Canada, the difference between high and low tides is as high as 14m. The Gulf Stream was discovered by **Ponce de Leon** in 1513.
- The Nile river in Africa is the longest river in the world, it drains into the Mediterranean sea forming a delta to the North of Cairo city.
- The river Amazon in South America, is the second longest river, and has the largest drainage basin of any river.
- The Yangtze river, which flows in China, is the longest river in Asia and the third longest river in the world
- The **Mississippi-Missouri** system in the United States is the fourth longest river system in the world.
- The continental shelf of the Eastern coast of India is much wider than that of the Western coast.
- The recent discovery of petroleum in the Godavari basin are examples of on shore drilling.

07

Soil and Natural Vegetation

(SOURCES)

Class-IXth New NCERT Chap 5 (Natural Vegetation and Wildlife), Class-VIII New NCERT Chap 2 (Land, Soil, Water, Natural Vegetation and Wildlife Resources), Class-XI Old NCERT Chap 7 (Soils) Class-XIth New NCERT Chap 5 (Geomorphic Processes), Tamil Nadu Board (Class XI), NIOS

Soil

- Soil is a mixture of many solid, liquid and gaseous substances.
- It forms the top most layer of the **Earth's** crust. Soils are indispensable for the growth of all plants.
- The soil consists of mineral matter such as sand and clay as well as **organic matter** such us decayed leaves, flowers, dead tissues of organisms, minute bacteria and earthworms.
- **Pedology** is the science of soil and **pedologist** is the soil scientist.

Soil Forming Process

The process of soil formation is called as **Pedogenesis.** Soil forming process includes various steps like:

- **Translocation** It is the movement of soil constituents within the profile or between horizons. Translocation of materials is primarily due to gradients in water potential and chemical concentrations within the soil pores.
- **Leaching** It is the removal of soluble components of the soil column. Leaching is the gravitational movement of water that affects the chemical composition of a soil by moving the soluble chemicals deeper into the soil profile.

  As water washes down through the soil, it can carry away bases as well as acidification through the substitution of hydrogen ions.
- **Eluviation** It is the removal of finer grained particles like clay particles from the top soil. It is the movement down the profile. The materials are moved in suspension by water which is percolating downward. The upper layer from which materials have been eluviated is called the **eluvial zone.**
- **Illuviation** The accumulation in the lower part of the profile of material eluviated from above is called illuviation. This is the deposition or accumulation of materials that have been washed down from the upper layer to the lower horizon of the soil through the process of eluviation. Illuviation sometimes leads to the formation of a hardpan or crust of laterite.
- **Calcification** It is the formation and accumulation of calcium carbonate and gypsum in arid and semi-arid regions. Here, parent materials in these climatic regions are rich in lime and gypsum. It occurs when the evaporation exceeds precipitation. Under such conditions, the material has an upward movement within the profile due to capillary action.
- **Salinisation/Alkalisation** This happens when temporary excess of water and extreme evaporation bring the underground salts to the surface and a whitish fluorescent crust is left behind.

  Alkalisation is the process by which soils with high exchangeable sodium and pH greater than 8.5 are formed. It is often sodium carbonate and sodium bicarbonate are formed in extreme cases of alkalisation. Such soils are called **sodic soils** or **alkali soils**.

- **Podzolisation/Cheluviation** It occurs in cool, humid climates where the bacterial activity is low through the influence of organic agents which are also referred to as chelating agents. The process involves plant acids rather than mere water as the case with **leaching**. During podzolisation or cheluviation, the upper horizons become rich in silica and the lower horizons rich in sesquioxides- mainly of iron.
- **Organic Changes** These changes occur mainly on the surface and follow a specific sequence. This process involves the accumulation of decaying plants and animal matter on the ground surface.

  The accumulated mass slowly breaks down to form humus which is a major component of the soil. Degrading or breakdown of the organic material by algae, fungi, insects and worms causes humification which leaves behind, a dark and amorphous humus.
- **Gleying** It is a soil forming process that occurs in waterlogged, anaerobic conditions. It occurs when iron compounds are reduced and either removed from the soil or segregated out as concretions in the soil. Under such conditions, some specialised bacteria flourish which use up the organic matter.
- **Desilication/Lateralisation** Such processes are common in hot, wet tropical and equatorial climates. Desilication (or desilicification) is the removal of silicon from a soil or soil horizon, relative to some less mobile component or components. High temperature leaves little or no humus on the surface.

Factors Influencing Soil Formation

Important factors that influence the formation of soil are as follows :

Parent Rock

- The material in which soil forms is called **parent material.**
- Soils are formed by the direct weathering of underlying rocks. Also soils form in materials that have moved in from elsewhere.
- These soils have the same general chemistry as the original rocks. The parent rock controls texture permeability and fertility of soil.

Climate

- The climate exercises influence temperature and rainfall. Temperature and moisture amounts cause different patterns of **weathering** and **leaching**.
- **Temperature** and **precipitation** influence how fast parent material weather. Thus, soil properties such as mineral composition and organic matter content also depend on it.
- Temperature directly influences the speed of chemical reactions. High temperature facilitates more bacterial activity, more weathering. Little organic activity, low temperature help in forming thicker, organic layers of soil.
- Precipitation governs water movement in the soil. The amount of water the soil receives and the amount of evapotranspiration influence water movement.

Biological Activity

- Plants and animals are the instruments of biotic activity. These include organisms that live in the soil, such as bacteria and gophers and vegetation growing on the surface.
- Organisms in the soil can speed up or slow down soil formation. Soils formed under forests tend to be more weathered because forests grow in higher rainfall areas.
- Plants form humus in the soil profile, which is basically a decayed plant material.

Topography

- Various aspects of topography have their own influence on the process of soil formation.
- Steep, long slopes mean water will run down faster and potentially erode the surfaces of slopes.
- The effect will be poor soils on the slopes and richer deposits at the foot of the slopes.

Time

- Soils take many years to form. Younger soils have some characteristics from their parent material.
- As the age increases, the addition of organic matter, exposure to moisture and other environmental factors may change its features.
- A more porous rock like sandstone or a less massive rock like glacial till may take less time in soil formation than an impervious rock or a more massive rock like dark basalt.

Soil Profile

- The soil profile is the vertical arrangement of horizons down to the parent material.
- A young soil means the soil where the factors of soil formation and **pedogenic processes** are still operative the processes have not made a distinct impression on the soil profile.
- A mature soil represents a steady state in respect of the parent material.
- A vertical section through different layers of the soil is called the soil profile. Each layer differs in feel (texture) colour, depth and chemical composition. These layers are referred to as **horizons.**
- Soil profiles differ from one location to another.
- The soil horizons depict the history of soil formation. There are five **master horizons** in the soil profile. These are designated by the capital letters **O, A, E, B.** Both **C, O** represents the organic horizon at the surface.

Properties of Soil

Physical, chemical and biological properties of soil are discussed as follows :

Physical Properties

- **Colour** The colour of the soil is defined by two factors, its organic content and the chemical nature of compounds found in the soil. Iron gives soil a brown, yellow or red colour and the organic matter gives a black or dark brown colour to it.
- **Texture** It refers to the mixture of different soil particles grading from fine to coarse and also the ability of the soil to retain water and to drain it to lower levels
- **Sandy** It contains large proportion of sand grains and has large pore spaces making it less water retentive
- **Clay** It contains large proportion of clay particles and a little proportion of sand and has small pore spaces making them more water retentive
- **Loamy** It has equal proportion of sand, silt and clay and hence, it is the best for plant growth and ploughing it is easier.

Chemical Properties

- **Acidic Soil** Soil with low lime content is called acidic in nature and they are indicated by **low pH values**, soils in humid regions tend to be acidic in nature.
- **Alkaline Soil** Soil with high lime content is called alkaline in nature and are indicated by **high pH values**, soils in arid and semi-arid regions tend to be alkaline.

Biological Properties

- **Respiration rate** CO_2 evolution under standard laboratory conditions or at the field.
- **Potential N/C mineralisation** Increase in mineral nitrogen or carbon content under standard laboratory conditions.
- **Earthworm** Density of earthworms.
- **Bacterial biomass** Total bacterial biomass for a given soil mass.
- **Bacterial diversity** It can be determined by functional groups, or describing genetic diversity.

Classification of Soil

The soil classification was first done by Russian pedologist, **Dokuchaev.**

Classification on the Basis of Parent Rock

On the basis of parent rocks and location of formation, soils can be classified as follows :

Azonal Soil

- Azonal soils are of recent origin and soil forming processes have not been operation for long. They are not linked to prevailling climate of that area and its horizons are not distinct.
- These are immature soils as a result of high altitude, low temperature and slow decay of organic matter. e.g. volcanic soil, till, loess sand, etc.

Intrazonal Soil

- Soils are found within the definite climatic belt, but it is different from normal because of dominance of any local factor.
- **Calcimorphic** or calcareous soils develop on limestone and **hydromorphic** soils develops in water abundance regions. **Halomorphic** soils are saline in nature due to high salt level and found in dry regions.

Zonal Soil

- Zonal soils are formed at the site of their parent rocks and the influence of parent rock and climate is clearly visible and are major determining factors.
- They are mature, have distinct profile and clear horizons. e.g. Tundra soil in Arctic, Mediterranean soil in Mediterranean climate, red yellow soil in desert and latosols in equatorial climates are zonal soils.

Classification on the Basis of Chemical Compositions

On the basis of chemical compositions, soils are broadly classified as follows:

Pedalfer

Pedalfer soils have abundance of aluminium and iron. These are of following types :

- **Podzol** They develop in the regions where precipitation exceeds evapotranspiration. These soils are sandy and develop in cooler climate or Tundra region and coniferous forest is found there. Leaching is intense, humus acidic and horizons are bleached as iron, aluminium and organic matter is removed. Soils are acidic and not encourage earthworm.
- **Grey Podzol** This soil is found in the Taiga coniferous region of the sub-Arctic climatic zone.
  - **A-horizon** is eluviated- bleached grey appearance (silica accumulation).
  - **B-horizon** is illuviated- hard clayey pan, sesquioxide rich, nodules and concretion of brown colour.

  This is acidic in nature (pH = 4) because of slow decomposition of organic matter and hence, unsuitable for agriculture.

- **Grey-Brown Podzol** This soil is found in the deciduous forest region of the mid-latitudes, rich in humus. It can be fertile by the use of manures and fertilisers and crop rotation. It is suitable for dairy farming and mixed farming practices.
- **Red-Yellow Podzol** This soil is formed by the processes of podzolisation and laterisation in the sub-tropical climatic region. Pronounced leaching because of high rainfall. It is devoid of humus since, warmer regions enhance pronounced bacterial activity. Productivity is fertiliser responsive and high crop yield.
- **Red Podzol or Terra Rossa** This soil found in the Mediterranean and Lime regions, is red in appearance due to presence of Fe_2O_3. It is devoid of humus because moist conditions enhance bacterial activity. They are deeply weathered, but lack distinct horizons. Low fertility and can be productive if used scientifically.
- **Laterite Soil** This soil is formed in the regions of high temperature, abundant rainfall and equatorial forests, where the process of leaching is dominant.
  Though humus is available in ample amount, yet due to consumption by microbes and the process of leaching, very little of it is left. Salts of Al and Fe_2O_3 are found in the upper layers of this soil. Crust formation near the surface, nodular concretions, induration. When dry, it becomes hard and forms a useful building material.

Pedocals

Pedocals have abundance of calcium. These are of following types :

- **Brown Earths** These are moderately or well-drained soil, found where precipitation exceeds potential evapotranspiration and particles move downward through the soil. They are main soil of UK and other warm temperate climate. The soil is reasonably fertile.
- **Chernozem** It is the most fertile soil. It needs very little fertilisers and irrigation. It is found in the Steppe region. It is black in colour due to abundance of humus. Lime is found in abundance in its lower layers.
- **Chestnut** It is dark brown soil found in the drier parts of Chernozem region. It contains less humus than the Chernozem. Lighter colour than Chernozem. Formation of $CaCO_3$ nodule in B-horizon. Red chestnut and red-brown soil is found in semi-arid parts of the Savanna region.
- **Prairie Soil** This is the soil having properties both of Chernozem and grey-brown podzol are found in the wet temperate tall grass region. Its colour is brown-black due to abundance of humus. It is a fertile soil. It is found in the **Prairie region** of USA, **Pampas** of South America, **Pustaz** of Hungary and **Downs** of Australia.
- **Sierozems** This is a basic soil (pH>8) found in the hot deserts of the mid-latitudes. Lime forms a deposition over the upper layer of the soil. Thin soils having poor in nitrogen and humus, near absence of humus or low humus content.
- **Red Desert Soil** This is the soil of hot deserts in the tropical region. It is characterised by deposition of lime near the surface and absence of humus. Moderate to high fertility depending on nitrogen (N) content. Productive if abundant irrigation is available and salt removed.

USDA Soil Classification

CF Marbut of USA gave an extensive scheme, called **USDA System** (US Department of Agriculture), for the classification of world soils in 1938. Under USDA system, world soils are divided into 10 orders, 47 sub-orders and 185 great soil groups.

- Alfisols
- Gelisols
- Histosols
- Entisols
- Oxisols
- Ultisols
- Andisols
- Aridisols
- Inceptisols
- Vertisols
- Spodosols
- Mollisols

Soil Conservation

- Soil conservation is a methodology to maintain soil fertility, prevent soil erosion and exhaustion. It also helps to improve the degraded condition of the soil.
- Experiments have been made to stabilise sand dunes in Western Rajasthan by the **Central Arid Zone Research Institute** (CAZRI).
- The **Central Soil Conservation Board**, set up by the Government of India, has prepared a number of plans for soil conservation in different parts of the country.
- Some methods of soil conservation are listed below:
  - **Mulching** The bare ground between plants is covered with a layer of organic matter like straw. It helps to retain soil moisture.
  - **Contour barriers** Stones, grass, soil is used to build barriers along contours. Trenches are made in front of the barriers to collect water.
  - **Rock dam** Rocks are piled up to slow down the flow of water. This prevents gullies and further soil loss. In bigger gullies, the erosive velocity of water may be reduced by constructing a series of check dams. Special attention should be made to control headward extension of gullies.
  - **Terrace farming** Broad flat steps or terraces are made on the steep slopes so that flat surfaces are available to grow crops. They reduce surface run-off and soil erosion. Finger gullies can be eliminated by terracing.

- **Intercropping** Different crops are grown in alternate rows and are sown at different times to protect the soil from rain wash.
- **Contour ploughing** Ploughing parallel to the contours of a hill slope to form a natural barrier for water to flow down the slope.
- **Shelter belts** In the coastal and dry regions, rows of trees are planted to check the wind movement to protect soil cover. In arid and semi-arid areas, efforts should be made to protect cultivable lands from encroachment by sand dunes through developing shelter belts of trees and ago-forestry.

Natural Vegetation

- A natural vegetation is a plant community that has been left undistributed for an extended period of time. They grow naturally in response to climatic variables.
- There is a close relationship between height of land and the character of vegetation. With the change in height, the climate changes. This ultimately changes natural vegetation. The growth of vegetation depends on **temperature** and **moisture**. It also depends on factors like **slope** and **thickness of soil**.
- Natural vegetation of the world is classified into three main categories :

– Forests – Grasslands – Deserts

1. Forest Vegetation

This can be further classified based on the climate, temperature and regions found in the world. They are :

– Tundra – Taiga – Equatorial

– Deciduous – Mangrove

Tundra Vegetation

- Tundra's are vast lowlands along the Arctic oceanic shores where the ground is frozen for the majority of the year. The ice caps are limited to lowland and the highlands of these latitude regions, where the ground is permanently covered in snow. With a few months of ice-free weather, the lowlands have tundra vegetation.
- The tundra climate is distinguished by a very low annual mean temperature. Temperatures can drop to 40° C – 50° C below freezing in the middle of winter. Summers are generally milder.
- The tundra is devoid of trees. Mosses, lichens, sedges and other low-level vegetation can be found. Polar bear, caribou, musk-ox and reindeer are the important animals of this region.
- This type of vegetation is found mainly in North of the Arctic Circle in the Northern Hemisphere and also in the North of Asia, Canada and Europe.
- They include the coastal strip of Greenland, the barren grounds of Northern Canada, Alaska and the Arctic seaboard of Eurasia.

Taiga (Coniferous) **Vegetation**

- Taiga accounts for lowest annual average temperatures after the tundra and permanent ice caps.
- They are found only in the Northern Hemisphere due to great East-West extent and absent in the Southern Hemisphere because of the narrowness in the high latitudes. They are found in the regions just below **Arctic Circle**.
- Here, annual precipitation typically ranges from 38 cm to 63 cm. Evergreen coniferous forest is the dominant vegetation. Conifers, which require little moisture, also found in this type of sub-Arctic climate.
- The taiga (a Russian word for coniferous forest) in **Siberia** is the **largest single band of coniferous forest**.
- The richest sources of softwood are the coniferous forest belts of Eurasia and North America.
- In contrast to equatorial rain forests, coniferous forests have a lower density and are more uniform. These forests have trees that grow straight and tall.
- The majority of conifers are evergreen. As with deciduous trees, there is no annual replacement of new leaves.
- It stretches from 50° N to 70° N across Central Canada, some parts of Scandinavian Europe and the majority of Central and Southern Russia. It merges with the Arctic tundra of Canada and Eurasia around the Arctic Circle to the North or polewards.
- As a result, this climate is also known as **'Sub-Arctic climate'**. It has characteristics of both the maritime and continental climates.

Equatorial Vegetation

- A lush tropical rainforest is supported by high temperatures and abundant rainfall. The forest in the Amazon lowlands is so dense that it is referred to as **selvas** (tropical rainforest with a dense canopy).
- Unlike in temperate regions, the growing season here lasts all year; seeding, flowering, fruiting and decay do not follow a seasonal pattern. It is dominated by Maritime Tropical air masses. The region is also a high energy region as it receives maximum insolation from the Sun which explains its rich *flora* and *fauna*.
- Major examples are rosewood, mahogany, ebony, etc. Trees will have greater heights upto 60m or above.
- The majority of the time, it is between 5° N and S of the Equator. Its greatest range is found in the Amazon, Congo, Malaysia and the East Indies lowlands.

- It can be found on three continents:
  - **South America** (Brazil, Bolivia, Colombia, Ecuador, Guyana, Peru, Suriname and Venezuela)
  - **Africa** (Congo, Burundi, Rwanda and Central African Republic, among others)
  - **Asia** (Indonesia, Malaysia, Laos, Cambodia, Thailand, etc.)

Deciduous Vegetation

This can be classified as Temperate and Tropical forests.

Temperate Deciduous

- This type of forest, dominated by broad-leaved deciduous trees, once covered the majority of temperate Europe, Eastern North America, Eastern Asia and small parts of South America and Australia.
- Temperate deciduous forest consists largely of trees that drop their leaves during the cold season.
- It is characteristic of the marine West coast and moist continental climate.
- There is a longer growing season, more intense light, and a moderate amount of precipitation of **50 to 150 cm per year**.
- Its climatic zone is not as extreme as that of the **boreal forest**.
- Soils of temperate forests are podzolic and fairly deep. Shedding begins in **autumn** (fall season) and growth begins in **spring**.
- Some of the common species include oak, elm, ash, birch, beech and poplar.

Tropical Deciduous

- This type of forests are also known as **monsoon forests**. They are found in the belt along the Equator between the Tropic of Cancer and Capricorn as well as in the humid sub-tropics.
- The lowlands carry both evergreen broad-leaved forests and deciduous trees (hardwood). Monsoon forest of the tropical latitude zone differs from tropical deciduous rainforest.
- Most of the trees of the monsoon forest shed their leaves due to stress during the long dry season, which occurs at the time of low Sun and cool temperatures.
- Most of the forests yield valuable timber like teak. Other kinds of timber are sal, acacia and eucalyptus.
- This region includes Eastern margins of the continents between 10°N to 30°N and 10°S to 30°S. It is most developed in India, Burma, Thailand, Laos, Cambodia, parts of Vietnam and South China and Northern Australia.

Mangrove Vegetation

- Mangroves are a group of broad-leaved trees (10-40 feet tall) that grow in muddy creeks and tidal estuaries. They are located on the transition zone between land and sea and are one of the best examples of an **ecotone.**
- They are found along tropical coastlines as they require warm saline water. Mangrove plants thrive in the saltwater zones that exist between the sea and the land.
- Mangroves are confined to only tropical and sub-tropical coastal waters.
- They provide habitat for a wide range of terrestrial and marine organisms. Because it is the meeting point of terrestrial and marine ecosystems, the area of mangroves has a **higher species diversity.**
- Mangroves occur worldwide in the tropics and sub-tropics, mainly between latitudes **25° N and 25° S.** In the warm waters of tropical oceans around the world, there are 15.9 million hectares of mangrove forests.
- They can be found in large numbers along the Atlantic coast from Florida to Argentina. Mangroves can be found on both Africa's Western and Eastern coasts. They extend into India, Myanmar and South-East Asia. In New Zealand and Australia, mangrove forests are also common.

Types of Mangroves

There are three major types :

- **Red mangroves** They grow along coastlines and are the hardiest of the three major mangrove plant types.
- **Black mangroves** They are named so because of their dark-bark. They usually grow at slightly higher elevations than red mangroves. They have access to more oxygen because the roots are more exposed.
- **White mangroves** They grow at higher elevations than red and black mangroves. Generally, they do not have aerial roots.

2. Grassland Vegetation

- Grasslands are **grass-dominated areas.** They account for roughly 20% of the land on the planet's surface. Grasslands occur in both tropical and temperate regions where rainfall is insufficient to support tree growth.
- Grasslands are known by different names around the world. Grasslands can be found in areas with distinct hot and dry, warm and rainy seasons.

Temperate Grasslands

- In Temperate grasslands, woody growth is absent or negligible. The geographical isolation of these areas has resulted in some species differentiation, but most of the other characteristics are similar.
- Tall grass Prairie is a ground cover made up of tall grasses and some broad-leaved herbs known as **forbs.**
- **Steppe,** also known as short-grass Prairie, is made up of sparse clumps of short grasses. In dry areas, steppe transitions to semi-desert and in wetter areas, steppe transitions to prairie.

- Steppe grassland is mostly found in the mid-latitudes of North America and Eurasia.
- Temperate grasslands are found on the outskirts of deserts, away from Mediterranean regions and in the interiors of continents.
- The grasslands are far more extensive and entirely continental in the Northern Hemisphere. They are known as the **Steppes** in Eurasia.
- The grasslands, known as **Prairies** in North America, are also quite extensive. In the case of Argentina and Uruguay's **Pampas**, the grasslands extend all the way to the sea and are heavily influenced by the sea.
- The grasslands of South Africa are divided into the more tropical **Bush-Veld** in the North and the more temperate **High-Veld** in the South, between the Drakensberg and the Kalahari Desert.

Tropical Grasslands

- Tropical grasslands are commonly called **Savannas**. Savannas form a complex ecosystem with scattered medium size trees in grasslands. Its vegetation ranges from woodland to grassland. The woodland has an open, park like appearance.
- In savanna woodland, the trees are spaced rather widely apart because there is not enough soil moisture during the dry season to support a full tree cover.
- The African savanna is widely known for the diversity of its large grazing mammals. With these grazers come a large variety of predators-lions, leopards, cheetahs, hyenas and jackals. Elephants are the largest animals of the savanna and adjacent woodland regions.
- For example, acacias are deciduous trees that shed their leaves during the cool, dry season to prevent excessive water loss through transpiration.
- Many trees are umbrella-shaped, with only a narrow edge exposed to the strong winds.
- It is located on either side of the Equator between 5° and 20° latitude. It is a type of climate that exists between equatorial forests and semi-arid and sub-tropical humid climates.
- The **Llanos** of Orinoco Valley, the **Campos** of Brazil, hilly areas of Central America, Southern Zaire and other savanna climate areas are particularly notable.

3. Desert Vegetation

- The climate of this region always has high temperatures and less rainfall. The lagging in moisture and excessive heat is favourable for plant growth.
- All deserts have some form of vegetation such as grass, scrub, herbs.
- Vegetation of both hot and mid-latitude desert is Xerophytic or drought resistant scrub.
- The major hot deserts of the world are located on the Western coasts of continents between latitudes 15°-30°N and S.
- They include the Sahara Desert, the Great Australian Desert and the other hot deserts like the Arabian Desert, Iranian Desert, Thar Desert, Kalahari and Namib Deserts.

Extra Facts From Tamil Nadu Board and NIOS

- The taiga biome is the largest terrestrial biome and extends across Europe, North America and Asia. This biome has short wet summer and long cold winters. Taiga is the home of some larger animals like moose, deer and bears, while smaller animals like bobcats, squirrels, chipmunks, ermine, and moles are also found.
- Animals common to Arctic tundra are the polar bear, Arctic wolf, Arctic fox, Arctic hare and Arctic weasel. Large herbivores such as musk oxen, caribou and reindeer are found. Insects like moths, butterflies, beetles, mosquitoes and black flies are common in the Arctic tundra.
- **Tropical deciduous Forest** In summer, the maximum temperature ranges from 38°C to 48°C. Summer season is warm and humid. In the dry winter season temperature ranges between 10° C to 27° C. The total amount of precipitation is 75 to 150 cm/year and this affects the natural vegetation of the tropical deciduous forest.
- Inhabiting the temperate deciduous forest are ants, insects, flies, bees, wasps, cicadas, walking sticks, moths, butterfly, dragon flies, mosquitoes and praying mantises.
- The animals in temperate grasslands include the bison, wolves of the Prairies of North America. The other animals and birds are coyotes, Prairie dog, foxes, mice, rabbits, badgers, rattle snakes, pocket gophers, weasel, grasshoppers, quails and hawks.
- The **A Horizon** is made up of decomposed organic matter, micro-organisms such as earthworms, fungi, bacteria, etc. The **B Horizon** consists of less humus, but more minerals. The **C Horizon** is made up of broken bed rocks and **R Horizon** is the compact bedrock region.
- On 5th December 2015, the Soil Health Card Scheme was introduced by the Ministry of Agriculture and Farmers Welfare, Government of India.
- It is being implemented through the Department of Agriculture of all the State and Union Territory Governments in India. Under the scheme, the card is provided to all farmers of the country at an interval of 3 years.
- **Soil Health Card** (SHC) is a printed report of a particular landholding which gives information on 12 soil parameters along with recommendation in dosage of nutrients to be utilised for different crops.
- India has 2.4% of the world's total land area, accounting for 7-8% of all recorded species, including species of animals and plants. According to state records, 23.28% of the total land area of India is under the forest cover.

Agriculture and Animal Husbandry

08

[SOURCES]

Class-VIII New NCERT Chap 3 (Agriculture), Class-IX Old NCERT Chap 8 (Human Occupations), Class-XI Old NCERT Chap 2 (Renewable Resources 'Forest and Fisheries'), Class-XI Old NCERT Chap 3 (Grasslands and Pastoralism), Class-XIth Old NCERT Chap 7 (Utilisation of Natural Resources), Class-XI Old NCERT Chap 8 (Major Crops of the World), Class-XII New NCERT Chap 4 (Primary Activities), Tamil Nadu Board (Class XII), NIOS

- Human activities which generate income are known as **economic activities**. Economic activities are broadly grouped into **primary**, **secondary**, **tertiary**, **quaternary** and **quinary activities**.
- Primary activities are directly dependent on environment as these refer to utilisation of Earth's resources such as land, water, vegetation, building materials and minerals.
- Thus, it includes hunting and gathering, pastoral activities, fishing, forestry, agriculture, mining and quarrying.

Hunting and Gathering

- The earliest human beings were depended on their immediate environment for their sustenance. They subsisted on animals which they hunted; and the edible plants which they gathered from forests in the vicinity.
- Primitive societies were depended on wild animals. People located in very cold and extremely hot climates survived on hunting.
- The people in the coastal areas still catch fishes though fishing has experienced modernisation due to technological progress.
- Gathering and hunting are the **oldest known economic activities**. These are carried out at different levels with different orientations.
- Gathering is practised in regions with harsh climatic conditions. It often involves primitive societies, who extract, both plants and animals to satisfy their needs for food, shelter and clothing.
- This type of activity requires a small amount of capital investment and operates at very low level of technology. The yield per person is very low and little or no surplus is produced.
- Gathering is practised in
  - **High latitude zones** such as Northern Canada, Northern Eurasia and Southern Chile.
  - **Low latitude zones** such as the Amazon Basin, tropical Africa, Northern fringe of Australia and the interior parts of South-East Asia.

Agriculture

- It is the most fundamental form of economic activities in any nation.
- In every continents, practically, exists all form of agricultural activities simultaneously.
- Before the advent of agriculture, all human beings were hunters, gatherers or fishers. The earliest agriculture called **vegeculture** was probably first practised in South-East Asia.
- 50% of the world population is involved in agriculture and allied activities.
- Land that is suitable for agricultural activities is called as **cultivable land**. In general words, agriculture is also known as **cultivation**.

Types of Agriculture

On the basis of geographical conditions, demand, labour and technology, agriculture can be divided into subsistence and commercial farming.

Subsistence Farming

- This type of farming is practised to meet the needs of the farmer's family. Traditionally, low levels of technology and household labour are used to produce on small output. Subsistence farming can be further classified as **primitive subsistence** and **intensive subsistence farming.**

Primitive Subsistence Agriculture

It includes shifting cultivation and nomadic herding

- **Shifting Cultivation** It is practised in the thickly forested areas of Amazon basin, tropical Africa, parts of South-East Asia and North-East India. These are the areas of heavy rainfall and quick regeneration of vegetation.

  A plot of land is cleared by felling the trees and burning them. The ashes are then mixed with the soil and crops like maize, yam, potatoes and cassava are grown. After the soil loses its fertility, the land is abandoned and the cultivator moves to a new plot. Shifting cultivation is also known as **slash and burn** agriculture.

Names of Shifting Cultivation in Different Parts of the World

Shifting Cultivation	Country	Shifting Cultivation	Country
Ladang	Malaysia	Roca	Brazil
Tamrai	Thailand	Konuko	Venezuela
Taungya	Burma	Masole	Zaire and Congo
Caingin	Philippines	Ray	Vietnam
Chena	Sri Lanka	Proka	Ghana
Hummah	Java	Tavy	Madagascar
Milpa	Mexico and Central America	Jhuming/ Bewar	India

- **Nomadic Herding** It is practised in the semi-arid and arid regions of Sahara, Central Asia and some parts of India, like Rajasthan and Jammu and Kashmir. In this type of farming, herdsmen move from place to place with their animals for fodder and water, along defined routes. This type of movement arises in response to climatic constraints and terrain. Sheep, camel, yak and goats are most commonly reared. They provide milk, meat, wool, hides and other products to the herders and their families.

Intensive Subsistence Agriculture

- This type of agriculture is largely found in densely populated regions of monsoon Asia, there are two types of intensive subsistence agriculture.
  (i) **Intensive subsistence agriculture dominated by wet paddy cultivation** This type of agriculture is characterised by dominance of the rice crop. Land holdings are very small due to the high density of population.

  Farmers work with the help of family labour leading to intensive use of land. Use of machinery is limited and most of the agricultural operations are done by manual labour. Farm yard manure is used to maintain the fertility of the soil. In this type of agriculture, the yield per unit area is high but per labour productivity is low.

  (ii) **Intensive subsistence agriculture dominated by crops other than paddy** Due to the difference in relief, climate, soil and some of the other geographical factors, it is not practical to grow paddy in many parts of monsoon Asia.

  Wheat, soyabean, barley and sorghum are grown in Northern China, Manchuria, North Korea and North Japan. In India, wheat is grown in Western parts of the Indo-Gangetic plains and millets are grown in dry parts of Western and Southern India. Most of the characteristics of this type of agriculture are similar to those dominated by wet paddy except that irrigation is often used.

Commercial Farming

- In this type of farming, the crops and livestock are raised to sell products in order to make money. It involves huge amount of capital investment.
- In commercial farming, most of the activities are highly mechanised. **Commercial grain farming, mixed farming, plantation agriculture** are the examples of commercial farming.

Commercial Grain Farming

- Farms are very large, ranging from 240 to 16000 hectares. The most important crop grown is wheat.
- Two types of wheat is grown in this farming i.e., **spring wheat** and the **winter wheat.**
- Cultivation is highly mechanised. Farmers invest heavily in labour saving devices such as tractors, ploughs, drills and combine harvesters. The output per unit of land is always low as compared to regions where intensive cultivation is the common practice.
- Despite low yields per unit of land, the farming is commercial because of a large surplus (the per capita production is high).
- Large scale commercial grain cultivation is found in only five countries – the United States, Canada, South Africa, Argentina and Australia.

Mixed Farming

- In this type of farming, holdings are of variable size, the farms have individual family ownership and are operated by family labour.
- The ratio of cropland to total agricultural land, is very high, but at the same time the intensity of livestock production is much higher.

- Most of the crops grown on a mixed commercial farm are fed to the animals rather than consumed directly by humans.
- Characterised by high expenditure on machinery and farm buildings, extensive use of manures and fertilisers and also by the input of technical skill by the farmers. Cereals dominate the crop land use; the leading grain varies with climate and soil.
- Mixed commercial farming is practised in Europe from Ireland to Russia, in North America, West of the Appalachians and East of the 98th meridian. It is also practised in South Africa, North-Eastern Argentina, South-Eastern Australia and New Zealand.

Plantation

- These crops are generally raised on large estates of more than 40 hectares. It is large scale, capitalised and often highly centralised cultivation of cash crops for export.
- Among the most important crops grown in plantations are cotton, sugarcane, coffee, rubber and tobacco.
- Plantation is a form of commercial agriculture found in the tropics and the subtropics of Latin America, Africa and Asia. Latin American plantations are most likely to grow coffee, sugarcane and bananas while Asian plantations may provide rubber and palm oil.

Other Types of Farming

Some of other types of farming are as follows

Mediterranean Agriculture

- In the bordering areas of Mediterranean sea, the two most important cash crops are **olives** and **grapes**. Two-thirds of the world's wine is produced in the Italy, France and Spain. Greece specialises in producing raisins and wine while Spain in oranges, olive oil and wine.
- In Land area, cereal crops are the most important in Mediterranean agriculture. Wheat, especially hard winter wheat is the principal foodgrain and barley is grown in the poorer areas.

Livestock Ranching

- It is the commercial grazing of livestock over an extensive area, which is associated with a very large land requirement and modest input of capital and human resources. The major types of livestock are sheep, cattle, goats and horses.
- Ranching is rare in Europe, except in Spain and Portugal. With the exception of humid Pampa and South Island of New Zealand, all regions are semi-arid.
- It is also practised in the Western United States and the adjacent parts of Canada and Mexico, the Llanos of Venezuela, Sertao of Brazil, the Pampa of Uruguay, the Chaco and Patagonia, the Karoo of South Africa.

Commercial Dairy Farming

- It is a **capital intensive** type of farming. The business of keeping animals is labour intensive and offers great scope for intensive employment of labour.
- In North-Western Europe, dairy farms occupy coastal and low-lying meadowlands of abundant precipitation, warm summers and cold winters (50° to 60°N latitudes). Other regions of dairy farming are the Eastern states of the South-Eastern part of Australia and the North Island of New Zealand (30° to 40°S latitudes).

Horticulture (Market Gardening or Truck Farming)

- The market gardens are located just outside the city in sub-urban areas or in areas where climatic and soil conditions are particularly favourable.
- Farmers in these regions specialise either in particular fruits or vegetables the scale of farming is small and intensive. The farming is **capital intensive** and **scientifically managed.**
- In addition to market gardening, a modern development in the industrial regions of Western Europe and North America is factory farming.
- Livestock, particularly poultry and cattle are raised entirely under one cover. This type of farming is called **truck farming** because trucks are used to transport the fruits and vegetables from the farm to the buyers.

Collective Farming

- The land of a collective farm is the state property, but it is leased to the association of the farm workers and is worked in the direction of a committee selected by the members farm. The collective farms are highly mechanised.
- Collective farming are called **Kolkhoz** in Soviet Union, **Communes** in China and **Kibbutzims** in Israel.

Types of Agriculture on the Basis of Organisation

Some types of agriculture on the basis of organisation are as follows

Cooperative Farming

- Cooperative farming refers to farming practices where farming operations are conducted by individuals with other members of a cooperative.
- These cooperatives are engaged in collection and purchase of agricultural inputs such as seeds, fertilisers, equipment, etc. They help the individual farmers in selling their agricultural produce.
- Farmers pool their land, livestock and other implements. The entire farm is managed by a single unit of management.

Community Supported Agriculture

- It is a system that connects the producer and consumers within the food system more closely by allowing the consumer to subscribe to the harvest of a certain farm or group of farms.
- This type of farming is known as **Kolkhoz** in Russia. It is an alternative socio-economic model of agriculture that allows the producer and consumer to share the risks of farming.

Sovkhoz

- This agricultural technique prevailing in communist nation is based on the model of the Soviet Union. It was first practiced in 1920s in **Siberia** and **Kazakhstan**.
- Under this, factors of production are govern by the government and labours are paid salaries. In this technique, machines are used at broader level. At present, this technique as become obsolete.

Organic Agriculture

- It is a production system that sustains the health of soils, ecosystems and people. It relies on ecological processes, biodiversity and cycles adapted to local conditions, rather than the use of inputs with adverse effects.
- Organic farming combines tradition, innovation and science to benefit the shared environment and quality of life.

Sustainable Agriculture

- It refers to the ability of a farm to produce food indefinitely, without causing severe and irreversible damage to ecosystem health.
- It involves two key issues i.e. bio physical issues that is the long-term effects of various practices on soil properties and processes essential for crop productivity, socio-economic issues those involve long-term ability of farmers to obtain inputs and manage resources.

Other Types of Agricultural Technique

Agricultural Technique	Description
Viticulture	Cultivation of grapes at commercial scale.
Pisciculture	Cultivation of fishes at commercial scale.
Sericulture	Silk production
Horticulture	Cultivation of fruits
Arboriculture	Cultivation of specialised trees and shrubs.
Apiculture	Production of honey at commercial scale.
Floriculture	Cultivation of flowers.
Silviculture	Branch of forestry dealing with the development care of forest.
Vegeculture	Primitive agriculture of trees practised by early man of South-East Asia.
Moriculture	Cultivation of mulberry plants.
Olericulture	Branch of horticulture dealing with the production, storage, processing and marketing of vegetable.
Mariculture	Production of sea animals at commercial scale.
Horsiculture	Rearing of hybrid horses and mules.

Major Crops of the World

- A large variety of crops are grown to meet the requirement of the growing population. Crops also supply raw materials for agro-based industries. Crops are broadly categorised as follows
  - **Food grains** Rice, Wheat and Maize
  - **Millets** Jowar/Ragi and Bajra
  - **Oil seeds** Mustard, Groundnut, Coconut and Sunflower
  - **Fibrous crops** Cotton and Jute
  - **Beverages** Tea and Coffee
  - **Commercial crops** Sugarcane and Rubber

Food Crops

Important food crops are discussed as follows

Rice

- It is a tropical humid crop of monsoonal climate. It is a labour intensive crop. 90% of the world's rice is grown in East and South Asia. Its different and new varieties are IR8, IR20, IR22, miracle rice, etc.
- **Miracle rice** is developed in Philippines at the Rice Research Institute of Manila. It is the principal food crop for half of the population of the world.

Geographical Conditions

- The rice plant (paddy) requires high temperature (27°-30°C) and high rainfall (about 100 cm) during its growth period. Clay, loam soil is best suited for its cultivation.
- Paddy is categorised into two groups–wet paddy and dry paddy. Floating rice can be grown in water upto 5 m deep.

Productions and Yields

- Thailand and Myanmar are the traditional leaders in rice exports in the world. In Malaysia, paddy occupies the second greatest cultivated acreage after rubber and nearly 95% of the paddy grown is wet paddy.
- **Bahagia** variety of rice produced in Malaysia.
- The largest production of rice is in China followed by India, Indonesia and Bangladesh. Rice yield is highest in Australia followed by Egypt, USA and Spain.
- East Asia covers nearly 25% of total world area under rice which contributes nearly 40% of total world production of rice.
- Brazil producing only 1.8% of the world's total rice production is the greatest rice growing nation in the Southern America.

- USA produces about 1% of the world's rice. The leading rice growing state in USA is Louisiana, followed by California, Texas and South Carolina.

Leading Producers

Its leading producers in the world are China, India, Indonesia, Bangladesh, Thailand, Japan, Myanmar, Vietnam and Malaysia. Its leading exporter in the world is Thailand.

Wheat

Wheat is produced in temperate and sub-tropical zone. According to growing seasons, it is divided into two groups,

1. **Winter Wheat** It is usually grown in regions of the middle latitudes.
2. **Spring Wheat** It is grown in the colder North of the Canadian Prairies and in parts of the continental steppes and Siberia.

Geographical Conditions

- It is mainly a crop of the temperate region. The annual rainfall is required between 40 to 75 cm. An average temperature of 16°C and clear sky are required at the time of ripening.
- Loam and chernozem soils are best suited for wheat cultivation. Over irrigation should be avoided as high humidity may cause a disease known as **Red-rot**.

Production and Yield

- The Wheat Crescent of the Pampas (in Argentina) Black Earth of USSR, Paris basin, the Lombardy plain of Italy, the lower Danube basin are famous for wheat production.
- Almost all the wheat from Canada is spring wheat and 95% of the total comes from the Prairie Provinces (Saskatchewan, Alberta and Manitoba).
- In USA, Nebraska separates the winter wheat belt from spring wheat belt.

Leading Producers

Its leading producers in the world are China, India, USA, Russia, Australia, Canada, France and Turkey. Its leading exporter in the world is USA.

Maize

- Maize is a sub-tropical zone crop. It is the third after wheat and rice in terms of area cultivated.
- Maize is known as *Makkah* in India, corn in the USA and Indian corn in Europe. It is originated from American continent.

Geographical Conditions

- Maize usually requires summer temperatures of between 18° and 27°C during the day and around 14°C during the night. The most essential climatic factor is a period of 140 frost free days.
- Rainfall varies from 30 cm to 100 cm annually. It grows in a wide range of soil types from the temperate podzols to the strangely leached red soils of the tropics. However, it grows best in deep nitrogen rich soils of the sub-tropics.

Leading Producers

Its leading producers in the world are USA, China, Brazil, Mexico, Russia, Romania, India and South Africa. Its leading exporter in the world is USA.

Millets

- They are also known as coarse grains and can be grown on less fertile and sandy soils.
- It is a hardy crop that needs low rainfall and high to moderate temperature and adequate rainfall.
- They require temperature of 20° to 27°C and rainfall 50 cm to 75 cm.
- Ragi, jowar, bajra, etc, are the important millets.

Leading Producers

Its leading producers in the world are China, USA, India, Nigeria, Ukraine, Thailand, Russia and Turkey. Its leading exporter in the world is USA.

Oil seeds

Edible oils are extracted from the oilseeds. Major oilseeds crops are mustard, groundnut, coconut, etc. Olive oil is extracted in Mediterranean countries and palm oil extracted from palm trees.

Rapeseed and Mustard

Rapeseed and Mustard comprise several oilseeds as Rau, sarron, toria and taranira. These are sub-tropical corps. These are frost sensitive crops and their yield fluctuates year-to-year. Low rainfall is needed for such crops to grow.

Sesame

- This crop is grown in the area of low rainfall. It require sandy soil and it is sown in Kharif season.
- It require light rainfall and excessive winters are harmful for its production.
- Oil is obtained from the seeds of sesame.
- Sesame is cultivated in India, China, Myanmar, Sudan, Egypt, Turkey, Sri Lanka, Vietnam, Thailand, Bangladesh, etc. India, China and Nigeria are the top three sesame producing countries.

Sunflower

- Sunflower was first cultivated in Southern United States and Mexico. In 19th century, it was cultivated as oil seed in Soviet Union.
- It is mainly cultivated for obtaining oil.
- It requires cold weather for germination and growth of plants. At the time of ripening, it requires normal temperature and cloudless sky.

- Although, it is cultivated in all types of soil but black soil is best suited for its production.
- The Leading producers of the sunflower are Ukraine, Russia, Argentina, Bulgaria, Romania, Turkey, Spain, United States of America, India and China, etc.

Soyabean

- It is kharif crop. Although it is also a edible crop but it mostly used for the production of oil.
- It best grows in all types of soils except sandy soil. Clayey soil is best suited for its production.
- Its leading producers are United States of America, China, Japan, Brazil, Argentina and Indonesia, etc.

Flax

- It is cultivated for both oil and fibre. Its oil is used in paints and varnishes. It required cold weather and alluvial and clayey soil.
- Its leading producers are India, Argentina, United States of America, Canada, Pakistan, France, etc. Its top three producers are Canada, China and Russia.

Groundnut

- It plants need well-drained sandy loam or clay loam soil. 20° to 25°C temperature and 50 to 75 cm rainfall is necessary for its growth.
- India, China, Nigeria, USA, Sudan, Senegal, Indonesia are important producers of groundnut. China is the leading producer, followed by India and Nigeria.

Coconut

- The coconut palm is referred to as '**Kalpavriksha**, the tree of heaven' as each and every part of the palm is useful to mankind in one way or other. It is essentially a tropical plant, growing mostly between 20°N and 20°S.
- A well distributed rainfall of about 200 cm per year is the best for proper growth. Indonesia, Philippines, India, New Guinea, Fiji, Sri Lanka, Malaysia, Mozambique are major coconut producing countries. Indonesia is the leading producer followed by Philippines and India.

Fibrous Crops

Important fibrous crops are discussed as follows

Cotton

- It is a product of tropical and temperate zone. Cotton is an ancient crop in India and Egypt.
- After the discovery of the cotton ginning machine in 1793, there was a revolutionary change in the production and utilisation of cotton. Cotton varieties are usually distinguished by the staple length. The longer the staple, the finer the fibres are.

Geographical Conditions

- Cotton is essentially a plant of dry climate.
- Cotton requires warm climate but temperature between 21°C and 27°C is ideal during the period of its growth.
- Cotton plant can tolerate as high temperature as 40°C but it should not be lower than 21°C.
- A light well drained soil capable of retaining moisture is ideally suited for the cultivation of the cotton.
- Volcanic, black and alluvial soils are most suitable for it. It requires intensive fertiliser use.
- It cannot tolerate frost. So, it needs 210 frost free days.
- Moderate to light rainfall is adequate for its production, that ranges from 50-100 cm which must be evenly distributed.

Types of Cotton

- **Long Staple Cotton** The longest staple cotton is the sea island cotton, which is now largely grown in the West Indies. The main producing regions are South coast of USA, Puerto Rico and other islands of West Indies. Egypt is one of the major producers of long staple cotton and has developed many varieties of it.
- **Medium Staple Cotton** It is produced in Nile basin, Soviet Central Asia and USA. It is also known as **Egyptian cotton**. American upland cotton is an example of this size.
- **Short Staple Cotton** It is the shortest and the coarsest of the cotton which is produced mainly in Asian countries and Brazil.

Production

- USA remained a major cotton producer for a long time. In India, cotton is produced in the black soil region.
- Sao-Paulo in Brazil, Nile delta in Egypt, Indus valley of Pakistan and Jazira of Sudan are cotton producing regions.
- The major cotton producing regions of Central Asia lie in Tajikistan, Kazakhstan, Turkmenistan and Uzbekistan.

Leading Producers

- Its leading producers in the world are China, USA, India, Brazil, Pakistan, Uzbekistan, Egypt and Turkey. Its leading exporter in the world is USA.

Jute

Jute is the fibre obtained from certain plant species of the Corchorus family. It is a coarse fibre and is thus, the second most important fibre crop.

Geographical Conditions

- Jute grows well in hot, tropical climatic conditions with plenty of moisture and heavy rainfall. It is suited to the same regions as wet paddy. It is often grown as a cash crop in paddy growing areas.
- It requires rich soils and thrives on river alluvium, especially where annual floods renew the fertility of the soil.

Leading Producers

Its leading producers in the world are India, Bangladesh, Brazil, Thailand, Myanmar, Indonesia, Taiwan and China.

Beverage Crops

Tea and coffee are the most important beverage crops.

Tea

It is a warm temperate crop. Tea is made from the leaves of a tropical shrub of the **Camellia family**. Tea cultivation is believed to have originated in the Chang-Jiang valley of China.

Variety of Tea

Major tea varieties are **black tea** (India and Sri Lanka), **green tea** (China), **Oolong tea** (Taiwan) and **yerba tea** (Paraguay). China tea or green tea is small-leaved-tea and Assam tea or black tea is large-leaved-tea.

Geographical Conditions

- It requires warm and humid climate but water should not stagnate near the roots. It grows best in the monsoon lands of the tropics and the sub-tropics.
- It is grown mainly in regions between 27° South and 43° North latitudes on hill slopes. It requires moderate temperature of about 25°C and a rainfall between 125 cm and 750 cm annually.
- Its plants grow well in fertile soils with high humus content and application of nitrogen fertilisers is essential to maintain soil fertility.
- The most suitable soils are slightly acidic and without calcium. The presence of iron in the sub-soil is desirable.

Leading Producers

Its leading producers in the world are India, China, Sri Lanka, Japan, Kenya, Indonesia, Bangladesh and Turkey. One of its leading exporter in the world is India.

Coffee

- It is the second most important beverage crop. Coffee grows in the tropical highlands at an altitude between 500 and 1500 m above the main sea-level.
- It is a tropical crop. One-third of the world population drinks coffee. It is the second largest beverage after tea.
- The coffee tree is a native of the highlands of Southern Ethiopia and the name coffee is derived from the highland district of Kaffa, where it was found. Generally, coffee grows in deep, porous and water retentive soils with high humus content.
- Well drained volcanic soils like the terra roxa of Brazil, which contain potash as well as organic material are the best.
- Large coffee plantation in Brazil is known as **Fazenda**. **Mocha coffee** is grown mainly in Yemen.
- In India, Karnataka is the largest producer of coffee.

Types of Coffee

There are three types of coffee plants—**arabica, robusta** and **liberica**. Robusta is the main variety produced in the world.

Other varieties are **mocha coffee** (Arabian peninsula), **blue mountain coffee** (in Jamaica and other West Indian islands) and **java coffee**. Both robusta and liberica are widely grown in Africa.

Geographical Conditions

- Temperature from 14° to 25°C and rainfall range of 40 to 80 cm is required to grow coffee.
- Coffee plant is very suscepitble to frost and cannot tolerate it. Hence, it is grown under shady trees.
- Shelter from sunlight is required especially for young plants.
- It requires highly humid conditions, sandy loam to clay loam, well drained, rich in organic matter soil. Coffee production is labour intensive, because mechanisation is not possible.

Leading Producers

Its leading producers in the world are Brazil, Colombia, Indonesia, Vietnam, Ivory-Coast, Mexico, Ghana, Cameroon and India. Brazil is the leading exporter of coffee in the world.

Cash Crops

Important cash crops are discussed as follows

Sugarcane

- It is a warm temperate crop. Sugarcane is a member of the grass family and is tall tropical variety with a hard, thick stem.
- The plant probably originated in Eastern Asia. The sugar mill must be near the farms because of sugar deterioration and expensive transportation.
- The sugar mills are also located near the fields as sucrose content decreases when transported to large distance.
- Sugarcane accounts for about 60% of the world's sugar requirements.

Geographical Conditions

- Sugarcane requires constantly high temperature ranging between 21°C and 27°C. Less than 20°C temperature restricts the growth of sugarcane. Frost is extremely harmful to this crop.
- It is a less water efficient crop. The hot and humid climate of tropical region is very good for its cultivation.
- It requires 75 to 120 cm of rainfall. Loam, clay and alluvial soils are suitable for sugarcane. Cuba is known as **sugar bowl of the world.**
- Brazil is the largest producer and exporter of sugar. It has the highest per capita consumption of it.

Leading Producers

Its leading producers in the world are Brazil, India, China, Pakistan, Thailand, Mexico, Cuba, Columbia. Its leading exporter in the world is Brazil.

Top Five Exporting and Importing Countries of Sugarcane (2022)

Exporting Country	Importing Country
Brazil	Indonesia
Thailand	China
India	USA
France	Italy
Germony	South Korea

Sugar Beet

- It is a temperate crop. Sugar beet is a root crop of the beet family. It is usually cultivated as a rotation crop. It thrives well in loams and clayey loams.
- It cannot survive on water logged soils. It is fertiliser intensive crop and requires high amount of nitrogenous fertiliser.

Geographical Conditions

It takes about 5 to 6 months to mature. It requires about 16° to 23°C temperature. It requires high moisture and rainfall around 60 cm.

Leading Producers

Its leading producers in the world are France, USA, Germany, Russia, China, Ukraine, Poland Turkey. Its leading exporter in the world is France.

Rubber

- It is a tropical wet zone crop. Rubber is the latex of the tree *Hevea brasiliensis*. It is widely found in the tropical forest of Amazon and Zaire basins.
- Rubber is obtained through gathering in the Amazon basin where rubber gatherers are called **Seringueiros.**
- After the discovery of vulcanisation, it became more useful. USA and china are one of the largest synthetic rubber producers.

Geographical Conditions

- Equatorial climate is best suited for it. It requires high temperature of about 27°C and rainfall of 150 cm evenly distributed throughout the year.
- Deep, friable, well drained soils are ideal and acidic soils are also suitable.

Leading Producers

Its leading producers in the world are Thailand, Indonesia, Malaysia, India, China, Sri Lanka, Liberia and Brazil. Its leading exporter in the world is Thailand.

Tobacco

- It is a crop of the tropical and sub-tropical zone. Tobacco is a broadleaved annual growing plant. It is a native plant of tropical America.
- It is now grown in almost every country with a warm temperate, sub-tropical or tropical climate.

Geographical Conditions

Temperature exceeding 18°C in the warmest month is ideal. The crop requires moderate rainfall and rich, regularly fertilised soil.

The plant requires a frost free period of 120 to 180 days and a warm growing season.

Leading Producers

Its leading producers in the world are China, USA, India, Brazil, Turkey, Japan, Bulgaria and South Korea. Its leading exporter in the world is USA.

Pulses

- Pulses are a source of supplementary protein to daily diets based on cereals and starchy food for essential minerals, vitamins, etc.
- Their cultivation enriches soil by adding nitrogen and the soil properties.

Geographic Conditions

- There are well suited to diverse environments and fit in various cropping systems owing to their wide adaptability, low input requirements, fast growth, nitrogen fixing and weed smothering ability.
- Dry beans, which include green gram and black gram are the most important pulse crops of the world.

Leading Producers

India is the biggest producer, as well as the largest consumer and importer of pulses. Worldwide major exporting countries are Canada, Brazil and USA.

Top three Producers of Major Crops of the World

Crop	First Rank	Second Rank	Third Rank	India's Rank
Wheat	China	India	Russia	Second
Rice	China	India	Indonesia	Second
Sugarcane	Brazil	India	China	Second
Cotton	India	China	USA	First
Banana	India	China	Indonesia	First
Coconut	Indonesia	Philippines	India	Third
Tobacco	China	India	Brazil	Second
Potato	China	India	Ukraine	Second
Jute	India	Bangladesh	China	First
Pulses	India	Canada	Myanmar	First
Barley	Russia	Germany	France	–
Sorghum	Nigeria	USA	Sudan	–
Soyabean	Brazil	USA	Argentina	Fifth
Groundnut	China	India	Nigeria	Second
Rapeseed	Canada	India	Australia	Second
Sunflower	Ukraine	Russia	Argentina	–
Apple	China	Turkiye	USA	Fifth
Spices	India	Turkiye	Bangladesh	First
Grapes	China	Italy	USA	Twelfth
Orange	China	Italy	Spain	Seventh

Animal Husbandry

- Animal husbandry is the science of caring and breeding of domestic animals and the development of genetic traits such as high yielding, disease resistance, etc. that are valuable to humanity.
- Animal husbandry involves breeding and raising livestock like buffaloes, cows, goats, camels, horses, sheep, etc. and even extended to poultry farming and fisheries. Some of the important practices of animal husbandry are as follows

Management of Farms and Farm Animals

This is a professional approach towards the conventional farm management practices, which gives the boost to food production.

- **Dairy Farm Management** This is the management of the animals that provide milk (milch animals). The goal is to enhance the quantity and quality of the milk produced. For this purpose, high yielding and disease resistant breeds are maintained in a strictly hygienic manner with proper housing, adequate water supply, and nutrient-rich fodder.

  Regular inspection and record keeping ensures that a good high quality yield is generated.
- **Poultry Farm Management** Poultry farming refers to the rearing of domesticated fowl (birds) for their meat and eggs. These birds include chicken, ducks, Turkey, geese, etc.

  Just like dairy farming, selection of disease free and suitable breeds, maintenance of hygienic farm conditions, providing proper food and water and health care, are the main goals of poultry farm management.

Animal Breeding

Another part of animal husbandry is animal breeding. Breeding of animals aims to develop high yielding animals and improve the desirable qualities of the produce.

- **Inbreeding** It refers to the practice of mating closely related superior males to superior females within the same breed for fourth to sixth generations.

  The superior males and females among the progenies are further mated for developing Mendelian pure lines, which are homozygous in nature.

  However, continued close inbreeding eventually decreases fertility and productivity, a phenomenon was known as inbreeding depression.
- **Out-breeding** It is the breeding of the unrelated animals that can be carried out in three different fashions. When two unrelated individuals of the same breed, which do not have a common ancestor for the past fourth to sixth generations are mated, it is called out-crossing.

  Mating between a superior male of one breed and a superior female of another breed to give a progeny with the combined qualities of both breeds is known as crossbreeding. When males and females across different related species are mated, it is known as interspecific hybridisation.
- Apart from conventional breeding techniques, controlled breeding experiments are conducted utilising artificial insemination to yield the desired mating. To improve the chances of obtaining successful hybrids, programmes like **Multiple Ovulation Embryo Transfer Technology** (MOET) are used.

Apiculture

Maintenance of hives of honeybees for the production of honey and beeswax is known as beekeeping or **apiculture beekeeping**. Honey is an age old food of high nutritional value and is also used in traditional medicines across various cultures.

Although it is not a labour intensive practice, an idea of the following points is necessary for successful beekeeping

- Selection of a suitable location for keeping the beehives.
- Nature and habits of bees.
- Catching and hiving of swarms.
- Handling and collection of honey and beeswax.
- Management of beehives during different seasons.

Fishing

Fishes are found in saline marine ecosystem, fresh water, in tropical as well as freezed zones.

Factors Affecting Fish Distribution

- Shallow coastal waters are ideal to fish since, there is plentiful food supply from the erosion of continents, which provide mineral and organic matter and there is enough Sunlight penetration.
- In areas of coastal upwelling high rates of primary production take place. Conventional mixing provides plenty of oxygen to sustain life in coastal zones as well as assuring a favourable dispersion of nutrients.
- Mixing of warm and cold water as on the **Newfoundland banks** and the **Sea of Japan**.
- Broken coastline with numerous indentations provides excellent berthing facility.
- Climatic condition, temperate climate with temperature less than 20°C is best regions for marine life.

Major Fishing Ground of the World

- **Coastal Margins of Middle Latitudes** These are the biggest fish producing areas where the largest concentrations of marketable species are found. The tropical waters produce many fish as well, but they are less desirable because of their higher oil content.
- **North-West Pacific Region** This region extends from the outer Aleutian islands in the North to the Central Pacific, North of the Philippine islands. Salmon, herring, halibut, cod and king crab are important catches of this region.
- **North-East Atlantic and Adjacent Waters of the Arctic** It extends from Iceland to Mediterranean including the European countries especially Norway, Denmark, Spain, Iceland and the United Kingdom.

  Shallow waters of the North Sea especially the most exploited Dogger Bank are important areas where fishing is carried out all round the year.
- **North-West Atlantic Region** It includes Grand Bank and the Georges Bank area of the North-West Atlantic. The convergence of the Gulf Stream and the Labrador current in that region enhances productivity. The major fish is the cod, but halibut, herring and mackerel are also important.
- **North-East Pacific Region** It extends from Alaska to California along the Western shores of North America. It comprises the world's best cod fishing ground alongwith herring and haddock. Salmon is the most valuable fish of this region, but tuna, halibut and sardines are also important.
- **South-East Pacific** Off the coast of South America is known for the anchovy harvest off the coast of Peru.

  The Northward flowing Peru current provides an ideal environment for the anchovy culture because it is associated with a coastal upwelling of nutrient rich colder water laden with plankton on which the anchovy feeds.

Fish Conservation

- Factors which are hindering the development of fishing in tropical latitudes are, a large variety of species all mixed up. This reduces the scope for large-scale commercial exploitation.
- High temperature does not support plankton population. The very warm climate does not allow fish preservation and the fish must be consumed quickly.

  Most of the tropical countries have inefficient and inadequate transportation and refrigeration facilities. The demand for fish is also very low in these countries.
- Humans get 23% of total protein received from animal by fishes. Thus, fish conservation is essential.

  Following the important ways to conserve fishes :
  - Over fishing should be stopped.
  - Pollution should be checked in estuaries.
  - It is essential to check oil spill from industrial and ship wrecks as it leads to huge fish loss.
  - Nuclear testing should banned as it is harmful for the oceanic organisms.
  - Oceanic transportation should be controlled and oceanic routes should be used efficiently.

Extra Facts From
Tamil Nadu Board and NIOS

- Present day gatherers and hunters are confined to a few pockets. Inuit in the Arctic region, Pygmies of Kalahari, Pintupi, Aborgines of Australia and Paliyans of South India are the example of foragers.
- Transhumance is the seasonal movement of people with their livestock between fixed summer and winter pastures. In mountain region, it implies movement between higher altitude pastures during summer and valleys in winter.
- The Net Sown Area (NSA), current fallows and land under tree crops and groves are included in agricultural land use. The agricultural land in India is little more than 50 per cent of the total geographical area in the country. This is the highest share of land in any country in the world.
- India is leading producer of milk in the world. It is due to initiative taken by government through **Operation Flood**.
- The largest number of livestock is found in Uttar Pradesh followed by the states of Rajasthan, Bihar and Madhya Pradesh. These four states account for 44% of total livestock of India.

Mineral Resources

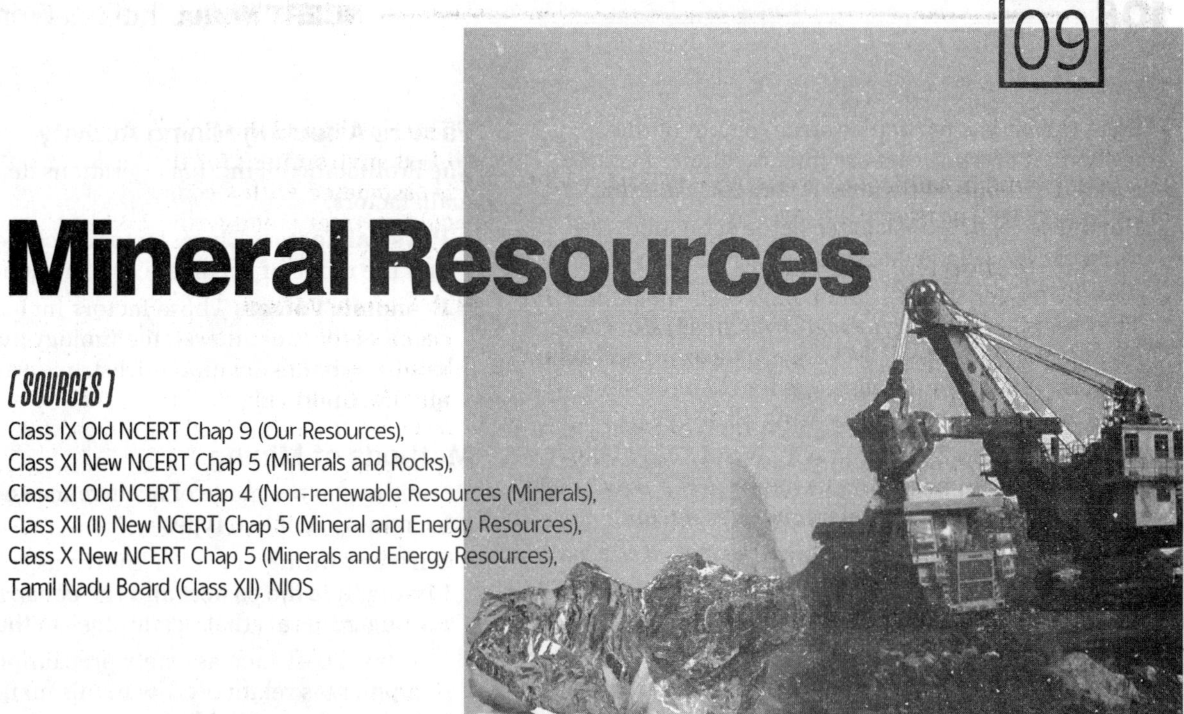

[SOURCES]

Class IX Old NCERT Chap 9 (Our Resources),
Class XI New NCERT Chap 5 (Minerals and Rocks),
Class XI Old NCERT Chap 4 (Non-renewable Resources (Minerals),
Class XII (II) New NCERT Chap 5 (Mineral and Energy Resources),
Class X New NCERT Chap 5 (Minerals and Energy Resources),
Tamil Nadu Board (Class XII), NIOS

- **The Earth is composed of various kinds of elements. These elements are in solid form in the outer layer of the Earth. They are in hot and molten form in the interior.**
- **About 98% of the total crust of the Earth is composed of eight elements like oxygen, silicon, aluminium, iron, calcium, sodium, potassium and magnesium.**
- **The rest is constituted by titanium, hydrogen, phosphorous, manganese, sulphur, carbon, nickel and other elements.**

Minerals

- **Mineral is a naturally occurring organic and inorganic substance, having an orderly atomic structure and a definite chemical composition and physical properties.**
- **A mineral is composed of two or more elements. But, sometimes single element minerals like sulphur, copper, silver, gold, graphite, etc., are found.**
- **The basic source of all minerals is the hot magma in the interior of the Earth.**
- **When magma cools, crystals of minerals appear and a systematic series of minerals are formed in sequence to solidify so as to form rocks.**
- **Minerals such as coal, petroleum and natural gas are organic substances found in solid, liquid and gaseous forms respectively.**

Physical Features of Minerals

- **External Crystal Form** It is determined by internal arrangement of the molecules; cubes, octahedrons, hexagonal prisms, etc.
- **Cleavage** It is tendency to break in given directions producing relatively plane surfaces; result of internal arrangement of the molecules; may cleave in one or more directions and at any angle to each other.
- **Fracture** The crystal will break in an irregular manner, not along planes of cleavage. It will break along random direction.
- **Lustre** It is appearance of a material without regard to colour, each mineral has a distinctive lustre like metallic, silky, glossy, etc.
- **Colour** Some minerals have characteristic colour determined by their molecular structure; malachite, azurite, chalcopyrite, etc. Some minerals are coloured by impurities as because of impurities quartz may be white, green, red, yellow, etc.
- **Streak** Colour of the ground powder of any mineral. It may be of the same colour as the mineral or may differ - malachite is green and gives green streak, fluorite is purple or green but gives a white streak.
- **Transparency** It can be shown as follows
  - **Transparent** Light rays pass through so that objects can be seen plainly.
  - **Translucent** Light rays pass through but will get diffused so that objects cannot be seen.
  - **Opaque** Light will not pass at all.

- **Structure** It is a particular arrangement of the individual crystals that are fine, medium or coarse grained, fibrous (separable, divergent, radiating).
- **Hardness** relative resistance being scratched, ten minerals are selected to measure the degree of hardness from 1 to 10.

  They are; (1) talc (2) gypsum (3) calcite (4) fluorite (5) apatite (6) feldspar (7) quartz (8) topaz (9) corundum (10) diamond. Compared to this for example, a fingernail is 2.5 and glass or knife blade is 5.5.
- **Specific gravity** Specific gravity is the ratio of the weight of a volume of the substance to the weight of an equal volume of the reference substance.
- There is no unit for specific gravity since, it is a ratio comparison.

Types of Minerals

There are over three thousand different minerals. On the basis of composition, minerals are classified mainly as metallic and non-metallic minerals.

Metallic Minerals

- Metallic minerals contain metal in raw form. Metals are hard substances that conduct heat and electricity and have a characteristic lustre or shine.
- It can be sub-divided into three sub-categories

1. **Precious Metals** They include gold, silver, platinum, etc.
2. **Ferrous Metals** They include iron and other metals often mixed with iron to form various kinds of steel.
3. **Non-ferrous Metals** They include metals like copper, lead, zinc, tin, aluminium, etc.

Non-metallic Minerals

- These minerals do not contain metal content. Limestone, mica and gypsum are examples of such minerals.
- The mineral fuels like coal and petroleum are also non-metallic minerals.

Mining

- The discovery of minerals in the history of human development is reflected in many stages in terms of Copper Age, Bronze Age and Iron Age.
- The use of minerals in ancient times was largely confined to the making of tools, utensils and weapons.
- The process of taking out minerals from rocks buried under the Earth's surface is called mining.
- The actual development of mining began with the industrial revolution and its importance is continuously increasing.

Factors Affecting Mining Activity

The Profitability of mining operations depends on two main factors.

- **Physical Factors** These factors include the size, grade and the mode of occurrence of the deposits.
- **Economic Factors** These factors include such as the demand for the mineral, technology available and used, capital to develop infrastructure and the labour and transport costs.

Methods of Mining

Depending on the mode of occurrence and the nature of ores, mining is of two types

- **Surface Mining** It is also known as Open Cast Mining, it is the easiest and the cheapest way of mining minerals that occur close to the surface.

  Overhead cost such as safety precautions and equipment is relatively low in this method. The output is both large and rapid.
- **Under Ground Mining** When the ore lies deep below the surface, Underground Mining Method has to be used. In this method, vertical shafts have to be sunk from where underground galleries radiate to reach the minerals. Minerals are extracted and transported to the surface through these passages.

Other Methods of Mining

- **Drilling** Petroleum and natural gas occur far below the Earth's surface. Deep wells are bored to take them out, this is called drilling.
- **Quarrying** Minerals that lie near the surface are simply dug out, by the process known as quarrying.

Distribution of Minerals

- Minerals occur in different types of rocks. Some are found in igneous rocks, some in metamorphic rocks while others occur in sedimentary rocks.
- Generally, metallic minerals are found in igneous and metamorphic rock formations that form large plateaus.
- Iron-ore deposits in North Sweden, copper and nickel deposits in Ontario, Canada; iron, nickel, chromite and platinum in South Africa are examples of minerals found in igneous and metamorphic rocks.
- Sedimentary rock formations of plains and young fold mountains contain non-metallic minerals like limestone.
- Limestone deposits of Caucasus region of France, manganese deposits of Georgia and Ukraine and phosphate beds of Algeria are some examples.
- Mineral fuels such as coal and petroleum are also found in the sedimentary strata.

Iron-ore

- It is a metallic mineral which is not found in pure form in nature but is available as ore or compound.
- There are different types of iron ores, Haematite, Magnetite, Limonite and Siderite.
- Iron is a symbol of modern civilisation. It is used in almost all types of machines, machine tools, construction of buildings and factories and in various means of transport.
- In comparison to other metals, it is the most widely used metal in the world mainly because of its certain qualities.
- It can be converted into different forms such as cast iron, sheets, magnetic iron and steel. Iron ore is mixed with coke and limestone and heated in a blast, furnance.
- This process is known as smelting. Hardness, strength and durability are other major characteristicks of iron.
- Different kinds of metals such as manganese, nickle vanadium and chromium are mixed in various proportions with iron to prepare different alloys.

Top 5 Iron-ore Producing Countries

Rank by Iron-ore production in 2020	Country
First	Australia
Second	China
Third	Brazil
Fourth	India
Fifth	Russia

Distribution of Iron-ore in the World

Country/region	Centre
China	• Shenyang region of Manchuria • Wuhan, Tai Yeh in Yangtze valley, Hainan, Hnan, Shandong peninsula, Hangzhou
USA	• Great Lakes region – Mesabi, Marquette, Vermillion, Gogebic and Cuyuna, Alabama state
Europe	• Sweden - Kiruna and Gallivare • France - Lorraine, Normandy and Pyrenees • Germany - Salzgitter and Seigen • Spain - Bilbao region • UK - Cleveland, Midland, Scotland • Ukraine - Kryvyi Rih, Kerch basin, Kremenchuk region
Russia	• Tula region : Kursic Magnetic Anomaly • Ural and Siberia region
Africa	• Liberia, South Africa, Algeria, Morocco
Australia	• Pilbara region, Mt. Goldsworthy, Mt. Tom Price, Mt. Newman, Tailoring peak
South America	• Brazil had largest reserve of Iron-ore • Orinoco valley in Venezuela and La Sarena in Chile
India	• Mayurbhanj, Keonjhar and Sundargarh in Odisha • Singhbhum region in Jharkhand • Bailadila range in Chhattisgarh • Chikmagalur, Chitradurga, Tumkur and Bellary in Karnataka

Copper

- Copper has been used by human being since ancient times. Copper occurs in pure state as well as in the form of compounds.
- It is used largely in the electrical industry because of its quality of electrical conductivity.
- Its increasing demand due to expansion of electrical industry in the 20th century, led to the development of such a technology which made it possible to extract copper from low grade ores.
- Copper has been proved useful due to its properties of malleability and ductility. Besides, these it is corrosion resistant and can be mixed with other metals to form copper alloys. The main copper ores are cuprite, malechite, calchocite and coveite.

Top 5 Copper Producing Countries

Rank by Copper production in 2020	Country
First	Chile
Second	Peru
Third	Democratic Republic of Congo
Fourth	China
Fifth	United States

Distribution of Copper in the World

Country/Region	Centre
Chile	Chuquicamata, El- Teniente Potreillous and Bradue
The USA	Arizona, Morence, Globe and Casa- Grande Western part from Canadian border in the North to Mexican border in the South
Canada	Sudbury, North and Ontario
Zaire	Karanja district
India	Singhbhum Hazaribagh in Jharkhand Khetri and Agunch- Rampur area in Rajasthan

Bauxite

- Bauxite is the ore of Aluminium. It is light and versatile metal.
- It has a wide industrial uses such as in aeroplane industry, machine tools, automobiles, electrical and utensils industry.
- Aluminium is the energy intensive industry because it is extracted from the ore using electrolyte mixing process.
- Bauxite is found mainly in tertiary deposits and is associated with laterite rock occuring extensively either on the plateau or hill ranges of peninsular India and also in the coastal tracts of the country.
- Bauxite is mainly mined in the tropical regions but aluminium is manufactured in developed countries where cheap electrical energy is abundantly available.

Top 5 Aluminium Producing Countries

Rank by Aluminium production in 2019	Country
First	China
Second	India
Third	Russia
Fourth	Canada
Fifth	UAE

Distribution of Bauxite in the World

- Australia is leading producer of Bauxite ores in the world. It is mined from Weipa lying East of the Gulf of Carpentaria and from Arnhem region.
- In USA, bauxite is mainly mined from Arkansas region. A small amount is mined from Georgia and Alabama. Production of bauxite is insufficient to meet the demand therefore it is imported from Jamaica, Suriname and Dominican Republic.
- Bauxite mining is not important in Russia and the aluminium industry is dependent from imports of bauxite from Guinea, Yugoslavia, Greece, Hungary and Caribbean Islands.
- China, Malaysia, India, Turkey and Indonesia are the leading producer of bauxite in the Asia.
- Odisha is the largest bauxite producing state in India.

Minerals in Antarctica

- The geology of Antarctica is sufficiently well known to predict the existence of a variety of mineral deposits, some probably large.
- Significant size of deposits of coal in the Trans Antarctic Mountains and iron near the Prince Charles Mountains of East Antarctica is forecasted.
- Iron ore, gold, silver and oil are also present in commercial quantities.

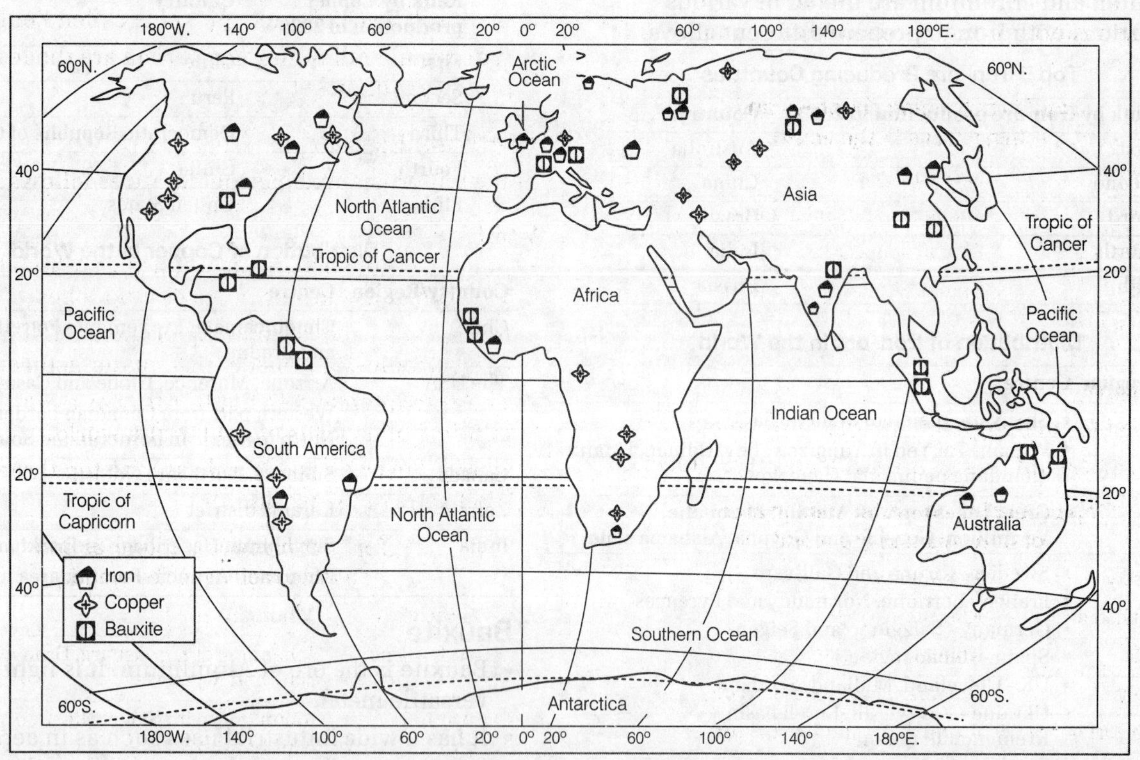

Manganese

- Manganese is an important raw material for smelting of iron-ore and also used for manufacturing ferro alloys.
- Manganese deposits are found in almost all geological formations, however, it is mainly associated with Dharwar system. South Africa, Australia, China and Brazil, etc., are the top producers of manganese.
- South Africa has the largest reserve of manganese.
- The leading exporters of lead in the world are Australia and Mexico and the chief importer is USA.

Top producing countries and mining areas of manganese in the world.

Country	Mining Area
China	Anshon Changeling, peking area (Southern and China)
South Africa	Postonashurg area, kimberley and kuram drop
Gabon	Franceville, comilang
Ukraine	Nikopol
Brazil	Anapa region
Georgia	chiatura

Mica

- Mica is a lustrous mineral and it is a bad conductor of heat and electricity. Due to this property, Mica finds applications in electric appliances.
- Mica occurs in the form of thick sheets that can be split into thin layers.
- India is the largest producer of the mica in the world.

Tin

- Tin is one of those important metals that are used for making alloys. It is a rather scarce metal in its world distribution.
- Most of the tin occurs in the form of placer deposits in alluvium, found prominently in South-East Asian region.
- The world's leading producers are China, Indonesia, Myanmar, Peru, Brazil, Bolivia and Malaysia.
- Leading importer countries of tin are Germany, Italy and France.

Top Tin producing countries and mining areas in the world.

Country	Mining Area
Malaysia	Panong island, Selangor Jelubi Valley
Indonesia	Banka, malacca, and Billiton
China	Yunan, Hunan and Kwanxi
Thailand	Uket

Chromium

- It is used for making high quality alloy steel.
- South Africa and Russia are the leading producers.

Top producing countries mining areas of Chromium in the world.

Country	Mining Area
Kazakhstan	Khrontau
Russia	Khalilobi, Kartali, Komaroro etc
Turkey	Guleman, Fethiye, Denili etc
South Africa	Rusten burg and Lyden burg
Zimbabe	Selewid and Kildonam
Philippines	Jambolage filld

Zinc

- Zinc occurs generally in association of lead and both these minerals are therefore mined together.
- The world leaders in production of zinc are China, Australia and Peru.
- Other important producers are Peru, Japan Mexico, Spain, Zaire and Poland.
- The chief exporters of zinc in the world are Canada, Australia, Peru, Mexico, Spain and Zaire.

Lead

- Lead is also an important mineral and the lead ore is a chemical mixture of pure metal and sulphur.
- The ore is found widely distributed in the world and leading countries are Australia, China, USA, Peru and Canada.
- Other important producers are **Kazakhstan**, **Russia** and **Yugoslavia**.

Cobalt

- Cobalt is a hard metal, mostly found in blue colour.
- The chemical properties of cobalt is similar to iron ore. The Democratic Republic of Congo has the **largest** cobalt reserves in the world.

Nickel

- Nickel is a metallic mineral and it is used for metal plating. The chief ore of nickel is called Pentlandite.
- Indonesia, Philippines and Russia are the leading producers of nickel.

Precious Metals

Some important precious metals are as follows :

Gold

- In nature, gold occurs in the form of Alluvial placer deposits or as reefs or underground lobes.
- It is mainly used for making ornaments. It is also used in electronics, pharmaceutical manufacturing etc.
- The **Witwatersand** in South Africa is the richest area in terms of deposits of gold in the world.
- China, Australia and Russia are the top three gold producers in the world.

Top gold producing countries and mining regions in the world.

Country	Mining Area
South Africa	Johannesburg, Boksburg, Drange free state and Kimberley
Australia	Mount morgan, Kalgoorlie, Coolgardie, New South Wales
USA	Carlin, Nerada, cortez
China	Shandong, Yunnan, Henan

Silver

- This metal has a wide range of uses and occurs in pure state as well as in combination with gold, lead and copper.
- It is used for making coins, ornaments, crafts, silver plating, electroplating, etc.
- Its Leading producer of silver in the world are Mexico, Peru, China, Australia and Chile.

Top Silver producing countries and mining regions in the world

Country	Mining Area
Mexico	Hindalo and Chinhua-hua
Canada	Quebee, Ontario, Saskatchewan and British Columbia
USA	Montana, Arizona, Nevada and Texas
Australia	Kalgoorlie, mount Isa, Brokenhill
South Africa	Natal province and Transvaal
Bolivia	Potsey

Diamond

- Diamond is the purest form of carbon and also the hardest substance.
- Diamond is used for cutting glasses, drilling in rocks, polishing the diamond and for making ornaments.
- The Republic of Congo is the largest producer of industrial diamonds.
- Other leading producers are South Africa, Australia, Ghana and Angola.

Platinum

- Platinum is a rare mineral. It is also called '**White Gold**.' It is used for making ornaments, laboratory instruments, etc.
- The melting point of platinum is 1550° C to 2700° C. Canada and South Africa are the leading producers of platinum.

Uses of Minerals

- Minerals which are used for gems are usually hard. These are then set in various styles for jewellery.
- Copper is another metal used in everything from coins to pipes. Silicon, used in the computer industry is obtained from quartz.
- Aluminium obtained from its ore bauxite is used in automobiles and airplanes, bottling industry, buildings and even in kitchen cookware.

Conservation of Minerals

- Minerals are a non-renewable resource. It takes thousands of years for the formation and concentration of minerals.
- The rate of formation is much smaller than the rate at which the humans consume these minerals.
- Economic development has brought with it increasing consumption of all types of minerals leading to increase in prices.
- It is necessary to reduce wastage in the process of mining. Recycling of metals is another way in which the mineral resources can be conserved.

Extra Facts From Tamil Nadu Board and NIOS

- Iron-ore are classified into four categories.
  - **Magnetite** - It is red in colour and has 72% of pure Iron.
  - **Haematite** - It is black in colour and has 70% of pure Iron.
  - **Limonite** - Its colour varies from dark brown to yellow and has 50% or pure Iron.
  - **Siderite** - It is brown in colour and contains only 30% of pure iron.
- Manganese is a kind of Ferro-alloy used to manufacture the special quality steel. A little manganese added to iron, removes gases and acts as a **Cleanser** in the manufacturing process.
- Nearly 6 kg of manganese is used for making 1 ton of steel. India is the **8th** largest producer of manganese in the world though it possesses the largest reservers of manganese in the world.
- The chief ore of copper is **copper pyrite**. It yields nearly 76% of the world production of copper.
- Bauxite is an impure raw material. It generally occurs as an ingredient of chemical compounds in highly complex minerals such as Cryolite, Corundum and Kaolin.
- Platinum in one of the densest metals almost twice as dense as lead. Platinum is found with other rare metals such as **Osmium, Palladium, Iridium** and **Rhodium**.
- Mica does not react to water, acids, oil or solvents. It can resists extremely high temperatures or sudden changes in temperature and is able to withstand high voltages and insulate with low power loss. It can absorb or reflect light, which enables a decorative effect and protects against Ultra Violet (UV) light.
- Phosphate occurs in the sedimentary rocks or as phosphate nodules. Another source is bird dropping of Guano. It is the most important source of phosphate. It is mainly used in fertiliser. China is the largest producer of Phosphate in the world. The other leading producers are **Morocco, USA, Russia** and **Peru**.
- It is estimated that India possesses over 20 per cent of the world's total reservers of iron-ore. The quality of ore found in India is very high, containg above 60% iron content.
- Limestone is useful in a wide range of industries. Approximately two-thirds of the country's total consumption is used in the cement industry. Iron and steel, chemical, sugar, paper, fertilisers and ferromanganese industries are some of the other areas where it is used in large quantities.

10

Energy Resources

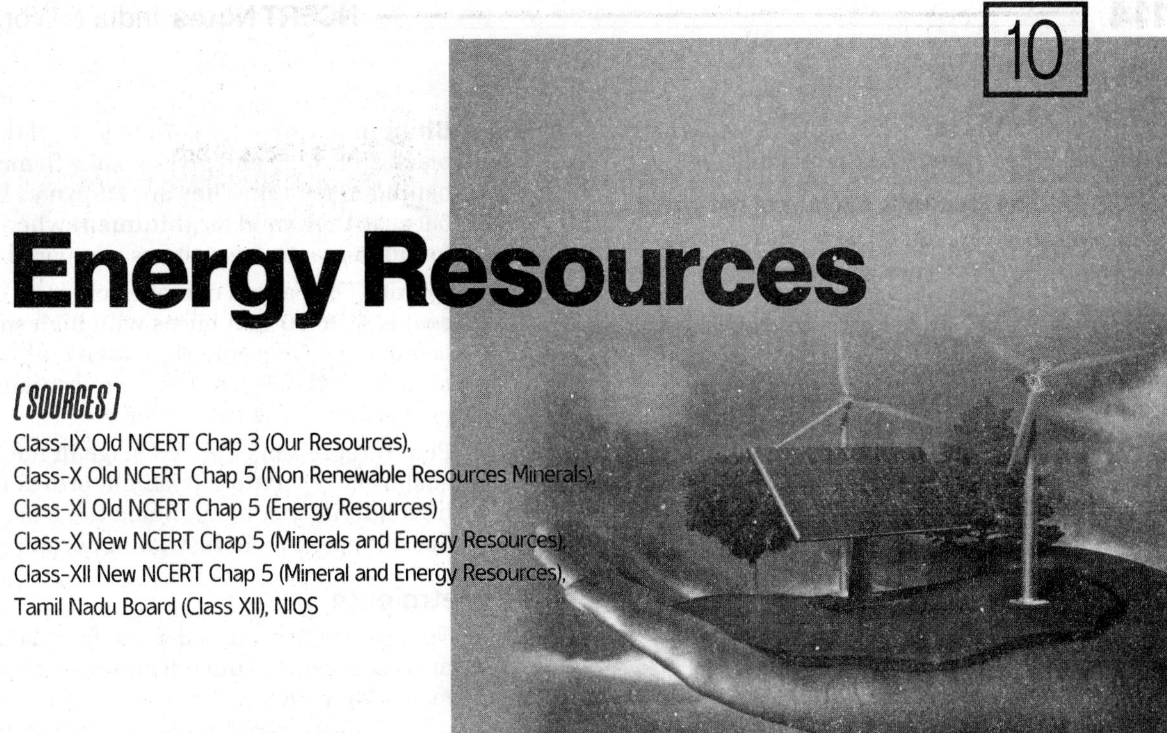

[SOURCES]

Class-IX Old NCERT Chap 3 (Our Resources),
Class-X Old NCERT Chap 5 (Non Renewable Resources Minerals),
Class-XI Old NCERT Chap 5 (Energy Resources)
Class-X New NCERT Chap 5 (Minerals and Energy Resources),
Class-XII New NCERT Chap 5 (Mineral and Energy Resources),
Tamil Nadu Board (Class XII), NIOS

- Energy is an important factor in development of an economy. The demand for energy has increased with socio-economic development in the world.
- Some of the energy resources are exhaustible or **non-renewable**, for example, coal and mineral oil but many are **renewable**, for example, water and solar energy.
- Potential of water energy is more in those regions where water discharge of the rivers is high, rainfall is heavy and running water is available throughout the year.
- Solar energy is more dependable and universally applicable. The increasing demand of the energy and the energy crisis of 1973 in the world have given impetus to research and development of non-conventional sources of energy.

Classification of Energy Resources

Energy plays a vital role in our lives. We need energy for industry, agriculture, transport, communication and defence. It may be broadly categorised as conventional and non-conventional resources.

Conventional Sources

- Conventional sources of energy are those, which have been in common use for long time. **Firewood** and **fossil fuels** are the two main conventional energy sources.
- Firewood and cattle dung cake are most common in rural India. According to an estimate, more than 70% energy requirement in rural households is met by firewood and cool.

Firewood

- It is widely used for cooking and heating. In our country more than 50% of the energy used by villagers comes from firewood.
- Remains of plants and animals, which were buried under the Earth for millions of years got converted by the heat and pressure into fossil fuels.
- Fossil fuel such as coal, petroleum and natural gas are the main sources of conventional energy. The reserves of these minerals are limited.
- The rate at which the growing world population is consuming them is far greater than the rate of their formation. So, these are likely to be exhausted soon.

Coal

- It is the most abundantly found fossil fuel. It is used as a domestic fuel, in industries such as iron and steel, steam engines and to generate electricity.
- It has been the basis of Industrial revolution and its importance as a source of energy has declined after the introduction of mineral oil and natural gas.
- It is found in the seams in sedimentary rocks. Its major quality is its combustibility and volatileness.
- Most of the coal has been formed during carboniferous period of geological history owing to the submergence of natural vegetation. It is therefore referred as **Buried Sunshine**.
- According to the latest estimates by International Energy Agency (IEA), top five producer of coal in 2021 were, China, India, Indonesia, Australia and USA.

- The coal producing areas of India are Raniganj, Jharia, Dhanbad and Bokaro in Jharkhand.

Coal Producing Regions of the World

Country/Region	Centre
China	Datong in Shansi province, Huo-LinGHe in Inner Mongolia, Huainan and Huaibei in Anhui Xuzhou in Jiangsu, Lipanshin in Guizhou and Kailuan in Heger Province
The USA	Western Pennsylvania to Alabama. Kentucky and Western Virginia Illinois, Utah, Montana, Wyoming, Colorado, Arizona and New Mexico
Europe	Franco-Belgian coalfields, Campine- Limburg coalfield, Rurh, Saar, Silesia Saxony and Pilsen, Penine ranges and Scottish highland
Australia	New South Wales, Queensland and Western Australia
India	Raniganj, Jharia, Giridih, Ramgarh in Jharkhand Wardha valley in Maharashtra, Umaria and Sohagpur region of Madhya Pradesh

Types of Coal

On the basis of carbon content, coal is divided into following types

- **Anthracite** It is very hard, shiny and free of impurities. It contains about 90% of carbon and gives off little smoke and leaves little ash after being burnt.
- There are very limited reserves of this type of coal.
- **Bituminous** It contains 70 to 90% of the carbon. It is black and shiny and gives smoky flame and leaves behind much ash. They are known as bituminous because they yield tar (**bitumen**) when heated. It is found in greater quantity as compared to other types.
- **Lignite** The carbon content in Lignite or Brown of coal is 45 to 70%. It burns with high smoky flames. It is much more recent origin than anthracite and bituminous coals and therefore contains higher proportion of vegetal matter.
- **Peat** It represents the first stage in the formation of coal from vegetation. It is light brown in colour with high humidity content. Being the most inferior coal, it doesn't have any industrial importance.

Petroleum

- The word petroleum is derived from Latin words '–Petra' meaning rock, 'oleum' meaning oil. So, petroleum means **rock oil**.
- It is found between the layers of rocks and is drilled from oil fields located in off-shore and coastal areas.
- This is then sent to refineries which process the crude oil produce a variety of products like diesel, petrol, kerosene, wax, plastics and lubricants.
- Petroleum and its derivatives are called Black Gold as they are very valuable.

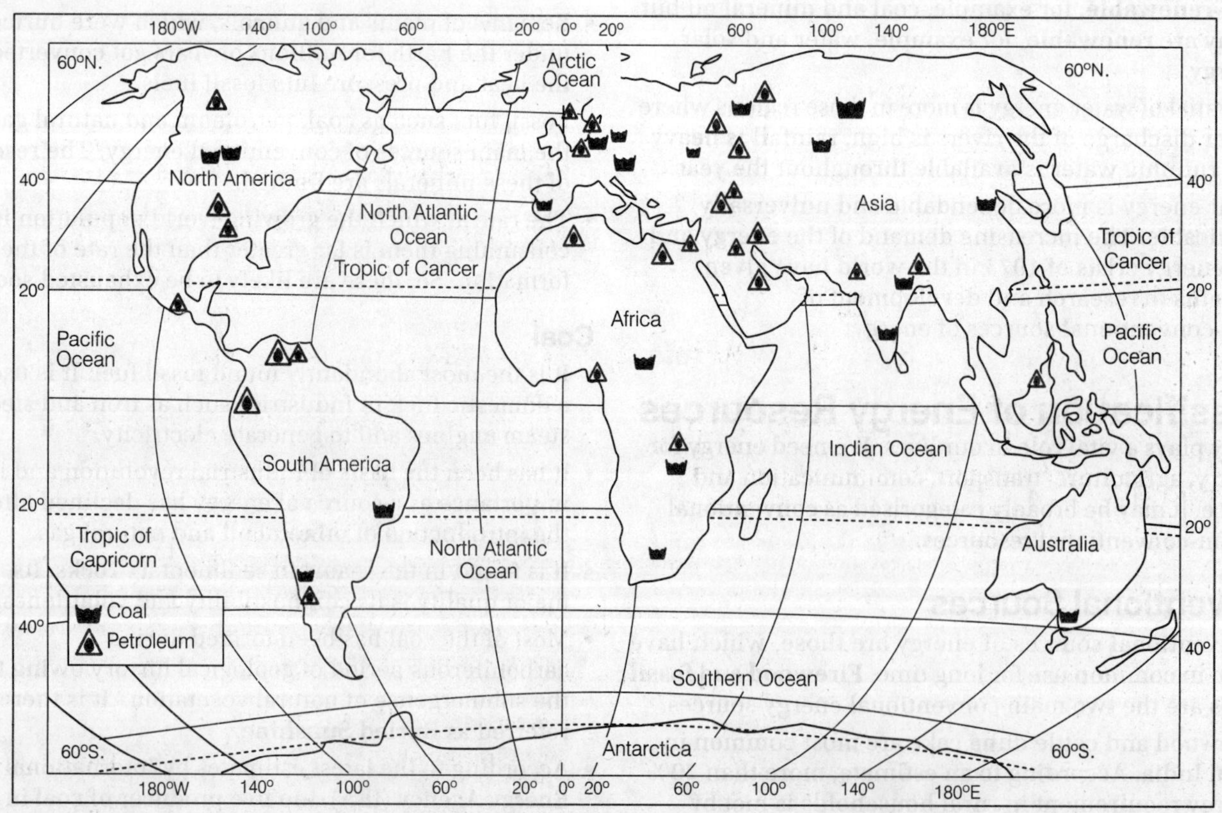

World Wide Distribution of Coal and Petroleum

Top 5 Petroleum Producing Countries

Rank by Petroleum production in 2022	Country
First	United States
Second	Saudi Arabia
Third	Russia
Fourth	Canada
Fifth	Iraq

Natural Gas

- Natural gas is found with petroleum deposits and is released when crude oil is brought to the surface.
- It can be used as a domestic and industrial fuel.
- It is used as a source of energy as well as an industrial raw material in the petrochemical industry.
- It is considered an environment friendly fuel because of low carbon dioxide emissions and is, therefore, the fuel for the present century.
- Russia, Norway, UK and the Netherlands are the major producers of natural gas.
- Domestically, large reserves of natural gas have been discovered in the Krishna-Godavari basin.
- Along the West coast the reserves of the Mumbai high and allied fields are supplemented by finds in the Gulf of Cambay.
- Andaman and Nicobar islands are also important areas having large reserves of natural gas.

Top 5 Natural Gas Producing Countries

Rank by Natural gas production in 2022	Country
First	United States
Second	Russia
Third	Iran
Fourth	Canada
Fifth	Algeria

Compressed Natural Gas

Compressed Natural Gas (CNG) is a popular eco-friendly automobile fuel as it causes less pollution than petroleum and diesel.

Electricity

- Electricity has such a wide range of applications in today's world that, its per capita consumption is considered as an index of development.
- It is generated mainly in two ways by running water which drives hydro turbines to generate hydro electricity; and by burning other fuels such as coal, petroleum and natural gas to drive turbines to produce thermal power.

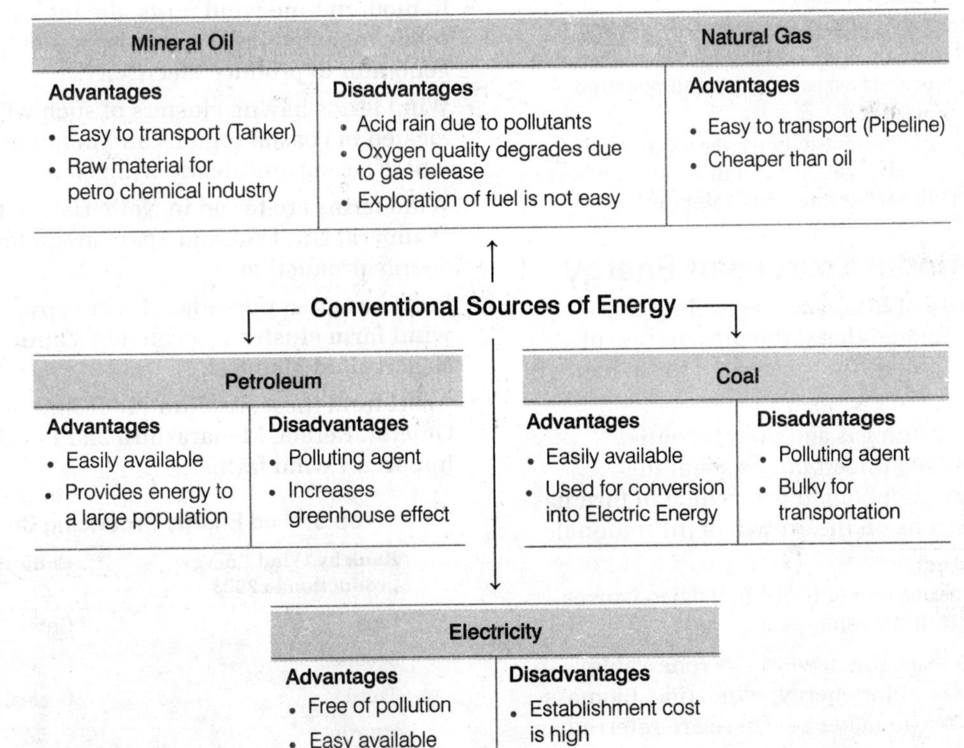

Thermal Power

- It is generated by using coal, petroleum and natural gas. The thermal power stations use non-renewable fossil fuels for generating electricity.
- There are over 310 thermal power plants in India.

Hydel Power

- Rain water or River water stored in dams is made to fall from heights.
- The falling water flows through pipes inside the dam over turbine blades placed at the bottom of the dam.
- The moving blades then turn the generator to produce electricity. It is called **hydroelectricity**.
- The water discharged after the generation of electricity is used for irrigation. One-fourth of the world's electricity is produced by hydel power.
- Hydel energy is the source of clean energy, which does not pollute the environment. It can be transmitted to the long distance through wires and cables but there could be transmission losses if transmitted for very long distance.
- The leading producers of hydel power in the world are Paraguay, Norway, Brazil and China.
- Some important hydel power stations in India are Bhakranangal, Gandhi Sagar, Nagarjunsagar and Damodar valley projects.

Facts About Hydel Energy

- **Norway** was the first country in the world to develop hydro electricity.
- The site of the world's first solar and wind powered bus shelter is in **Scotland**.
- Development of hydroelectricity power has made it possible to locate industries even in those areas where it was not possible earlier due to lack of power.

Non-Conventional Sources of Energy

- The increasing use of fossil fuels is leading to its shortage. It is estimated that if the present rate of consumption continues, the reserves of these fuel will get exhausted.
- Rising prices of oil and gas and their potential shortages have raised uncertainties about the security of energy supply in future, which in turn has serious repercussions on the growth of the national economy.
- Moreover, increasing use of fossil fuels also causes serious environmental problems.
- Hence, there is a pressing need to use renewable energy sources like solar energy, wind, tide, biomass and energy from waste material. These are referred as non-conventional sources of energy.

Solar Energy

- Solar energy is the most widely available and non-exhaustible source of energy.
- The solar energy can be directly converted into electricity with the help of Photovoltaic cell. These Photovoltaic cells are made up of silicon, which is commonly found element in the world.
- The technology of utilising solar energy benefits a lot of tropical countries that are blessed with abundant sun shine.
- Solar energy is also used in solar heaters, solar cookers, solar dryers besides being used for community lighting and traffic signals.

Top 5 Solar Energy Producing Countries

Rank by Solar Energy production in 2023	Country
First	China
Second	USA
Third	Japan
Fourth	Germany
Fifth	India

Wind Energy

- Wind is an inexhaustible source of energy. Wind mills have been used for grinding grain and lifting water since times immemorial.
- In modern time wind mills, the high speed winds rotate the wind mill, which is connected to a generator to produce electricity.
- Wind farms having clusters of such wind mills are located in coastal regions and in mountain passes where strong and steady winds flow.
- Wind farms are found in Netherlands, Germany, Denmark, UK, USA and Spain are noted for their wind energy production.
- India has great potential of wind power. The **largest wind farm cluster** is located in **Tamil Nadu** from Nagercoil to Madurai.
- Apart from these, Andhra Pradesh, Karnataka, Gujarat, Kerala, Maharashtra and Lakshadweep have important wind farms.

Top 5 Wind Energy Producing Countries

Rank by Wind Energy production in 2023	Country
First	China
Second	USA
Third	Germany
Fourth	India
Fifth	Spain

Biogas

- Organic waste such as dead plant and animal material, animal dung and kitchen waste can be converted into a gaseous fuel called biogas.
- The organic waste is decomposed by bacteria in biogas digesters to emit biogas, which is essentially a mixture of methane and carbon dioxide.
- Biogas is an excellent fuel for cooking and lighting and produces huge amount of organic manure each year.
- The plants using cattle dung are known as '**Gobar gas plants**' in rural India.
- These provide twin benefits to the farmer in the form of energy and improved quality of manure.
- Biogas also prevents the loss of trees and manure due to burning of fuel wood and cow dung cakes.

Geothermal Power

- Heat energy obtained from the Earth is called **Geothermal energy**.
- The temperature in the interior of the Earth rises steadily as we go deeper.
- Sometimes, this heat energy may surface itself in the form of hot springs. This heat energy can be used to generate power.
- Geothermal energy in the form of hot springs has been used for cooking, heating and bathing for several years.
- USA has the world's largest geothermal power plants followed by New Zealand, Iceland, Philippines and Central America.
- Two experimental projects have been set up in India to harness geothermal energy.
- One is located in the **Parvati valley** near **Manikaran** in Himachal Pradesh and the other is located in the **Puga valley, Ladakh**.

Tidal Energy

- Energy generated from tides is called tidal energy. Tidal energy can be harnessed by building dams at narrow openings of the sea.
- During high tide the energy of the tides is used to turn the turbine installed in the dam to produce electricity.
- The first tidal energy station was built in France. South Korea, France, United Kingdom and Canada are among the biggest producer of tidal energy in the world.
- In India the Gulf of Khambhat, the Gulf of Kutch in Gujarat on the Western coast and Gangetic delta in Sunderban regions of West Bengal provide ideal conditions for utilising tidal energy.

Nuclear or Atomic Energy

- Nuclear power is obtained from energy stored in the nuclei of atoms of naturally occurring radioactive elements like uranium and thorium.
- These fuels undergo nuclear fission in nuclear reactors and emit power.
- The greatest producers of nuclear power are **USA** and **Europe**. In India Rajasthan and Jharkhand have large deposits of Uranium. Thorium is found in large quantities in the Monazite sands of Kerala and in Andhra Pradesh.

Top 5 Nuclear Energy Producing Countries

Rank by Nuclear Energy production in 2020	Country
First	United States
Second	France
Third	China
Fourth	Japan
Fifth	Russia

Uranium

- There are two primary sources of uranium. **Pitchblende**, which has 50 to 80% uranium content and uraninite, in which Uranium content is 65 to 80%.
- Australia, Kazakhstan and Canada are the biggest producer of Uranium in the World. It is found in the Uranium City (Canada) on the Northern bank of Lake Athabasca and Port Radium of Great Bear. Colorado plateau of USA also has rich Uranium deposits.
- It is also found in Kazakhstan, South Africa, Zaire, Russia, Australia, Germany, Sweden, Spain and India.
- The Uranium deposits in India are found at **Gaya** and **Singhbhum** district of Bihar and Jharkhand, Udaipur and Jaipur district of Rajasthan, Nellore district of Andhra Pradesh and Palghat district of Kerala.

Countries with world's top Uranium producer and reserves

Top producing countries	Countries with top reserves
Kazakhstan	Kazakhstan
Canada	Canada
Australia	Russia

Thorium

- The major source of thorium are thorianite, allanite, and monazite. Monazite is a greyish mineral with yellowish lustre and is a constituent of granite and pegmatite.
- Globally, India has the largest reserve of thorium followed by Brazil, Australia and United States.

Nuclear Power Plants in India

Nuclear Power Plant	State
Kaiga	Karnataka
Kakrapar	Gujarat
Kudankulam	Tamil Nadu
Kalpakkam	Tamil Nadu
Narora	Uttar Pradesh
Rawatbhata	Rajasthan
Tarapur	Maharashtra

Top reservoir and producing nations of Thorium

Producing Country	Reservoir Country
India	India
USA	USA
Australia	Australia
Canada	Canada
South Africa	South Africa

Conservation of Energy Resources

- Energy is a basic requirement for economic development. Every sector of the national economy-agriculture, industry, transport, commercial and domestic-needs Inputs of energy.
- The economic development plans Implemented since Independence necessarily required increasing amounts of energy to remain operational. As a result, consumption of energy in all forms has been steadily rising all over the country.
- In this background, there is an urgent need to develop a sustainable path of energy development. Promotion of energy conservation and increased use of renewable energy sources are the twice planks of sustainable energy.

Extra Facts From Tamil Nadu Board and NIOS

- Most of the coal resources of the world were formed during the carboniferous period (280 to 350 million years ago).
- Out of the total coal reserves and production in India, Gondwana coal fields contribute 98% and the rest 2% is produced by tertiary coal fields.
- **Steam coal** It is used for producing steam and it has high Sulphur content.
- China is the largest producer of steam coal in the world followed by India. The other leading producers of steam coal are USA, Indonesia and South Africa.
- Coal is used for various purposes. It is used as a source of steam energy, electrical energy, domestic fuel, metallurgical coke, chemical industries and byproducts such as Ammonium Sulphate, Naphthalene, Phenol, Benzene, etc.
- OPEC is the short form of the 'Organisation of Petroleum Exporting Countries'. It was formed in 1960 at Bagdad convention. Initially it comprised of Saudi Arabia, Iran, Iraq, Kuwait and Venezuela. Later on added in eight countries Libya, Algeria, Qatar, UAE, Nigeria, Ecuador and Angola, Indonesia left from OPEC in recently.
- A powerful odourant, ethanethiol (commonly known as ethyl mercaptan) is added in natural gas, so that leaks can be detected easily. It is prepared by refining petroleum or wet natural gas.
- The world's first commercial nuclear power station Calder Hall at sellafield, England was opened in 1956.
- Noor Complex is the world's largest Concentrated Solar Power (CSP) plant, located in the Sahara Desert.
- The world's largest wind farm is in Altamont Pass in California.
- The largest tidal power station is at Sihwa lake in South Korea and it is the largest tidal power producer in the world.

11

Industries

[SOURCES]

Class-VIII New NCERT Chap 4 (Industries), Class-XI Old NCERT Chap 10 (Location of Industries and Major Industries of the World), Class-XII New NCERT Chap 5 (Secondary Activities) and Chap 6 (Tertiary and Quaternary Activities), Class-IX Old NCERT Chap 8 (Human Occupation), Tamil Nadu Board (Class XII), NIOS

- All economic activities namely **primary, secondary, tertiary** and **quaternary** revolve around obtaining and utilising resources necessary for survival.
- **Industry** refers to an economic activity that is concerned with production of goods, extraction of minerals or the provision of services.
- **Secondary activities** add value to natural resources by transforming raw materials into valuable products. It is therefore linked to the manufacturing, processing and construction activities.

Manufacturing

- Manufacturing involves a full array of production from handicrafts to moulding iron and steel and stamping out plastic toys to assembling delicate computer components or space vehicles.
- In each of these processes, the common characteristics are the application of power, mass production of identical products and specialised labour in factory settings for the production of standardised commodities. Manufacturing may be done with modern power and machinery or it may still be very primitive.

Characteristics of Modern Large Scale Manufacturing

Modern large scale manufacturing has the following characterstics :

- **Specialisation of Skills/Methods of Production** Under the 'craft' method, factories produce only a few pieces which are made-to-order. So the costs are high. On the other hand, mass production involves production of large quantities of standardised parts by each worker performing only one task repeatedly.
- **Mechanisation** It refers to using gadgets, which accomplish tasks. Automation (without aid of human thinking during the manufacturing process) is the advanced stage of mechanisation. Automatic factories with feedback and closed loop computer control systems where machines are developed to 'think', have sprung up all over the world.
- **Technological Innovation** Technological innovations through research and development strategy are an important aspect of modern manufacturing. It helps the manufacturing process by ensuring quality control, eliminating waste and inefficiency and combating pollution.

Manufacturing Industry

- Manufacturing literally means 'to make by hand'. However, now it includes goods 'made by machines'. It is essentially a process, which involves transforming raw materials into finished goods of higher value for sale in local or distant markets.
- Conceptually, an industry is a geographically located manufacturing unit maintaining books of accounts and records under a management system.
- As the term industry is comprehensive, it is also used as synonymous with 'manufacturing' When one uses terms like 'steel industry' and 'chemical industry' one thinks of factories and processes.
- But there are many secondary activities, which are not carried on in factories such as what is now called the '**entertainment industry**' and **Tourism industry**, etc.

- **Organisational Structure and Stratification** Modern manufacturing is characterised by :
  (a) a complex machine technology
  (b) extreme specialisation and division of labour
  (c) vast capital
  (d) large organisations
  (e) executive bureaucracy
- **Uneven Geographic Distribution** Major concentrations of modern manufacturing have flourished in a few numbers of places. These cover less than 10% of the world's land area.

Factors Influencing Location of Manufacturing Industries

Industries maximise profits by reducing costs.

Therefore, industries should be located at points where the production costs are minimum. Some of the factors influencing industrial locations are as under :

- **Access to Market** The existence of a market for manufactured goods is the most important factor in the location of industries. 'Market' means people who have a demand for these goods and also have the purchasing power (ability to purchase) to be able to purchase from the sellers at a place. Remote areas inhabited by a few people offer small markets.

  The developed regions of Europe, North America, Japan and Australia provide large global markets as the purchasing power of the people is very high.

  The densely populated regions of South and South-East Asia also provide large markets. Some industries, such as aircraft manufacturing, have a global market. The arms industry also has global markets.
- **Access to Raw material** Raw material used by industries should be cheap and easy to transport. Industries based on cheap, bulky and weight-losing material (ores) are located close to the sources of raw material such as steel, sugar and cement industries.

  Perishability is a vital factor for the industry to be located closer to the source of the raw material. Agro-processing and dairy products are processed close to the sources of farm produce or milk supply respectively.
- **Access to Labour Supply** Labour supply is an important factor in the location of industries. Some types of manufacturing still require skilled labour. Increasing mechanisation, automation and flexibility of industrial processes have reduced the dependence of industry upon the labours.
- **Access to Sources of Energy** Industries which use more power are located close to the source of the energy supply such as the aluminium industry.

  Earlier coal was the main source of energy; today hydroelectricity and petroleum are also important sources of energy for many industries.
- **Access to Transportation and Communication Facilities** Speedy and efficient transport facilities to carry raw materials to the factory and to move finished goods to the market are essential for the development of industries. The cost of transport plays an important role in the location of industrial units.

  Western Europe and Eastern North America have a highly developed transport system, which has always induced the concentration of industries in these areas. Modern industry is inseparably tied to transportation systems.

  Improvements in transportation led to integrated economic development and regional specialisation of manufacturing. Communication is also an important need for industries for the exchange and management of information.
- **Government Policy** Governments adopt 'regional policies' to promote 'balanced' economic development and hence, set up industries in particular areas.
- **Access to Agglomeration Economies/ Links between Industries** Many industries benefit from nearness to a leader-industry and other industries. These benefits are termed as agglomeration economies.

  Savings are derived from the linkages, which exist between different industries. These factors operate together to determine industrial location.

Foot Loose Industries

- Foot loose industries can be located in a wide variety of places.
- They are not dependent on any specific raw material, weight losing or otherwise. They largely depend on component parts, which can be obtained anywhere.
- They produce in small quantity and also employ a small labour force. These are generally not polluting industries.
- The important factor in their location is accessibility by road network.

Classification of Manufacturing Industries

Manufacturing industries are classified on the basis of their size, inputs/ raw materials output/ products and ownership.

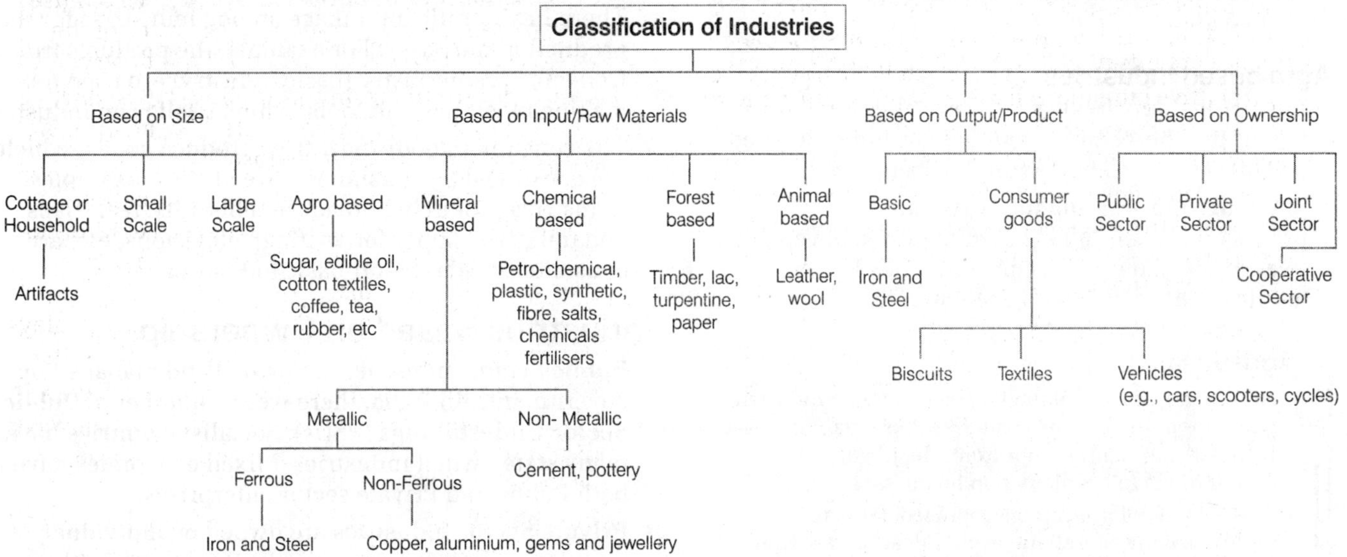

Industries based on Size

- The amount of capital invested, number of workers employed and volume of production determine the size of industry.
- Accordingly, industries may be classified into household or cottage, small-scale and large-scale.

Household Industries or Cottage Manufacturing

- It is the smallest manufacturing unit. The artisans use local raw materials and simple tools to produce everyday goods in their homes with the help of their family members or part time labour.
- Finished products may be for consumption in the same household or for sale in local (village) markets or for barter.
- Capital and transportation do not wield much influence as this type of manufacturing has low commercial significance and most of the tools are devised locally.
- Some common everyday products produced in this sector of manufacturing include foodstuffs, fabrics, mats, containers, tools, furniture and shoes.
- Besides these, figurines from wood lot and forest, shoes and other articles from leather; pottery and bricks from clays and stones are also produced in these industries.
- Goldsmiths make jewellery of gold, silver and bronze. Some artefacts and crafts are made out of bamboo, wood obtained locally from the forests.

Small Scale Manufacturing

- Small scale manufacturing is distinguished from household industries by its production techniques and place of manufacture (a workshop outside the home/cottage of the producer).
- This type of manufacturing uses local raw material, simple power-driven machines and semi-skilled labour. It provides employment and raises local purchasing power.
- Therefore, countries like India, China, Indonesia and Brazil, etc have developed labour-intensive small scale manufacturing in order to provide employment to their population.

Large Scale Manufacturing

- Large scale manufacturing involves a large market, various raw materials, enormous energy, specialised workers, advanced technology, assembly-line mass production and large capital.
- This kind of manufacturing developed in the last 200 years, in the United Kingdom, North-Eastern USA and Europe. Now it has diffused to almost all over the world.
- On the basis of the system of large scale manufacturing, the world's major industrial regions may be grouped under two broad types, namely:
  1. Traditional large-scale industrial regions, which are thickly clustered in a few more developed countries.
  2. High-technology large scale industrial regions, which have diffused to less developed countries.

Industries based on Inputs/Raw Materials

On the basis of the raw materials used, the industries are classified as:

Agro based Industries

- Agro processing involves the processing of raw materials from the field and the farm into finished products for rural and urban markets.
- Major agro-processing industries are food processing, sugar, pickles, fruits juices, beverages (tea, coffee and cocoa), spices and oils fats and textiles (cotton, jute, silk), rubber, etc.

Agri-business

- Agri-business is commercial farming on an industrial scale often financed by business whose main interests lie outside agriculture, for example, large corporations in tea plantation business.
- Agri-business farms are mechanised, large in size, highly structured, reliant on chemicals and may be described as 'agro-factories'.

Mineral based Industries

- These industries use minerals as a raw material. Some industries use ferrous metallic minerals, which contain ferrous (iron), such as iron and steel industries.
- But some use non-ferrous metallic minerals, such as aluminium, copper and jewellery industries.
- Many industries use non-metallic minerals such as cement and pottery industries.

Chemical based Industries

- Such industries use natural chemical minerals, e.g. mineral-oil (petroleum) is used in petrochemical industry. Salts, sulphur and potash industries also use natural minerals.
- Chemical industries are also based on raw materials obtained from wood and coal.
- Synthetic fibre, plastic, etc. are other examples of chemical based industries.

Forest based Raw Material using Industries

- The forests provide many major and minor products which are used as raw material.
- Timber for furniture industry, wood, bamboo and grass for paper industry, lac for lac industries come from forests.

Animal based Industries

- Leather for leather industry and wool for woollen textiles are obtained from animals. Besides, ivory is also obtained from elephant's tusks.

Industries Based on Output/ Product

- The industry whose products are used to make other goods by using them as raw materials are basic industries.
- There lies significant linkage among industries for the production purposes. For example, the products from Iron and Steel industry (basic industry) are used for making machines and tools, which itself is an industry.
- The consumer goods industries produce goods, which are consumed by consumers directly. For examples, industries producing breads and biscuits, tea, soaps and toiletries, paper for writing, televisions, etc. are consumer goods or non-basic industries.

Industries Based on Ownership

- **Public Sector** Industries are owned and managed by governments. In India, there were a number of **Public Sector Undertakings** (PSUs). Socialist countries have many state owned industries. Mixed economies have both Public and Private sector enterprises.
- **Private Sector** Industries are owned by individual investors. These are managed by Private organisations. In capitalist countries, industries are generally owned privately.
- **Joint Sector** Industries are managed by joint stock companies or sometimes the private and public sectors together establish and manage the industries.
- **Cooperative sector** Industries are owned and operated by the producers or suppliers of raw materials, workers or both Anand Milk Union Limited and Sudha Dairy are a success stories of a cooperative nature.

Industrial System

- An industrial system consists of inputs, processes and outputs. The inputs are the raw materials, labour and costs of land, transport, power and other infrastructure.
- The processes include a wide range of activities that convert the raw material into finished products. The outputs are the end product and the income earned from it.
- In case of the textile industry, the inputs may be cotton, human labour, factory and transport cost. The processes include ginning, spinning, weaving, dyeing and printing. The output is the shirt you wear.

Industrial Regions

- Industrial regions emerge when a number of industries locate close to each other and share the benefits of their closeness.
- Major industrial regions of the world are Eastern North America, Western and Central Europe, Eastern Europe and Eastern Asia.

- Major industrial regions tend to be located in the temperate areas, near sea ports and especially near coal fields.
- India has several industrial regions like Mumbai - Pune cluster, Bengaluru-Tamil Nadu region, Hugli region, Ahmedabad-Baroda region, Chhota Nagpur industrial belt, Vishakhapatnam-Guntur belt, Gurgaon-Delhi- Meerut region and the Kollam-Thiruvananthapuram industrial cluster.

Traditional large Scale Industrial Regions

- These are based on heavy industry, often located near coal-fields and engaged in metal smelting, heavy engineering, chemical manufacture or textile production.
- These industries are now known as **smokestack industries.** Traditional industrial regions can be recognised by following four factors :

1. High proportion of employment in manufacturing industry.
2. High-density housing, often of inferior type and poor services.
3. Unattractive environment, for example, pollution, waste heaps, and so on.
4. Problems of unemployment, emigration and derelict land areas caused by closure of factories because of a worldwide fall in demand.

World Industrial Regions

The world's major manufacturing regions are found in North America, Europe and East Asia. Other manufacturing centres are also found elsewhere.

North America

- Manufacturing in North America is concentrated in the North-Eastern quadrant of the United States and in South-Eastern Canada (called the **North American manufacturing** or **rust belt**).
- Only 5% of the land area of these countries contains one-third of the population and nearly two-third of the manufacturing output. This manufacturing belt has achieved its dominance through a combination of historical and environmental factors. Early settlement gave Eastern cities an advantage to become the country's dominant industrial centre.
- First settled in the 17th and 18th century, it is lined by a transportation system that includes the St Lawrence river and the Great lakes connected to the East coast and the Atlantic ocean by the Mohawk and Hudson rivers.
- The North-East also had essential raw materials and good transportation.
- The Great lakes and major rivers were supplemented in the 1800s by canals, railways and highways.
- In modern times, the New England district is developed for availability of highly skilled labour from nearby universities in Boston. Computer manufacturing and software development is now having greatest concentration in California.

Europe

The Western European industrial region appears as one of the major industrial regions on the world map. Location of manufacturing is in a North-South linear pattern from Scotland through England, mouth of the Rhine river valley, Germany and France, to Northern Italy.

In reality, four distinct districts have emerged primarily because European countries competed with one another to develop their own industrial areas. Eastern Europe has six major industrial regions. Four are entirely in Russia, one is in Ukraine and one is Southern Poland and Northern Czech Republic.

Factors for such development in Western Europe are :

- The **Industrial Revolution** started in the United Kingdom in 1750 based on iron and steel production and textile and woollen manufacturing.
- Germany and Japan with US assistance rebuilt, after World War II gaining industrial success against Great Britain.
- The **Rhine** river is the main waterway of European commerce emptying into the North sea at the Dutch city of Rotterdam-the world's largest port.
- Northern Italy has attracted manufacturing due to lower wages and cheap hydroelectricity from the Alps.

Mid-Rhine Belt

- The second most important industrial area in Western Europe includes South-Western Germany, North-Eastern France and the tiny Luxembourg. In contrast to the Rhine-Ruhr valley, the German portion of the Mid-Rhine region lacks abundant raw materials but it is at the centre of Europe's most important consumer market.
- The French portion of the Mid-Rhine region-Alsace and Lorraine-contains Europe's largest iron-ore field and is the production centre for two-thirds of France's steel. **Luxembourg** is also one of the world's leading steel producers because the Lorraine iron-ore field extends into the Southern part of the country.

United Kingdom Region

- The Industrial Revolution originated in the Midlands and Northern England and Southern Scotland because those areas contained a remarkable concentration of innovative engineers and mechanics during the late 18th century. The United Kingdom lost its international industrial leadership in the 20th century saddled with outmoded and deteriorating factories.

- The United Kingdom expanded industrial production in the late 20th century by attracting new high-tech industries that serve the European market.
- Today, British industries are more likely to locate in South-Eastern England near the country's largest concentrations of population, wealth and the Channel Tunnel.

Northern Italy Region

- A fourth important European industrial region lies in the Po river basin of Northern Italy.
- Modern industrial development in the Po basin began with establishment of textile manufacturing during the 19th century because of two key assets: numerous workers and inexpensive hydroelectricity.

Eastern Europe and Russia

Major manufacturing centres are clustered in European Russia and the Ukraine. Other centres were developed East of the Urals. The factors responsible for development of such region are as following :

- Moscow, the population centre of Russia, takes advantage of a large, skilled labour pool and a large market not only for textiles but also for iron and steel, transportation equipment, chemicals and motor vehicles.
- Eastern Ukraine to the South-West of Moscow benefits from rich coal deposits, attracting iron and steel producers.
- The linear Volga region to the East of Moscow is the principal location of substantial oil and gas deposits. It is also linked to the Black sea from the Volga river.
- Just East of Volga in the Urals region where the Urals mountains have the largest deposits of industrial materials in the former Soviet Union.
- The Kuznetsk basin is the chief industrial region to the East of the Urals.

East Asia

- Many industries in China are clustered in three centres near the East coast. In Japan, production is clustered along the South-East coast.

The Ruhr Coal-field, Germany

- This has been one of the major industrial regions of Europe for a long time. Coal, iron and steel formed the basis of the economy.
- But as the demand for coal declined, the industry started shrinking. Even after the iron ore was exhausted, the industry remained, using imported ore brought by waterways to the Ruhr.
- The Ruhr region is responsible for 80% of Germany's total steel production. Changes in the industrial structure have led to the decay of some areas and there are problems of industrial waste and pollution.
- The future prosperity of the Ruhr is based less on the products of coal and steel, for which it was initially famous and more on the new emerging industries.
- It includes the huge Opel car assembly plant, new chemical plants, universities. Out of town shopping centres, which have appeared in the region resulting in creation of a 'New Ruhr' landscape.
- Manufacturing contributes significantly to the world economy. Iron and steel, textiles, automobiles, petrochemicals and electronics are some of the world's most important manufacturing industries.

Industrial Disaster

In industries, accidents/disasters mainly occur due to technical failure or irresponsible handling of hazardous material. One of the worst industrial disasters of all time occurred in Bhopal on 3rd December, 1984 around 12:30 AM.

It was a technological accident in which highly poisonous Methyl Isocyanate (MIC) gas along with Hydrogen Cyanide and other reaction products leaked out of the pesticide factory of Union Carbide. It resulted into heavy casualties.

In another incident, on 23rd December, 2005, due to gas well blowout in Gao Qiao, Chongqing, China, 243 people died, 9,000 were injured and 64,000 were evacuated. Many people died because they were unable to run after the explosion.

Risk Reduction Measures

- Densely populated residential areas should be separated far away from the industrial areas.
- People staying in the vicinity of industries should be aware of the storage of toxins or hazardous substances and their possible effects in case if an accident occurs.
- Fire warning and fighting system should be improved.
- Storage capacity of toxic substances should be limited
- Pollution dispersion qualities in the industries should be improved.

Iron and Steel Industry

- The iron and steel industry forms the base of all other industries and therefore, it is called a **basic industry**.
- It is basic because it provides raw material for other industries such as machine tools used for further production. It may also be called a **heavy industry** because it uses large quantities of bulky raw materials and its products are also heavy.
- Iron is extracted from iron ore by smelting in a blast furnace with carbon (coke) and limestone. The molten iron is cooled and moulded to form pig iron, which is used for converting into steel by adding strengthening materials like manganese.
- The large integrated steel industry is traditionally located close to the sources of raw materials – iron, ore, coal, manganese and limestone – or at places where these could be easily brought. e.g., near ports.

- But in mini steel mills access to markets is more important than inputs. These are less expensive to build and operate and can be located near markets because of the abundance of scrap metal, which is the main input.
- Traditionally, most of the steel was produced at large integrated plants.
- The Indian iron and steel industry consists of large integrated steel plants as well as mini steel mills. It also includes secondary producers, rolling mills and ancillary industries.
- This industry is one of the most complex and capital-intensive industries and is concentrated in advanced countries of North America, Europe and Asia.

The Changing Location of the Iron and Steel Industry

- Before 1800 AD, iron and steel industry was located where raw materials, power supply and running water were easily available.
- Later the ideal location for the industry was near coal fields and close to canals and railways.
- After 1950, iron and steel industry began to be located on large areas of flat land near the ports.
- This is because by this time steel works had become very large and iron-ore had to be imported from overseas.

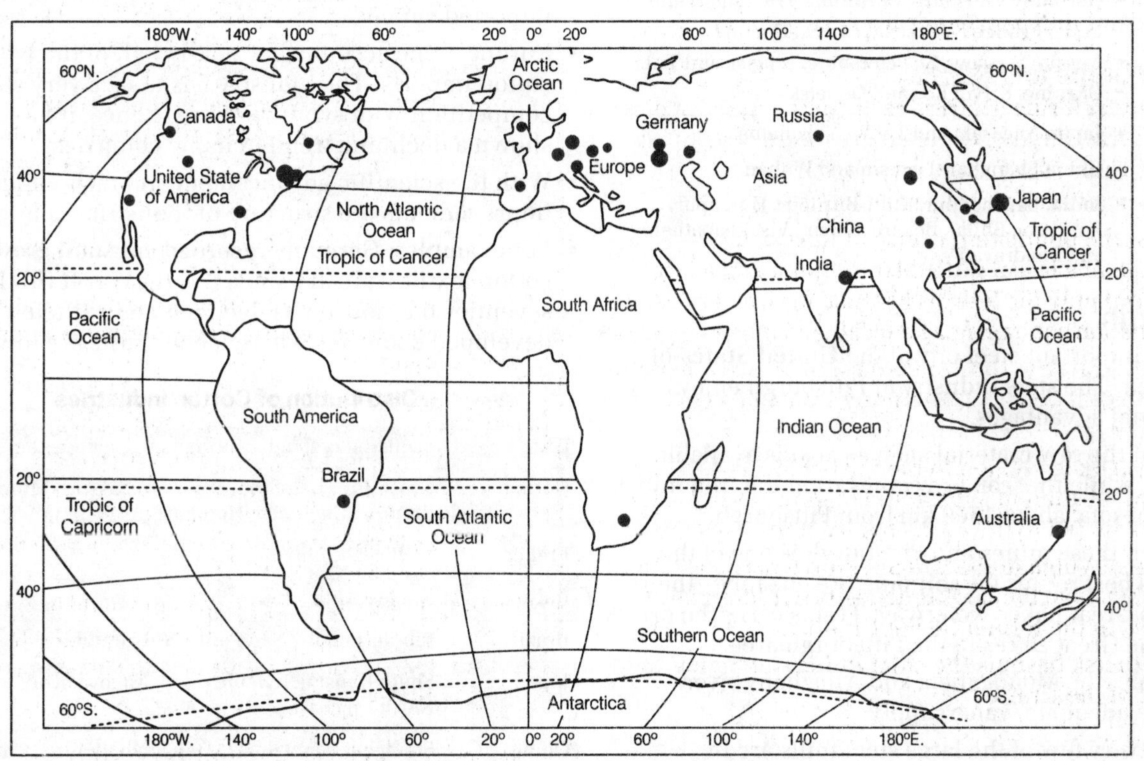

Famous Iron and Steel Industry

Jamshedpur

- Before 1947, there was only one iron and steel plant in the country **Tata Iron and Steel Company Limited** (TISCO).
- It was privately owned. After Independence, the government took the initiative and set up several iron and steel plants.
- TISCO was started in 1907 at **Sakchi**, near the confluence of the rivers **Subarnarekha** and **Kharkai** in Jharkhand. Later on Sakchi was renamed as Jamshedpur.
- Geographically, Jamshedpur is the most conveniently situated iron and steel centre in the country. Sakchi was chosen to set up the steel plant for several reasons.
- This place was only 32 km away from Kalimati station on the Bengal-Nagpur railway line. It was close to the iron ore, coal and manganese deposits as well as to Kolkata, which provided a large market.
- TISCO, gets coal from **Jharia coalfields** and iron ore, limestone, dolomite and manganese from Odisha and Chhattisgarh.
- The Kharkai and Subarnarekha rivers ensured sufficient water supply. Government initiatives provided adequate capital for its later development.
- In Jamshedpur, several other industrial plants were set up after TISCO. They produce chemicals, locomotive parts, agricultural equipment, machinery, tinplate, cable and wire.

Steel Producing Regions

Countries/ Regions	Major Steel Producing Regions
USA	• North Appalachian region (Pittsburgh) • Great Lake region (Chicago-Gary, Erie, Cleveland, Lorain, Buffalo and Duluth) • Atlantic coast (Sparrows Point and Morrisville) • The industry has also moved towards the Southern state of Alabama. Pittsburgh area is now losing ground and it has now become the **'rust bowl' of USA**
Europe	• **United Kingdom** Scun Thorpe, Port Talbot, Birmingham and Sheffield • **Germany** Duisburg, Dortmund, Dusseldorf and • **Essen France** Le Creusot and **St. Etienne** • **Russia** Moscow, St. Petersburg, Lipetsk and Tula • **Ukraine** Krivoi Rog and Donetsk
Asia	• **Japan** Nagasaki and Tokyo-Yokohama • **China** Shanghai, Tientsin and Wuhan • **India** Jamshedpur, Kulti-Burnpur, Durgapur, Rourkela, Bhilai, Bokaro, Salem, Visakhapatnam and Bhadravati

Pittsburgh

- It is an important steel city of the **United States of America**. The steel industry at Pittsburgh enjoys locational advantages.
- Some of the raw material such as coal is available locally, while the iron ore comes from the iron mines at Minnesota, about 1500 km from Pittsburgh.
- Between these mines and Pittsburgh is one of the world's best routes for shipping ore cheaply – the famous Great Lakes waterway. Trains carry the ore from the Great Lakes to the Pittsburgh area.
- The Ohio, the Monogahela and Allegheny rivers provide adequate water supply.
- Today, very few of the large steel mills are in Pittsburgh itself.
- They are located in the valleys of the **Monogahela** and **Allegheny** rivers above Pittsburgh and along the **Ohio river** below it.
- The Pittsburgh area has many factories other than steel mills. These use steel as their raw material to make many different products such as railroad equipment, heavy machinery and rails.

Cotton Textile Industry

- Cotton textile industry has three sub-sectors i.e., handloom, powerloom and mill sectors.
- Handloom sector is labour-intensive and provides employment to semi-skilled workers. It requires small capital investment.
- This sector involves spinning, weaving and finishing of the fabrics.
- The powerloom sector introduces machines and becomes less labour intensive and the volume of production increases.
- Cotton textile mill sector is highly capital intensive and produces fine clothes in bulk.
- Cotton textile manufacturing requires good quality cotton as raw material. India, China, USA, Pakistan, Uzbekistan, Egypt produce more than half of the world's raw cotton.
- The UK and other North-Western European countries and Japan also produce cotton textile made from imported yarn.
- Europe alone accounts for nearly half of the world's cotton imports. The industry has to face very stiff competition with synthetic fibres hence, it has now shown a declining trend in many countries.
- With the scientific advancement and technological improvements the structure of industries changes.
- For examples, Germany recorded constant growth in cotton textile industry since, World War II till the seventies but now it has declined and shifted to less developed countries where labour costs are low.

Distribution of Cotton Industries

UK	Scottish Lowland, Nottingham, Ireland, Lancashire
Germany	Great Ruhr industrial region, Frankfurt, Munich, Bremen, Chemnitz, Hamburg
France	Bedford, Kollmann, Nancy
Italy	Naples, Milan
Brazil	Rio-de-Janeiro, Sao-Paulo, Rio-Grande
Japan	South Kyushu, Kwanto plain, Nagoya, Kinki plain, Northern coast
China	Shanghai, Manchuria, Tien Shan, Beijing, Chuang, Nanchang, Lanchow
USA	New England and adjacent areas, Georgia, Florida, Carolina, Alabama, Virginia, Tennessee and Kentucky

Ahmedabad

- It is located in **Gujarat** on the banks of the **Sabarmati** river. The first mill was established in 1859.
- It soon became the second largest textile city of India, after Mumbai. Ahmedabad was therefore often referred to as the **Manchester of India**.
- Ahmedabad is situated very close to cotton growing area. This ensures easy availability of raw material.
- The climate is ideal for spinning and weaving. The flat terrain and easy availability of land is suitable for the establishment of the mills.

- The densely populated states of Gujarat and Maharashtra provide both skilled and semi-skilled labour.
- Well developed road and railway network permits easy transportation of textiles to different parts of the country, thus providing easy access to the market. Mumbai port nearby facilitates import of machinery and export of cotton textiles.
- In the recent years, Ahmedabad textile mills have been facing some problems. Several textile mills have closed down.
- This is primarily due to the emergence of new textile centres in the country as well as non-upgradation of machines and technology in the mills of Ahmedabad.

Osaka

- It is an important textile centre of Japan, also known as the **Manchester of Japan**.
- The textile industry developed in Osaka due to several geographical factors.
- The extensive plain around Osaka ensured that land was easily available for the growth of cotton mills. Warm humid climate is well suited to spinning and weaving.
- The river **Yodo** provides sufficient water for the mills. Labour is easily available. Location of port facilitates import of raw cotton and for exporting textiles.
- The textile industry at Osaka depends completely upon imported raw materials. Cotton is imported from Egypt, India, China and USA.
- The finished product is mostly exported and has a good market due to good quality and low price.
- Though it is one of the important textile cities in the country; the cotton textile industry at Osaka has been replaced by other industries, such as iron and steel, machinery, shipbuilding, automobiles, electric equipment and cement.

Woollen Textile Industry

- It is older than the cotton textile industry and has been developed at local and cottage industry level.
- The bulk of the wool is produced by a handful of developed countries. e.g., Russia, Austria, New Zealand, USA, Japan, UK, Germany, China, France and Italy.
- Raw wool is prepared in temperate and sub-tropical areas. The sheep rearing is a popular occupation in sub-tropical countries by nomadic herders. Most of the woollen product is generally consumed by high latitude people.
- Wool as a raw material is impure in nature. Most of the highly productive woollen industries are developed near the market e.g., at Western Europe while the wool producing areas in Southern hemisphere are not very developed in the manufacturing of woollen goods.

Distribution of Woollen Textile Industry

USA	New-England region, Massachusetts and Rhode island are the reputed centres, the other centres are Pennsylvania.
Japan	In Japan, major woollen goods producing centres are located within Tokyo-Yakohama, Nagoya, Kobe, Himeji, Osaka and Nagasaki.
UK	In United Kingdom, Yorkshire was the leading centre of woollen goods production, subsequently new centres were developed in Midland and Lancashire, later in Scottish lowland, South-Wales and Ireland.
Germany	Saxony, Westphalia and Great Ruhr
Italy	Naples and Po river valley
China	Shanghai and Canton
India	Ludhiana, Shimla, Kanpur, Bhatinda, Dhariwal and Jalandhar

Information Technology (IT)

- The Information Technology industry deals in the storage, processing and distribution of information. Today, this industry has become global.
- This is due to a series of technological, political and socio-economic events.
- The main factors guiding the location of these industries are resource availability, cost and infrastructure.
- The major hubs of the IT industry are the Silicon Valley, California and Bengaluru, India.
- There are other emerging information technology hubs in metropolitan centres of India such as Mumbai, New Delhi, Hyderabad and Chennai. Other cities such as Gurgaon, Pune, Thiruvananthapuram, Kochi and Chandigarh are also important centres of the IT industry.
- However, Bengaluru has always had a unique advantage, as a city with highest availability of middle and top management talent.

Major IT Hubs of the World

Some major IT Hubs of the world are as follows :

Bengaluru

- Bengaluru is located on the Deccan Plateau from where it gets the name 'Silicon Plateau'. The city is known for its mild climate throughout the year.
- It has some important public sector industries and research institutions and largest number of educational institutions and IT colleges in India.
- The Karnataka Government was first to announce an IT policy in 1992. The city has the largest and widest availability of skilled managers with work experience.

Silicon Valley

- Silicon Valley, is a part of **Santa Clara Valley**, located next to the Rocky Mountains of North America. The area has temperate climate with the temperatures rarely dropping below 0° centigrade.
- It is close to one of the most advanced scientific and technological centres in the world.
- Besides pleasant climate, it also has plenty of space for development and future expansion. It is located close to major roads and airports and enjoy good access to markets and skilled workforce.

> **'Being Bangalored..'**
> It means to lose one's job to someone in the city of Bengaluru. A few years ago many IT jobs in the USA were outsourced to countries like India where equally skilled labour was available at lower salaries.

Concept of High Technology Industry

- High technology, or simply high-tech, is the latest generation of manufacturing activities.
- It is best understood as the application of intensive research and development (R and D) efforts leading to the manufacture of products of an advanced scientific and engineering character.
- Professional (white collar) workers make up a large share of the total workforce.
- These highly skilled specialists greatly outnumber the actual production (blue collar) workers.
- Robotics on the assembly line, computer-aided design (CAD) and manufacturing, electronic controls of smelting and refining processes, and the constant development of new chemical and pharmaceutical products are notable examples of a high-tech industry.
- Neatly spaced, low, modern, dispersed, office-plant-lab buildings rather than massive assembly structures, factories and storage areas mark the high-tech industrial landscape.
- Planned business parks for high-tech start-ups have become part of regional and local development schemes.
- High-tech industries which are regionally concentrated, self-sustained and highly specialised are called **technopolies.**
- The Silicon valley near **San Francisco** and **Silicon Forest** near Seattle are examples of technopolies.

> **Sunrise Industry**
> Emerging industries are also known as 'Sunrise Industries'. These include Information technology, Wellness, Hospitality and Knowledge.

Industrial Machinery Industries

- The machine tool industry is a highly specialised industry which produces various tools and foundries used in the manufacture of various goods and in constructional activities.
- These industries are generally located in the clustered industrial region as often other industries are its main consumers.

Important Countries/Regions of Machine Tools

Countries	Region
USA	Ohio, Michigan, Connecticut, Illinois, Rhode island, New York. Cincinnati (Ohio) is the leading centre of production.
Russia	Moscow, Gorky, Tula, Lipetsk, Kursk, Rostov, Vladivostok.
Ukraine	Kiev, Lugansk
Germany	Rhine- Ruhr region, Dusseldorf, Frankfurt, Colonge, Stuttgart, Berlin, Dresden and Leipzig.
UK	Sheffield, Birmingham, Glasgow, London and Manchester.
Japan	Tokyo, Yokohama, Kobe, Osaka and Nagoya.

Important Countries/Regions of Textile Machinery

Country/Region	Fact
UK	• First country to manufacture cotton and woolen textiles with power driven machines. • Leicester and Nottingham produce machines for making hosiers. • Macclesfield makes silk machines. • Dundee specialises in Jute machines and Belfast specialises in machines for linen industries.
USA	• Half of all the textile machinery is manufactured in New England. • Important centres: Worcester, Lowell, Hydepark and Philadelphia.

Transport Equipment Industries

It includes Ship building, automobile, aircraft and railway equipment making industries.

These are given below

Important Countries/Regions of Ship Building Industry

Country/Region	Centre
Europe	The heavily industrialised sea ports of Europe also contains the largest shipyards Clydeside (Glasgow), Tyneside (New Castle), Merseyside (Liverpool), Rotterdam, Amsterdam, Dunkrik, Antwerp, Goteborg, Marseilles, Hamburg, Cadiz and Lisbon
North America	New York, Sparrows Point, Montred Chicago, Buffalo, Cleveland and Toledo
Japan	Tokyo, Yokohama, Kawasaki, Nagasaki and Kobe
India	Cochin, Mormugao, Kolkata and Vishakhapatnam

Important Countries/Regions of Automobile Industry

Country	Centre
USA	Detroit, Chicago, Atlanta
UK	Coventry Birmingham, London, Oxford
Japan	Tokyo
Germany	Stuttgart, Dusseldorf, Wolfsburg, Berlin,
India	Aurangabad, Chennai, Pune, Gurugram, Ahmedabad

Important Countries/Regions of Railway Equipment

Country/region	Centre
USA	Detroit, Chicago, New York and Philadelphia
UK	Derby, Glasgow, Doncaster and Manchester
India	Chittaranjan, Varanasi, Perambur, Kapurthala and Jamshedpur.

Important Countries/Regions of Aircraft Industries

Country/region	Centre
USA	California, Santa Monica, El Segundo, Long Beach, Hawthrone, Los Angeles, Texas, Wichita, Seattle, Baltimore, Long Island (New York)
UK	Birmingham, Conventry, Derby, Bristol and London
France	Paris, Amiens- St. Quentine and Reims, St. Nazare, Nantas, Bordeaux
Russia	Moscow, Gorky, Ulyanovsk, Kuibyshev, Saratov, Tomsk, Leninsk-Kuznetskiy, Komsomolsk, Khabarovsk
Italy	Savona, Turin, Trento, Gorizia
Sweden	Boras and Linkoping
Japan	Tokyo, Yokohama, and Kanazawa, Tachikawa, Tanaka, Mitaka, Giru, Nagoya, Akaishi and Nishinomiya
China	Shenyang, Beijing and Harbin
Australia	Melbourne, Parafield and Brisbane

Important Countries/Regions of Chemical Industry

Country/region	Centre
USA	New Jersey, New York, Illinois, Texas, Pennsylvania, Ohio and Michigan
Germany	The Ruhr region : Elberfeld, Essen, Cologne, Gelsenkirchen Northern Rhine region: Ludwigshafen, Manheim, Heidelberg and Stuttgart
Ukraine	Kiev, Dniprodzerzhynsk, Kharkov, Volgograd, Donetsk and Dnepropetrovsk
France	Norde, Pasde-Calais, Marseilles and Garonne region
Italy	Milan, Ferrara, Ravenna, Terni and Naples
UK	Willingham, Wilton, Huddersfield, Port Sunlight, St. Helens, Avon valley, Leeds, Birmingham and Glasgow
Japan	Osaka region, Kyoto, Nagoya region, Yokaichi, Nihama, Fushiki, Omuta, Hokkaido
China	Shanghai, Nanking, Yangtze valley and Northern China
India	Sindri, Durgapur, Jamshedpur, Rourkela, Bhilai, Neyveli, Kolkata, Alwaye, Chennai, Bengaluru, Trombay, Vadodara, Ahmedabad, Kanpur, Kota, Amritsar, Delhi, Hyderabad etc

Fertiliser Industry

Nitrogen, phosphate and potash fertilisers are prominent fertiliser industries.

Nitrogen Fertilisers

- China is the world largest producer of nitrogen fertiliser in the world. It is followed by India and USA at second and third position respectively.
- It is the crucial factor behind success of green revolution all over the world.

Phosphate Fertilisers

- China is the largest producer of Phosphate fertiliser, followed by USA and India.
- Other major producer of Phosphate fertilisers in the world are – Russia, Morocco, Brazil, Saudi Arabia and Egypt.

Potash Fertilisers

- It is a basic nutrient for plants and an important ingredient in fertiliser.
- Canada is the world's largest potash producer, accounting for 31.6% of the world's total in **2019**. Four countries- Canada, Russia, Belarus and China accounted for 80% of the world's potash production in **2019**.

Important Countries/Regions of Synthetic Rubber Industry

Country	Centre
USA	Connecticut, California, Indiana, Illinois, Pennsylvania, New Jersey, New York, Massachusetts, Ohio
UK	Fort Dunlop, Liverpool, Manchester,. Leicester
Germany	Hanover, Berlin, Duisburg, Halle
France	Clemont Ferrand and Paris
Russia	Moscow and St. Petersburg

Important Countries/Regions of Paper and Pulp Industry

Types of paper	Leading producer
Printing and writing paper	USA, Canada, Finland, Germany, China, Japan
Machine made paper and paper board	China, USA, Russia, Germany, Japan
Newsprint	Canada, USA, Japan, Sweden, China, Germany, France, Finland, UK
Wrapping and packaging paper	USA, China, Germany, Sweden, France, Canada, Brazil

Major Industrial Cities of the World

City	Country	Industry
Abadan	Iran	Oil-refining
Anshan	China	Iron and steel
Amsterdam	Netherlands	Diamond polish
Baku	Azerbaijan	Petroleum
Bangkok	Thailand	Ship-building
Belfast	Ireland	Ship-building
Birmingham	UK	Iron and steel
Buenos Aires	Argentina	Dairy
Cadiz	Spain	Cork
Chicago	USA	Iron and steel, meat packing
Dhaka	Bangladesh	Textiles
Darjeeling	India	Tea- processing
Detroit	USA	Automobiles
Dundee	Scotland	Linen manufacturing
Dresden	Germany	Optical
Dusseldorf	Germany	Iron and steel
Dortmund	Germany	Iron and steel
Essen	Germany	Iron and steel
Firozabad	India	Glass Industry
Geneva	Switzerland	Watches and light precision goods
Glasgow	UK	Ship Building
Gorky	Russia	Engineering goods
Havana	Cuba	Sugar and Cigar
Johannesburg	South Africa	Gold Mining
Kansas	USA	Meat Packaging
Kawasaki	Japan	Iron and steel
Kharkov	Ukraine	Machine building
Kiev	Ukraine	Engineering industry
Kimberley	South Africa	Diamond mining
Kobe	Japan	Iron and steel
Kirov Rog	Ukraine	Iron and steel
Leeds	UK	Woollen textiles
Leningrad	Russia	Ship building
Los Angeles	USA	Petrochemical, Films
Lyons	France	Silk industry
Manchester	UK	Cotton textiles
Melbourne	Australia	Food Processing
Meerut	India	Sports goods
Milan	Italy	Silk textiles
Munich	Germany	Lenses
Nagoya	Japan	Cotton textiles, Shipping, Engineering industry
New Orleans	USA	Coal mining, Iron and Steel
Nizhny Tagil	Russia	Iron and steel
Northampton	UK	Leather goods
Osaka	Japan	Textiles and Iron and steel
Oslo	Norway	Paper industry
Philadelphia	USA	Locomotives
Plymouth	USA	Ship building
Sheffield	UK	Cutlery
Tula	Russia	Iron and steel
Venice	Italy	Glass industry
Vienna	Austria	Glass industry
Vladivostok	Russia	Ship-building
Wellington	New Zealand	Dairy
Yenangyang	Myanmar	Oil drilling
Zurich	Switzerland	Light engineering industry

Extra Facts From Tamil Nadu Board and NIOS

- Maharashtra is the leading producer of cotton textile in the country. Mumbai has been the major center of textile mills. About a half of the Cotton textile mills are still located in Mumbai alone. Because of this reason, it is also called as 'Cottonopolis' of India.
- India exports products of the cotton industry to various countries. *For example*, it exports yarns to Japan, USA, UK, Russia, France, East European countries, Nepal Singapore, Sri Lanka and African countries as well.
- The first modern steel plant in India was set up at Kilti, Bengal in 1870 and production began in 1874.
- Detroit city in Michigan State, USA is known as the world's traditional automotive centre. In India Chennai is known as Detroit of India'. It has the world famous automobile industries such as GM, Ford, Hyundai and Mahindra. The city accounts of 60% of the country's automobile exports.

12

Transport and Communication

(SOURCES)

Class-XI Old NCERT Chap 11 (Transport and Communication), Chap 12 (International Trade Ports),
Class-XII New NCERT Chap 7 (Transport and Communication), Chap 8 (International Trade),

Transport

- Transport is a service or facility for the carriage of persons and goods from one place to the other using humans, animals and different kinds of vehicles.
- Such movements take place over land, water and air. **Roadways** and **railways** form part of land transport while **waterways** and **airways** are the other two modes.
- Transportation is an organised service industry created to satisfy the basic needs of society.
- It includes transport arteries, vehicles to carry people and goods and the organisation to maintain arteries and to handle loading, unloading and delivery.

Transport Network

Several places (nodes) joined together by the series of routes (links) to form a pattern.

Modes of Transportation

- The principal modes of world transportation i.e. land, water, air and pipelines are used for inter-regional and intra-regional transport and each one (except pipelines) carries both passengers and freight.
- The significance of a mode depends on the type of goods and services to be transported, costs of transport and the mode available.
- Modes of transportation can be understood by the following chart :

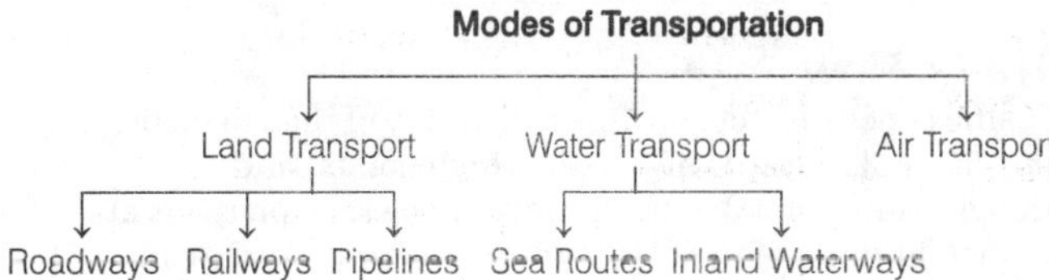

Land Transport

- Most of the movement of goods and services takes place over land. In early days, humans themselves were carriers. Later, they were supplemented by animals.
- The revolution in transport came about only after the invention of the steam engine in the 18th century.
- With the gradual development of railways, it opened up continental interiors for commercial grain farming, mining and manufacturing in USA.
- The invention of the internal **combustion engine** revolutionised road transport in terms of road quality and vehicles.
- Among the newer developments in land transportation are pipelines, **ropeways** and **cableways**. Liquids like mineral oil, water, sludge and sewers are transported by pipelines.
- Despite these developments, the old and elementary forms of transportation like human porter, pack animal, cart or wagon have not extinct at all.
- They are important in supplementing modern channels and carriers, which penetrate the interiors in large countries such as India and China.

Roads

- Road transport is the most economical for short distances compared to railways. Freight transport by road is gaining importance because it offers door-to-door service.
- The unmetalled roads, though simple in construction, are not effective and serviceable for all seasons. During the rainy season, these become unmotorable and even the metalled ones are seriously handicapped during heavy rains and floods.
- In such conditions, the high embankment of rail-tracks and the efficient maintenance of railway transport service is an effective solution.
- The quality of the roads varies greatly between developed and developing countries because road construction and maintenance require heavy expenditure.
- In developed countries, good quality roads are universal and provide long-distance links in the form of motorways, autobahns (Germany) and inter-state highways for speedy movement.
- The world's total motorable road length is only about 15 million km, of which North America accounts for 33%. This continent also has highest road density and the highest number of registered vehicles.

Traffic Flow

Traffic congestion occurs due to inability of road to meet the demands of the traffic. Peaks (high points) and troughs (low points) of traffic flow can be seen on roads at particular times of the day, for example, peaks occurring during the rush hour before and after work.

Highways

- Highways are metalled roads connecting distant places. They are constructed in a manner for unobstructed vehicular movement.
- In general, highways are 80 m wide, with separate traffic lanes, bridges, flyovers and dual carriageways to facilitate uninterrupted traffic flow.
- In developed countries, every city and port town is linked through highways.

Distribution of Highways in the World

- In **North America**, highway density is high, about 0.65 km per sq km. Every place is within 20 km distance from a highway. Cities located on the Pacific coast in West are well-connected with those of the Atlantic Coast in East.
- Important Highways of North America are :
  - The **Trans Canadian Highways** links Vancouver in British Columbia(West coast) to St. John's City in Newfoundland (East coast)
  - The **Alaskan Highway** links Edmonton (Canada) to Anchorage (Alaska)
  - The **Pan-American Highway** connects the countries of South America, Central America and USA-Canada.
- **Europe** has a large number of vehicles and a well-developed highway network. But highways face a lot of competition from railways and waterways.
- In **Russia**, a dense highway network is developed in the industrialised region West of the Urals with Moscow as the hub. The important **Moscow-Vladivostok Highway** serves the region to the East.
- In **China**, highways criss-cross the country connecting all major cities such as Tsungtso (near Vietnam boundary), Shanghai (central China), Guangzhou (South) and Beijing (North). A new highway links Chengdu with Lhasa in Tibet.
- In **India**, there are many highways linking the major towns and cities. For example, National Highway No. 44 (NH 44), connecting Kashmir with Kanyakumari, is the longest in the country.
  - The **Golden Quadrilateral** (GQ) or Super Expressway in India connects the major metropolitan cities — New Delhi, Mumbai, Bangalore, Chennai, Kolkata and Hyderabad.
- In **Africa**, a highway joins Algiers in the North to Conakry in Guinea. Similarly, Cairo is also connected to Cape Town.
  - The **Transcontinental Stuart Highway** connects Darwin (North coast) and Melbourne via Tennant Creek and Alice Springs in Australia.
  - **Aligners Conakry Highway** connects Aligners of Africa to the Conakry of Guinea.
- In **Australia**, all the states are connected with highways. Important highways of the Australia are :
  - **Australian Highway** connects all the coastal areas of the Australia. It is one of the longest highway of the world with the length of 1450 km.
  - **Stuart Highway** is the longest highway of the Australia. It connects Darwin in the Northern Territory, via Tennant Creek and Alice Springs, to Port Augusta in South Australia. Its length is 2720 km.

Border Roads

- Roads laid along international boundaries are called border roads. They play an important role in integrating people in remote areas with major cities and providing defence.
- Almost all countries have such roads to transport goods to border villages and military camps.

Railways

- Railways are a mode of land transport for bulky goods and passengers over long distances.
- The **first public railway line** was opened in 1825 between Stockton and Darlington in **Northern England**.
- The railway gauges vary in different countries and are roughly classified as broad (more than 1.5 m), standard (1.44 m), metre gauge (1 m) and smaller gauges. The standard gauge is used in the UK.

Europe

- Europe has one of the most dense rail networks in the world. There are about 4,40,000 km of railways, most of which is double or multiple-tracked.
- The industrial regions exhibit some of the highest densities in the world.
- The important rail heads are London, Paris, Brussels, Milan, Berlin and Warsaw. Belgium has the highest density of 1 km of railway for every 6.5 sq kms area.
- The **Channel Tunnel**, operated by Euro Tunnel Group through England, connects London with Paris.

North America

- North America has one of the most extensive rail networks accounting for nearly 40% of the world's total network.
- The most dense rail network is found in the highly industrialised and urbanised region of East Central USA and adjoining Canada.
- In **Canada**, railways come under the public sector and distributed all over the sparsely populated areas.
- Australia has about 40,000 km of railways, of which 25% are found in New South Wales alone. The West-East Australian National Railway line runs across the country from Perth to Sydney.

South America

- In **South America**, the rail network is the most dense in two regions, namely, the Pampas of Argentina and the coffee growing region of Brazil, which together account for 40% of South America's total route length.
- In South America, there is only one trans-continental rail route linking Buenos Aires (Argentina) with Valparaiso (Chile) across the Andes Mountains through the Uspallata Pass located at a height of 3,900 m.

Asia

- In **Asia**, rail network is the most dense in the thickly populated areas of Japan, China and India.
- In China, the train from Xining to Lhasa runs at an altitude of 4,000 m above sea level and the highest point is 5,072 m.

Africa

- Continent of **Africa** , despite being the second largest, has only 40,000 km of railways with South Africa alone. It accounts for 18,000 km due to the concentration of gold, diamond and copper mining activities.

Important Routes of Africa

- **Benguela Railway** through Angola to Katanga-Zambia Copper Belt.
- **Tanzania Railway** from the Zambian Copper Belt to Dar-es-Salaam on the coast.
- **Blue Train** from Cape Town to Pretoria in the Republic of South Africa.
- Railway through Botswana and Zimbabwe linking the landlocked states to the South African network.

Trans-Continental Railways

- **Trans- Siberian Railway** (9332 km) It connects Pacific coast in the Russia (East) to St. Petersburg (near European borders) in the West.

  It is a longest double-tracked and electrified trans–continental railway in the world. Important cities on this railway are Moscow, Ufa, Novosibirsk, Irkutsk, Chita and Khabarovsk.
- **Trans–Canadian Railway** (7050 km) It connects Halifax in the East to Vancouver on the Pacific Coast. It connects the Quebec-Montreal Industrial Region with the wheat belt of the Prairie Region and the Coniferous Forest region in the North. Important cities on this railway are Montreal, Ottawa, Winnipeg and Calgary.
- **Union and Pacific Railway** It connects New York on the Atlantic Coast to San Francisco on the Pacific Coast. The most valuable exports on this route are ores, grain, paper, chemicals and machinery. Important cities on this railways are Cleveland, Chicago, Omaha, Evans, Ogden and Sacramento.
- **Australian Trans-Continental Railway** It connects Perth on the West coast, to Sydney on the East coast. It passes through Kalgoorlie, Broken Hill and Port Augusta. Another major North-South line connects Adelaide and Alice Spring and to be joined further to the Darwin–Birdum line.
- **Orient Express** It connects Paris to Istanbul. The chief exports on this rail-route are cheese, bacon, oats, wine, fruits and machinery. Important cities on this railways are Strasbourg, Munich, Vienna, Budapest and Belgrade.
- **Trans-Andean Railways** It connects Valparaiso to Buenos Aries. It is the most important rail route of South America.
- **Northern Trans-Continental Railway** It connects Seattle to New York. It is an important rail route of the USA.

- **South Trans-Continental Railway** It connects Los Angeles to New York. It is also an important railway of the USA.
- **Cape to Cairo Railway** It connects Cape Town to Cairo. It is an important railway of Africa as it is the only mode to travel to Cairo from Cape Town.
- **Trans-Asian Railways Network** It is an integrated railway that will connect 28 Asian nations. It was started in 1992.
- **Beijing-Canton Railway** It connects Beijing to canton. This 2,350 km rail route is one of the most important railway of China.

Belt and Road Initiative

- More than 2,000 years ago, China's imperial envoy Zhang Qian helped to establish the Silk road, a network of trade routes that linked China to Central Asia and the Arab world. The name came from one of the China's most important exports–silk.
- In 2013, China's President ,Xi Jinping, proposed for establishing a modern equivalent, creating a network of railways, roads, pipelines and utility grids that would link China and Central Asia, West Asia and parts of South Asia. This initiative is called as Belt and Road Initiative (BRI).
- It aims to create the world's largest platform for economic cooperation, including policy coordination, trade and financing collaboration and social and cultural cooperation. This project is still in operation, once it is completed, it will be of great use to entire world.

Pipelines

- Pipelines are used extensively to transport liquids and gases such as water, petroleum and natural gas for an uninterrupted flow. Through the networks of pipelines cooking gas or LPG and liquefied coal is transported in many parts of world.
- In USA there is a dense network of oil pipelines from the producing areas to the oil consuming areas.
- In Europe, Russia, West Asia and India pipelines are used to connect oil wells to refineries and to ports or domestic markets.
- Turkmenistan is central Asia has extended pipelines to Iran and also to parts of China. The proposed Iran-India via Pakistan international oil and natural gas pipeline will be the longest in the world.

Important Pipelines of the World

- **Big Inch Pipeline** It is one of the oldest petroleum pipeline constructed from Texas to New Jersey in USA. Petroleum products had been transported from the oil fields of Texas to the North-Eastern United States.
- **Trans-Afghanistan Pipeline** It is also known as **Turkmenistan-Afghanistan-Pakistan-India Pipeline** (TAPI). It is a proposed natural gas pipeline being developed with the help of Asian Development Bank. This pipeline will transport Caspian sea natural gas from Turkmenistan through Afghanistan into Pakistan and then to India.
- **Keystone Pipeline** It starts from Alberta, Canada and gives Delivery in Illinois and Oklahoma, USA. It is Extensively used for of shale oil on North American continent. It allows for reduced need of oil from non-North American sources.
- **ESPO Pipeline** It starts from Russia and gives delivery in China (potentially also Japan). ESPO (Eastern Siberia-Pacific Ocean Oil Pipeline) has the impact of Connecting China into its strategic partnership with Russia as it draws more from its neighbour's energy reserves. If Japan remains out of the equation, it may serve to boost the China-Russia Partnership.

Water Transport

- One of the great advantages of water transportation is that it does not require route construction.
- All that is needed is to provide port facilities at the two ends.
- The oceans are linked with each other and are navigable with ships of various sizes.
- It is much cheaper because the friction of water is far less than that of land. The energy cost of water transportation is lower.
- Water transport is divided into **sea routes and inland waterways.**

1. Sea Routes

- The oceans offer a smooth highway traversable in all directions with no maintenance costs.
- Its transformation into a routeway by sea-going vessels is an important development in human adaptation to the physical environment.
- Compared to land and air, ocean transport is a cheaper means of haulage (carrying of load) of bulky material over long distances from one continent to another.
- Modern passenger liners (ships) and cargo ships are equipped with radar, wireless and other navigation aids.
- Further use of refrigerated chambers, tankers and containers have made cargo handling at the world's major ports easier.

Important Sea Routes

Sea Route	Description
The Northern Atlantic Sea Route	It links North-Eastern USA and North-Western Europe, the two industrially developed regions of the world. It is the busiest waterway and is also referred as **Big Trunk Route**. One fourth of the world's foreign trade moves on this route.
The Mediterranean–Indian Ocean Sea Route	Serves more countries and people than any other route. Port Said, Aden, Mumbai, **Colombo** and **Singapore** are some of the important ports on this route.
The Cape of Good Hope Sea Route	It connects the highly industrialised Western European region with West Africa, South Africa, South-East Asia and the commercial agriculture and livestock economies of Australia and New Zealand.
The Southern Atlantic Sea Route	It connects West European and West African countries with Brazil, Argentina and Uruguay in South America. The traffic is far less on this route because of the limited development and availability of similar products and resources in Africa and South America
The North Pacific Sea Route	This sea route links the ports on the West coast of North America with those of Asia. These are Vancouver, Seattle, Portland, San Francisco and Los Angeles on the American side and Yokohama, Kobe, Shanghai, Hong Kong, Manila and Singapore on the Asian side.
The South Pacific Sea Route	It connects Western Europe and North America with Australia, New Zealand and the scattered Pacific islands via the Panama Canal. This route is also used for reaching Hong Kong, Philippines and Indonesia.

Coastal Shipping

- It is a convenient mode of transportation with long coastlines.
- **Shenzhen** in Europe are most suitably placed for coastal shipping connecting one member's coast with the other.

Shipping Canals

The **Suez** and the **Panama canals** are two vital man-made navigation canals or waterways, which serve as gateways of commerce for both the Eastern and Western worlds.

The Suez Canal

- This canal had been constructed in 1869 in Egypt between Port Said in the North and Port Suez in the South linking the Mediterranean Sea and the Red Sea.
- It gives Europe a new gateway to the Indian Ocean and reduces direct sea-route distance between Liverpool and Colombo compared to the cape of good Hope route.
- It is a sea-level canal without locks, which is about 160 km and 11 to 15 m deep.
- A navigable fresh-water canal from the Nile also joins the Suez Canal in Ismailia to supply fresh-water to Port Said and Suez.

The Panama Canal

- It connects the Atlantic Ocean in the East to the Pacific ocean in the West.
- It has been constructed across the Panama Isthmus between Panama city and Colon by the US government, which purchased 8 km of area on either side and named it the Canal zone.
- It is about 72 km long and involves a very deep cutting for a length of 12 km. It shortens the distance between New York and San Francisco by 13,000 km by sea.
- The economic significance of this Canal is relatively less than that of the Suez. However, it is vital to the economies of Latin America.

Main Canals of the World

Canal	Description
Sault-Ste-Marie Canal	It joins Superior lake with Atlantic ocean.
Manchester Shipping Canal	It connects Manchester with Eastham.
North-Sea Canal	It joins North sea with Amsterdam.
Nicaragua Canal	It joins Caribbean sea to Pacific ocean.
Kiel Canal	It joins North sea with Baltic sea.
Stalin Cana (Volga Don Canal)	It connects Black sea and Caspian sea.
Gota Canal	It connects Stockholm to Gothenburg.

Ports

- The chief gateways of the world of international trade are the harbours and ports.
- The ports provide facilities of docking, loading, unloading and the storage facilities for cargo.
- In order to provide these facilities, the port authorities make arrangements for maintaining navigable channels, arranging tugs and barges and providing labour and managerial services.
- The quantity of cargo handled by a port is an indicator of the level of development of its hinterland.

Types of Ports on the Basis of Cargo Handled

- **Industrial Ports :** These ports specialise in bulk cargo-like grain, sugar, ore, oil and similar materials.
- **Commercial Ports :** These ports handle general cargo-packaged products and manufactured goods. These ports also handle passenger traffic.
- **Comprehensive Ports :** Such ports handle bulk and general cargo in large volumes. Most of the world's great ports are classified as comprehensive ports.

Types of Port on the Basis of Location

- **Inland Ports :** These ports are located away from the sea coast.
- They are linked to the sea through a river or a canal. Such ports are accessible to flat bottom ships or barges.

  For example, Manchester is linked with a canal; Memphis is located on the river Mississippi; Rhine has several ports like Mannheim and Duisburg and Kolkata is located on the river Hooghly, a branch of the river Ganga.
- **Out Ports :** These are deep water ports built away from the actual ports.

  These serve the parent ports by receiving those ships, which are unable to approach them due to their large size.

  For example, Athens and its out port Piraeus in Greece is a classic combination.

Types of Port on the Basis of Specialised Functions

- **Oil Ports :** These ports deal in the processing and shipping of oil.

  Some of these are tanker ports and some are refinery ports. Maracaibo in Venezuela, La Skhira in Tunisia, Tripoli in Lebanon are tanker ports. Abadan on the Gulf of Persia is a refinery port.
- **Ports of Call :** These are the ports which originally developed as calling points on main sea routes where ships used to anchor for refuelling, watering and taking food items. Later on, they developed into commercial ports. Aden, Honolulu and Singapore are good examples.
- **Packet Station :** These are also known as **ferry ports.** These packet stations are exclusively concerned with the transportation of passengers and mail across water bodies covering short distances.

  These stations occur in pairs located in such a way that they face each other across the water body, e.g., Dover in England and Calais in France across the English Channel.
- **Entrepot Ports :** These are collection centres where the goods are brought from different countries for export.

  Singapore is an entrepot for Asia. Rotterdam for Europe and Copenhagen for the Baltic region.
- **Naval Ports :** These are ports which have only strategic importance. These ports serve warships and have repair workshops for them. Kochi and Karwar are examples of such ports in India.

Important Ports with their Countries

Important Port	Country	Important Port	Country
Auckland	New Zealand	Lisbon	Portugal
Brisbane	Australia	Montreal	Canada
Boston	USA	Marseilles	France
Cape Town	South Africa	Port Said	Egypt
Chicago	USA	Rio de Janeiro	Brazil
Durban	South Africa	Santos (Coffee port of the world)	Brazil
Dar-es-Salaam	Tanzania	Shanghai (Busiest port of the world)	China
Glasgow	UK	Sydney	Australia
Havana	Cuba	Vancouver	Canada
Hamburg	Germany	Zanzibar	Tanzania
Los Angeles	USA		

2. Inland Waterways

- Rivers, canals, lakes and coastal areas have been important waterways since time immemorial.
- The development of inland waterways is dependent on the navigability width and depth of the channel, continuity in the water flow and transport technology in use.
- Rivers are the only means of transport in dense forests. Very heavy cargo like coal, cement, timber and metallic ores can be transported through inland waterways.
- Despite inherent limitations, many rivers have been modified to enhance their navigability by dredging, stabilising river banks and building dams and barrages for regulating the flow of water.

Important Inland Waterways

Inland Waterways	Description
The Rhine Waterways	It flows through Germany and the Netherlands. It is navigable for 700 km from Rotterdam (Netherland) to Basel (Switzerland). It connects the industrial areas of Switzerland, Germany, France, Belgium and the Netherlands with the North Atlantic sea Route.
The Danube Waterway	The Danube river rises in the Black Forest and flows Eastwards through many countries. It is navigable up to Turnu Severin. This waterway serves Eastern Europe.
The Volga Waterway	It is the most important waterways of Russia. It provides a navigable waterway of 11,200 km and drains into the Caspian Sea. The Volga-Moscow Canal connects it with the Moscow region and the Volga-Don Canal with the Black Sea.
The Great Lakes – St. Lawrence Seaway	The Great Lakes of North America Superior, Huron Erie and Ontario are connected by Soo Canal and Welland Canal to form an inland waterway. The ports on this route like Duluth and Buffalo are equipped with all facilities of ocean ports.
The Mississippi Waterways	It connects the interior part of USA with the Gulf of Mexico in the South.

Air Transport

- It is the fastest means of transportation and often the only means to reach inaccessible areas.
- Being fast it is favoured by the passenger for long distance trade as well as for movement of valuable articles.
- The frictions created by mountainous snow fields or inhospitable desert terrains have been overcome by the use of air transport.
- The manufacturing of aircrafts and their operations require elaborate infrastructure like hangars, landing, fuelling and maintenance facilities for the aircrafts.
- The construction of airports is also very expensive and has developed more in highly industrialised countries where there is a large volume of traffic.
- Airways also have great strategic importance. The air strikes by US and British forces in Iraq bear testimony to this fact. The USA is served by four large air corporations *viz.* The United Airlines, World Airlines, Pan American Airlines and Eastern Airlines.

Three types of services are performed by air transport :

Inter-Continental Air Route

This includes the longest services e.g.,

- New York–London–Paris–Rome Cairo–Delhi–Kolkata –Hong Kong– Tokyo
- New York–San Francisco–Honolulu–Hong Kong–Adelaide–Perth

Continental Air Route

- These services are performed among the countries within a continent e.g.,
  - New York–Chicago–Montreal Route
  - London–Frankfurt–Warsaw–Moscow
  - London–Paris–Frankfurt Prague–Warsaw
  - Delhi–Kolkata–Hong Kong–Tokyo

National Air Route

- Provide services for long distance within the country e.g.,
  - New York–Chicago–San Francisco
  - St. Petersburg–Moscow–Tashkent
  - Delhi–Mumbai–Chennai
  - Delhi–Kanpur–Patna–Kolkata
  - The World's busiest airports are (mostly by number of passengers) in USA.
  - Hartsfield-Jackson Atlanta International Airport is the busiest airport in the world.

Different Aircraft Companies

- Airbus is based in Blagnac, France.
  - Boeing is based in the Chicago, United States.
  - Bombardier is based in Quebec, Canada.
  - Embraer is based in Sao Paulo, Brazil.
  - Tupolve is Russian aerospace company based in Moscow.
  - The Russian Government merged Tupolev with five other companies as a new company named United Aircraft Corporation.

The International Air Transport Association (IATA)

The International Air Transport Association (IATA) is the trade association for the world's airlines, representing some 280 airlines or 33% of total air traffic. It support many areas of aviation activity and help formulate industry policy on critical aviation issues.

Communication

- Communication is the process of conveying messages to others. Human beings have used different methods of long-distance communications of which the telegraph and the telephone were important.
- During the early and mid 20th century, the **American Telegraph and Telephone** (AT and T) **Company** enjoyed a monopoly over USA's telephone industry.
- In developing countries, the use of cell phones is made possible by satellites. It is important for rural connectivity.
- In sector of telecommunication, there is phenomenal pace of development and competition. The first major breakthrough is the use of **Optic Fiber Cables** (OFC).
- Consequently, all major telephone companies of the world upgraded their copper cable systems to include optic fiber cables. It allowed large quantities of data to be transmitted rapidly, securely and are virtually error-free.
- With the digitisation of information in the 1990s, telecommunication slowly merged with computers to form integrated networks termed as Internet.

Satellite Communication

- Communication through satellites emerged as a new area in communication technology since the 1970s after USA and former USSR pioneered space research.
- Artificial satellites, now, are successfully deployed in the Earth's orbit to connect even the remote corners of the globe with limited onsite verification.
- These have rendered the unit cost and time of communication invariant in terms of distance. This means it costs the same to communicate over 500 km as it does over 5,000 km via satellite.
- India has also made great strides in satellite development. **Aryabhatta** was launched on 19th April, 1979, **Bhaskar-I** in 1979 and **Rohini** in 1980.
- On 18th June, 1981, **APPLE** (Ariane Passenger Payload Experiment) was launched through Ariane rocket.

- **Bhaskar Challenger** and **INSAT I-B** have made long distance communication, television and radio very effective.

Cyber Space : Internet

- Cyberspace is the world of electronic computerised space. It is encompassed by the Internet such as the **World Wide Web** (www).
- In simple words, it is the electronic digital world for communicating or accessing information over computer networks without physical movement of the sender and the receiver. It is also referred as **Internet**.
- The speed at which this electronic network has spread is unprecedented in human history.
- There were less than 50 million Internet users in 1995, about 400 million in 2000 AD and over two billion in 2010. In the last few years there has been a shift among global users from USA to the developing countries.

Top 10 Internet User's of the World (2020-21)

Country	Internet Users (in million)
China	765
India	391
United States of America	245
Brazil	126
Japan	116
Russia	109
Mexico	75.94
Germany	73.43
Indonesia	66.45
United Kingdom	62.35

Concept of Global Village

- As billions use the Internet each year, cyberspace will expand the contemporary economic and social space of humans through e-mail, e-commerce, e-learning and e-governance.
- Internet together with fax, television and radio will be accessible to more and more people cutting across place and time.
- It is these modern communication systems, more than transportation that has made the concept of global village a reality.

Global Positioning System (GPS)

- It was created by the **US Department of Defense** (DoD) and was originally run with 24 satellites. It became fully operational in 1994.
- GPS is a space-based satellite navigation system that provides location and time information about the Earth in all weather conditions.
- The maintenance is done by the United States Government and is freely accessible to anyone with a GPS receiver. The GPS programme provides critical information to military, civil and commercial users around the world. In addition, GPS is the backbone for modernising the global air traffic system.
- The GPS project was developed in 1973 to overcome the limitations of previous navigation systems, integrating ideas from several predecessors, including a number of classified engineering design, studies from the 1960s.
- In line with GPS, **Indian Space Research Organisation** (ISRO) has developed the indigenous Indian Regional Navigation Satellite System (IRNSS).
- The United States was the first country to introduce satellite technology with the Global Positioning System (GPS). But the US isn't the only country developing and advancing GPS technology. Japan, China, India, Russia and Europe are also developing new technologies similar to this.

Countries that Developed GPS Technology

Countries	Technology
USA	GPS (Global Positioning System)
Japan	QZSS (Quasi-Zenith Satellite System)
Russia	GLONASS (Russian Global Navigation Satellite System)
China	BeiDou Navigation Satellite System
European Union	Galileo
India	IRNSS

Extra Facts From Tamil Nadu Board and NIOS

- The Indian railway network is the fourth largest in the world after Russia, the USA and Canada. The first train steamed off in the country in 1853 from Mumbai to Thane, covering a distance of 34 km.
- There has been considerable development in the road length after independence. Route length of surfaced roads had increased from 1.57 lakh km (1950-51) to 41.16 lakh km in 2019
- The national highways comprises only about 2% of the total length of surfaced roads in India. They carry about 40% of goods and passenger traffic. Maharashtra has the highest share of National Highways (17,757 km) followed by Uttar Pradesh (11,737 km) and Rajasthan (10,342 km).
- The long coastline of India has 13 major ports managed by the central government and there are 200 minor ports operating under the jurisdiction of the state governments.
- The Airport Authority of India is responsible for providing safe and efficient air traffic services.
- It also provides aeronautical communication services for control of air traffic in the Indian air space. There are 131 operational airports in India.
- India's core digital economy has added 8.5% of Gross Value Added (GVA) in 2019. Its growth is 2.4 times faster than the Indian economy.

13

Population and Settlement

[SOURCES]

Class-VIII New NCERT Chap 5 (Human Resources), Class-IX Old NCERT Chap 7 (Our Growing Number), Class-XI Old NCERT Chap 14 (Settlements), Class-XII New NCERT Chap 2 (The World Population Distribution, Density and Growth), Chap 3 (Human Development), Class-XII (II) New NCERT Chap 2 (Human Settlements), Tamil Nadu Board (Class XII), NIOS

World Population

- The term **population geography** refers to the subject matter and the term **geography** refers to the perspective of investigation.
- The study of the human covering of the Earth and its various facets with regard to physical and cultural factors is referred to as population geography.
- People are the real wealth of the nation and that's why they are considered as a human resource.
- At the starting of 21st century, world population was more than 600 crore (6 billion). In January 2022, it increased to 790 crore (7.90 billion). Over the last 10000 years, population growth has accelerated at two distinct times i.e.,
  - When man began domesticating animals and plants, **Agricultural** revolution leads the population to grow at a steady rate.
  - When man discovered fossil fuels and invented the rail engine, there was an **Industrial** revolution in population demographics.
- **George B. Cressey** has stated that, "In Asia few people live at many places and many people live at few places". This is correct in reference to the pattern of population distribution.

Population Distribution in the World

The pattern of population distribution refers to how people are distributed across the Earth's surface. More than 90% of the world's population lives in about 30% of the land surface. The world's population distribution is extremely unequal.

Factors Affecting Population Distribution

There are many factors affecting the distribution. This can be divided as geographical, social, cultural and economical factors.

These are discussed as follows

Geographical Factors

- **Climate** Extreme climates, such as extremely hot or cold deserts, are unsuitable for human habitation.

  People prefer to live in areas with a pleasant climate and little seasonal variation. Population density is low in areas with heavy rainfall or extreme and harsh climates. Similarly, an extremely hot climate is harmful, it may increase intestinal diseases. Mediterranean regions have been inhabited since ancient times because of their pleasant climate.
- **Topography** People prefer to live on plains rather than mountains and plateaus because these areas are better suited for farming, manufacturing and service activities. The Ganga plains are the world's most densely populated area, while mountains such as the Andes, Alps and Himalayas are sparsely populated.
- **Fertility of the Soil** Soil quality is an important determinant of population density. The higher the fertility of the soil, the higher population density. Lateritic tropical soils do not lend themselves to improved cropping practises. The best soil for cultivation is alluvial soil. This soil is found in the

Indo-Gangetic region, Huang-He, Chang Jiang in China and Nile in Egypt. As a result, population density is extremely high there.

- **Availability of Water** Water availability is pre-requisite for higher population density. Human settlement is hampered by a lack of rainfall. Low rainfall areas are not conducive to agricultural development. Population density decreases with decreasing rainfall and increases with increasing rainfall.

  Water availability, however, is not solely determined by rainfall, rivers, springs or lakes. There may be artificial means of obtaining water. It is because of this that river valleys are among the most densely populated areas of the world. Population density is low in desert areas because there is insufficient water for humans, plants and animals to survive.
- **Landforms** People prefer flat plains and gentle slopes for living. This is due to the fact that such areas are ideal for crop production as well as the construction of roads and industries.

  Mountainous and hilly areas impede the development of transportation networks and as a result, do not initially favour agricultural and industrial development. As a result, these areas are typically less populated.

  The **Ganga plains** are among the world's most densely populated areas, whereas the **Himalayan Mountain zones** are sparsely populated.

Social, Cultural and Economical Factors

- **Urbanisation** Cities provide better employment opportunities, educational and medical facilities and better modes of transportation and communication. People are drawn to cities by good civic amenities and the allure of city life. It causes rural-to-urban migration and increases the size of cities. Every year, the world's mega cities attract a large number of migrants.
- **Social** Some places draw more visitors because they are religious or culturally significant. Similarly, people tend to avoid areas where there is social and political unrest. Governments frequently provide incentives for people to live in sparsely populated areas or to relocate away from overcrowded areas.
- **Industrialisation** Industrial belts create jobs and attract a large number of people. These include not only factory workers, but also bus drivers, shopkeepers, bank employees, doctors, teachers and other service providers. Because of the presence of a number of industries, the Kobe-Osaka region of Japan and Mumbai in India is densely populated. Industrial areas provide employment opportunities. Large number of people are attracted to these areas.

Continent-wise Population Distribution

Region	Population (2018)	Land Area (km^2)	Density (p/km^2)	World Share (In percentage)
Asia	4,545,133,094	31,033,123	146	59.5%
Africa	1,287,920,518	29,648,481	43	16.9%
Europe	742,648,010	22,134,900	34	9.7%
Latin America and the Caribbean	652,012,001	20,139,378	32	8.5%
Northern America	363,844,490	18,651,660	20	4.8%
Oceania	41,261,212	8,486,460	5	0.5%

Population Density

- Each block of land has a finite capacity to support the people who live on it. As a result, it is critical to comprehend the relationship between the number of people and the size of land.
- This ratio represents population density. It is usually expressed in terms of people per 52 km.
- This is calculated by dividing the number of persons of a country or region by the total land area.

$$\text{Density of population} = \frac{\text{Population}}{\text{Area}}$$

- In case the land area is small for a given population, the density will be high; but if the land area is large, then the density will be low.
- Many natural and human factors influence density, including soil, rainfall, climate, economic resources, economic growth stage and so on. Because these factors differ in different places, density will also vary. The degree of population concentration in a specific area is measured by density. The world can be divided into three sections based on population density. High density, medium density and low density areas.

High Density Areas

There are four distinct regions. China and the Far East, South and South-East Asia, Europe and the European part of the Soviet Union and North America's Eastern coastal plain.

Medium Density Areas

- The world's medium density population areas are not found in a continuous belt. These are found in areas between high and low density population areas where favourable economic opportunities drew people in and caused population density to rise.
- The Nile Valley Delta region, Morocco's Mediterranean coast, Algeria Tunisia in North, Brazilian coast South of the Amazon, the coasts of Argentina, Venezuela and Chile are the areas of medium density.

Low Density Areas

Africa and Asia have the most extensive paths with the lowest population density. A distinctively populated region stretches from the Western margins of the Sahara to the Eastern margins of desert plateaus and mountainous regions of Central Asia, passing through Saudi Arabia, Iran and Afghanistan.
There are various types of population density. They are

- **Arithmetic Density** The number of persons per sq mile or km is known as simple arithmetic density. In other words, arithmetic density is nothing but the man-land ratio. Arithmetic density is too crude a method for measuring the concentration of life.
- **Economic Density** While calculating the economic density of population, one has to keep in mind the productivity of the area under consideration. The index of population density can be realistic if it can be considered with respect to per sq mile of productive land of a region.
- Economic Density (ED) may be expressed by the following formula

$$\text{Economic Density (ED)} = \frac{PO}{PR} \times 100$$

  Where, PO means the index of population and PR is the index of production.
- **Agricultural Density** Agricultural density means the number of agricultural people' per unit of cultivable land. The agricultural density of India is approximately **435 persons per sq mile** of cultivable land. It varies from region to region in a country because of the differences in the availability of cultivable land.
- **Physiological Nutritional Density** It substitutes arable land for total area in the man-land ratio. It omits the unproductive land from consideration. Physiological density takes into account all types of population, whereas agricultural density takes into account only the agricultural population.
- **Critical Density (CD)** This density is proposed by Allan. He defines it as "the human carrying capacity of an area in relation to a given land-use system, expressed in terms of population per sq unit of area."

$$\text{Critical Density (CD)} = 100\,(C/F) \times (A/L),$$

  where,
  C is the extent of cultivated area,
  F is the extent of fallow land,
  A is per capita acreage planted,
  L is the percentage of land cultivable by traditional methods.

Most Densely Populated Countries (2019)

Country	Population Densely (per sq km)	Country	Population Densely (per sq km)
Monaco	26150	Bahrain	2159
Macau (China)	21420	Maldives	1770
Singapore	8292	India	460
Hong Kong (China)	7082	**World**	59
Gibraltar	3370		

Least Populated Countries (2019)

Country	Population Density (per sq km)
Greenland	0
Mongolia	2
Australia/Iceland/Namibia/Surinam	3
Botswana/Canada/Uganda/ Mauritania/Libya	4

Population Change

- The term population change refers to the change in the number of people over a specific period of time.
- The global population has not remained stable. For an extremely long time, until the 1800s, the world's population grew steadily but slowly.
- A large number of babies were born, but they all died at a young age. This was due to the lack of adequate health care facilities. There was not enough food to go around for everyone. Farmers were unable to produce enough food to meet the needs of all people. As a result, the overall population increase was very low.
- The world's population reached one billion in 1804. In 1959, the world's population had reached 3 billion people, 155 years later. This is commonly referred to as population explosion.
- In 1999, the population had more than doubled to 6 billion, 40 years later. The main reason for this increase was improvement in food and medicine as deaths were decreasing while births remained relatively high.

Components of Population Change

There are three components of population changes

- **Migration** When people move from one place to another, the place they move from is called the **place of origin** and the place they move from is called the **place of destination.**
- **Crude Birth Rate** (CBR) It is expressed as number of live births in a year per thousand of population.

$$\text{Crude Birth Rate} = \frac{\text{Live births during the year}}{\text{Mid-year population area}} \times 1000$$

- **Crude Death rate** (CDR) It plays an active role in population change, population growth occurs not only by increasing births rate but also due to decreasing death rate.

Crude Death Rate

$$= \frac{\text{Number of deaths}}{\text{Estimated mid - year population of that year}} \times 100$$

Growth Rate of Population

- This is the change of population expressed in percentage.
- **Natural Growth of Population** This is the population increased by difference between births and deaths in a particular region between two points of time.
  Natural Growth = Births – Deaths
  Actual Growth of Population = Births – Deaths + In Migration – Out Migration

Migration

- Migration is shifting of the home and not the house. In the context of migration, we come across two processes: **emigration and immigration.**
- Emigration refers to going out of a country, while immigration refers to coming into a country.
- Thus, emigration reduces the population of a country and immigration increases it.
- Migration implies the movement of people from one place to another.
- It is a highly selective process. It may be age-selective, occupation- selective or sex-selective.
- Generally, migration is male dominated, particularly in developing countries.
- Migration is not merely a process of shifting people from one place to another; it is a fundamental process to change the structure of population and it contributes a lot for the understanding of the space-content and space-relations of a particular geographical area.

Types of Migration

The different types of migrations which include

- **Rural to Urban Migration** It is more common in developing countries as industrialisation take effect (Urbanisation).
- **Urban to Rural** It is more common in developed countries due to higher cost of urban living.
- **Rural to Rural Migration** It mainly happens because of marriage of a rural girl to another rural area.
- **Urban to Urban Migration** It is mostly common in developed countries where people migrate from one area to another area.

Other types of migration include

- **Seasonal human Migration** Based on seasonal economy activity like agriculture and tourism, etc.
- **International Migration** Migration to other country.

Push and Pull Factors of Migration

- People migrate for a better economic and social life. There are two sets of factors that influence migration.
- Better economic opportunities more jobs and the promise of a better life often pull people towards a new region. The **Push** factors make the place of origin seem less attractive for reasons like unemployment, poor living conditions, political turmoil, unpleasant climate, natural disasters, epidemics and socio-economic backwardness.
- The **Pull** factors make the place of destination seem more attractive than the place of origin for reasons like better job opportunities and living conditions, peace and stability, security of life and property and pleasant climate.

Reasons for Migration

Following are some of the major reasons for migration :

- Availability of land
- Employment opportunities
- Hope wealth
- Religious tolerance
- Political freedom
- Post migration
- Other push and pull factors

International Migration Trends

- International comparisons of human development are interesting. Size of the territory and per capita income are not directly related to human development.
- Often smaller countries have done better than larger ones in human development. Similarly, relatively poorer nations have been ranked higher than richer nations in terms of human development.

Urbanisation and Migration

- Rural-to-Urban migration occurred in richer nations for centuries and continues to occur in poorer nations today.
- It has a significant impact on population growth because it affects a country's birth and death rates. As a country becomes more Urbanised, the birth rate rises while the death rate falls.

Trends in Population Growth

- According to 1st January, 2022, the population on the Earth is 790 crores (7.90 billion). It has grown to this size over centuries. In the early periods population of the world grew very slowly.
- It is only during the last few hundred years that population has increased at an alarming rate.

- After the evolution and introduction of agriculture about 12,000 to 8,000 years ago, the size of population was small – roughly 8 million.
- In the first century AD, it was below 300 million. The expanding world trade during the 16th and 17th centuries, set the stage for rapid population growth.
- Around 1750 AD, at the dawn of the Industrial Revolution, the world population was 550 million. World population exploded in the 18th century after the Industrial Revolution.
- Technological advancement achieved so far helped in the reduction of death rate and provided a stage for accelerated population growth.

Contribution of Science and Technology in Population Growth

Science and technology has contributed a lot in the growth of population. This can be understood by the following instance

- The steam engine replaced human and animal energy and also provided mechanised energy of water and wind. This increased agricultural and industrial production.
- Vaccination against epidemics and other communicable diseases, improvement in medical facilities and sanitation contributed to a rapid decline in death rates throughout the world.

Doubling Time of World Population

- Human population increased more than ten times in the past 500 hundred years.
- In the 20th century itself the population has increased four times.
- It took more than a million years for the human population to attain the one billion mark. But, it took only 12 years for it to rise from 5 billion to 6 billion.
- There is a great variation among regions in doubling their population.
- Developed countries take more time to double their population as compared to developing countries.
- Most of the population growth is taking place in the developing world, where population is exploding.
- According to January 2022, population growth in India is 0.99% per year. This rate is 0.4% in America and 1.1% in Canada.

Spatial Pattern of Population Growth

- Population growth in different parts of the world can be compared. The growth of population is low in developed countries as compared to developing countries.
- There is negative correlation between economic development and population growth.
- Although the annual rate of population change (1.4%) seems to be low it is actually not so. This is because :
  - When a small annual rate is applied to a very large population, it will lead to a large population change.
  - Even if the growth rate continues to decline, the total population grows every year. The infant mortality rate may have increased as has the death rate during childbirth.

Impact of Population Growth

- A small increase in population is desirable in a growing economy. However, population growth beyond a certain level leads to problems. Of these, the depletion of resources is the most serious. Population decline is also a matter of concern.
- It indicates that resources that once had supported a population are now insufficient to maintain the population.
- The deadly HIV/AIDS epidemics in Africa and Central Asian have pushed up death rates and reduced average life expectancy. This has slowed down population growth.

Demographic Transition

- The demographic transition refers to the change that populations undergo from high rates of births and deaths to low rates of births and deaths. Historically, high levels of births and deaths kept most populations from growing rapidly.
- In fact, many populations not only failed to grow but also completely died out when birth rates did not compensate for high death rates. Death rates eventually fell as living conditions and nutrition improved.
- The decline in mortality usually precedes the decline in fertility, resulting in population growth during the transition period. With the added benefit of medical advances, death rates fell more rapidly in the countries that began the transition in the 20th century.
- Fertility rates fell neither as quickly nor as dramatically as death rates and thus population grew rapidly. This can be represented best in the demographic transition model. The **Demographic Transition Model** attempts to show how population changes as a country develops.
- The Demographic Transition Theory is a generalised description of the changing pattern of mortality, fertility and growth rates as societies move from one demographic regime to another.
- The term was first coined by the American demographer **Frank W. Notestein** in the mid-20th century, but it has since, been elaborated and expanded upon by many others.

Stages of Demographic Transition

- There are four stages to the classical demographic transition model
  - **Stage 1 : Pre Transition** This stage is characterised by high birth rates and high fluctuating death rates. Population growth was kept low by Malthusian 'preventative' (late age at marriage) and 'positive' (famine, war, pestilence) checks.
  - **Stage 2 : Early Transition** During the early stages of the transition, the death rate begins to fall. As birth rates remain high, the population starts to grow rapidly.
  - **Stage 3 : Late Transition** Birth rates start to decline. The rate of population growth decelerates.
  - **Stage 4 : Post Transition** Post transitional societies are characterised by low birth and low death rates. Population growth is negligible or even enters a decline.

Stages of Demographic Transitional Model

Stage	Characteristics of the Stage
Stage 1	Birth rate and death rate are high - low natural increase - low total population.
Stage 2	Birth rate is high - death rate is falling - high natural increase (population growth).
Stage 3	Falling birth rate - low death rate high natural increase (population growth).
Stage 4	Birth rate and death rate is low - low natural increase - steady population.

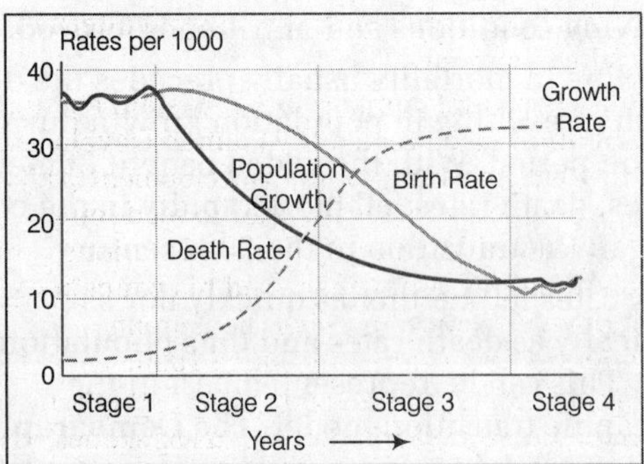

Population Structure

- This is an analysis of the population based on characteristics such as age and sex composition, birth rate, death rate, natural growth rate, Infant Mortality Rate, life expectancy, sex-ratio, crude population density, etc.

Population Control Measures

- **Thomas Malthus** in his theory (1798) stated that the number of people would increase faster than the food supply. Any further increase would result in a population crash caused by famine, disease and war. The preventive checks are better than the physical checks.
- For the sustainability of resources, it is essential to control the rapid population increase. Access to family planning services is a significant factor in limiting population growth and improving women's health.
- Use of contraceptives and tax disincentives for large families are some of the measures which can help in population control.

Age-Sex Composition of Population

- The population of an area includes persons of various ages. The age composition is important for understanding the natality and mortality of a community. Age differences may create social and economic differences.

Age Pyramids

- The age pyramid is useful for analysing a population's age composition. The most common method for graphically representing a population's age structure is to build 'Age Pyramids.'
- The vertical axis is graduated in groups of years, usually five, beginning with zero at the bottom and rising to 80 or 90 at the top. The horizontal axis shows either numbers or percentages of males and females within these groups.
- Under normal circumstances, the number of people at each age group will be lower than the previous year. As a result, the age structure of the population tends to take the shape of a pyramid when graphically represented.

Types of Age Pyramids

Three types of age pyramids are categorised as follows

- **Expanding/Growing Population** This type of population pyramid is in a triangular shape with a wide base. e.g., Nigeria, Bangladesh, Mexico. It is generally in less developed countries. A large base shows a high birth rate.
- **Constant/Stationary Population** It is shown in bell-shaped and tapered towards the top. The bell-shaped pyramid has birth and death rates almost the same and leading to a constant population. e.g., Australia.
- **Declining Population** A narrow base and tapered top of the pyramid show the low birth rate and death rate. e.g., Japan. Population growth in developed countries usually zero or even negative.

Percentage of Age Index in different Countries of the World (2023)

Country	0-14	15-64	65+
China	16.48	69.40	14.11
Japan	12.29	58.49	29.22
India	24.77	68.42	6.80
USA	18.15	63.72	18.12
UK	16.91	64.03	19.06
Germany	13.75	62.97	23.28
Finland	16.25	60.50	23.25
Mexico	23.76	68.22	8.02
Egypt	34.37	60.27	5.36
Ethiopia	38.91	57.55	3.54
Niger	49.70	47.60	2.70
Nigeria	40.69	55.95	3.36
UAE	16.32	81.77	2.00
World	24.70	65.20	10.10

Sex Composition

The number of women and men in a country is an important demographic characteristic. The ratio between the number of women and men in the population is called the sex ratio.

In some countries, it is calculated by using the formula

$$\frac{\text{Male Population}}{\text{Female Population}} \times 1000$$

or the number of males per thousand females.

In India, the sex ratio is worked out using the formula

$$\frac{\text{Female Population}}{\text{Male Population}} \times 1000$$

or the number of females per thousands males.

- The sex ratio is an important information about the status of women in a country. In regions where gender discrimination is rampant. The sex ratio is bound to be unfavourable to women.
- Such areas are those, where the practice of female foeticide, female infanticide and domestic violence against women are prevalent. One of the reasons could be lower socio-economic status of women in these areas.
- On an average, the world population reflects a sex ratio of 102 males per 100 females. The highest sex ratio in the world has been recorded in Latvia where there are 85 males per 100 females. In contrast, in Qatar there are 311 males per 100 females.
- The world pattern of sex ratio does not exhibit variations in the developed regions of the world. The sex ratio of favourable for females in 139 countries of the world and unfavourable for them in the remaining 72 countries listed by the United Nations. In general, Asia has a low sex ratio, Countries like China, Saudi Arabia, Pakistan, Afghanistan have a lower sex ratio.
- On the other extreme is greater part of Europe (including Russia) where males are in minority.

A deficit of males in the populations of many European countries is attributed to better status of women and an excessively male dominated out-migration to different parts of world in the past.

Human Development

- **Dr. Mahbub-ul-Haq** pioneered the concept of human development. Human development, according to Dr. Haq, is development that broadens people's options and improves their lives. According to this concept, people are at the heart of all development.
- These options are not fixed and are constantly changing. The fundamental goal of development is to create conditions that allow people to live meaningful lives.
- A meaningful life is more than just a long life. It has to be a meaningful life. This means that people must be healthy, capable of developing their talents, participating in society and free to pursue their dreams.
- Building people's capabilities in areas such as health, education and access to resources is thus critical to broadening their options.
- People's options become more limited if they lack skills in these areas. For example, an uneducated child cannot chosen to be a doctor because her options are limited due to her lack of education.
- Similarly, poor people are frequently unable to choose medical treatment for disease because their options are limited by a lack of resources.

Do You Know

- Dr. Mahbub-ul-Haq and professor Amartya Sen were close friends and have worked together under the leadership of Dr. Haq to bring out the initial Human Development Reports. Both these South Asian economists have been able to provide an alternative view of development.
- A man of vision and compassion, Pakistani economist Dr. Mahbub-ul-Haq created the Human Development Indax in 1990. According to him, development is all about enlarging people's choices in order to lead long, healthy lives with dignity. The United Nations Development Programme has used his concept of human development to publish the Human Development Report annually since 1990.
- Dr. Haq's flexibility of mind and ability to think out of the box can be illustrated from one of his speeches where he quoted Shaw saying, "you see things that are & ask why?" I dream of things that never were and ask why not?
- Nobel Laureate professor Amartya Sen saw an increase in freedom (or decrease in unfreedom) as the main objective of development. Interestingly, increasing freedoms is also one of the most effective ways of bringing about development. His work explores the role of social and political institutions and processes in increasing freedom.
- The works of these economists are path breaking and have succeeded in bringing people to the center of any discussion on development.

Four Pillars of Human Development

Human development is supported by the concepts of equity, sustainability, productivity and empowerment, just as any building is supported by pillars. These pillars are discussed below

- **Equity** It refers to providing everyone with equal access to opportunities. People's opportunities must be equal regardless of their gender, race, income or in the case of India, caste. However, this is not always the case and occurs in almost every society.

  For example, In India, a large number of women and people from economically and socially disadvantaged backgrounds drop out of school. This demonstrates how not having access to knowledge limits these groups' options.
- **Sustainability** The availability of opportunities must be consistent in order for sustainability to be achieved. To achieve long-term human development, each generation must have equal access to the same opportunities.

  All environmental, financial and human resources must be used with the future in mind. Any misuse of these resources will result in fewer opportunities for future generations.

  A good example is the significance of ensuring that girls attend school so that their career options would not be limited. This way each generation must ensure that future generations have access to options and opportunities.
- **Productivity** In the context of human development, productivity refers to human labour productivity or productivity in terms of human work. Such productivity must be constantly enhanced by developing people's capabilities.

  People are ultimately the true wealth of nations. As a result, efforts to increase their knowledge or provide better health care facilities result in increased work efficiency.
- **Empowerment** It entails having the ability to make decisions. Increased freedom and capability lead to increased power. To empower people, good governance and people-centered policies are required. It is especially important to empower socially and economically disadvantaged groups.

Approaches to Human Development

- **Income Approach** This is one of the oldest approaches to human development. Human development is seen as being linked to income.

  The idea is that the level of income reflects the level of freedom an individual enjoys. Higher the level of income, the higher is the level of human development.
- **Welfare Approach** This approach looks at human beings as beneficiaries or targets of all development activities. The approach argues for higher government expenditure on education, health, social secondary and amenities.

  People are not participants in development but only passive recipients. The government is responsible for increasing levels of human development by maximising expenditure on welfare.
- **Basic Needs Approach** This approach was initially proposed by the International Labour Organisation (ILO). Six basic needs i.e., health, education, food, water supply, sanitation and housing were identified.

  The question of human choices is ignored and the emphasis is on the provision of basic needs of defined sections.
- **Capability Approach** This approach is associated with Prof. Amartya Sen. Building human capabilities in the areas of health, education and access to resources is the key to increasing human development.

Measuring Human Development

- The **Human Development Index** (HDI) ranks the countries based on their performance in the key areas of health, education and access to resources.
- These rankings are based on a score between **0 to 1** that a country earns from its record in the key areas of human development.
- The indicator chosen to assess health is the life expectancy at birth.
- A higher life expectancy means that people have a greater chance of living longer and healthier lives.
- The adult literacy rate and the gross enrollment ratio represent access to knowledge.
- The number of educated adults and the number of children enrolled in schools show access to knowledge in a particular country.
- Access to resources is measured in terms of purchasing power (in US dollars). Each of these dimensions is given a weightage of 1/3.
- The Human Development Index is a sum total of the weights assigned to all these dimensions.
- The closer a score is to one, the greater is the level of human development.
- Therefore, a score of 0.983 would be considered very high while 0.268 would mean a very low level of human development.
- The Human Development Index measures attainments in human development.
- It reflects what has been achieved in the key areas of human development.

- Yet, it is not the most reliable measure. This is because it does not say anything about the distribution.
- The Human Poverty Index is related to the Human Development Index.

Inequality- Adjusted HDI (IHDI)

- This index is the actual level of human development while the HDI can be viewed as an index of the human development (are the maximum level of HDI) this could be achieved if there was no inequality.
- The loss in potential human development due to inequality is given by the difference between the HDI and the IHDI and can be expressed as a percentage.

Gender Inequality Index (GII)

- The Gender Inequality Index reflex women disadvantage in three dimensions i.e., reproductive health, empowerment and the labour market.
- The index shows the loss in human development due to inequality between female and male achievements in these dimensions.
- It ranges from 0 which indicates that women and men fair equally to 1, which indicate that women fair as poly as possible in all measured dimensions.

Gross Happiness Index, GHI

- Bhutan is the only country where Gross Happiness Index (GHI) is considered as an official parameter of development of the country.
- GHI encourages us to think about the spiritual, physical and qualitative constraints of development.

Settlement

- The form of settlement in any region reflects man's relationship with the environment.
- Settlements have gradually grown up and evolved over a long period of time and by studying the site, pattern and arrangement of settlement.
- We can see something of the history of man's exploitation of the surrounding land.
- Settlements reflect not only man's response to his environment, but also the religions and social customs of his society.

Classification of Settlements

Settlements can be classified based on spacing between the houses.

The main types of settlements are

- **Dispersed** In some areas, large members of scattered farms or homes are spread over an area to produce dispersion pattern of settlements.
- **Clustered/Nucleated** In some areas, farms and homes are built close to one another to form compact or nucleated settlements.
- **Isolated** It refers to areas either in long distance away from cities where there is lack of facilities as well as opportunities such as transportation, market training place, educational institutions, etc.

Factors Involved in the Formation of Settlement

Few settlements have grown up at random and the site on which people choose to build their town or village always, has some particular advantages.

- **Site** It refers to the actual piece of ground on which the settlement is built.
- **Location** It is also called position. It refers to the location of the village or town in relation to the surrounding areas. It is the chief function or role played by the village, town or settlement.

Settlement Patterns

- Different types of settlement patterns can be found due to the site and situation factors. Main patterns are
  - Rectangular pattern
  - Linear pattern
  - Circular and semi-circular pattern
  - Star-like pattern
  - Triangular pattern
  - Nebular pattern

Rural Settlement

- Rural geography means the study of social, economic, land use activities of place which could be described as countryside.
- In rural settlements, site is the most important aspect as the needs of village folks lie around the basic requirements of food, water, shelter and protection.

Rural Settlement Patterns

Patterns of rural settlements reflect the way the houses are sited in relation to each other.

The site of the village, the surrounding topography and terrain influence the shape and size of a village. Rural settlements may be classified on the basis of a number of criteria.

(i) **On the basis of setting** The main types are plain villages, plateau villages, coastal villages, forest villages and desert villages.

(ii) **On the basis of functions** There may be farming villages, fishermen's villages, lumberjack villages, pastoral villages etc.

(iii) **On the basis of forms or shapes of the settlements** These may be a number of geometrical forms and shapes such as linear, rectangular, circular star like, T-shaped village, double village cross-shaped village etc.

(a) **Linear pattern** In such settlements houses are located along a road, railways line, river canal edge of a valley or along a levee.

(b) **Rectangular pattern** Such patterns of rural settlements are found in plain areas or wide inter montane valleys.
The roads are rectangular and cut each other at right angles.

(c) **Circular pattern** Circular villages develop around lakes, tanks, etc. Sometimes the villages is planned circularly so that the central part remains open and is used for keeping the animals to protect them from wild animals.

(d) **Star like pattern** Where several roads converge, star shaped settlement developed by the houses built along the roads.

(e) **T–shaped, Y–shaped, Cross shaped or cruciform settlements** T-shaped settlements develop at tri-junctions of the roads (T) while (Y)–shaped settlements emerge as the places where two roads converge on the third one and houses are built along these roads. Cruciform settlements develop on the cross-roads and houses extend in all the four direction.

(f) **Double village** These settlements extend on both sides of a river where there is a bridge or a ferry.

Urbanisation

- Urbanisation is the process of percentage increase of urban areas and urban population. Each country has its own parameters to define any dwelling as urban or non-urban, but broadly, urban area could be defined as those where secondary and tertiary economic activities are in prominence.
- Study of urban areas is conducted under two heads :
1. Spacing between cities
2. Internal structure of cities

Urban Settlement

- Rapid urban growth is a recent phenomenon. Until recent times, few settlements reached the population size of more than a few thousand inhabitants. The first urban settlements to reach a population of one million was the city of London by around 1810 AD.
- By 1982 approximately 175 cities in the world had crossed the one million population mark.
- Presently 54% of the world's population lives in urban settlements compared to only 3% in the year 1800.

Percentage of World's Population Living In Urban Areas

Year	Percentage
1800	3
1850	6
1900	14
1950	30
1982	37
2001	48
2017	54
2020	56.2

Description of Continental Population

Continent/Subcontinent	Urbanisation in %
1. Europe	74.5
2. Latin America	80.7
3. Oceania	68.2
4. Asia	49.9
(i) East Asia	62.9
(ii) Central Asia	48.2
(iii) South Central Asia	36.2
(iv) South-East Asia	48.9
(v) Western Asia	71.6
5. Africa	42.5
6. North America	82.2
7. Australia	86.0
8. World	53.3

Classification of Urban Settlement

The definition of urban areas varies from one country to another. Some of the common basis of classification are size of population, occupational structure and administrative setup.

Population Size

- It is an important criteria used by most countries to define urban areas. The lower limit of the population size for a settlement to be designated as urban is 1500 in Columbia, 2000 in Argentina and Portugal, 2500 in USA and Thailand, 5000 in India and 30000 in Japan.
- Besides the size of population, density of 400 persons per sq km and share of non-agricultural workers are taken into consideration in India.
- Countries with low density of population may choose a lower number as the cut-off figure compared to densely populated countries.
- In Denmark, Sweden and Finland, all places with a population size of 250 persons are called **urban**. The minimum population for a city is 300 in Iceland, whereas in Canada and Venezuela, It is 1000 persons.

Occupational Structure

- In some countries, such as India, the major economic activities in addition to the size of the population in designating a settlement as urban area also taken as a criterion.
- Similarly, in Italy, a settlement is called urban. If more than 50% of its economically productive population is engaged in non-agricultural pursuits. India has set this criterion at 75%.

Administration

- The administrative setup is a criterion for classifying a settlement as urban in some countries. For example, in India, a settlement of any size is classified as urban, if it has a Municipality, Cantonment Board or Notified Area Council.
- Similarly, in Latin American countries, such as Brazil and Bolivia, any administrative centre is considered urban irrespective of its population size.

Location

- Location of urban centres is examined with reference to their function. For example, the sitting requirements of a holiday resort are quite different from that of an industrial town, a military centre or a seaport.
- Strategic towns require sites offering natural defence ; mining towns require the presence of economically valuable minerals and industrial towns generally need local energy supplies or raw materials. In the same way, tourist centres require attractive scenery or a marine beach, a spring with medicinal water or historical relics, ports require a harbour, etc.
- Locations of the earliest urban settlements were based on the availability of water, building materials and fertile land. These considerations nowadays still remain valid. Modern technology plays a significant role in locating urban settlements far away from the source of the materials.
- Piped water can be supplied to a distant settlement, building material can be transported from long distances.

Functions of Urban Centres

- The earliest towns were centres of administration, trade, industry, defence and religious importance. The significance of defence and religion as differentiating function has declined in general, but other functions have entered the list.
- Today several new functions, such as, recreational, residential transport, mining, manufacturing and most recently activities related to information technology are carried on in specialised towns.

  Some of these functions do not necessarily requires the urban centre to have any fundamental relationship with their neighbouring rural areas.

Classifications of Towns/Cities

Towns and cities can be classified as follows :

Administrative Towns

- National capitals, which house the administrative offices of Central Governments, such as New Delhi, Canberra, Beijing, Addis Ababa, Washington DC and London etc., are called administrative towns.
- Provincial (sub-national) towns can also have administrative functions, for example, Victoria (British Columbia), Albany (New York), Chennai (Tamil Nadu).

Trading and Commercial Towns

- Agricultural market towns, such as, Winnipeg and Kansas city; banking and financial centres like Frankfurt and Amsterdam; large inland centres like Manchester and St Louis and transport nodes such as, Lahore, Baghdad and Agra have been important trading centres.

Cultural Towns

- Places of pilgrimage, such as Jerusalem, Mecca, Jagnnath Puri and Varanasi, etc. are considered as cultural towns. These urban centres are of great religious importance.
- Additional functions which the cities perform are health and recreation (Miami and Panaji), industrial (Pittsburgh and Jamshedpur), mining and quarrying (Broken Hill and Dhanbad) and transport (Singapore and Mughal Sarai).

Types of Urban Settlements

Depending on the size and the services available and functions rendered, urban centres are designated as town, city, million city, conurbation and megalopolis.

- **Town** The concept of 'town' can be best understood with reference to 'village'. Population size is not the only criterion. Functional contrasts between towns and villages may not always be clear cut, but specific functions such as, manufacturing, retail and wholesale trade and professional services exist in towns.
- **City** A city may be regarded as a leading town, which has outstripped its local or regional rivals. In the words of Lewis Mumford, " the city is in fact the physical form of the highest and most complex type of associative life".

  Cities are much larger than towns and have a greater number of economic functions. They tend to have transport terminals, major financial institutions and regional administrative offices.

  When the population crosses the one million mark it is designated as a **million city**.

- **Conurbation** The term conurbation was coined by Patrick Geddes in 1915 and applied to a large area of urban development that resulted from the merging of originally separate towns or cities. Greater London, Manchester, Chicago and Tokyo are examples.
- **Million City** The number of million cities in the world has been increasing as never before. London reached the million mark in 1800, followed by Paris in 1850, New York in 1860 and by 1950 there were around 80 such cities. There were 162 million cities in mid 70s and there was threefold increase in 2005 and the number reached to 438. In 2016, there were 512 cities with at least 1 million inhabitants globally. By 2030, a projected 662 cities will have at least 1 million residents.
- **Megalopolis** This Greek word meaning 'great city', was popularised by **Jean Gottmann** (1957) and signifies 'super- metropolitan' region extending, as union of conurbations. The urban landscape stretching from Boston in the North to South of Washington in USA is the best known example of a megalopolis.

Distribution of Mega Cities

- A mega city is a general term for cities together with their sub-urbs with a population of more than 10 million people. New York was the first to attain the status of a mega city by 1950 with a total population of about 12.5 million.
- The number of mega cities is now 31 (according to NCERT). The number of mega cities has increased in the developing countries during the last 50 years vis-à-vis the developed countries.

Human Race

- A race is a group of people with similar, permanent distinguishing characteristics. People belonging to a particular race, have skin and hair colour have certain interpretations.
- Among humans, race has no cladistics significance- all human beings belong to the same hominid subspecies, ***Homo sapiens***, each differing from other populations in the relative commonness of certain hereditary trait.
- Generally, human races are categorised on the following basis :

1. **Outer Characteristics** Races can be distinguished on the basis of outer characteristics such as skin colour, hair texture, shape of eyes and lips, stature, etc.
2. **Inner Characteristics** Races can also distinguished on the basis of inner characteristics.
   For this, following two index are considered :
   - **Cephalic** (Cranial) **Index** In this index, human head is divided into three categories :
     Less than 78 – Long head
     Between 78-82 – Middle head
     More than 82 – Broad head

$$\text{Cephalic Index} = \frac{\text{Breadth of Head}}{\text{Length of Head}} \times 100$$

   - **Nasal Index** In this index, length-breadth of nose is measured. If Index is
     Less than 70 – Thin Nose
     Between 70-85 – Middle Nose
     More than 85 – Broad Nose

$$\text{Nasal Index} = \frac{\text{Breadth of Nose}}{\text{Length of Nose}} \times 100$$

Classification of Human Race

- The classification of racial groups is done on the basis of characteristics, physical features inherited from a common ancestor.
- The first classification of human race was done by Linnaeus in 18th century.

According to anthropologists, there are three major races in the world

Negroid

- They are commonly called as **Black People**. They have the darkest skin tone than other human races in the world. Black lives in Sub-Sahara Africa.
- This group includes African Negro, Nilotic Negro and Negrito (Pygmies) belonging to the primary sub-races.

Caucasoid

- The Caucasoid also known as **White People**.
- It is believed that their light skin tone is meant to receive more sunlight due to Europe's cold climate.
- It is also believed that Caucasoid nose structure is used to keep the nose moisture from getting dried by the wind. These people are living in Europe and the Middle East.

Mongoloid

Mongoloid facial structure likely to adapt to the cold mild wind. They live in East Asia. Native Americans and Eskimo are also Mongoloid.

Ethnic Groups of the World

- Ethnicity is defined as, Either a large or small group of people, who are united by a common inherited culture racial similarity, religion and belief in common history and ancestry. They also exhibit strong psychological sentiments of belonging to a group".
- The physical characteristics of the Indian population vary from region to region. Our present day population is a conglomeration of people belonging to different racial groups with different ethnic backgrounds.

Important Tribes of the World

Name	Description
Aborigines	Australoids, native people of Australia
Acliua	Pygmy of Belgium Congo
Acta	Negroid racial stock found in Philippine Islands
Bantu	Negroes of Central Africa
Beja	Pastoral nomads living between river Nile and Red sea
Berber	Gauge souls inhabiting region West of Tripoli in North Africa
Bora	Inhabitants of South-East Columbia and near portions of Brazil
Buryats	Central Asian inhabitants
Chukchi	Mongoloids inhabiting Chukchi peninsula
Dayak	Groups inhabiting Borneo
Fellah	Agricultural labourers of Nile valley in Egypt
Fulani	Cattle herders of Nigeria
Han	Original inhabitants of Nigeria
Hottentots	A group of Negroid racial stock known as **Khoi Khoi** found in South-West Africa. Their distinctive feature is the marked presence of steatopygia.
Inca	Inhabitants of Peru in Kulko valley
Inuit	Eskimos of North America
Kafir	Inhabitants of South African temperate lands
Kamasin	Samoyeds inhabiting the Northern part of Yennessey in Siberia
Kamha	Bantus of Central Kenya
Karakalpak	Inhabitants occupying region around Aral sea
Karod Kirghiz	Inhabitants resembling the Kyrgyz in and around Tien Shan and Pamir
Kubu	Inhabitants of Sumatra
Kurd	A nation in many countries - Iran, Iraq, Armenia, Turkey, Syria and Azerbaijan whose main activity is pastoral nomadism
Lapp	Caucasoid group of people found in Northern Scandinavia, Sweden, Northern Finland, Norway and North-Western region of Russia
Madhesi	Community found in Nepal
Maori	Original inhabitants of New Zealand
Mayal	A large group of American Indians living in the Highlands of Guatemala
Negrito	Sub-race of Negroid (found in Andamans)
Negro	A race of men distinguished by dark skin, fuzzy hair, broad and protruding lips, living in South-West and Central Africa
Nordic	Caucasoid group of people found in Baltic region, Northern Germany, Northern France, parts of Netherlands and Belgium
Papuan	Negroids of Papua New Guinea
Rohingya	Community belonging to Bangladesh
Red Indians	Race living in USA between the rocky mountains and the Missouri river. They are original inhabitants of America
Semang	Group of Negroes having a well built body with inesocephalic head, round face, short flattened and very broad nose but Without thick everted lips, found in Malayan Peninsula and East Sumatra
Shan	Inhabitants of south China, Assam, Myanmar
Swahili	Bantu speaking people in Zanzibar and nearby regions
Tatars	Siberian inhabitants
Tungus	Migratory tribes of East Siberia
Vedda	Short statured inhabitants of Sri Lanka with the smallest heads
Xinca	Zuks Lila people in Cape province of Africa
Yugeer	Nomads of North-East Asia
Yuit	Inhabitants of Siberia and St. Lawrence island of Alaska
Zulu	They are a Sub-negroid race in Natal (South Africa), having close ethnic, linguistic and cultural ties with the Swazis and the Bantus. They are Bantu speaking people

Various Tribes in the World and their Distributions

Tribes Names	Distribution
Aleuts	Alaska
Ainus	Japan
Bedouin	Sahara and Middle East
Bindibu or Aborigines	Australia
Bushman	Kalahari
Chukchi	NE Asia, USSR, North Siberia
Eskimos	Greenland, North Canada, Alaska, North Siberia
Fulani	Western Africa
Gobi Mongols	Gobi
Hausa	North Nigeria
Ibanas	Equatorial rain forest region of South-East Asia
India Tribes	Amazon Basin
Kalmuk	Central Asia
Lapps	N. Finland, Scandinavian country
Maoris	New Zealand
Orang Asli	Malaysia
Red Indian	North America
Tapiro	Papua New Guinea
Turregs	Sahara
Yokuts	Siberia
Zulus	South Africa

Life in Different Regions of the World

- The life of different region of the world are discussed below.
- **Life in Equatorial Region** This region stretches from 0 to 5 degrees latitude on both sides of the equator. It includes the Congo basin, the Amazon basin and the Eastern highlands.

  The tribal people who live here include Congo Basin Pygmies, Amazon Basin Boro, Sakai and Semang Malaysian and Papua of New Guinea framing.
- **Life in Tropical Deserts** Tropical deserts can be found along the Western margins of continents between 30 and 45 degrees North and South latitude. The main aborigines who live here are Kalahari desert Bushmen or San.
- **Life in Grasslands** Grassland can be found in low-rainfall areas. The people of the grasslands are pastoralists. These people are Maasai from East Africa and Khirghis from Central Asia.
- **Life in Tundra Region** People in the Tundra region are still in the early stages of development, leading semi-nomadic lives.

  In the harsh environment of the Arctic, they rely on hunting, fishing and gathering for their subsistence. Eskimos, Yuti, Chukchi, Yachts and Sai are the dominant groups.

Extra Facts From Tamil Nadu Board and NIOS

- Fertility Rate is the number of live births expected per 1000 women in their life times in a specified geographic area and for a specific point in time, usually a calendar year. Nigeria has the highest fertility rate of 6.49 while Singapore has the lowest fertility rate of 0.83.
- Among the ten largest countries worldwide, Nigeria is growing the most rapidly. Consequently, the population of Nigeria, currently the world's seventh largest, is projected to surpass that of the United States and become the third largest country in the world shortly before 2050.
- The current world population according to UN Department of Economic and Social Affairs, February, 2019 is 7,685,036,620.
- A city with million or more people is termed as the million city. London reached the million marks in 1800, followed by Paris in 1850, New York in 1860 and by 1950 there were around 80 such cities.
- According to 2011 census, 53 Indian cities have more than 1000000 population each. They are called the metropolitan or million plus cities. These 53 metropolitan cities alone account for 37.8% of the total India's population.
- According to the Census of India 2011, there are only 973 females per thousand males. So sex composition in India is unfavourable.
- According to Human Development Report 2021-2022, India ranks 132 out of 191 countries of the world. India was placed almost at the bottom of the table in the medium level category. Our neighbouring countries like China (78), Sri Lanka (73), Maldives (90) and Bhutan (127) remained well above the India's position.

Continents

[SOURCES]

Class-VI Old NCERT Unit 1 (Africa), Class-VI Old NCERT Unit 1 (South America), Class-VI Old NCERT Unit 4 (Australia), Class-VI Old NCERT Unit 5 (Antarctica), Class-VII Old NCERT Unit 3 (North America), Class-VII Old NCERT Unit 4 (Europe), Class-VIII Old NCERT Unit 2 (Asia), Class-VII New NCERT Chap 7 (Life in the Deserts)

- The large landmasses are known as the **continents.** Initially word 'continent' was used for peninsular regions or islands. Currently, large land areas above sea level are called **islands.**
- There are seven major continents in the world which are separated by large water bodies.
- These continents are; Asia, Europe, Africa, North America, South America, Australia and Antarctica.

Asia

- Asia is the **world's largest continent.** Its area is 4,45,57,000 sq km. It possesses one-third of the land area of the Earth.
- It contains more than **59% population** of the world as of 2024.
- The word **Asia** is used as a female name and means **sunrise.**
- It lies between 10°S and 80°N latitudes and thus, extends from the hottest to the coolest regions.
- Its latitudinal extension is from 10°S to 80°N but main land of the Asia lies North of the Equator.
- Its longitudinal extension is from 25°E to 17°W. Its East-West extension is about half of the surface of the globe.
- Therefore, its major land is situated on the Eastern Hemisphere but some part lies on the Western Hemisphere also.
- Asia is surrounded by oceans from three sides. **Pacific ocean** on East, **Indian ocean** on South and **Arctic ocean** on North.
- Ural mountain, Caspian ocean, Caucasus mountain and Black sea form boundary between Asia and Europe while New Guinea islands form boundary between Asian continent and Australian continent.
- Asian continent is also known as **continent of varieties.** Its highest temperature (54°C) is found at **Tirat Zvi**, Israel and lowest temperature (–69°C) is found at **Verkhoyansk**, Siberia.
- Asia's coastal length is 69000 km (except the coastal length of islands) and land extension from North to South is 6400 km and 9650 km from East to West.
- Three out of the four most populous countries in the world (China, India and Indonesia) are located in Asia.
- Japan has the longest life expectancy (80.9 years for men and 86.6 years for women) in world.

Major locations of Asian Continent

- Northernmost point- Chelyuskin, Russia (77°43'N)
- Southernmost point- Tanjung Piai, Malaysia (10°14'N)
- Easternmost point- Cape Dezhnev, Siberia (169°40'W)
- Westernmost point- Cape Bosporus, Turkey (26°4'E)

Physical Features

Asia may be divided into five major physical divisions. They are :

1. The Northern Lowlands
2. The Central Mountain Belt
3. The Southern Plateaus
4. The Great River Valleys
5. Island Groups of South-East and East Asia

The Northern Lowlands

- Ob, Yenisei and Lena are the rivers which flow through Siberian Plain (Northern part of the continent) from South to North and drain into the Arctic ocean.
- Water coming from the upper courses is blocked and inundates a large part of the flat plain, making it swampy and marshy due to severe winter of the polar region.
- **Lake Baikal** (world's deepest lake) is in this region, which account for 20% of water found in freshwater lakes.

The Central Mountain Belt

- **Pamir Plateau** in central Asia forms a mountain knot from which several mountain chains run out in different directions. These mountain chains enclose huge plateaus and desert basins. Two mountain chains which run Westward enclose the plateaus of Iran and Anatolia.
- The mountain chain of **Himalayas, Karakoram** and the **Kunlun** runs towards the East. The plateau of Tibet, enclosed by Himalayas and Kunlun is the highest and the largest plateau of the world.
- The vast cool **desert of Gobi** lies to the North-East.

The Southern Plateaus

- To the South of central mountain belt, there are some plateaus of very old rock. These are the plateau of Arabia, Deccan plateau and the plateau of Shan and Yunnan.
- The plateau of Arabia lies in the South-West part of the Asia. It is a dry sand desert, made up of ancient shells and is part of the **Gondwana land**.
- It is surrounded by Persian Gulf in East, Red sea in West and Arabian sea in the South.
- **Deccan plateau** in India is one of the oldest plateaus. This is bordered by the Western Ghats in the West, Eastern Ghats in the East and the Satpura, Maikal range and Mahadeo hills in the North.

The Great River Valleys

- Some of the important valleys are those made by Tigris-Euphrates, Indus, Ganga-Brahmaputra, Irrawaddy, Mekong, Sikiang, Changjiang and Hwang Ho. These fertile valleys are some of the most thickly populated regions.
- **Tigris-Euphrates valley** lies on the banks of rivers Tigris and Euphrates. Both these rivers originate in North from Torres mountain and falls in Persian sea in South. Mesopotamian civilisation (Iraq) began here.
- Before entering the Bay of Bengal, the Ganga along with the Brahmaputra forms the **largest delta of the world**. The coastline of delta is a highly indented area.

Island Groups of South-East and East Asia

- The important island groups consist of Indonesia, Philippines and Japan.
- Most of these islands are mountainous and are known for their volcanoes, which are active or have been active in the recent past.
- It is located primarily in the Eastern and Northern Hemispheres.
- The Equator, Tropic of Cancer and Arctic Circle passes through it. It is separated from Africa by the **Red sea** and **Suez canal**.
- It is separated from North America by **Bering Strait**.
- **Arabian Peninsula** is the largest Peninsula in the world.
- The deepest trench of the world **Mariana Trench** lies in the pacific ocean near Philippines.
- Pamir plateau is known as **Roof of the World** situated in the Central Asia.
- **Important Peninsulas** are Arabian Peninsula, Indo-Chinese Peninsula and Deccan Peninsula.
- **Important Island groups** are Andaman and Nicobar, Indonesia, Philippines and Japan.
- **Major Strait** are Malacca Strait, Palk Strait, Sunda Strait, Bering Strait, Bonne-Fasio Strait, Bosphorus Strait, Hormuz Strait, Makassar Strait, Tsungaru Strait and Formosa Strait.

Climate

- Asia has great range of climate due to large area and it possesses great difference in elevation.
- During winter, the central part of Asia has temperature below freezing point. The air over this region contracts, becomes heavy and thus forms a high pressure area.
- As this wind blows from the land, air flowing from this region is dry and pick up the moisture only when they flow over the sea.
- This causes rainfall in Japan, parts of South-East Asia, Southern-East coast of India and Sri Lanka receives rain from this wind during this season.
- During summer season, low pressure area is developed in the region as air is heated, expanded and thus become light. It draws air from the surrounding relatively cooler oceans. It causes rainfall to most part of the Asia.
- Annual rainfall in Asia varies greatly from area to area. For example, **Mawsynram** situated in East Khasi Hill district of Meghalaya (India) is the wettest place on the Earth.
- On the other hand, there are desert regions (Red sea to Mongolia), which don't receive a single drop of rain for many years.

Soil

- Most soils of South and South-East Asia belong to varying degrees of red or black colour. The soils are rich in aluminum and iron oxides, low in silica; are nearly structureless and generally of low fertility.
- In the Arabian desert and deserts in Central Asia, the soils are usually high in their content of unleached minerals but may be deficient in their content of nitrogen and humus.
- In the regions, where the water-table is high, evaporation salts have accumulated in excess near the surface, the soils are alkaline. Such red desert soils cover much of the Arabian Peninsula and North-West India, while higher desert soils cover the rest of South-West Asian countries.
- Large parts of Northern Asia are covered by **podzolic soils** of varying but generally low fertility. These soils cover the mid to high latitude locations in the region of well-distributed rainfall.
- The grasslands of Western Siberia, Manchuria and most of Anatolia plateau of Turkey are underlain by **black prairie soils** which have good texture and are of generally high fertility.
- The most important soils in Asia are the relatively immature soils of alluvial origin that are found in the river valleys.
- **Alluvial soils** cover the river valleys of the Tigris-Euphrates, the plains of Indus-Ganga rivers, the lower Irrawaddy basin, the deltas of the Mekong and the lower basins of Chang Jiang, Huang He Rivers.
- These are also found in the river plains of smaller rivers in India, Malaysia, Philippines, Taiwan, Korea and Japan.
- Several islands of Indonesia and Southern Philippines contain active volcanoes that periodically provide a new layer of rich basic soils of recently deposited volcanic materials.

Agriculture

- **Shifting agriculture** is practiced in some mountainous and forests area. A patch of forest is cleared by burning trees. It is mostly done by people in mountains of South and South-East Asia.
- **Intensive agriculture** involves a great deal of manual labour on a small piece of land. It is usually done in plains and river valleys. **Extensive agriculture** is used in some parts of Central Asia and West Siberia.
- Manual labour is not possible on such huge farms therefore machines are used for farming.

Crops

- **Rice** is the main crop of the Asian continent. More than 90% of the world's rice is grown here. The main producers are China, India, Japan, Bangladesh and countries of South-East Asia.
- **Wheat** is grown in sub-tropical and temperate lands of Russia, Ukraine, India, Pakistan and South-West Asia. Millets such as bajra, jowar and ragi are grown in semi-arid regions of Asia. Pulses and oilseeds are also grown along with cereals.
- The important cash crops of Asia are cotton, jute, sugarcane and tea. Cotton is grown in China, Kazakhstan, Azerbaijan, India, Pakistan and South-West Asia.
- **Jute** is produced in Ganga-Brahmaputra delta. Sugarcane is mainly grown in India, Indonesia and Pakistan. Tea is cultivated in India, Sri Lanka, China, Japan and Indonesia.

Vegetation

- The natural vegetation of Asia is closely related to climate. The belt of **Tundra vegetation** along the Northern coast of Asia is mostly covered with snow and ice for the major part of the year. Summer is short and cool here.
- Precipitation is 30 cm annually. Due to the cold weather conditions, plants do not attain much height and vegetation mainly consists of moss and lichen. Reindeer is the main animal of the region.
- **Taiga** (to the South of Tundra) is a much broader belt of coniferous forest. Here winters are severe and summers are warm. Precipitation is 25-30cm annually.
- The region is famous for softwood trees such as fir, spruce and pine. These are used as timber and in making paper pulp and rayon. Taiga is home to fur-bearing animals such as fox, sable and mink.
- **Steppe** is temperate grassland located on the further South. Winters are cold here and summers are fairly hot. Rainfall is between 20-40 cm. Due to evaporation, moisture is sufficient for grasses but not for trees. Antelope is a common animal of this region.
- Under **desert vegetation**, hot desert of Thar and Arabia are found in South-West while cold desert of Gobi and Tibet are found in North. Due to unfavourable conditions for plant growth, only shrubs, thorny bushes and poor grasses can grow. The common animals are camel, ass, gazelle, cheetah and yak (on the high plateau region).
- **Monsoon forests** are found in South, South-East and East Asia. The forest consists of many useful trees such as teak, sal and sandalwood. Elephant is a typical animal of monsoon forest.
- In North-Eastern Asia, as the climate becomes cooler, the monsoon forests changes into temperate wood lands. **Equatorial forests** are found in the extremely Southern part of Asia. Such forests are confined to Malaysian peninsula and island groups that are close to Equator. This forest is home to apes, monkeys and variety of animals.

Forest

- Asia has three main types of forest namely **coniferous forests, monsoon forests** and **equatorial forests**. Coniferous forests are found in Russia, Japan and Himalayan region. They provide softwood which is used as timber and for making paper pulp and rayon.
- Monsoon forests are found in India, Myanmar and parts of South-East Asia. They provide useful trees such as teak, sal and bamboo.
- Equatorial forests are found in Malaysia and Indonesia. Much of these forests are now been converted into rubber estates.
- **Thailand** is the largest producer and exporter of rubber in the world.

Minerals

- Important mineral resources found in Asia are iron, manganese, tungsten, bauxite, mica, tin, coal and oil.
- **Iron ore** is found in India, China, Russia and Azerbaijan.
- **Mica** deposits are mainly found in India. Malaysia is rich in Tin deposit. Large deposit of **coal** is found in China, Russia and India.
- Countries of South-West Asia possess large deposits of oil. While the leading producers of oil are Kuwait, Bahrain, Iraq, Iran and Russia.
- A good deal of oil is also produced in Myanmar, Indonesia and India also.

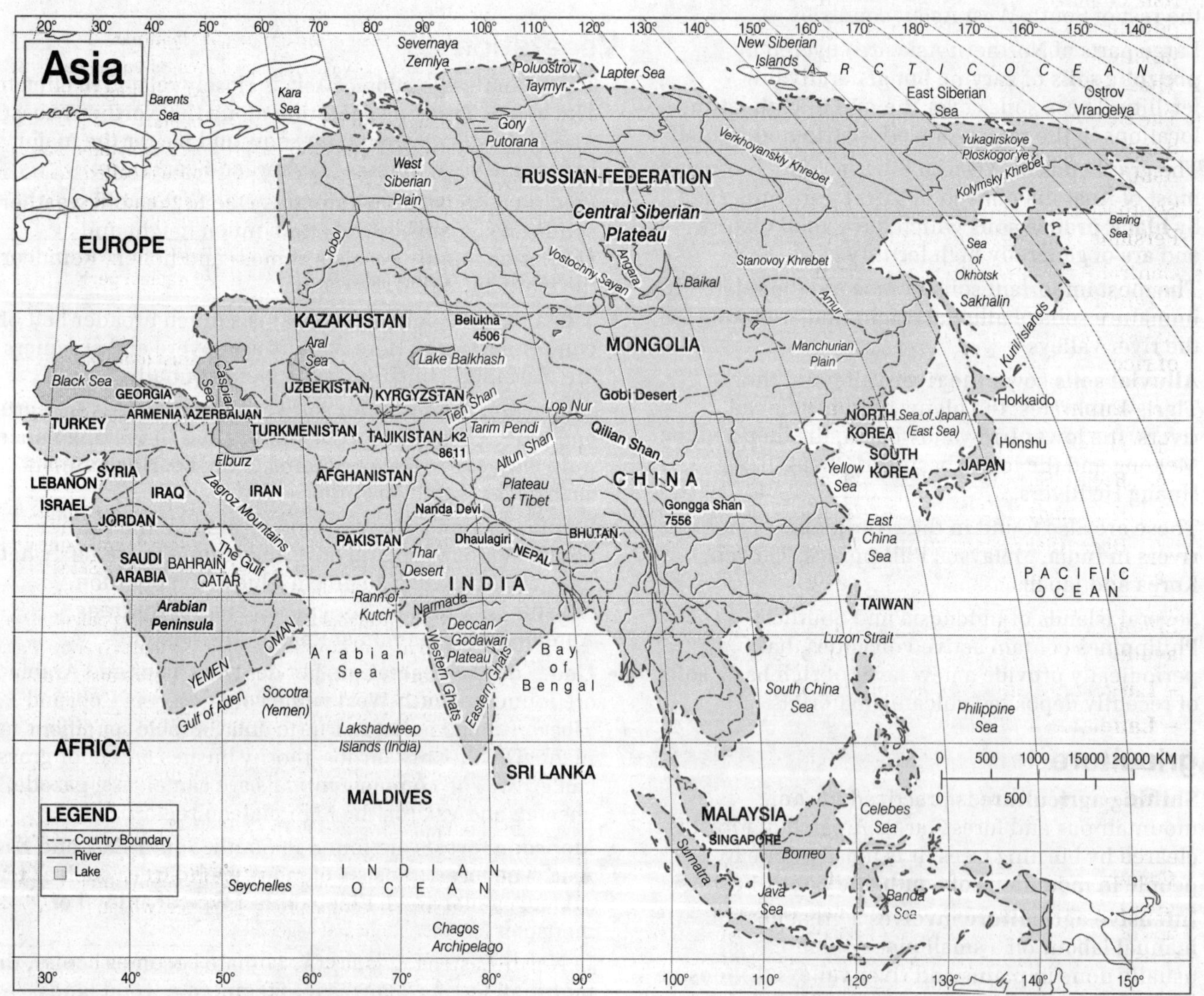

The People

- Asia is **most populated continent** of the world. Asia's population is equivalent to 59.76% of the total world population as of 2021.
- The average density of population in Asia is **150 persons per sq kilometre**.
- Northern and Eastern part of Siberia, the deserts and highlands of Asia, the Arabian desert, the plateau of Iran and Thar desert in India are the regions in which population is vary sparse.
- The most thickly populated parts of the Asia include the plains of India, Bangladesh, Java island in Indonesia, plains of China and Japan.
- The **yellow people** of Eastern and South-Eastern Asia constitutes more than one-third of the population of the continent. They include Chinese, Japanese, Koreans, Filipino, Malay, Indonesian, Thai, Myanmarese and people of other countries.
- The **brown people** belong to India, Pakistan, Bangladesh and some other countries of South Asia.
- South-West Asia inhabited by Arabs, Turks, Persians, Afghans and number of other groups.
- Central Asia has Mongols, Kazakhs, Uzbeks and Kirghiz.
- Asians eat upto 90% of the total world production of rice.

Asia's Top 10 Cities with Urban Population

1.	Shanghai (China)	2.	Karachi (Pakistan)
3.	Beijing (China)	4.	Mumbai (India)
5.	Delhi (India)	6.	Istanbul (Turkiye)
7.	Dhaka (Bangladesh)	8.	Tokyo (Japan)
9.	Manila (Philippines)	10.	Guangzhou (China)

- Singapore, South Korea and Japan have the highest average IQ (intelligence quotient) on the planet.
  - **Largest** city in terms of population **Tokyo**
  - **Land area** 44579000 km^2
  - **Largest Lake Baikal Lake**
  - **Religion Hinduism**, Islam, Buddhism

Major Countries of Asian Continent

Country	Description
Pakistan (Land of Canals)	• It is called country of canals. Its Swat valley is said to be heaven of Pakistan. Jacobabad, Pakistan is considered to be one of the hottest places (58°C) on Earth. • Salt range in Pakistan is famous for mayo salt, gypsum and lime stone. • Faisalabad is considered as Manchester of Pakistan.
Nepal (Himalayan Kingdom)	• Nepal had been established as a buffer state in the North of the India. It is a landlocked country. • World's highest mountain, Mount Everest (8848m) is situated in Nepal. • Devishali, Trishali and Koshi projects over here have been established by the support of Government of India. • Virat Nagar is the only industrial town here. • Shuklaphanta National Park is situated in Nepal.
Bhutan	• It is a landlocked country which is known as land of thunderbolt. • Gangkhar Puensum (7561m) is the highest peak of Bhutan. • It is the only country in the world, which measures its economic development through Gross National Happiness.
Myanmar	• It is called land of golden pagoda. • Doab of Saloni and Ervadi river are called rice bowl of the far East. • Ervadi river is the life line of Myanmar. • Mandalay is a historic city, located on the banks of Ervadi river. Pyu city is a World Heritage Site.
Bangladesh	• Bangladesh is called land of rivers. • Bangladesh is surrounded by India from three sides. Border between Bangladesh and Tripura is called 'Zero Line'. • Bangladesh produces 50% of jute and jute related material in world.
Sri Lanka (The Pearl of the East)	• It is also known as 'Pearl of East' and 'Heaven's Door'. Pidurutalagala (2524m) is the highest peak of Sri Lanka. • Mahaweli Ganga is the longest river which flows to North-East and falls into Bay of Bengal. • Kandy city is famous for Buddhist temples. In Asia, highest number of newspapers are circulated here.
Indonesia	• Borneo is the largest island of Indonesia which is locally called as Kalimantan. • Krakatoa, world famous volcano island is situated between Java and Sumatra. • After China, it is second largest producer of tin.
Malaysia	• Malaysia is world's leading producer and exporter of tin. Tin producing areas of Malaysia are Selangor, Penang and Jelebu valley. • Mount Kinabaku (4101) is the highest peak of Malaysia. • Pahang and Kinabatangan are the main rivers of Malaysia. • Sarawak Province of Malaysia resides maximum number of Chinese people.
China- (The Home of One-Fifth of Mankind)	• Its population is largest in the world and fourth in area wise. • Taklamakan desert is an isolated and cold desert which is situated in Tarim basin. • Huang Ho river in China is also known as 'Yellow River'. • Shanghai is known as Manchester of China. • China is leading producer of rice, wheat, tobacco, tea, groundnut and vegetables.
Japan- (The Land of the Rising Sun)	• Japan is called Nippon in Japanese which means 'Land of rising Sun'. • Honshu is the largest island of Japan where capital Tokyo, active volcano Fujiyama is situated. • Kyoto of Japan is known as 'city of small industries' and Osaka is known as 'Manchester of Japan'.

Africa

- Africa is the **second largest continent** in the world, both in size and population. It occupies about 20% of the land area of Earth.
- It is the **hottest continent** on the Earth.
- It has the **shortest coastline** despite being the second largest continent in the world.
- It is the **most centrally located continent** in the world. Both the Prime Meridian (0° longitude) and the Equator (0° degrees latitude) cut across it.
- The African continent terrain was inhabitable and remained unknown for thousands of years, earning it the name of **Dark Continent**.
- The African continent is separated from Europe by the **Mediterranean sea** and from Asia by the **Red sea**.
- It touches **Eurasia** at three different points namely the strait of Gibraltar in North-West, Suez Canal in North-East and the straits of Bab-el-Mandeb in East.
- The Equator passes through the middle of the African continent and it receives direct sunlight throughout the year. **Nigeria** has the highest population (154.7 million people) in Africa. This represents 18% of Africa's total population.
- Both the world's tallest and largest land animals come from Africa. They are the giraffe and African elephant, respectively.
- **Algeria** is the biggest country in Africa by land area.
- The world's hottest place, **Ethiopia** is in Africa.

Physical Features

- The highest peak of Africa is **Kilimanjaro** (5895m). It remains snow covered throughout the year.
- The **Great Rift Valley** in Africa running from the South of lake Malawi Northward to the Red sea and then through the Gulf of Suez and the Gulf of Aqaba to the Dead sea.
- About one-third of Africa is a desert land. The **Sahara** (located in the Northern part) is the largest desert in the world. The **Kalahari** desert in Southern Africa is another great desert.

Drainage System

- **Victoria** is the largest lake in Africa. It is the source of river Nile, longest river of the world. After a long journey through Sahara desert, it reaches the Mediterranean sea.
- **Zaire river** in Central Africa is known as **Congo** in later part. It carries greatest amount of water into Atlantic ocean.
- **Niger** in the Western part and the **Zambezi** and **Orange** in the Northern part are the other important rivers of Africa.
- Except **Nile** and **Zaire** river, few African rivers can be used for shipping because rivers falls from the higher plateaus to the coastal lowlands making waterfalls.
- **Victoria Falls** on the Zambezi is higher and wider than famous **Niagara Falls** of North America.

Climate and Vegetation

- Africa extends between 37° 14′ N to 34° 50′ S latitudes. A major part of the African continent lies within tropical zone.
- Africa is most tropical of all the continents. The highest temperature in the world has been recorded at **Al-Aziziyah** (Libya) as 58°C.
- The belt lying along the both sides of Equator is known as equatorial type of climate. It rains almost daily and there is only one season namely hot-wet summer. Because of abundance of heat and moisture, most of the region is covered with thick forest known as tropical rainforest. It has varied wildlife.
- In rainforests, there are regions of warm summers and mild winters. Most of the rain occurs in summer. There is less rainfall.
- This climate is known as **Sudan type of climate**, which is found in a very large part of the continent. Its vegetation is mostly grasses.
- The Temperate grasslands of South Africa are called the Velds. Velds are rolling plateaus with varying heights ranging from 600m to 1100m and It is bound by the Drakensburg mountains on the East. To its West lies the Kalahari desert.
- On the North-Eastern part, "high velds" are located that attain a height of more than 1600m, in some places.
- The animals of the velds are primarily lions, leopards, cheetah and kudu. There are extensive deserts in both Northern and Southern parts of Africa. Temperature is very high with almost no rainfall.
- The climate is hot and extremely dry, known as **desert type of climate**. Vegetation is either wholly absent or includes only scrub and bushes.
- The Sahara desert cover a large part of North Africa. It is the world's largest desert. It has an area of around 8.54 million sq km.
- The Sahara desert touches eleven countries. These are Algeria, Chad, Egypt, Libya, Mali, Mauritania, Morocco, Niger, Sudan, Tunisia and Western Sahara.
- The Northern and Southern coasts of Africa have mild and rainy winters and warm and dry summers. This is known as **Mediterranean type of climate**. The climate is cooler in the highlands of Southern and Eastern Africa.

Soil

In Africa, only 10% of the soil is suitable for crops. It includes **volcanic soils** of East Africa, **alluvial soil** of Nile valley and certain very fertile soils of the Savanna lands.

Forests

- Larger parts of Central Africa are covered with thick forests. They yield hardwood which may be used as timber. They have many valuable trees such as Mahogany, Ebony and Kapok. Rubber trees (native to South America) are growing wild in these forests.
- Africa exports rubber in large quantities as it is being planted properly. Coconut palm trees are found in the tropical islands such as Zanzibar and Pemba and along the equatorial coast such as Tanzania. They yield Copra from which coconut oil is obtained.
- Oil palm, from which palm oil is obtained, is common in West Africa. Date palm grows in the oases in the drier regions. Dates constitute an important food item for local people. Egypt exports a large amount of dates. Cocoa and kola trees provide beverages.
- Cocoa (used for making chocolate), grows well in the equatorial lowlands West African countries such as Ghana and Nigeria. Kola trees yields nuts which are used in preparing cola drinks and chewing gum.
- Tropical African region grows banana, pineapple, jackfruit and mango fruit trees. Citrus fruits such as lemon, orange and lime are also grown here.
- The Mediterranean region grows olives, apples, peaches and grapes. East Africa produces cashewnuts. Zanzibar and Pemba islands are the biggest producers and exporters of cloves in the world.

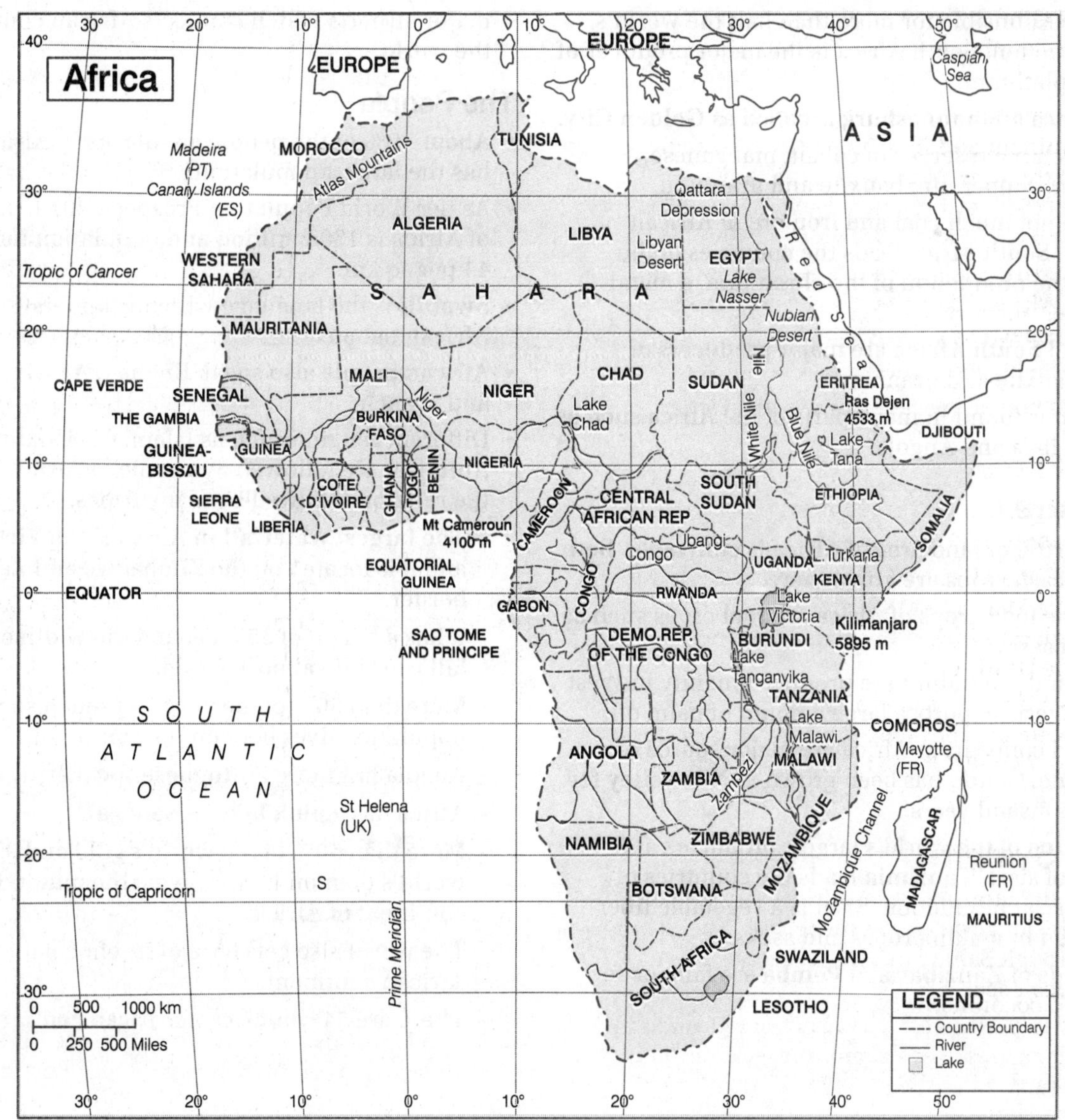

Wildlife

- Elephants, wild buffaloes, snakes, pythons, monkeys, hippopotamus and rhinoceros are some of the important animals found in the forests and swamps of Africa. Deer, stag, zebra and giraffe are found in open woodlands and grasslands.
- Camels are found in deserts. Ostrich is found in the Kalahari desert.
- In the higher Savanna regions of Africa, cattle grazing are very important which are owned by nomadic tribes. The major animals in Africa include cheetah, African elephant, lion, zebra, Egyptian mongoose, giraffe, addax.

Minerals and Energy Resources

- 95% of the world's diamond production comes from Africa.
- Africa is responsible for more than half the world's gold production. South Africa is the major producer of gold and platinum.
- South Africa's **Johannesburg** is called as **Golden City**.
- Africa has large reserves of cobalt, manganese, chromium, copper, tin, bauxite and uranium.
- There are not much coal and iron ore in African continent. South Africa leads the countries of the world in the production of the chromium, a metal which does not rust.
- **Congo** and **South Africa** are major producers of copper, bauxite and uranium.
- Petroleum is found in many parts of the Africa such as Nigeria, Libya and Angola.

Agriculture

- Only the 10% of land area of Africa is cultivable. Both food and cash crops are grown here.
- Most of the food crops of Africa are root crops such as yam and cassava.
- Palm oil and groundnut are produced mainly in West Africa. Nigeria exports a large amount of palm oil.
- Cocoa and coffee from Africa are major source of world trade. Cotton has been grown in Nile valley for several thousand years.
- Africa is one of the world's largest producers and exporter of sisal. **Tanzania** leads the countries of Africa in sisal production. Sisal is a vegetable fiber that is used in making ropes and sacks.
- The islands of **Zanzibar** and **Pemba** are famous for cloves and coconuts.

Industries

- South Africa's larger industrial complex is Pretoria, Johannesburg and virgin area where iron, steel, machinery, garments and chemical industries are situated.
- Cotton cloths industry is situated at Egypt, South Africa's Johannesburg, Durban and East London.
- Cement industry is situated at Johannesburg, Cairo (Egypt) and Nigeria.

Transportation

- Africa does not have enough means of transport. Extensive desert and thick forests hinder the construction of roads and railways.
- Major ports in African continent are Durban, Port of Richard bay, port Dar Es Salaam (Tanzania). Cairo, Johannesburg and Cape town are the major airports which connects African continent to the world.

The People

- About 70% of the people are blacks in Africa. **Nigeria** has the largest population.
- As per World Population Prospect, 2019, population of Africa is 1308 million and population density is 44 per sq km.
- **Swahili** is the language which is understood by many African people.
- African people also speak English, Arabic, Italian and French.
- Different religion such as Islam, Christianity and Animism are followed by people of Africa. Animism is the religion followed by many tribes.
  - The **largest waterfall** in Africa is the **Victoria Falls** and it is located on the Zimbabwe and Zambia border.
  - It has a height of 355 feet and the width of the water fall runs into almost a mile.
  - More than 50% of the world's French speaking population lives here on the continent.
  - Angola has more Portuguese speakers than Portugal.
  - Africa has a **pink lake** in **Senegal**.
  - More than 50% of the world's gold and 95% of the world's diamonds come from the mineral rich continent of Africa.
  - The world also gets 66% of its chocolate from the African continent.
  - There are 54 countries in African continent.

Major Countries of Africa

Country	Description
Zaire (Land of Forests)	• Democratic republic of Congo (Zaire) has been named after river Zaire. It crosses Equator twice. • It is also called as big zoo due to the vast variety of wild animals. • Matadi port on the bank of Zaire river is a major port.
Nigeria (Land of Oil and Cocoa)	• It is a country of lowlands and plateau. • Hot and dust-laden winds often blow from North-East is known as Harmattan. • Ibadan is main industrial city of Nigeria. • Lagos and Port Heart Court are the major industrial port.
Egypt	• The Arab republic of Egypt is situated in Africa but it is at the junction of two continents namely Africa and Asia. • Hot, dry and sand laden blown here are known as 'Khamsin'. • Farmers of Egypt are called as Faillah. • Suez canal links the Mediterranean sea with the Red sea. This canal is 173 km long.
South Africa (Country of Diamond and Gold)	• Pretoria is administrative capital and Cape Town is legislative capital of South Africa. • Drakensberg is the main mountain range. Wall and Orange rivers originates from here. • Limpopo is major river which cuts Tropic of Capricorn twice. • The plateau region in South Africa is covered with grasses. It is called "The Veld". It is called as triangle of maize. • The centre of diamond mining is Kimberley and centre of gold mining are near Johannesburg.

Australia

- Australia is the only country in the world that covers the entire continent. Australia was discovered by Captain **James Cook**, an English seaman, in 1770.
- Australia is the **smallest continent.** It lies entirely in Southern Hemisphere. Together with New Zealand and nearby islands, it is known as 'Australasia'.
- The country is divided into six self-governing states and two centrally administered territories.
- Tropic of Capricorn passes almost through the middle of this continent. Australia is known as **Island Continent** as it is surrounded by water on all sides.
- The continent of Australia is often called **Sahul**, **Australinea** or **Meganesia** to differentiate it from the country of Australia.
- Australia lies entirely on the South of the Equator and it is often called the country **down under**.
- Of all the continents in the world, Australia stands at the top of wool production and import. This is because the sheep population in the world's smallest continent is 14 times that of its human population.
- Australia is home to over 500 varieties of Eucalyptus trees. The world's largest coral reef, the Great Barrier Reef is around 2000 kilometres long.
- **Sydney Harbor Bridge** is the world's largest steel arch bridge and the Sydney Tower Center is the tallest building in the Southern Hemisphere.

Physical Features

- Australia can be divided into three major physical divisions namely Western plateau, Central lowlands and Eastern highlands.
- The Western plateau of Australia occupies nearly two-third of the continent. Most of the plateau is desert or semi-desert. It is rich in minerals such as Gold and Iron ore.
- The Central lowlands extend from Gulf of Carpentaria in North to Southern shores. The Murray and the Darling are the major rivers of Australia flowing through Central lowlands.
- The Eastern highlands form a long belt of elevated plateaus known as **Great Dividing Range**.
- **Mt. Kosciusko** (2234m) is the highest peak in Australia. Most of the rivers of Australia rise in Eastern highlands. World famous Great Barrier Reef is found along the North-East coast of Australia.

Climate

- Most of the Australia is dry. The Eastern, North-Eastern and South-Western parts of Australia come in the way of winds blowing from sea and thus receive heavy rainfall.
- Eastern highlands act as barrier to these rain bearing winds.
- Therefore very large part of Central and Western Australia has no rain at all.
- Thus a hot, desert type of climate is found in vast interior of Australia.
- The Southern coast of Australia enjoys the Mediterranean type of climate.
- The Island of Tasmania receives plenty of rain throughout the year from the winds blowing from the West.
- The Northern part of the Australia receives rains from the monsoon winds in Summer. This region is cool and dry in Winter and wet in Summer.

Forest and Grasslands

- Eucalyptus is the most common tree in Australia and is known as 'Gum trees'. Some of the varieties such Jarrah and Karri are valuable for their timber.
- Wattle is another common tree. It is tall and bears golden flowers in summer.

- The tropical grasslands of Australia are found in North. They are called **Savannas**. The temperate grasslands found in the Murray-Darling basin are called **Downs**. These grasslands are known for pastoral farming.
- The vegetation of semi-arid regions consists of salt bush and mulger plants. Cactus and thorny grass plants are found in more arid parts.

Wildlife

- Many of the animals of Australia are MARSUPIALS (pouch like fold of skin near stomach to carry baby).
- The Kangaroo and wallby are well known examples of marsupials. The kangaroo) lives on grass and leaves.
- **Kangaroo** is the symbol of Australia.
- Koala is another marsupial of Australia which resembles teddy bear.
- Dingo, wild dog and Platypus are also found in Australia. Emu, Kookaburra and Lyrebird are some of the birds of Australia.

Crops

- Wheat is the most important food crop of Australia. New South Wales and Western Australia are main wheat growing states.
- Barley, oats and maize are other food crops grown in Australia. Rice is cultivated in irrigated areas.
- Sugarcane, tobacco and cotton are important crops grown in Queensland.
- Pineapple, banana and papaya are grown in the tropical North whereas apple, oranges and grapes are grown in the temperate South.

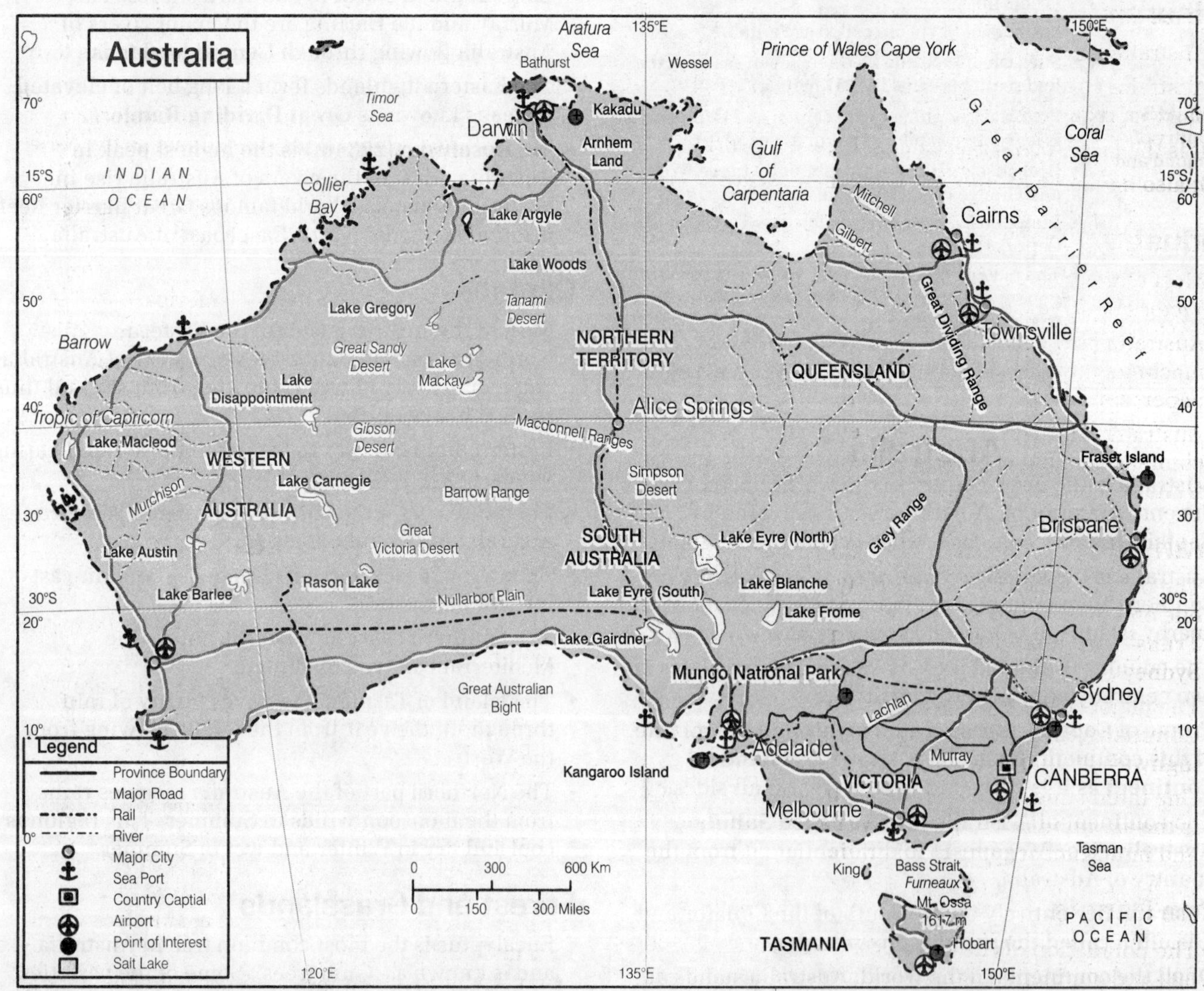

Sheep Rearing

- Australia has highest number of sheep in the world. Sheep are reared mainly for wool.
- The best sheep lands are the lands between the rivers **Murray** and **Darling**.
- Merino is the most important breed of the sheep producing the best wool. Large farms (sheep stations) are run by labours known as Jakaroos.

Cattle Rearing

- The finest beef producing cattle is reared on the grounds of Queensland and the Northern territory.
- The main areas of dairy farming are in the East and Southern-East part of the Australia. These regions have sufficient rainfall for the growth of grasses.

Minerals

- Australia produces a fairly good amount of gold.
- Australia possesses large reserve of coal, iron-ore, bauxite, manganese and tin.
- It is the largest producer of bauxite in the world.
- It also has some reserve of oil and natural gas.

Industry

- Most of the manufacturing industries are located in Victoria and New South Wales.
- Australia produces iron and steel, agricultural machinery, motor vehicles, electrical goods, chemicals, paper, ships, machine tools and refined oil.
- Australia produces cotton, woolen textiles, sugar, condensed and powdered milk, butter, cheese, tinned fruits and meat.

Transport

- The only transcontinental railway running from one end of the continent to the other is the **Trans-Australian Railway** (4000 km). It runs between Sydney and Perth.
- The major roads in Australia are called **Commonwealth highways**. They are like national highways in India.
- One interesting feature of the air transport in Australia is the air ambulance system. **Sydney** is the largest city and important seaport of Australia.

The People

- The population of Australia is approximately 23, 401, 892 and population density is 2 persons per sq km.
- Most of its population is concentrated in the Eastern coastal lowlands and South Eastern parts of the continent.
- Though Australia is mainly an agricultural and pastoral country, most of the Australians live in towns. 85% of the people live in eight capital cities.
- **Aborigines** are the native tribes of Australia. They originally spoke around 200 languages and dialects.

North America

- North America is the **third largest continent** of the world. It is located at 54.5260°N, 105.2551°W.
- North America stretches between Alaska in North, West Labrador in the North-East and Panama in South.
- To the North is the Arctic ocean where the continents breaks off into a series of cold and barren islands.
- It has extensive forest, rich farmlands, abundant minerals, huge water power resources and extensive coastal fishing grounds.
- North America has five time zones and is the only continent with every type of climate.
- North America was named after the explorer **Amerigo Vespucci** and is also known as the **New World**.
- The largest freshwater lake in the world, Lake Superior is located in this continent.
- The world's third longest river, the **Mississippi** (3778 km) is located in North America.
- When compared with the other continents, North America has the highest average per-person income. The average food intake of individuals is the highest on this continent.

Physical Features

North America has four major physical divisions which are as follows :

The Canadian Shield

- It covers nearly half of Canada in North. Its average height is 300 to 400 metres.
- A large part of it is covered with swamps and lakes like Great Bear, Winnipeg and the Great Lakes (Lake Superior, Lake Michigan, Lake Huron, Lake Erie and Lake Ontario).
- The Southern parts of the shield are lowlands of Great Lakes and St Lawrence river. St Lawrence river is the busiest inland waterway in North America. St Lawrence and the Great Lakes provides the largest inland waterways in the world as they link USA and Canada.
- The shield is a treasure house of valuable mineral resources like gold, silver, nickel, iron, copper, platinum, radium, cobalt and uranium.

The Appalachian Mountains or Eastern Highlands

- The height of this mountain varies from 1000 m in South-Western Pennsylvania to 1800 m in Mount Washington.
- The Hudson river flows through the Appalachian Mountains. It is joined to the Great Lakes by the Erie canal. A number of mineral resources such as coal, copper and lead are found here.

The Central Lowlands

- Central lowlands stretch about 2000 km between Western Cordilleras and Eastern highland.
- Its extension is more than 6000 km from the delta of river Mackenzie to coastal plain in Texas.
- The central and Southern parts are River basin of Missouri- Mississippi Rivers. This river basin has very fertile soil and has rich agricultural resources.

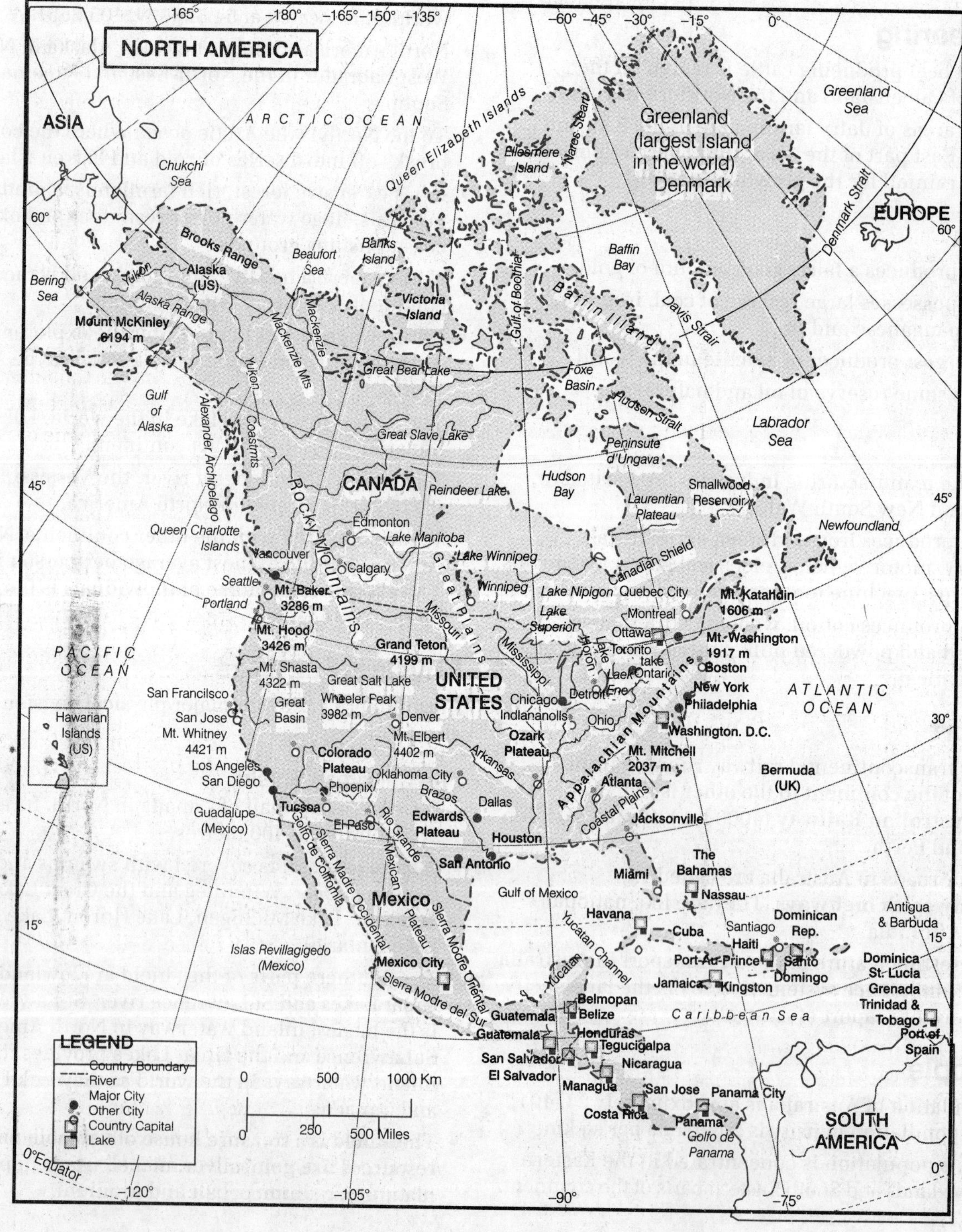

The Western Cordilleras

- Mountain region known as **Western Cordilleras** stretches from North to South along the entire length of the continent. Mt McKinley (6187m), in Alaska is the highest peak of Cordilleras. Most of the rivers of North America rise in Western Cordilleras.
- Rocky mountain, Coastal range and Sierra Nevada are the mountain ranges found in Western Cordilleras. The Great Basin is the largest intermontane plateau of this continent.
- South of the Great Basin is the Colorado plateau. The **Grand Canyon of Colorado** is the largest of its kind and famous all over the world for its beauty.
- The Western Cordilleras have many active volcanoes in Alaska and Mexico. The most famous Old Faithful geyser in Yellow Stone Park lies here.
- The Western Cordilleras is also rich in coal, lead, zinc, gold and copper.

Climate

- North America has varied climate extending between the tropical zone in South and frigid Zone in North.
- The Western highlands and Appalachian mountains provides cold winds from the North and warm winds from South.
- Summers are hot except at **Arctic zone** and **Western cordilleras**.
- The Western coast in the North faces the winds coming from West known as **Westerlies** and South-Eastern coast comes under the influence of **trade winds**.
- Both these winds bring heavy rainfall. However, parts of South-West United States and North-West Mexico remains extremely dry.
- Winters are cold over much of the North America. Winter temperature is much below the freezing point in the Northern and central parts. Temperature decreases from South to North.
- Chinook is a hot wind that blows in winter and therefore, raises the temperature within a short time. This incerease in temperature results in the melting of snow, making pasture land available for grazing of animals.

Vegetation and Animals

- In the extreme North of the continent, the climate is very cold and severe. This region is known as **Tundra**. Here snow covers the ground for eight to nine months.
- During this period, only mosses, lichens, grasses grow. Polar beer, caribou, musk-ox and reindeer are the important animals of this region.
- To the South of the Tundra region is a wide belt of coniferous forests known as **Taiga**. It stretches from Atlantic to the Pacific across Canada. The forest consists of balsam, fir and white and red pines. Similar forests are also found on the Western cordilleras.
- South of Taiga region (South-East Canada and North-East United States) has coniferous and deciduous forests. Trees like beech, birch, maple and oak are found here.
- Tropical forests are found in central America, Eastern Mexico and West Indies. Palm, mahogany and logwood are common trees found in North America.
- Grasslands are found in the interior plains of North America. They are known as Prairies. The Prairies are known for tall and nutritious grasses.
- It is a region of flat, gently sloping or hilly land. For the most part, Prairies are treeless but, near the low lying plains, flanking river valleys, woodlands can be found. Tall grass, upto two metres high dominates, the landscape. it is actually a "Sea of grass."
- The prairies cover parts of United State of America and parts of Canada. In the USA, the area is drained by the tributaries of Mississippi and the Canadian Prairies are drained by the tributaries of Saskatchewan Rivers.
- The grasslands of Praities were the home of native Americans often called "Red Indians". They were the actual habitant of the continent. The Prairies were home of other tribes also like the Apache, the crow, the cree and the Pawnee.
- The extreme South-West part of the United States and North-Western Mexico receives scanty rainfall. The natural vegetation consists of a variety of cactus plants.
- The **Mediterranean type of climate** is found on the West coast of California. Olive, pine, orange and cork oak trees are found here.
- The **Grand Bank** near the coast of Newfoundland is famous for fishing. On the Pacific coast, tuna and salmon are the main fish catches. The world's smallest owl, the Elf, is found on this continent.
- The moose and the elk, found in North America, are the first and second tallest animals on the continent.
- The other major animals of North America are brown bears, hummingbirds, bald eagles, brown bears, bullfrogs.

Crops

- Maize, wheat and barley are the important cereals grown in North America. The other important crops are cotton, tobacco, soyabean and linseed.
- Almost half of the world's maize is grown in North America. Here it is known as **corn**. Maize crop probably originated in South Mexico.

- Wheat is grown in the prairie region of Canada and United States. North America produces about one-fifth of the world's wheat.
- Cotton and tobacco are grown in the Southern parts of the Mississippi river basin.
- United States and Mexico are the leading producers of cotton in North America.
- Along the Gulf Coast, rice and sugarcane are grown. The tropical lowland of central America is famous for growing banana. West Indies is known for **sugarcane cultivation**.
- North America accounts for about one-fourth of the total cow's milk produced in the world. It is also a leading producer of meat.
- The world's largest producer of maize, wheat and soyabean is North America.
- The world's largest sugar exporter among the seven continents, Cuba, also called the **sugar bowl of the world** is located in North America.

Forest

- Coniferous forests cover most of Canada, Northern United States and the Western Cordilleras.
- These forests are great source of softwood which provides some very useful products such as pulp and paper, douglas fir and white pine (provides house building material), cellulose, resin, turpentine etc.
- In the Southern part of the temperate regions, deciduous trees, pineapple, oak and beech grow along with coniferous trees.
- White pine and spruce trees yield pulp for newspaper, the wood of oak and willow trees is used for furniture and the sap of the maple tree yields sugar.
- Tropical rain forests are found in Southern Mexico and countries of Central America.
- These forests yield good quality hardwoods such as mahogany and logwood.

Minerals

- North America is a major producer of petroleum, natural gas, nickel, zinc, asbestos, gold, silver, copper and iron ore.
- The **Canadian Shield** contains deposits of nickel, iron-ore, gold, platinum and copper.
- Lake Superior is the leading producer of high grade iron-ore, gold is found mainly in Ontario, which has the largest gold mine in the world.
- The **Appalachian highlands** produce a large amount of anthracite and high grade bituminous coal. They have the largest soft coal field in the world.
- The **Gulf Coast** and the **Atlantic coastal plain** produce much of the world's petroleum and natural gas.
- United States is the second largest producer of the natural gas in the world. Sulphur, phosphate and potash are also found here.
- **Western Cordilleras** have vast deposits of copper. This region also possesses mineral oil, natural gas, coal and rock phosphate.
- The largest deposits of lead and zinc in the world are found in British Columbia. Mexico has been leading producer of silver in world for many years.

Transport

- The Panama canal connects two great oceans –Atlantic and Pacific ocean. It is of great commercial and strategic importance.
- In North America, highways are known as **Freeways** or **Superways**.
- Mississippi and St Lawrence are the large navigational rivers. The **Great lakes** together with **St Lawrence** form the largest and busiest inland waterways in the world.
- The Kennedy airport in New York is the busiest international airport in the world.

Population

- The North American population consists of original inhabitants (the native Indians) and the people who came from different parts of the world.
- Total population of North America is 366 million (2019) and population density is 23 people per sq. km.
- 90% of Canada is still virtually uninhabited because of harsh climate.
- The majority of its people lives along the narrow Southern fringe.

Major Countries of North America

Country	Description
Canada	• Canada's coastline is world's longest (243, 042 km). • Wood Buffalo National Park is Canada's largest national park located in north Canada. • Wood cutters in Canada are known as 'Lumberjacks'. • Canada's biggest iron and steel industry is situated at Hamilton.
United States of America	• Washington DC, the capital of United States of America is situated on the river bank of river Potomac. • United States of America is the leading producer of aeroplanes in the world. • The leading production center of United States of America is Boston, New York, Philadelphia, Detroit and Chicago.

South America

- South America is the **fourth largest continent** of the world. Most part of South American continent lies in Southern hemisphere.
- Its Andes mountains are next only to Himalayas in their average height.
- South America, Central America, Mexico and West Indies together make up Latin America.
- South America is bounded by the Caribbean Sea to the North-West and North, the Atlantic Ocean to the North-East, East and South-East and the Pacific Ocean to the West.
- South America is connected to North America through the Isthmus of Panama.
- **Brazil** is the largest country in South America, encompassing around half of the continent's land area and population.
- The smallest country in South America is **Suriname**. It has the smallest population in the world.
- South America is home to the world's highest uninterrupted waterfall, **Angel Falls** in Venezuela.
- South America is also home to the highest single drop waterfall Kaieteur Falls in Guyana.

Physical Features

South America has following divisions :

The Western Coastal Strip

There is a narrow strip of lowland along the Pacific coast in Western part. It has great variations in its width from North to South.

The Western Mountains

- These mountains run from Caribbean sea to the Southern tip of South America. They are called **Andes**.
- Andes form the second highest mountain system in the world next to Himalayas.
- Andes are called young fold mountains as they have been formed recently in the Earth's history.
- **Lake Titicaca**, one of the largest lake of the South America is located on **Bolivian plateau**.
- **Mt. Aconcagua** (6962m) is the highest peak of Andes.
- **Cotopaxi** in Ecuador is the highest active volcano in the world.

The Central Plains

- Central plain lies between Andes and Eastern highlands.
- The central plain mainly consists of basins of Orinoco, Amazon and the Plata.
- **Amazon** is the largest river (6280 km) in the world. It rises in the Andes and after flowing through entire width of Brazil, falls into Atlantic ocean.

The Eastern Highlands

- The Guyana and the Brazilian highlands along the Eastern coast form the Eastern highlands.
- The Andes Falls is the highest waterfall in the world. It is located in the South-Eastern part of the Venezuela.

Climate

- The larger part of South America lies in tropical zone and hence, generally hot.
- The Amazon basin has equatorial type of climate. It is hot and wet all the year.
- On the other side of Amazon forests, Savanna type of climate is found. In this region, there is distinct dry period and rain occurs mainly in summer.
- In the low lands of Northern Argentina and Western Paraguay, it is dry during winter and wet during summer. The region experiences heavy rains.
- Parts of Southern Peru and Northern Chile have a typical hot, desert type of climate. This region is known as **Atacama desert**.
- In central Chile, Mediterranean type of climate is found. This region has rainy winters and warm and dry summers.
- In Southern Chile, there is oceanic or marine type of climate is found. Rainfall occurs here throughout the year and the climate is cool.
- South of the tropical grasslands of Southern Brazil lies the region of temperate grasslands.
- This region has warm climate with rain throughout the year (more in summer).
- On the Eastern side of Andes, desert of Patagonia is found. Its climate is dry because it lies in the rain shadow area of Western mountains.
- There are seven types of climate are found in South America-Equatorial Climate, Savanna type of climate, Prairie Climate, Tropical Climate, Desert Climate, Mediterranean Climate and Temperate Maritime Climate.

Vegetation

- The **Amazon basin** is covered with equatorial rain forests locally known as Selvas.
- Savanna type of climate is region of grasslands. In the North, in the Orinoco river basin, it is locally known as Llanos and in the South in central Brazil, it is known as Campos.
- Low lands of Northern Argentina and Western Paraguay is covered with thick forests and grasslands locally known as Gran Chaco.
- Desert type of climate consists of scrubs, prickly pear and cactus.
- Mediterranean type of climate consists of evergreen forests with trees such as oak, walnut, chestnut and fig.
- Ocean or Marine type of climate is region of temperate, mixed forests where beech and pine are valuable trees.
- Temperate grasslands in central Argentina are known as **Pampas**.

Forests

- A very large part of the South America is covered with forests. Most of these, in Amazon basin are tropical rain forests.
- They are storehouse of hardwood such as mahogany. Amazon basin is home of the rubber tree.
- The lightest wood in the world **Balsa** comes from Amazon rain forests.
- The Carnauba palm trees of Brazil yield wax. It is used for furniture polish, shoe polish and candles.
- Cinchona bark is used for medicine and quinine. **Chicle** is used for chewing gum.
- **Yerba** is an important tree of the Eastern highlands. Its leaves are brewed like tea.
- **Quebracho** meaning **Axe breaker** is an important hardwood tree of Gran Chaco. It yields tannic acid used for tanning leather.
- The forests along the Eastern slopes of Andes are known as **Montana**. They yield valuable softwood.

Crops

- Only 10% of the soil is suitable for farming. Most of the good farmland is found in Argentina and Uruguay.
- Wheat and maize are the important crops of South America.
- Wheat is grown in Argentina and Chile.
- Brazil and Argentina are the main producers of maize (native to the South America).
- Coffee, sugarcane, cocoa and banana are important cash crops of South America.
- Brazil, Colombia and Ecuador are among the leading producers of coffee in the world.
- Cotton is another important cash crop grown in Brazil.

Wildlife

- South American continent possesses about 1500 species of very colourful birds. **Candor** is the largest bird of prey in the world.
- Rhea is flightless bird. It is like Ostrich of Africa and Emu of Australia.
- The spider monkeys are known for their acrobatic skills. The owl monkeys are night lovers and squirrel monkeys are known for their gentleness.
- **Anaconda**, a very large python (about 10 m long) is found in South America.
- **Puma** is a dangerous animal of the Cat family. It is stronger than leopard, is found in South America.
- **Llamas** are found in the highlands of Andes. Being surefooted, they are used as beasts of burden in this mountainous region. These long necked animals belong to the family of camel and can go without water for many days.
- **Alpaca** is a smaller variety of Llama found on the high plateaus and Guanaco is a wild variety of Llama, found in the desert of Patagonia.
- South America accounts about one-fifth of the world's total fish production. Peru is one of the leading countries of the world in fishing industry.

Animal Rearing

- The most important cattle rearing areas in South America are the semi-humid parts of Argentina, Uruguay and Brazil.
- In this area, original grass is replaced by more valuable variety of grass called **Alfalfa**.
- The alfalfa is a leguminous plant which besides being nutritious, helps in maintaining the fertility of the soil.
- The sheep rearing areas are in Argentina and Chile. Argentina is one of the largest meat exporters.

Mineral

- About one-seventh of the world's mineral oil comes from South America.
- Venezuela and the island of Trinidad and Tobago have huge deposits of mineral oil.
- Much of the oil is being drilled from below the lake waters in Maracaibo in Venezuela.
- **Brazil** has one of the largest iron-ore deposits of the world. Asphalt or coal-tar is found in Trinidad.
- **Chile** is the major producer of copper in the world. Bolivia is world's fourth largest producer of tin.
- South America possesses rich deposits of nitrates (important source of manures and fertilisers) in the deserts of Atacama. Chile is the largest producer of nitrates.
- Guano islands, off the coast of Peru, has world's most concentrated single source of natural manure.
- South America possesses sizeable reserves of bauxite, manganese, silver and antimony.
- Surinam and Guyana are the major producers of bauxite in South America.

Population

- The total population of South America is 435, 375, 625 as of 2021 and population density is 25 persons per sq. km. The people of South America belong to three main racial groups namely American Indians, Blacks and Europeans.
- A large number of people of mixed races namely Mestizos (people of mixed Indian and European blood), Mulattos (people of mixed European and Black blood) and Zambo (people of mixed Black and Indian blood) are found in South America.
- Large areas of Amazon lowlands, Llanos, Gran Chaco, Guyana highlands, Atacama and Patagonia deserts are uninhabited.
- The major languages spoken on this continent are **Portuguese** and **Spanish**.
- The longest mountain range, the Andes (whose highest mountain is Aconcagua at 6962 m).
- The driest non-polar place on Earth, the Atacama Desert. The largest rainforest, the Amazon Rainforest.
- The highest capital city, **La Paz**, Bolivia.
- The highest commercially navigable lake in the world, **Lake Titicaca**.
- The world's Southernmost permanently inhabited community, Puerto Toro, Chile.
- The largest salt lake in the world is **Salar de Uyuni** (Bolivia and Chile).

Major Countries of South America

Country	Description
Brazil (Coffee pot of the World)	• In area, this is fifth largest country in the world. • Brazil got its present name from the redwood tree brasil. Brazilian forests are among the richest in the world because they provide many useful products. • Coffee is most common crop of Brazil. A very large coffee estate plantation in Brazil is called 'Fazenda'. • Some of the highest railways of the world are across the Andes in Chile.
Argentina (The land of Wheat and Cattle)	• Argentina is mainly a country of lowlands. The large grasslands known as Pampas are called heart of the Argentina. It is famous for wheat production. • Quebracho is the most important tree of Argentina. Tannin can be extracted from it bark used for tanning leather. • The lofty mountains of Andes form a boundary between Argentina and Chile. • The trans- Andean railway line between Chile and Argentina passes over some of the highest mountains of the world.

Europe

- Europe is a peninsula of the Eurasian continent.
- Among the seven continents it **ranks sixth** in area.
- Europe is most densely populated continent of the world.
- Its boundaries are Arctic ocean in North, Atlantic ocean in West and Mediterranean sea in South.
- In the East, it is separated from Asia by the Ural mountains, **Caucasus mountains** and **Caspian Sea**.
- Iceland, Norway, Sweden and Denmark are collectively known as Scandinavia.
- Estonia, Lithuania and Latvia are together known as the **Baltic States**.
- Belgium, Netherlands and Luxemburg are called Low Countries.
- Yugoslavia (Serbia and Montenegro), Slovenia, Croatia, Bosnia and Herzegovina, Macedonia, Bulgaria, Greece, Romania and Albania are known as Balkan States.
- **Vatican city** is a small and independent state in a part of Rome with a population of few hundred people. It is the seat of the Pope and headquarters of the **Roman Catholic Church**.
- The **British Isles** include the two main islands of **Ireland** (Northern Ireland and Irish Republic) and the **Great Britain** (Scotland, Wales and England) as well as a number of small islands.

Land

Europe may be divided into four major physical divisions :

The North-Western Highlands

- It extends from Finland through Sweden, Norway and British Isles to Iceland. The Northern part of this highland is called **Fenno-Scandian Shield.** These shields rocks are oldest in Europe.
- This area is fairly rich in metallic minerals such as iron and copper but almost without fossil fuels such as coal, oil and natural gas.
- Along the Norwegian coast, they reach into Atlantic ocean, creating Fjords.

The North European Plain

- It extends from the Urals in the East to the Atlantic coast in the West. It is bounded in the East by the White sea and North-Western highlands and in the South by central uplands. It has long been an important farming area.
- This plain is drained by large navigational rivers such as Seine and Rhine. Danube, Dnieper, Don and Volga are other important rivers.
- This plain is under laid with deposits of coal, oil and natural gas.

The Central Uplands

- The Meseta in Spain and Portugal, the Massif central and Jura mountains in France, the Black forest in Germany and several low ranges in Czech and Slovak republics are part of this region.
- Two major rivers in this region namely Rhine flows Northwards and Rhone flows Southward. Rhine-Rhone canal, connecting the two rivers, makes it possible to cross the continent through waterways.

The Alpine System

- It stretches from Atlantic ocean in west to the Caspian sea in East from where it further extends into Asia. Alps is most important mountain system. Mont Blanc (4807m) is the highest peak of the Alps. It is located in **France**.
- Other important mountain ranges are Pyrenees, Carpathian and Caucasus. The highest mountain peak of the Europe is Mount Elbrus (5633m) in Caucasus.

Plateaus/Mountain Ranges/Peninsulas

- **Major Plateaus of Europe** Iberian plateau, Central plateaus of France, the Vosages and Black Forest (Black Mountain) of Germany and Bohemian plateau.
- **Major Mountain ranges of Europe** Cantabrian, Pyrenees, Apennines, Dinaric Alps, Carpathian, Kjolen and Balkan ranges.
- **Major Peninsulas of Europe** Jutland and the Scandinavian, Iberian, Italian and Balkan peninsulas.

Climate

Major part of the Europe lies in temperate zone but Europe's climate is described as mild.

- **West European type** The moderating influence of westerlies and nearness to seas and oceans keeps summers warm and winters cool in Western Europe. The temperature remains equable and rainfall is well distributed throughout the year.
- **Mediterranean Type** In Southern Europe, summers are long, hot and dry. Winters are warm and wet.
- **Continental type** In central and Eastern Europe, summers are hot and winters are very cold and less rainfall as influence of ocean reduces Eastward.
- **Tundra Climate** In Northern Europe (the area North to the Arctic Circle), precipitation is very scanty and mostly in the form of snow.
- Summers are short with long and warm days. Sun is visible even at midnight for a brief period. For the major part of the year, land is covered with snow.

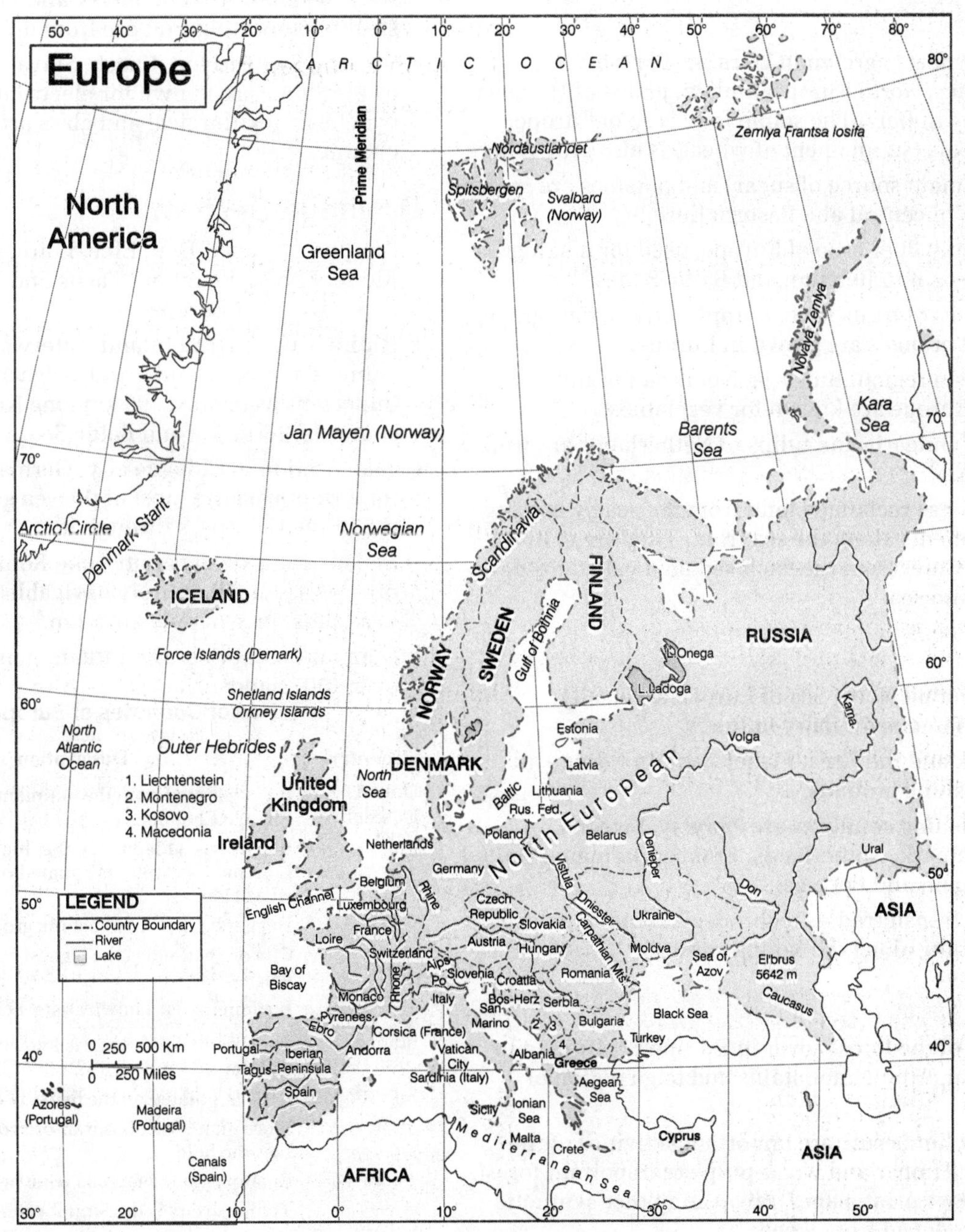

Vegetation

- Olive, fig, grapes and oranges are the most common fruits of Mediterranean region. Tundra type consists of lichens, moss and few stunted trees. Taiga, South of Tundra consists of pine, spruce, and fir.
- South of the above belt lies the belt of mixed forest. Oak, ash and poplar are common trees of this region.
- In the South-East part of the Europe, there is extensive grassland called **steppes**. This region extends from the Danube valley in Romania to Ukraine.

Crops

- In Europe, wheat is grown in Ukraine, Paris basin, Low Countries, North European plain, plains of Hungary and Po valley in Italy. The staple food crop of Europe, Barley and oats (supplement of wheat) is also grown here.
- Sugar-beet (main source of sugar) and potatoes are grown in the plains of central and Eastern Europe.
- Flax is the only fiber crop of Europe, used for making linen. It is grown in Belgium and Baltic States.
- Large varieties of fruits such as apple, olives, figs, grapes, peaches and oranges are grown in Europe.
- Mediterranean region, Bulgaria, Netherlands and Belgium of Europe are known for vegetables.
- The roses of Bulgaria and tulips of Netherlands are well known.
- Netherlands has reclaimed land from the sea by making big embankments along the sea front. They are called **Dykes**. The water from the enclosed land called **Polders** is pumped into sea.

Fisheries

- Countries around North Sea of Europe especially Denmark is famous for dairy industry.
- Dogger Bank and the Great Fisher Bank in Europe are important fishing grounds.
- The major fishing countries are Norway, Sweden, Iceland, Denmark, Netherlands, France, Germany, United Kingdom, Spain and Portugal.
- Norway has transferred its technology to India to develop deep sea fishing along the Kerala coast.

Forests

- A large part of the forest cover in Europe is confined to Scandinavian, Alpine mountains and taiga region of Russia.
- Logging and lumbering are important activities of the forest areas. Timber and wood-pulp are important forest products. News print, paper, rayon and other synthetic fibers are produced from wood.

Minerals

- Coal is found in Great Britain and mainland region of Europe (North-East France to Poland). Coal is also found in Spain, Ukraine and Russia.
- Petroleum is found in North Sea, Romania, Georgia, Armenia, Azerbaijan and Russia.
- Iron ore, Manganese, copper, bauxite, sulphur and potash are found in France, Ukraine, Azerbaijan, Sweden, United Kingdom, Germany, Russia and Spain.
- Italy, Belgium, Czech, Slovak and Poland make steel by importing iron ore from other countries.
- Austria, Switzerland, Czech, Slovak, Belgium and Netherlands are known for electronic instruments, watches, metallurgical and glass articles and chemicals.

Drainage System

- Danube, Dnieper, Don, Elbe, Loire, Oder, Po, Rhine, Rhone, Shannon, Tagus and Volga are the major rivers of Europe.
- **Rhine** is the busiest inland waterway of Europe. Seine, Thames, Danube and Volga are other important waterways. 99 km long **Kiel Canal** connects North Sea and Baltic Sea.
- The location of Cologne city (Germany) is very important because most of the sea going vessels on the Rhine river pass through it.
- In a medium sized country like Romania, there are nine ports on the entirely navigable river Danube over a distance of only 1075 km.
- Denmark comprises the Jutland peninsula and over 400 islands.

Major Countries of Europe

Country	Description
United Kingdom (UK)	• It is separated from the mainland of Europe by the English Channel. • Ben Nevis (1343m) is the highest peak of UK. London, its capital is situated on the banks of the river Thames. • Dogger bank is main fishing ground over here. • City of Sheffield is the biggest cutlery city of world. • Birmingham is known as steel city of UK.
France	• Paris, capital of France is known as city of fashion. • Paris is situated on the banks of the river Seine. • More than 90% of its iron-ore comes from the Loraine field. • Champagne is a famous wine here. • Toulouse city is the largest center for aerospace.

Country	Description
Germany	• Berlin, capital of Germany is situated on the banks of Spree river. • Ruhr is the biggest coal producing area of Europe. It is also called as heart of industrial Europe. • Dresden is known for its ceramics, Munich is known for breweries. • Germany is one of the largest producers of rye, potatoes and sugar beet.
Russia	• Area wise, it is the biggest country in the world. • Ural mountains, Ural river and Caspian sea divides Russia into Europe and Asiatic parts. • Mt. Elbrus (5633m) in the Caucasus Mountains is the highest peak of Russia. • Verkhoyansk, coldest place on Earth is situated at Tundra region of Russia. • Trans-Siberian Railway is the longest railway in the world. St Petersburg and Moscow are connected with the industrial centers of Siberia by the Trans-Siberian Railway. • Moscow is a port of five seas-Caspian sea, Black sea, Baltic sea, lake Ladoga and Arctic ocean through White sea.

The People

- According to **World Population Prospect, 2019**, the population of Europe is 747 million and population density is 34 persons per sq. kilometres.
- Europe is very unevenly distributed. The plains of Europe have a fairly high density of population.
- The industrial regions of UK, France, Germany and Italy have high density of population whereas Eastern and Southern Europe has moderate density while Northern Europe is thinly populated.
- London, Paris, Frankfurt, Berlin, Geneva, Rome, Moscow and Amsterdam are major international airports of Europe.
- Russia, Kazakhstan, Azerbaijan, Georgia and Turkey are transcontinental countries, partially located in both Europe and Asia.
- **Armenia** and **Cyprus** are politically considered European countries, through geographically they are located in the West Asia territory.
- Europe is surrounded by water-bodies from all three sides- Arctic Ocean in the North, Atlantic Ocean in the West and Mediterranean Sea in the South.
- Europe is separated from Asia by Caspian Sea and Ural mountains. Mt. Elbrus is the highest peak of Europe.
- Finland is called the **Land of Lakes** because several lakes are formed due to the melting of ice-sheets.
- Spain and Portugal together form the **Iberia**.

Antarctica

- Antarctica is **fifth largest continent** in size.
- Antarctica lies completely in Southern hemisphere with South Pole almost in its centre.
- It is the only continent which is completely frozen, therefore known as **White Continent**.
- It is coldest and loneliest continent on Earth.
- The mainland of this continent was first discovered in 1820, but real exploration began only in 20th century. Antarctica is called **a continent for science**.
- The highest peak of Antarctica is **Vinson Massif** (4892 m) and **Mount Erebus** is the only live volcano on it.

Land and Climate

- About 99% of the continent remains covered permanently with ice.
- Antarctica continent is surrounded by Southern ocean.
- It is a cold ocean where surface temperature of water rarely rising above 40°C.
- At South Pole, lowest temperature has been recorded at –95°C during winters.
- It is summer in Antarctica from November to February. The Sun never sets during this period.
- Midsummer temperature normally does not rise above 0°C.
- During winters (May, June, July and August), Sun never rises.
- Wind blow at high speed throughout the year which is relatively calm at the centre of the continent.

Resources

- Some amount of coal, iron and copper has been found but their commercial utilisation is not possible due to difficulties.
- About 70% of the world's supply of fresh water is stored in the ice caps and ice sheets of Antarctica.
- Huge masses of ice from these ice caps break away and float in the surrounding sea. These are called **icebergs**.
- The land surface is mostly barren and is a cold desert.
- Krill is very small fish (length up to six cm and weight, 1-105 gm) which provides fish meat, krill meat paste (used as bread spread) and krill protein.
- There is no time zone in Antarctica continent.

- Penguins, sea birds and seals are abundant. Whales are found in surrounding sea.
- The largest land animal in Antarctica is a 1.3 cm long insect known as **Belgica Antarctica**.
  - Till date, India has launched 40 scientific expeditions to Antarctica.
  - The Indian Antarctic expeditions began in 1981, led by **Dr. SZ Qasim**.
  - India has now credited to have built three permanent research base stations in Antarctica namely **Dakshin Gangotri**, **Maitri** and **Bharati**.
  - As of today, India has two operational research stations in Antarctica named Maitri and Bharati.
  - **The National Centre for Polar and Ocean Research** (NCPOR), Goa, manages the entire Indian Antarctic program.

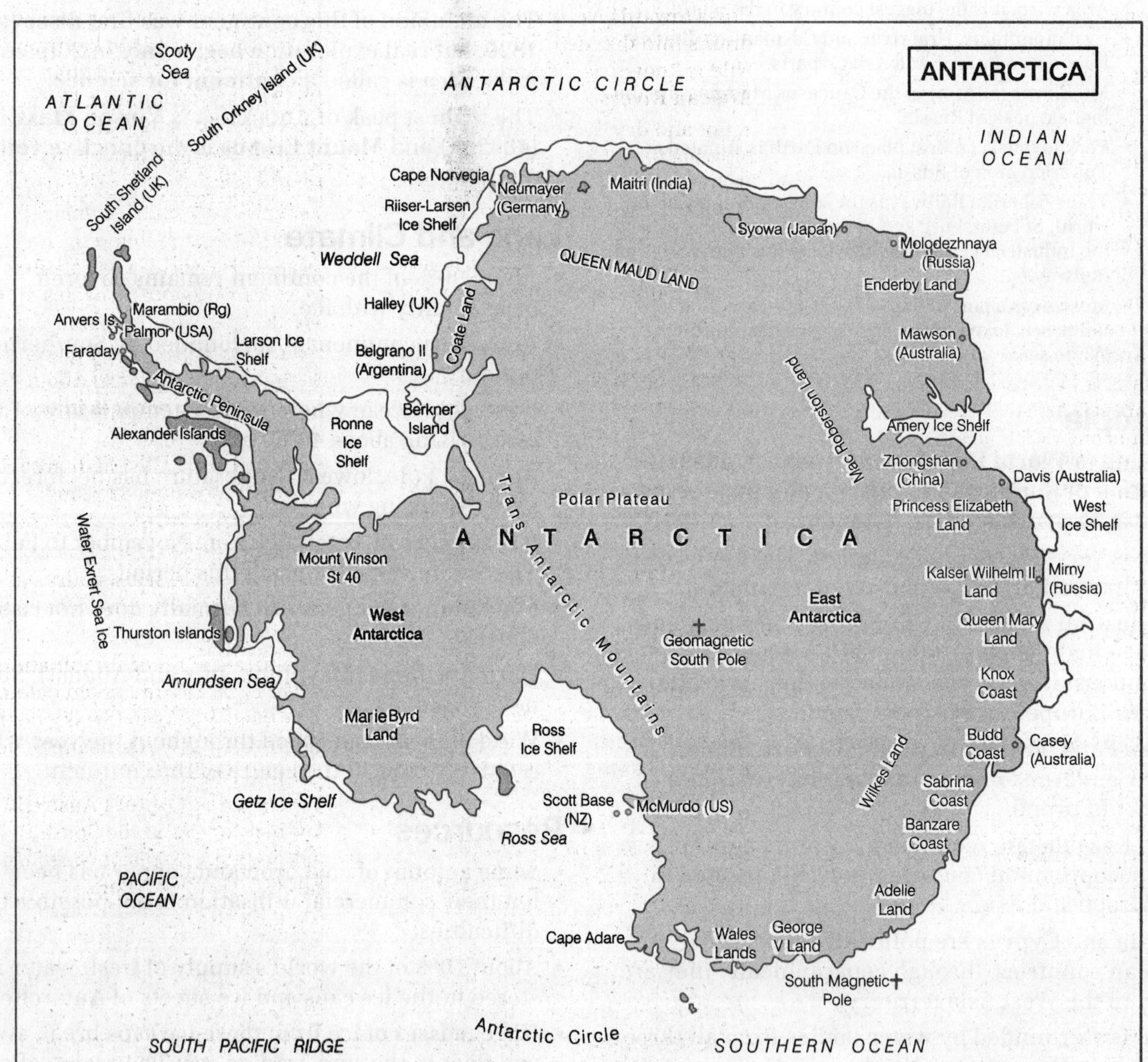

Extra Facts From Tamil Nadu Board and NIOS

- Africa is the only continent through which the major latitudes such as Tropic of Cancer, Equator and Tropic of Capricorn pass. Its North-South extent is 7623 km and East-West extent is 7260 km.
- The Prime Meridian passes near Accra the capital of Ghana in the West of this continent. It is located in all the four hemispheres.
- The North-Western African countries of Morocco, Algeria, Libya, Mauritania and Tunisia are collectively called 'Maghreb' which means West in Arabic language.
- Tropical dry grasslands with scattered trees are known as **Savanna.** It is located near the Equator and covers almost half of the area of Africa. The Serengeti Plain is one of the largest plains in Savanna. This is called the **Open Air Zoo.**
- A Rift valley is a large crack in the Earth's surface formed by the shifting of tectonic plates. It stretches from Northern Syria in Asia to Central Mozambique in Africa for a distance of 6400 kilometers.
- The African Great Lakes are a series of lakes found in the Rift valley. The water in the Great Lakes of Africa constitutes about 25% of the planet's unfrozen surface fresh water. There are seven major lakes in this region.
- The Nile is the longest river in the world with a length of 6650 km.
- It has two main tributaries. They are the White Nile, which originates from Burundi, and the Blue Nile, which originates from Ethiopia.
- These two join and form the Nile River at Khartoum, in Sudan. It flows towards Northward and drains into the Mediterranean sea. Nile is known as the **Father of African Rivers**.
- A hot and dry dusty local wind blowing from the Sahara desert to Guinea coast is called **Harmattan.** A hot local wind blowing from Sahara to Mediterranean sea is called **Sirocco.** Tropical rain forest is called the **Jewel of the Earth** and the 'World's Largest Pharmacy'.
- **Canberra** is the capital of Australia. Sydney, Brisbane, Adelaide, Hobart, Melbourne, Perth and Darwin are the other important cities of Australia.
- Rottnest Island, Magnetic Island, Fitzroy Island, Fraser Island, Phillip Island, Lord Howe Island, Kangaroo Island and Whitsunday Islands are the major Islands of Australia.
- Ayers rock or Uluru is the largest monolith rock in the world. It is 863 meters high above the sea level. It is one of the natural wonders of Australia. The pointed limestone pillars called pinnacles are common in this region.
- Australian Alps mountain range is the highest mountain range of **Australia**. It is covered with ice.
- The highest peak of this range is **Mt. Kosciuszko** (2230m) and is located in the New South Wales.
- The Great Artesian Basin is the region on the Earth's surface where water gushes out like a fountain. The Great Artesian Basin in Australia is the largest and deepest basin in the world.
- River Murray is the longest river in Australia. It runs 2508 km from Australian Alps to the Indian ocean. Darling, Murrumbidgee, Cooper creek Lachlan and Swan are the other important rivers of this continent.
- About 80 percent of animals in Australia are not found in the other parts of the world. Australia has almost 400 mammal species and about 140 species of marsupials.
- Antarctica is the largest piece of ice on the surface of Earth. About 70% of Earth's fresh water is in the Antarctic ice caps.
- Small red fish called **krill** are found in large shoals. It is the food for many warm blooded sea animals.
- The living creatures of this region include whales, seals, walrus and sea birds like penguins, albatross, polar Skua and Stout.
- A natural curtain of combination of bright pink, red and green colour light that appears in the sky near the North and South magnetic poles is called **Aurora.**
- It is also called Aurora Australis or Southern Lights in the South Pole and Aurora Borealis or Northern Lights in the North Pole.

15

Map Studies

(SOURCES)

Class-XI New NCERT Chap 1 (Introduction to Maps), Tamil Nadu Board (Class XI, XII), NIOS

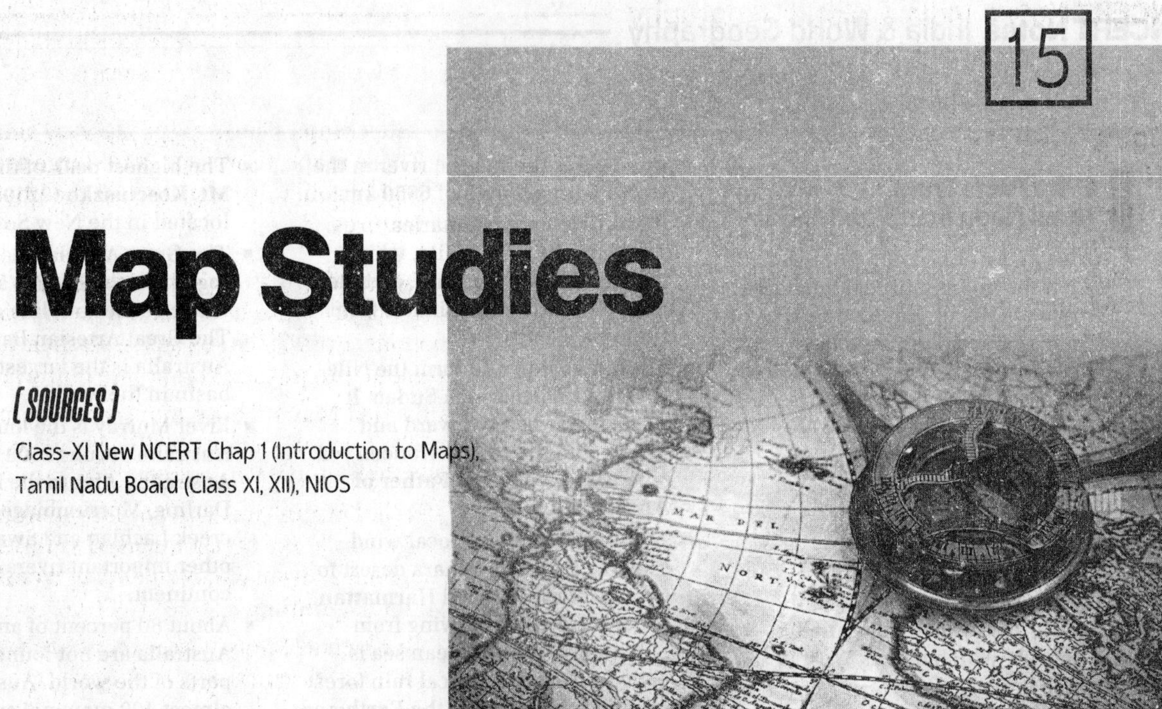

Map

- A map is a selective, symbolised and generalised representation of the whole or part of the Earth at a reduced scale.
- It is a two-dimensional form of the three-dimensional Earth. Hence, a map can be drawn by using a system of map projections.
- As it is impossible to represent all features of the Earth's surface in their true size and form, a map is drawn at a reduced scale.
- **Cartography** is an art, science and technology of making maps, charts, plans and other modes of graphical expression as well as their study and use.

History of Map Making

- The history of map making is very ancient. The oldest map was found in **Mesopotamia** drawn on a clay tablet that belongs to 2,500 BC.
- **Greek** and the **Arab** geographers laid the foundation of modern cartography.
- The measurement of the circumference of the Earth and the use of the system of geographical coordinates in map-making are some of the significant contributions of the Greeks and the Arabs.
- The foundation of map-making in India was laid during the Vedic period when the expressions of astronomical truths and cosmological revelations were made.
- The expressions were crystallised into **Sidhantas** or laws in classical treaties of **Aryabhata**, **Varahamihira** and **Bhaskara** and others. Ancient Indian scholars divided the known world into seven **dwipas**.
- The intensive topographical surveys for the preparation of up-to-date maps of the entire country, were taken up with the setting up of the **Survey of India** in 1767, which culminated with the map of Hindustan in 1785. Today, the Survey of India produces maps at different scales for the entire country.

Classification of Maps

Maps fulfill our different needs and show different important facts. Maps can be classified into following three types

- **Political Map** A political map is a type of map that represents political divisions or human-created boundaries of the world, continents and major geographic regions. Political features are characteristics such as country borders, roads, population centres and landform boundaries.
- **Physical Map** A physical map is a representation of natural features of the Earth such as mountains, plateaus, plains, rivers, oceans, etc. It is also called Relief maps.
- **Thematic Map** A thematic map is a type of map that portrays the geographic pattern of a particular subject matter (theme) in a geographic area. The theme corresponds to the data selected and the data is connected to a particular geographic location.

Components of Maps

There are three main components of maps are as follows:

- **Distance** It is a measurement between two points 'initial and final'. Distance is the major component of a map, which tells about time indirectly in the terms reaching at a particular place by fixed scale ratio of distance.
- This factor reduces the large area in the required work sheet as a map. On map a large distance is represented in small scale.
- **Direction** Maps are drawn normally with North orientation. North direction in a map is always towards the North Pole of the Earth. If we position ourselves looking at the North Pole, on our right will be the East, our left will be the West, at our back will be South. These four main directions are called the cardinal directions. Direction is usually indicated on a map by a North-South line, with the North direction represented by an arrow head.
- **Symbol** It is the third important component of a map. It is impossible to draw exact size of different features such as buildings, roads, bridges, trees, railway lines or a well on a map so, they are shown by using certain letters, shades, colours, pictures and lines.

Types of Maps

Maps can be classified on the basis of scale and function.

Types of Maps Based on Scale

On the basis of scale, maps may be classified into large-scale and small-scale.

- **Large-Scale Maps** Large scale maps are drawn to show small areas at a relatively large scale. These maps are further divided into the following types :
  - **Cadastral Maps** These are large scale maks, drawn at a scale of 1 : 500 to 1 : 4000 to show property boundaries, designating each parcel of land with a number.
  - **Topographical Maps** The topographical maps are based on precise surveys and are prepared in the form of series of maps made by the national mapping agencies of almost all countries of the world. For example, the Survey of India undertakes the topographical mapping of the entire country at 1 : 250,000, 1 : 50,000 and 1 : 25,000 scale.
- **Small-Scale Maps** These maps are drawn to show large areas. These maps are further divided into the following types :
  - **Wall Maps** These maps are generally drawn on large size paper or on plastic base for use in classrooms or lecture halls. The scale of wall maps is generally smaller than the scale of topographical maps but larger than Atlas maps.
  - **Atlas Maps** These maps are very small scale maps. These maps represent fairly large areas and present highly generalised picture of the physical or cultural features.

Types of Maps Based on Function

The maps may also be classified on the basis of their functions. Broadly, maps based on their functions may be classified into physical maps and cultural maps.

- **Physical Maps** These maps show natural features such as relief, geology, soils, drainage, elements of weather, climate and vegetation, etc.
  - **Relief Maps** These maps show general topography of an area like mountains and valleys, plains, plateaus, drainage, elements of **weather, climate** and **vegetation.**
  - **Geological Maps** These maps are drawn to show geological structures, rock types, etc
  - **Climatic Maps** These maps depict climatic regions of an area. Besides, maps are also drawn to show the distribution of temperature, rainfall, cloudiness, relative humidity, direction and velocity of winds and other elements of weather.
  - **Soil Maps** These maps are also drawn to show the distribution of different types of soil and their properties.
- **Cultural Maps** These maps show man-made features. These include a variety of maps showing population distribution and growth, levels of education attainment, occupational structure, location of settlements, distribution and flow of different commodities, etc.
  They can be categorised as follows :
  - **Political Maps** These maps show the administrative divisions of an area such as country, state or district. These maps facilitate the administrative machinery in planning and management of the concerned administrative unit.
  - **Population Maps** The population maps are drawn to show the distribution, density and growth of population, age and sex composition, distribution of religious, linguistic and social groups, occupational structure of the population, etc.

  Population maps serve the most significant role in the planning and development of an area.
  - **Economic Maps** Economic maps depict production and distribution of different types of crops and minerals, location of industries and markets, routes for trade and flow of commodities.
  - **Transportation Maps** These maps show roads, railway lines and the location of railway stations and airports.

Uses of Maps

- Geographers, planners and other resource scientists use maps. In doing so, they make various types of measurements to determine distances, directions and area.
- To study the maps, different types of measurements are considered. These are as follows

Measurement of Distance

- The linear features shown on the maps fall into two broad categories i.e., straight lines and erratic or zigzag lines.
- The measurement of straight line features like roads, railway lines and canals is simple.
- It can be taken directly with a pair of dividers or a scale placed on the map surface. Such as the coastlines, rivers and streams.
- The distances along all features can be measured by placing a thread at the starting point and carrying it along the line up to the end point.
- The thread is then stretched and measured to determine the distance.
- It can also be measured by using a simple instrument called **Rotameter**. The wheel of the 'Rotameter' is moved along the route to measure the distance.

Measurement of Direction

- Direction is defined as an imaginary straight line on the map showing the angular position to a common base direction. The line pointing to the North is **zero direction** or the **base direction** line. A map always shows the North direction.
- All other directions are determined into this relation. The North direction enables the map-user to locate different features with respect to each other.
- The four commonly known directions are North, South, East and West. These are also called the **Cardinal points**.
- In between the cardinal points, one may have several intermediate directions.

Measurement of Area

- The measurement of area of features like that of administrative and geographic units is also carried out over the surface of the map by map-users.
- There are different methods in which areas can be determined. One of the simplest but not very accurate method to determine the area is by means of **regular pattern of squares**.
- In this method, the area to be measured is covered by squares by placing a sheet of graph paper beneath the map on an illuminated tracing table or by tracing the area onto the square sheet.
- The total number of 'whole squares' are summed up, together with **partial squares**. The area can also be calculated by using a fixed area **polar planimeter.**

Essentials of Map Making

Cartography, being an art and science of mapmaking, does include a series of processes that are common to all the maps. These processes that may also be referred to as **essentials of maps** are:

Essentials of Map Making

- Scale
- Map Projection
- Map Generalisation
- Map Design
- Map Construction and Production

- **Scale** We know that all maps are reductions. The first decision that is taken for a map making is about the scale of the map. The choice of scale is of utmost importance.
  The scale of a map sets limits of information contents and the degree of reality with which it can be delineated on the map.
- **Projection** We also know that maps are a simplified representation of the three-dimensional surface of the earth on a plane sheet of paper. The transformation of all-side-curved- geoidal surface into a plane surface is another important aspect of the cartographic process.
  Such a radical transformation introduces some unavoidable changes in directions, distances, areas and shapes from the way they appear on a geoid.
  A system of transformation of the spherical surface to the plane surface is called a **map projection.**
  Hence, the choice, utilisation and construction of projections is of prime importance in map-making.
- **Generalisation** Every map is drawn with a definite objective. For example, a general purpose map is drawn to show information of a general nature such as relief, drainage, vegetation, settlements, means of transportation, etc.
- Similarly, a special purpose map exhibits information pertaining to one or more selected themes like population density, soil types or location of industries.
- It is, therefore, necessary to carefully plan the map contents while the purpose of the map must be kept in the forefront.
- As maps are drawn at a reduced scale to serve a definite purpose, the third task of a cartographer is to generalise the map contents.
- In doing so, a cartographer must select the information (data) relevant to the selected theme and simplify it as per the needs.

- **Map Design** The fourth important task of a cartographer is the map design. It involves the planning of graphic characteristics of maps including the selection of appropriate symbols, their size and form, style of lettering, specifying the width of lines, selection of colours and shades, arrangement of various elements of map design within a map and design for map legend.
- The map design is, therefore, a complex aspect of mapmaking and requires thorough understanding of the principles that govern the effectiveness of graphic communication.
- **Map Construction and Production** The drawing of maps and their reproduction is the fifth major task in the cartographic process.
- In earlier times, much of the maps construction and reproduction work used to be carried out manually.

  Maps were drawn with pen and ink and printed mechanically.

  However, the map construction and reproduction has been revolutionalised with the addition of computer assisted mapping and photo-printing techniques in the recent past.

Extra Facts From
Tamil Nadu Board and NIOS

- Prismatic compass measures the horizontal angle with reference to the magnetic North-line.
- Prismatic compass is a simple instrument comprising an aluminium ring graduated to 30 minutes held at the top of a broad magnetic needle set in balance on a hard steel pivot.
- Surveying is the science of measuring and recording distances, angles, heights and sizes of the Earth's surface to obtain data from which accurate plans and maps are made.
- Poles are straight lines equal in length to the Equator.
- Meridians are straight parallel lines, equally spaced and are half as long as the Equator. All meridians are of same length therefore, scale is true along all meridians.
- Parallels are straight, equally spaced lines which are perpendicular to the meridians and are equal to the length of the Equator.
- Length of the Equator on the map is the same as that on the globe but the length of other parallels on map is more than the length of corresponding parallels on the globe. So, the scale is true only along the Equator and not along other parallels. Distance between the parallels and meridians remain same throughout the map.

16

Indian Geography

Location and Structure of India

[SOURCES]

Class-VI New NCERT Chap 6 (Our Country : India),
Class-IX New NCERT Chap 1 (India : Size and Location),
Class-XI New NCERT Chap 1 (India : Location),
Class-XII Old NCERT Chap 1 (Introduction to India)

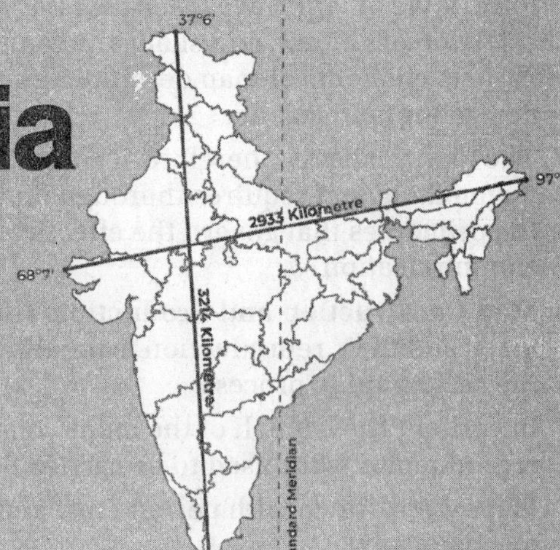

Geographical Location

- India is located latitudinally in the **Northern Hemisphere** and longitudinally in the **Eastern Hemisphere**.
- The Indian mainland extends between 8°4' North and 37°6' North latitudes and from 68°7' East and 97°25' East longitudes. Thus, the latitudinal and the North-South extent is **3214 km** and East-West extent is **2933 km**.
- The **82°30'E longitude** passes through **Mirzapur** (in Uttar Pradesh). This is the **Standard Meridian** of the country. The 82°30' East has been selected as Standard Meridian because there is a time lag of almost two hours between Gujarat and Arunachal Pradesh.
- Therefore, a **Central Meridian** is selected to determine the time for the whole country. **Indian Standard Time** (IST) is ahead of **Greenwich Mean Time** (GMT) by 5 hours and 30 minutes.
- There are some countries where there are more than one standard meridian due to their vast East to West extent. For example, the USA has seven time zones.
- India lies largely on the Indian Plate, the Northern portion of the **Indo-Australian Plate**, whose continental crust forms the Indian sub-continent physical divisions are marked by natural configuration.
- India is divided into six physiographic divisions on the basis of the varied physiographic features i.e., Northern and North-Eastern Mountain, Northern Plain, Peninsular Plateau, Indian Desert, Coastal Plains and Islands.
- The **Tropic of Cancer** (23°30' N) passes through eight states in India i.e., Gujarat (Jasdan), Rajasthan (Kalinjarh), Madhya Pradesh (Shajapur), Chhattisgarh (Sonhat), Jharkhand (Lohardaga), West Bengal (Krishnanagar), Tripura (Udaipur) and Mizoram (Champhai).

Extreme Points of India

- The **Southernmost point of the country** is the **Pygmalion Point** or **Indira Point** and is located at 6° 45' N latitude.
- The **Southernmost point of mainland** India is Kanyakumari.
- The **Northernmost point** is Indira Col in Kashmir.
- The **Westernmost point** is Guhar Moti in Rann of Kutch.
- The **Easternmost point** is Kibithu in Arunachal Pradesh.

Areas and Size

- India with its area of **3.28 million sq km** accounts for **2.4%** of the world's land surface area and stands as the **seventh largest country** in the world.
- India stands apart from the rest of Asia, marked off as it is by mountains and the sea, which gives the country a distinct geographical entity.
- India has a land boundary of about **15,200 km** and the total length of the coastline of the mainland, including Andaman and Nicobar and Lakshadweep, is **7,516.6 km.** At present, there are **28 States** and **8 Union Territories** in India.

Indian States and their Capitals

States	Capitals	States	Capitals
Andhra Pradesh	Amravati	Manipur	Imphal
Arunachal Pradesh	Itanagar	Meghalaya	Shillong
Assam	Dispur	Mizoram	Aizawl
Bihar	Patna	Nagaland	Kohima
Chhattisgarh	Raipur	Odisha	Bhubaneshwar
Goa	Panaji	Punjab	Chandigarh
Gujarat	Gandhinagar	Rajasthan	Jaipur
Haryana	Chandigarh	Sikkim	Gangtok
Himachal Pradesh	Shimla	Tamil Nadu	Chennai
Jharkhand	Ranchi	Telangana	Hyderabad
Karnataka	Bengaluru	Tripura	Agartala
Kerala	Thiruvanantha puram	Uttar Pradesh	Lucknow
Madhya Pradesh	Bhopal	Uttarakhand	Dehradun
Maharashtra	Mumbai	West Bengal	Kolkata

List of Union Territories and their Capitals

Union Territories	Capitales
Andaman and Nicobar Island	Port Blair
Chandigarh	Chandigarh
Dadra and Nagar Haveli and Daman and Diu	Daman
Delhi	Delhi
Ladakh	Leh
Lakshadweep	Kavaratti
Jammu and Kashmir	Srinagar
Puducherry	Puducherry

States/UTs with the Length of Coastline

States / Union Territories	**Length of the Coastline** (in kms)
Gujarat	1214.7
Andhra Pradesh	973.7
Tamil Nadu	906.9
Maharashtra	652.6
Kerala	569.7
Odisha	476.4
Karnataka	280
Goa	160.5
West Bengal	157.5
Puducherry	30.6

Top 5 States (According to Area)

State	**Area** (In Sq km)
Rajasthan	342239
Madhya Pradesh	308245
Maharashtra	307713
Uttar Pradesh	240928
Gujarat	196024

India and Its Neighbourhood

- India is part of **Asian continent**. India is surrounded by water from three sides. Arabian sea in West, Bay of Bengal in the East and Indian Ocean in the South.
- Towards its North-West is **Pakistan** and **Afghanistan. China, Bhutan, Tibet** and **Nepal** lie to its North. Bangladesh and Myanmar lie to its East. Sri Lanka and Maldives are located in the Indian Ocean towards its South.
- The Indian sub-continent, or simply the sub-continent, is a physiographic region in South Asia. It is situated on the Indian Plate and projecting Southwards into the Indian Ocean from the Himalayas.
- It generally includes Bangladesh, Bhutan, the British Indian Ocean Territory, India, Maldives, Nepal, Pakistan and Sri Lanka.
- A total of 9 countries share borders with India. Out of these, 7 countries share land borders while 2 countries share sea borders with India. Bhutan is the smallest neighbouring country of India in terms of land borders.

Neighbouring Countries of India

Neighbouring Countries	Name of the Border	Length of Border (in kms)	Bordering States
Afghanistan	Durand Line	106	Jammu and Kashmir
Bangladesh	Radcliffe Line	4096.7	West Bengal, Mizoram, Meghalaya, Tripura and Assam
Bhutan	N/A	699	Arunachal Pradesh, Assam, Sikkim and West Bengal
China	MacMahon Line	3488	Jammu and Kashmir, Himachal Pradesh, Uttarakhand, Sikkim and Arunachal Pradesh
Myanmar	N/A	1643	Arunachal Pradesh, Manipur, Mizoram and Nagaland
Nepal	N/A	1751	Sikkim, West Bengal, Bihar, Uttar Pradesh and Uttarakhand
Pakistan	Radcliffe Line	3323	Jammu and Kashmir, Punjab, Gujarat and Rajasthan
Sri Lanka	Palk Strait	Sea Border	Separated from India by Gulf of Mannar
Maldives	N/A	Sea Border	The South-West part of the Indian Ocean below the Lakshadweep Island

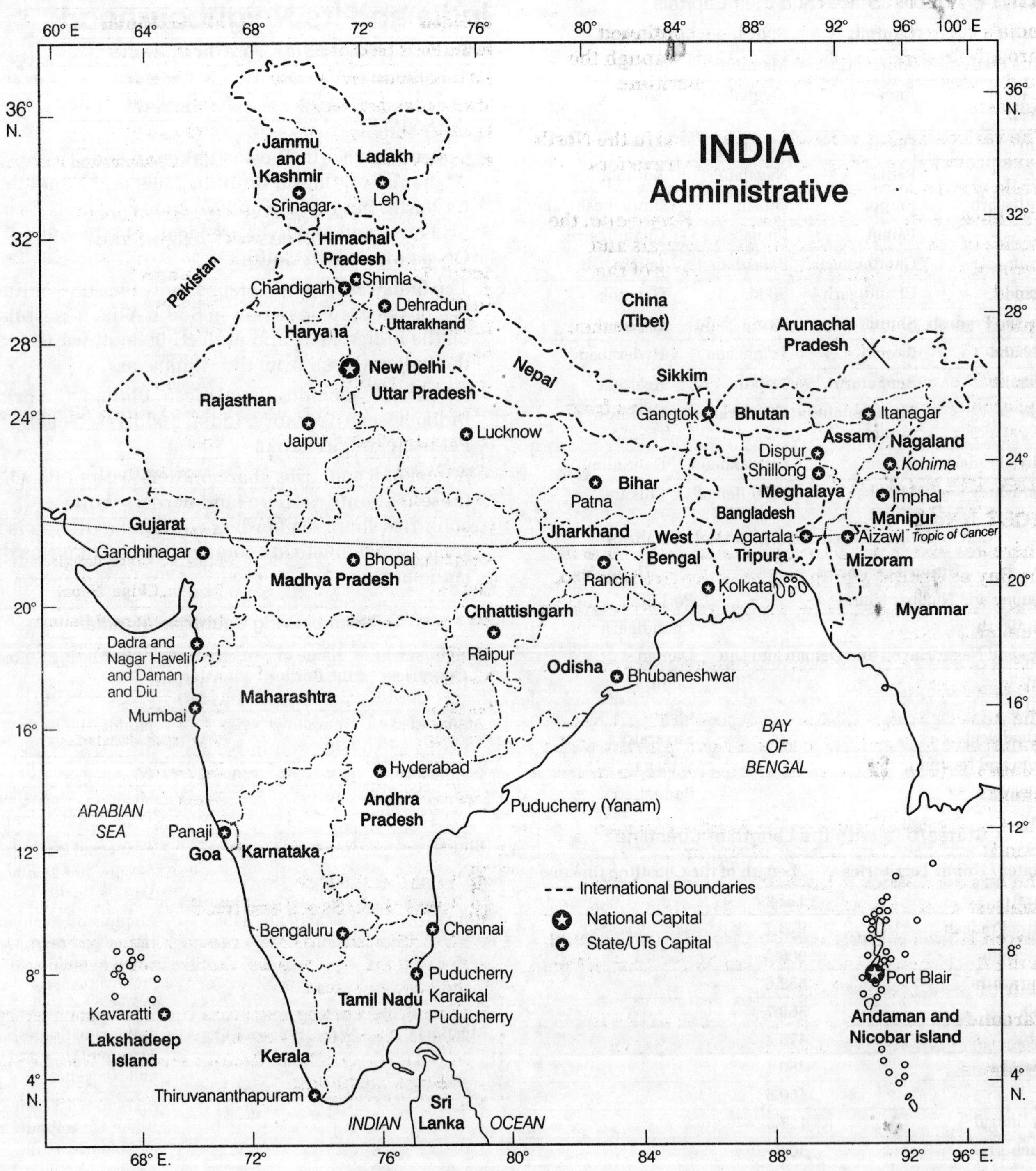
INDIA
Administrative
60° E
64°
68°
72°
76°
80°
84°
88°
92°
96°
100° E
36° N.
32°
28°
24°
20°
16°
12°
8°
4° N.
68° E.
96° E.
Jammu and Kashmir
Srinagar
Ladakh
Leh
Himachal Pradesh
Shimla
Chandigarh
Dehradun
Uttarakhand
Haryana
New Delhi
Uttar Pradesh
Lucknow
Pakistan
Rajasthan
Jaipur
China (Tibet)
Nepal
Sikkim
Gangtok
Bhutan
Arunachal Pradesh
Itanagar
Assam
Dispur
Shillong
Meghalaya
Nagaland
Kohima
Imphal
Manipur
Aizawl
Mizoram
Tripura
Agartala
Bangladesh
Tropic of Cancer
Myanmar
Bihar
Patna
Jharkhand
Ranchi
West Bengal
Kolkata
Gujarat
Gandhinagar
Bhopal
Madhya Pradesh
Chhattisgarh
Raipur
Odisha
Bhubaneshwar
Dadra and Nagar Haveli and Daman and Diu
Mumbai
Maharashtra
Hyderabad
Andhra Pradesh
Puducherry (Yanam)
BAY OF BENGAL
ARABIAN SEA
Panaji
Goa
Karnataka
Bengaluru
Chennai
Puducherry
Karaikal Puducherry
Tamil Nadu
Kerala
Thiruvananthapuram
Kavaratti
Lakshadeep Island
Sri Lanka
INDIAN OCEAN
Port Blair
Andaman and Nicobar island
International Boundaries
National Capital
State/UTs Capital

India and the World

- India's contacts with the world have continued through the ages, but its relationships through the land routes are much older than its maritime contacts.
- The various passes across the mountains in the North have provided passages to the ancient travellers while oceans restricted such interactions.
- The ideas of the *Upanishads* and the *Ramayana*, the stories of the *Panchtantra*, Indian numerals and decimal system have reached many parts of the world.
- **Spices, muslin** and other merchandise were taken from India to different countries.
- The influence of Greek sculpture and the architectural style of domes and minarets from West Asia can be seen in many parts of India.

Other Important Facts About India

- There are two major island groups in India – one in the **Bay of Bengal** and the other in the **Arabian Sea.**
- South Andaman and Little Andaman are separated by **Duncan Passage.**
- The Andaman and Nicobar Islands are also known as the **Emerald Islands.**
- The Adam's Bridge is situated between Tamil Nadu (India) and Sri Lanka. **Pamban Island** is a part of the **Adam's Bridge.** Rameshwaram is situated on this Island.
- The Coco Strait is between the North Andaman Islands and the Coco Islands of Myanmar.
- The **largest district** is **Kachchh** (Gujarat) and the **smallest district is Mahe** (Puducherry).
- **Barren Island** is India's only active volcano situated in the Andaman Sea about 135 km North-East of Port Blair in the Andaman Islands.
- **Narcondam Island** is a volcanic island which is situated in the Northern-Eastern part of North Andaman.

Important Straits/Channels

Location	Channel/Strait
Indira Point-Indonesia	Great Channel
Little Andaman and Nicobar	10° Channel
Minicoy-Lakshadweep	9° Channel
Maldives-Minicoy	8° Channel
India-Sri Lanka	Gulf of Mannar and Palk Strait

Countries Sharing International Boundaries with Indian State

State/UTs	Countries
Gujarat	Pakistan
Rajasthan	Pakistan
Punjab	Pakistan
Jammu and Kashmir	Pakistan
Ladakh	China, Pakistan, Afghanistan
Himachal Pradesh	China
Uttarakhand	China, Nepal
Uttar Pradesh	Nepal
Bihar	Nepal
West Bengal	Bhutan, Nepal, Bangladesh
Sikkim	Bhutan, China, Nepal
Arunachal Pradesh	Bhutan, China, Myanmar
Assam	Bhutan, Bangladesh
Nagaland	Myanmar
Manipur	Myanmar
Mizoram	Myanmar, Bangladesh
Meghalaya	Bangladesh
Tripura	Bangladesh

Extra Facts From Tamil Nadu Board and NIOS

- The Indian landmass has a central location between, the East and the West Asia and the Southward extension of the Asian continent.
- About **6,100 km** long coastline of India is surrounded by sides of the country by the Indian ocean in the South and its two arms namely the **Arabian sea in the West** and **Bay of Bengal in the East.**

Geological History and Physiography of India

[SOURCES]

Class-VIII Old NCERT Chap 12 (India : The Land),
Class-IX New NCERT Chap 2 (Physical Features of India),
Class-X Old NCERT Chap 1 (Physical Features),
Class-XI (II) New NCERT Chap 2 (Structure and Physiography),
Class-XII Old NCERT Chap 5 (Physical Divisions of India)

- India is mostly located on the Indian Plate, which is generally called the Northern portion of the **Indo-Australian Plate.**
- The Indian sub-continent, Australia, New Guinea, Tasmania and New Zealand, etc have a common geological history by virtue of being an integral part of the **Mesozoic Gondwana super-continent** until 160 million years ago.

Geological History of India

- In the **late Paleozoic period** (542 – 250 million years ago), supercontinent **Pangaea** was formed that existed during the Paleozoic and Mesozoic eras.
- Pangaea started to break up approximately 200 million years ago, before the component continents were separated into their current configuration.
- It first broke into **Northern Laurasia** (Angaraland) and **Southern Gondwanaland**.
- Later, the Laurasia and Gondwana drifted apart. Gondwana included Antarctica, South America, Africa, Madagascar, Australia-New Guinea and New Zealand, as well as Arabia.
- It also consisted the Indian sub-continent, which have now moved entirely into the Northern Hemisphere.

Thus, from geological history two main structural divisions of India are

1. **Himalayan Mountain Chain**, which is a part of Laurasia or Angaraland.
2. Southern part called Gondwanaland of which **Peninsular India** formed one of the blocks.

- The intervening space between the two giant continental blocks was filled with water. It was a shallow sea called **Tethys Sea**.
- During the subsequent geological periods, the Indian Peninsular block began drifting Northward leaving a huge gap filled with water, which truly came to be called the **Indian Ocean**.
- As the peninsular block continued its drift Northward, the Indian ocean continued to advance and filled up the depressions on either side of the landmass when it compressed the Tethys sea. Thus, the **Arabian Sea** and **Bay of Bengal** were formed.

Geological Aspects of India

The Geology of India started with the geological evolution of the Earth.

- India entirely falls under the Indian plate that was formed when it split off from the major tectonic plate of ancient continent **Gondwanaland**.
- It was an ancient landmass consisting of the Southern part of the supercontinent **Pangaea**.

Geological Structure of India

Geologically, India represents a monumental assemblage of rocks of different character belonging to different ages, ranging from **Pre-cambrian era** to the recent times.

The Geological Survey of India (by Sir T Holland) divides geological formations of India into four groups

1. **The Archaean Rock System** First half of the Pre-cambrian era (about 4000 million years ago).
2. **The Purana Rock System** Second half of the Pre-cambrian era (1400-600 million years old).
3. **The Dravidian Rock System** Cambrian to middle Carboniferous (600-300 million years old).
4. **The Aryan Rock System** Upper Carboniferous to the Pleistocene (300 million years old) to the present age.

Classification of Indian Rock System

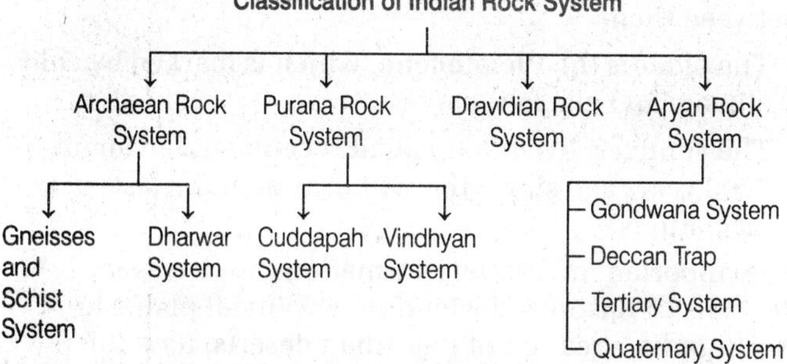

1. The Archaean Rock System

The word *Archaean* was first used by JD Dana for rock structure prior to the Cambrian system. These rocks do not contain fossils due to its ancient origin depicting absence of life forms. The term Archaean is also used for ancient. It includes the following two rock groups

- **The Gneisses and Schist System** This system contains the earliest formed rocks of the Earth. These rocks in the peninsula are found primarily in Tamil Nadu, Andhra Pradesh, Karnataka, Odisha, Meghalaya, Madhya Pradesh, Chhattisgarh and Chhota Nagpur plateau of Jharkhand. They also cover the whole of Bundelkhand in the North and to the North-West, they are formed in a number of isolated outcrops, extending from North of Vadodara to a long distance along the Aravallis in Rajasthan.
- **The Dharwar System** This system derives its name from the rocks that were first studied in the Dharwar district of Karnataka. These are the earliest formed sedimentary rocks, found today in metamorphic forms. The earliest rock deposits are over 3100 million years old and the latest one about 2300 million years old. They were metamorphorised around 1000 million years ago and are found in Karnataka, Madhya Pradesh, Jharkhand, Chhattisgarh, Odisha, Meghalaya and Rajasthan. They also occur in the Central and Northern Himalayas.

  Some of the rocks of this system are schist, slates, quartzites and conglomerates. This system carries minerals like gold, manganese ore, iron ore, chromium, copper, uranium, thorium, mica, etc and building materials like granites, marbles, etc.

2. The Purana Rock System

In India, the word 'Purana' has been used in place of Proterozoic.

This rock system includes two divisions

- **The Cuddapah System** A long interval of time elapsed before the rock system next to the dharwars and peninsular gneisses began to be deposited. A great thickness of unfossiliferous clay, slates, sandstones and limestone was deposited presumably in great synclinal basins.

  This formation is known as the **Cuddapah System**, from the occurrence of the most typical and first studied outcrops of these rocks in Cuddapah districts of Andhra Pradesh.
- **The Vindhyan System** This system of ancient sedimentary rocks stands over the Cuddapah rocks. Except a few traces of animal and vegetable life, this group do not contain any recognisable fossils. It covers a large area in Madhya Pradesh, Chhattisgarh, North of Bihar, Rajasthan, Karnataka and Andhra Pradesh.

  This system contains rocks like limestones, sandstones, shales and slates often over 4000 m thick which are useful as building materials.

3. The Dravidian Rock System

- These rocks do not occur in the Peninsular plateau as it was above the sea level at that time, but are found in continuous sequence in the Himalayas.
- Most rocks of this system are found in the extra peninsular region and in one or two patches of lower Permian age, near Umaria, Madhya Pradesh.
- The rocks belonging to the Dravidian System contain abundant fossils, which help in finding the inclusions of rocks of different periods like the rocks of Cambrian, Ordovician, Silurian, Devonian and Carboniferous periods.

4. The Aryan Rock System

- The marine sedimentary rocks belonging to late Paleozoic to tertiary periods are exposed today in the Northern part of the Central Himalayan axis extending from Kashmir to Sikkim.
- These rocks in the peninsula occur in several places in Gujarat, Rajasthan, Tamil Nadu and North-Eastern India. The divisions of this system are discussed below

The Gondwana System

- The peninsula during the Upper Carboniferous period experienced crustal movements, which led to the formation of basin-shaped depressions. These depressions had countless terrestrial plants and animals, which were buried to form coal deposits in India known as the **Gondwana rocks.**
- These rocks have also marks of the climatic changes from arctic cold to tropical and desert conditions. These rocks are found mainly in the **Damodar**, **Mahanadi** and **Godavari** valleys of the peninsula.

The Deccan Trap

- Towards the end of the Mesozoic era, intensive volcanic activity took place, which flooded vast areas of Maharashtra and other parts of the Deccan with lava, known as the Deccan Traps.
- The volcanic rocks contain some thin fossiliferous sedimentary layers found between the solidified lava flows. This indicates that the lava flow was not continuous.
- The volcanic activity led to two great events
  - Break up of the Gondwanaland.
  - Uplift of the Himalayas out of the Tethys sea.

The Tertiary System

The tertiary rocks were formed from **Eocene to Pliocene.** It is the most significant period in India's geological history because the Himalayas were born and India's present form came into being.

It is the age of the mammals. It is generally divided into three systems

- **The Eocene System** It is mainly found in Jammu and Kashmir, Himachal Pradesh, Rajasthan, Gujarat and in the North-Eastern part of India. Some Eocene deposits have recently been noticed in Puducherry.
- **The Oligocene System** It is very poorly developed in India. Rocks of the Oligocene period are found in the greater part of the Barail series of Assam, where they were overlain with a marked unconformity by lower Miocene rocks.
- **The Miocene System** It is fully developed in India and is found in all the tertiary areas of the extra-peninsula. It is also found in outcrop of Murre series in Jammu hills, in the Dagshai-Kasauli band of Shimla, in the coal measures of Assam and in the Garo hills.

Besides, some rocks of Kachchh in Gujarat, Mayurbhanj in Odisha, Durgapur in West Bengal and Kollam in Kerala also belong to this group.

Quaternary System

- It has two divisions without any clear cut boundary in between them
  - The older is the **Pleistocene**, which is marked by cold climate and glaciations.
  - The younger division is called **recent**, started about 1200 years ago since, the withdrawal of the last glaciations.
- The important quaternary formations are ice age deposits in Kashmir, formation of Alluvial plains in North India, creation of Rajasthan deserts, Rann of Kachchh, laterite formation in the peninsula and the formation of regur soils.

Physical Divisions of India

- India has the topographical diversity. The reasons for variation in the topography could be
  - Differences in the rock formations. These landmasses have been formed in different geological periods.
  - Number of processes such as weathering, erosion and deposition have modified these features to their present forms.
- India is a country of physical diversity. There are high mountain peaks in some areas while in others, lie the flat plains formed by rivers.
- On the basis of physical features, India can be divided into following six divisions
  1. The Northern Mountains or Himalayas
  2. The Northern Plains
  3. The Peninsular Plateau
  4. The Indian Desert
  5. The Coastal Plains
  6. The Islands

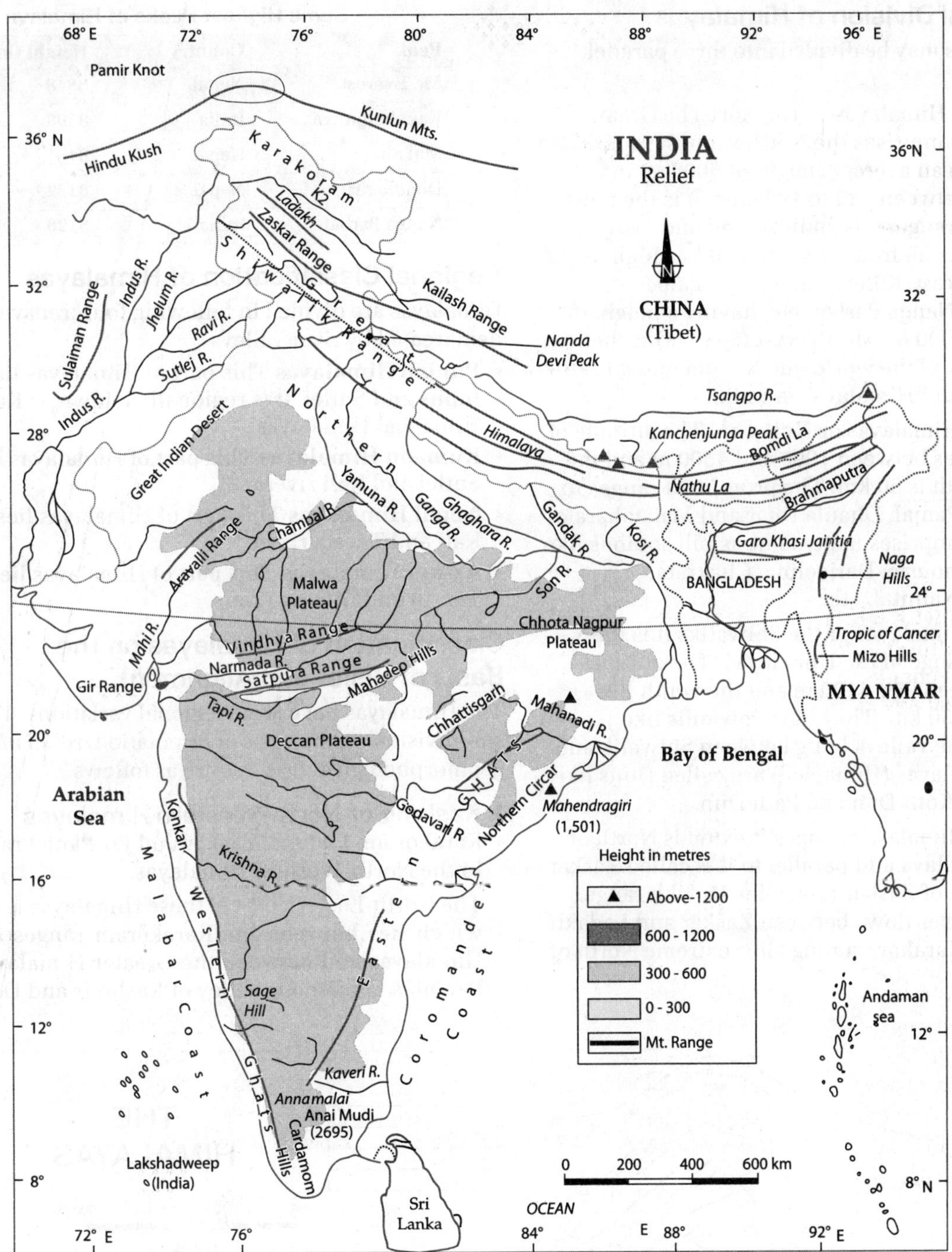

1. The Northern Mountains or Himalayas

- Himalayas are the young fold mountains. This is the highest mountain range in the world. The Himalayas act as a natural barrier.
- The extreme cold, snow and rugged topography discourage the neighbours from entering India through the Himalayas.
- They run from **West-East direction** from Indus to Brahmaputra along the Northern boundary of India covering a distance of **2500 km**. Their width varies from 400 in the West and 150 km in the East.

Longitudinal Division of Himalayas

The Himalayas may be divided into three parallel ranges

- The Greater Himalayas or Himadri The Greater Himalayas comprises the Northernmost ranges and peaks. It has an average height of 6000 m and width lies between 120 to 190 kms. It is the most continuous range. It is snow bound and many glaciers descend from this range. It has high peaks like Mt. Everest, Kanchenjunga, Makalu, Dhaulagiri, Nanga Parbat, etc. having a height of more than 8000 m. Mt. Everest (8848 m) is the highest peak of the world and Kanchenjunga is the highest peak of Himalayas in India.
- The Lesser Himalayas or Himachal The altitude of this range lies between 1000 and 4500 m and the average width is 50 km. The prominent ranges in this are Pir Panjal, Dhaula Dhar and Mahabharata ranges. It comprises many famous hill stations like Shimla, Dalhousie, Darjeeling, Chakrata, Mussoorie, Nainital, etc.
- The Outer Himalayas or the Shiwaliks It is the outermost range of the Himalayas. The altitude varies between 900-1100 m and the width lies between 10-50 km. They have low hills like Jammu Hills, etc. The valleys lying between Shiwalik and Lesser Himalayas (Himachal) are called Duns like Dehra Dun, Kotli Dun and Patli Dun.
- The Trans-Himalayan ranges It extends North of greater Himalaya and parallel to it is called Zaskar range. North of Zaskar range lies Ladakh range. The Indus river flows between Zaskar and Ladakh range. The Karakoram range lies extreme North of the country.

Some Highest Peaks of Himalaya

Peak	Country	Height (In Metre)
Mt. Everest	Nepal	8848
Kanchenjunga	India	8598
Makalu	Nepal	8481
Dhaulagiri	Nepal	8172
Nanga Parbat	India	8126

Regional Classification of Himalayas

Himalayas are divided in following four transverse regions demarcated by river valleys

- **Punjab Himalayas** This part of Himalayas lies between Indus and Sutlej. It is regionally known as Kashmir and Himachal Himalayas.
- **Kumaon Himalayas** This part of Himalayas lies between Sutlej and Kali rivers.
- **Nepal Himalayas** This part of Himalayas lies between Kali and Teesta rivers.
- **Assam Himalayas** This part of Himalayas lies between Teesta and Dihang rivers.

Classification of Himalayas on the Basis of Relief and Alignment

The Himalayas have large regional variations. Their sub-division on the basis of orientation, relief and other geomorphological features are as follows

1. Kashmir or North-Western Himalayas

- Karakoram, Ladakh, Zaskar and Pir Panjal ranges, etc., lie in the North-Western Himalayas.
- The North-Eastern part of these Himalayas is a Cold Desert which lies between the Karakoram ranges and Greater Himalayas and between the Greater Himalayas and Pir Panjal is the famous valley of Kashmir and Dal lake.

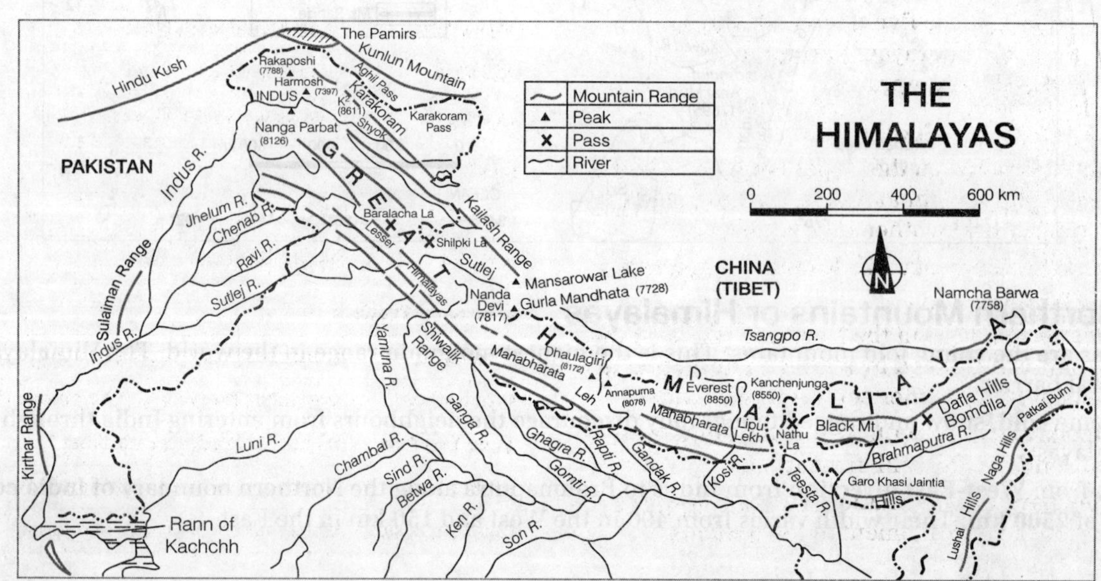

- Important glaciers of Asia such as Baltoro and Siachen can be located in this region.
- Important passes in this region Zoji La (Great Himalayas), Banihal (Pir Panjal), Photu La (Zaskar), Khardung La (Ladakh).
- Some of the important freshwater lakes are Wular and Dal. Saltwater lakes are Pangong Tso and Tso Moriri.
- This region is drained by the Indus and its tributaries like Jhelum and Chenab.
- Famous places of pilgrimage in this region are Vaishno Devi, Amarnath Cave, Charar-e-Sharif, etc.
- The Southern part of this region has longitudinal Valleys called Duns. e.g., Jammu and Pathankot Duns.
- This region is famous for **Karewa formations**, which are useful for the cultivation of **Zafran** (a local variety of Saffron).

2. Himachal and Uttarakhand Himalayas

- This region lies between the Ravi and Kali rivers and is drained by two major river systems, that is the Indus and the Ganga. Major tributaries are the Ravi, Beas and Sutlej of the Indus system, Yamuna and Ghaghara of the Ganga system.
- The Northernmost part of this region is an extension of the Ladakh cold desert, which lies in the district of Lahaul and Spiti.
- Some of the important places such as Dharamshala, Mussoorie, Shimla, Kausani, Kasauli, Almora, etc. are in this region.
- This region also has Duns such as Chandigarh-Kalka Dun, Nalagarh Dun, Dehra Dun, Hari-ke-dun, etc.
- Some of the important places of pilgrimage such as the Gangotri, Yamunotri, Kedarnath, Badrinath and Hemkund Sahib are in this region.
- This region also has the five famous Prayags i.e., Devprayag, Rudraprayag, Karnaprayag, Nandaprayag and Vishnuprayag.

3. The Darjeeling and Sikkim Himalayas

- This region lies between the Nepal Himalayas in the West and the Bhutan Himalayas in the East. It is very small in comparison to other subdivisions.
- The High mountain peaks like Kanchenjunga and Deep valleys reside here.
- **Lepcha tribes** live here in the Northern part and the Southern part is inhabited by a mixed population of Nepalis, Bengalis and other central Indian tribes.
- These Himalayas along with Arunachal Himalayas have an absence of Shiwalik formation.
- Rather they have dual formation. Hence, these are important for the development of tea gardens.

Important Passes of Himalayas

Name	Connects
Jammu and Kashmir	
Mintaka Pass	Kashmir with China
Parpik Pass	Kashmir with China
Khunjerab Pass	Kashmir with China
Aghil Pass	Ladakh region of India with the Xinjiang (Sinkiang) Province of China
Banihal Pass	Jammu and Srinagar
Chang La	Ladakh with Tibet
Khardung La	Near Leh in the Ladakh range
Lanak La	India with China (Akasai-Chin area of Jammu and Kashmir)
Pir Panjal Pass	Across the Pir Panjal range
Qara Tag La	Indo-China border across the Karakoram range
Imis La	Ladakh region of India with Tibet in China
Pensi La	Vital link between the Kashmir Valley and Kargil
Zoji La	Important road link between Srinagar on one side and Kargil and Leh on the other side
Himachal Pradesh	
Baralacha La	Himachal Pradesh and Jammu and Kashmir
Rohtang Pass	Acts as road link between Kullu, Lahaul and Spiti Valleys
Shipki La	Himachal Pradesh with Tibet
Uttarakhand	
Lipu Lekh	Trijunction of Uttarakhand (India), Tibet (China) with Nepal borders
Mana Pass	Uttarakhand with Tibet
Niti Pass	Uttarakhand with Tibet
Muling La	Uttarakhand with Tibet
Sikkim	
Nathu La	Sikkim with Tibet
Jelep La	Sikkim-Bhutan border
Arunachal Pradesh	
Bom Di La	Arunachal Pradesh with Bhutan
Dihang Pass	Arunachal Pradesh with Myanmar
Yong Yap Pass	Arunachal Pradesh with Tibet
Dipher Pass	Trijunction of India, China and Myanmar
Chankan Pass	Arunachal Pradesh with Myanmar

4. The Arunachal Himalayas

- This region extends from East of the Bhutan Himalayas to the Diphu Pass (Arunachal Pradesh – tripoint of China-India-Burma).
- The general direction of this region is from South-West to the North-East.
- Some of the important mountain peaks of this region are Kangtu and Namcha Barwa.
- Some of the important rivers of this region are the Kameng, Subansiri, Dihang, Dibang and Lohit.
- This subdivision has a high potential for hydro-electric power.
- Some of the important tribes of this region are the Monpa, Abor, Mishmi, Nyishi and Nagas.
- Most of the people here practice **Jhumming**, which is also known as **Shifting** or **Slash** and **Burn agriculture.**

5. The Eastern Hills and Mountains

- These Himalayas are in the North-South direction.
- They have their local names in different regions such as Patkai Bum, Naga hills, the Manipur hills and Mizo or Lushai hills.
- People in these areas practice **Jhum cultivation** too.
- **Loktak Lake** in Manipur is in this region. Mizoram is known as the **Molasses basin**, which is made up of soft unconsolidated deposits.

Important Glaciers in Himalayas

Name	Length (in km)	State/UT	Mountain Range
Siachen Glacier	72	Jammu and Kashmir	Karakoram Mountain Range
Hispar Glacier	60	Jammu and Kashmir	Karakoram Mountain Range
Batura Glacier	58	Jammu and Kashmir	Karakoram Mountain Range
Baltoro Glacier	58	Jammu and Kashmir	Karakoram Mountain Range
Bara Shigri Glacier	27	Himachal Pradesh	Pir Panjal Range of the Inner Himalayas
Gangotri Glacier	26	Uttarkashi, Uttarakhand	Himalayas
Zemu Glacier	26	Sikkim	Eastern Himalaya Located on Kanchenjunga Peak
Sunderdhunga Glacier	24	Uttarakhand	Kumaon-Garhwal
Godwin Austen Glacier	16	Ladakh	Karakoram
Chorabari Glacier	14	Uttarakhand	Kumaon-Garhwal
Satopanth Glacier	13	Uttarakhand	Kumaon-Garhwal
Bandarpunch Glacier	12	Uttarakhand	Western Edge of the High Himalayan Range
Sonapani Glacier	11	Himachal Pradesh	Pir Panjal
Pindari Glacier	9	Nanda Devi, Uttarakhand	Upper Reaches of The Kumaon Himalayas

State-wise Highest Mountain Peaks in India

Peak	Range/Region	State	Height
Arma Konda	Eastern Ghats	Andhra Pradesh	1680 m
Kangto	Eastern Himalaya	Arunachal Pradesh	7060 m
Someshwar Fort	West Champaran District	Bihar	880 m
Bailadila Range	Dantewada District	Chhattisgarh	1276 m
Sonsogor	Western Ghats	Goa	1166 m
Girnar	Junagadh District	Gujarat	1069 m
Karoh Peak	Morni Hills	Haryana	1467 m
Reo Purgyil	Western Himalaya	Himachal Pradesh	6816 m
Parasnath	Parasnath Hills	Jharkhand	1370 m
Mullayanagiri	Western Ghats	Karnataka	1930 m
Anaimudi	Western Ghats	Kerala	2695 m
Dhupgarh	Satpura	Madhya Pradesh	1350 m
Kalsubai	Western Ghats	Maharashtra	1646 m
Mount Iso	Senapati District	Border of Manipur and Nagaland	2994 m
Shillong Peak	Khasi Hills	Meghalaya	1965 m
Phawngpui	Saiha District	Mizoram	2157 m
Mount Saramati	Naga Hills	Nagaland	3826 m
Deomali	Eastern Ghats	Odisha	1672 m
Guru Shikhar	Aravalli Range	Rajasthan	1722 m
Kanchenjunga	Eastern Himalaya	Sikkim	8586 m
Doddabetta	Nilgiri Hills	Tamil Nadu	2637 m
Doli Gutta	Deccan Plateau	Border of Telangana and Chhattisgarh	965 m
Betlingchhip	Jampui Hills	Tripura	930 m
Amsot Peak	Shiwalik Hills	Uttar Pradesh	945 m
Nanda Devi	Garhwal Himalaya	Uttarakhand	7816 m
Sandakphu	Eastern Himalaya	West Bengal	3636 m

2. The Northern Plains

- The Northern Plains are located between South of the Himalayas and North of the Peninsular plateau.
- It is formed by the deposition of the sediments brought by three main river systems namely, the **Indus**, **Ganga** and **Brahmaputra**.
- From West to East, this plain is about 3200 km long.
- Its width varies from about 300 km in the West to about 150 km in the East. It mainly includes the states of Punjab, Haryana, Uttar Pradesh, Bihar, West Bengal and Assam.
- This plain is very fertile due to alluvial sediments brought by the rivers from the Himalayas. This plain is one of the largest and most fertile plains of the world.
- Major crops such as wheat, rice, sugarcane, pulses, oil seeds and jute are grown here.
- Due to proper irrigation, the plain makes a significant contribution in the production of food grains.

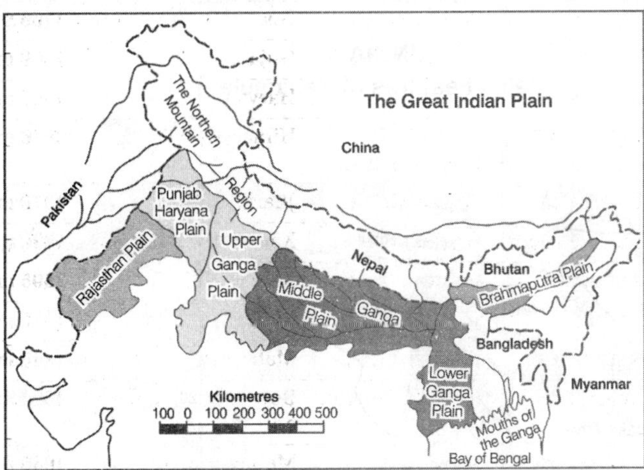

On the basis of characteristics of the alluvium, surface gradient, drainage channels and regional traits, this plain is divided into the following four parts

- **Bhabar region** This region is found along the foothills of Shiwaliks from Indus to Teesta without any break. Its width is 8-16 km. Since, it is made up of stones and pebbles, it is highly porous, which make rivers disappear beneath the ground in this region.
- **Terai region** This region is found to the South of the Bhabhar region. The underground streams of the Bhabar re-emerge on the surface and give birth to marshy area. The speed of river flow in this region is slow. This is the region of dense forests and high biological diversity.
- **Khadar region** It is made up of new alluvium. In this region, floods bring new alluvium every year. Khadar region is generally found in the delta regions. e.g. the Ganga-Brahmaputra delta spread in India and Bangladesh is a Khadar region.
- **Bhangar region** It is that higher part of the plains, where the flood water cannot reach. It is made up of old alluvium. It is often seen in the structure of a terrace.

Reh or Kollar

- Reh or Kollar comprises saline efflorescences of drier areas in Haryana.
- Reh areas have spread in recent times with increase in irrigation (capillary action brings salts to the surface).

Parts of Northern Plains

- **The Northern Plain** This lies to the West of the Indus river. It is mainly made up of the old alluvium i.e. Bhangar. Dhoros and Dhands are important feature here. Dhoros are depressions formed by the former rivers and Dhands are alkaline lakes.
- **Punjab-Haryana Plain** This plain is located to the East and North-East of the Great Indian Desert (Thar) and West of the Yamuna river. A part of this plain is made-up of doabs from East to West. Intensive agriculture is practiced in this region.
- **Ganga Plain** It is very vast and the largest unit of the Great Plain of India. According to convenience, it is divided into three sub-divisions, namely, Upper Ganga Plain, Middle Ganga Plain and Lower Ganga Plain. Upper Ganga Plain comprises course of Yamuna river, Middle Ganga Plain comprises Eastern Uttar Pradesh and Bihar and Lower Ganga Plain covers some districts of Bihar and whole of West Bengal.
- **Rajasthan Plain** Thar or **Great Indian Desert** covered by sand dunes is the Westernmost region of Great Indian Plains in the Western Rajasthan. A semi-arid plain, lying to the East of Thar desert is known as **Rajasthan Bagar**.

  The Luni is the only South-West flowing river of this region. The Sambhar (largest), Kuchaman and Didwana are important lakes situated to the North of Luni Basin.
- **Brahmaputra Plain** The low plains formed by the Brahmaputra river system is situated between Eastern Himalaya (Arunachal Pradesh) in the North, Patkai and Naga hills in the East, Garo-Khasi-Jaintia, Mikir hills, lower Ganga plain and Indo-Bangladesh border in the West.

Doab

It refers to a tract of land lying between two converging or confluent rivers. In the Western region of seven rivers, where Aryan settled first, the sequence of doabs from West to East are is Sindhu Sagar doab of Indus and Jhelum, Chhaj doab of Jhelum and Chenab, Rechna doab of Chenab and Ravi, Bari doab of Ravi and Beas, Bist doab of Beas and Sutlej.

3. The Peninsular Plateau

- It is part of an ancient landmass called **Gondwana land**. It covers an area of nearly 5,00,000 sq.km.
- It is spread over the states of Gujarat, Maharashtra, Bihar, Karnataka and Andhra Pradesh.

Narmada river divides the peninsular plateau into two parts

(i) The Central Highlands

- It extends from Narmada river and the Northern plains.
- Aravalli is an important mountain range which extends from Gujarat through Rajasthan to Delhi. The highest peak of the Aravalli hills is **Guru Shikhar** (1722m) near Mount Abu.
- The Malwa Plateau and Chhota Nagpur plateau are parts of the central highlands.
- The River Betwa, Chambal and Ken are the important rivers of Malwa plateau while Mahadeo, Kaimur and Maikal are the important hills of Chhota Nagpur plateau.
- The valley of Narmada lies between the Vindhyas and the Satpura which flows East to West and joins the Arabian sea.

(ii) The Deccan Plateau

- The Deccan plateau is separated by a fault (A fracture in the rock along which rocks have been relatively replaced), from Chhota Nagpur plateau.
- The black soil area in the Deccan plateau is known as **Deccan trap**.
- It is formed due to volcanic eruptions.This soil is good for cotton and sugarcane cultivation.
- The Deccan plateau is broadly divided into the Western and Eastern ghats.

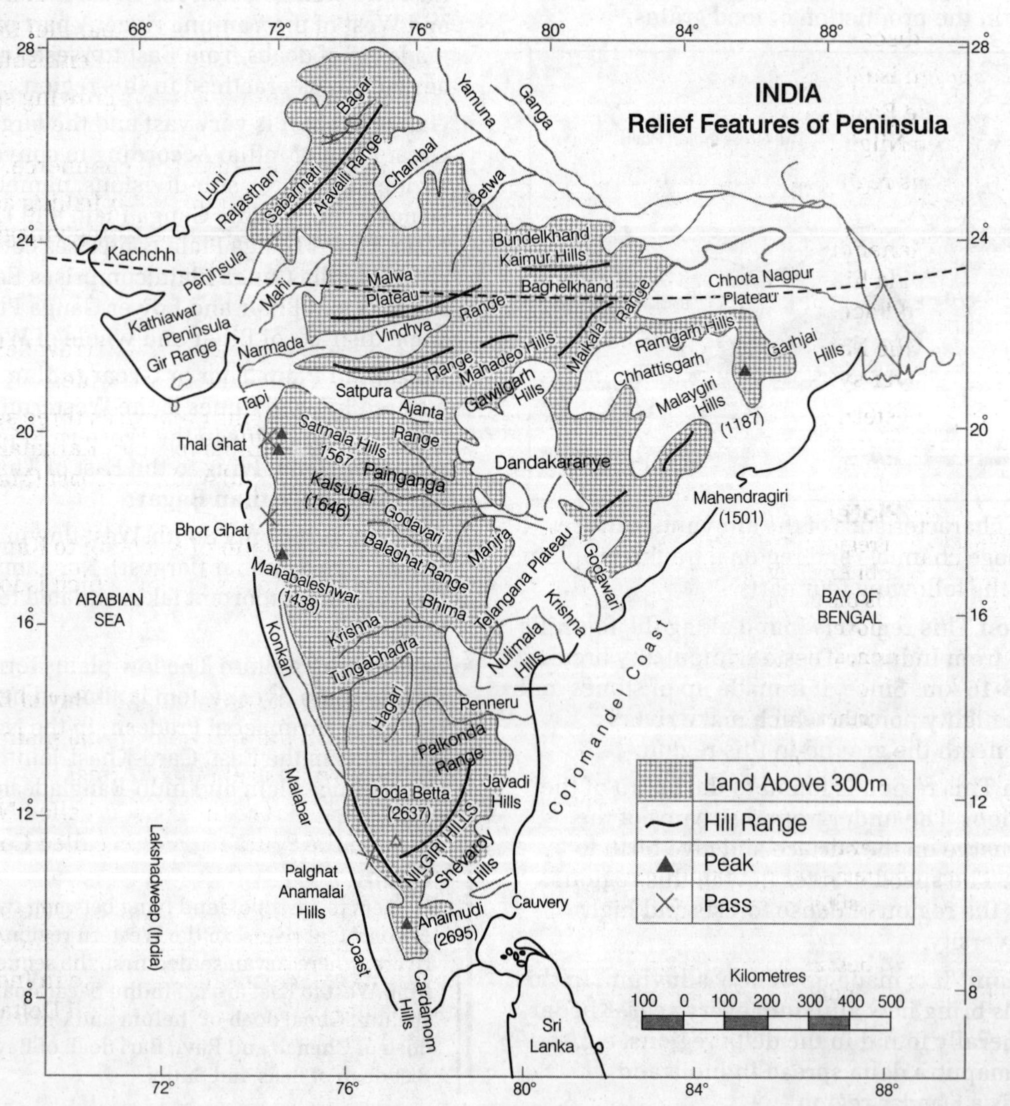

The Western Ghats

- The Western Ghats or Sahyadris lie on the Western edge of the Deccan plateau.
- It runs parallel to the Western coast for about 1600 km.
- The average elevation of the Western ghats is 1500 m.
- The famous peaks in this area are Dodabetta, Anaimudi and Makurti.
- The highest peak in this region is **Anaimudi (2695 m)**.
- Western ghats are continuous and can be crossed through passes like Pal ghat, Thal ghat and Bhor ghat.
- The rivers like Godavari, Bhima and Krishna flow Eastward while the river Tapti flows Westward.
- The streams form rapids and water falls before entering the Arabian sea.
- The famous waterfalls are Jog Falls on Sharavathi, Shiva Samudram falls on Cauvery, etc.

The Eastern Ghats

- The Eastern ghats are discontinuous low belts.
- Their average elevation is 600 m.
- They run parallel to the East coast from South of Mahanadi valley to the Nilgiri hills.
- The highest peak in this region is **Mahendragiri** (1501 m).
- The famous hills are Mahendragiri hills, Niyamgiri hills in Odisha, Nallamala hills in Southern Andhra Pradesh, Kollimalai and Pachaimalai in Tamil Nadu.
- The area is drained by the Mahanadi, Godavari, Krishna and Cauvery river systems.
- The Nilgiri hills join Western and Eastern Ghats in the South.

The North-Eastern Plateau

The North-Eastern plateau region consists of the Meghalaya plateau and Karbi Anglong plateau (Assam). It is believed that this region is the extension of the main peninsula. But, due to the movement of the Indian plate in the North-Eastward direction, at the time of Himalayan origin, they got detached.

The Meghalaya plateau is further divided into three

- The Garo hills,
- The Khasi hills
- The Jaintia hills

These names were given after the tribes living in those regions. The Meghalaya plateau is also rich in mineral resources like coal, iron-ore, sillimanite, uranium and limestone.

This region receives the highest amount of rainfall in comparison to other parts of India.

4. The Indian Desert

- The Indian Desert lies towards the Western margin of Aravalli hills.
- It is also called **Thar Desert**.
- It is a land of undulating topography dotted with longitudnal dunes and **barchans**.
- It is the **ninth largest desert** in the world. It spreads over the states of Gujarat and Rajasthan.
- This region has semi-arid and arid weather conditions. It receives less than 150 mm of rainfall per year.
- The vegetation cover is low with thorny bushes.
- **Luni** is the main river in this area.
- All other streams appear only at the time of rainfall otherwise they disappear into the sand.

5. The Coastal Plains

- The coastal plains in India run parallel to the Arabian sea and Bay of Bengal along the Peninsular plateau.
- The coastal plains are belts for growing spices, rice, coconut, pepper, etc.
- They are centres of trade and commerce.
- The coastal areas are known for fishing activities, therefore a large number of fishing villages have developed along the coasts.

Western Coast

- The Western coastal plain is a narrow belt along the Arabian sea of about 10-20 km wide.
- Western coastal plains comprises three sectors - Konkan Coast (Mumbai to Goa), Karnataka coast from Goa to Mangalore and Malabar Coast (Mangalore to Kanyakumari).
- It stretches from Rann of Kachchh to Kanyakumari.
- Vembanad is a famous lagoon which is located at Malabar coast.

Eastern Coast

- The Eastern coast runs along the Bay of Bengal.
- It is wider than the Western coastal plain.
- Its average width is about 120 kms.
- The Northern part of the coast is called **Northern Circar** and the Southern part is called **Coromandel Coast.**
- Eastern coastal plain is marked by Deltas made by the rivers Mahanadi, Godavari, Krishna and Cauvery.
- The **Chilika**, largest salt water lake in India in Odisha is located to the South of Mahanadi Delta.

6. The Islands

There are two major island groups in India – one in the Bay of Bengal and the other in the Arabian sea.

Bay of Bengal Island Group

- The Bay of Bengal island group consists of about 572 islands/islets.
- These are situated roughly between 6°-14°N and 92°-94°E.
- The two principal groups of islets include the Ritchie's archipelago and the Labyrinth Island.
- The entire group of islands is divided into two broad categories – the Andaman in the North and the Nicobar in the South.
- They are separated by a water body which is called the 10° channel.

Arabian Sea Island Group

- The islands of the Arabian Sea include Lakshadweep and Minicoy.
- These are scattered between 8°-12°N and 71°-74°E longitude.
- These islands are located at a distance of 280 km - 480 km off the Kerala coast. The entire island group is built of coral deposits.
- They cover an area of 32 sq. km. Kavaratti is the capital of Lakshadweep.
- There are approximately 36 islands, of which 11 are inhabited.
- Minicoy is the largest island with an area of 453 sq. km.
- The entire group of islands is broadly divided by the 11° channel, North of which is Amini island and to the South is Cannanore island.

Extra Facts From
Tamil Nadu Board and NIOS

- The area covered by Himalayan mountain system is about 5,00,000 square km.
- Kanchenjunga is the highest peak of Himalayas in India.
- Himachal (Lesser or middle Himalaya) The breadth of Himachal range is **60 to 80 km** and the height varies from 1000 m to 4500 m.
- The average height of the Shiwalik range is very low, about 600 m only.
- **Purvanchal** The average height of these hills from sea level is 500 to 3000 m.
- The area of Indian plain is more than 7,00,000 sq. km.
- **Central Highlands** The height of these hills is about 1500 m in South-West while near Delhi they are hardly 400 m high.

Drainage System of India

(SOURCES)

Class-IX New NCERT Chap 3 (Drainage),
Class-X New NCERT Chap 3 (Water Resources),
Class-XI New NCERT Chap 3 (Drainage System),
Class-XII Old NCERT Chap 2 (Relief and Drainage)

- **Drainage Pattern** refers to the system of flow of surface water mainly through the forms of rivers and basins.
- It refers to a design which a river and its tributaries form together from its source to its mouth. The drainage pattern of an area is the outcome of
  - the geological time period
  - nature and structure of rocks
  - amount of water flowing
  - the periodicity of the flow
  - topography
  - slope

Types of Drainage Pattern

As per the lie of channels, drainage systems can fall into one of several categories, known as drainage patterns. These depend on the topography and geology of the land.

- **Antecedent Drainage** The drainage pattern was already present before a period of uplift and folding that formed the present structure. As the uplift took place, the rivers were able to cut down at approximately the same rate and that's why maintained their courses. This process is called antecedence and the drainage system thus developed is called **antecedent drainage**.

  Many of the Himalayan rivers have antecedent origin i.e. these rivers existed even before the Himalayan ranges were uplifted.
- **Superimposed Drainage** The drainage pattern developed on rock strata that have since, been removed by erosion. The drainage pattern thus developed is called **superimposed drainage** (or Epigenetic or Superinduced Drainage). Its examples are the Damodar, Subarnarekha, Chambal, Banas.
- **Discordant Drainage** A pattern of drainage that bears no relation to the structure of the underlying rock.
- **Concordant Drainage** (also called accordant drainage) The pattern of drainage which arises from and closely follows the trends of the underlying strata is called concordant drainage.
- **Dendritic Drainage Pattern** It is the most common form and resembles the branching pattern of tree roots. The dendritic pattern develops where the river channel follows the slope of the terrain.

  The pattern develops in areas where the rock beneath the stream has no particular structure and can be eroded equally easily in all directions.

  Tributaries join larger streams at acute angles (less than 90°). Its examples are the rivers of the Northern plains; Indus, Ganga and Brahmaputra.
- **Parallel Drainage Pattern** It develops in regions of parallel, elongated landforms where there is a pronounced slope to the surface. Tributary streams tend to stretch out in a parallel-like pattern following the slope of the surface. e.g., the rivers originate in the Western ghats; Godavari, Cauvery, Krishna and Tungabhadra.
- **Trellis Drainage Pattern** Trellis drainage develops in folded topography where hard and soft rocks exist parallel to each other. Down-turned folds called **synclines** form valleys in which reside the main channel of the stream.

Such a pattern is formed when the primary tributaries of main rivers flow parallel to each other and secondary tributaries join them at right angles. e.g., the rivers in the upper part of the Himalayan region; Indus, Ganga and Brahmaputra.

- **Rectangular Drainage Pattern** The rectangular drainage pattern is found in regions that have undergone faulting. It develops on a strongly joined rocky terrain. Streams follow the path of least resistance and thus are concentrated in places where exposed rock is the weakest.

  The tributary streams make sharp bends and enter the main stream at high angles. e.g. Streams found in the Vindhya mountain range; Chambal, Betwa and Ken.
- **Radial Drainage Pattern** The radial drainage pattern develops around a central elevated point and is common to conically shaped features such as volcanoes.

  When the rivers originate from a hill and flow in all directions, the drainage pattern is known as **Radial**. e.g. the rivers originating from the Amarkantak range; Narmada and Son (tributary of Ganga).
- **Centripetal Drainage Pattern** It is just the opposite of the radial as streams flow toward a central depression. During rainy season, these streams feed ephemeral lakes, which evaporate away during dry periods. Sometimes, salt flats are also created in these dry lake beds as salt dissolved in the lake water precipitates out of solution and is left behind when the water evaporates away. e.g., Loktak lake in Manipur.

Basic Terminology related to Drainage System

- **Distributary** The small river that branches out from the main river and then never meets again. It thus decreases the river's water volume. Distributaries are commonly found on deltas but are also important in the formation of alluvial fans and cones.
- **Tributary** A stream or smaller river which joins a larger stream or river and thus increases its water volume.
- **Mouth** The point where the river comes to the end, usually when entering a sea.
- **River Basin** All the area drained by a river and its tributaries.
- **Catchment area** It refers to all the area of land over which rain falls and is caught to serve a river basin.
- **Watershed** As a water divide, it refers to an elevated line from where the water flows in different directions into different river basins.
- **River Profile** It refers to the cross-section of a river from its source to mouth representing the height of the river at various points.

Classification of Drainage Systems of India

- **Drainage Systems Based on the Size of the Catchment Area** On the basis of catchment area, rivers in India can be classified as follows

Division	Size of catchment area in sq km
Major river	20,000
Medium river	20,000 – 2,000
Minor river	2,000 and below

- **Drainage Systems Based on the Type of Drainage** The river systems of India can be classified into the following
  - Himalayan rivers, Deccan rivers and Coastal rivers that drain into the sea.
  - Rivers of the inland drainage basin (endorheic basin).
  - Streams like the Sambhar in Western Rajasthan are mainly seasonal in character, draining into the inland basins and salt lakes. In the **Rann of Kachchh**, the only river that flows through the salt desert is the Luni.
- **Drainage Systems Based on Orientation to the Sea** The Bay of Bengal drainage (Rivers that drain into Bay of Bengal), (East flowing rivers) Arabian sea drainage (Rivers that drain into Arabian sea), (West flowing rivers).

Difference between Bay of Bengal and Arabian Sea Drainage

Bay of Bengal Drainage	Arabian Sea Drainage
It includes rivers that drain into Bay of Bengal.	It includes rivers that drain into Arabian sea.
Its rivers are East flowing rivers.	Its rivers are West flowing rivers.
Its 77% of the drainage area of the country is oriented towards the Bay of Bengal.	Its 23% of the drainage area of the country is oriented towards the Arabian sea.
The Ganga, the Brahmaputra, the Mahanadi, the Godavari, the Krishna, the Cauvery, the Penneru, the Pannaiyar, the Vaigai, etc.	The Indus, the Narmada, the Tapi, the Sabarmati, the Mahi and the large number of swift flowing Western coast rivers descending from the Sahyadris.

The area covered by the Bay of Bengal drainage and Arabian Sea drainage are not proportional to the amount of water that drains through them. Over 90% of the water drains into the Bay of Bengal; The rest is drained into the Arabian sea or forms inland drainage.

- **Drainage Systems Based on Origin** The drainage systems of India are mainly controlled by the different relief features of the subcontinent. Accordingly, the Indian rivers are divided into two major groups
  - The Himalayan rivers
  - The Peninsular rivers

There is no clear-cut line of demarcation between these two drainage systems, as many of the peninsular rivers like the Chambal, Betwa, Sind, Ken and Son are much older in age and origin than the Himalayan rivers.

Drainage System of India

Drainage System of India can be classified into Himalayan and peninsular Drainage systems.

1. Himalayan Drainage System

- During the **Miocene** period, **Shiwalik** or **Indo-Brahma** river traversed the entire longitudinal extent of the Himalaya river Assam to Punjab and to Sind and finally it discharged into the Gulf of Sind near lower Punjab.
- The continuity of the Shiwalik and its alluvial deposits consisting of sands, silt, clay, boulders and conglomerates support this viewpoint. Himalayan rivers later got dismembered into three major systems.
- It mainly includes the Cranga, the Indus and the Brahmaputra river basins.
- These rivers form deep gorges and **v-shaped** valleys.
- This dismembered was probably due to the **Pleistocene upheaval** in the Western Himalayas, including the uplift of the **Potwar Plateau** (Delhi Ridge), which acted as the water divide between the Indus and Ganga drainage systems.
- These rivers form depositional features like flat valleys, **ox-bow** lakes, **flood** plains, etc., while entering the plain.
- During the **mid-Pleistocene period**, the down-thrusting of the **Malda gap** (Garo-Rajmahal Gap) area between the Rajmahal hills and the Meghalaya plateau diverted the Ganga and the Brahmaputra systems to flow towards the Bay of Bengal.

Indus River System

- It is one of the largest river basins of the world. It is also known as the **Sindhu** and is the Westernmost of the Himalayan rivers in India.
- It originates from a glacier near **Bokhar Chu** in the Tibetan region in the Kailash Mountain range and falls into Arabian **sea in Karachi.**
- In Tibet, it is known as **Singi Khamban** or Lion's mouth.

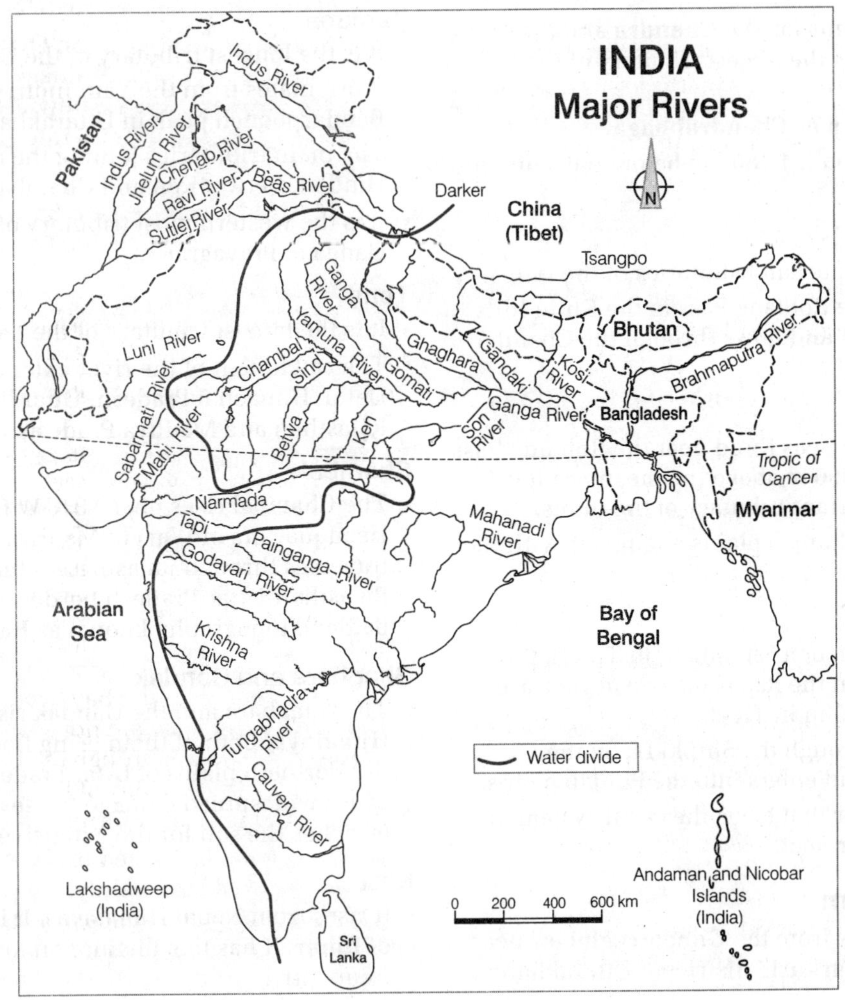

- It forms spectacular grorge near Gilgit in Jammu and Kashmir and cuts across the Ladakh range.
- The Indus flows in India only through the Leh district in the Union Territory of Ladakh.
- Its **right bank tributaries** are Shyok, Gilgit Hunza, Nubra, Kabul, Khurram, Tochi, Gomal, Sangar, Kunar.
- Its **left bank tributaries** are Zaskar, Sutlej, Beas, Ravi, Chenab and Jhelum.

Note *'Panjnad' joins Indus a little above Mithankot. The Panjnad is the name given to the five rivers of Punjab-Sutlej, Beas, Ravi, Chenab and Jhelum.*

Tributaries of Indus

Important tributaries of Indus are as follows

Jhelum

- The Jhelum, an important tributary of the Indus, rises from a spring at Verinag situated at the foot of the Pir Panjal.
- The Jhelum flows through Srinagar and the Wular lake before entering into Pakistan.
- Jhelum joins the Chenab near Jhang in Pakistan.

Chenab

- Formed by two streams i.e. the **Chandra** and the **Bhaga**, the Chenab is the largest tributary of the Indus.
- Chenab is also known as **Chandrabhaga**.
- The Chenab flows about 1,180 km before entering into Pakistan.

Ravi

- Ravi is one of the important tributaries of the Indus.
- It originates from the Rohtang Pass in the Kullu hills of Himachal Pradesh and flows through the Chamba valley of the state.

Beas

- Originating from the Beas Kund near the Rohtang Pass at an elevation of 4,000 m above the mean Sea level, Beas is also an important tributary of the Indus.
- Beas enters into the Punjab plains and meets with the Sutlej near Harike.

Sutlej

- Also popular as Langchen Khambab (in Tibet), the Sutlej originates from the Rakas lake near Mansarovar at an altitude of 4,555 m in Tibet.
- The Sutlej passes through the Shipki La on the Himalayan ranges and enters into the Punjab plains.
- The Sutlej is the river that feeds the canal system of the Bhakra Nangal project.

Ganga River System

- The Ganga originates from the **Gangotri glacier** near **Gaumukh** in the **Uttarkashi** district of Uttarakhand.
- However, the river, when it originates from the Gangotri glacier, is known as the **Bhagirathi**.
- At Devprayag, the Bhagirathi merges with another river, i.e., the **Alaknanda**; and from here, it is known as the **Ganga**.
- The Alaknanda originates from the **Satopanth glacier** above Badrinath. The Ganga enters the Northern plains at Haridwar. Ganga flows through the states of Uttarakhand, Uttar Pradesh, Bihar and West Bengal.
- Ganga flows into the Bay of Bengal near the Sagar island.
- Its flow is minimum during January to June and maximum during August-September. In Farakka, maximum average flow of Ganga is 55,000 cusec and minimum flow is 1,300 cusec.
- The total length of the Ganga in India is **2,525 km**, which is shared by Uttarakhand (110 km); Uttar Pradesh (1,450 km); Bihar (445 km); and West Bengal (520 km).
- The **Ganga river** system is the **largest river** system in India.

Tributaries of Ganga

Important tributaries of Ganga are as follows

Yamuna

- It is the longest tributary of the Ganga river.
- It originates from the Yamunotri glacier, at the Bandarpoonch peak in Uttarakhand.
- The main tributaries joining the river include the Sin, Hindon, Betwa, Ken and Chambal.
- It is the western most tributary of Ganga. It joins Ganga at Prayagraj.

Tons

- It is the largest tributary of the Yamuna.
- The catchment of the river extends to the states of Delhi, Himachal Pradesh, Uttar Pradesh, Haryana, Rajasthan and Madhya Pradesh.

Chambal

- The Chambal rises near MHOW (Military Headquarters of War) in Madhya Pradesh and traverses through Rajasthan to finally join Yamuna at Rajasthan-Uttar Pradesh border. It is famous for its badland topography known as **Ravines**.

Ghaghara and Gandak

- The Ghaghara and the Gandak rise in the **Nepal Himalaya**. Both of them bring floods to the parts of the Northern plains of Uttar Pradesh every year. They cause widespread damage to life and property but enriches the soil for the extensive agricultural lands.

Kosi

- It rises from Nepal Himalayas. It is known as **Sorrow of Bihar**. It has this distinction for changing its path frequently.

- It brings huge amount of sediments and as it reaches the Bihar plains. These sediments get deposited blocking the path of the river and consequently, it changes course.

Mahananda

- It is another tributary of the Ganga rising in the Darjeeling hills.

Son

- A large bank tributary Son originates from the radial drainage site of Amarkantak plateau. After forming a series of waterfalls, it joins Ganga at Arrah in Bihar.

Ramganga

- It rises in **Kumaon Himalayas** near Nainital. Its total length is 696 km. It joins the left bank of Ganga near Farukkhabad.

Sharda or Saryu

- It originates from **Milap Glacier** of Nepal Himalayas as **Gauriganga**. In India, it is known by the name of **Kali** river and joins Ghaghara river.

Panch Prayag

- **Vishnuprayag** It is a place where the river Alaknanda meets river Dhauli Ganga.
- **Nandprayag** It is a place where river Alaknanda meets river Mandakini.
- **Karnaprayag** It is a place where river Alaknanda meets river Pindar.
- **Rudraprayag** It is a place where river Alaknanda meets river Mandakini.
- **Devprayag** It is a place where river Alaknanda meets river Bhagirathi.

Brahmaputra River System

- The Brahmaputra originates from the **Chemayungdung** glacier of the Kailash range near the Mansarovar.
- In Tibet, the Brahmaputra is known as the **Tsangpo** (means 'the purifier'). The river emerges from the foothills of Himalayas under the name of Siang or Dihang.
- The **Rango Tsangpo** is the major right bank tributary of the Brahmaputra in Tibet.
- The Brahmaputra enters into India near the West of Sadiya town in Arunachal Pradesh.
- Major **left bank tributaries** of the Brahmaputra are Lohit, Dibang or Sikang, Burhi Dihing and Dhansari.
- Major **right bank tributaries** of the Brahmaputra are the Subansiri, Kameng, Manas and Sankosh.
- The Teesta joins the Brahmaputra on its right bank in Bangladesh and from here, the river is known as the Yamuna.
- It is one of the largest rivers of the world and has its origin in the **Chemayungdung glacier** (Kailash range) near the Mansarovar lake.
- In Bangladesh, it merges with the river **Padma**, which falls in the Bay of Bengal.

2. Peninsular Drainage System

- Geologists believe that the Sahyadri-Aravali axis was the main water divide in the past.
- According to one hypothesis, the existing peninsula is the remaining half of a bigger landmass.
- The Western ghats were located in the middle of this landmass. So, one drainage was towards East flowing into Bay of Bengal and the other towards West draining into Arabian sea.
- The Western part of the Peninsula cracked and submerged in the Arabian sea during the early Tertiary period (coinciding with the formation of Himalayas).
- During the collision of the Indian plate, the Peninsular block was subjected to subsidence in few regions creating a series of rifts (trough, faults).
- The peninsular rivers are characterised by fixed course, absence of meanders and non-perennial flow of water.
- There is lack of alluvial and deltaic deposits.
- The drainage system is older than the Himalayan one.
- The Western ghats running close to the Western coast act as the water divide between the major Peninsular rivers.
- Most of the major Peninsular rivers except Narmada and Tapi flow from West to East.
- The other major river systems of the Peninsular drainage are Mahanadi, Godavari, Krishna and Cauvery.

Narmada River System

- The Narmada is a river located in Central India.
- It rises to the summit of the Amarkantak hill in Madhya Pradesh state.
- It outlines the traditional frontier between North India and South India.
- It is one of the major rivers of peninsular India. Only the Narmada, the Tapti and the Mahi rivers flow from East to West.
- Since, the river flows through a narrow valley confined by precipitous (dangerously high or steep) hills, it does not have many tributaries.
- The absence of tributaries is especially noted on the right bank of the river where the Hiran is the only exception.

- The other **right bank tributaries** are the Orsang, the Barna and the Kolar.
- The river flows through the states of Madhya Pradesh, Gujarat and Maharashtra.
- Its flow is minimum during January to July but maximum in the month of August. It drains into the Arabian sea in the Bharuch district of Gujarat.

Tapi River System

- It is a Central Indian River. It is one of the most important rivers of peninsular India with the run from East to West. It originates in the Eastern Satpura Range of Southern Madhya Pradesh state.
- It flows in a Westward direction. It drains historic places like Madhya Pradesh's Nimar region, East Vidarbha region and Maharashtra's Khandesh region and South Gujarat before falling into the Gulf of Cambay of the Arabian sea.
- The River Basin of **Tapi River** lies mostly in Eastern and Northern districts of Maharashtra state.
- The river also covers some districts of Madhya Pradesh and Gujarat as well.
- Its **right bank tributaries** are the Suki, the Gomai, the Arunavati and the Aner.
- Its **left bank tributaries** are the Vaghur, Amravati, Buray, Panjhra, Bori, Girna, Purna, Mona and Sipna.

Godavari River System

- The Godavari river is the second-longest course in India with brownish water.
- It is largest peninsular river system. Its length is about 1500km.
- The river is often referred to as the **Dakshin** (South) **Ganga** or **Vridha Ganga.**
- It is a seasonal river, dried during the summers and widens during the monsoons.
- This river originates from Trimbakeshwar, near Nasik in Maharashtra.
- It flows South-East across South-Central India through the states of Madhya Pradesh, Telangana, Andhra Pradesh and Odisha and drains into the Bay of Bengal.
- The river forms a fertile delta at **Rajamahendravaram.**
- The banks of this river have many pilgrimage sites, Nasik(MH), Bhadrachalam(TS), and Trimbak. Some of its tributaries include Pranahita (Combination of Penuganga and Warda), Indravati river, Bindusara, Sabari and Manjira.
- Asia's third longest rail-cum-road bridge (RCRB) which links **Kovvur** and **Rajamahendravaram** is located on the River **Godavari**.
- Godavari's flow is minimum in May and maximum in July-August.
- Its **left bank tributaries** are Dharna, Penganga, Wainganga, Wardha, Pranahita [conveying the combined waters of Penganga, the Wardha and Wainganga], Pench, Kanhan, Sabari, Indravati, etc.
- Its right bank tributaries are Pravara, Mula, Manjra, Peddavagu, Maner.

Krishna River System

- Krishna is one of the longest rivers of India, which originates from Mahabaleshwar in Maharashtra.
- It is the second largest East flowing peninsular river.
- It flows through Sangli and drains the sea in the Bay of Bengal.
- The river flows through the states of Maharashtra, Karnataka, Telangana and Andhra Pradesh.
- Its **right bank tributaries** are the Ghatprabha, the Malprabha and the Tungabhadra.
- Its **left bank tributaries** are the Bhima, the Musi and the Munneru.

Cauvery River System

- The Cauvery is also known as Ganga of South India **Dakshin Bharat ki Ganga.**
- It originates from **Talakaveri** located in the Western ghats. It is a famous pilgrimage and tourist place in the Kodagu district of Karnataka.
- The headwaters of the river are in the Western ghats range of Karnataka state and from Karnataka through Tamil Nadu.
- The river drains into the Bay of Bengal. The river supports irrigation for agriculture and is considered as a means of support of the ancient kingdoms and Modern cities of South India.
- Its **left bank tributaries** the Harangi, the Hemavati, the Shimsha and the Arkavati.
- Its **right bank tributaries** Lakshmantirtha, the Kabbani, the Suvarnavati, the Bhavani, the Noyil and the Amaravati join from right.
- The River Cauvery makes second biggest waterfall in India, known as Shivanasamudra falls.

The Mahanadi River System

- The Mahanadi originates from the Satpura range of central India and it is a river in Eastern India.
- It flows East to the Bay of Bengal. The river drains the state of Maharashtra, Chhattisgarh, Jharkhand and Odisha.
- The largest dam, the **Hirakud Dam**, is built on the river.
- Its **left bank tributaries** are the Seonath, the Hasdeo, the Mand and the Ib.
- Its **right bank tributaries** are the Ong, the Tel and the Jonk.

Percentage Contribution of Water by Various Rivers

- Brahmaputra - 40
- Ganga -25
- Godavari - 6.4
- Mahanadi - 3.5
- Krishna - 3.4
- Narmada - 2.9
- Rest - 20

West Flowing Small Rivers

- **Mahi** The river originates from Dhar district of Madhya Pradesh. The river flows through Madhya Pradesh, Rajasthan and Gujarat. The river drains in the Gulf of Cambay. Mahi Bajaj Sagar Dam and Kadana Dam are the major Hydro Power stations situated on this river.
- **Sabarmati River** Sabarmati river is a combination of two streams the Sabar and Hathmati. The river is flowing through Rajasthan and Gujarat. It originates from **Tepur** in the **Udaipur** district of Rajasthan. The **Wakal**, the **Hathmati**, the **Vatrak** and the **Sei** are the major tributaries of Sabarmati river.

  Sabarmati reservoir, Hathmati reservoir and Meshwo reservoir project are the major projects situated on this river.
- **Luni** Luni is an endorheic river. It is also known as the **Sagarmati**. It originates from the Western slopes of the Aravalli ranges near Ajmer.
- **Tawa River** The river rises from the Satpura Range of Betul in Madhya Pradesh. This river is the longest tributary of River Narmada.
- **Sharavati River** This is an important river in the state of Karnataka flowing towards the West.

  The Sharavati River originates from the **Shimoga** district of **Karnataka**. The river drains a catchment area of 2,209 sq. km. The Jog falls is created by the Sharavati river.

East Flowing Small Rivers

- **Pennar River** The Pennar river (also known as Uttara Pinakini) is one of the major rivers of the peninsula. The Pennar rises in the Chennakesava hill of the Nandidurga range, in Chikkaballapura district of Karnataka and flows towards East eventually draining into the Bay of Bengal.
- **Subarnarekha River** The Subarnarekha river originates from the Ranchi Plateau in Jharkhand forming the boundary between West Bengal and Odisha in its lower course. It joins Bay of Bengal forming an estuary between the Ganga and Mahanadi deltas. Its total length is 395 km.
- **Brahmani River** The Brahmani river comes into existence by the confluence of the Koel and the Shankh rivers near Rourkela.

  It has a total length of 800 km. The basin is bounded in the North by Chhota Nagpur plateau, in the West and South by the Mahanadi basin and in the East by the Bay of Bengal. The basin flows through Jharkhand, Chhattisgarh and Odisha States and drains into Bay of Bengal.
- **Ponnaiyar River** The Ponnaiyar river is a small stream which is confined to the coastal area only. It covers a small area in the state of Tamil Nadu, Karnataka and Andhra Pradesh.

  The Basin is bounded on the North -West and South by various ranges of the Eastern ghats like the Velikonda Range, the Nagari hills, the Javadi hills, the Shevaroy hills, the Chitteri hills and the Kalrayan hills and in the East by the Bay of Bengal.
- **Vaigai River** South of the Cauvery delta, there are several streams, of which the Vaigai is the longest. The Vaigai basin is an important basin among the 12 basins lying between the Cauvery and Kanyakumari.

  This basin is bounded by the Varusanadu hills, the Andipatti hills, the Cardamom hills and the Palani hills on the West and by the Palk strait and Palk Bay on the East. The Vaigai drains an area of 7,741 Sq. km, which entirely lies in the state of Tamil Nadu.

Difference between Himalayan and Peninsular River System

Characteristics	Himalayan River	Peninsular River
Place of origin	Himalayan mountains (covered with glaciers).	Peninsular plateau and central highland.
Nature of flow	Perennial; receive water from glaciers and rainfall.	Seasonal; dependent on monsoon rainfall.
Type of drainage	Antecedent and consequent leading to dendritic pattern in plains.	Superimposed, rejuvenated resulting in trellis, radial and rectangular patterns.
Nature of river	Long course, flowing through the rugged mountains experiencing headward erosion and river capturing; In plains, meandering and shifting off course.	Smaller, fixed course with well adjusted valleys.
Catchment area	Very large basin.	Relatively smaller basin.
Age of the river	Young and youthful, active and deepening in the valleys	Old rivers with graded profile and have almost reached their base levels.

River Basin and their Area

Basin Code	Basin Name	Area (sq.km)
1.	Indus (Up to border)	3,21,289
2. A	Ganga	8,61,452
2. B	Brahmaputra	1,94,413
2. C	Barak and others	41,723
3.	Godavari	3,12,812
4.	Krishna	2,58,948
5.	Cauvery	81,155
6.	Subarnarekha	29,196
7.	Brahmani and Baitarani	51,822
8.	Mahanadi	1,41,589
9.	Pennar	55,213
10.	Mahi	34,842
11.	Sabarmati	21,674
12.	Narmada	98,796
13.	Tapi (Tapti)	65,145
14.	West flowing rivers from Tapi to Tadri	55,940
15.	West flowing rivers from Tadri to Kanyakumari	56,177
16.	East flowing rivers between Mahanadi and Pennar	86,643
17.	East flowing rivers between Pennar and Kanyakumari	1,00,139
18.	West flowing rivers of Kachchh and Saurashtra including Luni	3,21,851
19.	Area of inland drainage in Rajasthan	
20.	Minor rivers draining into Myanmar and Bangladesh	36,202

List of Major Waterfalls in India

Name	Location
Talakona Falls	Andhra Pradesh (Tirupati)
Tirathgarh Falls	Chhattisgarh (Mugabahar river)
Bundla Falls	Himachal Pradesh (Bundla stream)
Chulia Falls	Rajasthan (Chambal river)
Hundru Falls	Jharkhand (Subarnarekha river)
Lodh Falls	Jharkhand (Burha river)
Dasam Falls	Jharkhand (Subarnarekha river)
Dudhsagar Falls	Goa (Mandovi river)
Barkana Falls	Karnataka (Sita river)
Unchalli Falls	Karnataka (Aghanashini river)
Gokak Falls	Karnataka (Ghataprabha river)
Gersoppa (Jog) Falls (Highest)	Karnataka (Sharavathi river)
Shivanasmudra Falls	Karnataka (Cauvery river)
Palaruvi Falls	Kerala
Chachai Falls	Madhya Pradesh (Bihad river)
Rajat Prapat Falls	Madhya Pradesh (Pachmarhi river)
Dhuandhar (Marble) Falls	Madhya Pradesh (Narmada river)
Kune Falls	Maharashtra
Nohkalikai Falls	Meghalaya
Elephant Falls	Meghalaya
Vantawng Falls	Mizoram (Lau river)
Barehipani Falls	Odisha (Budhabalanga river-Simlipal National Park)
Khandadhar Falls	Odisha (Kaprani stream)
Catherine Falls	Tamil Nadu
Kutralam Falls	Tamil Nadu (Siruvani river)
Thalaiyar Falls	Tamil Nadu (near Kodaikanal)
Birthi Falls	Uttarakhand (Pancholi peak)
Vasudhara Falls	Uttarakhand (near Badrinath)
Kapildhara Falls	Madhya Pradesh (Narmada river)

Lakes

- A lake is defined as an area of variable size filled with water, localised in a basin, that is surrounded by land, apart from any other river or outlet surrounded by the lake.
- They lie on land and not part of the ocean and are usually bigger than ponds. They have still water.
- They can be broadly split into two, natural lakes and artificial lakes.

Natural Lakes

- They are generally found in mountainous areas and rift zones. They form due to a number of processes like
  - A tectonic movement of mountain range
  - Landslides or global leakages
  - Spits and bars form lagoons

Artificial Lakes

- They are constructed or man-made, for industrial or agricultural purposes.
- It is also used for irrigation, hydro power supply, domestic water supply and so on. Lakes can be further classified into the following
  - Freshwater Lakes
  - Saltwater Lakes
  - Natural Lakes
  - Oxbow Lakes
  - Artificial Lakes
  - Crater Lakes

Some Important Facts about Lakes

- Wular lake one of the biggest freshwater lakes of Asia.
- Upper lake in Madhya Pradesh is the largest artificial lake in Asia.
- Chilika lake in Odisha is the largest saline water lake in India.
- Vembanad lake in Kerala is the longest lake in India.
- Cholamu lake in Sikkim is the highest lake in India.

Important Lakes in India

Name	State/UT	Type	Details
Pulicat Lake	Andhra Pradesh	Brackish Water	It encompasses Pulicat Lake Bird Sanctuary; Satish Dhawan Space Centre is located here
Kolleru Lake	Andhra Pradesh	Freshwater	Home to migratory birds
Nagarjuna Sagar	Andhra Pradesh	Freshwater	Artificially constructed, Krishna river
Haflong Lake	Assam	Freshwater	High altitude lake
Deepor Beel	Assam	Freshwater	Under Ramsar Convention
Kanwar Lake	Bihar	Oxbow (freshwater)	Asia's largest freshwater oxbow lake
Hamirsar Lake	Gujarat	Artificial	Situated in centre of Bhuj
Blue Bird Lake	Haryana	Freshwater	Migratory Birds, Wetland Habitat
Chandra Taal	Himachal Pradesh	Fresh water	Ramsar wetland site
Suraj Taal	Himachal Pradesh	Fresh water	Bhaga River inflow
Maharana Pratap Sagar	Himachal Pradesh	Freshwater	Ramsar site
Prashar Lake	Himachal Pradesh	Holomitic	It has a floating Island
Renuka lake	Himachal Pradesh	Freshwater	It is designated as the Ramsar site
Dal Lake	Jammu and Kashmir	Warm monomitic	Remnants of past glacial period
Pangong Tso	Ladakh	Endorheic Lake (saline water)	Indo-China Border
Wular Lake	Jammu and Kashmir	Tectonic Lake (fresh water)	Largest freshwater lake in India
Tso Moriri	Ladakh	Saltwater	High altitude lake
Bellandur Lake	Karnataka	Freshwater	–
Ashtamudi Kayal	Kerala	Brackish water	Ramsar wetland site
Kuttanad	Kerala		Backwater paddy cultivation
Vembanad	Kerala	Brackish water	Ramsar wetland, boat race
Sasthamkotta	Kerala	Freshwater	Ramsar wetland
Bhojtal	Madhya Pradesh	Freshwater	Ramsar site; largest artificial lake in India
Salim Ali	Maharashtra	Freshwater	Birdwatching
Shivsagar	Maharashtra	Freshwater	Koyna dam
Lonar Lake	Maharashtra	Crater lake	National Geo-Heritage monument
Loktak lake	Manipur	Lenticular freshwater	Ramsar wetland; Phumdis (Floating Islands); Multipurpose project
Chilika Lake	Odisha	Brackish water	India's largest brackish water lake; lagoon
Harike	Punjab	Freshwater	Ramsar wetland site
Rupar	Punjab	Freshwater	Manmade riverine lake
Kanjli	Punjab	Freshwater	Ramsar wetland site
Sambhar Lake	Rajasthan	Saltwater	Ramsar wetland; largest inland saltwater lake in India
Rajsamand	Rajasthan	Freshwater	–
Kodaikanal Lake	Tamil Nadu	Artificial lake	Boat club, boathouse, and boat service
Govind Ballabh Pant Sagar	Uttar Pradesh	Man-made lake	Rihand dam
Bhimtal	Uttarakhand	Freshwater	Medium altitude lake
East Calcutta Wetlands	West Bengal	Brackish water	Ramsar wetland

Extra Facts From Tamil Nadu Board and NIOS

- Length of Indus river is about 2,880 km (Only 1,114 km is in India).
- The Ganga river system is the largest drainage system of India. It extends over an area of 8,61,404 sq km.
- The length of Brahmaputra river is about 2,900 km (900 km in India).
- It enters into India through a gorge in Arunachal Pradesh namely Dihang.
- Tapti river rises near Multai tank in the Betul district of Madhya Pradesh at an elevation of about 752 m.
- Narmada, Tapti, Mahi and Sabarmati rivers confluence with the Arabian sea.
- Mahanadi, Godavari, Krishna and Cauvery are the major East flowing rivers and drain into Bay of Bengal.

19

Climate in India

[SOURCES]

Class-IX New NCERT Chap 4 (Climate),
Class-X Old NCERT Chap 2 (Climate),
Class-XI New NCERT Chap 4 (Climate)

- **Climate** is a measure of the average pattern of variation in temperature, humidity, atmospheric pressure, wind, precipitation, atmospheric particle count and other meteorological variables in a given region over long periods of time.
- Any independent study of each of these elements does not put forward any comprehensive view of climate. On the basis of these elements, there could be many types of climates in the world.

Climate and Weather

- Weather consists of the short-term (minutes to months) changes in the atmosphere while climate is the average of weather over an extended time.
- In most places, weather can change from minute-to-minute, hour-to-hour, day-to-day and season-to-season.
- However, climate, is the average of weather over an extended time.

Climate of India

- The climate of India belongs to the 'tropical monsoon type' indicating the impact of its location in the tropical belt and the monsoon winds.
- Huge part of the country lies North of the Tropic of Cancer and thus, falls in the Northern temperate zone.
- The presence of the Himalayas and the Indian ocean in the South play a significant role in providing India a distinctive climatic characteristics.

Salient Features of Indian Climate

Following are the salient features of the Indian climate

- **Reversal of Winds** The Indian climate is characterised by the complete reversal of wind systems with the change of season in a year.During the winter season, winds generally blow from North-East to South-West in the direction of trade winds. These winds are dry and devoid of moisture. They are characterised by low temperature and high pressure conditions over the country. During summer season, complete reversal in the direction of the winds is observed and these blow primarily from South-West to North-East.
- **Formation of alternatively high and low pressure areas over the land** There is a change in the atmosphere pressure conditions with the change of season. During the winter season, due to low temperature conditions, high pressure areas are formed over the Northern part of the country. On the other hand, the intense heating of the land during summer season leads to the formation of a thermally induced low pressure cell over the North-Western part of the country. These pressure areas control the direction and intensity of wind.
- **Seasonal and Variable Rainfall** In India, over 80% of annual rainfall is obtained in the latter part of the summer whose duration ranges from 1-5 months in different parts of the country. Since, the rainfall is in the form of heavy downpour, it creates problems of floods and soil erosion. Sometimes there is continuous rain for many days and sometimes, there is a long spell of dry period.

Similarly, there is a spatial variation in the general distribution of rainfall. **Mawsynram** has received in a single day an amount equal to 10 years of rainfall at **Jaisalmer**, Rajasthan. The Indian climate is characterised by climatic extremes and varieties.

- **Plurality of seasons** The Indian climate is characterised by constantly changing weather conditions. There are three main seasons but on broader consideration. But their number goes to a six year (winter, fall of winter, spring, summer, rainy and autumn).
- **Unity of Indian Climate** The Himalayas and the associated mountain ranges extend to the North of India from East to West. These tall mountain ranges prevent the cold northerly winds of Central Asia from entering into India.

  Therefore, even the parts of India extending North of the Tropic of Cancer experience a tropical climate. Due to this the entire country comes under the influence of the monsoon winds. In this manner, the climate in the entire country becomes monsoon type.
- **Diversity of Indian Climate** In spite of the unity of Indian climate, it is characterised by regional differences and variations. For example, while in the summer, the mercury occasionally touches 55°C in the Western Rajasthan, it drops down to as low or minus 45°C in winter around Leh.

  These differences are visible in terms of winds, temperature, rainfall, humidity and aridity, etc.

  These are caused by differences in the location, altitude, distance from the sea, distance from mountains and general relief conditions at different places.
- **Characterised by Natural Calamities** Due to its peculiar weather conditions especially rainfall, the Indian climate is characterised by natural calamities like floods, droughts, famines and even epidemics.

Factors Determining the Climate of India

- India's climate is controlled by a number of factors which can be broadly divided into two groups
  - Factors related to location and relief
  - Factors related to air pressure and winds

Factors Related to Location and Relief

Factors related to location and relief are as follows

Latitude

- The Tropic of Cancer passes through the central part of India in East-West direction.
- Thus, the Northern part of India lies in a sub-tropical and temperate zone and the part lying South of the Tropic of Cancer falls in the tropical zone.
- The tropical zone being nearer to the equator, experiences high temperatures throughout the year with small daily and annual range.
- Areas which are North of the Tropic of Cancer experience extreme climate with a high daily and annual range of temperature as they are away from the Equator.

Himalayan Mountains

- The lofty Himalayas in the North along with its extensions act as an effective climatic divide between Central Asia and the Indian sub-continent.
- The cold and chilly winds that originates near the **Arctic Circle** are obstructed by the Himalayas and give a distinctive taste to the climate of India.

Distribution of Land and Water

- India is surrounded by the Indian ocean on three sides in the South and girdled by a high and continuous mountain-wall in the North.
- As compared to the landmass, water heats up or cools down slowly. This differential heating of land and sea creates different air pressure zones in different seasons in and around the Indian sub-continent.

Distances from the Sea

- With a long coastline, large coastal areas have an equable climate. Areas in the interior of India are far away from the moderating influence of the sea. Such areas have extremes of climate.
- That is why, the people of the **Konkan coast** have hardly any idea of extremes of temperature and the seasonal rhythm of weather.
- On the other hand, the seasonal contrasts in weather at places in the interior of the country such as **Kanpur** and **Amritsar** affect the entire sphere of life.

Altitude

- Temperature decreases with height. Due to thin air, places in the mountains are cooler than places on the plains.
- For example, Agra and Darjeeling are located on the same latitude, but the temperature of Agra in January is 16°C, whereas it is only 4°C in Darjeeling.

Relief

- The physiography or relief of India also affects the temperature, air pressure, direction and speed of wind and the amount and distribution of rainfall.
- The windward sides of Western ghats and Assam receive high rainfall during June-September whereas the Southern plateau remains dry due to its leeward situation along the Western ghats.

Factors Relating to Air Pressure and Winds

The mechanism of air pressure and wind in context of the Indian climate, can be understood with reference to winter and summer seasons of the year separately.

Weather Conditions in Winter Season

Weather conditions in winter season are as follows

Surface Pressure and Winds

- During the Northern hemisphere's winter, high pressure is built up in Central and West Asia.
- This centre of high pressure gives rise to the flow of air at the low level from the North towards the Indian sub-continent, South of the Himalayan mountain range, in the form of a dry continental air mass. These continental winds come in contact with trade winds over North-Western India.
- The contact zone is not stable and sometimes it shifts up to the middle Ganga valley thus bringing the entire North-Western India under the influence of the North-Westerly winds.

Jet Stream and Upper Air Circulation

- A different pattern of air circulation is observed at a height of about 3 km above the surface. Direction and velocity of winds at this height are different from those of the surface winds.
- All of the Western and Central Asia remains under the influence of westerly **winds along the altitude** of 9-13 km from West to East.
- These winds blow across the Asian continent at latitudes North of the Himalayas roughly parallel to the Tibetan highlands. These are known as **Jet Streams**.
- Tibetan highlands act as a barrier in the path of these jet streams. As a result, jet streams get bifurcated – one to the South and other to the North of this mountain chain along 25° N latitude.
- This jet stream is responsible for bringing Western disturbances from the Mediterranean region into the Indian sub-continent.
- Winter rain and hail storms in North-Western plains and occasional heavy snowfall in hilly regions are caused by these disturbances.

Western Cyclonic Disturbance and Tropical Cyclones

- The Western cyclonic disturbances which enter the Indian sub-continent from the West and the North-West during the winter months originate over the Mediterranean sea and are brought into India by the westerly jet stream.
- An increase in the prevailing night temperature generally indicates an advance in the arrival of these cyclone disturbances. It brings little rain in winter months.
- This rain is considered to be a very good for wheat crops in Northern plains.
- Tropical cyclones originate over the Bay of Bengal and the Indian ocean. These tropical cyclones have very high wind velocity and heavy rainfall and hit the Tamil Nadu, Andhra Pradesh and Odisha coast. Most of these cyclones are very destructive due to high wind velocity and torrential rain that accompanies it.

Weather Conditions in the Summer reason

Weather conditions in summer season are as follows

Surface Pressure and Winds

- As the summer sets in the Sun shifts Northward, the wind circulation over the sub-continent undergoes a complete reversal at both, the lower as well as the upper levels.
- By the middle of July, the low pressure belt nearer the surface, termed **Inter Tropical Convergence Zone** (ITCZ), shifts Northwards, roughly parallel to the Himalayas between 20° N and 25° N. It extends from Punjab to the Chhotanagpur plateau.
- By this time, the westerly jet stream withdraws from the Indian region. There is a cause and effect relationship between the Northward shift of the ITCZ and the withdrawal of the westerly jet stream from over the North Indian Plain.
- Being an area of low pressure, the ITCZ attracts winds from all around. The **maritime tropical air mass** (mT) from the Southern hemisphere, after crossing the Equator, rushes to the low pressure area in the South-West direction.
- These winds cross the Equator between 40°E and 60°E longitudes. Blowing over the ocean for a long distance, they pick up a large amount of moisture. It is this moist air current which is popularly known as the **South-West monsoon.**

Jet Streams and Upper Air Circulation

- At the upper layers of the troposphere, the winds blow in a direction reverse to that of the surface winds.
- An **easterly jet stream** flows over the Southern part of the Peninsula in June and has a maximum speed of 90 km per hour. In August, it is confined to 15° N latitude and in September up to 22° N latitudes.

Tropical Cyclones

- The easterly jet stream steers the tropical depressions into India. These depressions play a significant role in the distribution of monsoon rainfall over the Indian sub-continent.
- The tracks of these depressions are the areas of highest rainfall in India. Their frequency, direction and intensity determine the rainfall pattern during the South-West monsoon period.

Inter Tropical Convergence Zone (ITCZ)

- It is a zone between the Northern and Southern hemisphere where winds blowing equator-ward from the mid-latitudes and winds flowing poleward from the tropics meet.
- It shifts from North and South seasonally according to the movement of the Sun.
- For example, when the ITCZ is shifted to North of the Equator, the South-East trade wind changes to a South-West wind as it crosses the Equator.
- The ITCZ shifts only between 40° to 45° of latitude North or South of the equator based on the pattern of land and ocean.

Indian Monsoon

- India's climate is 'tropical monsoon' type. The word 'monsoon' has been derived from the Arabic word '*Mausim*' which means 'season'.
- Originally, this word was used by Arab traders to describe a system of seasonal reversal of winds along the shores of the Indian ocean.
- Monsoons are especially prominent within the tropics on the Eastern sides of the great landmass, but in Asia, it occurs outside the tropics in China, Korea and Japan.
- Monsoon is a complex meteorological phenomenon. Experts of meteorology have developed a number of concepts about the origin of the monsoon.
- Some of the important concepts about the origin of monsoon have been given as follows

Thermal Concept

- **Halley**, a noted astronomer in 1866 hypothesised that the primary cause of the annual cycle of the Indian monsoon circulation was the differential heating effects of the land and the sea.
- According to this concept, monsoons are the extended land breeze and sea breeze on a large scale.
- During winter, the huge landmass of Asia cools more rapidly than the surrounding oceans with the result that a strong high pressure centre develops over the continent.
- On the other hand, the pressure over adjacent oceans is relatively lower. As a consequence, the pressure-gradient is directed from land to sea.
- Therefore, there is an outflow of air from the continental landmass towards the adjacent oceans so that it brings cold, dry air towards the low latitudes.
- In summer, the temperature and pressure conditions are reversed.
- Halley's concept is criticised because it fails to explain the intricacies of monsoon such as sudden burst of monsoon, breaks in monsoon, spatial and temporal distribution of monsoon.
- Also, the low pressure areas are not stationary and the rainfall is not only convectional but a mix of orographic, cyclonic and convectional rainfall.

Dynamic Concept

- The Dynamic concept about the origin of monsoons was put forward by a German meteorologist **Flohn** in 1951. According to this concept, monsoon is the result of seasonal migration of planetary winds and pressure belts.
- The **equatorial Westerlies** become South-West or summer monsoons. As the Earth rotates, the trade winds of the Southern hemisphere after crossing the equator turn towards their right (Coriolis effect).
- The Northern Inter-Tropical Convergence Zone (NITCZ) is associated with numerous atmospheric storms (cyclones), which yield heavy rainfall during wet monsoon months (July to September).

Modern Concept about the Origin of Indian Monsoon

After World War II, the upper atmospheric circulation has been studied significantly. It is now believed that the differential heating of sea and land alone can't produce the monsoon circulation. Apart from it, the recent concept of monsoon relies heavily on the role of

- Himalayas and Tibetan plateau as a physical barrier and a source of high-level heat.
- Circulation of upper air jet streams in the troposphere.
- Existence of upper air circum-polar whirl over North and South poles in the troposphere.
- The occurrence of **ENSO** (El-Nino and Southern Oscillation) in the South Pacific ocean.
- **Walker cell** in the Indian ocean.
- Indian ocean Dipole

Nature of Indian Monsoon

Systematic studies of the causes of rainfall in the South Asian region help to understand the salient features of the monsoon, particularly some of its important aspects, such as

- Onset and advance of monsoon
- Rain-bearing systems and the relationship between their frequency and distribution of monsoon rainfall.
- Break in the monsoon
- Retreat of the monsoon

1. Onset and Advance of Monsoon

- The differential heating of land and sea is still believed to be the primary cause of the monsoon by many meteorologists. Low pressure at ITCZ which is located over North India in the month of May becomes so intense that it pulls the trade winds of the Southern hemisphere Northwards. These South-East trade winds cross the Equator and enter the Bay of Bengal. The Arabian sea, is only surrounded by air circulation over India. Passing over the equatorial warm currents, they bring with them moisture in abundance. With the Northwards shift of ITCZ, an easterly jet stream develops over 15° N.
- The rain in the South-West monsoon season begins rather abruptly. It can substantially bring down the temperature. This sudden onset of the moisture-laden winds associated with violent thunder and lightning, is often termed as the **break** or **burst** of the monsoons. South-West monsoon first of all reaches the Andaman and Nicobar Islands on 15th May. Kerala coast receives, it on 1st June. It reaches Mumbai and Kolkata between 10th and 13th June. By 15th of July, South-West monsoon covers the whole of India.

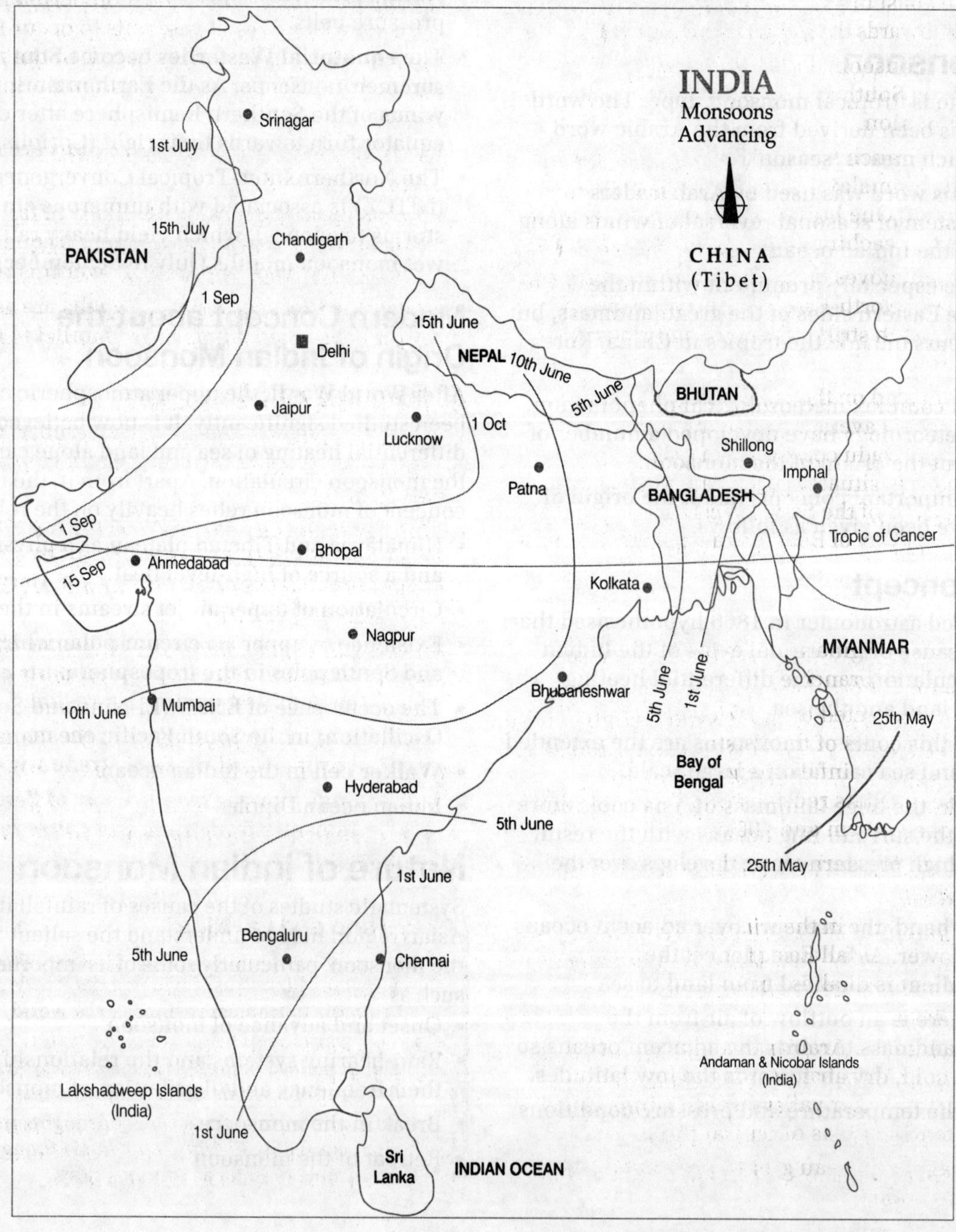

2. Rain Bearing Systems and Distribution of Rainfall

The South-West monsoon splits into two branches, the Arabian sea Branch and the Bay of Bengal Branch near the Southernmost end of the Indian peninsula.

Bay of Bengal Branch

- The first branch originates in the Bay of Bengal causing rainfall over the plains of North India. The Bay of Bengal branch strikes the coast of Myanmar and part of South-East Bangladesh. But, the Arakan hills along the coast of Myanmar deflect a big portion of this branch towards the Indian sub-continent.
- Therefore, the monsoon, enters West Bengal and Bangladesh from South and South-East instead of the South-West direction.
- From here, this branch splits into two under the influence of the Himalayas and the thermal low is North-West India. One branch moves Westward along the Ganga plains reaching as far as the Punjab plains.

  The other branch moves up the Brahmaputra valley in the North and the North-East, causing widespread rains. Its sub-branch strikes the Garo and Khasi hills of Meghalaya.

  Mawsynram, located on the crest of Khasi hills, receives the highest average annual rainfall in the world. The Tamil Nadu coast remains dry during this season because it is situated in the rainshadow area of Arabian sea branch of the South-West monsoon and lies parallel to the Bay of Bengal branch of South-West monsoon.

Arabian Sea Branch

The monsoon winds originating over the Arabian sea further split into three branches

- One branch is obstructed by the **Western ghats**. These winds climb the slopes of the Western ghats and as a result of orographic rainfall phenomenon, the windward side of Ghats receives very heavy rainfall ranging between 250 cm and 400 cm.

  After crossing the Western ghats, these winds descend and get heated up.

  This reduces humidity in the winds. As a result, these winds cause little rainfall East of the Western ghats. This region of low rainfall is known as the **rain-shadow area.**
- Another branch of the Arabian sea monsoon strikes the coast North of Mumbai. Moving along the Narmada and Tapi river valleys, these winds cause rainfall in extensive areas of central India.
- The Chhotanagpur plateau gets 15 cm rainfall from this part of the branch.
- Thereafter, they enter the Ganga plains and mingle with the Bay of Bengal branch.
- A third branch of this monsoon wind strikes the Saurashtra Peninsula and the Kutch.
- It then passes over West Rajasthan and along the Aravallis, causing only a scanty rainfall.
- In Punjab and Haryana, it too joins the Bay of Bengal branch. These two branches, reinforced by each other, cause rains in the Western Himalayas.

3. Break in the Monsoon

- During the South-West monsoon period after having rains for a few days, if rain fails to occur for one or more weeks, it is known as **break in the monsoon.** These dry spells are quite common during the rainy season.
- These breaks in the different regions are due to different reasons
  - In Northern India rains are likely to fail if the rain-bearing storms are not very frequent along the monsoon trough or the ITCZ over this region.
  - Over the West coast the dry spells are associated with days when winds blow parallel to the coast.

4. Retreat of Monsoon

- Monsoon starts retreating in September. On the first of September, it starts retreating from North-Western part of India.
- This day is the last day of the rainy season in Jaisalmer and Barmer in Rajasthan. By 15th September, monsoon leaves Punjab, Haryana, Rajasthan and Gujarat.
- The area under the monsoon influence shrinks slowly and the monsoon retreats from all parts of India except the Southern peninsular region.
- Monsoon winds in most parts of the country are replaced by the North-Easterly trade winds.
- These winds blowing over the Bay of Bengal pick up moisture from there and cause rainfall in Tamil Nadu.

El-Nino and La-Nina

- Weather conditions in India are also influenced by *El-Nino* which causes widespread floods and droughts in tropical regions of the world.
- This warming of tropical Pacific waters affects the global pattern of pressure and wind systems including the monsoon winds in the Indian ocean.
- It is believed that the severest droughts in India have been caused by *El-Nino*. *La-Nina* is thought to be favourable to India as it brings rains.

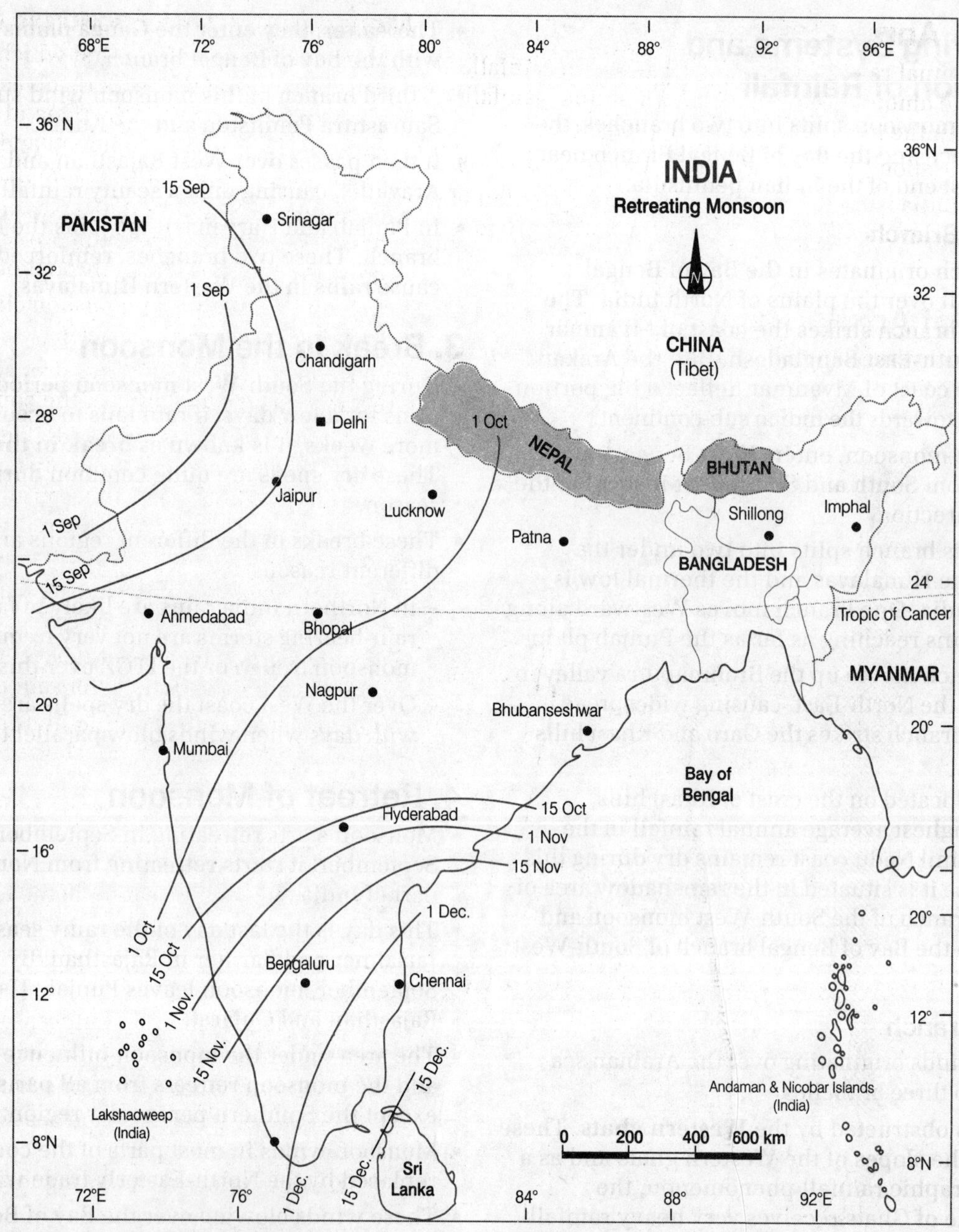

Features of Monsoon Rainfall

- Monsoon rain is seasonal in character which occurs between June and September. Spatial distribution of rainfall is largely governed by relief or topography.
- For instance, the windward side of the Western ghats registers a rainfall of over 250 cm.
- Again, the heavy rainfall in the North-Eastern states can be attributed to their hill ranges and the Eastern Himalayas. Rainfall ranges from 20 cm in Western Rajasthan to more than 400 cm in certain parts of Western ghats and North-East India.
- The monsoon rainfall has a declining trend with increasing distance from the sea.
- Rainfall decreases from East to West in plains as one branch of monsoon enters from Eastern side.
- Kolkata receives 119 cm, Prayagraj 76 cm and Delhi 56 cm only.
- Breaks in rainfall are related to the cyclonic depressions mainly formed at the head of the Bay of Bengal and their crossing into the mainland.
- Besides the frequency and intensity of these depressions, the passage followed by them determines the spatial distribution of rainfall.
- The rains sometimes end considerably earlier than usual, causing great damage to standing crops and making the sowing of winter crops difficult.

Variability of Annual Rainfall

- Variability of annual rainfall refers to variations in rainfall from the average amount. The variability of annual rainfall is computed with the help of the following formula
- Coefficient of Variation CV = (Standard Deviation / Mean) × 100
- The rainfall in India is highly variable. The actual rainfall of a place in a year deviates from its average rainfall by 10 to over 60%.

Distribution of Annual Rainfall

The distribution of average annual rainfall in India is shown in the below figure

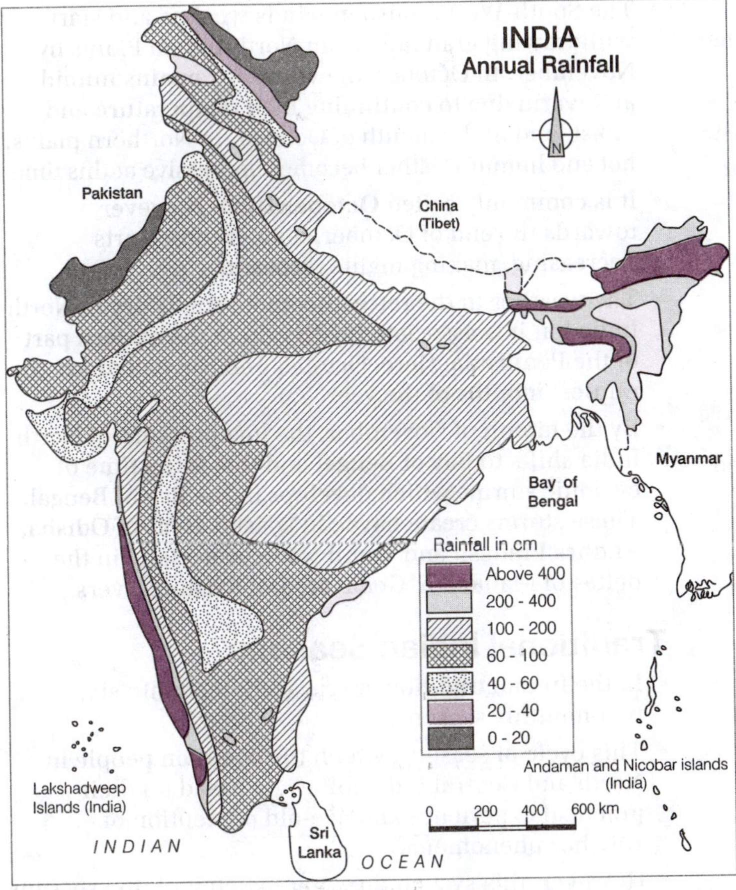

Distribution of Rainfall in Different Regions

Category	Rainfall in cms	Regions
Heavy Rainfall	More than 200 cm	Western coast, Western ghats, Sub-himalayan region of North- East, Garo, Khasi and Jaintia hills of Meghalaya. In some parts, rain exceeds 1000 cm.
Moderate Rainfall	Between 100 to 200 cm	100 cm isohyet extends from Gujarat to South up to Kanyakumari parallel to Western ghats. Northern Andhra Pradesh, Eastern part of Maharashtra, Madhya Pradesh, Odisha, some parts of Jammu and Kashmir
Low Rainfall	Between 60 to 100 cm	Most parts of Tamil Nadu, Karnataka, Andhra Pradesh, Eastern Rajasthan, South-Western Uttar Pradesh
Inadequate Rainfall	Less than 60 cm	Punjab, Haryana, North-Western Rajasthan, Kachchh, Kathiawar

Monsoons and the Economic Life in India

- Monsoon is that axis around which the entire agricultural cycle of India revolves. It is because about 64% people of India depend on agriculture for their livelihood and agriculture itself is based on South-West monsoon.
- Except the Himalayas all the parts of the country have temperatures above the threshold level to grow the crops or plants throughout the year.
- Regional variations in monsoon climate help in growing various types of crops.
- Variability of rainfall brings droughts or floods every year in some parts of the country.
- Agricultural prosperity of India depends very much on timely and adequately distributed rainfall. If it fails, agriculture is adversely affected particularly in those regions where means of irrigation are not developed.
- Sudden monsoon bursts create a problem of soil erosion over large areas in India.
- Winter rainfall by temperate cyclones in North India is highly beneficial for rabi crops.
- Regional Climatic variation in India is reflected in the vast variety of food, clothes and house types.

Seasons

Seasons are a special feature of the Indian climate. Temperature, pressure, wind direction and the amount and duration of rain varies from one season to the other.

- Meteorologists identify four seasons in India
  - The cold weather season or winter season,
  - The hot weather season or summer season,
  - The South-West monsoon season or Rainy season
  - The season of the retreating monsoon.

1. Winter Season

- During the winter season, the temperature decreases with increasing latitude in India from 25°C in the South to near zero temperature in the North. This season is characterised by fog and frost in North and North-West India.

  There is light rainfall in this region due to Western disturbances. There is a sustained snowfall on the higher slopes of the Himalayas.
- In India, rains occur in winter due to the North East Monsoon. During the winter season, North-East trade winds prevail over India. They blow from land to sea and that is why for most parts of the country, it is a dry season.

- A part of North-East trade winds blow over Bay of Bengal. They gather moisture which causes rainfall in the Coromandel coast while the rest of the country remains dry.
- In the Northern part of the country, the weather is marked by clear sky, low temperatures and low humidity. The winter rainfall is very important for the cultivation of **Rabi** crops.

2. Summer Season

- By the end of February, the temperature starts rising and there is a hot weather season in India from March to May.

  During these months, the central part of peninsular India experiences extreme hot weather and an elongated low pressure belt which is called **monsoonal trough** created, which extends from Jaisalmer in Western Rajasthan to Jharkhand and parts of Odisha to the East.
- However, over the Indian ocean South of the equator high pressure belt begins to develop in this season.
- In North-West India, afternoon dust storms are common. During summer, very hot and dry winds blow over North Indian plains. They are locally called **Loo**.
- Hot, dry and oppressing winds (Loo) blowing in the Northern plains from Punjab to Bihar with higher intensity between Delhi and Patna.
- At the same time, localised thunderstorms, associated with violent winds, torrential downpours, often accompanied by hail occur in many parts of India. In West Bengal and Assam region it is known as nor wester these storms are known as the **Kaal Baisakhi** (calamity for the month of Baisakh).

Pre-Monsoon Showers

- Towards the close of the summer season, pre-monsoon showers are common, especially in Kerala and Karnataka, which help in the early ripening of mangoes and are often referred to as 'mango showers'.
- The thunderstorms which occurs during summer to bring some rainfall in Karnataka are also known as Cherry Blossom Showers.

3. Rainy Season or South-West Monsoon Season (June-September)

- June to September are the months of advancing South-West monsoon season.
- By the end of May, the monsoon trough further intensifies over North India due to high temperature.
- The general direction of the wind during this season is from South-West to North-East. These winds are strong and blow at an average velocity of 30 km per hour.
- These moisture laden winds first hit the Andaman and Nicobar islands in the last week of May and Kerala coast in the first week of June with violent thunder and lightning. This South-West monsoon that flows into India brings about a major change in its weather.

4. Retreating Monsoon Season

- October and November are the months of post (or retreating) monsoon season.
- The temperatures during September-October start decreasing in North India. Monsoonal trough also becomes weak over North-West India. This is gradually replaced by a high pressure system.
- The South-West monsoon winds weaken and start withdrawing gradually from North Indian Plains by November. In October, the weather remains humid and warm due to continuing high temperature and moist land in the month of October. In Northern plains, hot and humid weather becomes oppressive at this time.
- It is commonly called **October Heat**. However, towards the end of October, temperature starts decreasing, making nights pleasant.
- The weather in the retreating monsoon is dry in North India but it is associated with rain in the eastern part of the Peninsula. Here, October and November are the rainiest months of the year.
- By the month of November, the low pressure of North India shifts to Bay of Bengal and this is the time of cyclonic storms which develops in the Bay of Bengal. These storms create havoc in coastal areas of Odisha, Andhra Pradesh and Tamil Nadu, especially in the deltas of Mahanadi, Godavari and Krishna rivers.

Traditional Indian Seasons

- In the Indian tradition, a year is divided into six, two-monthly seasons.
- This cycle of seasons, which the common people in North and Central India follow, is based on their practical experience and age-old perception of weather phenomena.
- However, this system does not match with the seasons of South India where there is little variation in the seasons.

Traditional Indian Seasons

Season	Months according to Indian Calendar	Months according to English Calendar
Vasanta	Chaitra-Vaisakha	March-April
Grishma	Jyaistha-Asadha	May-June
Varsha	Sravana-Bhadra	July-August
Sharada	Asvina-Kartika	September-October
Hemanta	Margashirsa-Pausa	November-December
Shishira	Magha-Phalguna	January-February

Climatic Regions of India

- India is often referred to as a country with tropical monsoon type of climate. However, there is a great variations in the distribution of temperature and precipitation in India. It is due to the large latitudinal extent, the presence of Himalayas in the North and the Indian ocean in the South have resulted in.
- The climate of North is different from that of South and so is the climate of East from that of the West. To study the variations of climate in various parts, India is divided into a large number of climatic regions of small size.
- A climatic region is that area which possesses a broad uniformity of climatic conditions caused by the combined effects of climatic elements – temperature, pressure, winds, humidity and precipitation.
- Temperature and rainfall are two important elements which are considered to be decisive in all the schemes of climatic classification. There are different schemes of classification of climate.
- **Koeppen Scheme** of Climatic classification is based on monthly values of temperature and precipitation. India's climate is divided into the following climatic regions
  - **Monsoon Type With Short Dry Season** (Amw) The Western coastal region South of Goa experiences this type of climate.
  - **Monsoon Type With Dry Season in Summers** (AS) The region of this type of climate extends along the Coromandel coast.
  - **Tropical Savanna Type** (Aw) Almost the entire peninsular region except for some coastal parts experiences this type of climate.
  - **Semi-arid Steppe Climate** (BShw) This climatic region includes the interior parts of the peninsular plateau and some parts of Gujarat, Rajasthan, Haryana, Punjab and Jammu and Kashmir.
  - **Hot desert type** (BWhw) This type of climate is found only in the Western part of Rajasthan.
  - **Monsoon type with dry winters** (Cwg) Largely Northern plains of India experiences this type of climate.
  - **Cold-humid Winter Type with Short Summer** (Dfc) This climate is characterised by a short summer season. This region covers the North-Eastern parts of India.
  - **Polar Type** (E) This type of climate is experienced in Jammu and Kashmir and the neighbouring mountain ranges.

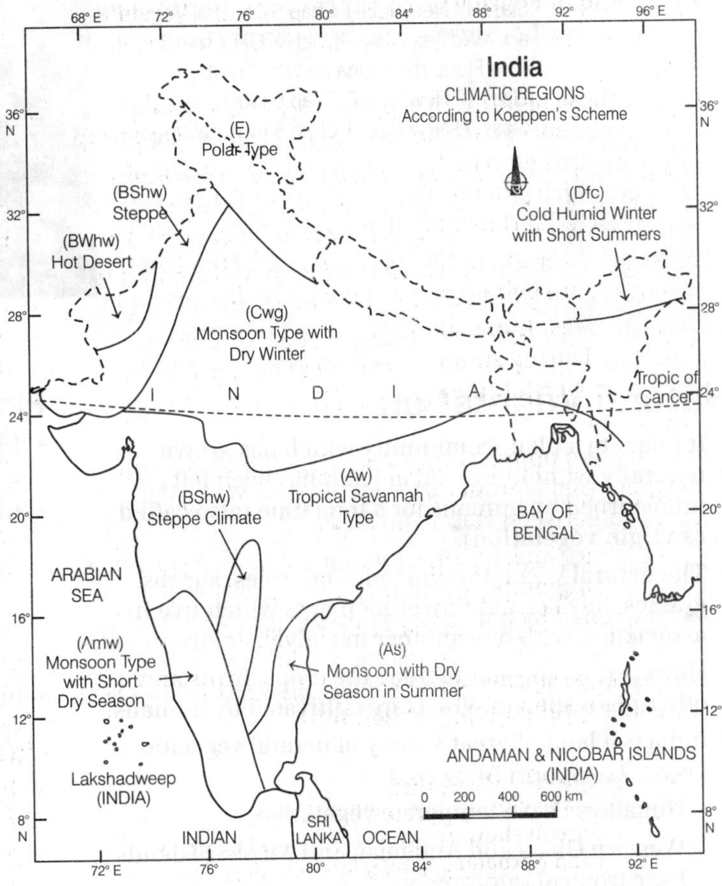

Extra Facts From Tamil Nadu Board and NIOS

- When the altitude increases the temperature decreases. Temperature decreases at the rate of 6.5°C for every 1000 m of ascent. It is called normal lapse rate.
- According to the **Jet Stream Theory,** the onset of South-West monsoon is driven by the shift of the sub-tropical westerly jet streams from the plains of India towards the Tibetan plateau.
- According to the Dynamic Concept, Monsoon wind originates due to the seasonal migration of planetary winds and pressure belts following the postion of the Sun.
- During Summer Solstice, the Sun's rays fall vertically over the Tropic of Cancer. Therefore, all the pressure and wind belts of the globe shift Northwards.
- The Easterly jet stream, created due to the Tibetan plateau's heating, takes the place of the Westerly stream.
- It caused the formation of an Easterly, chilly jet stream that was blowing over peninsular India and was focused at 15°N latitude. It aids in the monsoons' quick arrival.
- The Southern oscillation is a pattern of meteorological changes often observed between the Indian and Pacific oceans.
- It has been noticed that whenever the surface level pressure is high over the Indian ocean, it is low over the Pacific ocean and *vice-versa.*

20

Natural Vegetation and Soil in India

[SOURCES]

Class-IX New NCERT Chap 5 (Natural Vegetation and Wildlife), Class-X Old NCERT Chap 3 (The Flora, the Fauna and the Soils), Class-XI New NCERT Chap 6 (Soils), Class-XI New NCERT Chap 5 (Natural Vegetation)

Natural Vegetation

- It refers to a plant community which has grown naturally without human aid and has been left undisturbed by humans for a long time (also called as **virgin vegetation**).
- The natural vegetation includes tall trees, shrubs, grasses, bushes and flowering plants which live in association with one another in a given environment.
- However, it does not include the crops, fruits and other plant species which are cultivated by humans.
- India is a land of great variety of natural vegetation i.e.,
  - Himalayas have temperate vegetation
  - Western Ghats and Andaman and Nicobar Islands have tropical rainforests
  - Deltaic regions have tropical forests and mangroves
  - Desert and semi-desert areas of Rajasthan are known for cacti and a wide variety of bushes and thorny vegetation.
- The vegetation which is native in India are known as **endemic** or **indigenous species** but those which have come from outside India are termed as **exotic species.**
- **Lantana** and **water hyacinth** are used as the ornamental plants in the gardens.
- Water hyacinth is also known as **Terror of Bengal** as it spread in almost all water routes, rivers, ponds, etc., these are examples of exotic species.

Floristic Regions

- Floristic regions are the areas recognised by the plant geographers for the district plant life.
- In 1898, **CB Clarke**, divided into six floristic regions :
  - Himalayas region
    (a) Eastern Himalaya (b) Western Himalaya
  - Arid
  - Malabar
  - Coromandel
  - Ganga Plain
  - Assam Region
- In 1939, **D Chatterjee**, on the basis of indigenous plant species in different parts of the country, divided India into eight main floristic regions :
  - Eastern Himalaya
  - Western Himalaya
  - Assam Region
  - Ganga Plain
  - Indus Plain
  - Deccan Region
  - Malabar Region
  - Andaman-Nicobar Region

Factors Influencing Natural Vegetation

The climatic conditions of a country highly influence the type of natural vegetation of that country. This is because each plant species has different and in few cases even unique requirements for its growth. The various factors that influence the natural vegetation are :

- **Land** The nature of the land, whether it is a mountainous region or plateaus or plains, influences the type of natural vegetation. For example, the mountain regions have hydrophilous vegetation which have the ability to withstand the humid and cold climatic conditions while the vegetation in plains does not possess such abilities.

- **Soil** The nature of the soil and the nutrients present in it, provide a basis for different types of natural vegetation.
  For example, the sandy soil has very few nutrients and poor water holding capacity and hence, it is not suitable for vegetation, whereas the loamy soil which is rich in nutrients and possesses an ability to retain moisture is suitable for vegetation.
- **Precipitation** Rainfall is an important factor which influences natural vegetation. Areas with rainfall over 200 cm and above have a dense and evergreen vegetation when compared to ones which receive less than 50 cm rainfall.
  The natural vegetation in India is highly determined by the advancing South-West monsoon and retreating North-East monsoon, which brings maximum rainfall to the country.
- **Temperature** Along with the nature of soil and precipitation, the temperature of a region determines the character and extent of the natural vegetation. Particularly the vegetation in hills and mountains is highly influenced by the temperature.
  For example, in the Himalayas, tropical evergreen vegetation can be found in lower altitudes. However, as the altitude increases, the temperature falls and thus the nature of vegetation changes from evergreen to alpine.
- **Photoperiod** Another crucial factor which determines the natural vegetation of a region is the amount of sunlight received by them.
  Photoperiod i.e., duration of light exposure and the intensity of the light influences a process called photosynthesis which enables the plants to carry out necessary physiological processes for their survival.

Classification of Natural Vegetation of India

Classification of Natural Vegetation of India is primarily based on spatial and annual variations in rainfall. Temperature, soil and topography are also considered.

India's vegetation can be divided into five main types and 16 sub-types as given below :

Classification of Natural Vegetation in India

Moist Tropical Forests
- Tropical Wet Evergreen
- Tropical Semi-Evergreen
- Tropical Moist Deciduous
- Littoral and Swamp

Montane Sub-tropical Forests
- Sub-tropical broad leaved hill
- Sub-tropical moist hill (pine)
- Sub-tropical dry evergreen

Alpine Forests
- Sub-Alpine
- Moist Alpine scrub
- Dry Alpine scrub

Dry Tropical Forests
- Tropical Dry Evergreen
- Tropical Dry Deciduous
- Tropical Thorn

Montane Temperate Forests
- Montane Wet Temperate
- Himalayan Moist Temperate
- Himalayan Dry Temperate

Percentage of Different Types of Forests in India

Forest Type in India	% of Total Area
Tropical Moist Deciduous	37
Tropical Dry Deciduous	28
Tropical Wet Evergreen	8
Sub-Tropical Moist Hill	6
Tropical Semi-Evergreen	4
Rest below 4 %	

A. Moist Tropical Forests

There are following types of moist tropical forests :

1. Tropical Wet Evergreen Forests

- These forests are found where the annual rainfall exceeds 250 cm, the annual temperature is about 25°-27°C and the average annual humidity exceeds 77%.
- The dry season is distinctly short in these forests.
- Due to high heat and high humidity, the trees of these forests do not shed their leaves together and hence, are evergreen.
- Plants are **mesophytic**, i.e., adapted to neither too dry nor too wet type climate.
- The trees are lofty and often reach 45 - 60 metres in height. From the air, the tropical rain forest appears like a thick canopy of foliage, broken only where it is crossed by large rivers or cleared for cultivation.
- All plants struggle upwards (most **epiphytes**) for sunlight resulting in a peculiar layer arrangement. The entire morphology looks like a green carpet when viewed from above.
- The sunlight cannot reach the ground due to the thick canopy.
- The undergrowth is formed mainly of bamboos, ferns, climbers, orchids, etc.
- They are found in the Western side of the Western Ghats (500 to 1370 metres above sea level), some regions in the Purvanchal hills and in the Andaman and Nicobar Islands.

Mesophytes

- Unlike hydrophytic plants, such as water lily or pondweed, that grow in saturated soil or water, or xerophytic plants, such as cactus, that grow in extremely dry soil, mesophytes are ordinary plants that exist between the two extremes.
- Mesophytic environments are marked by average to hot temperatures and soil that is neither too dry nor too wet.

- The timber of these forests is fine-grained, hard and durable.
- It has high commercial value, but it is highly challenging to exploit due to dense undergrowth, absence of pure stands and lack of transport facilities.
- The important species of these forests are mahogany, mesua, white cedar, jamun, canes, bamboo, etc.

2. Tropical Semi-Evergreen Forests

- They are transitional forests between **tropical wet evergreen forests and tropical deciduous forests**.
- They are comparatively drier areas compared to tropical wet evergreen forests.
- These forests are found where the annual rainfall is between 200-250 cm, the mean annual temperature varies from 24°C to 27°C and the relative humidity is about 75%. Here the dry season is not short like in tropical evergreen forests.
- They are found in the Western coast, Assam, lower slopes of the Eastern Himalayas, Odisha and Andamans.
- The semi-evergreen forests are less dense.
- These forests are characterised by many species.
- The important species are laurel, rosewood, mesua, thorny bamboo in Western Ghats and white cedar, Indian chestnut, champa, mango, etc in Himalayan region.
- Timber industry in these forests is better than in evergreen forests.

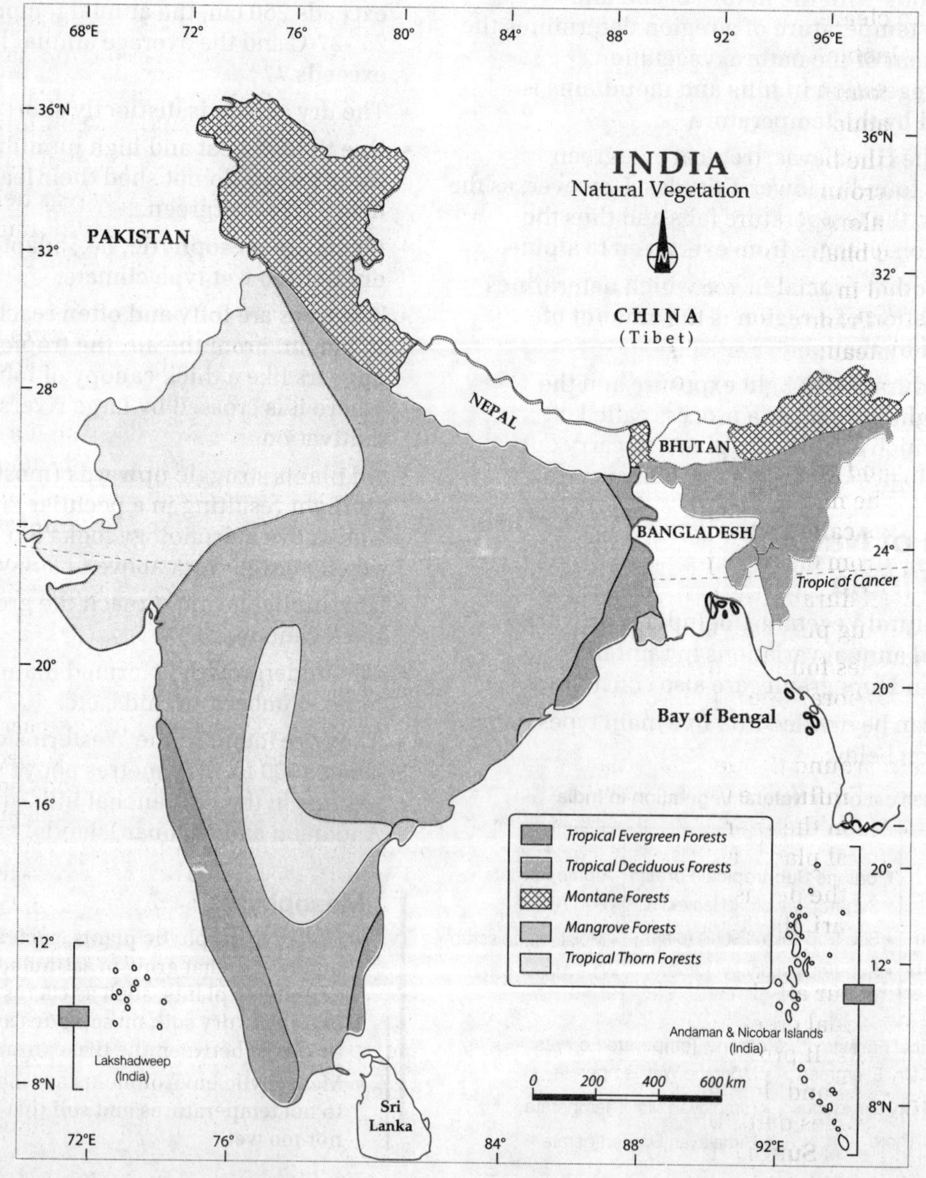

3. Tropical Moist Deciduous Forests

- These forests are found where the annual rainfall is between 100 to 200 cm, the mean annual temperature of about 27°C and the average annual relative humidity of 60 to 75%.
- The trees drop their leaves during the spring and early summer when sufficient moisture is not available.
- The general appearance is with leaves in extreme summers (April-May). The Tropical moist deciduous forests present irregular top canopy i.e., 25 to 60 m.
- They have heavily buttressed trees and fairly complete undergrowth.
- These forests occupy a much larger area than the evergreen forests, but large tracts under these forests have been cleared for cultivation.
- These provide valuable timber like **Teak**.
- The main species found in these forests are teak, sal, laurel, rosewood, amla, jamun, bamboo, etc.
- They are found in the belt running along the **Western Ghats** surrounding the belt of evergreen forests and a strip along the **Shiwalik range** including terai and bhabar from 77° E to 88° E.
- They are also found in Manipur and Mizoram, hills of Eastern Madhya Pradesh and Chhattisgarh, Chhota Nagpur Plateau, most of Odisha, parts of West Bengal and Andaman and Nicobar Islands.

4. Littoral and Swamp Forests

- They can survive and grow both in fresh as well as **brackish water** (The mixture of seawater and fresh water in estuaries is called brackish water and its salinity can range from 0.5 to 35 ppt).
- It provides hard and durable timber which is used for construction, building purposes and making boats.
- The important species found in these forests are Sundri, agar, rhizophora, screw pines, canes and palms, etc.
- They occur in and around the deltas, estuaries and creeks prone to tidal influences (delta or tidal forests) and littoral (on the shore of the sea or a lake) forests occur at several places along the coast.
- They are confined to the deltas of the Ganga, the Mahanadi, the Godavari, the Krishna and the Cauvery.
- Dense mangroves occur all along the coastline in sheltered estuaries, tidal creeks, backwaters, salt marshes and mudflats. It provides useful fuel wood.
- The most pronounced and the densest is the Sunderban in the Ganges delta where the predominant species is **Sundri** (Heriteera).

B. Dry Tropical Forests

Dry tropical forests can be further classified as follows :

1. Tropical Dry Evergreen Forests

- They are found in the following along the coasts of Tamil Nadu.
- These forests occur in the areas where the annual rainfall is around 100 cm [mostly from the North-East monsoon winds in October-December], the mean annual temperature is about 28°C and the mean humidity is about 75%.
- The growth of evergreen forests in areas of such low rainfall is a bit strange.
- They have short statured trees, up to 12 m high, with complete canopy.
- Bamboos and grasses are not conspicuous.
- The important species are jamun, tamarind, neem, etc.
- Most of the land under these forests has been cleared for agriculture or **casuarina plantations.**
- It reduces damage in the event of natural calamities.
- Line planting in the coastal areas helps in controlling the wind force. It is also used for tourism promotion in view of its ornamental appearance.
- It provides top quality firewood.
- The wood is suitable for paper pulp and useful raw material for the manufacture of paper for writing, printing and wrapping.
- The characteristics which make it a suitable species for wasteland development include adaptability to a wide range of habitats, fast growth, salt tolerant, drought resistant, ability to reclaim land and stabilise sand dunes.
- **Intercrops** such as groundnut, cucumber, watermelons, sesamum and **pulses** can also be raised along with the plantation.

Casuarina Plantation

- It resembles feathery conifer in general appearance.
- They are rapid-growing, carefree species for sites and climates as varied as coastal sand dunes, high mountain slopes, hot humid tropics and semi-arid regions.
- They have the ability to fix atmospheric nitrogen. It grows 15 to 25 m in height on average.
- Casuarina is the most popular farm forestry in the states of Andhra Pradesh, Tamil Nadu, West Bengal, Odisha, Maharashtra, Gujarat and Karnataka.

2. Tropical Dry Deciduous Forests

- These forests are found in the areas where the annual rainfall is between 70-100 cm.
- These are similar to moist deciduous forests and shed their leaves in the dry season.

- The major difference is that they can grow in areas of comparatively less rainfall.
- They represent a transitional type – **moist deciduous** on the wetter side and **thorn forests** on the drier side.
- They have a closed but uneven canopy. The forests are composed of a mixture of a few species of deciduous trees rising up to a height of 20 m.
- Enough light reaches the ground to permit the growth of grass and climbers.
- Large tracts of this forest have been cleared for agricultural purposes. These forests suffer from over grazing, fire, etc.
- The important species are teak, axlewood, rosewood, common bamboo, red sanders, laurel, satinwood, etc.
- They occur in an irregular wide strip running from the foothills of the Himalayas to Kanyakumari except in Rajasthan, Western Ghats and West Bengal.

3. Tropical Thorn Forests

- These forests are found in the areas where the annual rainfall is less than 50 cm, humidity is less than 50% and the mean temperature is 25°-30°C.
- The trees are low (6 to 10 m maximum) and widely scattered.
- **Acacias** and **Euphorbias** are very prominent in these forests.
- The Indian wild date is common. Some grasses also grow in the rainy season.
- They degenerate into desert type in the **Thar desert**.
- The important species are neem, babul, cactii, etc.
- They are found in Rajasthan, South-Western Punjab, Western Haryana, Kachchh and neighbouring parts of Saurashtra.
- Such forests also grow on the leeside of the Western Ghats covering large areas of Maharashtra, Karnataka, Telangana, Andhra Pradesh and Tamil Nadu.

C. Montane Sub-Tropical Forests

There are following types of montane sub-tropical forests:

1. Sub-tropical Broad-leaved Hill Forests

- These forests are found in the areas where the mean annual rainfall is 75 cm to 125 cm, the average annual temperature is 18°-21°C and humidity is 80%.
- They are found in the **Eastern Himalayas** to the East of 88°E longitude at altitudes varying from 1000 to 2000 m.
- They are forests of evergreen species.
- The commonly found species are evergreen oaks, chestnuts, ash, beech, sals and pines.
- Climbers and epiphytes (a plant that grows non-parasitically on a tree or other plant) are common. These forests are not so distinct in the Southern parts of the country.
- They occur only in the Nilgiri and Palni hills at 1070-1525 m above sea level.
- The higher parts of the Western Ghats such as Mahabaleshwar, the summits of the Satpura and the Maikal Range, highlands of Bastar and Mt. Abu in the Aravalli Range carry sub-types of these forests.

2. Sub-tropical Moist Pine Forests

- Chir or Chil is the most dominant tree which forms pure stands.
- It provides valuable timber for furniture, boxes and buildings.
- It is also used for producing resin and turpentine.
- They are found in Western Himalayas between 73°E and 88°E longitudes at elevations between 1000 to 2000 m above sea level. They are also found in some hilly regions of Arunachal Pradesh, Manipur, Naga Hills and Khasi Hills.

3. Sub-tropical Dry Evergreen Forests

- They are found in the Bhabar, the Shiwaliks and the Western Himalayas up to about 1000 m above sea level.
- These forests are found in the areas where the annual rainfall is 50-100 cm (15 to 25 cm in December-March). The summers are sufficiently hot and winters are very cold.
- They have low scrub forest with small evergreen stunted trees and shrubs. Olive, acacia modesta and pistacia are the most predominant species.

D. Montane Temperate Forests

Montane temperate forests are of following types:

1. Montane Wet Temperate Forests

- These forests are found at a height of 1800 to 3000 m above sea level in the areas where the mean annual rainfall is 150 cm to 300 cm, the mean annual temperature is about 11°C to 14°C and the average relative humidity is over 80%.
- They are found in the higher hills of Tamil Nadu and Kerala, in the Eastern Himalayan region.
- These are closed evergreen forests. Trunks have large girth. Their branches are clothed with mosses, ferns and other epiphytes.
- The trees rarely achieve a height of more than 6 metres. Deodar, Chilauni, Indian chestnut, birch, plum, machilus, cinnamomum, litsea, magnolia, blue pine, oak, hemlock, etc. are important species.

2. Himalayan Moist Temperate Forests

- These forests are found in the areas where the annual rainfall varies from 150 cm to 250 cm.
- They are found in the temperate zone of the Himalayas between 1500 and 3300 m.
- They cover the entire length of this mountain range in Kashmir, Himachal Pradesh, Uttarakhand, Darjeeling and Sikkim.
- They are mainly composed of **coniferous species.**
- Trees are 30 to 50 m high. Pines, cedars, silver fir, spruce, etc, are the most important trees.
- They form high but fairly open forest with shrubby undergrowth including oaks, rhododendrons and some bamboos.
- They provide fine wood which is of much use for construction, timber and railway sleepers.

3. Himalayan Dry Temperate Forests

- The precipitation is below 100 cm and is mostly in the form of snow.
- They are coniferous forests with xerophytic shrubs in which deodar, oak, ash, olive, etc. are the main trees.
- Such forests are found in the inner dry ranges of the Himalayas where South-West monsoon is very feeble like Ladakh, Lahaul, Chamba, Kinnaur, Garhwal and Sikkim.

E. Alpine Forests

- The altitude ranges between 2,900 to 3,500 m.
- These forests can be divided into sub-alpine, moist alpine scrub and dry alpine scrub.
- The sub-alpine forests occur in lower alpine scrub and grasslands.
- It is a mixture of coniferous and broad-leaved trees in which the coniferous trees attain a height of about 30 m while the broad-leaved trees reach only 10 m.
- Fir, spruce, rhododendron, etc are important species.
- The moist alpine scrub is a low evergreen dense growth of rhododendron, birch, etc. which occurs from 3,000 m and extends up to the snowline.
- The dry alpine scrub is the uppermost limit of scrub xerophytic, dwarf shrubs, over 3,500 m above sea level and found in the dry zone. Juniper, honeysuckle, Artemisia, etc., are important species.

Types and Distribution of Forest

- It is difficult to manage, control and regulate forest resources.
- In India, much of its forests are either owned or managed by the government through the Forest Department or other government departments.
- These are classified under the following categories:

(i) **Reserved Forests** More than half of the total forest land has been declared reserved forests. Reserved forests are regarded as the most valuable as far as the conservation of forest and wildlife resources are concerned. Madhya Pradesh has the largest area under permanent forests, constituting 75% of its total forest area. Jammu and Kashmir, Andhra Pradesh, Uttarakhand, Kerala, Tamil Nadu, West Bengal, and Maharashtra have large percentages of reserved forests of its total forest area.

(ii) **Protected Forests** Almost one-third of the total forest area is protected forest, as declared by the Forest Department. This forest land is protected from any further depletion. Bihar, Haryana, Punjab, Himachal Pradesh, Odisha and Rajasthan have a bulk of area under protected forests (6.98%).

(iii) **Unclassed Forests** These are other forests and wastelands belonging to both government and private individuals and communities. All North-Eastern states and parts of Gujarat have a very high percentage of their forests as unclassed forests managed by local communities.

Medicinal Plants

India is known for its herbs and spices from ancient times. Some 2,000 plants have been described in Ayurveda and at least 500 are in regular use.

The World Conservation Union's Red List has named 352 medicinal plants of which 52 are critically threatened and 49 endangered.

The commonly used plants in India are:

- **Sarpagandha** Used to treat blood pressure; it is found only in India.
- **Jamun** The juice from ripe fruit is used to prepare vinegar, which is carminative and diuretic, and has digestive properties. The powder of the seed is used for controlling diabetes.
- **Arjun** The fresh juice of leaves is a cure for earache. It is also used to regulate blood pressure.
- **Babool** Leaves are used as a cure for eye sores. Its gum is used as a tonic.
- **Neem** Has high antibiotic and antibacterial properties.
- **Tulsi** Is used to cure cough and cold.
- **Kachnar** Is used to cure asthma and ulcers. The buds and roots are good for digestive problems.

Forest Conservation

- Forests have an intricate interrelationship with life and environment. These provide numerous direct and indirect advantages to our economy and society.
- Hence, conservation of forest is of vital importance to the survival and prosperity of humankind.

- Accordingly, the Government of India proposed to have a nation-wide forest conservation policy and adopted a **Forest Policy in 1952**, which was further modified in 1988.
- According to the **New Forest Policy**, the Government will emphasise sustainable forest management in order to conserve and expand forest reserve on the one hand and to meet the needs of local people on the other.
- The forest policy aimed at :
  - Bringing 33% of the geographical areas under forest cover.
  - Maintaining environmental stability and to restore forests where ecological balance was disturbed.
  - Conserving the natural heritage of the country, its biological diversity and genetic pool.
  - Checks soil erosion, extension of the desert lands and reduction of floods and droughts.
  - Increasing the forest cover through social forestry and afforestation on degraded land.
  - Increasing the productivity of forests to make timber, fuel, fodder and food available to rural population dependent on forests, and encourage the substitution of wood.
  - creating of a massive peoples movement involving women to encourage planting of trees, stop felling of trees and thus, reduce pressure on the existing forest.
- Based on the forest conservation policy the following steps were initiated:

Social Forestry

- Social forestry means the management and protection of forests and afforestation on barren lands with the purpose of helping in the environmental, social and rural development.
- The **National Commission on Agriculture** (1976) has classified social forestry into three categories :

Urban Forestry

- Urban forestry pertains to the raising and management of trees on public and privately owned lands in and around urban centres such as green belts, parks, roadside avenues, industrial and commercial green belts, etc.

Rural Forestry

Rural forestry lays emphasis on promotion of agro-forestry and community-forestry.

- **Agro-forestry** is the raising of trees and agriculture crops on the same land inclusive of the waste patches. It combines forestry with agriculture, thus, altering the simultaneous production of food, fodder, fuel, timber and fruit.
- **Community forestry** involves the raising of trees on public or community land such as the village pasture and temple land, roadside, canal bank, strips along railway lines and schools etc.

  Community forestry programme aims at providing benefits to the community as a whole. Community forestry provides a means under which the people of landless classes can associate themselves in tree-raising and thus, get those benefits which otherwise are restricted for landowners.

Farm Forestry

- Farm forestry is a term applied to the process under which farmers grow trees for commercial and non-commercial purposes on their farm lands.
- Forest departments of various states distribute seedlings of trees free of cost to small and medium farmers.
- Several lands such as the margins of agricultural fields, grasslands and pastures, land around homes and cow sheds may be used for raising trees under non-commercial farm forestry.

Initiatives for the Conservation of Forests

- **Chipko Movement** The famous Chipko movement in the Himalayas has not only successfully resisted deforestation in several areas but has also shown that community afforestation with indigenous species can be enormously successful.
- **Beej Bachao Andolan and Navdanya** Attempts to revive the traditional conservation methods or developing new methods of ecological farming are now widespread. Farmers and citizen's groups like the Beej Bachao Andolan in Tehri and Navdanya have shown that adequate levels of diversified crop production without the use of synthetic chemicals are possible and economically viable.
- **Joint Forest Management** (JFM) In India, JFM programme furnishes a good example for involving local communities in the management and restoration of degraded forests.
- The programme has been in formal existence since 1988 when the state of Odisha passed the first resolution for joint forest management. JFM depends on the formation of local (village) institutions that undertake protection activities mostly on degraded forest land managed by the forest department.
- In return, the members of these communities are entitled to intermediary benefits like non-timber forest produces and share in the timber harvested by 'successful protection'.

Community and Conservation

- Conservation strategies are not new in our country. In some areas of India, local communities are struggling to conserve these habitats along with government officials, recognising that only this will secure their own long-term livelihood.
- In **Sariska Tiger Reserve**, Rajasthan, villagers have fought against mining by citing the Wildlife Protection Act. In many areas, villagers themselves are protecting habitats and explicitly rejecting government involvement.
- The inhabitants of five villages in the Alwar district of Rajasthan have declared 1,200 hectares of forest as the **Bhairodev Dakav 'Sonchuri'**, declaring their own set of rules and regulations which do not allow hunting, and are protecting the wildlife against any outside encroachments.

Cultural Significance of Forests

- Certain societies revere a particular tree which they have preserved from time immemorial. The Mundas and the Santhal of Chhotanagpur region worship mahua (*Bassia latifolia*) and kadamba (*Anthocaphalus cadamba*) trees.
- The tribals of Odisha and Bihar worship the tamarind (*Tamarindus indica*) and mango (*Mangifera indica*) trees during weddings. To many of us, peepal and banyan trees are considered sacred.

Forest Cover in India

- Indian government released its 17th **India State of Forest Report** (ISFR) on 13th January, 2022.
- According to the report, **total forest cover** in India is 71.37 million hectare (7137898 sq km) which 21.71% of the total geographical area.
- According to the report, **tree cover** in India is 9.57 million hectare (95748 sq km) which is 2.9% of the total geographical area.
- Total **forest and tree cover** in India is 80.93 million hectare (809537 sq km) which is 24.62% of the total geographical area.
- In ISFR 2021, maximum growth in forest cover was achieved by **Andhra Pradesh** (647 sq km) and minimum growth in forest cover was achieved by **Jharkhand** (110 sq km).
- On the basis of tree cover, states with maximum area under forest are **Maharashtra, Rajasthan** and **Madhya Pradesh** while **Sikkim, Manipur** and **Tripura** have minimum area under forest tree cover.
- On the basis of percentage of geographical area, state with maximum tree cover is **Kerala**.
- According of ISFR 2021, 17 states/UTs in India consist 33% of forests on their total geographical area.
- State with maximum forest cover is **Madhya Pradesh** and minimum forest cover is **Haryana.**

Top Five States with Maximum Forest Area

State	Area
Madhya Pradesh	77493
Arunachal Pradesh	66431
Chhattisgarh	55717
Odisha	52156
Maharashtra	50798

Top Five States/UTs with Maximum Forest Percentage

State/UTs	Forest %
Lakshadweep	90.33
Mizoram	84.53
Andaman and Nicobar Islands	81.74
Arunachal Pradesh	79.39
Meghalaya	76.00

Soil

- Soil is the topmost layer of the continental crust having weathered particles of rocks. The soils of India are the product of physical factors as well as human factors.
- Soil can be simply defined as a mixture of small rock particles and organic materials that supports the growth of plants.

Factors influencing Soil Formation

Factors that influence soil formation are as follows:

- **Parent Material/Rock** Soil is made up from erosion of soft rocks. It provides soil material, texture, porosity and pH value. Soft rocks means better soil formed than hard rocks.
- **Relief/Topography** Steep gradient gives underdeveloped soil and plain area gives well developed soil.
- **Climate** Wind, water, glaciers are agents of erosion. Climate determines the type of erosion and its intensity.
- **Natural Vegetation and Biological Factors** Microbes enrich the soil. Roots from plants help in weathering of rocks and humus content from plants enriches the soil.
- **Time** Soil formation is a long-term process. Time decides the maturity of the soil.

Soil Types in India

The first scientific classification of soil was done by **Vasily Dokuchaev**. In India, the **Indian Council of Agricultural Research** (ICAR) has classified soils into 8 categories.

1. Alluvial Soil
2. Black Cotton Soil
3. Red Soil
4. Laterite Soil
5. Mountainous or Forest Soil
6. Arid or Desert Soil
7. Saline and Alkaline Soil
8. Peaty and Marshy Soil/Bog Soil

This classification scheme is based on constitutional characteristics – colour and the resource significance of the soils.

Classification of Soils as per the USDA Soil Taxonomy

Order	Area (in Thousand Hectares)	Percentage
Inceptisols	130372.90	39.74
Entisols	92131.71	28.08
Alfisols	44448.68	13.55
Vertisols	27960.00	8.52
Aridisols	14069.00	4.28
Ultisols	8250.00	2.51
Mollisols	1320.00	0.40
Others	9503.10	2.92
Total		**100**

Source : Soils of India, National Bureau of Soil Survey and Land Use Planning. Publication Number 94

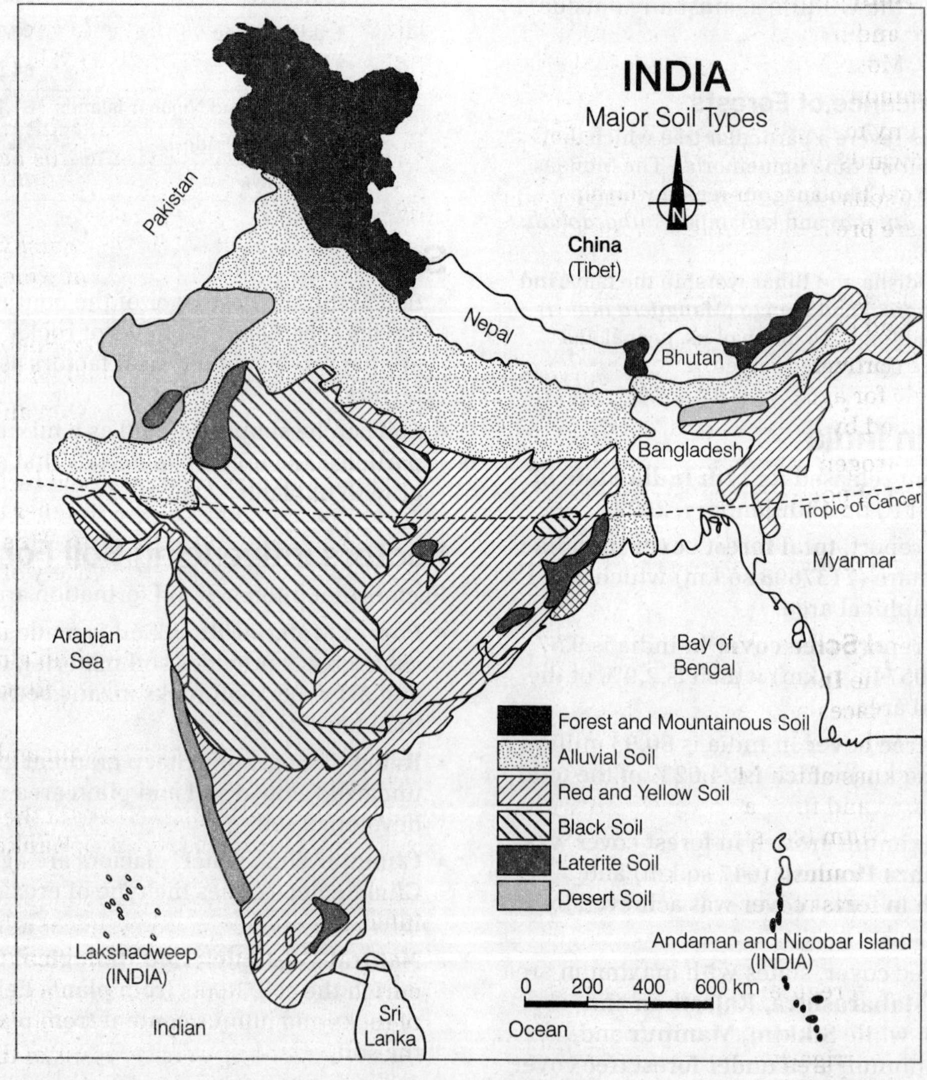

1. Alluvial Soils

- Alluvial soils are formed mainly due to silt deposited by **Indo-Gangetic-Brahmaputra** rivers. In coastal regions, alluvial deposits are formed in deffas of East coast and in the river valleys.
- Rocks of the Himalayas form the parent material. Thus, the parent material of these soils is of transported origin.
- They are the largest soil group covering about 15 lakh sq km or about 40% of the total area.
- They support more than 40% of India's population by providing the most productive agricultural lands.
- The colour of the alluvial soils varies from the light grey to ash grey.

Characteristics of Alluvial Soils

- They are immature and have weak profiles due to their recent origin. Most of the soil is sandy and clayey soils are not uncommon.
- They vary from loamy to sandy-loam in drier regions and clayey-loam towards the delta.
- Pebbly and gravelly soils are rare. Kankar (calcareous concretions) beds are present in some regions along the river terraces.
- The soil is porous because of its **loamy** (equal proportion of sand and clay) nature.
- Porosity and texture provide good drainage and other conditions favorable for agriculture. These soils are constantly replenished by the recurrent floods.
- The proportion of nitrogen is generally low in these soils. The proportion of potash, phosphoric acid and alkalis are adequate.
- The proportion of iron oxide and lime vary within a wide range.

Distribution of Alluvial Soils in India

- They occur all along the **Indo-Gangetic-Brahmaputra** plains except in few places where the top layer is covered by desert sand.
- They also occur in deltas of the Mahanadi, the Godavari, the Krishna and the Cauvery, where they are called deltaic alluvium (coastal alluvium).
- Some alluvial soils are found in the Narmada, Tapi valleys and Northern parts of Gujarat.

Crops in Alluvial Soils

- They are mostly flat and regular soils and are best suited for agriculture.
- They are best suited to irrigation and respond well to the canal and well/tube-well irrigation.
- They yield splendid crops of rice, wheat, sugarcane, tobacco, cotton, jute, maize, oilseeds, vegetables and fruits.

Geological Divisions of Alluvial soils

Geologically, the alluvium of the **Great Plain of India** is divided into newer or younger **khadar** and older **bhangar** soils.

Bhabar

- The bhabar belt is about 8-16 km wide running along the Shivalik foothills. It is a porous, Northern-most stretch of **Indo-Gangetic plain.**
- Rivers descending from the Himalayas deposit their load along the foothills in the form of alluvial fans. These alluvial fans (often pebbly soils) have merged together to build up the bhabar belt.
- The porosity of bhabar is the most unique feature. The porosity is due to deposition of a huge number of pebbles and rock debris across the alluvial fans.
- The streams disappear once they reach the bhabar region because of this porosity. Therefore, the area is marked by dry river courses except in the rainy season.
- The area is not suitable for agriculture and only big trees with large roots thrive in this belt.

Terai

- Terai is an ill-drained, damp (marshy) and thickly forested narrow tract (15-30 km wide) to the South of Bhabar running parallel to it.
- The underground streams of the Bhabar belt re-emerge in this belt. It is a swampy lowland with silty soils.
- The terai soils are rich in nitrogen and organic matter but are deficient in phosphate.
- These soils are generally covered by tall grasses and forests but are suitable for a number of crops such as wheat, rice, sugarcane, jute, etc. This thickly forested region provides shelter to a variety of wildlife.

Bhangar

- The Bhangar is the older alluvium along the river beds forming terraces higher than the floodplain (about 30 metres above the flood level).
- It is of a more clayey composition and is generally dark-coloured.
- A few meters below the terrace of the bhangar are beds of lime nodules known as **Kankar.**

Khadar

- The Khadar is composed of newer alluvium and forms the flood plains along the river banks.
- The banks are flooded almost every year and a new layer of alluvium is deposited with every flood. This makes them the most fertile soils of the Ganges.
- They are sandy clays and loams, drier and leached, less calcareous and carbonaceous (less kankary). A new layer of alluvium is deposited by river floods almost every year.

Alluvial Regions with Rainfall

- **Above 100 cm** – Suitable for paddy
- **B/w 50-100 cm** – Suitable for wheat, sugarcane, tobacco and cotton
- **Below 50 cm** – Coarse grains (millets)

2. Black Soils

- They are formed due to weathering of these basaltic rocks which emerged during fissure eruption of the Cretaceous period.
- The parent material for most of the black soil are the volcanic rocks that were formed in the Deccan Plateau (Deccan and the Rajmahal trap).
- In Tamil Nadu, gneisses and schist form the parent material. The former are sufficiently deep while the later are generally shallow.
- These are the regions of high temperature and low rainfall. It is, therefore, a soil group typical to the dry and hot regions of the Peninsula.
- Its extent is 15 % of the total soil area. This soil have feature called self-ploughing because of slow absorption and loss of moisture, during dry season.

Characteristics of Black Soils

- A typical black soil is highly argillaceous (containing clay) with a large clay factor, 62% or more.
- In general, black soils of uplands are of low fertility while those in the valleys are very fertile.
- The black soil is highly retentive of moisture. It swells greatly on accumulating moisture. Strenuous effort is required to work on such soil in rainy season as it gets very sticky.
- In summer, the moisture evaporates and the soil shrinks and is seamed with broad and deep cracks. The lower layers can still retain moisture. The cracks permits oxygenation of the soil to sufficient depths and the soil has extraordinary fertility.
- The black colour is due to the presence of a small proportion of titaniferous magnetite or iron and black constituents of the parent rock. In Tamil Nadu and parts of Andhra Pradesh, the black colour is derived from crystalline schist and basic gneisses.
- Various tints of the black colour such as deep black, medium black, shallow black, a mixture of red and black may be found in this group of soils.
- When dry, it develops cracks and has blocky structure which increases its self-ploughing capacity.

The chemical composition of black soils is as follows :

- 10% of alumina,
- 9-10% of iron oxide,
- 6-8% of lime and magnesium carbonates,
- Potash is variable (less than 0.5%) and
- phosphates, nitrogen and humus are low.
- They are rich in iron and lime but deficient in humus, nitrogen and phosphorous content.

Distribution of Black Soils

- It is found in the Deccan lava plateau region of India.
- Spread over 46 lakh sq km (16.6% of the total area) across Maharashtra, Madhya Pradesh, parts of Karnataka, Telangana, Andhra Pradesh, Gujarat and Tamil Nadu.

Crops Grown in Black Soils

- These soils are best suited for cotton crops. Hence, these soils are called as regur and black cotton soils.
- Other major crops grown on the black soils include wheat, jowar, linseed, Virginia tobacco, castor, sunflower and millets.
- Rice and sugarcane are equally important where irrigation facilities are available.
- Large varieties of vegetables and fruits are also successfully grown on the black soils.
- This soil has been used for growing a variety of crops for centuries without adding fertilisers and manures, with little or no evidence of exhaustion.

3. Red Soil

- This soil developed on Archean granite occupies the second largest area of the country. The presence of ferric oxides makes the colour of soil red, ferric oxides occurring as thin coatings on the soil particles.
- The top layer of the soil is red in colour due to wide diffusion of iron in crystalline and metamorphic rocks and the horizon below is yellowish when it occurs in hydrated form.
- Its extent is 18.5 % of the area. Its texture ranges from sandy to clayey and loamy. This soil is also known as the omnibus group.

Characteristics of Red Soils

- These are well drained soil and the structure is sandy.
- Once irrigated and added with humus, it gives a high yield because the mineral base is rich.
- They are rich in iron and potash but deficient in other minerals.

Types of Red Soil

Rainfall is highly variable. Thus, the soil has developed 3 sub-types :

1. **Red & Yellow Soil** The required rainfall is 200 cm. They are found in Nagaland, Mizoram, Manipur Hills, parts of Malabar coast. They require quick drainage.
2. **Red Sandy Soil** It is found in drier plateaus like Karnataka, Tamil Nadu, Telangana, Rayalaseema. The required rainfall is 40-60 cm.

3. **Red Alluvial Soil** It is found along river valleys and has good fertility.

Generally, these soils are deficient in phosphate, lime, magnesia, humus and nitrogen.

Distribution of Red Soils

They are mainly found in the Peninsula from Tamil Nadu in the South to Bundelkhand in the North and Raj Mahal in the East to Kathiawad in the West.

Crops Grown in Red Soil

- It supports rice, sugarcane, cotton cultivation.
- Millets and pulses are grown in drier areas.
- Kaveri and Vaigai basins are famous for red alluvium and if irrigated well, are suitable for paddy.
- Large regions of Karnataka and Kerala have developed Red soil regions for rubber and coffee plantation farming.

4. Laterite Soil

This soil has emerged in those regions where the following conditions are fulfilled :

- There must be laterite rock or structure (Laterites are rich in iron and aluminium content).
- Alternating dry and wet periods are more suitable for the development of laterite soils.

Characteristics

- It is brown in colour.
- It is composed essentially of a mixture of hydrated oxides of aluminium and iron.
- Iron oxides are found in nodules form.
- It is rich in iron and aluminium but poor in nitrogen, phosphorous, potash, lime and magnesia.
- Its humus and water-retaining capacities are moderate.
- Bacterial activities have been very high and heavy precipitation develops leaching of humus as a result humus content is moderate to low.

Distribution

- It is found in patches in Western Ghats (Goa and Maharashtra).
- Belgaum district of Karnataka and in laterite plateau of Kerala, the state of Orissa, in the Eastern Ghats, Amarkantak plateau region of MP, Panchmahal district of Gujarat and Santhal Pargana divisions of Jharkhand.

Crops Grown in Laterite Soil

- It is famous for crops like groundnut, cashew nut, etc.
- Laterite soil of Karnataka is given to coffee, rubber, and spices farming.

5. Forest Soil/ Mountain Soil

It is principally found on mountains with steeper slopes, high relief, shallow profiles.

Characteristics

- It is thin layered and the profiles and horizons are poorly developed. Due to fast drainage, it has been vulnerable to soil erosion.
- It is rich in organic content – humus content is also adequate but other nutrients are deficient. It is a loamy soil when sand, silt and clay are in mixed form.
- Large area also given to shifting agriculture where the soil fertility deteriorates after 2-3 years.
- Due to less scope of agriculture, silvi pastoral farming (forest+grasses) can be sustained.

Distribution

- These are generally found over 900 m altitude.
- Himalayas, Himalayan foothills, mountain slopes of Western Ghats, Nilgiri, Annamalai and Cardamom hills.

Crops Grown in Forest Soil

- It is very helpful to those crops which need favourable air and water drainage which is provided by this soil by virtue of being on slopes.
- Generally used for rubber plantation, bamboo plantation and also tea, coffee and fruits farming.

6. Desert Soil

This soil is deposited by wind action and mainly found in the arid and semi-arid areas like Rajasthan, West of the Aravallis, Northern Gujarat, Saurashtra, Kachchh, Western parts of Haryana and Southern part of Punjab.

Characteristics

- It lacks moisture content. Humus content is less and nitrogen is originally low, but some of it is available in the form of nitrates.
- They are sandy with low organic matter. Living microorganisms are low in content.
- It is rich in iron contents. Phosphorus content is nearly adequate, rich in lime and bases.
- It has low soluble salts and moisture with very low retaining capacity.
- If irrigated, this soil gives a high agricultural return.

Crops Grown in Desert Soil

These are suitable for less water-intensive crops like bajra, pulses, fodder and guar.

Distribution

Western Rajasthan, Rann of Kachchh, in patches in South Haryana and South Punjab.

7. Saline and Alkaline Soil

- It is both natural and anthropogenic.
- **Natural** includes dried up lakes of Rajasthan and Rann of Kachchh. It has emerged in the Palaya basin (a clay basin in the midst of the desert).
- **Anthropogenic** is developed in Western Uttar Pradesh and Punjab due to faulty agriculture.

Characteristics

- It lacks of moisture, humus and living microorganisms, as a result, humus formation is almost absent.
- It is alkali soil contains a large content of NaCl and is infertile. These are also called Reh, Usar, Kallar, Rakar, Thur and Chopan.
- Sodium chloride and sodium sulphate are present in this soil. It is suitable for leguminous crops.

Distribution

These are mainly found in Rajasthan, Haryana, Punjab, Uttar Pradesh, Bihar and Maharashtra.

8. Peaty and Marshy Soil/Bog Soil

This soil originates from the areas where adequate drainage is not possible. It is rich in organic matter and has high salinity. They are deficient in potash and phosphate.

Characteristics

- Dominance of clay and mud which make it heavy.
- Rich in moisture content but at the same time, greater content of salt and every day inundation by high tide has made it infertile soil.
- No organic activity due to excessive moisture content.

Distribution

- It is characteristic of the delta region of India.
- Besides the delta region, it is also found in Alleppey (Kerala) (known as Karri along the backwaters or Kayals of Kerala) and Almora (Uttarakhand).

Crops Grown in Peaty Soil

- Over Bengal delta, it is suitable for jute and rice and over Malabar, it is suitable for spices, rubber, big sized rice.
- It has to some extent been favorable to the Mangrove forests of India.

Characteristics of Indian Soils

- Most soils are old and mature. Soils of the peninsular plateau are much older than the soils of the great Northern plain.
- Indian soils are largely deficient in nitrogen, mineral salts, humus and other organic materials.
- Plains and valleys have thick layers of soils while hilly and plateau areas depict thin soil cover.
- Some soils like alluvial and black soils are fertile while some other soils such as laterite, desert and alkaline soils lack fertility and do not yield good harvest.
- Indian soils have been used for cultivation for hundreds of years and have lost much of their fertility.

Problems of Indian Soils

The following are the problems of Indian soils :

- Soil erosion in Himalayan region, Chambal Ravines, etc. Deficiency in fertility in the Red, lateritic and other soils.
- Desertification around the Thar desert, rain-shadow regions like parts of Karnataka, Telangana, etc.
- Waterlogging in Punjab-Haryana plain.
- Salinity and alkalinity in excessively irrigated regions of Punjab, Haryana, Karnataka, etc.
- Wasteland and overexploitation of soils due to increase in population. Encroachment of agricultural land due to urban and transport development.

Soil Erosion

- Soil erosion is the loosening and displacement of topsoil particles from the land. Soil erosion is a natural process that occurs on all lands.
- Soil erosion may occur at a slow or fast rate. Soil erosion in nature maybe :
  - a slow process (or geological erosion) or
  - a fast process promoted by deforestation, floods, tornadoes or other human activities.

Types of Soil Erosion

Soil erosion is classified on the basis of the physical agent responsible for erosion.

The various types of soil erosion are consequently referred to as:

1. Water erosion
2. Wind erosion

1. Water Erosion

Running water is one of the main agents, which carries away soil particles. Soil erosion by water occurs by means of raindrops, waves, or ice.

Soil erosion by water is termed differently according to the intensity and nature of erosion which are as follows:

- **Raindrop erosion** Raindrops behave like tiny bombs when falling on exposed soil, displace soil particles and destroy soil structure.

  Average size of a raindrop is approximately 5 mm in diameter, falling through the air hits the soil at a velocity of 32 km/hr.

  Presence of vegetation on land prevents raindrops from falling directly on the soil thus erosion of soil in areas covered by vegetation is prevented.

- **Sheet erosion** The detachment and transportation of soil particles by flowing rainwater is called sheet or wash off erosion. This is a very slow process and often remains unnoticed.
- **Rill erosion** In rill erosion, finger-like rills appear on the cultivated land after it has undergone sheet erosion. These rills are usually smoothened out every year while forming.

  Each year the rills slowly increase in number and become wider and deeper. When rills increase in size, they are called gullies. Ravines are deep gullies.
- **Stream-bank erosion** The erosion of soil from the banks (shores) of the streams or rivers due to the flowing water is called bank erosion.
- **Landslide** A sudden mass movement of soil is called a landslide. Landslides occur due to instability or loss of balance of land mass with respect to gravity.
- **Coastal erosion** Coastal erosion of soil occurs along seashores. It is caused by the wave action of the sea and the inward movement of the sea into the land.

Consequences of Water Erosion

- Erosion removes the most fertile part of the soil. The less fertile subsoil is left.
- The fine particles of the topsoil which contain the bulk of nutrients and organic matter needed by the plants are lost from soil erosion.
- Erosion may result in the removal of seeds or seedlings so that the soil becomes bare. Bare soil is more vulnerable to erosion both by wind and water.
- Removal of seeds and seedlings reduces the ability of soil to store water.
- Sheet, rill, gully and stream bank erosion also cause siltation of rivers, streams and fields.
- Deposition of silt results in damage of crops and pastures and sedimentation of water bodies like streams, dams, reservoirs, etc.
- Sedimentation of water bodies deteriorates water quality and damages aquatic habitats and organisms.
- Coastal erosion causes the adjourning land to become covered by sand.

2. Wind Erosion

Soil erosion by wind is more common in areas where the natural vegetation has been destroyed. Such conditions occur mainly in arid and dry areas along the sandy shores of oceans, lakes and rivers.

The loose soil particles are blown and transported from wind by following three ways:

- **Siltation** blown by the wind in a series of short bounces.
- **Suspension** transported over long distances in the form of suspended particles.
- **Surface creep** transported at ground level by high-velocity winds.

Consequences of Wind Erosion

- Wind erosion removes the finer soil material including organic matter, clay, silt etc. It leaves behind coarser and less fertile material.
- The productive capacity of the soil is lost as most of the plant nutrients which remain attached to smaller colloidal soil fractions are lost.
- Wind erosion also damages roads and fertile agricultural fields by depositing large quantities of air blown soil particles.

Soil Erosion Caused by Human Activity

Certain human activities like deforestation, farming, mining, developmental work, human settlements and transport accelerate soil erosion.

Deforestation

- Deforestation includes cutting and felling of trees, removal of forest litter, etc. Browsing and trampling by livestock, forest fires, also leads to deforestation.
- Deforestation leads to erosion. It further leads to land degradation, nutrient and the disruption of the delicate soil-plant relationship.

Farming

- Agriculture is a major human activity that causes soil erosion. Crops are grown, harvested, land re-ploughed, exposed to wind and rain intermittently.
- All this prevents replenishment of moisture. Agriculture also causes the worst type of soil erosion on farmland in the form of wash off or sheet erosion.
- The following agricultural practices can lead to accelerated soil erosion:
  - **Tilling** or ploughing increases the chances of erosion because it disturbs the natural soil surface and protective vegetation.
  - **Continuous cropping** Continuous cropping of the same land and extending of cultivation of marginal and sub-marginal lands encourages soil erosion.
  - **Cultivation on mountain slopes** Cultivation on mountain slopes without appropriate land treatment measures such as bounding, terracing and trenching cause soil erosion and loss of soil nutrients.
  - **Monoculture** A monoculture crop is harvested all at one time, which leaves the entire fields bare exposing it to both water and wind.
    Without vegetation natural rainfall is not retained by the soil and flows rapidly over the surface rather than into the ground. It also carries away the topsoil which results in soil erosion and degradation.
  - **Overgrazing** It means too many animals are allowed to feed on a piece of grassland. Trampling and grazing by cattle destroy the vegetation of the area.

In the absence of adequate vegetative cover, the land becomes highly susceptible to both wind and water erosion.

- **Economic activities** Soil erosion also occurs due to economic activities. The extraction of useful natural resources such as metals, minerals and fossil fuels, etc., from the land causes serious disturbance to the land leading to soil erosion and drastic changes in the landscape.
- **Developmental activities** Soil erosion may also occur because of various developmental activities such as housing, transport, communication, recreation, etc. Building construction also promotes soil erosion because accelerated soil erosion takes place during the construction of houses, roads, rail tracks, etc.

  The construction of such facilities causes massive disturbance to the land, resulting in soil erosion and disruption of the natural drainage system.

Land/Soil Degradation

- Degraded land is classified on the basis of the productive capacity of the land. Slight degradation refers to the condition where crop yield potential is reduced by 10%.
- Moderate degradation refers to 10-50% reduction in yield potential and in severe degradation means that the land that has yield potential is lost more than 50% of its potential yield capacity (productive capacity).
- Some causes of land degradation are :
  - Use of agrochemical (chemical fertilisers and pesticides)
  - Excessive irrigation
  - Cultivation of high yielding plant varieties

Agrochemical and Their Harmful Effects on Land

Excess use of chemical fertilisers and pesticides leads to the following problems:

- Most of the chemical fertilisers used in modern agriculture contain macronutrients like nitrogen, phosphorus and potassium (NPK).
- The excessive addition of NPK to the soil however, causes the plants to absorb more micronutrients from the soil.
- As a result, the soil becomes deficient in micronutrients like zinc, iron, copper, etc and the soil productivity decreases.
- Fertiliser which is not used by plants is washed down with rainwater and carried into water bodies, resulting in eutrophication or algal bloom leading to the death of aquatic life.
- About one-fourth of the applied fertiliser is not used by the crop plants and is leached down into the soil and underground water aquifer.
- Excess nitrates in water are harmful especially in bottle-fed infants who cause the disease, methemoglobinemia.

Problems due to Excessive Irrigation

Excessive irrigation of soil may lead to waterlogging and accumulation of salt in the soil. Both these degrade the soil.

- **Waterlogging** Excessive irrigation of land without proper drainage raises the water table. This causes the soil to become drenched with water or waterlogged.

  This waterlogged soil cannot support good plant growth due to a lack of air, particularly oxygen in the soil, which is essential for the respiration of plant roots.

  Waterlogged soils lack mechanical strength and cannot support the weight of plants that fell down and got logged thus becoming submerged in the mud.
- **Salt affectation** In areas of high temperature, excessive irrigation of land usually causes the accumulation of salt in the soil. This is because water evaporates fast leaving behind traces of salt in the soil.

  As cycles of irrigation are repeated the leftover salt accumulates and forms a thick layer of grey or white effervescence on the surface.

  The productivity of salt-affected soil is low. Plants in saline soil are unable to absorb nutrients and so face water stress (lack of water) even when moisture is abundant in the soil.

Impact of High Yielding Plant Varieties on Leads to Soil Degradation

- High Yielding Varieties (HYV) have helped to increase food production but at the same time, they have greatly impacted the environment are man-made varieties of agricultural plants, fodder plants, forest trees, livestock and fishes.
- The HYVs require adequate irrigation and extensive use of fertilisers, pesticides to be successful.
- As we have already seen about land degradation due to agrochemicals.

Measures for Preventing Soil Erosion and Land Degradation

- To prevent soil erosion by wind, trees should be planted in such a way so that they break the force of the wind.
- The trees not only cover soil from the Sun, wind and water, they also help to hold the soil particles.
- Cultivation, farming and agricultural techniques help in the prevention of soil erosion and land degradation.

Cultivation and Farming Techniques

- **Ploughing style** The ploughing style substantially reduces the amount of erosion. Tilling the field at right angles to the slope called counter ploughing in the soil of the land helps prevent or reduce soil erosion.

  The ridges that are created act like tiny dams and hold the water and help its seepage into the soil instead of let it run down freely the slopes causing soil pollution.

  Contour ploughing can reduce soil erosion by up to 50%.
- **Strip Farming** This is another controlling method of soil erosion. This involves planting the main crops in widely spaced rows and filling in the spaces with another crop to ensure complete ground cover.
  The ground is completely covered so it retards water flow which thus soaks down into the soil, consequently reducing erosion problems.
- **Terracing** It is another method of reducing or preventing soil erosion on mountain slopes. In this method, terraces are created on the steep slopes.

  Terracing is usually done on slopes, by leveling off areas on the slope to prevent the flow of water down it.

  There are disadvantages to terracing, however, in that the terraces themselves can be easily eroded and they generally require a lot of maintenance and repair.
  The time or season at which a field is tilled can also have a major effect on the amount of erosion that takes place during the year. If a field is ploughed in the fall, erosion can take place all winter long, however, if the ground cover remains until spring, there is not as much time for the erosion to take place.
- **No-till cultivation** Is also used as a preventive method for soil erosion. Specialised machinery is available that can loosen the soil, plant seeds and take care of weed control all at once with minimum disturbance to the soil.

  However, there is an adverse effect due to this practice as weed and insect populations can increase since they are not continuously being removed and so can compete or destroy crops.
- **Polyvarietal cultivation** Also helps in controlling soil erosion. In this method, the field is planted with several varieties of the same crop.

  As the harvest time varies for different varieties of the crops, they are selectively harvested at different times. As the entire field is not harvested at one time and so it is not bare or exposed all at once and the land remains protected from erosion.
- **Addition of organic matter** To the soil is also an important method for reducing soil erosion. This is achieved by ploughing in crop residues or entire the crop grown specifically for being ploughed into the ground.

  Microbes in the soil decompose the organic matter and produce polysaccharides which are sticky and act in gluing in the soil particles together and thus help the soil to resist erosion.

Agriculture Techniques

- **Organic farming or green manures** Instead of applying chemical fertiliser for supplementing the nitrogen content of the soil, we can use the natural process that involves the use of nitrogen-fixing bacteria in the legume root nodules.

  In addition to this, the use of organic forms of fertilisers such as cow dung, agricultural wastes also improves the nutrients status of soils.

  This may also help to reduce the excessive and prolonged use of chemical fertilisers and thus minimise their toxic effects.
- **Biofertilisers** Micro-organisms are important constituents of fertile soils. They participate in the development of soil structure, add to the available nutritional elements and improve the physical conditions of the soil. A large variety of microorganisms are being used as biofertilisers for improving the nutritional status of the crop fields.
- **Biological pest control** (biological control) The natural predators and parasites of pests play a significant role in controlling plant pests and pathogens. They are nowadays used by farmers to control or eliminate plant pests.

  The biological control agents of pests do not enter in the food chain or poison animals and so are not likely to harm mankind.

Extra Facts From Tamil Nadu Board and NIOS

- **Alluvial soil** has sediments deposited by streams and rivers when they slowly loose.
- **Black soil** consists of calcium and magnesium carbonates, high quantities of iron, aluminium, lime and magnesia.
- **Red soil** formed by decomposition of ancient crystalline rocks like granite and gneiss.
- **Laterite soils** is formed by the process of leaching.
- Forest and mountain soil is formed due to mechanical weathering caused by **snow, rain** and **temperature** variation.

Natural Resources of India

(SOURCES)

Class-X New NCERT Chap 1 (Resources and Development), Chap 3 (Water Resources), Class-X Old NCERT Chap 4 (Land Use and Water Resources), Class-XII New NCERT Chap 3 (Land Resources and Agriculture), Class-XII Old NCERT Chap 1 (Natural Resources of India), Tamil Nadu Board (Class XII), NIOS

Natural Resources

- Natural resources are resources that exist without any actions of humankind. This includes the sources of valued characteristics such as commercial and industrial use, aesthetic value, scientific interest and cultural value.
- On Earth, it includes sunlight, atmosphere, water, land, all minerals alongwith all vegetation and animal life.
- Natural resources are naturally occurring substances that have been considered valuable in their natural form. Its value rests in the amount available and demands for it.

Classification of Resources

Natural resources may be further classified as follows:

- **On the basis of origin** Biotic and abiotic
- **On the basis of exhaustibility** Renewable and non-renewable
- **On the basis of ownership** Individual, community, national and international
- **On the basis of status of development** Potential, developed stock and reserves.

On the Basis of Origin

On the basis of origin, natural resources can be categorised as follows :

- **Biotic Resources** These resources include all living elements of the environment. Forests and forest products, crops, birds, wildlife, fishes and other marine lives are the examples of biotic resources. These resources reproduce and regenerate themselves, hence, are renewable. Coal and mineral oil are also biotic resources but they are non-renewable.
- **Abiotic Resources** These resources include all non-living elements of the environment. Land, water, air and minerals. e.g., iron, copper, gold, silver etc., are abiotic resources.
- They are exhaustible and non-renewable as they cannot be regenerated or reproduced.

On the Basis of Exhaustibility

On the basis of exhaustibility, natural resources can be categorised as follows :

Renewable Resources

- Renewable resources can be replenished naturally. Some of these resources, like sunlight, air, wind, water, etc., are continuously available and their quantities are not noticeably affected by human consumption.
- Though many renewable resources do not have such a rapid recovery rate, these resources are susceptible to depletion by over-use.
- Resources from a human use perspective are classified as renewable so long as the rate of replenishment/ recovery exceeds that of the rate of consumption. They replenish easily compared to non-renewable resources.

Non-renewable Resources

- Non-renewable resources either form slowly or do not naturally form in the environment.
- Minerals are the most common resource included in this category.

- From the human perspective, resources are non-renewable when their rate of consumption exceeds the rate of replenishment/recovery; a good example of this are fossil fuels, which are in this category because their rate of formation is extremely slow (potentially millions of years), meaning they are considered non-renewable.
- Some resources naturally deplete in amount without human interference, the most notable of these being radio-active elements such as uranium, which naturally decay into heavy metals.
- Of these, the metallic minerals can be re-used by recycling them, but coal and petroleum cannot be recycled.
- Once they are completely used, they take millions of years to replenish.

On the Basis of Ownership

On the basis of ownership, natural resources can be categorised as follows :

- **Individual Resources** These are also owned privately by individuals. Many farmers own land which is allotted to them by government against the payment of revenue. In villages there are people with land ownership but there are many who are landless.
  Urban people own plots, houses and other property. Plantation, pasture lands, ponds, water in wells etc., are some of the examples of resources ownership by individuals.
- **Community Owned Resources** There are resources which are accessible to all the members of the community. Village commons (grazing grounds, burial grounds, village ponds, etc), public parks, picnic spots, playgrounds in urban areas are de facto accessible to all the people living there.
- **National Resources** Technically, all the resources belong to the nation. The country has legal powers to acquire even private property for public good. You might have seen roads, canals, railways being constructed on fields owned by some individuals. Urban Development Authorities get empowered by the government to acquire land.
  All the minerals, water resources, forests, wildlife, land within the political boundaries and oceanic area up to **12 nautical miles** (22.2 km) from the coast termed as territorial water and resources therein belong to the nation.
- **International Resources** There are international institutions which regulate some resources.
  The oceanic resources beyond **200 nautical miles** of the Exclusive Economic Zone belong to open ocean and no individual country can utilise these without the concurrence of international institutions.

On the Basis of Status of Development

On the basis of status of development, natural resources can be categorised as follows :

- **Potential Resources** Potential resources are those that may be used in the future. For example, petroleum in sedimentary rocks that, until drilled out and put to use remains a potential resource.
- **Actual Resources** Those resources that have been surveyed, quantified and qualified and are currently used in development, such as wood processing and are typically dependent on technology.
- **Reserve Resources** The part of an actual resource that can be developed profitably in the future.
- **Stock Resources** Those that have been surveyed, but cannot be used due to lack of technology e.g., hydrogen.

Land Resource in India

- Land is an important resource as humans live on it and obtain most of their needs from land. It is a mother of biotic resources or biosphere.
- The utilisation of land depends upon physical factors like topography, soil and climate as well as upon human factors such as the density of population, duration of occupation of the area, land tenure and technical levels of the people.
- There are spatial and temporal differences in land utilisation due to the continued interplay of physical and human factors.
- In India, various types of physical features are found like mountain, plateau, plains, islands, etc. Around 43% land area is plain which is suitable for agriculture. Mountain constitute 30% and 27% are plateaus.

Land Use Pattern

- **Net Sown Area** is 46% of the total geographic area because of the extensive availability of flat terrain in India. About 22% of the country is under forest cover.
- **Barren and unculturable waste land** amounts to about 8.5%.
- About 5.5% land is under **non-agricultural uses** like houses, industries, etc.
- Rest of the area is under tree crops, grooves, permanent pastures and grazing lands, etc.

Land Use Categories

- Land use records are maintained by the land revenue department.
- The land use categories add up to the reporting area, which is somewhat different from the geographical area.

- The difference between the two concepts is that while the former changes somewhat depending on the estimates of the land revenue records, the latter does not change and stays fixed as per Survey of India measurements.
- The **Survey of India** is responsible for measuring the geographical area of administrative units in India.

The land use categories as maintained in the Land Revenue Records are as follows :

1. Forests

- It is important to note that the area under actual forest cover is different from the area classified as forest. The latter is the area which the Government has identified and demarcated for forest growth.
- The land revenue records are consistent with the latter definition. Thus, there may be an increase in this category without any increase in the actual forest cover.
- Area under forest cover was 40.41 million hectares in 1950-1951 which increased to 69 million hectares in 1999-2000. The total forest cover of the country is 7137898 sq km which is 21.71% of the geographical area of the country according to the **India State of Forest Report** (ISFR) 2021.
- Tree and forest cover together made up 24.62% (809537 sq km) of India's area. In the last assessment, it was 24.56%. However, 24.39% of forest land to the total reporting area is not sufficient for a tropical country like India where about 33% of the total land should be under forests.
- This will require massive tree plantations, vigorous restrictions on the reckless felling of trees, reclaiming of forest area, etc.
- The increase in share under forest can be accounted for by an increase in demarcated area under forest rather than the actual increase in forest cover in the country.

2. Land put to Non-agricultural Uses

- Land under settlements (rural and urban), infrastructure (roads, canals, etc) industries, shops, etc., are included in this category.
- The rate of increase is the highest in the case of areas under non-agricultural uses. This is due to the changing structure of the Indian economy.
- An expansion of area under both urban and rural settlements has added to the increase in area under non-agricultural uses. Thus, the area under non-agricultural uses is increasing at the expense of wastelands and agricultural land.
- The largest amount of land in this category is in Andhra Pradesh followed by Rajasthan, Himachal Pradesh, Maharashtra, Madhya Pradesh, Gujarat, Uttar Pradesh and Bihar.

3. Barren and Wastelands

- The land which may be classified as a wasteland such as barren hilly terrains, desert lands, ravines, etc., normally cannot be brought under cultivation with the available technology.
- As the pressure on land increased, both from the agricultural and non-agricultural sectors, the wastelands and culturable wastelands have witnessed a decline over time. The amount of this land has been variable right from 1950-51 to 2010-11, the data for which are available. It accounted for 13.8% of the total reported area in 1999-2000.
- The largest amount of land in this category of land is in Andhra Pradesh followed by Rajasthan, Himachal Pradesh, Maharashtra, Madhya Pradesh, Gujarat, Uttar Pradesh and Bihar.

4. Area under Permanent Pastures and Grazing Lands

- Most of this type of land is owned by the village 'Panchayat' or the Government. Only a small proportion of this land is privately owned. The land owned by the village panchayat comes under **Common Property Resources.**
- A total area of 10.3 million hectares is devoted to permanent pastures and other grazing lands. This amounts to about 4% of the total reporting area of the country.
- Grazing takes place mostly in forests and other uncultivated lands wherever pasturage is available.
- The area presently under pastures and other grazing lands is not sufficient keeping in view the large population of livestock in the country.
- About one-third of the reporting area in Himachal Pradesh is under pastures. The proportion varies from 4 to 10% in Madhya Pradesh, Karnataka, Gujarat, Rajasthan, Maharashtra and Odisha. It is less than 3% in the remaining parts of the country.
- The decline in land under pastures and grazing lands can be explained by pressure from agricultural land. Illegal encroachment due to the expansion of cultivation on common pasture lands is largely responsible for this decline.

5. Area under Miscellaneous Tree Crops and Groves (Not included in net sown area)

- Land under miscellaneous tree crops and groves include all cultivable land which is not included under net area sown but is put to some agricultural use. Land under casuarina trees, thatching grass, bamboo, bushes, other groves for fuel, etc., which are not included under orchards are classed under this category.

- Most of this land is privately owned. Land under this category declined sharply from 198 million hectares in 1950-51 to only 4.46 million hectares in 1960-61 and further to 4.29 million hectares in 1970-71.
- After that juncture, the area under miscellaneous tree crops and groves has shown varying trends and stood at 3.21 million hectares of the total reporting area in 1999-2000.
- Odisha has the largest area in this category followed by Uttar Pradesh, Bihar, Karnataka, Andhra Pradesh Assam and Tamil Nadu.

6. Culturable Wasteland

- The 'wasteland survey and reclamation committee' defines 'culturable waste' as the land available for cultivation but not used for cultivation for one reason or the other.
- This land was used in the past but has been abandoned for some reason. It is not being used at present due to such constraints as lack of water, salinity or alkalinity of soil, soil erosion, waterlogging, an unfavorable physiographic position, or human neglect.
- Any land which is left fallow (uncultivated) for more than five years is included in this category. It can be brought under cultivation after improving it through reclamation practices.
- *Reh, bhur, usar* and *khola* tracts of Uttar Pradesh, Punjab and Haryana as well as in several other parts of the country are examples of such lands.
- Rajasthan has 4.3 lakh hectare of cultivable wasteland which is about 36% of the total wasteland of India. The other states with considerable culturable wasteland are Gujarat (43.6%), Madhya Pradesh (10.2%), Uttar Pradesh (6.93%) and Maharashtra (6.83%).
- The land under this category has declined considerably from about 22.9 million hectare in 1950-51 to 13.8 million hectare in 1999-2000.
- This decline in the wasteland is due to some land reclamation schemes launched in India after Independence.
- For long-term conservation and maintenance of eco balance, this land should be put under afforestation and not under crop farming.
- As the pressure on land increased, both from the agricultural and non-agricultural sectors, the wastelands and culturable wastelands have witnessed a decline over time.

7. Current Fallow

- Fallow of one year is called **current fallow**.
- There has been an increase in the area under current fallow from 10.68 to 14.70 million hectare from 1950-1951 to 1999-2000.
- Andhra Pradesh with about 2.2 million hectares has the largest area as current fallow. This is followed by over 1.3 million hectares in Rajasthan, 1.2 million hectares in Bihar.
- Fallowing is a cultural practice adopted for giving the land rest. The land recoups the lost fertility through natural processes.
- The trend of current fallow fluctuates a great deal over years, depending on the variability of rainfall and cropping cycles.

8. Fallow other than Current Fallow

- This is also a cultivable land which is left uncultivated for more than a year but less than five years.
- There had been a sharp decline in fallow lands other than current fallow from 17.4 million hectare to 11.18 million hectare from 1950-1951 to 1999-2000.
- The largest area of over 1.7 million hectare of fallow land other than current fallow is in Rajasthan followed by 1.5 million hectares in Andhra Pradesh and over one million hectares in Maharashtra.

9. Net Sown Area

- The physical extent of land on which crops are sown and harvested is known as net sown area.
- This area has a special significance in an agricultural country like India because agricultural production largely depends upon this type of land.
- The net sown area in 1950-51 was 118.7 million hectares which increased to 141.58 million hectares in 2010-11 as it was in 2000-01.
- The per capita cultivated land has gone down drastically from 0.53 hectares in 1951 to 0.11 hectares in 2011-12.
- It may be noted that agricultural prosperity does not depend as much on the total net sown area as it does on the percentage of net sown area to the total reporting area.
- There are large variations in the proportion of net sown area to total reporting area from one state to another. Punjab and Haryana had some of the highest proportions of 82.6% and 80.5% respectively while Arunachal Pradesh had 3%.
- The decline in the net sown area is a recent phenomenon that started in the late nineties, before which it was registering a slow increase.
- There are indications that most of the decline has occurred due to the increase in area under non-agricultural use.
- The **Cropping Intensity** (CI) is calculated as follows :

$$\text{Cropping Intensity} = \frac{\text{Gross Cropped Area (GCA)}}{\text{Net Sown Area (NSA)}} \times 100$$

Changes in Pattern of Land Use

- The agricultural land use has also recorded some substantial changes in the cropping pattern. The area under wheat and rice has increased at the cost of pulses, millets and fodder while the area under oilseeds, sugarcane, vegetables and orchards has increased.
- Unfortunately, about 70% of the good quality agricultural land has gone out of agriculture (Urbanisation, industrialisation and development of roads and railways, etc.,) and the former fallow land, pastures and degraded forests areas have been brought under agriculture.

Changes in Pattern of Land Use in India

- Land use change represents almost 25% of total global emissions. It can be a factor in CO_2 (carbon dioxide) atmospheric concentration and is thus a contributor to global climate change.
- Land degradation is affecting 3.2 billion people worldwide – Ecosystem services e.g., forest, agriculture, grassland tourism, etc., worth $10.6 trillion are lost due to land degradation annually.
- A report analysis done by the Food and Agriculture Organisation of the United Nations, states that by 2050, over 500 million hectares of new agricultural land will be needed to meet the global food demand.
- According to the **Intergovernmental Platform on Biodiversity and Ecosystem Services** (IPBES), over 70% of all-natural, ice-free land in the world is affected by human use and this could further rise to 90% by 2050.

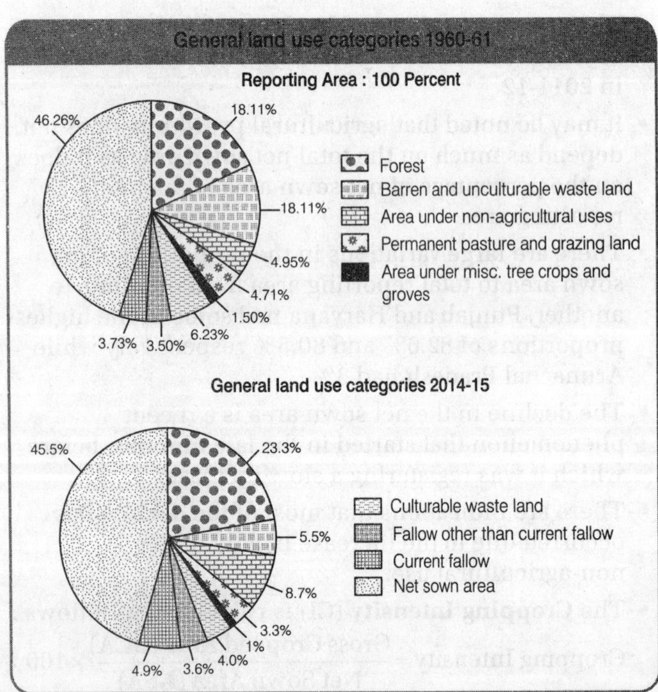

Reasons for the Changes in Land Use Pattern

- **Population Growth** In India, the rapidly growing population and the consequent high pressure on the existing resources have an adverse effect on the land resources. The cities are expanding and getting urbanised far beyond their formal limits.
- **Land Encroachment and Extensive use of Forest Resources** An increase in food and shelter demands have resulted in expansion by encroaching the uncultivated land areas and forest, shrubs and wetlands. The IPCC report on climate change and land has stated that agricultural land for food, animal feed and fiber are behind the land-use change.
- **Overgrazing** The farmers are abandoning their cultivated land for grazing purposes due to decline in its soil fertility status. Thus, we can conclude that there are two types of land-use change – one is direct anthropogenic and the other is indirect changes. Examples of anthropogenic changes include deforestation, reforestation and afforestation, agriculture and urbanisation, while the indirect changes include climate change or change in CO_2 concentration that leads to change in vegetation and land use patterns.

Common Property Resources

- Common Property Resources are usually non-exclusive resources to which rights of use are distributed among a number of co-owners, generally identified by their membership in a community or a village.
- In the context of Indian villages, common property resources include community forests, common grazing grounds, tanks and their beds, foreshores, threshing grounds, rivers and riverbeds, where well-defined property regimes may not exist.
- In pre-British India, a large part of the country's natural resources was freely available to the rural population. These resources were largely under the control of the local communities.
- Gradually, the extension of state control over these resources resulted in decay of the community management system and in this process, the common property resources available to the villagers declined substantially over the years.

Land Degradation and Desertification

- Land degradation is caused by multiple forces, including extreme weather conditions, particularly drought. It is also caused by human activities that pollute or degrade the quality of soils and land utility.
- Land degradation within dry land regions (arid, semi-arid and dry sub-humid regions) is termed as 'desertification'.

- Desertification is the process by which the biological productivity of drylands is reduced due to natural or manmade factors. It does not mean the expansion of existing deserts.

Statewise Data

- Around 23.79% of the area undergoing desertification/ land degradation with respect to TGA of the country was contributed by **Rajasthan, Maharashtra, Gujarat, Karnataka, Ladakh, Jharkhand, Odisha, Madhya Pradesh** and **Telangana**.
- India witnessed an increase in the level of desertification in 28 of 31 states and Union territories between 2011-13 and 2018-19.

Causes of Land Degradation

- **Loss of Soil Cover** Loss of soil cover, mainly due to rainfall and surface runoff, is one of the biggest reasons for desertification. It is responsible for 11.01% of the desertification in the country. Cutting forests adversely affect the soil and cause degradation. As urbanisation increases, the demand for resources is also increasing.
- **Vegetation Degradation** Vegetation degradation is defined as, 'the temporary or permanent reduction in the density, structure, species composition or productivity of vegetation cover'. It is found to be responsible for 9.15% of desertification in the country.
- **Water Erosion** It results in badland topography which itself is an initial stage of desertification. Badlands are a type of dry terrain where softer sedimentary rocks and clay-rich soils have been extensively eroded. In 2011-13, water erosion was responsible for 10.98% of desertification in the country.
- **Wind Erosion** Sand encroachment by wind reduces fertility of the soil making the land susceptible to desertification. It was found to be responsible for 5.46% of the desertification in India.
- **Climate Change** It may exacerbate desertification through alteration of spatial and temporal patterns in temperature, rainfall, solar radiation and winds.

Impact of Land Degradation

- **Economic Impact** Land degradation threatens agricultural productivity. It reduces soil health, thus in turn impacting the livelihood of rural people.
- **Climate Change** It is exacerbating climate change events, which in turn, are causing even greater degradation.

  For example, degraded land loses its capacity to absorb carbon dioxide (CO_2), a Greenhouse Gas (GHG) that is the biggest factor in worsening global warming.
- **Water Scarcity** Land degradation has resulted in a deterioration in the quantity and quality of both surface and groundwater resources. The dryland population vulnerable to water stress and drought intensity is projected to reach 178 million under the most ideal conditions of 1.5° C warming by 2050.

Water Resource

- Water is a **cyclic resource** with abundant supplies on the globe. Approximately, 71% of the Earth's surface is covered with it but freshwater constitutes only about 3% of the total water.
- India accounts for about 2.45% of the world's surface area, 4% of the world's water resources and about 16% of the world's population.
- The total water available from precipitation in the country in a year is about 4,000 cubic km.
- India experiences an average precipitation of 1170 mm per year. The availability from surface water and replenishable groundwater is 1,869 cubic km.
- Out of this only 60% can be put to beneficial uses. Thus, the total utilisable water resource in the country is only 1,122 cubic km.

Water Resources of India

Water resources of India can be classified in the following categories :

Surface Water Resources

- There are four major sources of surface water. These are rivers, lakes, ponds and tanks.
- The mean annual flow in all the river basins in India is estimated to be 1,869 cubic km.
- However, only about 690 cubic km (37%) of the available surface water can be utilised because :
  - Over 90% of annual flow of the Himalayan rivers occur over a four-month period.
  - Potential to capture such resources is complicated and limited by suitable storage reservoir sites.

Groundwater Resources

- The total replenishable groundwater resources in the country are about 432 cubic km.
- Ganga and the Brahmaputra basins, have about 46% of the total replenishable groundwater resources.
- The level of groundwater utilisation is relatively high in the river basins lying in North-Western region and parts of South India.
- The groundwater utilisation is very high in the states of Punjab, Haryana, Rajasthan and Tamil Nadu. However, there are States like Chhattisgarh, Odisha, Kerala, etc., which utilise only small proportion of their groundwater potentials.

- India also relies excessively on groundwater resources, which accounts for over 50% of irrigated area with 20 million tube wells installed.
- India has built nearly 5,000 major or medium dams, barrages, etc., to store the river waters and enhance ground water recharging.

Lagoons and Backwaters

- India has a vast coastline and the coast is very indented in some states. Due to this, a number of **lagoons** and **lakes** have formed.
- The States like Kerala, Odisha and West Bengal have vast surface water resources in these lagoons and lakes.
- Although, water is generally brackish in these water bodies, it is used for fishing and irrigating certain varieties of paddy crops, coconut, etc.

Water Demand and Utilisation

- India has traditionally been an agrarian economy and about two-third of its population have been dependent on agriculture.
- Development of irrigation to increase agricultural production has been assigned a very high priority in the Five Year Plans and multipurpose river valleys projects, like the Bhakra-Nangal, Hirakud, Damodar Valley, Nagarjuna Sagar, Indira Gandhi Canal Project, etc., have been taken up.

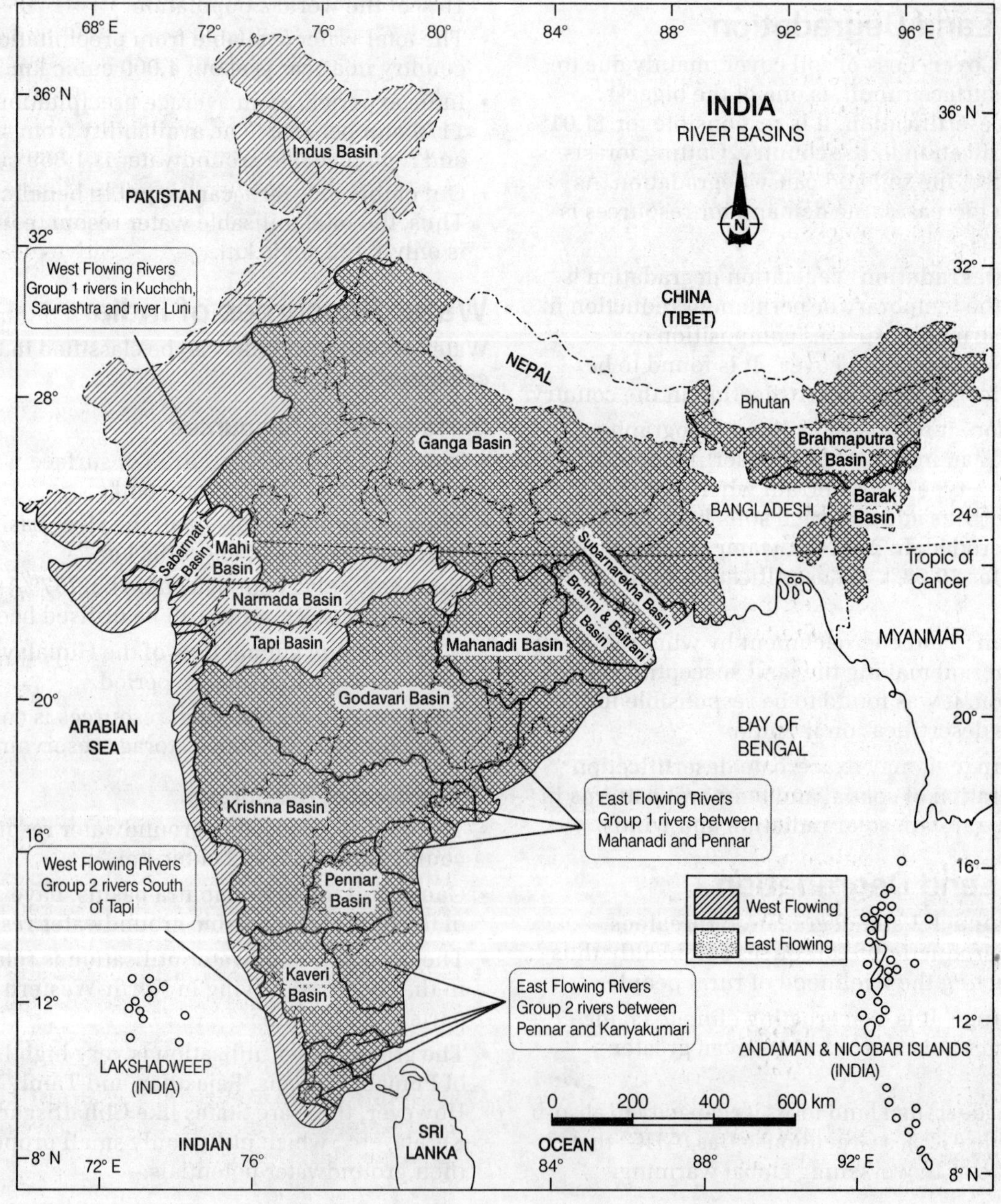

- In fact, India's water demand at present is dominated by irrigational needs. Agriculture accounts for most of the surface and groundwater utilisation, it accounts for 89% of the surface water and 92% of the groundwater utilisation.
- The share of industrial sector is limited to 2% of the surface water utilisation and 5% of the groundwater, the share of domestic sector is higher (9%) in surface water utilisation as compared to groundwater.
- The share of agricultural sector in total water utilisation is much higher than other sectors. However, in future, with development, the shares of industrial and domestic sectors in the country are likely to increase.

Demand of Water for Irrigation

- In agriculture, water is mainly used for irrigation. Irrigation is needed because of spatio-temporal variability in rainfall in the country.
- The large tracts of the country are deficient in rainfall and are **drought prone**. Winter and summer seasons are **more or less dry** in most part of the country. Hence, it is difficult to practise agriculture without assured irrigation during dry seasons.
- Even in the areas of ample rainfall like West Bengal and Bihar, breaks in monsoon or its failure creates dry spells detrimental for agriculture.
- Provision of irrigation makes **multiple cropping** possible. It has also been found that irrigated lands have higher agricultural productivity than unirrigated land. Further, the high yielding varieties of crops need regular moisture supply, which is made possible only by a developed irrigation systems.
- Green revolution strategy of agriculture development in the country has largely been successful in Punjab, Haryana and Western Uttar Pradesh.
- In these states, more than 85% of their net sown area is under irrigation.
- Of the total net irrigated area 76.1% in Punjab and 51.3% in Haryana are irrigated through wells and tubewells. The over-use of groundwater resources has led to decline in groundwater table in these states.
- In some states, like Rajasthan and Maharashtra, over withdrawals of water has increased fluoride concentration in groundwater and this practice has led to increase in concentration of **arsenic** in parts of West Bengal and Bihar.

Deterioration of Water Quality

- With the growing demand of water, its quality has been degrading day by day.
- Water quality refers to purity of water, or water without unwanted foreign substances.
- Water gets polluted by foreign matters, such as micro-organisms, chemicals, industrial and other wastes. Such matters deteriorate the quality of water and render it unfit for human use.
- When toxic substances enter lakes, streams, rivers, ocean and other water bodies, they get dissolved or lie suspended in water.
- This results in pollution of water, whereby quality of water deteriorates affecting aquatic systems.
- Sometimes, these pollutants also seep down and pollute groundwater.
- The Ganga and the Yamuna are the two highly polluted rivers in the country.

Water Conservation and Management

- With the declining availability of freshwater and increasing demand, the need has arisen to conserve and effectively manage this precious life giving resource for **sustainable development**.
- Water availability from sea/ocean, due to high cost of **desalinisation**, is considered negligible.
- India has to take quick steps and make effective policies and laws and adopt effective measures for its conservation.
- Besides developing water-saving technologies and methods, attempts are also to be made to prevent the pollution.
- There is need to encourage **watershed development**, rainwater harvesting, water recycling and reuse and conjunctive use of water for sustaining water supply in long run.
- The **Central Pollution Control Board** (CPCB) in collaboration with State Pollution Control Boards has been monitoring water quality of national aquatic resources at 507 stations.
- The data obtained from these stations show that organic and bacterial contamination continues to be the main source of pollution in rivers.
- The Yamuna river is the most polluted river in the country between Delhi and Etawah.
- Other severely polluted rivers are: the Sabarmati at Ahmedabad, the Gomti at Lucknow, the Kali, the Adyar, the Cooum (entire stretches), the Vaigai at Madurai and the Musi of Hyderabad and the Ganga at Kanpur and Varanasi.
- Groundwater pollution has occurred due to high concentrations of heavy/toxic metals, fluoride and nitrates at different parts of the country.
- The legislative provisions such as **the Water (Prevention and Control of Pollution) Act, 1974** and **Environment Protection Act 1986** have not been implemented effectively.

- The result is that in 1997, 251 polluting industries were located along the rivers and lakes. **The Water Cess Act, 1977**, meant to reduce pollution has also made marginal impacts.
- There is a strong need to generate public awareness about importance of water and impacts of water pollution.
- The public awareness and action can be very effective in reducing the pollutants from agricultural activities, domestic and industrial discharges.

Recycle and Reuse of Water

- Fresh water availability can be improved by recycle and reuse of water. Use of water of lesser quality such as reclaimed wastewater would be an attractive option for industries for cooling and firefighting to reduce their water cost.
- In urban areas, water after bathing and washing utensils can be used for gardening.
- Water used for washing vehicle can also be used for gardening. This would conserve better quality of water for drinking purposes.

Watershed Management

- Watershed management basically refers to efficient management and conservation of surface and groundwater resources.
- It involves prevention of runoff and storage and recharge of groundwater through various methods like percolation tanks, recharge wells, etc.
- In broader sense, watershed management includes conservation, regeneration and judicious use of all resources – natural (like land, water, plants and animals) and human with in a watershed.
- Watershed management aims at bringing about balance between natural resources on the one hand and society on the other. The success of watershed development largely depends upon community participation.
- The Central and State Governments have initiated many watershed development and management programmes in the country.
- **Haryali** is a watershed development project sponsored by the Central Government which aims at enabling the rural population to conserve water for drinking, irrigation, fisheries and afforestation. The Project is being executed by Gram Panchayats with people's participation.
- **Neeru-Meeru** (Water and You) programme (in Andhra Pradesh) and **Arvary Pani Sansad** (in Alwar, Rajasthan) have taken up constructions of various water-harvesting structures such as percolation tanks, dug out ponds (Johad), check dams, etc., through people's participation.
- Tamil Nadu has made water harvesting structures in the houses compulsory. No building can be constructed without making structures for water harvesting.
- There is a need to generate awareness regarding benefits of watershed development and management among people in the country and through this **Integrated Water Resource Management** approach water availability can be ensured on sustainable basis.

Rainwater Harvesting

- In ancient India, along with the sophisticated hydraulic structures, there existed an extraordinary tradition of water harvesting system.
- People had in-depth knowledge of rainfall regimes and soil types and developed wide ranging techniques to harvest rainwater, groundwater, river water and flood water in keeping with the local ecological conditions and their water needs.
- In hill and mountainous regions, people built diversion channels like the **'guls'** or **'kuls'** of the Western Himalayas for agriculture.
- 'Rooftop rainwater harvesting' was commonly practised to store drinking water, particularly in Rajasthan. In the flood plains of Bengal, people developed inundation channels to irrigate their fields.
- In arid and semi-arid regions, agricultural fields were converted into rain fed storage structures that allowed the water to stand and moisten the soil like the **Khadins** in Jaisalmer and **Johads** in other parts of Rajasthan.
- In the semi-arid and arid regions of Rajasthan, particularly in Bikaner, **Phalodi** and **Barmer**, almost all the houses traditionally had underground tanks or tankas for storing drinking water.
- The tankas were built inside the main house or the courtyard. They were connected to the sloping roofs of the houses through a pipe. Rain falling on the rooftops would travel down the pipe and was stored in these underground 'tankas'.
- Rainwater or **palar pani** is considered the purest form of natural water in Rajasthan. In a remote backward village in Mysuru, Karnataka, Gendathur, villagers have installed rainwater harvesting system in their household's rooftop to meet their water needs.
- **Rooftop rainwater harvesting** is the most common practice in Shillong, Meghalaya. Cherapunjee and Mawsynram are situated at a distance of 55 km from Shillong. Although, they receive the highest rainfall in the world, yet the state capital Shillong faces acute shortage of water.
- Nearly every household in the city has a rooftop rainwater harvesting structure. Nearly 15-25% of the total water requirement of the household is fulfilled from rooftop water harvesting.

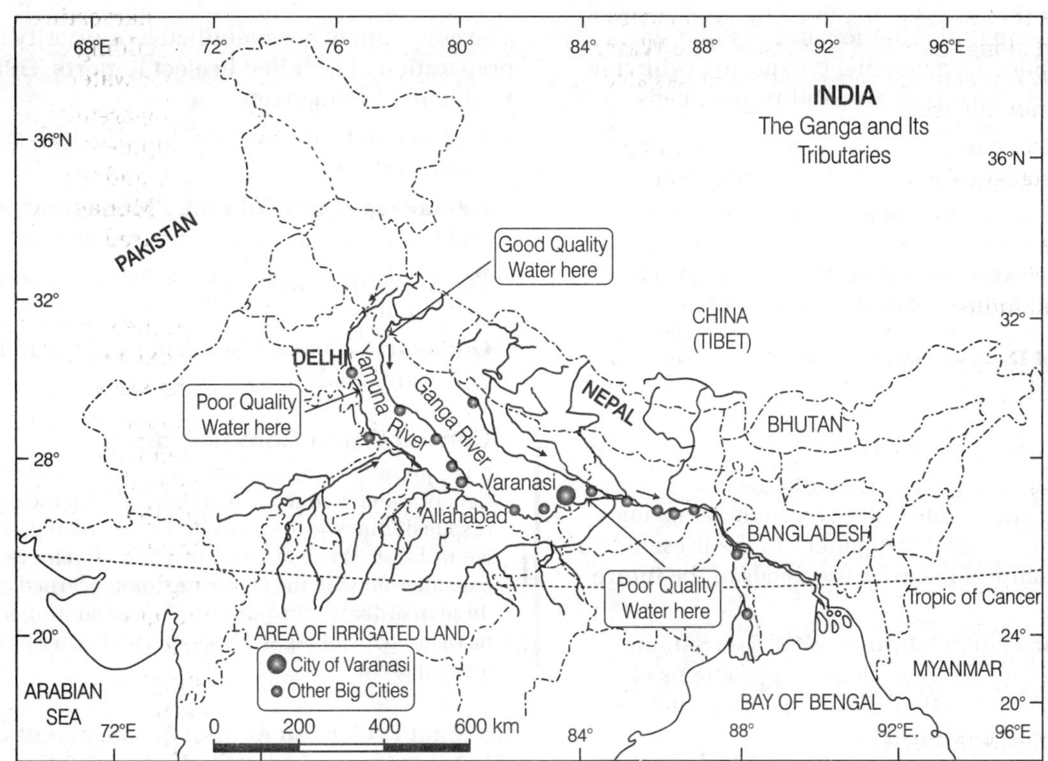

Bamboo Drip Irrigation System

- In Meghalaya, a 200-year-old system of tapping stream and spring water by using bamboo pipes, is prevalent.
- About 18-20 litres of water enters the bamboo pipe system, gets transported over hundreds of metres.
- Finally, it reduces to 20-80 drops per minute at the site of the plant.

Watershed Development in Ralegan Siddhi

- Ralegan Siddhi is a small village in the district of Ahmednagar, Maharashtra. It has become an example for watershed development throughout the country. In 1975, a youth group called **Tarun Mandal**, repaired village tank that could not hold water.
- The embankment wall leaked. The seven wells below it swelled with water in summer for the first time in the living memory of the people.
- The cultivation of water-intensive crops like sugarcane was banned.
- Crops such as pulses, oilseeds and certain cash crops with low water requirements were encouraged. People volunteered to help each other in agricultural operation.
- At present, water is adequate; agriculture is flourishing, though the use of fertilisers and pesticides is very high.

National Water Policy, 2002

It was adopted by the National Water Resources Council on 1st April, 2002.

The salient features of National Water Policy, 2002 are as follows:

- In the allocation of water, first priority should be given for drinking water, followed by irrigation, hydro-power, ecology, agro-industries and non-agricultural industries, navigation and other uses, in that order.
- The exploitation of groundwater should be regulated with reference to recharge possibilities and consideration of social equity. Both surface water and ground water should be regularly monitored for quality.
- Water should be made available to water short areas by transfer from other areas including transfer from one river basin to another, after taking into account the requirements of the areas/basins.
- Planning of water resources development projects should, be multipurpose with an integrated and multi-disciplinary approach having regard to human and ecological aspects including those of disadvantaged sections of the society.
- Adequate emphasis needs to be given to the physical and financial sustainability of existing water resources facilities.
- Needs of drought-prone areas should be given priority in the planning of project for development of water resources. These areas should be made less vulnerable through various measures.

- The water sharing /distribution amongst the states should be guided by a national perspective with due regard to water resources availability and needs within the river basin.

Day Zero Instances

- Day Zero is a situation when taps in a region start running dry.
- **Day Zero instances in India** It has been reported that Shimla, Himachal Pradesh and Udupi and Mangaluru in coastal Karnataka are on the verge of becoming Tier 2 cities which would have a 'Day Zero' situation soon.

Sustainable Development

- Sustainable economic development means development should take place without damaging the environment and development in the present should not compromise with the needs of the future generations.
- **Rio de Janeiro Earth Summit, 1992** The Summit was convened for addressing urgent problems of environmental protection and socio-economic development at the Global level.
- The Rio Convention endorsed the Global Forest Principles and adopted Agenda 21 for achieving Sustainable Development in the 21st century.
- It is the declaration signed by world leaders in 1992 at the United Nations Conference on Environment and Development (UNCED), which took place at Rio de Janeiro, Brazil. It aims at achieving global sustainable development. It is an agenda to combat environmental damage, poverty, disease through global co-operation on common interest, mutual needs and shared responsibilities. One major objective of the Agenda 21 is that every local government should draw its own local Agenda 21.

Government's Efforts for Water Conservation

- **NITI Aayog Composite Water Management Index** With the objective of achieving effective utilisation of water, NITI Aayog has developed the Composite Water Management Index. The index revolves around issues ranging from water scarcity and related morass like deaths due to lack of access to safe water, its projected increase in demand over the years and finding ways for its effective conservation.
- **Interlinking of Rivers Project** The interlinking of river project is a civil engineering project, which aims to connect Indian rivers through reservoirs and canals. The farmers will not have to depend on the monsoon for cultivation and also the excess or lack of water can be overcome during floods or drought.

  The government has identified four priority links for the preparation of **Detailed Project Reports** (DPR) under the Peninsular Component
  - **Ken Betwa Link Project** (Uttar Pradesh and Madhya Pradesh)
  - **Daman Ganga Pinjal Link Project** (Maharashtra and Gujarat)
  - **Par Tapi Narmada Link Project** (Maharashtra and Gujarat)
  - **Godavari Cauvery Link Project** (Andhra Pradesh and Tamil Nadu)

Central Water Commission (CWC)

It is a premier technical organisation in the country in the field of water resources. It is charged with the general responsibilities of initiating and coordinating, schemes for control, conservation and utilisation of water resources in consultation with the Governments concerned states. They do so in order to, the purpose of flood control, irrigation, navigation, drinking water supply and water power development.

- **National Project on Aquifer Management** (NAQUIM) It is being implemented by the **Central Ground Water Board** (CGWB). NAQUIM envisages mapping of aquifers(water bearing formations), their characterisation and development of Aquifer Management Plans to facilitate sustainable management of groundwater.
- **MGNREGA for Water Conservation** Mahatma Gandhi National Rural Employment Guarantee Act is one of the biggest government funded employment schemes in the world. The huge workforce employed under the MGNREGA has enabled the government to introduce water conservation as a project under the Act. The government aims to improve groundwater harvesting and build water conservation and storage mechanisms through MGNREGA.
- **Jal Kranti Abhiyan** (2015-16) The government is making active efforts to revolutionise villages and cities through block-level water conservation schemes.

  For example; the Jal Gram Scheme under the Jal Kranti Abhiyan is aimed at developing two model villages in water-starved areas to lead the other villages towards water conservation and preservation.
- **National Water Mission** The Government of India has launched the National Water Mission with the objective of conservation of water, minimising wastage and ensuring more equitable distribution both across and within states through integrated water resources development and management. One of the objectives of the Mission is to increase the water use efficiency by 20%.

- **National Rural Drinking Water Programme** It seeks to provide every rural person with adequate safe water for drinking, cooking and other basic domestic needs on a sustainable basis.
- **Jal Shakti Ministry and Jal Jeevan Mission** The efforts like the formation of Jal Shakti Ministry (to tackle water issues holistically) and the goal to provide piped water to all rural households by 2024, under the Jal Jeevan Mission, are steps in the right direction.
- **Multi-Purpose River Projects and Integrated Water Resources Management** Archaeological and historical records show that from ancient times we have been constructing sophisticated hydraulic structures like dams built of stone rubble, reservoirs or lakes, embankments and canals for irrigation.
- **Hydraulic Structures in Ancient India** In the first century B.C., Sringaverapura near Allahabad had sophisticated water harvesting system channelling the flood water of the river Ganga.
- During the time of Chandragupta Maurya, dams, lakes and irrigation systems were extensively built.
- Evidences of sophisticated irrigation works have also been found in Kalinga, (Odisha), Nagarjunakonda (Andhira Pradesh), Bennur (Karnataka), Kolhapur (Maharashtra), etc.
- In the 11th century, the tank in Hauz Khas, Delhi was constructed by Iltutmish for supplying water to Siri Fort area.

Traditional Water Conservation Systems around India

Traditional System	Description
Phad	It is a community-managed irrigation system in the Tapi river basin in Maharashtra. It starts with a check dam built across a river and canals to carry water to agricultural blocks with outlets to ensure excess water is removed from the canals.
Zing	It is found in Ladakh, are small tanks that collect melting glacier water. A network of guiding channels brings water from the glacier to the tank.
Kuhls	They are surface water channels found in the mountainous regions of Himachal Pradesh. The channels carry glacial waters from rivers and streams into the fields.
Zabo or Ruza System	It is practised in Nagaland. Rainwater that falls on forested hilltops is collected by channels that deposit the runoff water in pond-like structures created on the terraced hillsides.
Jackwells	The Shompen tribe of the Great Nicobar Islands uses this system, in which bamboos are placed under trees to collect runoff water from leaves and carries it to Jackwells which are pits encircled by bunds made from logs of hardwood.
Pat System	It is developed in Madhya Pradesh, in which the water is diverted from hill streams into irrigation channels by diversion bunds. They are made across the stream by piling up stones and teak leaves and mud.
Eri	It is a tank system, widely used in Tamil Nadu which acts as flood-control systems, prevents soil erosion and wastage of runoff during periods of heavy rainfall and also recharges the groundwater.
Johads	They are small Earthen check dams used to conserve and recharge ground water, mainly constructed in an area with naturally high elevation.
Panam Keni	The Kuruma tribe (a native tribe of Wayanad) uses wooden cylinders as a special type of well, which are made by soaking the stems of toddy palms and immersing them in groundwater springs.
Ahar Pynes	They are traditional flood water harvesting systems indigenous to South Bihar. Ahars are reservoirs with embankments on three sides and Pynes are artificial rivulets led off from rivers to collect water in the ahars for irrigation in the dry months.
Jhalara	Jhalaras are typically rectangular-shaped stepwells that have tiered steps on three or four sides in the city of Jodhpur.
Bawari	Bawaris are unique stepwells that were once a part of the ancient networks of water storage in the cities of Rajasthan.
Tanka	It is a cylindrical paved underground pit into which rainwater from rooftops, courtyards or artificially prepared catchments flows. It is indigenous to the Thar desert region of Rajasthan.
Khadin	Also called Dhora, is a long Earthen embankment that is built across the hill slopes of gravelly uplands. It is indigenous to the Jaisalmer region and similar to the irrigation methods of Ur region (Present Iraq).
Kund	It is a saucer-shaped catchment area that gently slopes towards the central circular underground well. It is found in the sandier tracts of Western Rajasthan and Gujarat.

Extra Facts From Tamil Nadu Board and NIOS

- Solar wind, geothermal energy, tidal energy, bio-gas etc. are the examples of renewable sources of energy.
- China is the largest producer of hydroelectricity in the world, followed by Canada.
- Wind energy is now the second fastest growing source of electricity in the world.
- Geothermal energy is derived from the natural heat of the Earth. The United States is its world's largest producer.
- The dense forest plants were converted into coal due to intense pressure and heat inside the Earth by the process of carbonisation.
- China was the largest producer of coking coal in the world in 2016 followed by Australia.
- Natural gas is considered as an environment friendly fuel because of its low carbon dioxide emissions. Therefore, this is the only fuel for the present century and it is also called green energy.
- USA has the largest reserve and is the leading producer of natural gas in the world.

22

Indian Agriculture and Irrigation

[SOURCES]

Class-VIII Old NCERT Chap 6 (Agriculture), Class XII New NCERT Chap 3 (Land Resources and Agriculture), Class XII Old NCERT Chap 2 (Main Features of Agriculture), Chap 5 (Regional Development), Tamil Nadu Board (Class XII), NIOS

Agriculture

- Agriculture is made up of two words –'*Ager*' + '*cultura*'. '*Ager*' means field and '*cultura*' means cultivation or growing.
- Agriculture is defined as the art, science and business of producing crops and livestock for economic purposes. Livestock, fisheries and poultry come under the **allied agricultural activities.**
- Two-third of the livelihood of the Indian population is directly or indirectly dependent on agriculture.
- **70%** of the labour force is directly or indirectly involved in agriculture. Agricultural sector accounts for **18.3%** of India's GVA according to 2022-23.

Types of Indian Agriculture/ Farming Systems

Based primarily on nature of land, climatic characteristics and available irrigational facilities, the farmers in India practice different types of farming.

Subsistence Farming

- Subsistence agriculture occurs when farmers grow food crops to meet the needs of themselves and their families on small holdings.
- Subsistence agriculturalists target farm output for survival and for mostly local requirements, with little or no surplus.
- Majority of farmers in the country practice subsistence farming.
- It is characterised by small and scattered land holdings and the use of primitive tools.
- As the farmers are poor, they do not use fertilisers and a high-yielding variety of seeds in their fields to the extent they should do.
- Facilities like electricity and irrigation are generally not available to them.
- The whole family works on the farm, most of the work is done manually.
- The farms are small, yield is not very high, most of the yield is consumed by the family with a very little surplus for the family.

Shifting Cultivation/Land Rotation/Jhumming

- Shifting cultivation is called so because of the shifting of the land after the cultivation of a crop when the soil losses its fertility (generally in 2 to 3 years).
- In shifting cultivation forest land is cleared and cultivated. It is also called land rotation because the same crop (generally rice) is grown on a different piece of land.
- Due to the cultivation of the same crop on the same cleared forest land year after year, soil productivity is lost.
- After the land fertility is lost, the crop is shifted to other slashed and burnt land. Shifting cultivation leads to soil erosion.
- It is because clearing of forest land leads to the clearing of vegetation over the soil which in turn leads to soil erosion.

- Shifting cultivation is practiced in North-Eastern states of India, Chhota Nagpur plateau of Jharkhand, Madhya Pradesh and in Hilly areas of the Himalayas, the Western ghats and the Eastern ghats.
- This practice is known by different names in different regions of India like:
  - Jhum in Assam
  - Ponam in Kerala
  - Podu in Andhra Pradesh and Odisha
  - Bewar, Masha, Penda and Bera in various parts of Madhya Pradesh

Crop Rotation

- Crop rotation is the reverse of land rotation (Shifting Cultivation)
- Crop rotation is the practice of planting different crops sequentially on the same plot of land to improve soil health, optimise nutrients in the soil and combat pest and weed pressure.
- In crop rotation, there is repeated cultivation of crops and fallow land which is done in a certain sequence in a scientific manner to conserve the fertility of the land.
- Suitable crop rotation is the key of modern scientific agriculture which aims to produce maximum yield by maintaining soil productivity.

Commercial Farming

- In areas where irrigation has been possible, the farmers use fertilisers and pesticides on a large scale. They have also brought their land under a high yielding variety of seeds.
- They have mechanised agriculture by introducing machines in various processes of farming.
- Also known as **industrial agriculture**, it is characterised by a low fallow ratio and higher use of inputs such as capital and labour per unit land area. This is in contrast to traditional agriculture in which the inputs per unit land are lower.

Plantation Agriculture

- Plantation agriculture is a type of commercial farming in which a single crop is grown for the entire year.
- The major crops grown during plantation agriculture are Tea, Coffee, Sugarcane, Cashew, Rubber, Banana or cotton. Major plantations are found in the tropical regions of the world. Plantations exist on every continent possessing a tropical climate.
- Rubber cultivation in Malaysia, coffee cultivation in Brazil, Tea cultivation in India and Sri Lanka are the examples of plantation agriculture.
- It is capital intensive agriculture and demands good managerial ability, technical know-how, machinery, fertilisers, irrigation and transport facilities. Plantation agriculture is **export-oriented** agriculture.

Sustainable Agriculture/Eco-Farming

- The concept of sustainable agriculture has come up because yields from modern farming techniques are reaching a plateau and the environmental problems due to excessive use of chemicals and fertilisers and pesticide residue in the food chain.
- The high use of modern farming techniques has led to the degradation of land and has led to various ecological problems like eutrophication, land degradation, etc., which has depleted the quality of land as a sustainable resource.
- A system of agriculture which produces sufficient food to meet the needs of the present generation without eroding the ecological assets and productivity of life supporting systems of the future generation.
- Sustainable agriculture is a system of cultivation with the use of manures, crop rotation and minimal tillage.
- Sustainable agriculture also involves agro-forestry (growing trees near the crops), multi-level cultivation (growing trees of different heights in sequence) and integrated animal husbandry (growing crops with animal rearing practices).
- The term sustainability denotes the characteristic of a process that can be maintained indefinitely.
- Here with the help of sustainable farm practices, the needs of the present generation can be met out without compromising the needs of future generations.

Types of Agriculture and Their Objectives

Types of Agriculture	Objectives	Quantity of Inputs	Outputs
Subsistence Agriculture	To sustain life and family need	Low	Low
Commercial Farming	To obtain high income	High	High
Sustainable Agriculture	Ecological balance	Low	High

Zero Budget Natural Farming (ZBNF)

- Zero Budget Natural Farming, a type of farming that involves the elimination of chemical pesticides, sustaining agriculture with eco-friendly processes and restoring soil fertility and organic matter.
- It is a unique chemical-free method that involves agroecology. For the zero-net expenditure of manufacturing, yields are known as the **term zero budget**.
- ZBNF reduces farming expenses and promotes the use of natural fertilisers, biological pesticides and local seeds.

Dryland and Wetland Farming

- **Dryland Farming** It is practiced in the region receiving low rainfall, like Rajasthan, some parts of Gujarat and Maharashtra, etc. The soil is sandy and has low water retention capacity. Crops like peas, millets, grams and other drought-resistant crops or varieties can be grown. Dryland farming helps in soil and water conservation.
- **Wetland Farming** It is practiced in the regions receiving high annual rainfall, mainly done in river plains, North-East India, the Ghats of India, etc., Crops requiring high irrigation can be easily grown. Types of crops under wetland farming in India are rice, sugarcane, cotton, jute, etc.

Cropping Seasons in India

There are three distinct crop seasons in the Northern and interior parts of the country, namely Kharif, Rabi and Zaid.

- **The Kharif season** The crops which are grown in the Kharif season require a good amount of water, thus the sowing of Kharif crops largely coincides with the onset of the South-West Monsoon.
- **The Rabi season** The sowing of Rabi crops begins with the onset of winter in October-November and the harvesting is done in March-April. The celebration of the festival Holi can be related to a good harvest in the month of March-April.
- **The Zaid season** It is a short duration summer cropping season beginning after harvesting of rabi crops. The cultivation of watermelons, cucumbers, vegetables and fodder crops during this season is done on irrigated lands. However, this type of distinction in the cropping season does not exist in Southern parts of the country due to high temperature. The same crop can be grown thrice a year.

Cropping Seasons	Major Crops cultivated	
	Northern States	Southern States
Kharif June-September	Rice, cotton, bajara, maize, jowar, tur	Rice, maize, ragi, jowar, groundnut
Rabi October-March	Wheat, gram, rapeseeds and mustard, barley	Rice, maize, ragi, groundnut, jowar
Zaid April-June	Vegetables, fruits, fodder	Rice, vegetables, fodder

Note *There are some crops that are grown in both Kharif and Rabi seasons like maize, jowar and groundnut.*

Major Crops Grown in India

India grows almost each and every crop.

The major crops are discussed in detail as follows :

Food Grains

Rice, wheat, millets and pulses are the prominent food grains grown in India.

Rice

Rice is the most important food crop of India. It is predominantly a Kharif or Summer crop. Maximum population of India is rice consumer.

It covers about one-third of the total cultivated area of the country and provides food to more than half of the Indian population.

Some of the geographical conditions are as follows:

- **Temperature** Rice requires hot and humid conditions. The temperature should be fairly high i.e., 24°C mean monthly temperature with average temperature of 22°C to 32°C.
- **Rainfall** It requires good amount of rainfall ranging between 150-300 cm in areas of Punjab, Haryana and Western Uttar Pradesh where rainfall is less than 100 cm, rice is cultivated with the help of irrigation.
- **Soil** Rice is grown in varied soil conditions but deep clayey and loamy soil provides the ideal conditions. Rice is primarily grown in plain areas. It is also grown below sea level at Kuttanad (Kerala), hill terraces of North-Eastern part of India and valleys of Kashmir.
- **Labour** Rice cultivation requires easily available cheap labour because most of the activities associated with it are labour oriented and are not very well suited for mechanisation.
- **Distribution** Rice is grown in almost all the states of India. The main rice producing states are Tamil Nadu, West Bengal, Andhra Pradesh, Bihar, Jharkhand, Uttarakhand, Chhattisgarh, Punjab, Odisha, Uttar Pradesh, Karnataka, Assam and Maharashtra. It is also grown in Haryana, Madhya Pradesh, Kerala, Gujarat and Kashmir Valley.
- In west Bengal, farmers grow three crops of rice called **Aus, Aman,** and **Boro.**

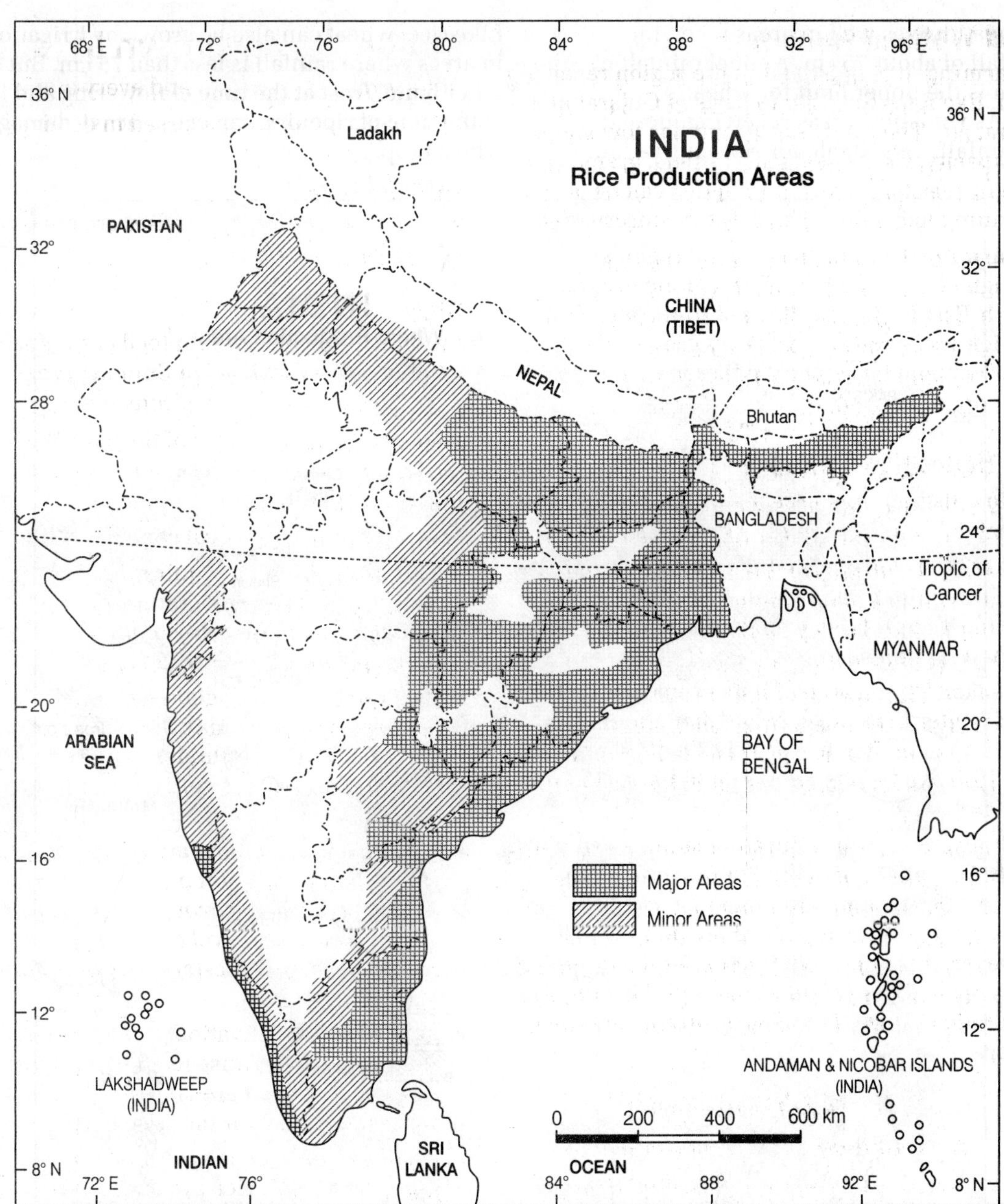

Wheat

Wheat is the second most important food crop of India next to rice. It is a Rabi or Winter crop. It is sown in the beginning of winter and harvested in the beginning of summer. Normally (in North India) the sowing of wheat begins in the month of October-November and harvesting is done in the month of March-April.

This is the staple food of millions of people particularly in the Northern and North-Western regions of India. Unlike rice, wheat is grown mostly as a Rabi or Winter crop.

India Produces about 13.1 Percent of total wheat production of world.

Some of the geographical conditions needed for wheat production are as follows:

- **Temperature** It is primarily a crop of mid-latitude grassland. It requires a cool climate. The ideal temperature is between 10°C to 15°C at the time of sowing and 21°C to 26°C at the time of ripening and harvesting.

- **Rainfall** Wheat thrives well in areas receiving annual rainfall of about 75 cm. Annual rainfall of about 100cm is the upper limit for wheat cultivation. As you know areas receiving more than 100 cm of rainfall are suitable for rice cultivation. Like rice, wheat can also be grown by irrigation method in areas where rainfall is less than 75 cm. But on the other hand, frost at the time of flowering and hailstorm at the time of ripening can cause heavy damage to the wheat crop.

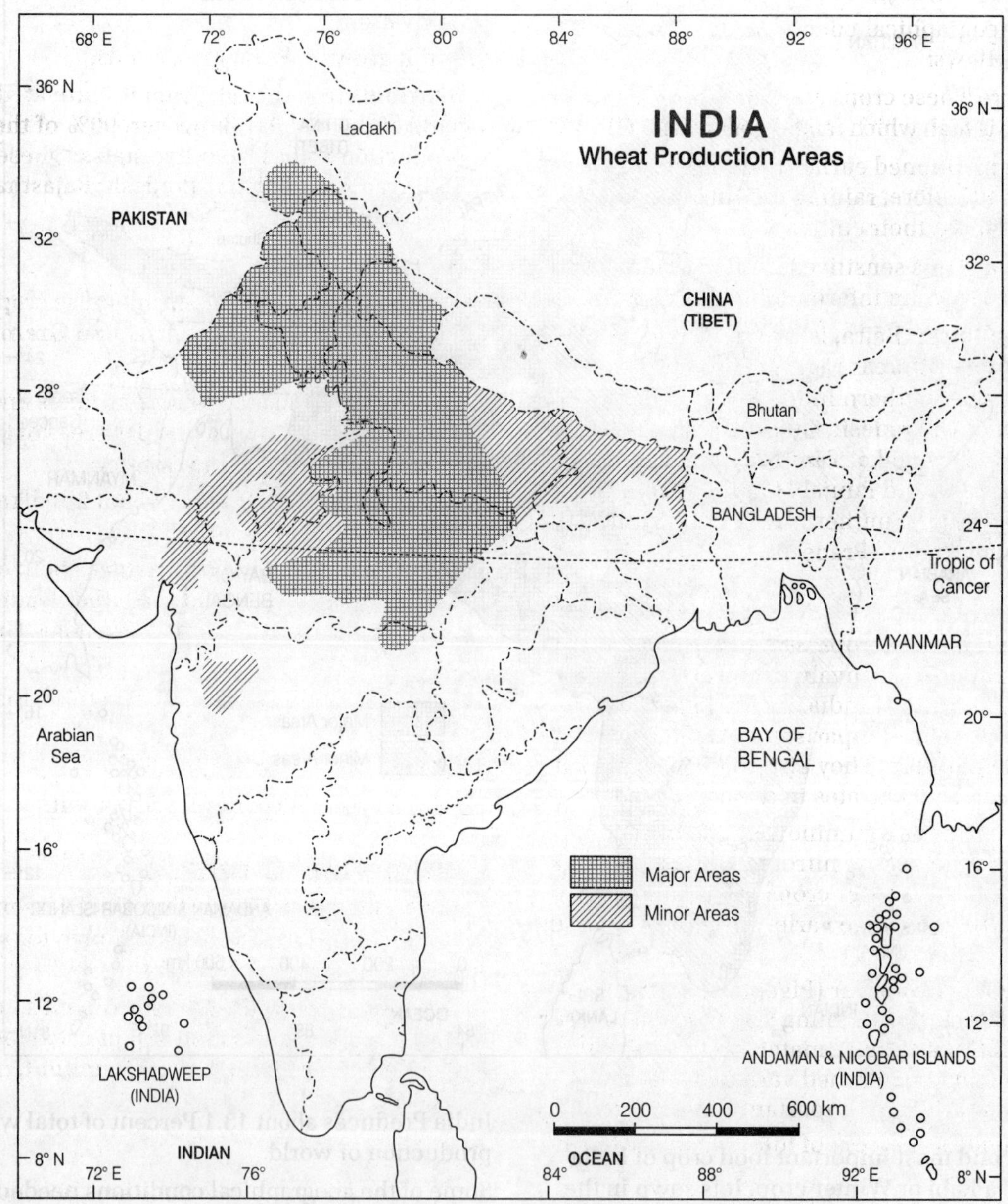

- **Soil** Although wheat can be grown in a variety of soils but well drained fertile loamy and clayey loamy soil is best suited for wheat cultivation. Plain areas are very well suited for wheat production.
- **Labour** Wheat is highly mechanised and requires less labour.
- **Distribution** The main regions of wheat production in India are Uttar Pradesh, Punjab, Haryana, Rajasthan, Madhya Pradesh, Gujarat, Maharashtra. Uttar Pradesh, Punjab and Haryana together produce more than 66% of the total wheat of the country.

Millets

- Millets are short duration warm weather crops. These are coarse grain crops and are used for both food and fodder. These are kharif crops.
- These are sown in May-August and harvested in October-November.

- Today millets are mostly consumed by poor people as their staple food.
- In India, lots of millet is grown and these are known by various local names.
- Some of these are Jowar, Bajra, Ragi, Korra, Kodon, Kutki, Hraka, Bauti, Rajgira.

  Some of the geographical conditions for growing these crops are as follows:
  - **Temperature** These crops are grown where the temperature is high which ranges between 27°C to 32°C.
  - **Rainfall** As mentioned earlier that millets are 'dry land crops', therefore, rainfall ranging from 50 to 100cm is ideal for their cultivation.
  - **Soil** Millets are less sensitive to soil deficiencies. They can be grown in inferior alluvial or loamy soil.
  - **Distribution** Jowar, Bajra, is grown both in North and South India whereas ragi is generally concentrated in Southern India. Jowar, Bajra, is grown in Madhya Pradesh, Gujarat, Rajasthan, Maharashtra, Karnataka, Tamil Nadu, Andhra Pradesh, Haryana and Punjab. Ragi is generally concentrated in the Southern India i.e., Tamil Nadu, Karnataka and Andhra Pradesh.

Pulses

- It includes a number of crops which are mostly leguminous and provide invaluable proteins to the vegetarian population of India. As they have fewer sources of proteins in comparison to those who consume meat and fish. They also serve as excellent forage and grain concentrates in the cattle feed.
- Apart from that, these leguminous crops have the capacity to fix atmospheric nitrogen in the soil and are normally rotated with other crops to maintain and restore soil fertility. A large variety of pulses are found in India.
- These are gram, tur or arhar (Pigeon Pea or Red Gram), urad (black gram), mung (green gram), masur (lentil), kulthi (horse gram), matar (peas) etc., But among these above-mentioned varieties only gram and tur or arhar are more important pulses.
- It occupies about 11 Percent of total cropped area in the country.

Gram

It is the most important of all the pulses. It accounts for about 37% of the production and about 30% of the total area of pulses in India. It is a rabi crop which is sown between September and November and is harvested between February and April. It is either cultivated as a single crop or mixed with wheat, barley, linseed or mustard. It covers about 2.8% of total cropped area.

Some of the geographical conditions for growing pulses are as follows :

- **Temperature** It is grown in a wide range of climatic condition. Mild cool and comparatively dry climate with 20°C-25°C temperature.
- **Rainfall** 40-45 cm rainfall is favourable for gram cultivation.
- **Soil** It grows well on loamy soils.
- **Distribution** Although gram is cultivated in several parts of the country, however, 90% of the total production comes from five states. These states are Madhya Pradesh, Uttar Pradesh, Rajasthan, Haryana and Maharashtra.

Tur (Arhar)

(i) Tur is the second important pulse crop in the country. It is also known as **Red Gram** or **Pigeon pea**.

(ii) It is cultivated over Marginal lands and under rainfed conditions in the dry areas of Central and Southern states of the country.

(iii) This crop occupies only about 2% of total cropped area of India.

(iv) Maharashtra alone contributes about one-third of the total production of tur. Other leading producer states are Uttar Pradesh, Karnataka, Gujarat and Madhya Pradesh.

(v) Temperature needed for growth of this crop is 20°C – 25°C .

(vi) **Rainfall** – 40-80 cm,

Soil type – Alluvial and Black soil.

Commercial Crops

As mentioned in the beginning of the lesson, commercial crops are those crops which are grown for sale either in raw form or semi processed form.

In this section we will learn more about selected cash crops i.e., sugarcane, cotton and jute; two beverages- tea and coffee; three oil seeds i.e., groundnut, mustard and rapeseed.

Sugarcane

It is a Kharif crop. It is the main source of **sugar, gur** and **khandsari**. It also provides raw material for the manufacturing of alcohol. Bagasse, the crushed cane residue, has also multiple uses. It is used for manufacturing paper. It is also an efficient substitute for petroleum products and a host of other chemical products. India accounts for 19 percent of world production of sugarcane.

A part of it is also used as fodder. Some of the geographical conditions for the growth of sugarcane are as follows :

- **Temperature** It requires a hot and humid climate with an average temperature of 21°C to 27°C.
- **Rainfall** 75-150 cm rainfall is favourable for sugarcane cultivation. Irrigation is required in those areas where rainfall is less than the prescribed limit.
- **Soil** It can grow in a variety of soils. In fact sugarcane can tolerate any kind of soil that can retain moisture. But deep rich loamy soil is ideal for its growth. The soil should be rich in nitrogen, calcium and phosphorus but neither should it be too acidic nor alkaline. Flat, plain and level plateau is an advantage for sugarcane cultivation because it facilitates irrigation and transportation of cane to the sugar mills. Sugarcane cultivation requires heavy manures and fertilisers because it exhausts the fertility of soils quickly and extensively.
- **Labour** It is a labour oriented cultivation and requires cheap labour. Ample human hands are required at every stage i.e.. sowing, hoeing, weeding, irrigation, cutting and carrying sugarcanes to the factories.
- **Distribution** India has the largest area under sugarcane cultivation in the world and is the second largest producer next to Brazil. As far as distribution of sugarcane cultivation in India is concerned, there are three distinct geographical regions in the country. These regions are :
  - The Sutlej-Ganga plain from Punjab to Bihar contains 51% of the total area and 60% of the country's total production.
  - The tropical Sugarcan region consists of sugarcane ogro climate zone 4 (Penin sular zone) and 5 (coastal zone) which includes the states of Maharashtra. Andhra Pradesh, Tamil Nadu, Karanatka, Gujarat, Madhya Pradesh, Goa, Pondicherry and Kerala.

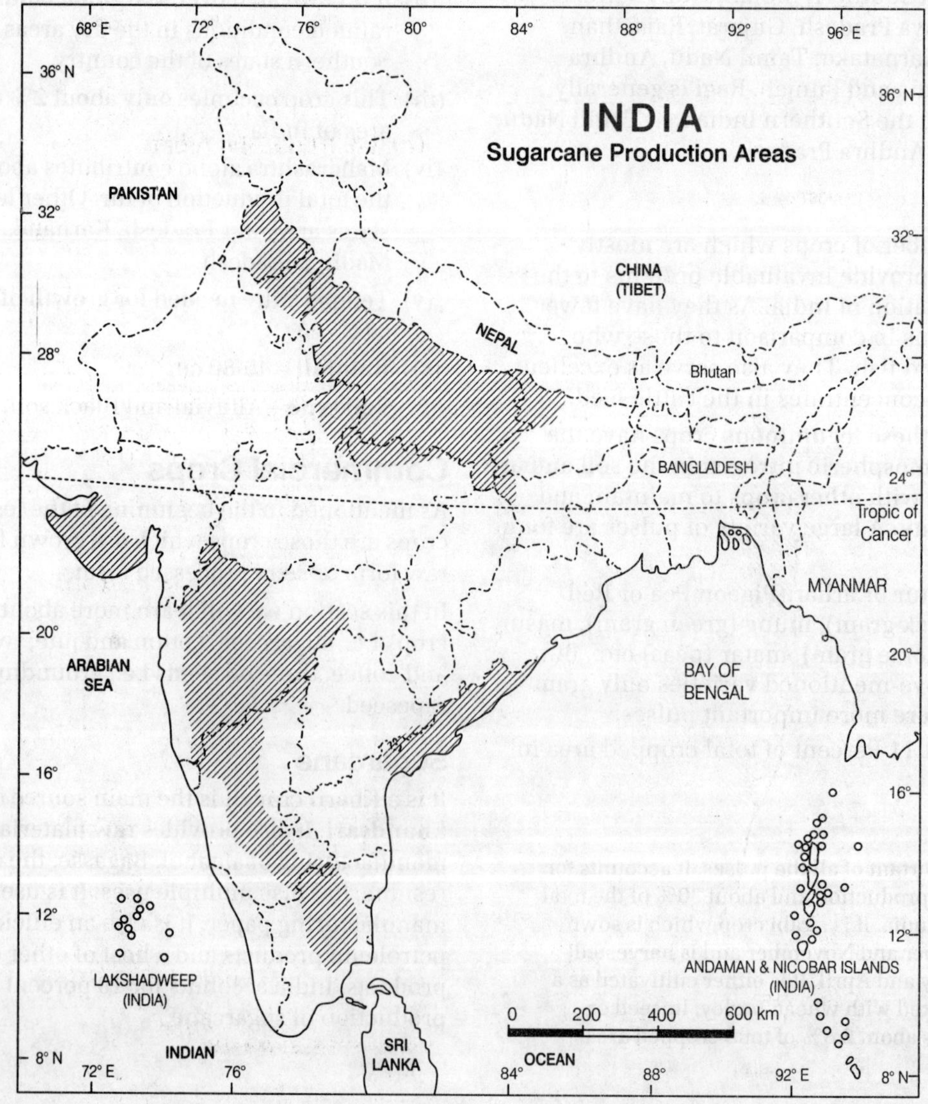

Cotton

Cotton is the most important fibre crop not only for India but also for the entire world. It not only provides raw material for cotton textile industry but also its seed is used in Vanaspati oil industry. The cotton seed is also used as part of fodder for milch cattle for better milk production. Cotton is basically a kharif crop and grown in tropical and sub-tropical areas.

India Produces about 23.7 Percent of world's total production of cotton.

Some of the geographical conditions are as follows :

- **Temperature** Cotton is the crop of tropical and sub-tropical areas and requires uniformly high temperature varying between 21°C and 30°C.
- **Rainfall** It grows mostly in the areas having at least 210 frost free days in a year. It requires a modest amount of rainfall of 50 to 100cm. However, cotton is successfully grown with the help of irrigation in the areas where rainfall is less than 50 cm. High amount of rainfall in the beginning and sunny and dry weather at the time of ripening are very useful for a good crop.
- **Soil** Cotton cultivation is very closely related to Black soils of Deccan and Malwa plateau. However, it also grows well in Alluvial soils of the Sutlej-Ganga plain and Red and Laterite soils of the Peninsular region.
- **Labour** As picking of cotton has not been mechanised till now, therefore a lot of cheap and efficient labour is required at the time of picking.
- **Distribution** India has the largest area under cultivation and third largest producer of cotton next only to China and the USA. Within the country, two third of total area and production is shared by four states. The main states for cotton production are Punjab, Maharashtra, Gujarat and Haryana.

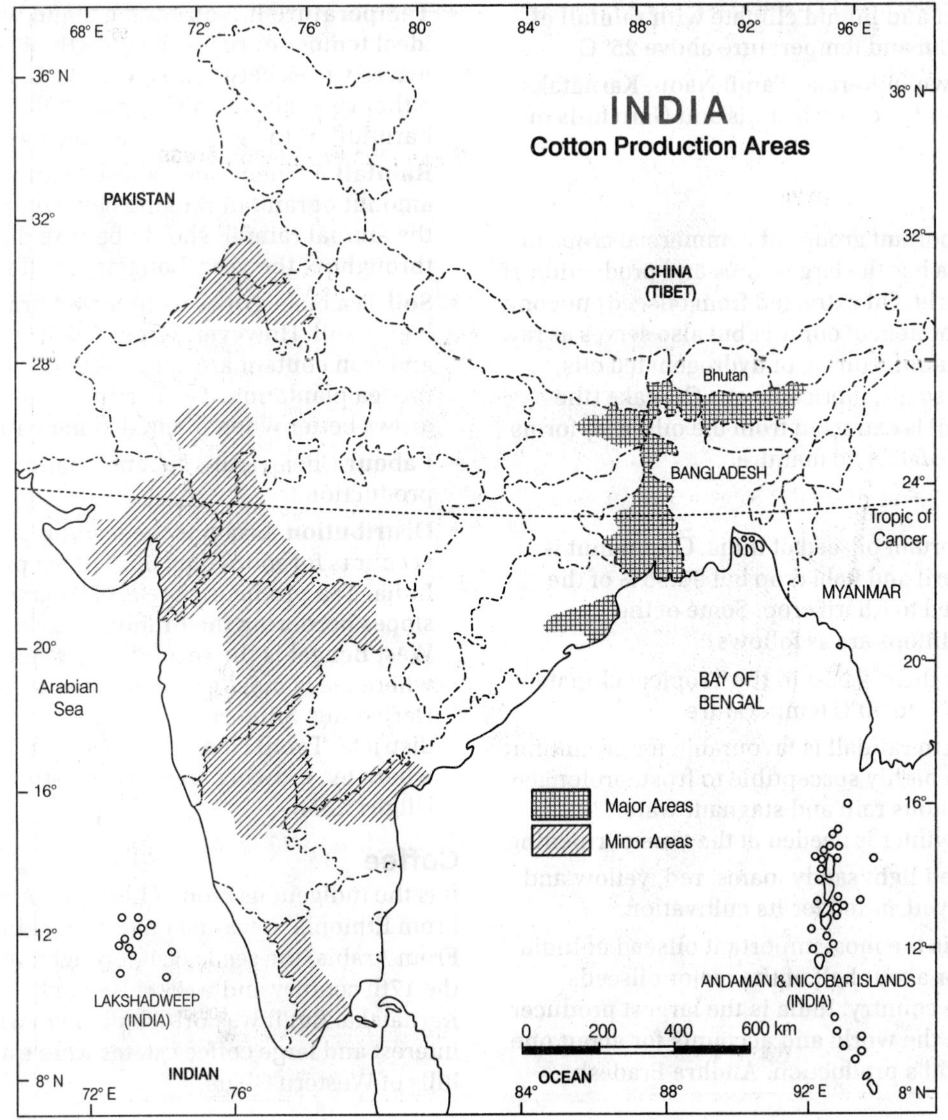

Jute

- Jute is used for making coarse cloth, bags, socks and decorative items.
- It is a cash crop in West Bengal and adjoining Eastern parts of the country.
- India produces about three-fifth of jute production in the world.
- West Bengal accounts for about three-fourth of the production in the country.
- **Temperature** 24 – 35°C
- **Rainfall** 125 – 200 cm
- **Soil** Sandy and Loamy

Rubber

- It is an Equatorial crop, grown under special conditions. It is also grown in Tropical and Sub-tropical areas.
- It requires moist and humid climate with rainfall of more than 200 cm and temperature above 25° C
- It is mainly grown in Kerala, Tamil Nadu, Karnataka and Andaman and Nicobar Islands and Garo hills of Meghalaya.

Oilseeds

It is one of the important groups of commercial crops in India. In fact, India has the largest area and production of oilseeds in the world. Oil extracted from oilseeds not only forms an important item of our diet but also serves as raw material for the manufacturing of hydrogenated oils, paints, varnishes, soaps, lubricants etc. Oil-cake (the residue after the oil is extracted from the oilseeds) forms an important cattle feed and manure.

Groundnut

It is the most important oilseed of India. Groundnut is grown both as kharif and Rabi crop but 90-95% of the total area is devoted to Kharif crop. Some of the geographical conditions are as follows :

- **Temperature** It thrives best in the Tropical climate and requires 20°C to 30°C temperature.
- **Rainfall** 50-75 cm rainfall is favourable for groundnut cultivation. It is highly susceptible to frost, prolonged drought, continuous rain and stagnant water. Therefore, dry winter is needed at the time of ripening.
- **Soil** Well drained light sandy loams, red, yellow and black soils are well suited for its cultivation.
- **Distribution** It is the most important oilseed of India and accounts for about half of the major oilseeds produced in the country. India is the largest producer of groundnut in the world and accounts for about one third of the world's production. Andhra Pradesh, Tamil Nadu and Gujarat are three main producers of groundnut in India and account for about 60% of the total production. Another 30% of the total production comes from Maharashtra, Karnataka and Odisha.

Beverage Crops

Tea and Coffee are the important **beverage crops.**

Tea

India is famous for its tea gardens. The tea plantations in India were started by the Britishers in 1923 when wild tea plants were discovered by them in the hilly and forest areas of Assam. Tea is made from tender sprouts of tea plants by drying them. At present, India is the leading tea producing country in the world. China and Sri Lanka are respectively the second and third largest producers of tea.

Some of the geographical conditions for the growth of tea are as follows :

- **Temperature** It requires a hot and wet climate. The ideal temperature for the growth of tea bushes and leaves varies between 20°C to 30°C. If the temperature either rises above 35°C or goes below 10°C, it would be harmful for the growth of tea bushes and leaves.
- **Rainfall** As mentioned above tea requires a good amount of rainfall ranging between 150-300 cm and the annual rainfall should be well distributed throughout the year. Long dry spell is harmful for tea.
- **Soil** Tea bush grows well in well drained, deep, friable loamy soil. However, virgin forest soils rich in humus and iron content are considered to be the best soils for the tea plantation. Tea is a shade loving plant and grows better when planted along with shady trees.
- **Labour** Cheap and efficient labour is required for tea production.
- **Distribution** Assam is the leading producer that accounts for more than 50% of tea production in India. Tea producing areas of Assam are the hill slopes bordering the Brahmaputra and Surma valleys. West Bengal is the second largest producer of tea where tea is mostly grown in the districts of Darjeeling, Siliguri, Jalpaiguri and Cooch Behar districts. Tamil Nadu is the third largest producer where tea growing areas are mostly restricted to Nilgiri hills.

Coffee

It is the indigenous crop of Ethiopia (Abyssinian Plateau). From Ethiopia, it was taken to Yemen in the 11th century. From Arabia, the seeds were brought by Baba Budan in the 17th century and were raised in Baba Budan hills of Karnataka. But it was British planters who took keen interest and large coffee estates were established in the hills of Western Ghats.

Some of the geographical conditions for the growth of coffee are as follows :

- **Temperature** It requires a hot and humid climate with temperature varying between 15°C and 28°C. It is generally grown under shady trees. Therefore, strong sunshine, high temperatures above 30°C, frost and snowfall are harmful for coffee cultivation. Dry weather is necessary at the time of ripening of berries.
- **Rainfall** It rainfall between 150 to 250 cm.
- **Soil** Well drained, rich friable loamy soil containing a good deal of humus and minerals like iron and calcium are ideal for coffee cultivation. The soil must be properly manured to retain and replenish fertility and to increase productivity.
- **Labour** Like tea, coffee cultivation also requires plenty of cheap and skilled labour for various purposes like sowing, transplanting, pruning, plucking, dying, grading and packing of coffee.
- **Distribution** Karnataka, Kerala and Tamil Nadu are the main states of coffee production in India.

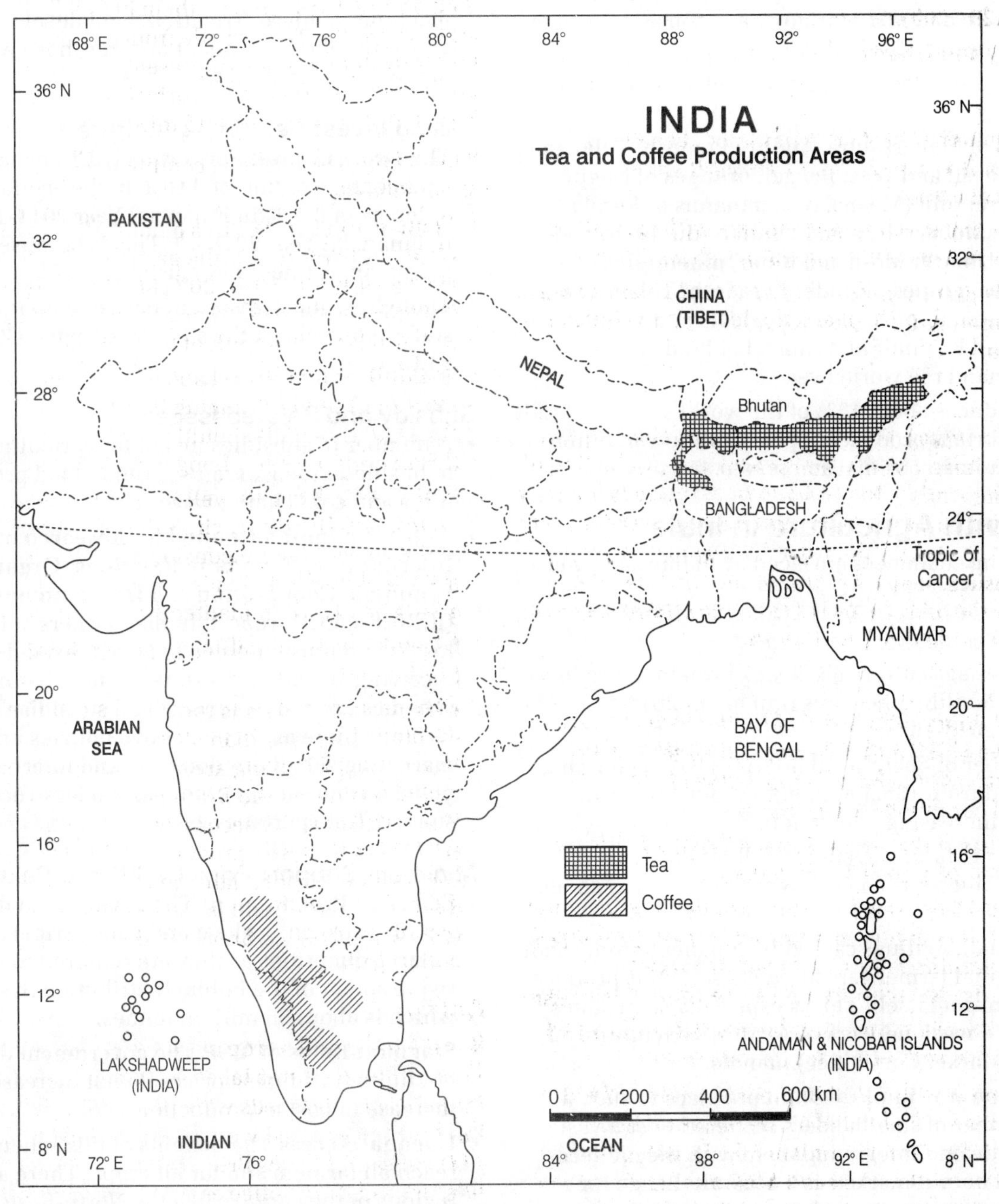

Horticulture

- Horticulture is the branch of agriculture concerned with intensively cultured plants directly used by man for food, medicinal purposes and aesthetic gratification.
- In simpler words, it is cultivation, production and sale of vegetables, fruits, flowers, herbs, ornamental or exotic plants.
- The term 'Horticulture' is derived from the Latin words hortus (garden) and cultura (cultivation).
- **LH Bailey** is considered as the Father of American Horticulture and **MH Marigowda** is considered as the Father of Indian Horticulture.
- India is a producer of tropical as well as temperate fruits.
- **Mangoes** of Maharashtra, Andhra Pradesh, Telangana, Uttar Pradesh and West Bengal, **oranges** of Nagpur and Cherrapunji (Meghalaya), **bananas** of Kerala, Mizoram, Maharashtra and Tamil Nadu, **litchi** and **guava** of Uttar Pradesh and Bihar, **pineapples** of Meghalaya, **grapes** of Andhra Pradesh, Telangana and Maharashtra, **apples**, **pears**, **apricots** and **walnuts** of Jammu and Kashmir and Himachal Pradesh are in great demand the world over.
- India produces about 13% of the world's vegetables. It is an important producer of pea, cauliflower, onion, cabbage, tomato, brinjal and potato.

Issues with Agriculture in India

The following challenges are faced by Indian agriculture sector :

Land Size

- Area under agriculture has been shrinking, it reduced from 159.5 million hectares (mn ha) in 2010-11 to 157 mn ha in 2015-16.
- The number of operational holdings has been rising (increased from 138.3 million to about 146 million) owing to increasing population.
- This leads to falling average landholdings' size of farmers, which has come down from 1.2 ha to about 1.08 ha.
- Due to small holdings caused by fragmentation, small and marginal farmers are forced to sell their produce at the farm gate itself. This is especially so in states that have a weak network of APMC (Agricultural Produce Market Committee) mandis.
- Bringing new technologies and practices to such a large number of smallholders scattered over a vast countryside and integrating them with the modern input and output markets is a huge challenge for Indian agriculture.

More Farm Labourers than Farmers

- A farmer is usually a farm owner, while employees of the farm are farm labourers, farmhands, etc.
- As per recent estimates from the Labour Bureau, 45% of India's workforce is employed in agriculture.
- According to Census 2011, 55% of the agri-workforce comprises agri-labourers.
- It is tough to drive or sustain growth in agriculture since farm labourers get no policy support or incentive to invest in farming.
- All benefits like seed kit, fertilisers, pesticides, farm machinery, micro-irrigation, land development assistance etc., are meant only for those who can prove land ownership.

Falling Investment in Agriculture

- The **Gross Capital Formation** (GCF) in agriculture as a percentage of the total GCF in the economy has fallen from 8.5 % in Financial Year 2011-12 to 6.5 % in Financial Year 2018-19. This is because the share of private investment has shrunk.
- Though public investment has gone up it is not sufficient to check the slide or keep the GCF at FY12 level.

Subsidy and Related Issues

- A number of subsidies meant for agriculture also flow to businesses, e.g., grants given to food processing units and cold chain projects.
- As per the **Indian Council** for **Research** on **International Economic Relations- Organisation** for **Economic Cooperation** and **Development** (ICRIER-OECD) report, Indian farmers suffered net losses and thus emerged to be net taxed despite receiving subsidies. Despite the fact that many schemes are run to support and subsidise Indian farmers, there are of regressive policies on the marketing side (both domestic and international trade policies) and the deficit of basic infrastructure for storage, transportation etc.,

Minimum Support Price (MSP) and Related Issues

- **Selective Procurement** The government declares MSP for 23 crops, only wheat and paddy (rice) are procured in large quantities as they are required to meet the requirement of the Public Distribution System (PDS), which is about 65 million tonnes.
- **Stagnant Rates of MSP** The government declaration of Minimum support prices do not increase at par with increase in cost of production.
- **Unequal Access** The benefits of this scheme do not reach all farmers and for all crops. There are many regions of the country like the North-Eastern region where the implementation is too weak.

- **Non Scientific Practices** MSP leads to non-scientific agricultural practices whereby the soil, water are stressed to an extent of degrading ground water table and salinisation of soil.

Effect of Globalisation on Agriculture

- After globalisation in 1990, Indian farmers are facing many challenges.
- Despite of being major producers of rice, cotton, rubber, tea, coffee, jute and spices, Indian agriculture is unable to compete with developed nations. These countries are provided high subsidy.
- Due to Green Revolution, quality of land degraded as use of chemical fertilisers led to loss of diversity and drying of aquifers.
- At present, organic farming has emerged as a potential solution to this problem in which agriculture is practiced with the use of chemicals.

Agricultural Development in India

- Indian agricultural economy was largely subsistence in nature before Independence.
- It had dismal performance in the first half of 20th century.
- After Independence, the immediate goal of the Government was to increase foodgrains production by
  - switching over from cash crops to food crops
  - intensification of cropping over already cultivated land
  - increasing cultivated area by bringing cultivable and fallow land under plough.
- This strategy helped in increasing food grains production, but agricultural production stagnated during late 1950s.
- To overcome this problem, **Intensive Agricultural District Area Programme** (IAAP) was launched. But two consecutive droughts during mid 1960s resulted in food crisis in the country. Consequently, foodgrains were imported from other countries.
- New seed varieties of wheat (Mexico) and rice (Philippines) known as **High Yielding Varieties** (HYVs) were available for cultivation by mid-1960s.
- India took advantage of this and introduced package technology comprising HYVs, along with chemical fertilisers in irrigated areas of Punjab, Haryana, Western Uttar Pradesh, Andhra Pradesh and Gujarat.
- Assured supply of soil moisture through irrigation was a basic pre-requisite for the success of this new agricultural technology.
- This strategy of agricultural development paid dividends instantly and increased the foodgrains production at very fast rate.
- This spurt of agricultural growth came to be known as **Green Revolution**.
- The **Planning Commission of India** focused its attention on the problems of agriculture in rainfed areas in 1980s.
- It initiated agro-climatic planning in 1988 to induce-regionally balanced agricultural development in the country.
- It also emphasised on the need for diversification of agriculture and harnessing of resources for the development of dairy farming, poultry, horticulture, livestock rearing and aquaculture.
- Initiation of the policy of liberalisation and free market economy in 1990s influenced the course of development of rural infrastructure.
- Withdrawal of subsidies and price support, and impediments in availing of the rural credits have lead to inter-regional and inter-personal disparities in rural areas.

Bhoodan-Gramdan

- Mahatma Gandhi declared **Vinoba Bhave** as his spiritual heir.
- He also participated in Satyagraha as one of the foremost satyagrahis. He was one of the votaries of Gandhi's concept of **Gram Swarajya**.
- After Gandhiji's martyrdom, Vinoba Bhave undertook *padyatra* to spread Gandhiji's message, covered almost the entire country.
- Once when he was delivering a lecture at **Pochampalli** in Andhra Pradesh, some poor landless villagers demanded some land for their economic well-being.
- Vinoba Bhave could not promise it to them immediately but assured them to talk to the Government of India regarding provision of land for them if they undertook cooperative farming.

  Suddenly, **Shri Ram Chandra Reddy** stood up and offered 80 acres of land to be distributed among 80 land-less villagers. This act was known as **Bhoodan**.
- Later he travelled and introduced his ideas widely all over India. Some zamindars, owners of many villages offered to distribute some villages among the landless. It was known as **Gramdan**.
- However, many land-owners chose to provide some part of their land to the poor farmers due to the fear of Land Ceiling Act.
- This Bhoodan-Gramdan movement initiated by Vinoba Bhave is also known as the **Blood-less Revolution**.

Kisan Credit Card (KCC)

- Kisan Credit Card (KCC), Personal Accident Insurance Scheme (PAIS) are some other schemes introduced by the Government of India for the benefit of the farmers.
- Moreover special weather bulletins and agricultural programmes for farmers were introduced on the radio and television.
- The government also announces Minimum Support Price, remunerative and procurement prices for important crops to check the exploitation of farmers by speculators and middlemen.

National Agriculture Policy, 2000

- The Government of India announced its new agriculture policy on 28th July, 2000. Its envisages a growth rate of 4% in the agriculture sector for the next two decades. This agriculture policy has been described as rainbow revolution.

Rainbow Revolution

Revolutions	Related Areas
Green	Foodgrains
White	Milk
Yellow	Oilseeds
Red	Meat/Tomato
Pink	Prawn
Round	Potato
Silver	Eggs
Golden	Fruits
Grey	Manure
Blue	Fish

Agro-Climatic Regions

- The Planning Commission of India has divided India into 12 major agro-climatic regions, delineated on the basis of a commonality of agro-climatic factors like soil, rainfall, temperature, water resources, etc.
  - **West Himalayan Region** Jammu and Kashmir, Ladakh, Himachal Pradesh, Uttarakhand.
  - **East Himalayan Region** Sikkim, Darjeeling (West Bengal), Meghalaya, Arunachal Pradesh.
  - **Sutlej-Yamuna Plain** (Trans Ganga Plain) Punjab, Haryana, Chandigarh, Delhi, Western Uttar Pradesh.
  - **Upper Ganga Plain** Western Uttar Pradesh, Haridwar, Uttaranchal.
  - **Middle Ganga Plain** Eastern Uttar Pradesh, Bihar.
  - **Lower Ganga Plain** Eastern Bihar, West Bengal, Assam.
  - **Aravalli-Malwa Highlands** Nagpur plateau, Mahabharat plateau, Vindhyan Hills, Chhattisgarh, Bundelkhand, Baghelkhand, Malwa.
  - **Maharashtra Plateau** Deccan Plateau.
  - **Eastern Plateau and Hills** Chhotanagpur Plateau, Rajmahal Hills, Chhattisgarh and Dandakaranya.
  - **Southern Plateau and Hills** Southern Maharashtra, Karnataka, Western Andhra Pradesh, Northern Tamil Nadu.
  - **East Coast Plains and Hills** Coromandel Coast, Utkal, North Circar.
  - **West Coast Plains and Hills** Konkan, Karnataka and Malabar Coast.

Animal Husbandry/Cattle Rearing/Livestock Farming

- Animal husbandry refers to livestock raising and selective breeding. It is the management and care of animals in which the genetic qualities and behaviour of animals are further developed for profit.
- A large number of farmers depend upon animal husbandry for their livelihood. It supports the livelihood of almost 55% of the rural population.
- As per the Economic Survey 2022-23, the contribution of Livestock in total agriculture and allied sector Gross Value Added (at Constant Prices) has increased from 24.32% (2014-15) to 80.1% in (2020-21).
- India is the highest livestock owner of the world.
- As per the 20th Livestock Census, the total Livestock population is 535.78 million in the country showing an increase of 4.6% over Livestock Census-2012.
- Animal rearing has multidimensional potential.

Buffaloes

- Buffaloes are an important source of milk supply in India contributing about 52.6% of the country's total production of milk although these constitute only 20% of the country's total livestock.
- Uttar Pradesh has the highest number of buffaloes followed by Andhra Pradesh, Rajasthan, Madhya Pradesh, Gujarat, Bihar, Maharashtra, Haryana and Punjab. The main buffaloes breeds include **Murrah, Bhadawari, Jaffarabadi, Surti, Mehsana, Nagpuri, Rohtak, Nili Ravi** and Deccan etc.

Goat Rearing

- It is the main source of meat for the country (18.99%), the annual production being 4.88 lakh tonnes.
- About 90% of the goats are of desi breed. Other important breeds include **Himalaya or Angora breed** (Himachal Pradesh, Haryana and Jammu and Kashmir), **Jamunapari-Barbari** (Western Uttar Pradesh, Haryana and Delhi), **Marwari Mehsana, Kathiawari** and **Zalwadi** and **Surti** (Rajasthan, Gujarat and Madhya Pradesh) and **Deccani (Peninsula)**.

Sheep Rearing

- Sheep are an important source of mutton and wool in the country. In India, sheep are mainly found in low rainfall zones of the plateaus and hills. Andhra Pradesh accounts for one-third of the total sheep population of the country followed by Rajasthan (16.36%), Karnataka (11.80%), Tamil Nadu (9.10%) and Jammu and Kashmir (5.55%).
- The important sheep breeds are the **Deccani, Nellore, Mandya, Bellary, Yalag** and **Bandur**.
- The country's best quality sheep are found in the Kashmir, Kullu, Chamba and Kangra valleys at an altitude of 2,000 m.

Poultry Farming

- Poultry includes domestic fowls like chickens, ducks, geese, turkeys, etc., which are reared to obtain meat, eggs and feathers.
- The largest number of poultry population is found in Andhra Pradesh followed by Tamil Nadu, West Bengal, Maharashtra, Karnataka.
- Poultry farms are being developed around almost all the important urban centres of the country.
- In case of ducks, West Bengal occupies the foremost place followed by Assam, Tamil Nadu, Kerala, Andhra Pradesh, Bihar and Odisha.

Sericulture

- Sericulture includes the rearing of silk worm for silk production. Silk worm thrives on the leaves of mulberry, mahua, sal, ber and kusum trees.
- India is the second largest producer of silk in the world. Here 17% of the world's silk is produced.
- India is unique country producing all the four varieties of silk, viz, mulberry, tasar, eri and munga. Karnataka is the largest producer of raw silk in the country (34.93%), followed by Andhra Pradesh, West Bengal, Assam and Tamil Nadu.

Fishing Industry in India

- Fisheries and aquaculture are an important source of food production, nutritional security, employment, and income in India.
- The fisheries sector is a direct source of livelihoods for more than 20 million fishers and fish farmers contributes INR 1.75 trillion annually to the gross value added to India's economy and is a major export earner, with fish being one of the most important agricultural commodities to be exported from India.
- **Blue Revolution** or the **Neel Kranti Mission** has the vision to achieve economic prosperity of the fishers and fish farmers. It also aims to contribute towards food and nutritional security through full potential utilisation of water resources for fisheries development in a sustainable manner, keeping in view the bio-security and environmental concerns.
- India is the world's second-largest fish producer with exports worth more than ₹ 47,000 crore.
- It has a marine fisher population of 3.5 million; 10.5 million people are engaged in inland fishery and fish farming.
- Andhra Pradesh stands at the top in terms of inland fisheries production with 34.5 lakh tonnes. Gujarat lead marine fisheries production with 7.01 lakh tonnes.

White Revolution

- The phenomenal increase in the milk production of the country has been termed as **white revolution**.
- White revolution started with the launching of **Operation Flood I** in July 1970 under the guidance of **Verghese Kurien, Chairman National Daily Development Programmes** (NDDB). Under this project (NDDB), were started in 10 states of the country which includes the development of infrastructural facilities for the procurement of the milk from rural areas, its processing, marketing, provision of cattle feed, factory, animal healthcare facilities, artificial insemination and extension services.
- The **Operation Flood II** (1979-85) involves to cover about one crore rural milk producer families. Under this project steps were taken to improve the quality of catttle feed, increase pasture facilities, promote animal health care facilities, improve cattle breed and provide better facilities to milk producers.
- The **Operation Flood III** which was completed in April 1996, helped in the organisation of 73,300 dairy cooperative societies under 173 milksheds involving over 9.4 million farmer members.
- White Revolution is as important to dairy development as Green Revolution has been to the foodgrains production. Its outcome is based on the improvement in cattle breeding and adoption of new technology. The rural cooperative societies have played pivotal role in the success of White Revolution.

Irrigation

- Irrigation is the artificial application of water to the soil or agricultural field. It is the replacement or supplementation of rainwater with another source of water. It is used in dry areas and during periods of inadequate rainfall.
- The main idea behind irrigation systems is to assist in the growth of agricultural crops and plants by maintaining the minimum amount of water required, suppressing weed growth in grain fields, preventing soil consolidation etc.

Types of Irrigation System

The different types of irrigation systems are as follows :

- **Well and Tube Well Irrigation** Wells are mainly found in Uttar Pradesh, Bihar, Tamil Nadu, etc. Deep wells are more suitable for the purpose of irrigation as water from them is available throughout the year. At places where groundwater is available, a Tube-well can be installed near the agricultural area.

  A deep tube well worked by electricity, can irrigate a much larger area (about 400 hectares) than a surface well (half hectares). Tube wells are mostly used in Uttar Pradesh, Haryana, Punjab, Bihar and Gujarat.
- **Canal Irrigation** The main concentration of canal irrigation is in the Northern plain of India, especially the areas comprising Uttar Pradesh, Haryana and Punjab. Most of the canals in India are perennial.
- **Tank Irrigation** Tank comprises an important source of irrigation in the Karnataka Plateau, Madhya Pradesh, Maharashtra, Odisha, Kerala, Bundelkhand area of Uttar Pradesh, Rajasthan and Gujarat.
- **Drip Irrigation** In drip irrigation, water is applied near the plant root through emitters or drippers, on or below the soil surface, at a low rate varying from 2-20 liters per hour. The soil moisture is kept at an optimum level with frequent irrigation. Among all irrigation methods, drip irrigation is the most efficient and can be practiced for a large variety of crops, especially in vegetables, orchard crops, flowers and plantation crops.
- **Sprinkler Irrigation** In this method, water is sprayed into the air and allowed to fall on the ground surface somewhat resembling rainfall. The spray is developed by the flow of water under pressure through small orifices or nozzles. The sprinkler irrigation system is a very suitable method for irrigation on uneven lands and on shallow soils.

  Nearly all crops are suitable for sprinkler irrigation systems except crops like paddy, jute, etc. The dry crops, vegetables, flowering crops, orchards, plantation crops like tea, coffee are all suitable and can be irrigated through sprinklers.
- **Furrow Irrigation** Furrow irrigation is a type of surface irrigation in which trenches or 'furrows' are dug between crop rows in a field. Farmers flow water down the furrows and it seeps vertically and horizontally to refill the soil reservoir. Flow to each furrow is individually controlled. One of the difficulties of furrow irrigation is ensuring uniform dispersion of water over a given field. Another difficulty with furrow irrigation is the increased potential for water loss due to runoff.
- **Surge Irrigation** Surge irrigation is a variant of furrow irrigation where the water supply is pulsed on and off in planned time periods. The wetting and drying cycles reduce infiltration rates resulting in faster advance rates and higher uniformities than continuous flow.
- **Ditch Irrigation** It is a rather traditional method, where ditches are dug out and seedlings are planted in rows. The plantings are watered by placing canals or furrows in between the rows of plants. Siphon tubes are used to move the water from the main ditch to the canals.
- **Sub Irrigation or Seepage Irrigation** It is a method of irrigation where water is delivered to the plant root zone from below the soil surface and absorbed upwards. The excess may be collected for reuse. Its advantages are water and nutrient conservation, and labor-saving. The outfitting cost is relatively high. Potential problems, such as the possibility of increased presence of disease in recycled water.

Net Area Under Irrigation by Sources

Source	Approx . Irrigated Area
Tubewells and other wells	62%
Tanks	3%
Canals	26%
Other Sources	9%

Multipurpose Projects

A multipurpose project serves several purposes such as flood control, irrigation, hydroelectric generation, navigation, fishing, tourism and supply of drinking water. Some of the important multi-purpose projects are as follows :

Bhakra Nangal Project

- It is the joint venture of Punjab, Haryana and Rajasthan. The project comprises of :
  - Two dams at Bhakra and Nangal
  - Nangal hydel channel
  - Power houses
  - Electricity transmission lines
  - Bhakra canal system for irrigation

Damodar Valley Project

It consists of four dams. These are as follows :

1. **Tilaiya Dam** It has been constructed on Barakar river.
2. **Konar Dam** It has been constructed on Konar river in Hazaribagh district of Jharkhand.
3. **Maithon Dam** It has been constructed on Barakar river, a little upstream from the confluence of river Damodar and Barakar.

4. **Panchet Dam** This is an earthen dam with a concrete spill-way, which has been constructed on the river Damodar.

Hirakud Dam Project

- It is an ambitious project of the state of Odisha, which consists of a dam on the river Mahanadi at Hirakud about 14 km upstream off the city of Sambalpur.
- The area served by the Hirakud is very rich in minerals like iron ore, bauxite, mica, manganese, which require large supply of hydroelectricity.

Kosi Project

- The entire project consists of three units such as a barrage near Hanuman Nagar in Nepal, flood embankment on both sides of the river and construction of irrigation canal.
- It has two major canals for irrigation purpose. They are :
  1. The Eastern Kosi canal
  2. Western Kosi canal

Rihand Valley Project

- It consists of a straight gravity dam across the Rihand river in Mirzapur district of Uttar Pradesh.
- The reservoir created by this dam is named as **Govind Ballabh Pant Sagar**.
- It is the largest man-made reservoir in India.
- Flood control in Son valley, fishing in Govind Ballabh Pant Sagar, tourism, prevention and control of soil erosion in Baghelkhand region are some of the benefits of the project.

Chambal Valley Project

- It is a joint venture of Rajasthan and Madhya Pradesh on the Chambal river, a tributary of Yamuna.
- The project aims at harnessing the Chambal river for irrigation, power generation and for prevention and control of soil erosion in the valley.
- The project is executed in three successive stages. These are as follows :
  1. **The First Stage** It consists of the construction of the Gandhi Sagar dam at the border of Madhya Pradesh and Rajasthan.
  2. **The Second Stage** It consists of the construction of the Rana Pratap Masonry dam at Rawatbhata (Rajasthan).
  3. **The Third Stage** It consists of the construction of the long gravity dam known as **Jawahar Sagar dam** or **Kota dam**.

Tungabhadra Multipurpose Project

- It is a joint undertaking of Andhra Pradesh and Karnataka.
- It consists of a straight gravity masonry dam across the Tungabhadra (a tributary of Krishna river) at Mallapur in Bellary district of Karnataka.

Gandak Project

- It is a joint venture of Bihar and Uttar Pradesh. Nepal also derived some benefits from this project according to an agreement signed in 1959.
- It consists of two major canals such as the main Western canal and the main Eastern canal.

Narmada Valley Project

- It is proposed on the Narmada river and the purpose is to harness the Narmada river for the economic prosperity of the concerned areas.
- This is one of the largest river valley projects of the world because the entire project includes the construction of 30 major, 135 medium and 3000 minor dams on the river.
- Some of the important dams of the Narmada valley projects are Sardar Sarovar dam, Maheshwar dam, Omkareshwar dam, etc.
- It is a joint venture of Madhya Pradesh and Gujarat. This project is under controversy due to the opposition from the farmers of the affected areas regarding environmental concerns, resettlement and rehabilitation.

Nagarjuna Sagar Project

- It consists of a concrete dam on Krishna river in Nalgonda district about 114 km to the South-East of Hyderabad. Two canals have been taken from it; one from either side of the dam.
- The **Jawahar canal** on the right side is irrigating the districts of Guntur, Prakasam, Nellore is whereas, **Lal Bahadur canal** is on the left side of the districts of Khammam, West Godavari and Krishna district.

Tehri Dam

- The Tehri dam is situated at the confluence of the Bhagirathi and the Bhilangana rivers in Garhwal district of Uttarakhand.
- This is a rock-fill dam with the purpose of generation of electricity and irrigation of the arid land between the Ganga and Yamuna.

Beas Project

- It is a joint venture of the Punjab, Haryana and Rajasthan. The main components of the project are :
  - Sutlej-Beas link
  - Pong dam at Beas

List of the Projects, States, Locations and their Purposes

Name of the Project	Location	State/Union Territories	Purpose
Nagarjuna Sagar Multipurpose Project	River Krishna	Andhra Pradesh and Telangana	Irrigation, Hydroelectricity
Pochampadu Project	River Godavari	Telangana	Irrigation
Lower Sileru Project	River Sileru (Godavari)	Andhra Pradesh	Hydroelectricity
Kakrapar Project	River Tapi	Gujarat	Irrigation
Kothagudem Project	Singareni Coalfields	Telangana	Thermal power
Kosi Project	River Kosi	Bihar	Flood control, Irrigation, Hydroelectricity
Gandak Project	River Gandak	Uttar Pradesh, Bihar	Irrigation, Hydroelectricity
Dhuvaran Power Station	Kheda district	Gujarat	Thermal power
Sabarigiri (Pamba-Kakki) Project	River Pamba-Kakki	Kerala	Hydroelectricity
Idukki Project	River Periyar	Kerala	Hydroelectricity
Chambal Project	River Chambal	Rajasthan, Madhya Pradesh	Irrigation, Hydroelectricity
Tawa Project	River Tawa (Narmada)	Madhya Pradesh	Irrigation
Korba Project	Near Korta Coalfields	Chhattisgarh	Thermal power
Satpura Power Station	Patharkata Coalfields	Madhya Pradesh	Thermal power
Koyna Project	River Koyna	Maharashtra	Hydroelectricity
Nagpur Power Station	Koradi, near Nagpur city	Maharashtra	Thermal power
Tungabhadra Multipurpose Project	River Tungabhadra	Karnataka, Andhra Pradesh	Irrigation, Hydroelectricity
Upper Krishna Project	River Krishna	Karnataka	Irrigation
Sharavathi Project	River Sharavathi, near Jog Falls	Karnataka	Hydroelectricity
Hirakud Multipurpose Project	River Mahanadi	Odisha	Irrigation, Hydroelectricity
Mahanadi Delta Project	River Mahanadi	Odisha	Irrigation
Bhakra Nangal Multipurpose Project	River Sutlej	Himachal Pradesh, Punjab, Haryana	Irrigation, Hydroelectricity
Indira Gandhi Canal Project	River Sutlej and Beas in Punjab	Rajasthan, Punjab	Irrigation
Kundah Project	River Bhavani	Tamil Nadu	Hydroelectricity
Ramganga Multipurpose Project	Chuisot Stream near Kalagarh	Uttarakhand	Irrigation, Hydroelectricity
Matatila Multipurpose Project	River Betwa	Uttar Pradesh, Madhya Pradesh	Irrigation, Hydroelectricity
Rihand Scheme	River Rihand	Uttar Pradesh	Hydroelectricity
Damodar Valley Project	River Damodar	Jharkhand, shared with West Bengal	Flood control, Irrigation
Ukai Project	River Tapi	Gujarat	Irrigation
Mahi Project	River Mahi	Gujarat	Irrigation
Ghataprabha Project	River Ghataprabha	Andhra Pradesh and Karnataka	Irrigation
Bhima Project	River Bhima	Maharashtra	Irrigation
Sardar Sarovar Project	River Narmada	Gujarat and Madhya Pradesh	Irrigation and Hydroelectricity
Bansagar Project	River Son	Madhya Pradesh, Chhattisgarh	Irrigation
Dul Hasti Project	River Chenab	Jammu and Kashmir	Hydroelectricity

Name of the Project	Location	State/Union Territories	Purpose
Salal Project	River Chenab	Jammu and Kashmir	Hydroelectricity
Thein Dam Project	River Ravi	Punjab	Irrigation, Hydroelectricity
Malaprabha Project	River Malaprabha	Karnataka	Irrigation
Jayakwadi Project	River Godavari	Maharashtra	Irrigation
Beas Project	River Beas	Punjab and Haryana	Hydroelectricity
Sharda Sahayak	River Ghaghara and Sharda	Uttar Pradesh	Irrigation
Mayurakshi Project	River Mayurakshi	West Bengal	Irrigation, Hydroelectricity
Rana Pratap Sagar Project	River Chambal	Rajasthan	Hydroelectricity
Mettur Project	River Cauvery	Tamil Nadu	Hydroelectricity
Pallivasal Project	River Munnar Abuja	Kerala	Hydroelectricity
Papanasam Project	River Thamirabarani	Tamil Nadu	Hydroelectricity
Loktak Project	Lake Loktak	Manipur	Hydroelectricity
Tehri Project	River Bhagirathi (Ganga)	Uttarakhand	Hydroelectricity
Farakka Project	Ganga	West Bengal	Irrigation
Daman Ganga	River Daman Ganga	Gujarat	Irrigation and River Link
Gima Project	River Gima (Tributary of Tapi)	Maharashtra	Irrigation and River Link
Pamba Project	River Pamba	Kerala	River Conservation and Irrigation
Tapovan-Vishnugad	River Dhauliganga	Uttarakhand	Hydroelectricity
Omkareshwar	River Narmada	Madhya Pradesh	Hydropower and Irrigation

Extra Facts From Tamil Nadu Board and NIOS

- **Shifting Agriculture** is performed by tribal people in a piece of forest land after clearing the trees through felling and burning the trunks and branches.
- **Mixed Farming** is defined as a system of farming which includes crop production, raising livestock, poultry, fisheries, bee keeping etc. to sustain and satisfy as many of the farmer as possible.
- **Terrace Farming** is practiced specially in hilly areas, where lands are of sloping nature.
- The **tank irrigation** is popular in the peninsular India due to the undulating relief and hard rocks make difficult to dig canals and wells, absence of perennial rivers.
- Tank irrigation is used to collect and store water for irrigation and other purposes. Irrigation by tanks is a very old system in India.
- **Perennial River** A river that flows continuously through its river bed for a year is known as a perennial river.
- Canals are the effective source of irrigation in areas of low level relief, deep, fertile soils, perennial source of water and extensive command area.
- Well irrigation is unavoidable in the region of low rainfall and becomes an essential one where the canals and tank irrigation are not available.

23

Energy and Mineral Resources in India

(SOURCES)

Class-X New NCERT Chap 5 (Mineral and Energy Resources),
Class-X Old NCERT Chap 5 (Mineral and Power Resources),
Class-XII New NCERT Chap 5 (Mineral and Energy Resources),
Class-XII Old NCERT Chap 1 (Natural Resources of India),
Tamil Nadu Board (Class XII), NIOS

Mineral Resources

- India is endowed with a rich variety of mineral resources due to its varied geological structure. Bulk of the valuable minerals are products of **Pre-Paleozoic age** and are mainly associated with metamorphic and igneous rocks of Peninsular India.
- The vast alluvial plain tract of North India is devoid of minerals of economic use. The mineral resources provide the country with the necessary base for industrial development.

Types of Mineral Resources

Mineral resources are categorised as follows

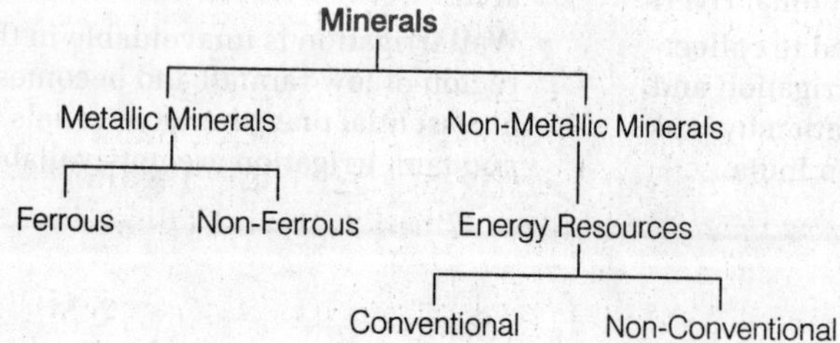

Metallic Minerals

These minerals contain metal. Iron ore, Copper, Manganese, Nickel, etc., are important examples of metallic minerals. Metallic minerals are further subdivided into Ferrous and Non-ferrous minerals.

- **Ferrous Minerals** These minerals have iron content. Iron-ore, manganese, chromite, pyrites, tungsten, nickel, cobalt, etc., are important examples of ferrous minerals.
- **Non-ferrous Minerals** These minerals do not have iron content. Gold, silver, copper, lead, bauxite, tin, magnesium, etc., are important examples of non-ferrous minerals.

Non-Metallic Minerals

- These minerals do not contain metal. Limestone, nitrate, potash, dolomite, mica, gypsum, etc., are important examples of non-metallic minerals.
- Coal and petroleum are also non-metallic minerals. They are used as fuel and are also known as **mineral fuels.**

Other Classification of Minerals

The wide varieties of minerals that have been explored by man for general and commercial purposes to satisfy his needs are classified into the following groups:

- **Industrial Metallic Minerals** Iron-ore
- **Ferroalloy Metallic Minerals** Manganese, chromium, Cobalt, molybdenum, vanadium, nickel, etc.
- **Precious Metallic Minerals** gold (Au), silver (Ag) and platinum (Pt).
- **Non-Metallic Minerals** Salt, tin, potash, asbestos and sulphur.
- **Power Minerals (Mineral fuels)** Coal, petroleum and natural gas which are non-metallic minerals derived from vegetable remains
- **Other** Uranium

Distribution of Minerals in India

- Most of the metallic minerals in India occur in the Peninsular plateau region in the old Crystalline rocks. Over 97% of coal reserves occur in the valleys of **Damodar, Son, Mahanadi** and **Godavari**.
- Petroleum reserves are located in the sedimentary basins of Assam, Gujarat and Mumbai High i.e., off-shore region in the Arabian Sea.
- New reserves have been located in the Krishna-Godavari and Kaveri basins. Most of the major mineral resources occur to the East of a line linking Mangalore and Kanpur.
- Minerals are generally concentrated in three broad belts in India. These belts are :

The North-Eastern Plateau Region

- This belt covers Chhota Nagpur (Jharkhand), Odisha Plateau, West Bengal and parts of Chhattisgarh.
- It has a variety of minerals viz. iron ore, coal, manganese, bauxite, mica.

The South-Western Plateau Region

- This belt extends over Karnataka, Goa and contiguous Tamil Nadu uplands and Kerala.
- This belt is rich in ferrous metals and bauxite.
- It also contains high grade iron ore, manganese and limestone.
- This belt packs in coal deposits except Neyveli lignite.
- This belt does not have as diversified mineral deposits as the North-Eastern belt.
- Kerala has deposits of monazite and thorium, bauxite, clay. Goa has iron ore deposits.

The North-Western Region

- This belt extends along Aravalli in Rajasthan and part of Gujarat and minerals are associated with the Dharwar system of rocks.
- Copper, zinc have been major minerals. Rajasthan is rich in building stones i.e. sandstone, granite, marble.
- Dolomite and limestone provide raw materials for the cement industry. Gujarat is known for its petroleum deposits.
- Gujarat and Rajasthan both have rich sources of salt.
- The Himalayan belt is another mineral belt where copper, lead, zinc, cobalt and tungsten are known to occur.
- They occur in both the Eastern and Western parts. Assam valley has mineral oil deposits.
- Besides, oil resources are also found in off-shore-areas near Mumbai Coast (Mumbai High).

Ferrous Mineral

- Ferrous minerals such as iron ore, manganese, chromite, etc., provide a strong base for the development of metallurgical industries.
- Our country is well-placed in respect of ferrous minerals both in reserves and production.

Iron Ore

- India is endowed with fairly abundant resources of iron ore. It has the **largest reserve of iron ore** in Asia.
- The two main types of ore found in our country are **haematite** and **magnetite**.
- It has great demand in the International market due to its superior quality.
- The Iron ore mines occur in close proximity to the coal fields in the North-Eastern plateau region of the country which adds to their advantage.
- The total reserves of iron ore in the country were about 20 billion tonnes in the year 2004-05.
- About 95% of total reserves of iron ore is located in the states of Odisha, Jharkhand, Chhattisgarh, Karnataka, Goa, Andhra Pradesh and Tamil Nadu.
- In **Odisha**, iron ore occurs in a series of hill ranges in Sundergarh, Mayurbhanj and Kendujhar.
- The important mines are Gurumahisani, Sulaipet, Badampahar (Mayurbhaj), Kiruburu (Kendujhar) and Bonai (Sundergarh).
- Similar hill ranges, Jharkhand has some of the oldest iron ore mines and most of the iron and steel plants are located around them.
- Most of the important mines such as **Noamundi** and **Gua** are located in Poorbi and Pashchimi Singhbhum districts.
- This belt further extends to **Durg, Dantewada** and **Bailadila**. Dalli and Rajhara in Durg are the important mines of iron ore in the country.
- In **Karnataka**, iron ore deposits occur in **Sandur-Hospet** area of Bellary district, **Baba Budan hills** and **Kudremukh** in **Chikmagalur** district and parts of Shimoga, Chitradurg and Tumkur districts.
- The districts of Chandrapur, Bhandara and Ratnagiri in Maharashtra, Karimnagar, Warangal, Kurnool, Cuddapah and Anantapur districts of Andhra Pradesh, Salem and Nilgiris districts of Tamil Nadu are other iron mining regions.
- Gua has also emerged as an important producer of iron ore.

Major Iron-ore Reserves in India

States	Regions	Important Mines
Odisha	• Sundergarh	Bonai
	• Mayurbhanj	Gurumahisani, Sulaipat, Badampahar
	• Jhar	Kiriburu
Jharkhand	• Poorbi Singhbhum	Noamundi
	• Pashchimi Singhbhum	Gua
Chhattisgarh	• Durg	Dalli Rajhara
	• Bastar	Dantewada, Bailadila
Karnataka	• Ballari district	Sandur-Hospet
	• Chikkamagaluru district, Shivamogga, Chitradurga, Tumkur	Baba Budan hills and Kudremukh

Manganese

- Manganese is an important raw Material for smelting of iron ore and also used for manufacturing ferro alloys. Manganese deposits are found in almost all geological formations; however, it is mainly associated with the **Dharwar system**.
- **Odisha** is the leading producer of manganese. Major mines in Odisha are located in the central part of the iron ore belt of India, particularly in Bonai, Kendujhar, Sundergarh, Gangpur, Koraput, Kalahandi and Bolangir.
- **Karnataka** is another major producer and here the mines are located in Dharwad, Bellary, Belgaum, North Canara, Chikmagalur, Shivamogga, Chitradurga and Tumkur.
- **Maharashtra** is also an important producer of manganese which is mined in Nagpur, Bhandara and Ratnagiri districts. The disadvantage to these mines is that they are located far from steel plants.
- The manganese belt of **Madhya Pradesh** extends in a belt in Balaghat-Chhindwara-Nimar-Mandla and Jhabua districts.
- **Andhra Pradesh**, **Goa** and **Jharkhand** are other minor producers of manganese.

Non-Ferrous Minerals

India is poorly endowed with non-ferrous metallic minerals except bauxite.

Bauxite

- Bauxite is the ore which is used in manufacturing Aluminium.
- Bauxite is found mainly in tertiary deposits and is associated with laterite rocks occurring extensively either on the plateau or hill ranges of peninsular India and also in the coastal tracts of the country.
- Odisha happens to be the largest producer of Bauxite. Kalahandi and Sambalpur are the leading producers.
- The other two areas which have been increasing their production are Bolangir and Koraput. The patlands of Jharkhand in Lohardaga have rich deposits.
- Gujarat, Chhattisgarh, Madhya Pradesh and Maharashtra are other major producers. Bhavanagar and Jamnagar in Gujarat have major deposits.
- Chhattisgarh has bauxite deposits in Amarkantak plateau while Katni-Jabalpur area and Balaghat in Madhya Pradesh have important deposits of bauxite. Kolaba, Thane, Ratnagiri, Satara, Pune and Kolhapur in Maharashtra are important producers. Guntur district of Andhra Pradesh, Hassan district of Karnataka and South Arcot district of Tamil Nadu are minor producers of bauxite.

Major Bauxite Reserves in India

States	Regions
Jharkhand	Palamau, Ranchi and Lohardaga districts
Gujarat	Bhavnagar, Junagadh and Amreli
Madhya Pradesh	Mandla, Shahdol and Balaghat and Katni district
Chhattisgarh	Surguja, Raigarh and Bilaspur in Amarkantak plateau
Maharashtra	Kolhapur, Raigarh, Thane, Satara and Ratnagiri districts
Karnataka	North-Western parts of Belgaum district

Copper

- Copper is an indispensable metal in the electrical industry for making wires, electric motors, transformers and generators.
- It is alloyable, malleable and ductile.
- It is also mixed with gold to provide strength to jewellery.
- The Copper deposits mainly occur in Singhbhum district in Jharkhand, Balaghat district in Madhya Pradesh and Jhunjhunu and Alwar districts in Rajasthan.
- Minor producers of copper are Agnigundala in Guntur district (Andhra Pradesh), Chitradurga and Hasan districts (Karnataka) and South Arcot district (Tamil Nadu).

Non-metallic Minerals

Among the non-metallic minerals produced in India, mica is the important one. The other minerals extracted for local consumption are limestone, dolomite and phosphate.

Mica

- Mica is mainly used in the electrical and electronic industries. It can be split into very thin sheets which are tough and flexible.
- Mica in India is produced in Jharkhand, Andhra Pradesh and Rajasthan followed by Tamil Nadu, West Bengal and Madhya Pradesh.

- In **Jharkhand**, high quality mica is obtained in a belt extending over a distance of about 150 km, in length and about 22 km, in width in lower Hazaribagh plateau.
- In **Andhra Pradesh**, Nellore district produces the best quality mica. In **Rajasthan**, the mica belt extends for about 320 kms from Jaipur to Bhilwara and around Udaipur.
- Mica deposits also occur in Mysore and Hasan districts of Karnataka, Coimbatore, Tiruchirapalli, Madurai and Kanyakumari in Tamil Nadu, Alleppey in Kerala, Ratnagiri in Maharashtra, Purulia and Bankura in West Bengal.

Diamond

- Diamond is the purest form of carbon and is the hardest element found in nature.
- The world famous **Kohinoor** diamond was extracted from the **Golconda mines** in Andhra Pradesh.
- Diamond regions in India include Panna and Satna districts of Madhya Pradesh; Raichur, Gulbarga of Karnataka; Anantpur district and Krishna basin of Andhra Pradesh.

Gypsum

- Gypsum is a mineral commonly found in Earth crust. Its major ores are selenite, satin spar, alabaster, gibbsite, etc.
- It is formed in the sedimentary rocks. Its largest producer is Rajasthan (90%). The largest producing region in Rajasthan is Hanumangarh district.
- The other regions are Bikaner, Jodhpur, Nagpur and Jaisalmer. Also, gypsum is produced in Doda district in Jammu and Kashmir and Kutch district in Gujarat. Gypsum is mainly used in making ammonium sulphate fertiliser and in cement industry.

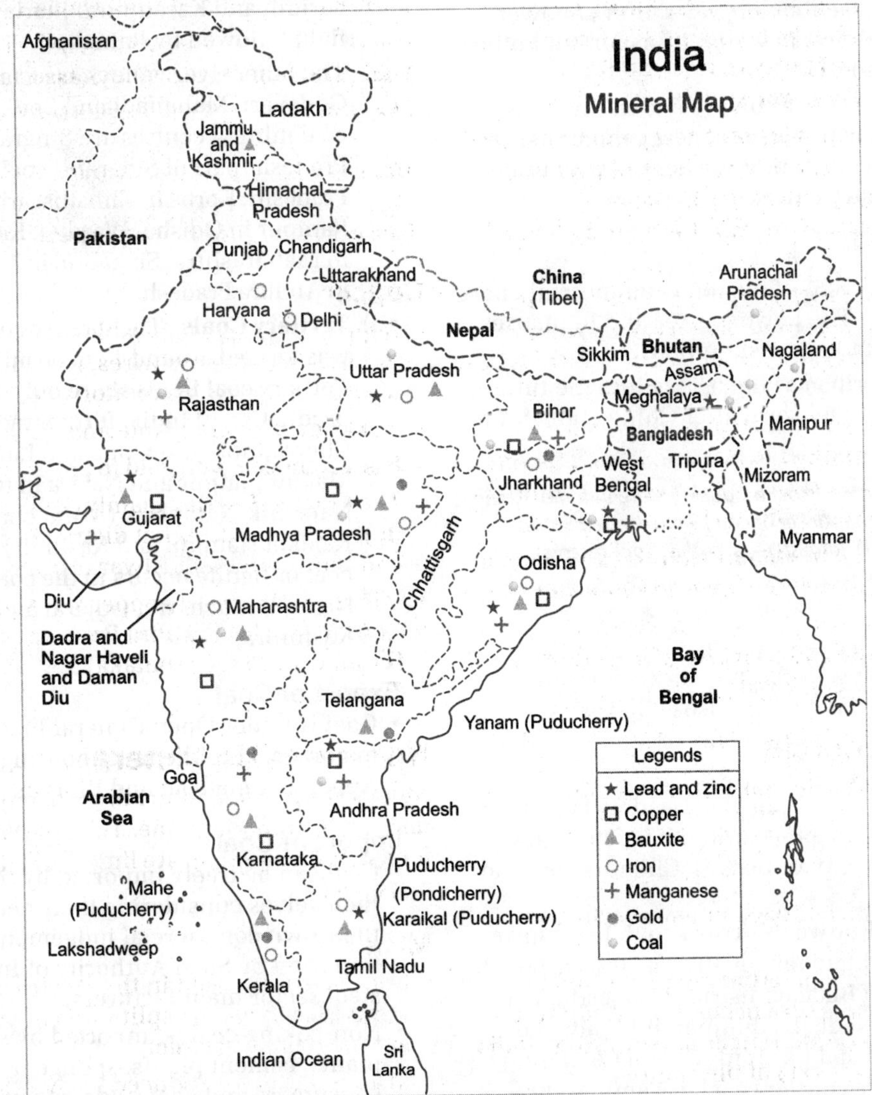

Non-Metallic Mineral Mines

Non-Metallic Mineral	Mines
Limestone	Andhra Pradesh, Rajasthan, Madhya Pradesh, Gujarat, Chhattisgarh
Dolomite	About 90% of the dolomite is found in Madhya Pradesh, Chhattisgarh, Odisha, Gujarat, Karnataka, West Bengal
Asbestos	Rajasthan, Andhra Pradesh and Karnataka
Gypsum	Found in Rajasthan and Jammu and Kashmir
Graphite	Occurs in Kalahandi, Belangir (Odisha) and Bhagalpur (Bihar)

Energy Resources

Energy resources can be categorised as conventional and non-conventional energy resources.

Conventional Energy Resources

- Mineral fuels are essential for generation of power, required by agriculture, industry, transport and other sectors of the economy.
- Mineral fuels like coal, petroleum and natural gas (known as fossil fuels), nuclear energy minerals, are the conventional sources of energy. These conventional sources are exhaustible resources.

1. Coal (Black Gold)

- It constitutes about 70% of the total commercial energy consumed in India. The power sector and industries account for 94% of total consumption.
- Coal has been described as the bridge into the future. India ranks third in the world after China and USA in coal production.

Note *Jharkhand is the largest coal producing state in India. China is the world's largest producer of coal, while United States contains the world's largest 'recoverable' coal reserves.*

Types of Coal

There are four major types of coal as follows

(i) **Anthracite Coal** It is the best quality of coal and contains 80% to 95% carbon, also called as **'Smokeless Fuel'**. It is found only in Jammu and Kashmir in small quantity.

(ii) **Bituminous Coal** This is the most widely used coal and contains 40% to 80% carbon. It is found in Jharkhand, Odisha, West Bengal, Chhattisgarh and Madhya Pradesh.

(iii) **Lignite It is also known as brown coal**. It is a lower grade coal and contains about 40% to 50% carbon. It is found in Palana of Bikaner district in Rajasthan, Neyveli of Tamil Nadu, Lakhimpur of Assam and Kerewa of Jammu and Kashmir. Over 90% of the lignite reserves are concentrated in Tamil Nadu. Neyveli is the largest lignite coal mine of India.

(iv) **Peat** It is the first stage of transformation of wood into coal and contains less than 40% carbon. It is found in Jharkhand state of India. Jharia area of Dhanbad district is the rich reserve of peat coal in the country.

Distribution of Coal Fields in India

Coal is one of the important minerals, which is mainly used in the generation of thermal power and smelting of iron-ore. About 80% of the coal deposits in India are of bituminous type and of **non-cooking grade**. Coal occurs in rock sequences mainly of two geological ages. These are as follows :

(i) **Gondwana Coal** The Gondwana coal is mature coal. The most important Gondwana coal fields of India are located in Damodar valley and Jharkhand-Bengal coal belt. The important coal fields in this region are Raniganj, Jharia, Bokaro, Giridih and Karanpura. Jharia is the largest coal field followed by Raniganj.

The other river valleys associated with coal are Godavari, Mahanadi and Son. The most important coal mining centres are Singrauli in Madhya Pradesh (part of Singrauli coal field lies in Uttar Pradesh); Korba in Chhattisgarh, Talcher and Rampur in Odisha, Wardha, Kamptee and Bhander in Maharashtra; Singareni in Telangana and Pandur in Andhra Pradesh.

(ii) **Tertiary Coals** The tertiary coal is young coal. It was formed around 15 to 60 million years ago. Tertiary coal fields share only 1% of coal production of India. It is extracted from Darangiri, Cherrapunji, Mewlong and Langrin (Meghalaya); Makum, Jaipur and Nazira in upper Assam; Namchik-Namphuk (Arunachal Pradesh) and Kalakot (Jammu and Kashmir). Besides, the brown coal or lignite occurs in the coastal areas of Tamil Nadu, Puducherry, Gujarat and Jammu and Kashmir.

Export of Coal

- Coal is under Open General Licence list. India exports coal to the neighbouring countries such as Nepal, Bangladesh and Bhutan.

Import of Coal

- Coal can be freely imported by the consumers themselves considering their needs and exercising their own commercial judgements. Coking coal is imported by Steel Authority of India Ltd. and other steel sector manufacturers.
- Non-coking coal is imported by sectors like power plants, cement plants, sponge iron plants, industrial consumers and coal traders to minimise transport expenses and against export entitlements.

2. Petroleum

- Crude petroleum consists of **hydrocarbons** of liquid and gaseous states varying in chemical composition, colour and specific gravity. It is an essential source of energy for all internal combustion engines in automobiles, railways and aircraft. Its numerous by-products are processed in petrochemical industries such as fertiliser, synthetic rubber, synthetic fibre, medicines, Vaseline, lubricants, wax, soap and cosmetics.
- **Crude petroleum** occurs in sedimentary rocks of the tertiary period. Oil exploration and production was systematically taken up after the Oil and Natural Gas Commission was set up in 1956. Till then, the Digboi in Assam was the only oil producing region.
- In recent years, new oil deposits have been found at the extreme Western and Eastern parts of the country. In **Assam**, Digboi, Naharkatiya and Moran are important oil producing areas.
- The major oil fields of Gujarat are Ankaleshwar, Kalol, Mehsana, Nawagam, Kosamba and Lunej.
- **Mumbai High** which lies 160 km off Mumbai was discovered in 1973 and production commenced in 1976.
- Oil and Natural gas have been found in exploratory wells in Krishna-Godavari and Kaveri basin on the East coast. Oil extracted from the wells is crude oil and contains many impurities.
- It cannot be used directly. It needs to be refined. There are two types of refineries in India-field based and market based. **Digboi** is an example of field based and **Barauni** is an example of market based refinery.

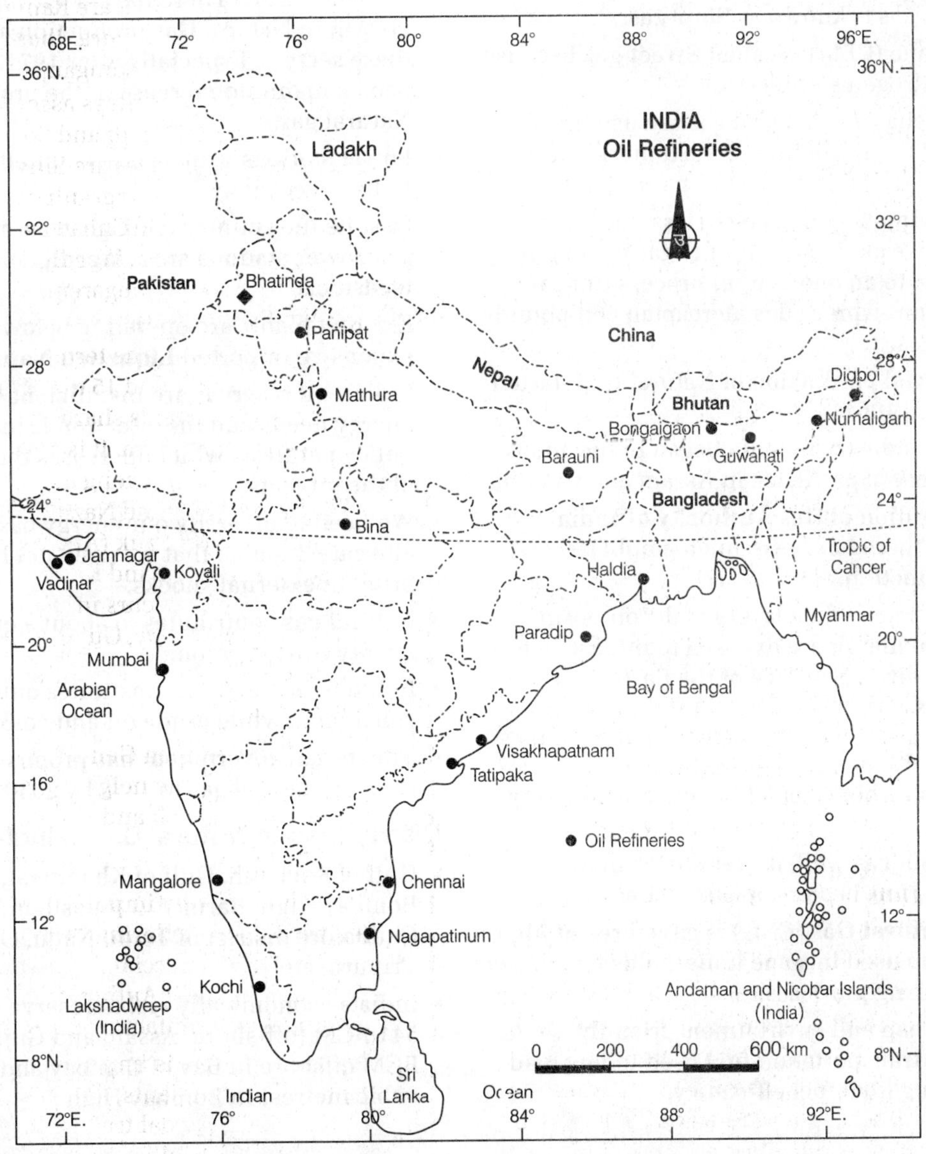

3. Natural Gas

- Natural gas (also called **Fossil gas**; sometimes just gas) is a naturally occurring hydrocarbon gas mixture consisting primarily of methane, but commonly including varying amounts of other higher alkanes, and sometimes a small percentage of carbon dioxide, nitrogen, hydrogen sulfide, or helium.
- Natural Gas is also a fossil fuel and is found in the same geological structure where petroleum is found.
- Sometimes, the pressure of natural gas forces oils up to the surface. Such natural gas is known as **'Associated gas'** or **'Wet gas'**.
- Some reservoirs contain gas and no oil. This gas is termed **Non-associated** gas or **Dry gas**.
- Often natural gases contain substantial quantities of hydrogen sulfide or other organic sulfur compounds. In this case, the gas is known as **Sour gas**.
- Coal-Bed Methane (CBM) is called **Sweet gas** because of its lack of hydrogen sulfide.
- In practice, purchases of natural gas are usually denoted as MBTUs (millions of British thermal units (BTU or Btu)) = ~1,000 cubic feet of natural gas.
- Natural gas is **odourless** and colourless; the slightly sour smell that we associate with the gas coming from a stovetop is due to an odorisation process (for safety and leak detection) which adds mercaptan compounds to the end-use gas.
- India's commercial production of Natural Gas started much later (since 1961).
- The natural gas industry in India began in the 1960s with the discovery of gas fields in Assam and Gujarat.
- After the constitution of **Gas Authority of India** (GAIL) in 1984, there has been much emphasis on natural gas production.
- Natural gas is formed when layers of decomposing plant and animal matter are exposed to intense heat and pressure under the surface of the Earth over millions of years.

Uses of Natural Gas

- It is used to turn turbines for Wind and Solar energy generation.
- It is a domestic fuel as well. It fires stoves in our houses and also runs heaters, ovens, boilers, etc.
- **Compressed Natural Gas** (CNG) is gas stored at high pressure and also used in some households for heating and cooking purposes.
- CNG is also a cheap and environment-friendly alternative for a transportation fuel used in low load vehicles requiring high fuel efficiency.
- **Liquefied Natural Gas** (LNG) is used to power vehicles such as off-road trucks and trains.
- Many buses and commercial automotive fleets now operate on CNG.
- It is an ingredient in dyes and inks. It is used in electric power generation and rubber compounding operations.
- Ammonia is manufactured using Hydrogen derived from Methane. Ammonia is used to produce chemicals such as Hydrogen cyanide, Nitric acid, urea and a range of fertilisers.

Importance of Natural Gas in India

- Currently, the largest share of Natural gas, about 40%, is consumed in the production of **fertilisers.**
- About 30% is used in power generation and 10% is used in LPG. There have been complimentary growth in Natural Gas production and all of these sectors. Especially after 1971, there has been a manifold increase in the production of Natural gas.
- Power stations using gas accounted for nearly 10% of India's electricity.
- Despite the country reeling under a power crisis, gas power stations are lying idle due to a lack of feedstock.
- Existing plants are operating below capacity on expensive imported **Liquefied Natural Gas** (LNG).
- India's oil reserves are insufficient for its growing energy needs and the situation is made worse by policy paralysis which increases the gestation period of the projects.
- We need to diversify our energy basket through alternate fuels so that we need not have to bear the brunt of external shocks.
- Natural gas contributes to about a quarter of global energy consumption.
- In India, however, it constitutes only 6% of the energy consumed, while crude oil and coal dominate.
- The Indian government has promised to raise the share of natural gas to 15% by 2030.

Distribution of Natural Gas in India

- Gulf of Kachchh, Gulf of Khambhat, Bassein field, Bombay High, Barmer in Rajasthan, KG basin, Cuddalore district of Tamil Nadu, Odisha, Assam, Tripura, etc.
- India's economically viable reserve of natural gas is 541 BCM (off-shore, Assam and Gujarat), besides 190 BCM offshore in Bay of Cambay and 190 BCM(billion cubic metres) in Bombay High.

- Recently a huge reserve of 400 BCM has been reported in the Tripura Basin.
- Besides them, 72 BCM is in the Rava structure and a huge reserve is reported around Andaman and Nicobar island. On the basis of remote sensing information, Andaman and Nicobar reserves are estimated to be around 1700 BCM.
- Its economic viability is yet to be established, that's why production has not yet started.
- This reserve will solve the problem or need of India for 100 years.
- This may produce an Economic Revolution in Eastern India.

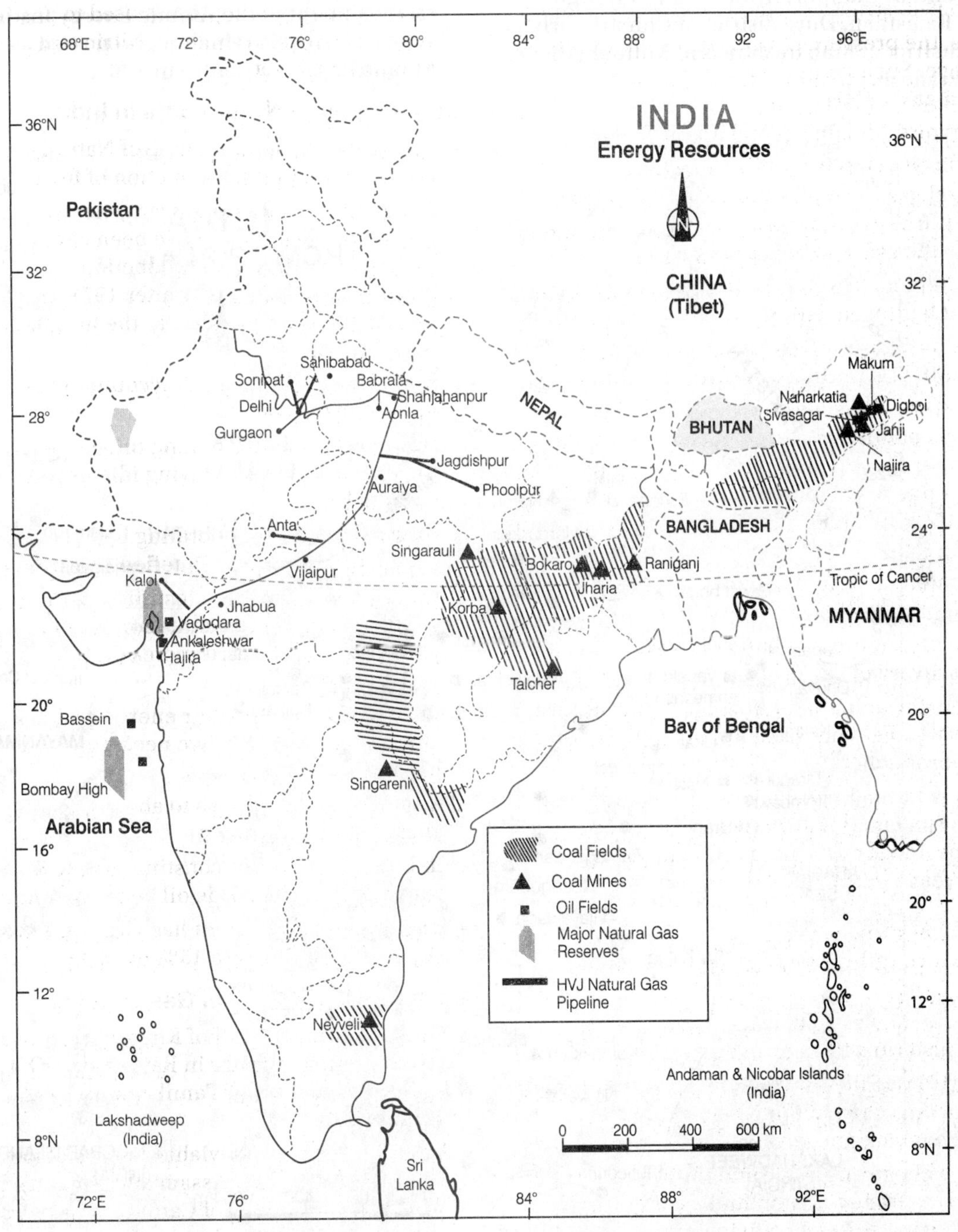

4. Nuclear Energy Resources

- Nuclear energy has emerged as a viable source in recent times. Important minerals used for the generation of nuclear energy are Uranium and Thorium.
- Uranium deposits occur in the Dharwar rocks. Geographically, Uranium ores are known to occur in several locations along the Singhbhum Copper belt.
- It is also found in Udaipur, Alwar and Jhunjhunu districts of Rajasthan, Durg district of Chhattisgarh, Bhandara district of Maharashtra and Kullu district of Himachal Pradesh.
- Thorium is mainly obtained from monazite and Ilmenite in the beach sands along the coast of Kerala and Tamil Nadu.
- World's richest monazite deposits occur in **Palakkad** and **Kollam** districts of Kerala, near Visakhapatnam in Andhra Pradesh and Mahanadi river delta in Odisha.
- The **Atomic Energy Commission** was established in 1948, progress could be made only after the establishment of the Atomic Energy Institute at Trombay in 1954 which was renamed as the Bhabha Atomic Research Centre in 1967.

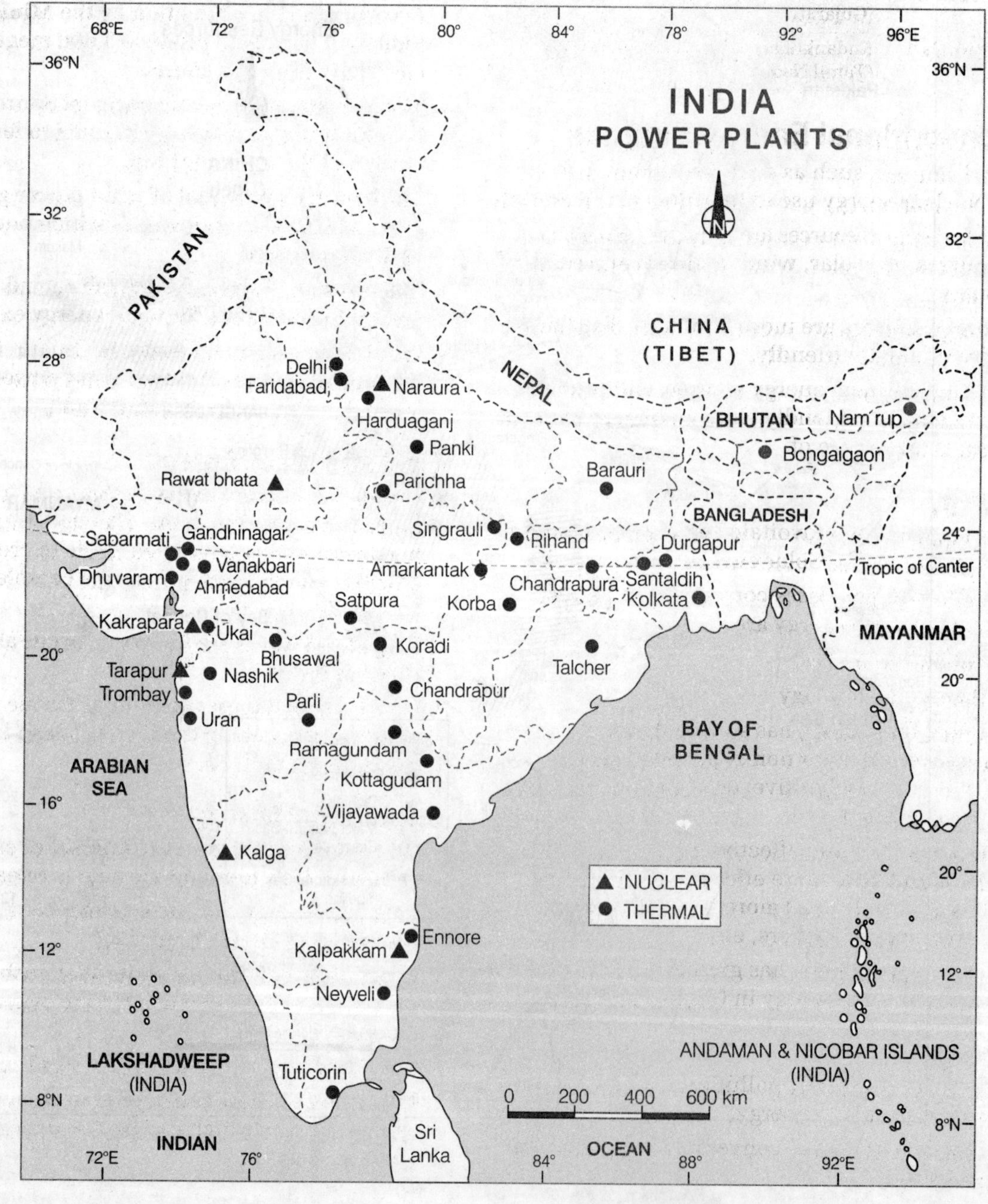

Important Nuclear Power Projects

Power Plant	Location	Total Power Production (MW)
Tarapur Nuclear Power	Tarapur (Maharashtra)	1400 (MW)
Rajasthan Nuclear Power	Rawatbhata, Kota (Rajasthan)	1180 (MW)
Madras Nuclear Power	Kalpakkam, Chennai (Tamil Nadu)	440 (MW)
Kaiga Nuclear Power	Kaiga (Karnataka)	880 (MW)
Narora Nuclear Power	Narora, Bulandsher (Uttar Pradesh)	440 (MW)
Kakarapara Nuclear Power	Kakarapara, Surat (Gujarat)	440 (MW)
Kudankulam Nuclear Power	Kudankulam (Tamil Nadu)	1000 (MW)

Non-Conventional Energy Sources

- Fossil fuel sources, such as coal, Petroleum, natural gas and Nuclear energy use exhaustible raw materials.
- Sustainable energy resources are only the Renewable energy sources like solar, wind, hydro-geothermal and biomass.
- These energy sources are more equitably distributed and environmentally friendly.
- The Non-conventional energy sources will provide more sustained, eco-friendly cheaper energy after the initial cost is taken care of.

Solar Energy

- Sun rays tapped in photovoltaic cells can be converted into energy, known as 'Solar energy'.
- The two effective processes considered to be very effective to tap solar energy are :
  - Photovoltaic technology
  - Solar thermal technology
- Solar thermal technology has some relative advantages over all other non-renewable energy sources. It is cost competitive, environment friendly and easy to construct.
- Solar energy is 7% more effective than coal or oil based plants and 10% more effective than nuclear plants. It is generally used more in appliances like heaters, crop dryers, cookers, etc.
- The Western part of India has greater potential for the development of solar energy in Gujarat and Rajasthan.

Wind Energy

- Wind energy is absolutely pollution free, an inexhaustible source of energy.
- The mechanism of energy conversion from blowing wind is simple.
- The kinetic energy of wind through turbines is converted into electrical energy.
- The permanent wind systems such the trade winds, Westerlies and seasonal wind like monsoon have been used as a source of energy.
- Besides these, local winds, land and sea breezes can also be used to produce electricity.
- India has already started generating wind energy.
- It has an ambitious programme to install 250 wind-driven turbines with a total capacity of 45 megawatts, spread over 12 suitable locations, especially in coastal areas.
- According to the estimation by the **Ministry of Power**, India will be able to produce 3,000 megawatts of electricity from this source.
- The Ministry of Non-conventional Sources of Energy is developing wind energy in India to lessen the burden of the oil import bill.
- The country's potential of wind power generation exceeds 50,000 megawatts, of which one-fourth can be easily harnessed.
- In Rajasthan, Gujarat, Maharashtra and Karnataka, favorable conditions for wind energy exist.
- Wind power plant at **Lamba** in Gujarat in Kachchh is the **largest in Asia**. Another wind power plant is located at **Tuticorin** in Tamil Nadu.

Tidal and Wave Energy

- Ocean currents are the store-house of infinite energy. Since the beginning of the 17th and 18th century, persistent efforts have been made to create a more efficient energy system from the ceaseless tidal waves and ocean current.
- Large tidal waves are known to occur along the West Coast of India.
- Hence, India has great potential for the development of tidal energy along the Coasts but so far these have not yet been utilised.

Geothermal Energy

- When the magma from the interior of earth comes out on the surface, tremendous heat is released.
- This heat energy can successfully be tapped and converted to electrical energy.
- Apart from this, the hot water that gushes out through the geyser wells is also used in the generation of thermal energy.
- It is popularly known as Geothermal energy.
- This energy is now considered to be one of the key energy sources which can be developed as an alternate source.

- The Hot springs and Geysers have been used since the medieval period.
- In India, a geothermal energy plant has been commissioned at **Manikaran** in Himachal Pradesh.

Bio-energy

- Bio-energy refers to energy derived from biological products which includes agricultural residues, municipal, industrial and other wastes.
- Bio energy is a potential source of energy conversion. It can be converted into electrical energy, heat energy or gas for cooking. It will also process the waste and garbage to produce energy.
- This will improve the Economic life of Rural areas in developing Countries, reduce Environmental pollution, enhance self-reliance and reduce pressure on fuel wood.
- One such project converting municipal waste into energy is in **Okhla** in Delhi.

Conservation of Resources

- The challenge of Sustainable development requires integration of the quest for Economic development with Environmental concerns.
- Traditional methods of resource use result in generating enormous quantities of waste as well as create other Environmental problems. Hence, **Sustainable development** calls for the protection of resources for the future generations.
- There is an urgent need to conserve the resources. The alternative energy sources like solar power, wind, wave, geothermal energy are Inexhaustible resources.
- These should be developed to replace the Exhaustible resources.
- In case of metallic minerals, use of scrap metals will enable **recycling of metals.**
- Use of scrap is especially significant in metals like copper, lead and zinc in which India's reserves are meagre.
- Use of substitutes for scarce metals may also reduce their consumption.
- Export of strategic and scarce minerals must be reduced, so that the existing reserve may be used for a longer period.

Extra Facts From
Tamil Nadu Board and NIOS

- Minerals are generally found in 'Ores'. It is actually an accumulation of any mineral mixed with other elements.
- Minerals generally occur in the cracks, crevices, faults and joints of the Igneous and Metamorphic rocks.
- Alluvial deposits are found in the sands of valley floor and at the foothills. These deposits consist of the minerals such as Gold, Silver and Platinum.
- Australia is the largest producer of Iron ore in the world. Other leading producers are China, Brazil, India and Russia. The majority of Iron ore (84%) is produced by 5 countries alone.
- Manganese is used for special quality steel-making; it makes steel anti-corrosive, hard and clean. It helps to increase toughness, strength and durability to resist oxidation.
- India is the 8th largest producer of manganese in the world though it possesses the largest reserves of manganese in the world.
- India's first attempt to harness tidal power for generating electricity would be in the form of a 3MW plant at the Durgaduani Creek in Sunderbans delta of West Bengal.

Transport and Communication in India

[SOURCES]

Class-XI Old NCERT Chap 11 (Transport and Communication), Class-X New NCERT Chap 7 (Lifelines of National Economy), Class-XII New NCERT Chap 7 (Transport and Communication), Class-XII Old NCERT Chap 4 (Transport Systems), Class-X Old NCERT Chap 8 (Transport, Communications and International Trade)

Transport

- Transport is a facility or a service for the carriage of persons and goods from one place to another using humans, animals and different kinds of vehicles.
- It is an organised service industry that handles loading, unloading and delivery.
- Several places (nodes) joined together by a series of routes (links) to form a pattern is called a '**transport network**'.

Modes of Transportation

- The main modes of transportation are land, water, air and pipelines.
- These are used for inter-regional and intra-regional transport and each one (except pipelines) carries both passengers and goods.

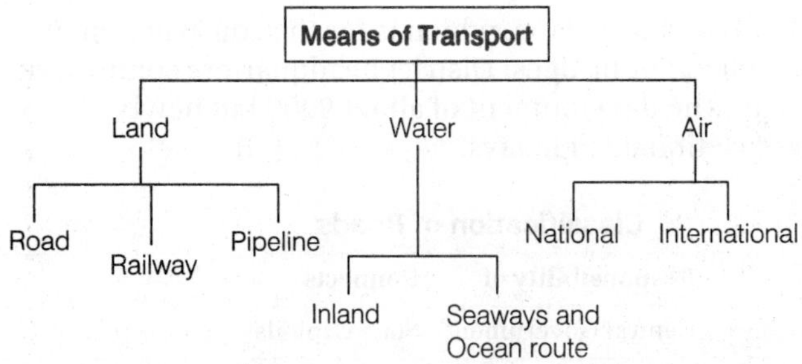

- The transport system in India includes rail transport, road transport, air transport, water transport and portal connectivity.

Land Transport

- The modes of land transport were in use since ancient times. Roadways and railways are the chief modes of land transport.
- With the economic and technological development, metalled roads and railways were developed to move large volumes of goods and people from one place to another.
- India has one of the largest road networks in the world, the largest railway system in Asia and the second largest in the world.

1. Road Transport in India

- The pathways and unmetalled roads have been used for transportation in India since ancient times. Roads are the most popular mode of transportation.
- India has one of the largest road networks in the world with a total length of 66.71 lakh km as of 31st December, 2023. About 85% of passengers and 70% of freight traffic are carried by roads every year.
- Road transport is relatively suitable for shorter distance travel.
- For the purpose of construction and maintenance, roads are classified as :
  - National Highways (NH)
  - State Highways (SH)
  - Major District Roads
  - Rural Roads

National Highways

- The main roads which are constructed and maintained by the Central Government are known as the **National Highways**.
- These roads are meant for inter-state transport and movement of defence men and material in strategic areas.
- These also connect the state capitals, major cities, important ports, railway junctions, etc.
- India has 146145 km of National Highways as of November, 2023. The National Highways constitute only 2% of the total road length but carry 40% of the road traffic.
- **NH-44** (Earlier NH-7) is the longest national highway in India with total length of 3,745 km.

Some Important National Highways

Highway Number	States through which it passes
NH1	Jammu and Kashmir
NH2	Assam, Nagaland, Manipur, Mizoram
NH3	Punjab, Himachal Pradesh, Jammu
NH4	Andaman and Nicobar
NH5	Punjab, Chandigarh, Haryana, Himachal Pradesh
NH6	Meghalaya, Assam, Mizoram
NH7	Punjab, Chandigarh, Haryana, Himachal Pradesh, Uttarakhand
NH8	Assam
NH9	Punjab, Haryana, Delhi, Uttar Pradesh
NH10	Sikkim, West Bengal
NH11	Rajasthan
NH12	West Bengal
NH19	Delhi, Haryana, Uttar Pradesh, Bihar, Jharkhand, West Bengal
NH20	Bihar, Jharkhand
NH21	Rajasthan, Uttar Pradesh
NH24	Gujarat, Rajasthan, Madhya Pradesh, Uttar Pradesh, Bihar, West Bengal, Assam
NH44 (Longest NH in India)	Jammu and Kashmir, Himachal Pradesh, Punjab, Haryana, Delhi, Uttar Pradesh, Madhya Pradesh, Maharashtra, Telangana, Andhra Pradesh, Karnataka, Tamil Nadu
NH48	Delhi, Haryana, Rajasthan, Gujarat, Maharashtra, Karnataka, Tamil Nadu
NH53	Gujarat, Maharashtra, Chhattisgarh, Odisha

National Highway Development Project

National Highways Authority of India (NHAI) has started following projects in different phases.

- **Golden Quadrilateral** It comprises construction of 5,846 km long 4/6 lane, high-density traffic corridor, to connect India's four big metro cities of Delhi-Mumbai-Chennai-Kolkata. With the construction of the Golden Quadrilateral, the time-distance and cost of movement among the megacities of India has been considerably minimised.
- **North-South and East-West Corridor** North-South corridor aims at connecting Srinagar in Jammu and Kashmir with Kanyakumari in Tamil Nadu (including Kochi-Salempur) with a 4,076 km long road.
- The **East-West Corridor** has been planned to connect Silchar in Assam with the port town of Porbandar in Gujarat with 3,640 km of road length.

State Highways

- These are constructed and maintained by State Governments Public Works Departments (PWDs). They join the state capitals with district headquarters and other important towns.
- These roads are connected to the National Highways.
- These constitute 4% of the total road length in the country.

District Roads

- These roads are the connecting link between district headquarters and the other important nodes in the district.
- They account for 14% of the total road length of the country.

Rural Roads

- These roads are vital for providing links in the rural areas.
- About 80% of the total road length in India are categorised as rural roads.
- There is regional variation in the density of rural roads because these are influenced by the nature of the terrain.

Bharatmala is an umbrella scheme for:

(i) Development of State roads along coastal border areas, including connectivity of non-major ports;

(ii) Backward areas religious and tourist places connectivity programme;

(iii) Setubharatam Pariyojana, which is for the construction of about 1500 major bridges; District headquarters connectivity scheme for the development of about 9000 km newly declared National Highways.

Classification of Roads

Name	Responsibility of	Connects
National Highways	Central Government	State Capitals
State Highways	State Government	State Capital to District HQ
District Roads	Zila Parishad	District HQ to Tehsil and Blocks
Village Roads	Gram Panchayat	Villages to neighbouring towns

Atal Tunnel

The world's longest Highway tunnel - **Atal Tunnel** (9.02 km) has been built by **Border Road Organisation.** This tunnel connects Manali to Lahaul-Spiti valley throughout the year.

Earlier the valley was cut off for about six months each year owing to heavy snowfall. The tunnel is built with ultra-modern specifications in the Pir Panjal range of Himalayas at an altitude of 3000 m from the Mean Sea Level (MSL).

Other Roads – Border Roads and International Highways

- Other roads include Border Roads and International Highways. The **Border Road Organisation (BRO)** was established in May, 1960 for accelerating economic, development and strengthening defence preparedness through rapid and coordinated improvement of strategically important roads along the Northern and North-Eastern boundary of the country.
- It is a premier multifaceted construction agency. It has constructed roads in high altitude mountainous terrain joining **Chandigarh** with **Manali** (Himachal Pradesh) and **Leh** (Ladakh). This road runs at an average altitude of 4,270 m above the mean sea level.
- Apart from the construction and maintenance of roads in strategically sensitive areas, the BRO also undertakes snow clearance in high altitude areas.
- The international Highways are meant to promote a harmonious relationship with the neighbouring countries by providing effective links with India. The distribution of roads is not uniform in the country.

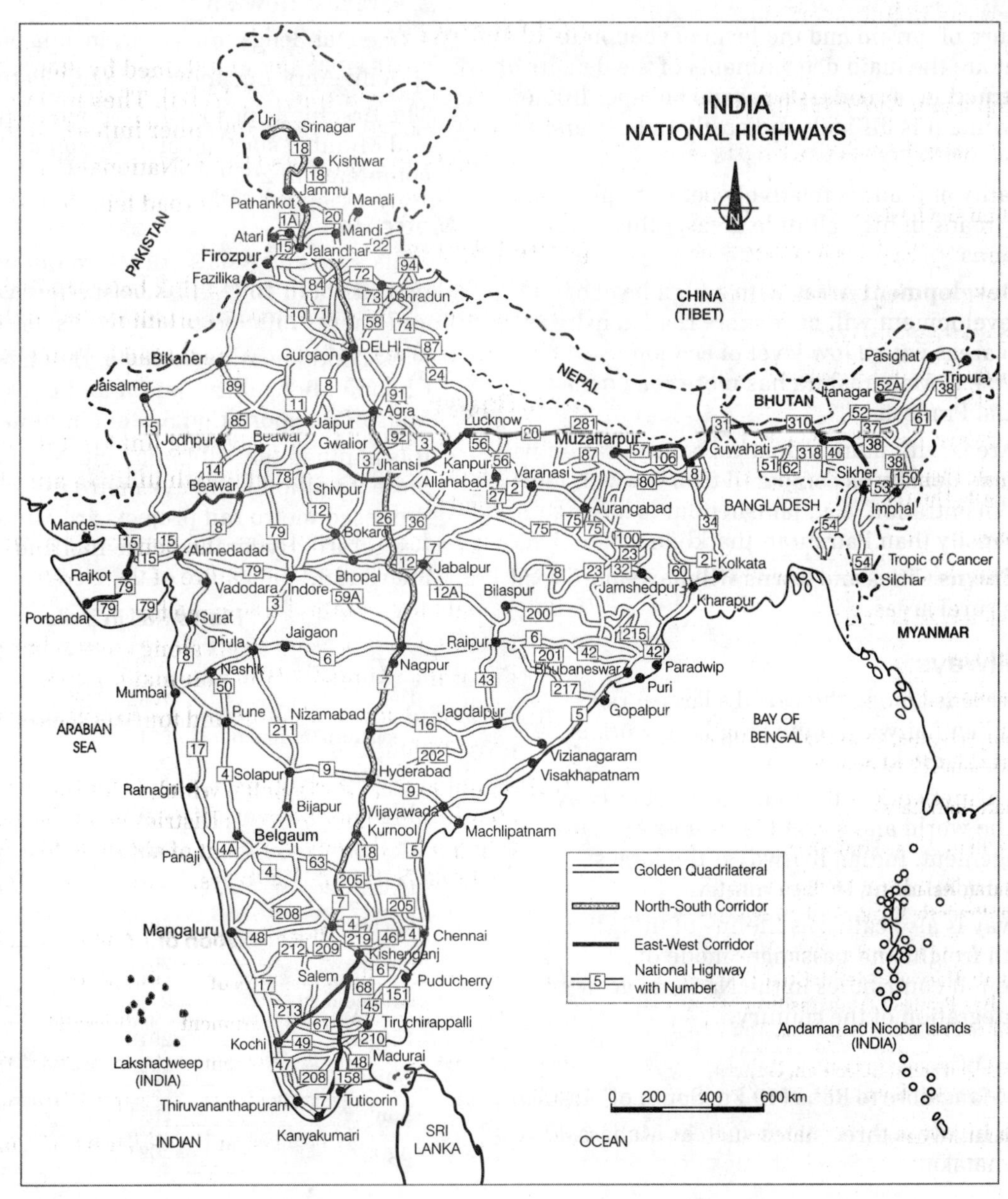

- The density of roads (length of roads per 100 sq km of area) varies from only 12.14 km in Jammu and Kashmir to 517.77 km in Kerala with a national average of 142.68 km in 2011.
- The density of roads is high in most of the Northern states and major Southern states. It is low in the Himalayan region, North-Eastern region, Madhya Pradesh and Rajasthan.

Roadways in India (2023)

Types of Roadways	Length (in km)
National Highway	146145
State Highway	179535
Other Roads	63,45,403
Total	66.17 lakh

Factors Influencing Roadways

- **Terrain** Nature of terrain and the level of economic development are the main determinants of the density of roads. Construction of roads is easy and cheaper in the plain areas while it is difficult and costly in hilly and plateau areas.
- **Climate** Quality of roads is relatively better in plains as compared to roads in high altitude areas, rainy and forested regions.
- **Economic Development** Areas with a high level of economic development will have more road density as compared to areas with a low level of economic development. e.g. Maharashtra has more road density than Himachal Pradesh.
- **Industries** Areas with more industrial concentration will have more road density as compared to areas with low industrial concentration. e.g., Jamshedpur is having more road density than Patratu in Jharkhand.
- **Cities and Towns** Cities and towns will have more road density than rural areas.

2. Indian Railways

- Indian Railways is among the world's largest rail networks. Indian Railways route length network is spread over 1,23,236 km.
- India's railway network is the fourth largest railway network in the world and second largest in Asia, under single management. Indian Railway is the largest government undertaking in the country.
- Indian Railway is also called as lifeline of India which provides both freight and passenger mode of transportation. It contributes in the National growth and economic integration of the country.

Konkan Railways

- It runs from Mangalore to Roha (40 km South of Mumbai).
- The network involves three states such as Maharashtra, Goa and Karnataka.
- It has a total length of 738 km. Almost 10% of the line passes through tunnels.

Bullet Train in India

- Railway Ministry in its white paper 'Vision 2020' envisages the implementation of regional high speed rail projects to provide services at 250-350 km/h.
- Six corridors have been identified for technical studies
  - Delhi-Chandigarh-Amritsar
  - Pune-Mumbai-Ahmedabad
  - Hyderabad-Vijayawada-Chennai
  - Howrah-Haldia
  - Nagaur-Mumbai
  - Delhi-Ahmedabad
  - Varanasi-Howrah
  - Chennai-Bengaluru-Thiruvananthapuram
  - Delhi-Agra-Lucknow-Varanasi-Patna
- The first high speed corridor between Ahmedabad and Mumbai started construction in 2017. It was completed in 2022.

Metro Rail

- India's 1st and Asia's 5th Metro rail was introduced in Kolkata in 1972. It is a cost effective, eco-friendly and energy efficiency mass transport system.
- Now 7 Indian cities (Kolkata, Delhi, Mumbai, Chennai, Bengaluru, Jaipur and Lucknow) have Metro Transportation System in India.
- It is planned that all Indian cities having population more 2 million will have metro rail system. Proposed metro rail projects are Mumbai, Bengaluru, Hyderabad, Chennai and Kochi metro rail.

Metro Rail in India

City	Start	Length (km)
Delhi	2002	348
Bengaluru (Namma)	2011	42.3
Gurgaon	2013	11.7
Jaipur	2015	11.9
Chennai	2015	45.1
Hyderabad	2015	69
Kochi	2017	27.8
Lucknow	2017	23.7
Ahmedabad	2019	6.5
Nagpur	2019	13.5
Noida	2019	29.7
Kanpur	2021	32
Agra	2024	29.65

Growth and Development of Indian Railways

- The **first railway line** in India was opened for public traffic on 16th April, 1853 between Mumbai and Thane over a distance of 34 km.
- Meanwhile, the construction of the railway lines was going on in the Eastern part of the country and the first section of the East Indian Railway, from Howrah to Hugli, a distance of 37 km was inaugurated on 15th August, 1854.
- In 1870, the all-rail route between Kolkata and Mumbai started functioning and the main line from Mughal Sarai to Lahore (now in Pakistan) was completed.
- In 1871, the Mumbai-Chennai route was also opened.
- Thus, within a short span of 18 years from 1853 to 1871, most of the important cities of India were connected by rail.
- At present, India has the **second largest railway network in Asia** and the **fourth largest in the world** after the USA (2, 27,736 km), Russia (2, 22,293 km), and China (87,157 km).
- But, India tops the world's leading countries with regard to passenger/km earned.

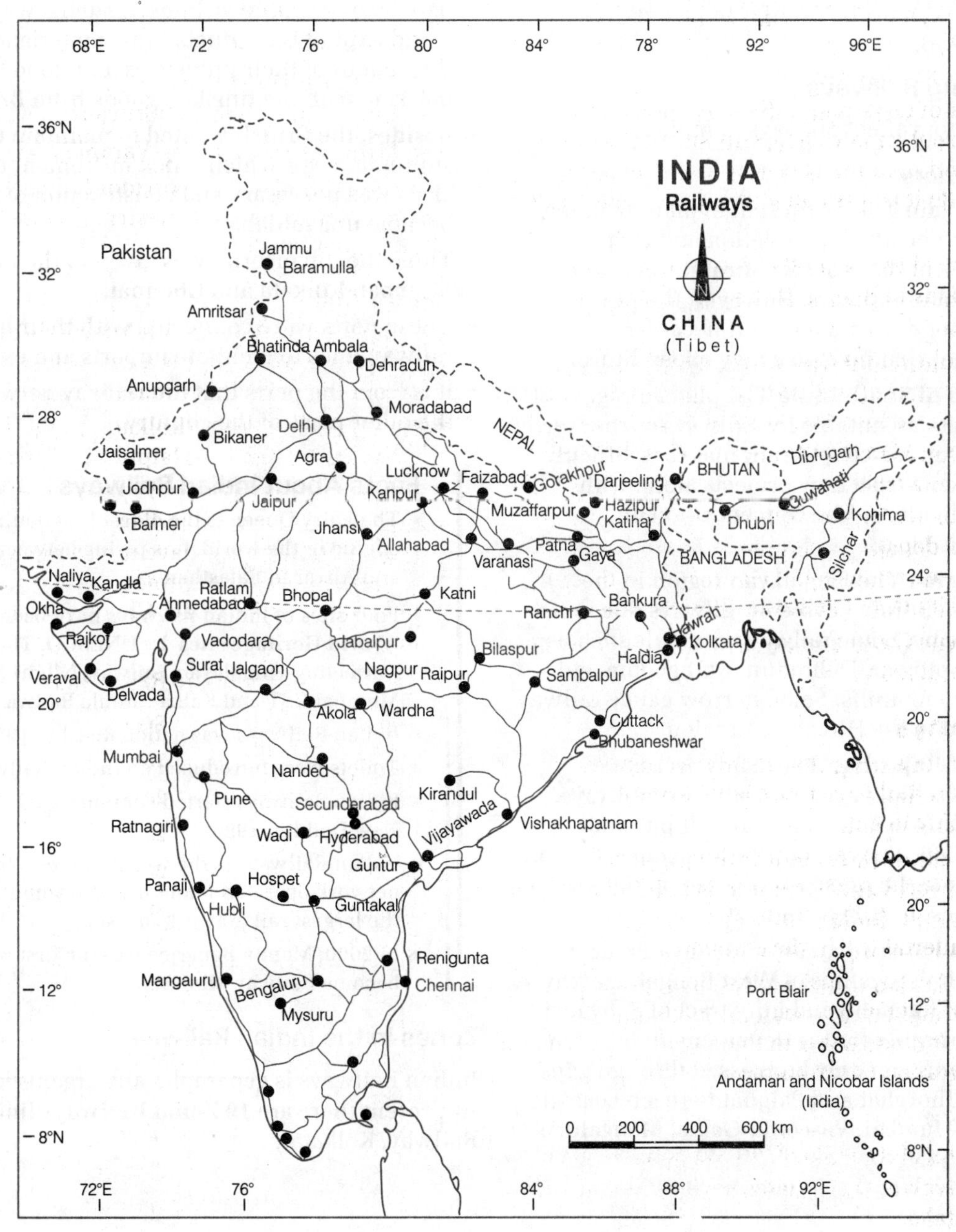

- The railway is the **largest Public Sector Undertaking** of the country comprising a vast network route length of 68,426 km.
- Today Indian Railways is operating in one of the most difficult terrains in the world. For example 55 km long rail route-length between Jammu and Udhampur, 837 km route length is added with the completion of the Konkan railway route.
- Indian railway is the largest government undertaking and is the largest employer with more than 10 lakh employees working in operational and commercial sections of railways.
- The **longest rail route in India** is from Dibrugarh in Assam to Kanyakumari in Tamil Nadu, covering distance 4,282 km.

Factors Affecting Railways

The following factors affect railways in India :

Geographical Factors

- **North Indian Plain** The North Indian plain with its level land, high density of population and rich agriculture present the most **favourable** conditions for the development of railways. However, the presence of a large number of rivers makes it necessary to construct bridges that involve heavy expenditure.
- **Plateau Region of South India** The plateau region of South India is not as suitable for railways as the North plain area. The undulating terrain makes it difficult for railways to construct new projects along with operational difficulties. The concentration of population is also less.
- **Himalayan Region** The Himalayan region in the North is almost entirely devoid of railways due to its rugged topography. Some railway terminals such as Jammu Tawi, Kotdwar, Dehradun, Kathgodam, etc. are found on the foothills. Some narrow gauge railway tracks are found in the Himalayan region.
- **Sandy Areas of Rajasthan** The sandy areas of Rajasthan are also not very favourable for railways. There was no railway line between Jodhpur and Jaisalmer till 1966. The reasons for less concentration of railway include the presence of less population, lack of industries, hostile terrain, etc.
- **Forested Areas** Forested areas of Madhya Pradesh and Odisha, deltaic swamps of West Bengal, marshy areas of Rann of Kachchh and hilly tract of Sahyadri are also **unfavourable** for the development of railways. Sahyadri can only be crossed through gaps like Thalghat, Bhorghat and Palghat to reach coastal trailheads like Mumbai, Vasco-da-Gama, Mangaluru and Kochi.

Economic Factors

- Railways develop more in economically advanced areas where the need for railway networks is felt more. e.g. Delhi, Northern Plains, Mumbai, etc.
- This is because of the economic linkages that we find the highest density of railways near big urban and industrial centers like Jamshedpur and in areas that are rich in mineral and agricultural resources.

Political and Administrative Factors

- The present railway system in India is the legacy of British rule.
- The British administration planned the direction and pattern of the railway lines in such a way that they could exploit the valuable raw materials of India for the benefit of their industries and flood the Indian markets with the finished goods from Britain.
- Besides, the British wanted to maintain their military supremacy, for which quick movement of troops and arms was necessary and construction of railways became unavoidable.
- Thus, the top priority was given to the big ports of Mumbai, Kolkata and Chennai.
- These ports were connected with their hinterlands by railway lines to facilitate imports and exports.
- It is from the ports that the railway network spread to the other parts of the country.

Facts About Indian Railways

- The Fairy Queen is the oldest functioning steam engine in the world. It is plying between New Delhi and Alwar in Rajasthan.
- Four sites of Indian Railways have been declared as **'World Heritage sites'** by UNESCO. They are Darjeeling-Himalayan Railway, Nilgiri Mountain, Mumbai CST and Kalka-Shimla Railways.
- Indian Railways was nationalised in 1951.
- Toilets were introduced on Indian Railways in 1909.
- Indian Railways started computerised reservations in New Delhi in 1986.
- Indian Railways is the world's second largest network operated under a single administration and the largest rail network in Asia.
- In 2000, Mamta Banerjee was the first woman to become Railway Minister.

Zones in the Indian Railway

Indian Railways is geographically organised into zones. At present there are **19 Zonal Railways** (including Metro Railway, Kolkata).

Zones in Indian Railway

Zones	Routes (Km)	Headquarters	Divisions
Central (CR)	3905	Mumbai	Mumbai, Bhusawal, Pune, Solapur, Nagpur
East Central (ECR)	3628	Hajipur	Danapur, Dhanbad, Mughal Sarai, Samastipur, Sonpur
East Coast (ECoR)	2572	Bhubaneswar	Khurda Road, Sambalpur, Visakhapatnam
Eastern (ER)	2414	Kolkata	Howrah, Sealdah, Asansol, Malda
North Central (NCR)	3151	Prayagraj	Prayagraj, Agra, Jhansi
North-Eastern (NER)	3667	Gorakhpur	Izzatnagar, Lucknow, Varanasi
North Western (NWR)	5459	Jaipur	Jaipur, Ajmer, Bikaner, Jodhpur
North-East Frontier (NFR)	3907	Guwahati	Alipurduar, Katihar, Rangia, Lumding, Tinsukia
Northern (NR)	6968	Delhi	Delhi, Ambala, Firozpur, Lucknow, Moradabad
South Central (SCR)	5803	Secunderabad	Secunderabad, Hyderabad, Guntakal, Guntur, Nanded, Vijayawada
South-East Central (SECR)	2447	Bilaspur	Bilaspur, Raipur, Nagpur
South-Eastern (SER)	2631	Kolkata	Adra, Chakradharpur, Kharagpur, Ranchi
South-Western (SWR)	3177	Hubli	Hubli, Bengaluru, Mysuru
Southern (SR)	5098	Chennai	Chennai, Tiruchirappalli, Madurai, Palakkad, Salem, Trivandrum
West Central (WCR)	2965	Jabalpur	Jabalpur, Bhopal, Kota
Western (WR)	6182	Mumbai	Mumbai Central, Ratlam, Ahmedabad, Rajkot, Bhavnagar, Vadodara
South Coast (SCoR)	3496	Visakhapatnam	Waltair, Vijaywada, Guntur, Guntakal
Konkan Railway (KR)	756.25	Navi Mumbai	Karwar, Ratnagiri
Kolkata Metro	24.5	Kolkata	—

Railway Gauges

The Indian railway has 4 different types of gauges.

- **Broad Gauge** Width 1.676 m
- **Meter Gauge** Width 1 m
- **Narrow Gauge** Width .762 m
- **Lift Gauge** Width .610 m

Freight Traffic

- Railway Freight traffic is vital for economic and industrial progress of the country since Freight traffic consists of around 65% of the total revenue of Indian Railways.
- But the problem is that only one-third of the total trains running daily on Indian Railway are freight trains.

Diamond Quadrilateral

- It is a project of the Indian railways to establish a high speed rail network in India connecting across the four mega cities i.e. Delhi, Mumbai, Kolkata and Chennai, similar to the Golden Quadrilateral expressways.
- Six corridors under it connecting the metropolitan cities include
  1. Delhi-Mumbai
  2. Mumbai-Chennai
  3. Chennai-Kolkata
  4. Kolkata-Delhi
  5. Delhi-Chennai diagonal
  6. Mumbai-Kolkata diagonal

3. Ports and Waterways

- Water transport is the cheapest and the oldest mode of transport.
- It operates on a natural track and hence does not require huge capital investment in the construction and maintenance of its track except in case of canals.
- Water transport has played a very significant role in bringing different parts of the world closer and is indispensable to foreign trade.
- The following are the advantages of water transport
  - **Cheapest Means of Transport** Rivers are a natural highway that does not require any cost of construction and maintenance. Even the cost of construction and maintenance of canals is much less or they are used, not only for transport purposes but also for irrigation, etc. Moreover, the cost of operation of inland water transport is very low.
    Thus, it is the cheapest mode of transport for carrying goods from one place to another.
  - **Least Consumption of Energy** Waterways are a fuel-efficient and environment-friendly mode of transportation. The boats and steamers, even if mechanised, consume much lesser fuel and do not pollute the surrounding.
  - **Suitable for Heavy Bulky Goods** Waterway can carry much larger quantities of heavy and bulky goods such as coal and timber, etc.
  - **No Friction** Since the boats and steamers flow in the direction of water the friction force is less as compared to road and railways.
  - **Eco-friendly** The boats and steamers consume much lesser fuel and do not pollute the surrounding.

Types of Waterways

Important types of waterways are as follows

Inland Waterways

- Inland Water Transport consists of transport by rivers, canals and lakes. Inland waterway is a network of rivers, canals, backwaters and creeks that can be utilised for transportation instead of or in addition to roads and rails.
- Some of the facts related to the Inland Waterway are
  - It is the cheapest mode of transport.
  - Water diversion from the rivers causes navigation difficult making the Inland Waterway less competitive.
  - The total navigable length of the Inland Waterway is 14500 km, out of which about 5200 km of river and 4000 km of canals can be used by mechanised crafts Account for 1% of transport.
  - Out of 3700 km of navigable rivers which are available for transport, only 2000 km is actually used.
  - Canals are controlled by the **Inland Waterway Authority.**
  - The **Inland Waterways Authority of India Act**, 1985 empowers the Government to declare waterways with potential for the development of shipping and navigation as National Waterways.

Ocean-Transport

- Ocean Transport is indispensable for foreign trade. It has brought the different parts of the world closer and has knitted together all the nations of the world into one big world market.
- It operates on a natural track, i.e., the sea, and does not require any investment in the construction and maintenance of its track. Ocean Transport includes coastal shipping and overseas shipping.

Limitations of Inland Waterways in India

- In India, it rains heavily during monsoons, so the water current is so torrential that it is difficult to ply boats.
- During the dry winter and summer season, most rivers run dry, not even have sufficient water for irrigation, so navigation is hindered.
- Rivers of South India flow through rocky areas. Hence, they are not fit for playing boats because of waterfalls.
- As compared to boats, railways are quicker and reliable means of transport. Since, Indian rivers fall from the shallow and sandy delta's so ships cannot sail from seashores to Inland parts.
- But inland water transport has the inherent advantage of cheap means of transport, especially for more load and long journey's.
- One horsepower can carry 4000 kg load in water whereas it can carry 150 kg and 500 kg load by road and rail respectively, moreover, water transport is less polluting.

National Waterways

The National Waterways Act came into effect in 2016. It proposed 106 additional National Waterways and merges 5 existing Acts which were declared the 6 National Waterways which are as follows

National Waterways 1	It starts from Allahabad(Prayagraj) to Haldia with a distance of 1620 km. The NW 1 runs through the Ganges, Bhagirathi and Hooghly river system with fixed terminals at Haldia, Farakka and Patna and floating terminals at most of the riverside cities like Kolkata, Bhagalpur, Varanasi and Allahabad. It is the longest National Waterways in India.
National Waterways 2	It is a stretch on the Brahmaputra river from Sadia to Dhubri in Assam state. The NW 2 is one of the major freight transportation waterways of North-East India and the third-longest Waterways with a total length of 891 km.
National Waterways 3 or the West Coast Canal	It is located in Kerala state and runs from Kollam to Kottapuram. The 205 km long West Coast Canal is India's first waterway with an all-time navigation facility. The NW3 consists of the West Coast Canal, Champakara Canal, and Udyogamandal Canal and runs through Kottappuram, Cherthala, Thrikkunnapuzha Kollam and Alappuzha.
National Waterway 4	It is connected from Kakinada to Puducherry through Canals, Tank and River Godavari along with Krishna river. The NW 4 the second-longest waterway of India with a total length of 1095 km in Andhra Pradesh and Tamil Nadu.
National Waterway 5	It connects Odisha to West Bengal using the stretch on Brahmani river, East Coast Canal, Matai river and Mahanadi river delta. The 623 km long canal system will handle the traffic of cargo such as coal, fertiliser, cement and iron.
National Waterway 6	It is the **proposed waterway** in Assam state and will connect Lakhipur to Bhanga in river Barak. The 121 km long waterway will help in trading between the town of Silchar to Mizoram State.

Role of Inland Water Transport in Regional Development

- The river water transport can contribute significantly to the regional development of the country. This is the cheapest mode of transport and except in the maintenance of ports, jetties, canals, not much money is involved in its maintenance.
- During the pre-colonial period, Inland Water Transport played a major part in the **Growth of trade** and 'regional development in North India. Even today it can play an important role in reducing the production cost of industries.'

- There are some regions like the deltaic regions of Ganga where it is difficult and costly to construct roads and bridges across numerous distributaries, river waterway can be a good mode of transport, facilitating the economic development of the region.
- In fact, **Rural Water Transport** (RWT), a specific sub-sector of **Inland Water Transport** (IWT) is particularly important due to its potential to help reduce isolation and poverty.
- It mostly consists of small family-owned boats that operate on river's and canal networks, such boats transport service, employment and promote fishing and additional employment is generated in boat making.

Ocean Routes and Ports

- India has a coastline of about 7,517 km.
- There are 13 major ports and 200 minor ports. 95% of India's foreign trade and 70% of the value is trade takes place through seaways.
- Over 7500 km of coastline with 13 major and 60 operational non-major ports.
- 90% of the country's trade by volume and 70% by value are moved through maritime transport.
- There are 13 major ports in India that handle approximately 58% of cargo traffic.
- Cargo handled at major ports is bulk (44% iron-ore, coal and fertiliser), liquid (33% petrol, oil and lubricants) and container (23%).
- There are 13 major ports in the country; 7 on the Eastern coast and 6 on the Western coast. Further, there are about 200 non-major ports.

Major Ports of India

- **Kolkata Port** Only riverine major port in India. Known for twin dock systems viz, **Kolkata Dock System** (KDS) on the Eastern bank and **Haldia Dock Complex** (HDC) on the Western bank of river Hooghly.
- **Paradip Port** It is an artificial, deep-water port on the East coast of India in the Jagatsinghpur district of Odisha. It is located at the confluence of river Mahanadi in Bay of Bengal in Odisha. It was the first major port on the East Coast commissioned in independent India.
- **New Mangalore Port** It is located at a side called Panambur in Karnataka at Gurupura river confluence with the Arabian sea.
- **Cochin Port** It is located on the Willington Island on the South–West coast of India. It is located on the crossroads of the East-West Ocean trade. The port is called the natural gateway to the vast industrial and agricultural produce markets of South–West India.
- **Jawaharlal Nehru Port** It is also known as **Nhava Sheva**. It is the largest container port in India, handling around half of the containers of all major ports. It is located on the Eastern shore of Mumbai harbour off Elephanta Island and is accessed via Thane Creek.
- **Vadhavan Port** This will be the 13th major port in India. With the development of this port, India will become one of the countries in the top-10 container ports in the world.
  The port will be developed on the landlord model. Vadhavan port has been planned by the Jawaharlal Nehru Port Trust (JNPT) as an **All Weather, All Cargo** satellite port to enhance capabilities in handling deep draft ships and larger vessels.
- **Mumbai Port** One of the oldest modern ports of India. Initially, the location was used by the navies of Shivaji.
- **Kandla Port** Kandla port was built after partition as the Karachi port on the Western coast had gone to Pakistan. It is known for handling much of the crude oil imports of India.
- **Visakhapatnam Port** This port is located in Andhra Pradesh and is known for the bulk of cargo handling on the East coast.
- **Chennai Port** This is the largest port in the Bay of Bengal and the second largest port of India after JNPT. It is the largest port at the East coast.
- **Tuticorin Port** This port has been renamed as **VO Chidambaranar Port.** It is located in the Gulf of Mannar. It is an artificial port. Tuticorin is the only port in South India to provide a direct weekly container service to the United States.
- **Ennore Port** This port is now named Kamarajar Port Limited. It is the first corporate port of India and is registered as a public company with 68% stake held by the government.
- **Mormugao Port** This port in Goa is the leading iron-ore exporting port of India.

The Sagar Mala Project

- On 15th August, 2005, Prime Minister Atal Bihari Vajpayee announced this plan. Under Sagar Mala Project, all major ports will be connected with the Golden Quadrilateral through high-speed expressways.
- The rail connectivity to such ports will also be strengthened, so that adequate line capacity and speed of movement are available.
- Besides 12 major ports, there are 200 minor ports, also in India. Maharashtra has highest 53 minor ports followed by Gujarat, 42 minor ports. Lakshadweep has 10 and Andaman and Nicobar Islands has 23 minor ports.

Sethusamudram Shipping Canal Project

- This project envisages dredging of a ship channel across the Palk strait between India and Sri Lanka. The projects that allow ships sailing between the East and West coasts of India to have a straight passage through India's territorial waters, instead of having circumvent Sri Lanka.
- This will lead to a saving of upto 424 nautical miles (780 km) and upto 30 hours in sailing time. Two channels will be created
  - Across North of Adam's bridge (the chain of Islets and shallows linking India with Sri Lanka) South-East of Pamban Island.
  - Through the shallows of Palk bay, deepening the Palk strait.
  - The total length of these two channels would be 89 km.

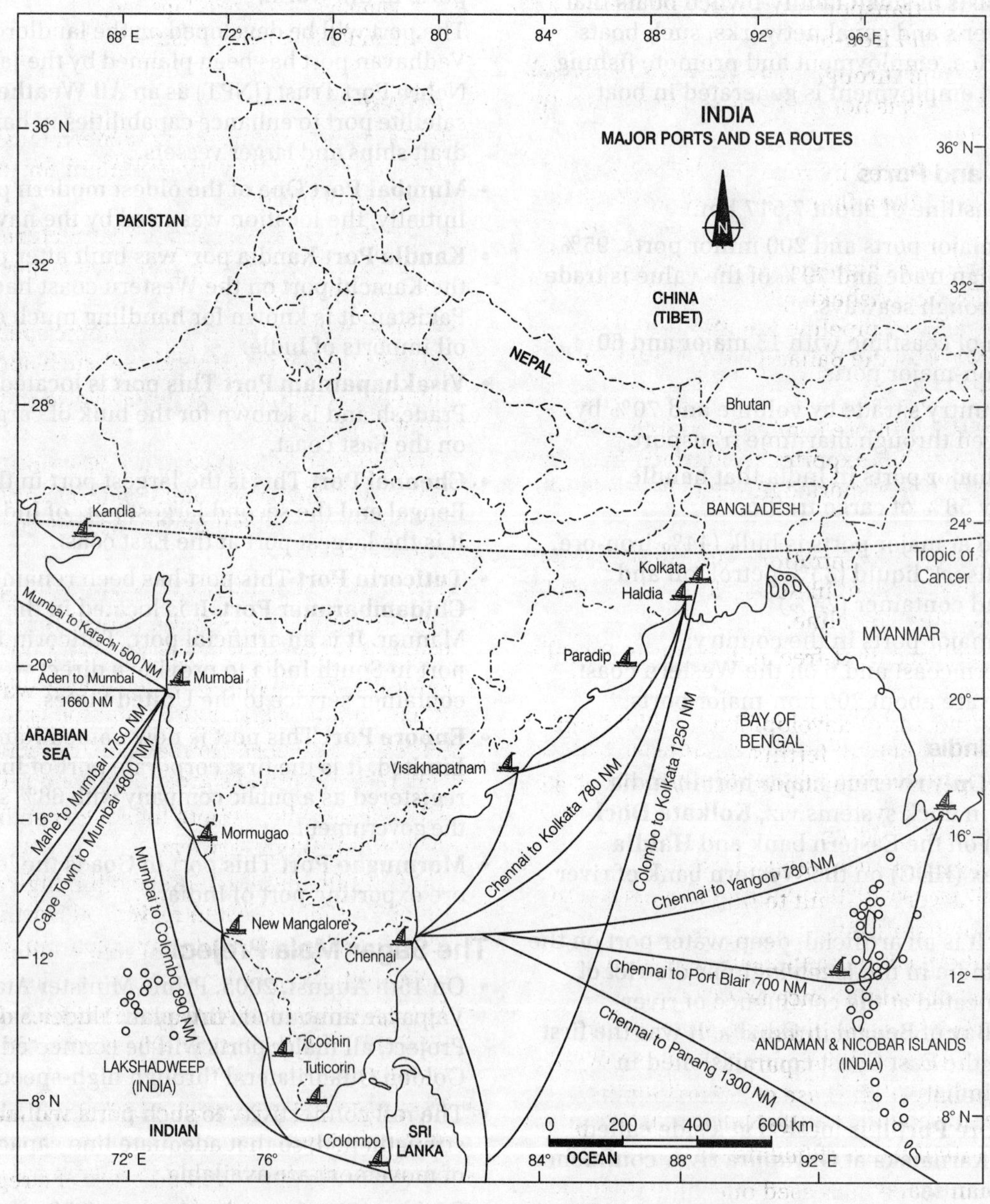

4. Pipelines

- Pipelines are the most convenient and suitable mode of transportation for petroleum products and gases in bulk for longer distances.
- The products which can be transported through pipelines are
  - Petroleum products- Crude oil, jet fuel
  - Liquid products- Water, Anhydrous Ammonia
  - Gases- Natural Gas, LPG, butane
  - Solid products- Coal, mineral, solid wastes,

Advantages of Pipelines

- Pipelines consume very little energy in comparison to another mode of transportation.
- Transit losses are minimal in transportation through pipelines.
- The running cost of the materials through pipelines is very low. It is less than 10 times more than surface transportation.
- The wastage of the transportation material is very less. e.g. slurry of coal and iron-ore.
- Pipelines can be laid through difficult terrains as well as underwater which is not possible in another mode of transportation.
- Pipelines are not affected by seasonal variations and climatic hostilities like a flood, snowfall, rainfall, etc. Examples
  - (i) Bailadila produces high-grade ore which was exported through Vishakhapatnam Port. Now a 270 km long slurry pipeline is constructed to bring the ore from the Bailadila mine to Vizag Steel Plant.
  - (ii) At Kudremukh iron-ore is mined on large scale for export, which is exported from New Mangalore port, where it is transported through 70 km slurry pipelines.
  - (iii) Rock phosphate concentration from Maltos mines to Debari smelter plant in Rajasthan is transported through the slurry pipeline.
- Pipelines are safe, accident-free and environmentally friendly.
- It brings about industrial development in adjoining areas. e.g. establishment of fertiliser industries at the places of gas pipeline (Jagdishpur, Shahjahanpur, etc).

Disadvantages of Pipelines

- Pipelines are prone to distortions in case of earthquakes. It is very difficult to find leakages and cracks in case of distortions.
- The initial cost of laying pipelines is very high. Though the cost of maintenance is low.
- The Pipelines face security threats from terrorist organisations, which could jeoparadise a country's economy, especially in the case of Transboundary pipeline. The oil pipelines in the North-East are often blasted by anti-nationalist elements.
- The capacity cannot be increased once the pipelines are laid. For increasing the capacity the new pipelines need to be laid.
- The repair of pipelines is also very difficult, particularly in case of leakages; detection of leakages is quite difficult.

Major Pipelines of India

- Naharkatia-Nunmati-Barauni Pipeline
- Mumbai High-Mumbai Pipeline
- Ankleshwar-Koyali Pipeline
- Salaya-Koyali-Mathura Pipeline
- Mathura-Delhi-Panipat-Ambala-Jalandhar Pipeline
- Haldia-Kolkata Pipeline
- Hajira-Bijapur-Jagdishpur (HBJ) Gas Pipeline
- Jamnagar-Loni LPG Pipeline
- Kandla-Bhatinda Pipeline

5. Airways

- Airways play a vital role as modern means of transportation. It is very important for the growth of trade and commerce.
- Rapid speed is the most peculiar feature of Air Transport. The aircrafts can fly at a speed of 500 km/h without any difficulty.
- Some planes can fly at a supersonic speed. No other means of transport can move at such speed.
- India holds 9th position in the world in the civil aviation market.
- The supreme advantage of air transport is its high speed. It is the fastest mode of transport and thus it is the most suitable means where time is an important factor.
- The significance of the aviation sector also increases because of the size of India which makes the aviation sector indispensable for faster communication.
- Aircrafts are capable of making their way everywhere. It has no physical barriers as in the case of other modes of transport. No roads, no railways, no ships can cross the world's great mountain ranges.
- The inaccessible, remote locations can be easily accessed through Airways.
- For example, deserts of Rajasthan, high altitude regions of Leh, forested regions of North-East India.
- Aviation plays an important role in international travel and transport.
- The significance of Airways multiplies during wartime situations and disaster management, natural calamities.
- The cargo (freight) services are based mainly on the aviation sector.
- Airway is the index of modernity of a region.
- Airways are free gift of nature and no capital is spent in their construction or maintenance.
- Air services promote tourism and to cater to the needs of tourists, basic infrastructure i.e. roads, transportation also gets the boost.

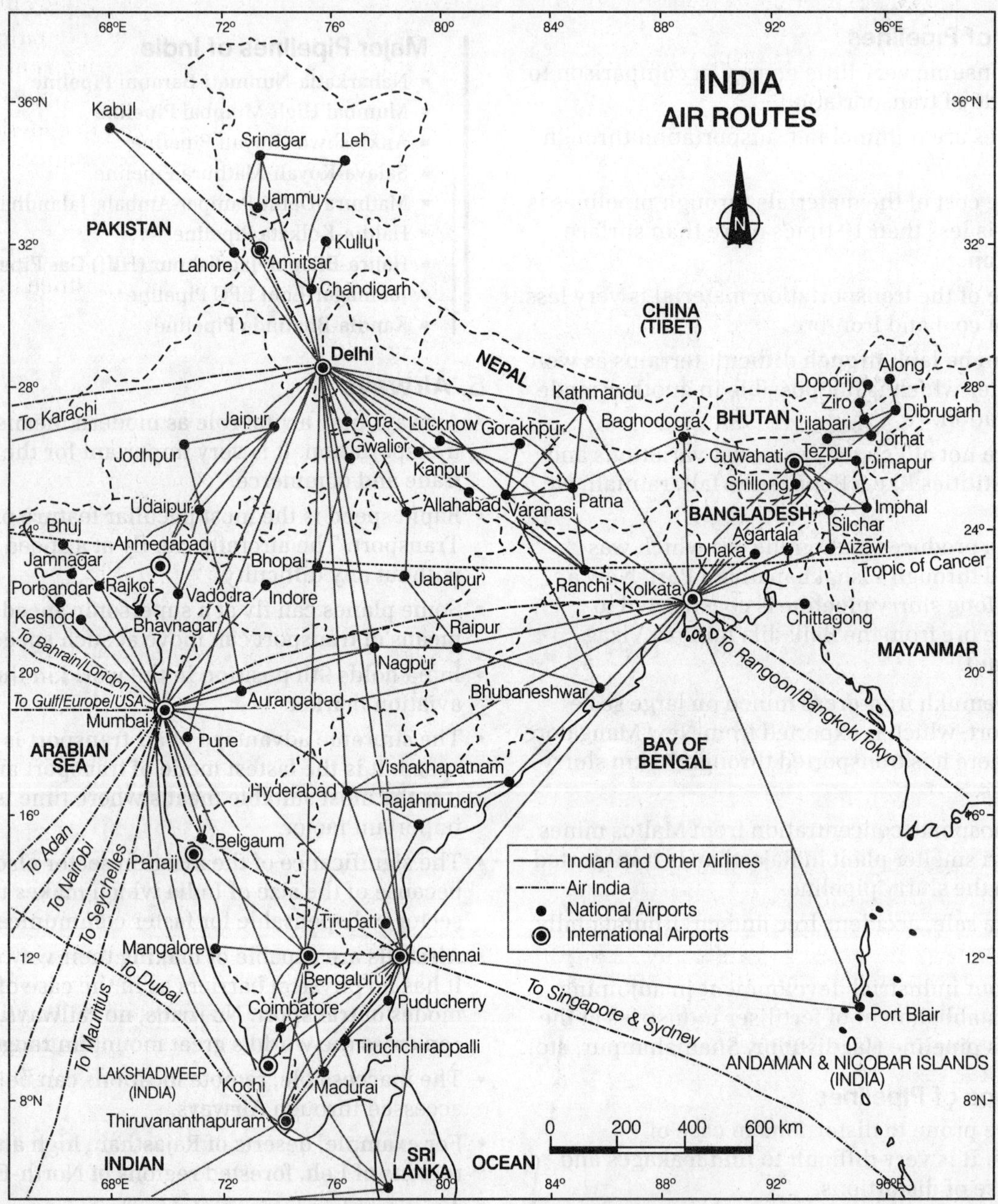

Growth and Development of Aviation Sector in India

- The humble beginning of the aviation sector started in 1911 when airmail operation started between **Prayagraj** and **Naini**.
- The British, French and Dutch carried forward the aviation set up of India between 1920 and 1930.
- **Indian National Airways** was formed in 1933. By the end of World War II the major cities were connected with air services.
- After independence a lot of companies came into the field of aviation and changed the face of the whole aviation sector.
- In 1953, **Indian Airlines Corporation** was formed as domestic aviation services. Air India International was formed in the same year for international services.
- **Vayudoot** was set up in 1981 to augment the air transport in the country.
- **Pawan Hans Limited** was established in 1985. It provides helicopter services to the petroleum sector including ONGC, Oil India Ltd. and Enron Oil and Gas, Mumbai High and connects remote and inaccessible areas.
- **International Airports Authority of India** and **National Airports Authority** were merged on 1st April, 1995 to form **Airports Authority of India** (AAI).

- This authority is responsible for providing safe and efficient air traffic services and aeronautical communication services for effective control of air traffic in the Indian Air Space.
- Today a lot of private companies like **SpiceJet**, **Indigo**, **Jet Airways** have entered into the aviation sector providing quality services to passengers.
- The **Ministry of Civil Aviation** is the nodal ministry that oversees the aviation sector in India.

Factors for Development of Air Transport in India

- The weather conditions in India are also quite congenial to Air Transport. Poor visibility due to clouds, fog and mist hinders air transport but India is lucky to have clear weather for most part of the year except for a short duration in rainy season.
- The central location of India which has Europe West Asia on the Western side and South-East Asia and East Asia on the Eastern side.
- India has extensive plains which provide suitable landing sites in India. The need for airways is high due to the larger size of India.

Communication

- Communication is an act of exchanging information. From the very beginning of time, humans used various means of communication.
- The pace of change has been rapid in modern times. Today, long distance communication is far easier without physical movement of the communicator or receiver. **Personal communication** and **mass communication** are the major means of communication in the country.
- **Communication Networks** In earlier times, the messages were delivered by beating the drum or hollow tree trunks, giving indication through smoke or fire or with the help of fast runners. Horses, camels, dogs, birds and other animals were also used to send messages.
- Invention of post-office, telegraph, printing press, telephone satellite, etc has made the communication much faster and easier.
- On the basis of scale and quality, the mode of communication can be divided into following categories

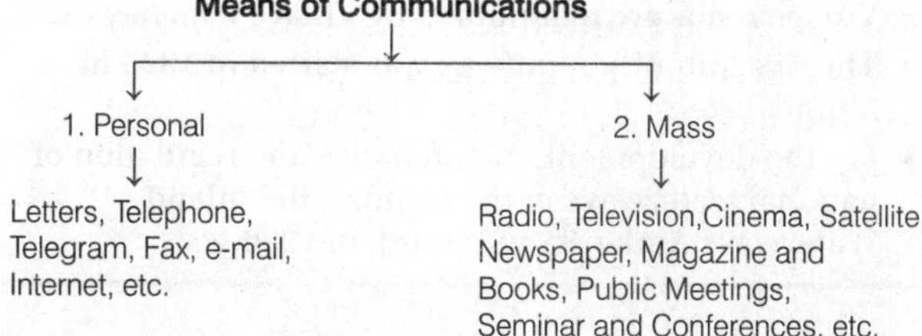

1. Personal Communication

It is the process of transferring or transmitting a message between two people. Mobile phones, postal letters are examples of personal communication.

Indian Post

- Postal services in India and started in 1776 AD by **Lord Clive**. It was opened for general public in 1837 AD. The Indian Postal Network, handled by the Department of Post under the **Ministry of Communication and Information Technology** (Government of India) is the largest in the world.
- It handles parcels as well as personal written communications. Mails in India are categorised *viz*, first-class mail and second-class mail.
- Postcards, inland letter forms and envelopes are considered **first-class mail**. They are airlifted between stations where air and land facilities are available.
- **Second-class mail** includes book packets, registered newspapers and periodicals. They are carried by surface mail, covering land and water transport.

Mail Channels

- To facilitate quick delivery of mail in large towns and cities, certain mail channels have been introduced.
- These are Rajdhani Channel, Metro Channel, Green Channel, Business Channel, Bulk Mail Channel and Periodic Channel.

Telecom Networks

- To improve telephonic communications, the government has made special provision to extend 24 hours Subscriber Trunk Dialing (STD) facility to every village in the country.
- This has been made possible due to the integration of developments in space technology with communication technology.

Mobile Telephony

- Telephones (both static and mobile) belong to the category of personal communication. This can be done by calling on the telephone, taking a conference call or by any other means.
- India has one of the fastest growing mobile networks in the world and one of the largest telecom networks in Asia. Mobile telephony has changed the way Indians conduct business.
- Now, even low income group people like vegetable vendors, plumbers and carpenters get better business because they are connected through mobile phones.

2. Mass Communication

- It is a process of transferring or transmitting a message to a large group of people, which requires the use of some forms of media.
- It provides entertainment and creates awareness among people about various national programmes and policies.
- These media include radio, television, newspapers, internet, periodicals and magazines, books and films.

Radio

- Radio broadcasting started in India in 1923 by the **Radio Club of Bombay**. Since then, it gained immense popularity and changed the socio-cultural life of people. Within no time, it made a place in every household of the country.
- Government took this opportunity and brought this popular mode of communication under its control in 1930 under the Indian Broadcasting System.
- It was changed to All India Radio in 1936 and to **Akashwani** in 1957. All India Radio broadcasts a variety of programmes related to information, education and entertainment.
- Special news bulletins are also broadcast at specific occasions like Sessions of Parliament and State Legislatures.

Television (TV)

- Television broadcasting has emerged as the most effective audio-visual medium for disseminating information and educating masses. Initially, the TV services were limited only to the National Capital where it began in 1959.
- After 1972, several other centres became operational. In 1976, TV was delinked from **All India Radio** (AIR) and got a separate identity as **Doordarshan** (DD).
- After INSAT-IA (National Television-DD1) became operational, Common National Programmes (CNP) were started for the entire network and its services were extended to the backward and remote rural areas.

Satellite Communication

- Satellites are modes of communication in themselves as well as they regulate the use of other means of communication.
- However, the use of satellites in getting a continuous and synoptic view of a larger area has made satellite communication very vital for the country due to economic and strategic reasons. Satellite images can be used for the weather forecast, monitoring of natural calamities, surveillance of border areas, etc.
- On the basis of configuration and purposes, Satellite systems in India can be grouped into two categories, **Indian National Satellite System** (INSAT) and Indian Remote Sensing Satellite System (IRS).
- The INSAT, which was established in 1983, is a multi-purpose satellite system for telecommunication, meteorological observation and for various other data and programmes.
- The IRS satellite system became operational with the launching of IRS-IA in March, 1988 from Baikonur in Russia.
- India has also developed her own Launching Vehicle PSLV (Polar Satellite Launch Vehicle).
- These satellites collect data in several spectral bands and transmit them to the ground stations for various uses.
- The **National Remote Sensing Centre** (NRSC) at Hyderabad provides facilities for acquisition of data and its processing. These are very useful in the management of natural resources.

Films

- India is the largest producer of feature films in the world. It also produces short films, video feature films and video short films.
- The **Central Board of Film Certification** is the authority to certify both Indian and foreign films exhibited in India.

Extra Facts From
Tamil Nadu Board and NIOS

- With the discovery of wheel, transport was made easier and gradually different means of transport were developed.
- Shershah Suri built the shahi (Royal) road to strengthen and consolidate his empire from the Indus valley to the Sonar valley in Bengal. This road from Kolkata to Peshawar was renamed as **Grand Trunk** (GT) road during the British period.
- Road density is the highest in **Kerala** and lowest in **Jammu and Kashmir**.
- State roads are administered and financed by State Governments.
- District roads are constructed and maintained by the Public Works Department of the states.
- Village roads are maintained by Village Panchayats.
- The first sub-urban railway was started in 1925 in Mumbai.
- For the development, maintenance and regulation of national waterways in the country, the Inland Waterways Authority was setup in 1986.

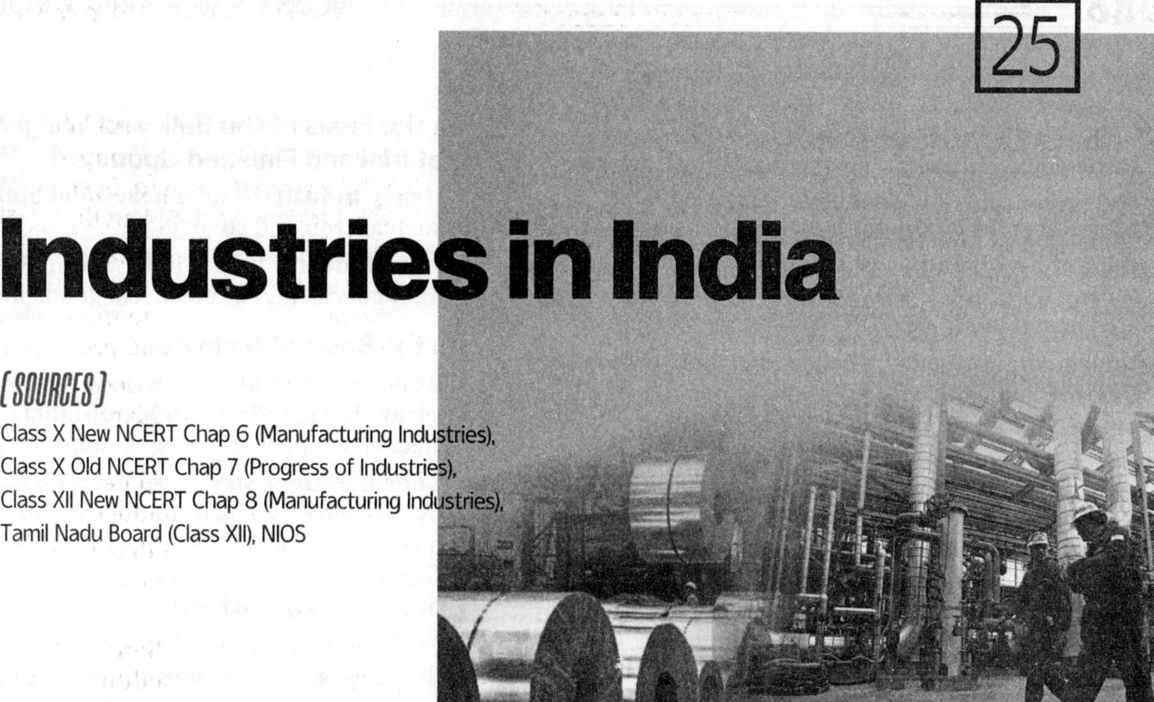

25

Industries in India

[SOURCES]

Class X New NCERT Chap 6 (Manufacturing Industries),
Class X Old NCERT Chap 7 (Progress of Industries),
Class XII New NCERT Chap 8 (Manufacturing Industries),
Tamil Nadu Board (Class XII), NIOS

- An industry is a manufacturing unit, which converts raw materials into usable goods. (goods can be classified as final goods or capital goods.), this is called the **secondary sector of the economy**.
- The industry is at the heart of a country's economy; it includes the **manufacturing** of goods, **extraction of metals** and **provision of services.**
- All the products available for use in the market are finished products and are the result of some industries.
- These industries are set up based on economic activities known as **Primary, Secondary, Tertiary, Quaternary** and **Quinary activities.**

Importance of Manufacturing

Manufacturing sector is considered as the backbone of development in general and economic development in particular mainly because

- Manufacturing industries not only help in modernising agriculture, they also reduce the heavy dependence of people on agricultural income by providing them jobs in secondary and tertiary sectors.
- Industrial development is a pre-condition for eradication of unemployment and poverty from our country. This was the main philosophy behind public sector industries and joint sector ventures in India.
- It was also aimed at bringing down regional disparities by establishing industries in tribal and backward areas.
- Export of manufactured goods expands trade and commerce, and brings in much needed foreign exchange.
- Countries that transform their raw materials into a wide variety of finished goods of higher value are prosperous. India's prosperity lies in increasing and diversifying its manufacturing industries as quickly as possible.
- Agriculture and industry are not exclusive to each other. They move hand in hand. For example instance, the agro-industries in India have given a major boost to agriculture by raising its productivity.
- They depend on the latter for raw materials and sell their products such as irrigation pumps, fertilisers, insecticides, pesticides, plastic and PVC pipes, machines and tools, etc. to the farmers.

Types of Industries

Industries are classified in a number of ways as follows

On the Basis of Ownership

- **Public Sector Industry** It is owned and operated by government agencies. e.g., BHEL, SAIL, etc.
- **Private Sector Industry** It is owned and operated by individuals or a group of individuals. e.g., TISCO, Bajaj Auto Ltd, Dabur Industries.
- **Joint Sector Industry** It is jointly run by the state and individuals or a group of individuals. Oil India Ltd. (OIL) is jointly owned by the public and private sector.
- **Cooperative Sector Industry** It is owned and operated by the producers or suppliers of raw materials, workers or both. They pool in the resources and share the profits or losses proportionately. Such examples are the sugar industry in Maharashtra, the coir industry in Kerala.

On the Basis of the Use of their Products

- **Basic Goods Industry** This industry provides raw material for the other industries. e.g., cotton production for textile industry.
- **Capital Goods Industry** This industry produces those capital goods that are used by other industries. e.g., machine industry.
- **Intermediate Goods Industry** This industry produces intermediate goods for other industries to make final products. e.g., producing tyres for cycle manufacturing company.
- **Consumer Goods Industry** It produces those goods that are consumed by consumers. e.g., edible oil, etc.

On the Basis of Source of Raw Materials Used

- **Agro Based Industry** It obtains raw materials from agricultural activities. e.g., raw cotton, wool, jute, silk textile, rubber, sugar, tea, coffee and edible oil, etc.
- **Forest Based Industry** It obtains raw materials from forest. e.g., paper industry
- **Mineral Based Industry** It obtains raw materials from minerals. e.g., iron and steel, cement, aluminium, machine tools and petrochemicals, etc.
- **Industrially Processed Raw Material Industry** It obtains raw materials from cottage and small industries. e.g., automobile industry

On the Basis of Nature of the Manufactured Products

- **Metallurgical Industry** e.g., Iron and steel Industry.
- **Mechanical Engineering Industry** e.g., Automobile Industry.
- **Chemical and Allied Industry** e.g., Fertiliser Industry.
- **Textile Industry** e.g., Cotton textile.
- **Food Processing Industry** e.g., Fishery
- **Electricity Generation Industry** e.g., Transformer manufacturing
- **Electronics Industry** e.g., Laptop manufacturing
- **Communication Industry** e.g., Telephone manufactuing

On the Basis of Capital Investment

- **Small Scale Industry** It is defined with reference to the maximum investment allowed on the assets of a unit. This limit has changed over a period of time. At present, the maximum investment of one crore is allowed.
- **Cottage Industry** In this industry, production of goods is done by family members with capital investment.
- **Large Scale Industry** In this industry, production of goods is done on large scale with the help of machine. It requires huge capital investment.

On the Basis of the Bulk and Weight of Raw Material and Finished Goods

- **Heavy Industry** It uses heavy and bulky raw materials such as iron and steel.
- **Light industry** It uses light raw materials and produce light goods such as electrical goods industries.

On the Basis of Main Role

- **Basic or Key Industry** This industry supplies its products as raw materials to manufacture other goods e.g. iron and steel and copper smelting, aluminium smelting.
- **Consumer Industry** It produces goods for direct use by consumers – sugar, toothpaste, paper, sewing machines, fans, etc.

Location of Industries

- Location of industries is influenced by several factors like access to raw materials, power, market, capital, transport and labour, etc. Relative significance of these factors varies with time and place.
- There is a strong relationship between raw material and type of industry. It is economical to locate the manufacturing industries at a place where cost of production and delivery cost of manufactured goods to consumers are the least.
- Transport costs, to a great extent, depend on the nature of raw materials and manufactured products. A brief description of factors influencing the location of industries are given below

Raw Materials

- Industries using weight-losing raw materials are located in the regions where raw materials are located.
- Similarly, the locations of pulp industry, copper smelting and pig iron industries are located near their raw materials. In iron and steel industries, iron-ore and coal both are weight-losing raw materials. Therefore, an optimum location for iron and steel industries should be near raw material sources.
- This is why most of the iron and steel industries are located either near coalfields (Bokaro, Durgapur, etc.) or near sources of iron-ore (Bhadravati, Bhilai and Rourkela).
- Similarly, industries based on perishable raw materials are also located close to raw material sources.

Power

- Power provides the motive force for machines and therefore, its supply has to be ensured before the location of any industry.
- However, certain industries, like aluminium and synthetic nitrogen manufacturing industries tend to be located near sources of power because they are power intensive and require huge quantum of electricity.

Market

- Markets provide the outlets for manufactured products. Heavy machines, machine tools and heavy chemicals are located near the high demand areas as these are market orientated.
- Cotton textile industry uses a non-weight losing raw material and is generally located in large urban centres, e.g. Mumbai, Ahmedabad, Surat, etc.
- Petroleum refineries are also located near the markets as the transport of crude oil is easier and several products derived from them are used as raw material in other industries.
- Koyali, Mathura and Barauni refineries are typical examples. Ports also play a crucial role in the location of oil refineries.

Transport

- The reasons for the concentration of industries in Mumbai, Chennai, Delhi and Kolkata was due to the fact that they initially became the nodal point having transport links.
- The industries shifted to interior locations, only when railway lines were laid. All major industrial plants are located on the trunk rail routes.

Labour

- Industries require skilled labour. In India, labour is available in large numbers due to our large population.

Historical Factors

- Mumbai, Kolkata and Chennai emerged as industrial nodes because these locations were greatly influenced by our colonial past.
- During the initial phase of colonisation, manufacturing activities received new impetus provided by the European traders.
- Places like Murshidabad, Dhaka, Bhadohi, Surat, Vadodara, Kozhikode, Coimbatore, Mysuru, etc., emerged as important manufacturing centres.
- In the subsequent industrial phase of colonialism, these manufacturing centres experienced rapid growth due to competition from the goods manufactured in Britain and the discriminatory policies of colonial power.

Industrial Policy

- India, being a democratic country aims at bringing about economic growth with balanced regional development.
- Establishment of iron and steel industry in Bhilai and Rourkela were based on the decision to develop backward tribal areas of the country.
- At present, the government of India provides lots of incentives to industries locating in backward areas.

Major Industries

The iron and steel industry is basic to the industrial development of any country. The cotton textile Industry is one of our traditional industries. The sugar industry is based on local raw materials, which prospered even in the British period. Petrochemical industry is also one of the important industries in India.

Iron and Steel Industry

- The development of the iron and steel industry opened the doors to rapid industrial development in India. Almost all sectors of the Indian industry depend heavily on the iron and steel industry for their basic infrastructure.
- The other raw materials besides iron-ore and coking coal, essential for iron and steel industry are limestone, dolomite, manganese and fire clay.
- All these raw materials are gross (weight-losing), therefore, the best location for the iron and steel plants is near the source of raw materials.
- In India, there is a crescent shaped region comprising parts of Chhattisgarh, Northern Odisha, Jharkhand and West Bengal, which is extremely rich in high grade iron ore, good quality coking coal and other supplementing raw materials.
- The Indian iron and steel industry consists of large integrated steel plants as well as mini steel mills. It also includes secondary producers, rolling mills and ancillary industries.

The various integrated steel plants in India are as follows:

TISCO

- The Tata Iron and Steel plant lies very close to the Mumbai-Kolkata railway line and about 240 km away from Kolkata, which is the nearest port for the export of steel. The Rivers **Subarnarekha** and **Kharkai** provide water to the plant.
- The iron ore for the plant is obtained from **Noamundi** and **Badam Pahar**. Coal is brought from **Joda mines** in Odisha. Coking coal comes from **Jharia** and **West Bokaro** coalfields.

IISCO

- The Indian Iron and Steel Company (IISCO) set up its first factory at **Hirapur** and later on another at **Kulti**.
- In 1937, the **Steel Corporation of Bengal** was constituted in association with IISCO and set up another iron and steel producing unit at Burnpur (West Bengal).
- All the three plants under IISCO are located very close to Damodar valley coalfields (Raniganj, Jharia and Ramgarh). Iron-ore comes from **Singhbhum** in Jharkhand. Water is obtained from the **Barakar River**, a tributary of the Damodar.

- All the plants are located along the Kolkata-Asansol railway line. Unfortunately, steel production from IISCO fell considerably in 1972-1973 and the plants were taken over by the government.

Visvesvaraya Iron and Steel Works Ltd. (VISL)

- The third integrated steel plant, the Visvesvaraya Iron and steel works was initially called the **Mysore Iron** and **Steel Works**. It is located close to an iron-ore producing area of **Kemmangundi** in the Baba Budan hills.
- Limestone and manganese are also locally available. But this region has no coal. At the beginning, charcoal obtained by burning wood from nearby forests was used as fuel till 1951. Afterwards, electric furnaces were installed, which use hydroelectricity from the Jog Falls hydel power project.
- The Bhadravati river supplies water to the plant. This plant produces specialised steels and alloys.

Rourkela Steel Plant

- The Rourkela Steel Plant was set up in 1959 in the **Sundargarh** district of Odisha in collaboration with Germany.
- The plant was located on the basis of proximity to raw materials, thus, minimising the cost of transporting weight-losing of raw material.
- This plant has a unique locational advantage, as it receives coal from Jharia (Jharkhand) and iron-ore from Sundargarh and Kendujhar.
- The **Hirakud project** supplies power for the electric furnaces and water is obtained from the Koel and Shankh rivers.

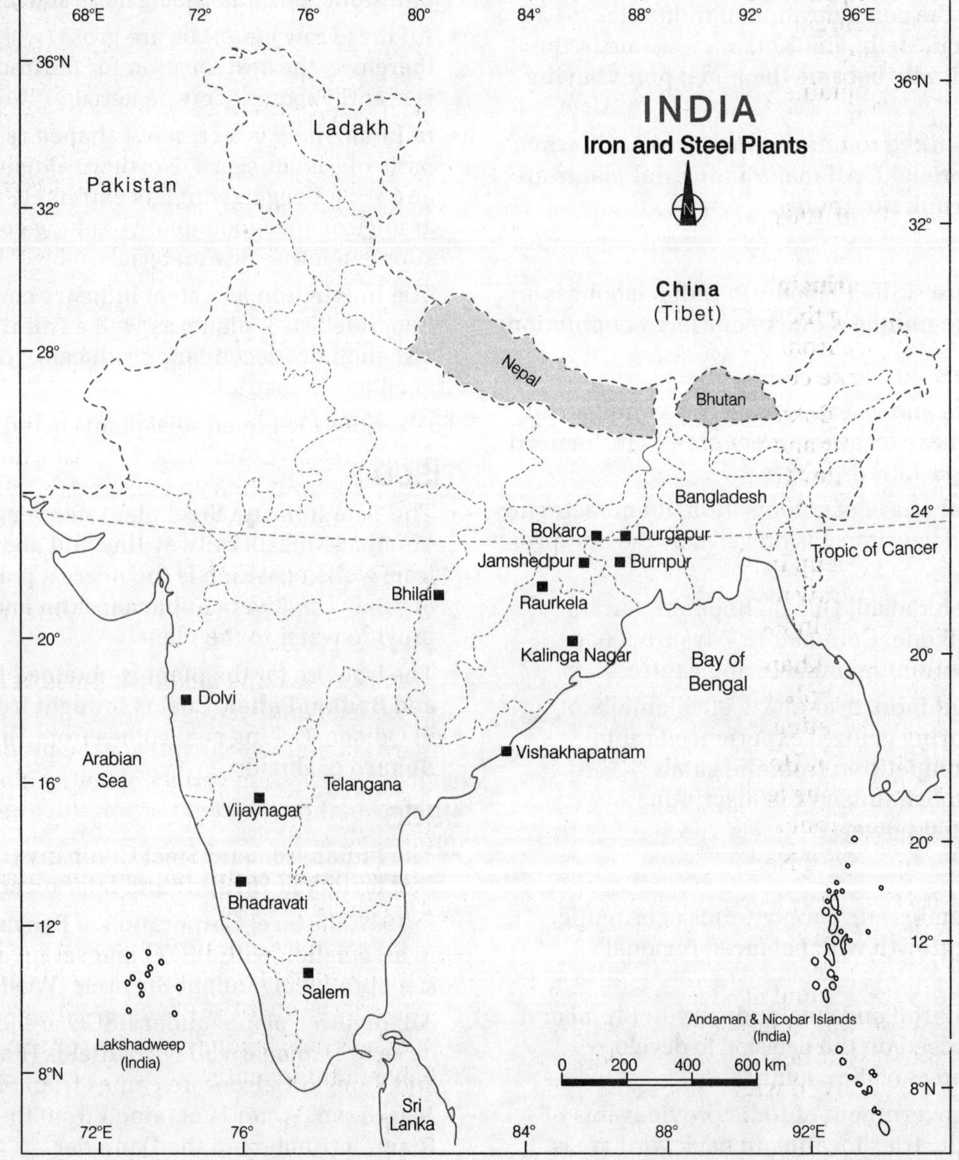

Bhilai Steel Plant

- The Bhilai Steel Plant was established with Russian collaboration in **Durg** district of Chhattisgarh and started production in 1959.
- Iron-ore comes from **Dalli-Rajhara mine** and coal from Korba and Kargali coal fields. Water comes from the Tandula dam and the power from the Korba Thermal Power Station.
- This plant also lies on the Kolkata-Mumbai railway route. The bulk of the steel produced goes to the Hindustan Shipyard at Visakhapatnam.

Durgapur Steel Plant

- Durgapur Steel Plant in West Bengal was set up in collaboration with the government of the United Kingdom and started production in 1962.
- This plant lies in **Raniganj-Jharia coal belt** and gets iron-ore from Noamundi. Durgapur lies on the main Kolkata-Delhi railway route.
- Hydel power and water is obtained from the **Damodar Valley Corporation** (DVC).

Bokaro Steel Plant

- This steel plant was set up in 1964 at Bokaro with Russian collaboration.
- This plant was set up on the **principle of transportation cost minimisation** by creating the Bokaro-Rourkela combine. It receives iron ore from the Rourkela region and the wagons on return take coal to Rourkela.
- Other raw materials come to Bokaro from within a radius of about 350 km. Water and hydel power is supplied by the Damodar Valley Corporation.

Other Steel Plants

New steel plants which were set up in the Fourth Plan period are away from the main raw material sources. All three plants are located in South India.

- The **Vizag Steel Plant**, in Visakhapatnam in Andhra Pradesh is the first port-based plant which started operating in 1992. Its port location is of advantage.
- The **Vijayanagar Steel Plant** at Hospet in Karnataka was developed using indigenous technology. This uses local iron-ore and limestone.
- The **Salem Steel Plant** in Tamil Nadu was commissioned in 1982.

Aluminium Smelting

- Aluminium smelting is the second most important metallurgical industry in India. It is a light, resistant to corrosion, a good conductor of heat, malleable and becomes strong when it is mixed with other metals.
- It is used to manufacture aircraft, utensils and wires. It has gained popularity as a substitute of steel, copper, zinc and lead in a number of industries.
- Aluminium smelting plants in the country are located in Odisha, West Bengal, Kerala, Uttar Pradesh, Chhattisgarh, Maharashtra and Tamil Nadu.
- Bauxite, the raw material used in the smelters, is a very bulky, dark reddish coloured rock.
- Regular supply of electricity and an assured source of raw material at minimum cost are the two prime factors for location of the industry.

Aluminium Plants in India

Company	Supporting Country	Units
Indian Aluminium Company Limited (INDALCO)	-	Muri (Jharkhand), Alwan (Kerala), Belur (West Bengal), Belgaum (Karnataka)
Hindustan Aluminium Corporation Limited (HINDALCO)	USA	Renukoot (Uttar Pradesh)
Madras Aluminium Company Limited (MALCO)	Italy	Mettur (Tamil Nadu)
Bharat Aluminium Company Limited (BALCO)	Soviet Union	Korba (Chhattisgarh)
National Aluminium Company Limited (NALCO)	France	Angul (Odisha)

Textile Industry

Textile industry plays and important role in the Indian economy. Cotton woollen and silk textile are the important textile industries.

Cotton Textile Industry

- The cotton textile industry is one of the traditional industries of India.
- In the ancient and the medieval times, it used to be only a cottage industry.
- India was famous worldwide for the production of muslin, a very fine variety of cotton cloth, calicos, chintz and other different varieties of fine cotton cloth.
- The development of this industry in India was due to several factors.
- One, it is a tropical country and cotton is the most comfortable fabric for a hot and humid climate. Second, a large quantity of cotton was grown in India.
- Abundant skilled labour required for this industry was available in this country.

Mumbai as the Centre

- In 1854, the first modern cotton mill was established in **Mumbai**. This city had several advantages as a cotton textile manufacturing.
- It was very close to the cotton producing areas of Gujarat and Maharashtra. Raw cotton used to be brought to Mumbai port to be transported to England. Therefore, cotton was available in Mumbai city itself.
- Moreover, Mumbai even then was the financial centre and the capital needed to start an industry was available there. As a large town, providing employment opportunities attracted labour in large numbers. Hence, cheap and abundant labour too was available locally. The machinery required for a cotton textile mill could be directly imported from England.

Features of Indian Cotton Industry

- The cotton textile industry in India can be broadly divided into two sectors, the **organised sector** and the **unorganised sector**.
- The decentralised sector includes cloth produced in **handlooms** (including *Khadi*) and **powerlooms**.
- The production of the organised sector has drastically fallen from 81% in the mid 20th century to only about 6% in 2000. At present, the power looms on the decentralised sector produce more than the handloom sector.
- Cotton is a 'pure' raw material, which does not lose weight in the manufacturing process. So other factors, like, power to drive the looms, labour, capital or market may determine the location of the industry.
- At present the trend is to locate the industry at or close to markets, as it is the market that decides what kind of cloth is to be produced.
- Presently, the major centres of the cotton textile industry are **Ahmedabad, Bhiwandi, Solapur, Kolhapur,** Nagpur, Indore and Ujjain. All these centres are the traditional centres and are located close to the cotton producing regions.
- Maharashtra, Gujarat and Tamil Nadu are the leading cotton producing states. West Bengal, Uttar Pradesh, Karnataka, and Punjab are the other important cotton textile producers.
- Tamil Nadu has the largest number of mills and most of them produce yarn rather than cloth.
- **Coimbatore** has emerged as the most important centre with nearly half of the mills located there. Chennai, Madurai, Tirunelveli, Tuticorin, Thanjavur, Ramanathapuram and Salem are the other important centres.
- In Karnataka, the cotton textile industry has developed in the cotton producing areas in the North-Eastern part of the state. Davangere, Hubballi, Ballari, Mysuru and Bengaluru are important centres.
- The cotton textile industry is located in the cotton producing **Telangana region**, where most of the mills are spinning mills producing yarn. The important centres are Hyderabad, Secunderabad and Warangal in Telangana and Guntur in Andhra Pradesh.
- In Uttar Pradesh, Kanpur is the largest centre. Some of the other important centres are Modinagar, Hathras, Saharanpur, Agra and Lucknow.
- In West Bengal, the cotton mills are located in the Hugli region. Howrah, Serampore, Kolkata and Shyamnagar are the important centres.
- Production of cotton cloth increased almost five times since independence.

Woollen Textile Industry

- The first woollen textile mill was set-up in 1876 at Kanpur, because Kanpur was the principal depot for the **British Indian Army**. But the industry did not flourish because of a short winter and long summer in India leading to an inadequate demand.
- Also, the textiles produced were of poor quality. After Independence, there was rapid development of the industry mainly as an export oriented industry.
- The organised woollen textile industries provide employment to about 12 lakh people, while the decentralised or unorganised sector provides employment to about 4 lakh people.
- The woollen textile industry in India can be divided into cottage industry and factory industry.

Geographical Distribution

- Most of the woollen textile mills are situated in Punjab along the **Amritsar-Gurdaspur-Ludhiana** belt and at **Patiala** and **Dhariwal**.
- The concentration in Punjab is due to its proximity to the high demand region in Northern India in general and the hilly areas in particular.
- Also, because Punjab is close to the sheep-rearing regions of Jammu and Kashmir (where the Bakerwals are associated with sheep rearing) and Himachal Pradesh (where the Gaddis rear sheep).

  The state-wise survey of other centres in the country is given below :

  - **Uttar Pradesh** Kanpur, Mirzapur
  - **Rajasthan** Jaipur, Jodhpur, Bikaner
  - **Madhya Pradesh** Gwalior
  - **Gujarat** Jamnagar, Ahmedabad, Vadodara
  - **Maharashtra** Mumbai
  - **Karnataka** Bengaluru
  - **Jammu and Kashmir** The state is a large producer of woollen products

Silk Industry

- Indian silk industry got great patronage during the medieval period.
- The famous 'Silk-Route' passed through India and Indian silk found markets worldwide.
- India is **second largest producer** of silk in the world.
- India is the only country producing all the five known commercial varieties of silk *viz* mulberry, tasar, oak tasar, eri and muga.
- **Karnataka** is the foremost silk producing state in India, which accounts for 50% of mulberry silk of country followed by Madhya Pradesh and Tamil Nadu.

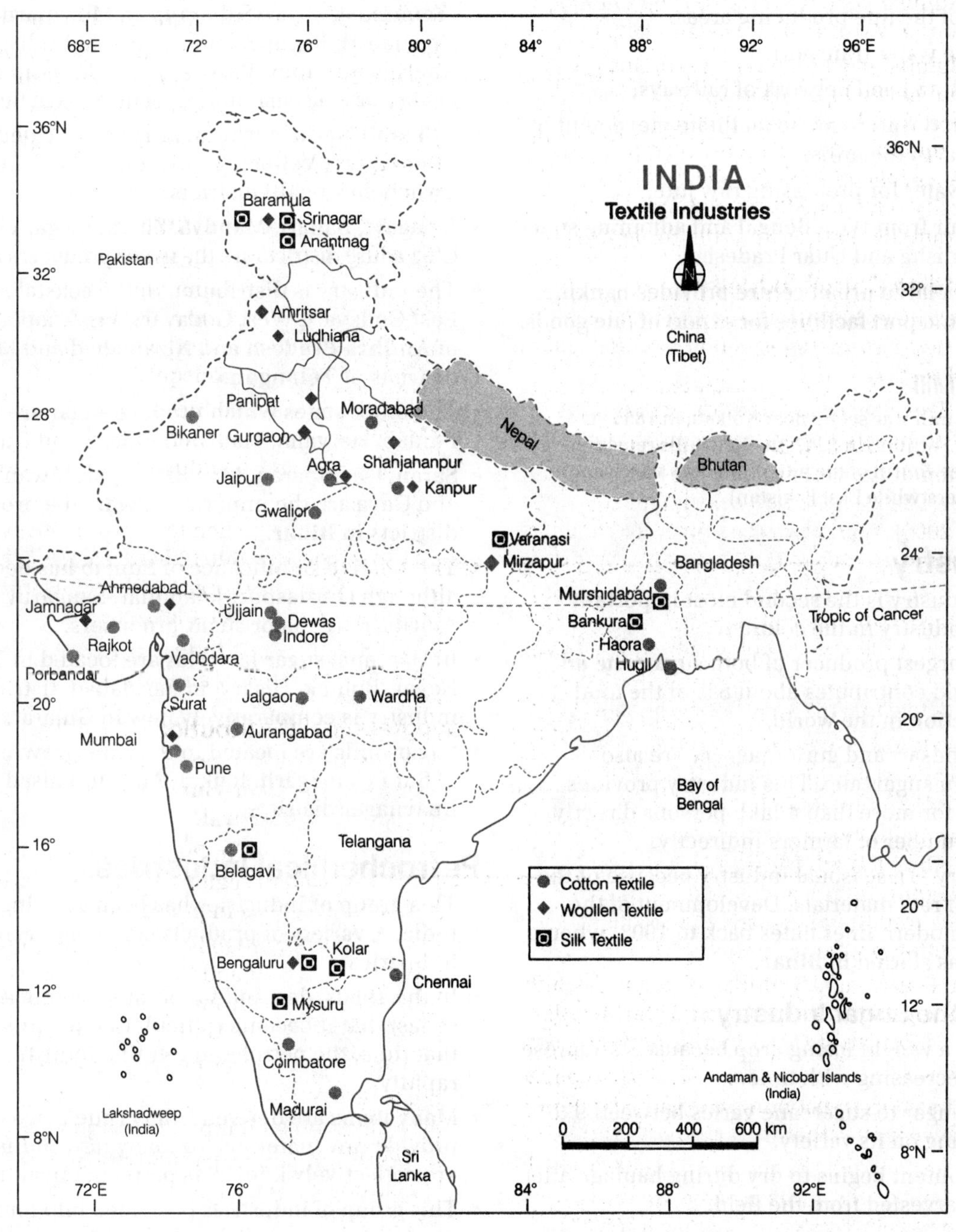

Jute Textiles

- India is the largest producer of raw jute and jute goods and stands at second place as an exporter after Bangladesh. Most of the mills are located in West Bengal, mainly along the banks of the Hugli river, in a narrow belt. Factors responsible for their location in the Hugli basin are:
  - proximity of the jute producing areas,
  - inexpensive water transport,
  - supported by a good network of railways,
  - roadways and waterways to facilitate movement of raw material to the mills,
  - abundant water for processing raw jute,
  - cheap labour from West Bengal and adjoining states of Bihar, Odisha and Uttar Pradesh.
  - Kolkata as a large urban centre provides banking, insurance and port facilities for export of jute goods.

First Jute Mill

The first jute mill was set up near Kolkata in 1855 at **Rishra**. After Partition in 1947, the jute mills remained in India but three-fourth of the jute producing area went to Bangladesh (erstwhile East Pakistan).

Sugar Industry

- The sugar industry is the second most important agro-based industry in the country.
- India is the largest producer of both sugarcane and cane sugar and contributes about 8% of the total sugar production in the world.
- Besides, khandsari and gur or jaggery are also prepared from sugarcane. This industry provides employment for more than 4 lakh persons directly and a large number of farmers indirectly.
- Sugar industry is a seasonal industry because of the seasonality of raw materials. Development of the industry on modern lines dates back to 1903, when a sugar mill was started in **Bihar**.

Location of the Sugar Industry

- Sugarcane is a weight losing crop because its sucrose content on decreasing with time.
- The ratio of sugar to sugarcane varies between 9 to 12% depending on its variety.
- Its sucrose content begins to dry during haulage after it has been harvested from the field.
- Better recovery of sugar is dependent upon its being crushed within 24 hours of its harvesting. Sugar factories hence, are located within the cane producing regions.
- **Maharashtra** has emerged as a leading sugar producer in the country and produces more than one-third of the total production of the sugar in the country.
- Uttar Pradesh is the second largest producer of sugar.
- The sugar factories are concentrated in two belts – the **Ganga-Yamuna doab** and the **terai region.**
- The major sugar producing centres in the Ganga -Yamuna doab are Saharanpur, Muzaffarnagar, Meerut, Ghaziabad, Baghpat and Bulandshahr districts; while Kheri Lakhimpur, Basti, Gonda, Gorakhpur, Bahraich are important sugar producing districts in the Terai region.
- In **Tamil Nadu**, sugar factories are located in Coimbatore, Vellore, Tiruvannamalai, Villupuram and Tiruchchirappalli districts.
- Belagavi, Ballari, Mandya, Shivamogga, Vijayapura and Chitradurg districts are the major producers in **Karnataka.**
- The industry is distributed in the coastal regions i.e. East Godavari, West Godavari, Visakhapatnam districts of **Andhra Pradesh** and Nizamabad and Medak districts of **Telangana.**
- The other states which produce sugar are Bihar, Punjab, Haryana, Madhya Pradesh and Gujarat.
- Saran, Champaran, Muzaffarnagar, Siwan, Darbhanga, and Gaya are the important sugarcane producing districts in **Bihar.**
- The relative significance of Punjab has declined, although Gurdaspur, Jalandhar, Sangarur, Patiala and Amritsar are major sugar producers.
- In Haryana, sugar factories are located in Yamuna Nagar, Rohtak, Hisar and Faridabad districts. Sugar industry is comparatively new in Gujarat.
- Sugar mills are located in the cane growing tracts of Surat, Junagarh, Rajkot, Amreli, Valsad and Bhavnagar districts.

Petrochemical Industries

- This group of industries has been growing very fast in India. A variety of products come under this category of industries.
- In the 1960s, demand for organic chemicals increased so fast that it became difficult to meet this demand. At that time, the petroleum refining industry expanded rapidly.
- Many items are derived from crude petroleum, which provide raw materials for many new industries, these are collectively known as petrochemical industries.
- This group of industries is divided into four sub-groups:
  - polymers
  - synthetic fibres
  - elastomers
  - surfactant intermediate

- Mumbai is the hub of the petrochemical industries.
- Cracker units are also located in Auraiya (Uttar Pradesh), Jamnagar, Gandhinagar and Hajira (Gujarat), Nagothane, Ratnagiri (Maharashtra), Haldia (West Bengal) and Visakhapatnam (Andhra Pradesh).
- Three organisations are working in the petrochemical sector under the administrative control of the Department of Chemicals and Petrochemicals.
- The **Indian Petrochemical Corporation Limited** (IPCL) is a public sector undertaking. It is responsible for the manufacture and distribution of the various petrochemicals like polymers, chemicals, fibres and fibre intermediates.
- The **Petrofils Cooperative Limited** (PCL), a joint venture of the Government of India and weaver's cooperative societies. It produces polyester filament yarn and nylon chips at its two plants located at Vadodara and Naldhari in Gujarat.
- The **Central Institute of Plastic Engineering and Technology** (CIPET), involved in imparting training in the petro-chemical industry. Polymers are made from ethylene and propylene. These materials are obtained in the process of refining crude oil. Polymers are used as raw materials in the plastic industry.
- Among polymers, polyethylene is a widely used thermoplastic. Plastic is first converted into sheets, powder, resin and pellets and then used in manufacturing plastic products.
- Industries manufacturing nylon and polyester yarns are located at Kota, Pimpri, Mumbai, Modinagar, Pune, Ujjain, Nagpur and Udhna. Acrylic staple fibre is manufactured at Kota and Vododara.

Other Important Industries

Other important industries in India are

Fertiliser Industry

- The fertiliser industry is centred around the production of nitrogenous fertilisers (mainly urea), phosphatic fertilisers and Di Ammonium Phosphate (DAP) and complex fertilisers, which have a combination of nitrogen, phosphate and potash (NPK).
- The third, i.e. potash is entirely imported as the country does not have any reserves of commercially usable potash or potassium compounds in any form. After the **Green Revolution**, the industry expanded to several other parts of the country.
- Gujarat, Tamil Nadu, Uttar Pradesh, Punjab and Kerala contribute towards half of the fertiliser production. Other significant producers are Andhra Pradesh, Odisha, Rajasthan, Bihar, Maharashtra, Assam, West Bengal, Goa, Delhi, Madhya Pradesh and Karnataka.

Cement Industry

- Cement is essential for construction activity such as building houses, factories, bridges, roads, airports, dams and for other commercial establishments.
- This industry requires bulky and heavy raw materials like limestone, silica and gypsum. Coal and electric power are needed apart from rail transportation.
- The industry has strategically located plants in Gujarat that have suitable access to the market in the Gulf countries.
- The first cement plant was set up in **Chennai** in 1904.
- After Independence, the industry expanded. Improvement in the quality has found the produce a readily available market in East Asia, Middle East, Africa and South Asia apart from a large demand within the country.

Automobile Industry

- Automobiles provide vehicles for quick transport of good services and passengers.
- Trucks, buses, cars, motor cycles, scooters, three-wheelers and multi-utility vehicles are manufactured in India at various centres.
- After the liberalisation, the coming in of new and contemporary models stimulated the demand for vehicles in the market, which led to the healthy growth of the industry including passenger cars, two and three-wheelers.
- The industry is located around Delhi, Gurugram, Mumbai, Pune, Chennai, Kolkata, Lucknow, Indore, Hyderabad, Jamshedpur and Bengaluru.

Engineering Industries

- The engineering sector is the largest sector among the industrial segments in India and provides direct and indirect employment to over 4 million skilled and non-skilled workers. Though a diverse industry, it can be divided into two broad categories :
  1. **Heavy Engineering Segment** This accounts for bulk of all engineering goods production in India and is responsible for the production of high-value products like heavy electrical, heavy engineering and machine tools and automotive parts.
  2. **Light Engineering Segment** This segment is responsible for medium to low technology products like casting and forging components, medical and surgical equipments and industrial fasteners (high tensile and mild tensile steel fasteners).
- Leading Companies in the engineering industry are :
  - Bharat Heavy Electrical Limited, (BHEL)
  - Engineers India Limited, Hindustan Aeronautics Limited, Crompton Greaves

- Elgi Equipments
- Hindustan Machine Tools (HMT)
- Kirloskar Oil Engines Limited (KOEL)
- Larsen and Toubro Limited (L & T)
- Thermax Limited, Cummins India Limited
- Alfa Laval (India) Limited
- Asea Brown Boveri Ltd (ABB) and Siemens Limited

Railway Equipment Industry

- India is self-sufficient and a major exporting country in railway equipments.
- **Chittaranjan Locomotive Works**, a PSU set-up in 1950 in Bardhaman district, West Bengal now producing electric locomotives.
- **Diesel Locomotive Works** set up at Varanasi in 1961 to manufacture diesel locomotives.
- **Diesel Component Works** has its locomotive parts manufacturing units at Patiala, Kanpur, Bengaluru, Haridwar and Bhopal. New factories were also set up at Marhowra (Saran, for diesel locomotive) and Madhepura (electric locomotives).
- **Tata Engineering and Locomotive Works** at Jamshedpur manufacture spare parts.
- **Integral Coach Factory set-up** with Swiss collaboration at Perambur, Chennai manufacture railway coaches.
- **Rail Coach Factory** is located at Kapurthala.
- Two more PSUs manufacturing rails, wagons and coaches are **M/S Jessops Company Limited** at Kolkata and **Bharat Earth Movers Limited** at Bengaluru. A new coach factory is being established at Raebareli, Uttar Pradesh.
- A wheel and Axel plant has been set up at Bengaluru.

Shipbuilding Industry

Indian shipbuilding is mainly centred around 27 Shipyards (8 in public sectors and 19 in private sector) with global market share of 1.3%.

Important Shipyard/Shipbuilding Industries

Industry	Location
Hindustan Shipyard Limited	Visakhapatnam
Cochin Shipyard Limited	Cochin
The Garden Reach Shipbuilding and Engineers Limited	Kolkata
The Mazagaon Dock (Naval Equipment)	Mumbai
The Goa Shipyard Limited (Advanced off shore Petrol Vehicles)	Vasco-da-Gama
ABG Shipyard	Magdalla, Dahej
Bharati Shipyard	Ratnagiri

Air Craft Industry

- The first air craft industry in India was established by **Walchand Hirachand** in 1940 as **Hindustan Air Craft Limited** (HAL) in Bengaluru.
- In 1942, this company was undertaken by government of India and renamed as Hindustan Aeronautics Limited. Its headquarters is at Bengaluru (Karnataka).

Paper Industry

- It is a vital and core industry for any country.
- The raw materials for the paper industry include bamboo, salai and salai grasses, wastepaper, rags, pulp and bagasse.
- The location of the industry is influenced by raw material and to a lesser extent by market.
- The first paper mill in the country was setup at Serampore (Bengal) in 1832, which failed.
- In 1870, a fresh venture was started at Ballygunge near Kolkata.
- The planned development of paper and paper based industry began after Independence.
- **Geographical distribution** West Bengal, Maharashtra, Andhra Pradesh, Madhya Pradesh, Karnataka, Uttar Pradesh, Bihar, Odisha, Haryana, Tamil Nadu, Gujarat and Kerala.

Electronic Industry

- Electronic industry includes production of electronic products such as television, telephone, cellphone, computer, etc.
- **Bengaluru** is developed as the **Electronic Capital of India**. The main centres of electronic industry are Mumbai, Delhi, Hyderabad, Pune, Chennai, Kolkata and Lucknow.
- Maximum concentration of this industry is in Bengaluru, Noida, Mumbai, Chennai, Hyderabad and Pune.

Knowledge based Industries

- The advancement in information technology has had a profound influence on the country's economy.
- The Information Technology (IT) revolution opened up new possibilities of economic and social transformation.
- The IT and IT Enabled services Business Process Outsourcing (ITESBPO) services continue to be on a growth path.
- The Indian software industry has emerged as one of the fastest growing sectors in the economy.
- The software industry has surpassed electronic hardware production.

- The Indian Government has created a number of software parks in the country.
- India's software industry has achieved a remarkable distinction for providing quality products.
- A large number of Indian software companies have acquired international quality certification.
- A majority of the multinational companies operating in the area of information technology have either software development centres or research development centres in India.
- A major impact of this growth has been on employment creation, which is almost doubled every year.

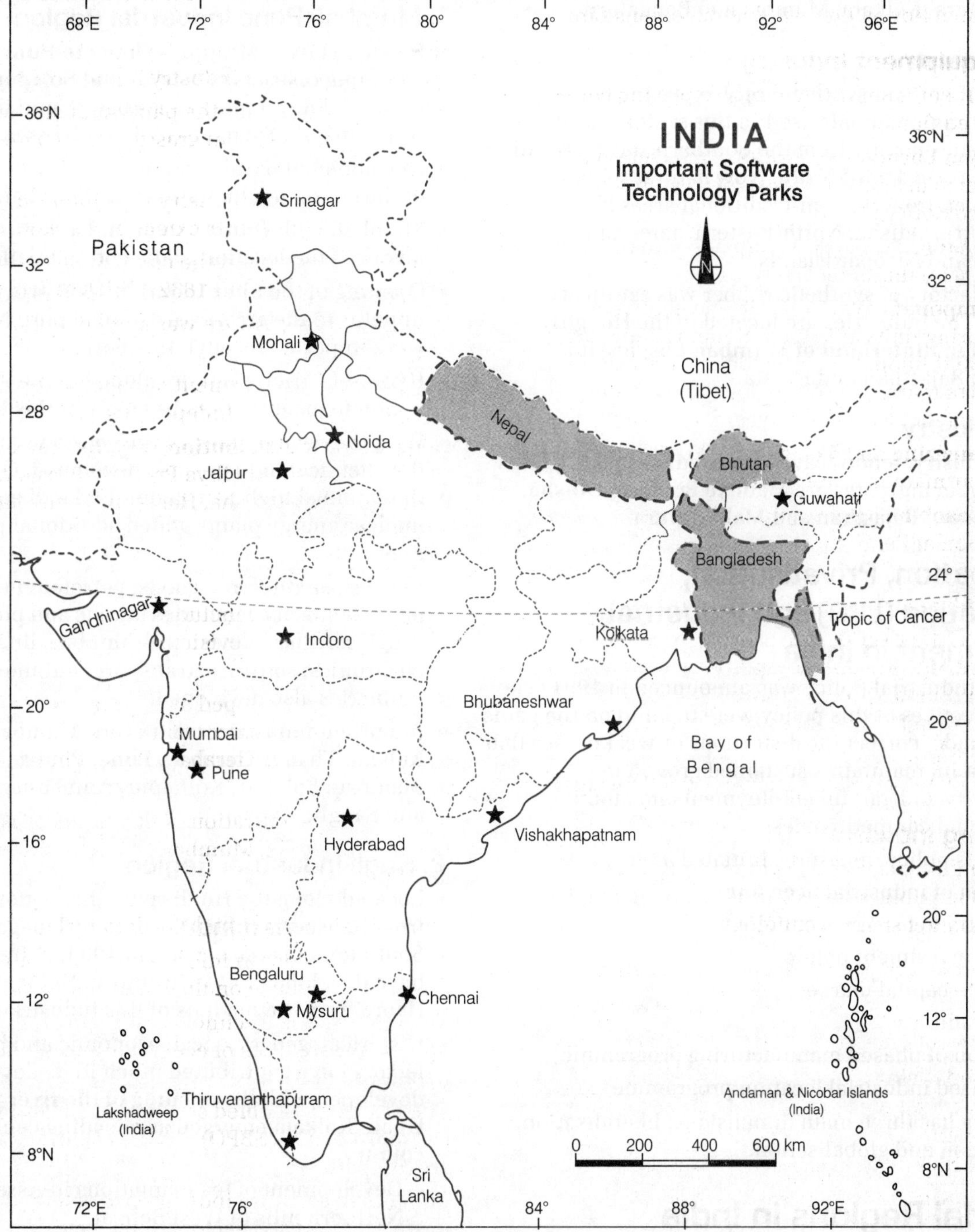

Leather Industry

- In India, different types of animals are found. According to 2020, India consists 33.38% of world cattle.
- Indian leather industry has two components : lather tanning and production of leather products like shoes, belts, purse, etc.
- In India, main centres of leather shoe production are Kanpur, Agra, Kolkata, Mumbai and Bengaluru.

Rubber Industry

- Natural rubber and synthetic rubber are the two important raw materials used in this sector. Natural rubber comes mainly from the Southern states– **Kerala**, **Karnataka** and **Tamil Nadu**. Now natural rubber is coming even from the non-traditional areas like Maharashtra, Odisha, North-Eastern states and Andaman and Nicobar islands.
- The first factory of synthetic rubber was set-up at **Bareilly**. The industries are located in the **Hooghly basin** and in **hinterland of Mumbai**. Besides, it is located in Rajasthan and Kerala.

Tendu Industry

- In this industry, tendu leaves are used for making bidis. Major producing states are Madhya Pradesh, Odisha, South-Eastern Rajasthan and Maharashtra.

Liberalisation, Privatisation, Globalisation (LPG) and Industrial Development in India

- The new Industrial Policy was announced in 1991. The major objectives of this policy were to build on the gains already made, correct the distortions or weaknesses that have crept in, maintain a sustained growth in productivity and gainful employment and attain international competitiveness.
- Within this policy, measures initiated are :
  - abolition of industrial licensing
  - free entry to foreign technology
  - foreign investment policy
  - access to capital market
  - open trade
  - abolition of phased manufacturing programme
  - liberalised industrial location programme
- The policy has three main dimensions: liberalisation, privatisation and globalisation.

Industrial Regions in India

- Industries are not evenly distributed in the country. They tend to concentrate on certain locations because of the favourable locational factors.
- Several indices are used to identify the clustering of industries. important among them are :
  - the number of industrial units,
  - number of industrial workers,
  - quantum of power used for industrial purposes,
  - total industrial output, and
  - value added by manufacturing, etc.

1. Mumbai-Pune Industrial Region

- It extends from **Mumbai-Thane to Pune** and in adjoining districts of Nashik and Solapur. Besides, industrial development has been rapid in Kolaba, Ahmednagar, Satara, Sangli and Jalgaon districts.
- Development of this region started with the location of the cotton textile industry in Mumbai.
- Mumbai, with cotton hinterland and moist climate favoured the location of the cotton textile industry.
- Opening of the **Suez Canal** in 1869 provided impetus to the growth of Mumbai port. Machineries were imported through this port.
- Hydro-electricity was developed in the Western Ghat region to meet the requirements of this industry.
- With the development of the cotton textile industry, the chemical industry also developed. Opening of the Mumbai high petroleum field and erection of nuclear energy plants added additional pull to this region.
- Besides, engineering goods, petroleum refining, petrochemicals, leather, synthetic and plastic goods, drugs, fertilisers, electrical, shipbuilding, electronics, software, transport equipment and food industries also developed.
- Important industrial centres are Mumbai, Kolaba, Kalyan, Thane, Trombay, Pune, Pimpri, Nashik, Manmad, Solapur, Kolhapur, Ahmednagar, Satara and Sangli.

2. Hugli Industrial Region

- Located along the Hugli river, this region extends from Bansberia in the North to Birlanagar in the South for a distance of about 100 km. Industries also have developed in **Medinipur** in the West. Kolkata-Haora from the nucleus of this industrial region.
- Historical, geographical, economic and political factors have contributed much to its development. It developed with the opening of the river port on Hugli. Kolkata emerged as a leading centre of the country.
  - Development of tea plantations in Assam and Northern hills of West Bengal,
  - The processing of indigo earlier and jute later coupled with the opening of coalfields of the Damodar Valley

- Iron-ore deposits of the Chhota Nagpur plateau many factor contributed to the industrial development of the region such as :
- Cheap labour available from thickly populated parts of Bihar, Eastern Uttar Pradesh and Odisha also contributed to its development.
- The establishment of the first jute mill at **Rishra** in 1855, ushered in the era of modern industrial clustering in this region. The major concentration of jute industry is at Howrah and Bhatapara.
- Cotton textile industry also grew along with jute industry, paper, engineering, textile machinery, electrical, chemical, pharmaceuticals, fertiliser and petrochemical industries have also developed within this region.
- Factory of the **Hindustan Motors Limited** at Konnagar and the Diesel Engine Factory at Chittaranjan are landmarks of this region.
- Location of petroleum refinery at Haldia has facilitated the development of a variety of industries. Important industrial centres of this region are Kolkata, Haora, Haldia, Serampore, Rishra, Shibpur, Naihati, Kakinara, Shamnagar, Titagarh, Sodepur, Budge Budge, Birlanagar, Bansberia, Belgurriah, Triveni, Hugli, Belur, etc.

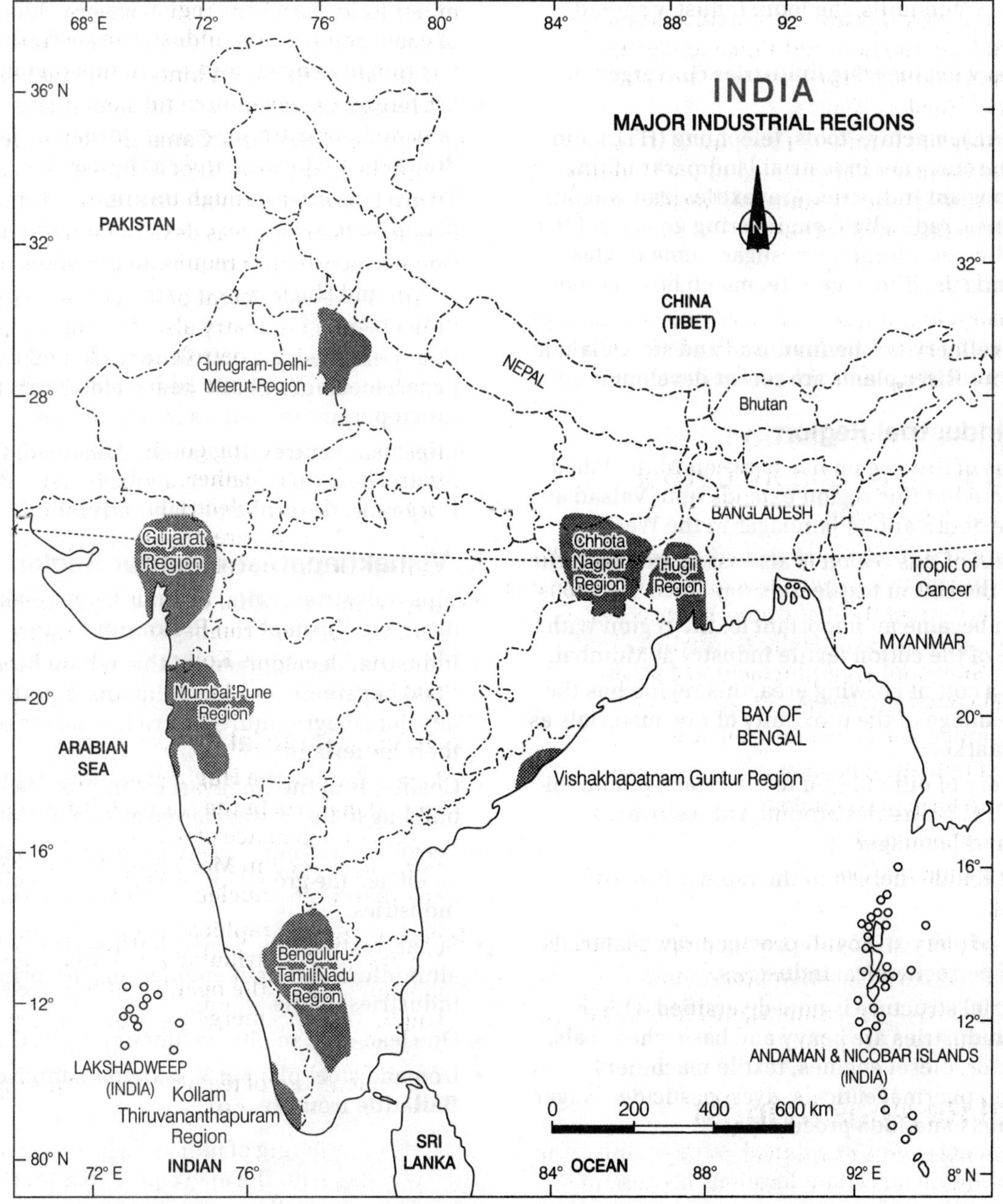

3. Bengaluru-Chennai Industrial Region

- This region witnessed the most rapid industrial growth in the post-independence period.
- Till 1960, industries were confined to Bengaluru, Salem and Madurai districts but now they have spread over all the districts of **Tamil Nadu** except **Viluppuram**.
- Since, this region is away from the coalfields, its development is dependent on the **Pykara hydroelectric** plant, which was built in 1932.
- Cotton textile industry was the first to take roots due to the presence of cotton growing areas.
- Along with cotton mills, the loom industry spread very rapidly.
- Several heavy engineering industries converged at Bengaluru.
- Aircraft (HAL), machine tools, telephone (HTL) and Bharat Electronics are industrial landmarks of this region. Important industries are textiles, rail wagons, diesel engines, radio, light engineering goods, rubber goods, medicines, aluminium, sugar, cement, glass, paper, chemicals, film, cigarette, match box, leather goods, etc.
- Petroleum refinery at **Chennai**, iron and steel plant at Salem and fertiliser plants are recent developments.

4. Gujarat Industrial Region

- The nucleus of this region lies between Ahmedabad and Vadodara but this region extends upto Valsad and Surat in the South and to Jamnagar in the West.
- Development of this region is also associated with the location of the cotton textile industry since the 1860s.
- This region became an important textile region with the decline of the cotton textile industry at Mumbai.
- Located in a cotton growing area, this region has the double advantage of the proximity of raw materials as well as of market.
- The discovery of oilfields led to the establishment of petrochemical industries around **Ankleshwar**, Vadodara and Jamnagar.
- The port at Kandla helped in the rapid growth of this region.
- Petroleum refinery at **Koyali** provided raw materials to a host of petrochemical industries.
- The industrial structure is now diversified. Other important industries are heavy and basic chemicals, motor, tractor, diesel engines, textile machinery, engineering, pharmaceuticals, dyes, pesticides, sugar, dairy products and food processing.
- The **largest petroleum refinery** has been set up at **Jamnagar**.
- Important industrial centres of this region are Ahmedabad, Vadodara, Bharuch, Koyali, Anand, Khera, Surendranagar, Rajkot, Surat, Valsad and Jamnagar.

5. Chhota Nagpur Region

- This region extends over Jharkhand, Northern Odisha and Western West Bengal and is known for the **heavy metallurgical industries**.
- This region owes its development to the discovery of coal in the Damodar valley and metallic and non-metallic minerals in Jharkhand and Northern Odisha. Proximity of coal, iron-ore and other minerals facilitated the location of heavy industries in this region.
- Six large integrated iron and steel plants at Jamshedpur, Burnpur-Kulti, Durgapur, Bokaro and Rourkela are located within this region.
- To meet the power requirement, thermal and hydroelectric plants have been constructed in the Damodar valley.
- Densely populated surrounding regions provide cheap labour and Hugli region provides vast market for its industries.
- Heavy engineering, machine tools, fertilisers, cement, paper, locomotives and heavy electricals are some of the important industries in this region.
- Important centres are Ranchi, Dhanbad, Chaibasa, Sindri, Hazaribag, Jamshedpur, Bokaro, Rourkela, Durgapur, Asansol and Dalmianagar.

6. Vishakhapatnam-Guntur Region

- This industrial region extends from Visakhapatnam district to **Kurnool** and **Prakasam** districts in the South.
- Industrial development of this region hinged upon Visakhapatnam and Machilipatnam ports and developed agriculture and rich reserves of minerals in their hinterlands.
- Coalfields of the Godavari basin provide energy. Ship building industry was started at Visakhapatnam in 1941.
- Petroleum refinery based on imported petroleum facilitated the growth of several petrochemical industries.
- Sugar, textile, jute, paper, fertiliser, cement, aluminium and light engineering are principal industries of this region.
- One lead-zinc smelter is functioning in **Guntur** district.
- Iron and steel plant at Visakhapatnam uses the **Bailadila** iron-ore.

- Visakhapatnam, Vijayawada, Vijayanagara, Rajahmundry, Guntur, Eluru and Kurnool are important industrial centres.

7. Gurugram-Delhi-Meerut Region

- Industries located in this region have shown very fast growth in the recent past.
- This region is located far away from the mineral and power resources, and therefore, the industries are light and market-oriented.
- Electronics, light engineering and electrical goods are major industries of this region.
- Besides these, cotton, woollen and synthetic fabrics, hosiery, sugar, cement, machine tools, tractor, cycle, agricultural implements, chemical and vanaspati industries, have been developed on large scale. Software industry is a recent addition.
- To the South lies the Agra-Mathura industrial area, which specialises in glass and leather goods.
- Mathura with an oil refinery is a petrochemical complex.
- Among industrial centres, mention be made of Gurugram, Delhi, Faridabad, Meerut, Modinagar, Ghaziabad, Ambala, Agra and Mathura.

8. Kollam-Thiruvananthapuram Region

- This region includes Thiruvananthapuram, Kollam, Ernakulam, Kochchi and Alapuzza districts of Kerala.
- In this region, there is concentration of horticulture and hydroelectricity.
- Important industries of this region are cotton textiles, sugar, rubber, matches, glass, chemical fertilisers and fishery.
- Food processing, paper, coconut, fibre production, aluminium and cement industry are also prominent in this region.

Minor Industrial Regions and Districts

Minor Industrial Regions (13)

- Ambala-Amritsar
- Jaipur-Ajmer
- Middle Malabar
- Bhojpur-Munger
- Bilaspur-Korba
- Allahabad-Varanasi-Mirzapur
- Indore-Dewas-Ujjain
- Northern Malabar
- Adilabad-Nizamabad
- Durg-Raipur
- Brahmaputra Valley
- Kolhapur-South Kannada
- Saharanpur-Muzaffarnagar-Bijnor

Industrial Districts (15)

- Kanpur
- Nagpur
- Lucknow
- Gorakhpur
- Purnia
- Hyderabad
- Gwalior
- Jalpaigudi
- Aligarh
- Jabalpur
- Agra
- Bhopal
- Cuttak
- Kota
- Bareilly

Extra Facts From Tamil Nadu Board and NIOS

- Manufacturing industries help in modernising agriculture which is the backbone of the Indian economy.
- As industries employ a large number of the population, industrial development is one of the preconditions for eradication of unemployment and poverty from our country.
- Cotton textile industries are located mostly in Western India, Gujarat, Maharashtra, Western Part of Madhya Pradesh, Tamil Nadu, West Bengal and Uttar Pradesh.
- Sholapur, Kolhapur, Nagpur, Pune, Aurangabad and Jalgaon are other important centres in Maharashtra.
- India exports products of the cotton industry to various countries. For example, it exports yarns to Japan, U.S.A., U.K., Russia, France, East European countries, Nepal, Singapore, Sri Lanka and African countries as well.
- The first modern steel plant in India was set up at Kulti, Bengal in 1870 and production began in 1874.
- Steel industry was delicensed in 1991 and de-controlled in 1992. Steel Authority of India Ltd. (SAIL) is the authority through which public sector undertakings market their steel.

Population and Human Settlement

[SOURCES]

Class-VI New NCERT Chap 1 (The Earth in the Solar System), Class-VI Old NCERT Chap 1 (The Earth in our Solar System), Class-XI New NCERT Chap 2 (The Origin and Evolution of the Earth), Tamil Nadu Board (Class XII), NIOS

Human Settlement

- A human settlement is defined as a place which is inhabited permanently.
- It means cluster of dwellings of any type or size where human beings live.
- There may be some settlements which are temporary and are occupied for short periods, or for a season.

Types of Settlements

The different type of human settlements are as follows :

- Temporary settlements
- Rural settlements (Countryside)
- Permanent settlements
- Urban settlements (Towns and cities)

Rural Settlement

- Rural settlements are most closely and directly related to land.
- They are dominated by primary activities such as agriculture, animal husbandry, fishing, etc.
- The rural settlement size is relatively small.

Types of Rural Settlements

- The sparsely located small settlements are called **Villages**, specialising in agriculture or other primary activities.
- Rural settlements in India can broadly be put into the following four types :

Rural Settlements

- (Clustered/Agglomerated/ Nucleated/Settlements)
- (Semi-Clustered or Fragmented Settlements)
- (Hamleted Settlements)
- (Dispersed or Isolated Settlements)

1. Clustered Settlements (Agglomerated or Nucleated)

- The clustered rural settlement is a compact or closely built up area of houses.
- In this type of village, the general living area is distinct and separated from the surrounding farms, barns and pastures.
- The closely built-up area and its intervening streets present some recognisable pattern or geometric shape.
- Such settlements are generally found in fertile alluvial plains and in the North-Eastern states. Sometimes they develop along river valleys. Communities living in such settlements are closely connected and share common occupations.

2. Semi-Clustered (Fragmented) Settlements

- **Semi-clustered** or **fragmented settlements** may result from the tendency of clustering in a restricted area of dispersed settlement.
- More often such a pattern may also result from segregation or fragmentation of a large compact village.
- Such settlements are widespread in the Gujarat plain and some parts of Rajasthan.

3. Hamleted Settlements

- These units are locally called panna, para, palli, nagla, dhani, in various parts of the country.
- This segmentation of a large village is often motivated by social and ethnic factors.

4. Dispersed (Isolated) Settlements

- Dispersed or isolated settlement patterns in India appear in the form of isolated huts or hamlets of few huts in remote jungles or on small hills with farms or pasture on the slopes.
- Many areas of Meghalaya, Uttarakhand, Himachal Pradesh and Kerala have this type of settlement.
- A cultural feature such as a place of worship or a market, binds the settlement together. Factors affecting the location of rural settlements areas follows:
  - **Land** People choose to settle near fertile lands suitable for agriculture.
  - **Upland** Upland which is not prone to flooding was chosen to prevent damage to houses and loss of life.
  - **Defense** During the times of political instability, war, hostility of neighbouring groups villages were built on defensive hills and islands.
  - **Planned Settlements** Sites that are not spontaneously chosen by villagers themselves, planned settlements are constructed by governments by providing shelter, water and other infrastructures on acquired lands.
  - The scheme of villagisation in Ethiopia and the canal colonies in the Indira Gandhi canal command area in India are some good examples.
- **Water Supply** Usually rural settlements are located near water bodies such as rivers, lakes and springs where water can be easily obtained. Sometimes the need for water drives people to settle in otherwise disadvantaged sites such as islands surrounded by swamps or low-lying river banks.

  Most water based 'wet point' settlements have many advantages such as water for drinking, cooking and washing. Rivers and lakes can be used to irrigate farm land. Water bodies also have fish which can be caught for diet and navigable rivers and lakes can be used for transportation.
- **Building Material** The availability of building materials- wood, stone near settlements is another advantage. Early villages were built in forest clearings where wood was plentiful.

Patterns of Rural Settlement

The various patterns of rural settlements are as follows:

- **Linear pattern** In such settlements houses are located along a road, railway line, river, canal edge of a valley or along a levee.
- **Rectangular pattern** Such patterns of rural settlements are found in plain areas or wide intermontane valleys. The roads are rectangular and cut each other at right angles.
- **Circular pattern** Circular villages develop around lakes, tanks and sometimes the village is planned in such a way that the central part remains open. It is used for keeping the animals to protect them from wild animals.
- **Star like pattern** Where several roads converge, star shaped settlements develop by the houses built along the roads.
- **T-shaped, Y-shaped, Cross-shaped or Cruciform settlements** T-shaped settlements develop at tri-junctions of the roads. Y-shaped settlements emerge as the places where two roads converge on the third one and houses are built along these roads. Cruciform settlements develop on the cross-roads and houses extend in all the four directions.
- **Double village** These settlements extend on both sides of a river where there is a bridge or a ferry.

Problems of Rural Settlements

- Rural settlements in the developing countries are large in number and poorly equipped with infrastructure.
- They represent a great challenge and opportunity for planners.
- Supply of water to rural settlements in developing countries is not adequate. People in villages, particularly in mountainous and arid areas have to walk long distances to fetch drinking water.
- Water borne diseases such as *Cholera* and *Jaundice* tend to be a common problem.
- The countries of South Asia face conditions of drought and flood very often. Crop cultivation sequences, in the absence of irrigation, also suffer.
- The general absence of toilet and garbage disposal facilities cause health related problems.
- The houses made up of mud, wood and thatch, remain susceptible to damage during heavy rains and floods, and require proper maintenance every year. Most house designs are typically lack proper ventilation.
- Unmetalled roads and lack of modern communication networks creates a unique problem. During the rainy season, the settlements remain cut off and pose serious difficulties in providing emergency services.
- It is also difficult to provide adequate health and educational infrastructure for their large rural population.

Urban Settlements

- Urban settlements are generally compact and larger in size. They are engaged in a variety of non-agricultural, economic and administrative functions.
- Cities are functionally linked to rural areas around them. Thus, exchange of goods and services is performed sometimes directly and sometimes through a series of market towns and cities.
- Cities are connected directly as well as indirectly with the villages and also with each other

Evolution of Towns in India

- Towns flourished since prehistoric times in India. Even at the time of Indus Valley civilisation, towns like Harappa and Mohenjodaro were in existence.
- On the basis of their evolution in different periods, Indian towns may be classified as:
  - **Ancient Towns** There are number of towns in India having historical background spanning over 2000 years. Most of them developed as religious and cultural centres.
  - Varanasi is one of the important towns among these. **Prayag** (Allahabad), **Pataliputra** (Patna), **Madurai** are some other examples of ancient towns in the country.
  - **Medieval Towns** About 100 of the existing towns have their roots in the medieval period. Most of them developed as headquarters of principalities and kingdoms.
  - These are fort towns which came up on the ruins of ancient towns. Important among them are Delhi, Hyderabad, Jaipur, Lucknow, Agra and Nagpur.
  - **Modern Towns** The British and other Europeans have developed a number of towns in India. Starting their foothold on coastal locations, they first developed some trading ports such as Surat, Daman, Goa, Puducherry, etc.
  - The British later consolidated their hold around three principal nodes – Mumbai (Bombay), Chennai (Madras) and Kolkata (Calcutta) – and built them in the British style.
- Rapidly extending their domination either directly or through control over the princely states, they established their administrative centres, hilltowns as summer resorts, and added new civil administrative and military areas to them.
- Towns based on modern industries also evolved after 1850. **Jamshedpur** can be cited as an example.
- After independence, a large number of towns have been developed as administrative headquarters, e.g., Chandigarh, Bhubaneswar, Gandhinagar, Dispur, etc., and industrial centres, such as Durgapur, Bhilai, Sindri, Barauni.
- Some old towns also developed as satellite towns around metropolitan cities, such as Ghaziabad, Rohtak, Gurugram around Delhi.
- With increasing investment in rural areas, a large number of medium and small towns have developed all over the country.

Difference Between Rural and Urban Settlement

- It is widely accepted that settlements can be differentiated in terms of rural and urban, but there is no consensus on what exactly defines a village or a town.
- Although population size is an important criterion, it is not a universal criterion since, many villages in densely populated countries of India and China have populations exceeding that of some towns of Western Europe and United States.

Urbanisation in India

- The level of urbanisation is measured in terms of percentage of urban population to total population.
- The level of urbanisation in India in 2011 was 31.16%, which is quite low in comparison to developed countries.
- Total urban population has increased eleven-fold during the twentieth century. Enlargement of urban centres and emergence of new towns have played a significant role in the growth of urban population and urbanisation in the country.
- But the growth rate of urbanisation has slowed down during last two decades.

Trends of Urbanisation in India (1901-2011)

year	Number of Towns	Urban Population (in thousands)	% of Total Population	Decennial Growth (%)
1901	1,827	2,58,51.9	10.84	—
1911	1,815	2,59,41.6	10.29	0.35
1921	1,949	2,80,86.2	11.18	8.27
1931	2,072	3,34,56.0	11.99	19.12
1941	2,250	4,41,53.3	13.86	31.97
1951	2,843	6,24,43.7	17.29	41.42
1961	2,365	7,89,36.6	17.97	26.41
1971	2,590	1,09,114	19.91	38.23
1981	3,378	1,59,463	23.34	46.14
1991	4,689	2,17,611	25.71	36.47
2001	5,161	2,85,355	27.78	31.13
2011	6,166	3,77,000	31.16	31.08

Classification of Towns on the basis of Population Size

- Census of India classifies urban centres into six categories. Urban centre with population of more than 1 lakh is called a **City or Class I town.**
- Cities accommodating population size between 1 to 5 million are called **Metropolitan cities** and more than 5 million are **Mega cities.**
- Majority of metropolitan and mega cities are urban agglomerations.
- An urban agglomeration may consist of any one of the following three combinations:
  - (i) a town and its adjoining urban outgrowths
  - (ii) two or more contiguous towns with or without their outgrowths
  - (iii) a city and one or more adjoining towns with their outgrowths together forming a contiguous spread. More than 60 % of urban population in India lives in Class I towns. Out of 468 cities, 53 cities/ urban agglomerations are metropolitan cities. Six of them are mega cities with population over five million each.

More than one-fifth (21.0%) of urban population lives in these mega cities. Among them, Greater Mumbai is the largest agglomeration with 18.4 million people. Delhi, Kolkata, Chennai, Bengaluru and Hyderabad are other mega cities in the country.

Class-Wise Number of Towns and Cities and their Population in India (2011)

Class	Population Size	Number of Cities	Total Urban Population (in thousand)	% of Total Urban Population
I.	1,00,000 and more	468	2,27,899	60.45
II.	50,000-99,999	474	41,328	10.96
III.	20,000-49,999	1,373	58,174	15.43
IV.	10,000-19,999	1,683	31,866	8.45
V.	5,000-9,999	7,749	15,883	4.21
VI.	Less than 5,000	424	1,956	0.51

Functional Classification of Towns

On the basis of dominant or specialised functions, Indian cities and towns can be broadly classified as follows:

- **Administrative towns and cities** Towns supporting administrative headquarters of higher order are administrative towns, such as Chandigarh, New Delhi, Bhopal, Shillong, Guwahati, Imphal, Srinagar, Gandhinagar, Jaipur, Chennai, etc.
- **Industrial towns** Industries constitute prime motive force of these cities, such as Mumbai, Salem, Coimbatore, Modinagar, Jamshedpur, Hugli, Bhilai, etc.
- **Transport Cities** They may be ports primarily engaged in export and import activities such as Kandla, Kochchi, Kozhikode, Vishakhapatnam, etc., or hubs of inland transport, such as Agra, Dhulia, Mughalsarai, Itarsi, Katni, etc.
- **Commercial towns** Towns and cities specialising in trade and commerce are kept in this class. Kolkata, Saharanpur, Satna, etc., are some examples.
- **Mining towns** These towns have developed in mineral rich areas such as Raniganj, Jharia, Digboi, Ankaleshwar, Singrauli, etc.
- **Garrison Cantonment towns** These towns emerged as garrison towns such as Ambala, Jalandhar, Mhow, Babina, Udhampur, etc.
- **Educational towns** Starting as centres of education, some of the towns have grown into major campus towns, such as Roorkee, Varanasi, Aligarh, Pilani, Allahabad, etc.
- **Religious and cultural towns** Varanasi, Mathura, Amritsar, Madurai, Puri, Ajmer, Pushkar, Tirupati, Kurukshetra, Haridwar, Ujjain came to prominence due to their religious/cultural significance.
- **Tourist towns** Nainital, Mussoorie, Shimla, Pachmarhi, Jodhpur, Jaisalmer, Udagamandalam (Ooty), Mount Abu are some of the tourist destinations. The cities are not static in their function.

Definitions of rural and Urban Areas by Census of India

Rural Settlement

- Population is less than 5000
- Population density is less than 400 persons/sq. km.
- More than 75 % of people are engaged in Agricultural and associated primary activities
- Run by Gram-Panchayats.

Urban Settlement

- Population is greater than 5000
- Population density is greater than 400 persons/ Sq. km. or 1000 persons/sq. mile
- More than 75 % of people are engaged in Non-agricultural activities
- Run by the Municipality, Cantonment Board, Corporation, etc.

Schemes for Rural/Urban Development

Important schemes for rural/urban development as follows :

Swachh Bharat Abhiyan

- Swachh Bharat Abhiyan was launched on 2nd October, 2014 by Prime Minister Narendra Modi.
- It is a national campaign to clean the streets, roads and infrastructure of the country.
- It covers 4,041 statutory towns. This campaign accomplished the vision of a **Clean India** by 2nd October, 2019, the 150th birthday of Mahatma Gandhi.
- The Union Government initiated the **Swachhata Udayami Yojana** to achieve the overall goal of the cleanliness campaign under the scheme.
- **Nirmal Bharat Abhiyan** was re-launched in name of Swachh Bharat Abhiyan.

Shyama Prasad Mukherji Rurban Mission (SPMRM)

- The SPMRM is a new initiative from the Modi government that aims to set up 300 rural clusters by 2020. It was formally launched on 16th August, 2015 by the Union Cabinet.
- Prime Minister Narendra Modi launched this scheme as National Rurban Mission on 22nd February, 2016.
- The scheme of Providing Urban Amenities in Rural Areas (PURA) is merged with Shyama Prasad Mukherjee Rurban Mission.
- Rurban development model of urbanisation of the rural areas, through which people living in the rural areas can get efficient civic infrastructure and associate services. It was proposed in the budget speech of 2014-15.

Amrut

- The Government has renewed the 10-year-old Jawaharlal Nehru National Urban Renewal Mission (JNNURM) and named it after the first BJP Prime Minister.
- The renewed scheme is known as **Atal Mission for Rejuvenation and Urban Transformation** (AMRUT). AMRUT for 500 Tier 2 and Tier 3 cities was also launched alongwith smart city project.
- The states have been asked to recommend cities which can be included under this scheme.
- For the selected cities, Central Government will provide 30% of the overall cost, if the city has a population of more than 10 lakh and 50% if under 10 lakh.

Smart Cities Mission

- The objective of the Smart Cities Mission is to promote cities that provide core infrastructure, a clean and sustainable environment and give a decent quality of life to its citizens.
- One of the features of Smart Cities is to apply smart solutions to infrastructure and services in order to make them better. For example, making areas less vulnerable to disasters, using fewer resources and providing cheaper services. The focus is on sustainable and inclusive development.

Top Five States with Maximum Urban Population

State	Percentage (in %)
Goa	62.2
Mizoram	52.1
Tamil Nadu	48.4
Kerala	47.7
Maharashtra	45.2

Top Five States with Minimum Urban Population

State	Percentage (in %)
Himachal Pradesh	10.0
Bihar	11.3
Assam	14.1
Odisha	16.7
Meghalaya	20.1

Top Five States with Maximum Urban Population

State	Population
Maharashtra	50818259
Uttar Pradesh	44495063
Tamil Nadu	34917440
West Bengal	29093002
Andhra Pradesh	28219075

Top Four States with Minimum Urban Population

State	Population
Sikkim	153578
Arunachal Pradesh	317369
Nagaland	570966
Mizoram	571771

Population

- Demographics refer to statistical data relating to the population in a region.
- This covers various factors like population growth rate, the percentage of different age groups within the population, the literacy rates, the sex ratio, urban-rural population ratios, etc.

- According to the 2011 Census, India has a 1.21 billion population. It comprises 17.5% of the world's population with 2.4 % of the world's land area.
- At present with 1.427 billion population, India is the largest country of the world.
- Despite its growth rate declining, India continues to be a high-growth country.
- Approximately one out of every six people in the world is from India. India's population is almost equal to the combined population of the USA, Indonesia, Brazil, Pakistan, Bangladesh and Japan together.
- India's population is a little over twice the population of Latin America and 1.2 times the population of the whole of Africa.
- In terms of area, India stands seventh, preceded by Russia, Canada, China, The United States of America, Brazil and Australia.
- It can also be revealed from the fact that the total population of North America, South America, and Australia added together is less than the population of India.
- On top of it, we are adding over 17 million people each year. It is more than the total population of Australia. In fact, the net addition to the Chinese population each year is less than ours.

Natural Growth of Population

- This is the population increase by difference between births and deaths in a particular region between two points of time.

Natural Growth = Births – Deaths

Actual Growth of Population = Births – Deaths + In Migration – Out Migration

- **Positive Growth of Population** This happens when the birth rate is more than the death rate between two points of time or when people from other countries migrate permanently to a region.
- **Negative Growth of Population** If the population decreases between two points of time it is known as negative growth of population. It occurs when the birth rate falls below the death rate or people migrate to other countries.

Crude Birth Rate and Death Rate

- Crude Birth Rate (CBR) is expressed as the number of live births in a year per thousand of population.
- Crude Death Rate (CDR) is the number of deaths in a particular year per thousand of population in a particular region.

The magnitude and Rate of India's Population Growth

Year	Total Population (In Million)	Absolute Increase in the Decade (In million)	Annual Growth Rate (%)
1951	361.0	42.43	1.25
1961	493.2	78.15	1.96
1971	548.2	108.92	2.20
1981	683.3	135.17	2.22
1991	846.4	163.09	2.16
2001	1028.7	182.32	1.97
2011	1210.6	181.46	1.64

Population in India

- Population data are collected through Census operations held every 10 years in our country.
- The first population Census in India was conducted in 1872 but its first complete Census was conducted only in 1881.

Growth of Population

- Population growth has two components namely; natural and induced. While the natural growth is analysed by assessing the crude birth and death rates, the induced components are explained by the volume of inward and outward movement of people in any given area.
- The annual growth rate of India's population is 1.64% (2011).

India's Population Growth Rates During 1951-2011

The growth rate of population in India over the last one century has been caused by annual birth rate and death rate and rate of migration and thereby shows different trends.

There are four distinct phases of growth identified within this period:

- **Phase I** The period from 1901-1921 is referred to as a period of stagnant or stationary phase of growth of India's population, since in this period growth rate was very low, even recording a negative growth rate during 1911-1921.
- Both the birth rate and death rate were high keeping the rate of increase low. Poor health and medical services, illiteracy of people at large and inefficient distribution system of food and other basic necessities were largely responsible for a high birth and death rates in this period.

- **Phase II** The decades 1921-1951 are referred to as the period of steady population growth.

  An overall improvement in health and sanitation throughout the country brought down the mortality rate. At the same time better transport and communication system improved distribution system.

  The crude birth rate remained high in this period leading to higher growth rate than the previous phase. This is impressive at the backdrop of Great Economic Depression, 1920s and World War II.
- **Phase III** The decades 1951-1981 are referred to as the period of population explosion in India, which was caused by a rapid fall in the mortality rate but a high fertility rate of population in the country.

  The average annual growth rate was as high as 2.2%.
- In this period, developmental activities were introduced through a centralised planning process and economy started showing up ensuring the improvement of living condition of people at large.
- Consequently, there was a high natural increase and higher growth rate. Besides, increased international migration bringing in Tibetans, Bangladeshis, Nepalies and even people from Pakistan contributed to the high growth rate.
- **Phase IV** In the post 1981 till present, the growth rate of country's population though remained high, has started slowing down gradually. A downward trend of crude birth rate is held responsible for such a population growth.

  This was, in turn, affected by an increase in the mean age at marriage, improved quality of life particularly education of females in the country.

  However, the growth rate of population is, still high in the country and it has been projected by the World Development Report that population of India will touch 1,350 million by 2025.

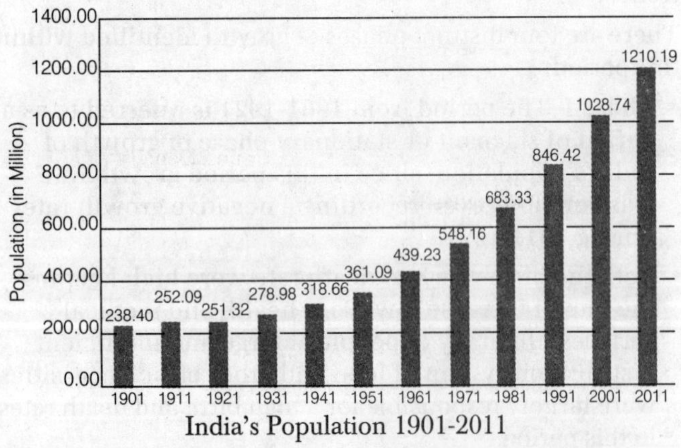

India's Population 1901-2011

Demographic Composition

The demographic composition of India's population is discussed below :

Density of Population

- It is defined as the number of persons per sq km area. It is an important index of population, which shows concentration of population in a particular area.
- In Indian topography, fertility of the soil and availability of water determine the extent of the concentration of population.
- However, in contemporary time the concentration of population is also influenced by the migration factor.

Density of Population According to Census

- As per the population totals of Census 2011, the population density of India has gone up to 382 persons per sq km from 325 persons per sq km in 2001.
- Among the ten most populous countries of the world, only Bangladesh has a higher population density compared to India.
- At the beginning of the 20th century i.e. in 1901, the density of India was as low as 77 persons per sq km.
- This steadily increased in each decade to reach 382 persons per sq km in 2011.
- It constitutes a 17.5% increase over 2001, but the rate of increase has slowed down.
- Nagaland is the only state, where density of population has decreased in 2011 Census (119) from its 2001 Census value (120).
- The States and Union Territories of our country vary widely in terms of their density due to differences in climatic conditions, geo-physical characteristics, availability of resources, etc.
- The **National Capital Region** (NCR) area of Delhi possesses the highest of the population density in India having a statistics of 11,320 per sq km.
- The State of Arunachal Pradesh has the lowest record of population density having just 17 per sq km as per the Census 2011.
- On the other hand, states of Mizoram, Sikkim and Nagaland follow Arunachal Pradesh in terms of least densely populated states.
- Excluding North-Eastern states, Himachal Pradesh becomes the least populated state with population density of 123.
- Among Union Territories, Andaman and Nicobar islands have got least density of 46 persons per sq km.

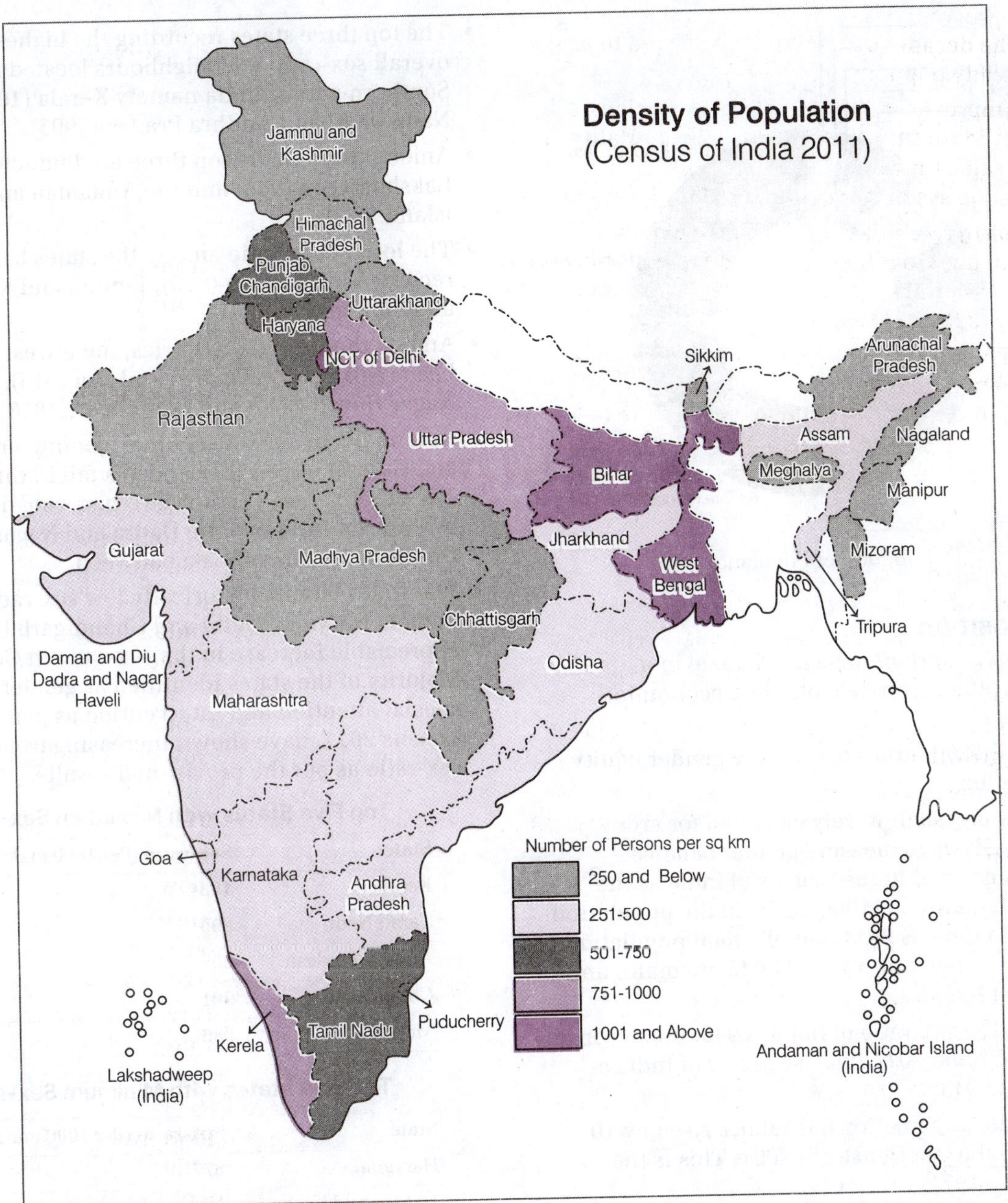

Top Five States with Maximum Population Density

State	Population Density/sq km
Bihar	1102
West Bengal	1029
Kerala	859
Uttar Pradesh	829
Haryana	573

Top Five States with Minimum Population Density

State	Population Density/sq km
Arunachal Pradesh	17
Mizoram	52
Sikkim	86
Nagaland	119
Manipur	122

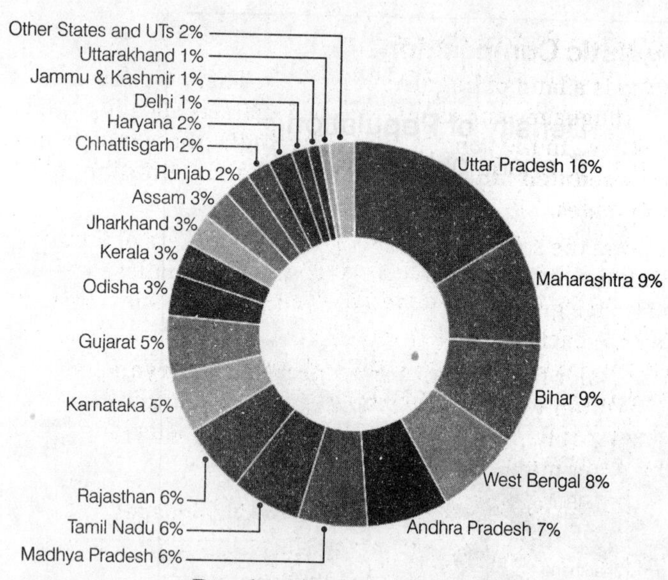

Distribution of Population

Sex Composition

- Distribution pattern of male and female in a population affects relative roles and economic relationships.
- There are different tools to measure gender equity in a population.
- **Sex-ratio** is one such widely used tool for cross sectional analysis to measure gender balance. Sex-ratio is defined in the Census of India as the number of females per 1000 males in the population. According to Census 2011, out of a total population of 1,21,01,93,422 persons, 62,37,24,248 are males and 58,64,69,174 females.
- As per this, the sex-ratio of India is 940. But according to Census of India 2011 final, sex-ratio of India's population is 943.
- The sex-ratio at the national level has risen by 10 points since the last Census in 2001. This is the highest since 1971.
- The sex-ratio in India has been unfavourable to females. In the pre-independence period, the sex-ratio declined consistently upto 1951, when it rose marginally.
- In the post-Independence period, the trend continued and the sex-ratio slipped down for two consecutive decades 946 in 1951 to reach 930 in 1971.
- After 1971 Census, trends were not consistent, showing increase in one decade and decline in the next.

Patterns of Sex-ratio (2011)

- The patterns in sex-ratio among the States and Union Territories are distinct.
- The top three states recording the highest value of overall sex-ratio are neighbours located in the Southern part of India namely Kerala (1084), Tamil Nadu (996) and Andhra Pradesh (993).
- Among the UTs the top three are Puducherry (1037), Lakshadweep (946) and the Andaman and Nicobar islands (878).
- The lowest sex-ratio among the states has been recorded in Haryana (879), Jammu and Kashmir (889) and Sikkim (890).
- Among the Union Terriotries, the lowest sex-ratio has been registered in Daman and Diu (618), Dadra and Nagar Haveli (774) and Chandigarh (818).
- Among the major states, Bihar, Jammu and Kashmir and Gujarat have experienced a fall in the sex-ratio. The other Union Territories registering decline in overall sex-ratio include Dadra and Nagar Haveli, Daman and Diu and Lakshadweep.
- The states having historically low sex-ratio such as Punjab, Haryana, Delhi and Chandigarh have shown appreciable increase in the sex-ratio in Census 2011. Majority of the states identified as gender critical for special attention and intervention as part of the Census 2011, have shown increasing trend in the sex-ratio as per the provisional results.

Top Five States with Maximum Sex-ratio

State	Sex-ratio (Per 1000 male-female)
Kerala	1084
Tamil Nadu	995
Andhra Pradesh	992
Chhattisgarh	991
Meghalaya	986

Top Five States with Minimum Sex-ratio

State	Sex-ratio (Per 1000 male-female)
Haryana	877
Jammu and Kashmir	883
Sikkim	889
Punjab	893
Uttar Pradesh	912

Literacy

- Literacy rate and educational development are considered to be key variables in improving quality of life.
- They directly relate to life expectancy, infant mortality, learning levels and nutritional levels of children. For the purposes of Census, a person aged 7 and above, who can both read and write with understanding in any language, is treated as literate.

- A person, who can only read, but cannot write, is not literate.
- The number of literates and illiterates aged 7 and above in India as per the population totals of Census 2011 is 77,84,54,120 and 27,29,50,015 respectively. There has been a marked improvement in the proportion of literates in the last decade.

Top Five States with Maximum Literacy Rate

State	Literacy Rate
Kerala	94.0%
Mizoram	91.3%
Goa	88.7%
Tripura	87.2%
Himachal Pradesh	82.8%

Top Five States with Minimum Literacy Rate

State	Literacy Rate
Bihar	61.8%
Arunachal Pradesh	65.40%
Rajasthan	66.1%
Jharkhand	66.4%
Andhra Pradesh	67.0%

Ethnic Composition

India is a country with huge racial and ethnic diversity. Indian people can be divided into six main ethnic groups. These include :

- **Negritos** They are originally from Africa. They were the earliest people to have come to India. They have survived in their original habitat in Andaman and Nicobar islands.
- **Austrics** They laid the foundation of Indian civilisation. They cultivated rice and vegetables and made sugar from sugarcane. Now these people are found in some parts of India, Myanmar and the islands of South-East Asia. Their languages have survived in the Central and Eastern India.
- **Mongoloids** They are found in the North-Eastern part of India.
- **Mediterranean** or **Dravidians** They are the people of South India. They have been believed to come before the Aryans. They are reputed to have built up the city civilisation of the Indus valley.
- **Western Brachycephalics** They include the broad headed people living mainly on the Western side of the country such as the Ganga valley.
- **Nordics** These were the last one to immigrate to India. They came to India somewhere between 2000 and 1500 BC. They are now mainly found in the Northern and Central part of India.

Linguistic Composition

- India is a land of linguistic diversity. There are around 179 languages and as many as 544 dialects spoken in the country. In the context of modern India, there are about **22 scheduled languages** and a number of **non-scheduled languages.**
- Among the scheduled languages, the speakers of **Hindi** have the highest percentage (40.42). The smallest language groups are **Kashmiri** and **Sanskrit** speakers (0.01% each).
- The major families are **Indo-European** or **Aryan** and **Dravidian** with 73% speakers and 20% speakers respectively, whereas Austric and Sino-Tibetan constitute the other major families.

Classification of Modern Indian Languages

Family	Sub-Family	Branch/ Group	Speech Areas
Austric (Nishada) 1.38%	Austro-Asiatic	Mon-Khmer	Meghalaya, Nicobar Islands
		Munda	East Bengal, Bihar, Odisha, Assam, Madhya Pradesh, Maharashtra
	Austro-Nesian		Outside India
Dravidian (Dravida) 20%		South-Dravidian	Tamil Nadu, Karnataka, Kerala
		Central Dravidian	Andhra Pradesh, Madhya Pradesh, Odisha, Maharashtra
		North Dravidian	Bihar, Odisha, West Bengal, Madhya Pradesh
Sino-Tibetan (Kirata) 0.85%	Tibeto-Myanmari	Tibeto-Himalayan	Jammu and Kashmir, Himachal Pradesh, Sikkim
	Siamese-Chinese	North Assam	Arunachal Pradesh
		Assam-Myanmari	Assam, Nagaland, Manipur, Mizoram, Tripura, Meghalaya
Indo-European (Aryan) 73%	Indo-Aryan	Iranian	Outside India
		Dardic	Jammu and Kashmir
		Indo-Aryan	Jammu and Kashmir, Punjab, Himachal Pradesh, Uttar Pradesh, Rajasthan, Haryana, Madhya Pradesh, Bihar, Odisha, West Bengal Assam, Gujarat, Maharashtra, Goa

Migration

- Migration is the movement of people in and out of an area. Actually migration was recorded beginning from the **first Census of India** conducted in 1881.
- This data was recorded on the basis of place of birth.

- However, the first major modification was introduced in the 1961 Census by bringing in two additional components *viz;* place of birth i.e., village or town and duration of residence (if born elsewhere).
- Migration is another way by which population size changes. People may move within a country or between countries.
- Emigrants are people who leave a country, Immigrants are those who arrive in a country.

Causes of Migration

- Generally, people are emotionally attached to their place of birth. But millions of people leave their places of birth and residence. There could be a variety of reasons of it.
- These reasons can be put into two broad categories- **push factors,** which cause people to leave their place of residence of origin; **pull factors**, which attract people from different places.
- In India, people migrate from rural to urban areas mainly due to poverty, high population pressure on the land, lack of basic infrastructural facilities like health care, education, etc.
- Apart from these factors, natural disasters such as, flood, drought, cyclonic storms, earthquake, tsunami, wars and local conflicts also give extra push to migrate.
- On the other hand, there are pull factors which attract people from rural areas to cities. The most important pull factor for the majority of the rural migrants to urban areas is the better opportunities, availability of regular work and relatively higher wages.
- Better opportunities for education, better health facilities and sources of entertainment, etc are also quite important pull factors.
- It can be seen that the reasons for migration of males and females are different. For example, work and employment have remained the main cause for male migration 38% while it is only 3% for the females.
- Contrary to this, about 65% of females move out from their parental houses following their marriage.
- This is the most important cause in the rural areas of India except in Meghalaya where reverse is the case.

Consequences of Migration

Migration is a response to the uneven distribution of opportunities over space. People tend to move from a place of low opportunity and low safety to a place of higher opportunity and better safety.

This in turn, creates both benefits and problems for the areas people migrate from and migrate to.

Consequences can be observed in economic, social, cultural, political and demographic terms.

- **Economic Consequences** A major benefit for the source region is the remittance sent by migrants. Remittances from international migrants are one of the major sources of foreign exchange.
- **Demographic Consequences** Migration leads to the redistribution of the population within a country. Rural urban migration is one of the important factors contributing to the population growth of cities.
- Age and skill selective migration from the rural area have adverse effect on the rural demographic structure.
- **Social Consequences** Migrants act as agents of social change. The new ideas related to new technologies, family planning, girl's education, etc., get diffused from urban to rural areas through them. Migration leads to intermixing of people from diverse cultures.
- **Environmental Consequences** Overcrowding of people due to rural-urban migration has put pressure on the existing social and physical infrastructure in the urban areas. This ultimately leads to unplanned growth of urban settlement and formation of slums shanty colonies.
- Apart from this, due to over-exploitation of natural resources, cities are facing the acute problem of depletion of groundwater, air pollution, disposal of sewage and management of solid wastes.
- **Others Consequences** Migration of 'women' either for education or employment enhances their autonomy and role in the economy but also increases their vulnerability. If remittances are the major benefits of migration from the point of view of the source region, the loss of human resources particularly highly skilled people is the most serious cost.
- The market for advanced skills has become truly a global market and the most dynamic industrial economies are admitting and recruiting significant proportions of the highly trained professionals from poor regions.
- Consequently, the existing under development in the source region gets reinforced.

Tribes of India

- India is the home to large number of indigenous people, who are still untouched by the lifestyle of the modern world with more than 104.2 million. India has the largest population of the tribal people in the world.
- These tribal people are also known as the Adivasi and some of them are still dependent on hunting, agriculture and fishing.
- Some of the major tribal groups in India include Gonds, Santhals, Khasis, Angamis, Bhils, Bhutias and Great Andamanese. All these tribal people have their own culture, tradition, language and lifestyle.

Major Tribal Groups in India (Zone-Wise)

From the point of view of distribution and diversity of the tribal population, India can be divided into seven zones :

- **North Zone** This zone covers Himachal Pradesh, Punjab, Uttarakhand, Sub-Himalayan, Uttar Pradesh and Bihar. The prominent tribes here are Khasi, Tharu, Bhoksa, Bhutias and Gujjars. The major problems of the tribes of this zone are inaccessibility, lack of communication, poverty, illiteracy and land alienation.
- **North-Eastern Zone** This zone includes the seven North-Eastern states and the major tribal groups here are Nagas, Khasi, Garo, Mishmi, Miri, Karbi and the Apatanis.
- These tribes mainly belong to the Mongoloid stock which gives them a distinct ethnic identity. These tribes have a very high rate of literacy and conversions to Christianity, mainly because of the missionary activities during the colonial rule.
- **Central Zone** This zone, which has the maximum tribal concentration, stretches from Southern Madhya Pradesh to South Bihar across Northern Odisha.
- **Southern Zone** This region comprises the Nilgiris together with the adjoining hilly regions in Andhra Pradesh and Karnataka, which are the home land of probably the smallest, the most backward and the most isolated tribal communities on the mainland. Among the prominent tribes of this zone are the Toda, Koya, Chenchu and Allars.
- **Eastern Zone** This zone includes West Bengal, Odisha and tribes such as Paraja, Kondhs, Bondas, Bhumij, Gadabas, Bhutias and Saoras.
- **Western Zone** This zone includes Rajasthan and Gujarat and tribes such as the Bhils, Garasiya and Meenas. The Bhils are regarded as a violent tribe.
- The Meenas are a very advanced and well educated tribe and they have entered in the main stream of the society.
- **Island Region** This zone includes Andaman and Nicobar Islands, Lakshadweep and Daman and Diu. The tribes include the great Andamanese, Sentinelese, Jarawas, Onges, Nicobaris and Shompen.

States/UTs with Maximum Scheduled Tribe Population

State	Population	Percentage (%)
Madhya Pradesh	1,53,16,784	21.1
Maharashtra	1,05,10,213	9.4
Odisha	95,90,756	22.8
Rajasthan	92,38,534	13.5
Gujarat	89,17,174	14.8

States/UTs with Maximum Scheduled Tribe Percentage

State	Percentage (%)
Lakshadweep	94.8
Mizoram	94.4
Nagaland	86.5
Meghalaya	86.1
Arunachal Pradesh	68.8
Manipur	35.1

States/UTs with Minimum Scheduled Tribe Percentage

State	Percentage (%)
Uttar Pradesh	0.6
Tamil Nadu	1.1
Bihar	1.3
Kerala	1.5
Uttarakhand	2.9

Major Tribes of India

Tribe	States	Major Trade
Adi, Apatami	Arunachal Pradesh	Cultivation
Angami, Ao	Nagaland	Cultivation
Badaga	Tamil Nadu	Cultivation
Baiga	Madhya Pradesh, Rajasthan and Gujarat	Cultivation
Bhil	Madhya Pradesh, Gujarat and Rajasthan	Cultivation
Bhotia	Uttarakhand	Shepherding, goat herding and farming
Bhutia	Sikkim	Cultivation
Birhor	Jharkhand	Cultivation
Bodo	Assam	Sericulture
Chenchu	Andhra Pradesh, Odisha	Hunting
Chutia	Assam	Agriculture
Gaddi	Himachal Pradesh	Shepherding
Garo	Meghalaya	Cultivation
Gond	Madhya Pradesh, Odisha, Jharkhand and Andhra Pradesh	Cultivation
Great Andamanese	Andaman Islands	Nomadic hunting, fishing and gathering
Irula	Tamil Nadu	Nomadic gathering
Jaintia	Meghalaya	Agriculture
Jarawa	Little Andamans	Nomadic hunting, fishing and gathering
Kanis	Kerala	Handicraft
Kacharis, Karbi	Assam	Agriculture
Khamti	Arunachal Pradesh	Cultivation

Tribe	States	Major Trade
Khasi	Meghalaya, Assam	Jhum cultivation
Khond	Odisha	Agriculture
Kol	Madhya Pradesh	Farming and forestry
Kota	Tamil Nadu, Karnataka	Artisans
Kuki	Manipur, Assam	Agriculture
Lepcha or Rongpa	Sikkim	Hunting and fishing
Meena	Rajasthan	Agriculture
Miri	Arunachal Pradesh	Agriculture
Mishing	Assam	Agriculture
Muria	Madhya Pradesh	Agriculture
Mikir	Assam	Slash and burn cultivation
Munda	Jharkhand	Cultivation
Oaron	Jharkhand, Odisha	Tea cultivation
Onge	Little Andamans	Hunters and gatherers
Rabha	Assam	Agriculture
Rengma	Nagaland	Jhum cultivation
Santhal	West Bengal, Jharkhand	Hunting, gathering and cultivation
Naga	Nagaland	Cultivation
Tiwa or Lalung	Assam	Cultivation
Khamti	Assam	Agriculture
Dimasas	Assam	Agriculture
Sentinelese	Andaman and Nicobar Island	Hunters and gatherers
Shompen	Great Nicobar Island	Hunters and gatherers
Tagin	Arunachal Pradesh	Weaving
Toda	Tamil Nadu	Cattle herding and dairy work
Urali	Kerala	Agriculture
Zeliang	Nagaland	Weaving

Tribe	States	Major Trade
Agaria	Madhya Pradesh	Agriculture
Saharia	Rajasthan and Madhya Pradesh	Forest gathering and wood cutting
Limbu	Sikkim	Agriculture
Dongria Kondh	Niyamgiri hills of Odisha	Forest gathering
Bonda	Odisha	Agriculture
Changpa	Jammu and Kashmir	Animal rearing
Mishmi	Arunachal Pradesh	Agriculture
Kotwalia	Gujarat	Bamboo handicraft
Hmar	Meghalaya, Mizoram, Assam,Tripura	Handicraft
Pawi	Mizoram	Cultivation

Extra Facts From Tamil Nadu Board and NIOS

- Physiological or Nutritional density is the ratio between total population and total cropped area.
- The total arable land in the world is 13.3% and the nurtitional density of the world is 325 per sq. km of land.
- Eastern Asia including China, Japan and Republic of Korea, Southern Asia comprising India, Bangladesh and Sri Lanka, North-Eastern part of the United States of America, Central and North Western Europe have high density in world.
- Amazon forest region of South America and Congo forest region of Africa, Arctic area of Canada, Greenland and the polar regions, Great deserts of the world i.e. Sahara, Kalahari, Arabia, Great Desert of Australia, Atacama Desert of South America, desert regions of Western United States and Thar Desert of India have low density.
- Australia with an average density of population of 2 persons per sq. km is one of the most sparsely populated countries of the world.

Environment

[SOURCES]

New NCERT Class-VI Chap 5 (Major domains of the Earth),
New NCERT Class-VII Chap 1 (Environment),
New NCERT Class-XI Geography Chap 15 (Life on Earth),
New NCERT, Class-X Scince Chap 13 (Our Environment),
New NCERT Class-XII Biology Chap 12 (Ecosystem),
Tamil Nadu Board (Class XI), NIOS

Environment

- Environment is derived from French word *'Environer/ Environner'* meaning 'neighbourhood'. Environment is our basic life support system. It provides the air we breathe, the water we drink, the food we eat and the land where we live.
- The place, people, things and nature that surround any living organism is called Environment. It is a combination of **natural** and **human-made phenomena**.

Types of Environment

The various types of environment are as follows :

- **Natural Environment** The non-human-made surroundings and conditions in which all living and non-living organisms exist on Earth are referred to as the 'Natural environment'. Water (Hydrosphere), Air (Atmosphere), Land (Lithosphere), Living things (Biosphere) comprises natural environment.
- **Man-made Environment** The surroundings created by humans to provide facilities for satisfying human requirements are referred to as a Human-made or Man-made environment. Man-made environment is comprised of buildings, parks, bridges, road, industries, monuments, etc.
- **Social or Cultural Environment** Humans interact with their surroundings and adapt them to suit their needs. Adapting to their circumstances was a natural process for early humans. Community, religion, educational, economic and political situation constitute social or cultural environment.

Components of Environment

There are two components of environment :

- **Abiotic Environment** It is also known as Physico-chemical factors. It includes all the physical and chemical aspects of an ecosystem. It is non-living parts of the environment that have influence on living organism.
  Abiotic factors include rainfall, temperature, sunlight, atmospheric humidity, soil conditions, inorganic substances (carbon dioxide, water, nitrogen, calcium, phosphorus, potassium, etc.). All the factors are interrelated to each other.
- **Biotic Environment** It is known as the world of living organisms. They are producers, consumers and decomposers. Biotic factors include the producers, the consumers (primary, secondary, tertiary) and the decomposers.
  The producers include all the green plants, which manufacture their own food through photosynthesis.

Parts of Environment

The various parts of environment are as follows :

Biosphere

- The Biosphere (Bios means life) is the narrow zone where we find land, water and air together, which contains all forms of life.
- All the living organisms including humans are linked to each other and to the biosphere for survival.

- The organisms in the biosphere may broadly be divided into the plant kingdom and the animal kingdom.
- Many ecologists regard the entire biosphere as a Global ecosystem, as a composite of all local ecosystems on Earth.
- The annual net primary productivity of the whole biosphere is approximately 170 billion tonns (dry weight) of organic matter.

Lithosphere

- The solid portion of the Earth on which we live is called the Lithosphere (*Lithos* means Stone).
- It comprises the rocks of the Earth's crust and the thin layers of soil that contains nutrient elements which sustain organisms.
- The Earth's surface is divided into two sections.
- The continents are the massive landmasses and the ocean basins are the vast bodies of water.
- Lithosphere is the domain that provides us forests, grasslands for grazing, land for agriculture and human settlements. It is also a source of mineral wealth.

Continents

- There are seven major continents. These are separated by large water bodies.
- These continents are-Asia, Europe, Africa, North America, South America, Australia and Antarctica.
- **Asia** is the largest continent. It covers about one third of the total land area of the Earth. The continent lies in the Eastern Hemisphere.

  The Tropic of Cancer passes through this continent. Asia is separated from Europe by the ural mountains on the West.
- **Europe** is much smaller than Asia. The continent lies to the West of Asia. The Arctic Circle passes through it. It is bound by water bodies on three sides. Look at the map of the world and locate it.
- **Africa** is the second largest continent after Asia. The Equator or 0° latitude runs almost through the middle of the continent. A large part of Africa lies in the Northern Hemisphere.
- **North America** is the third largest continent of the world. It is linked to South America by a very narrow world. It is linked to South America by a very narrow strip of land called the Isthmus of Panama. The continent lies completely in the Northern and Western Hemisphere.

Hydrosphere

- Water covers a very big area of the Earth's surface and this area is called the Hydrosphere. The Hydrosphere comprises water in all its forms, i.e., ice, water and water vapour. More than 71% of the Earth is covered with water. That is why it is called the **Blue planet**.
- Oceans are the major part of hydrosphere. They are all interconnected. The ocean waters are always moving. The three chief movements of ocean waters are the waves, the tides and the ocean currents.
- The five major oceans are Pacific Ocean, Atlantic Ocean, Indian Ocean, Southern Ocean and Arctic Ocean, in order of their size.
  - The **Pacific ocean** is the largest ocean. It is spread over one-third of the Earth. **Mariana Trench**, the deepest part of the Earth, lies in the Pacific Ocean.
  - The **Atlantic ocean** is the second largest ocean in the world. It is 'S' shaped. It is flanked by the North and South America on the Western side and Europe and Africa on the Eastern side.
  - The **Indian ocean** is the only ocean named after a country, that is, India. The shape of ocean is almost triangular. In the North, it is bound by Asia, in the West by Africa and in the East by Australia.
  - **Southern ocean** is comprises the Southernmost waters of the world ocean. It is also known as **Antarctic ocean.**
  - The **Arctic ocean** is located within the Arctic circle and surrounds the North pole. It is connected with the Pacific ocean by a narrow stretch of shallow water known as **Bering strait**.

Atmosphere

- The Earth is surrounded by a layer of gas called the Atmosphere. This thin blanket of air is an integral and important aspect of the planet. The density of the atmosphere varies with height.
- It is maximum at the sea level and decreases rapidly as we go up. The temperature also decreases as we go upwards. The atmosphere exerts pressure on the Earth. This varies from place-to-place.
- Some areas experience high pressure and some areas low pressure.
- Air moves from high pressure to low pressure. Moving air is known as **Wind.** The atmosphere is divided into five layers based on composition, temperature and other properties.
- These layers starting from Earth's surface are called the **Troposphere**, the **Stratosphere**, the **Mesosphere**, the **Thermosphere** and the **Exosphere**.

Layers of Atmosphere

Troposphere	The troposphere is the Earth's atmosphere's lowest layer. The troposphere contains the majority of the atmosphere's mass (about 75-80%). The troposphere is home to the majority of clouds and it is also where practically all weather happens.
Stratosphere	The stratosphere is the second layer of the atmosphere of the Earth. The stratosphere extends from the top of the troposphere to about 50 km (31 miles) above the ground. The ozone layer is found within this layer.
Mesosphere	The mesosphere is a layer of the atmosphere that surrounds the Earth. The mesosphere is located between the stratosphere and the thermosphere. It reaches a height of 50 to 85 kilometres (31 to 53 miles) above our Earth. The temperature drops with altitude in the mesosphere.
Thermosphere	The thermosphere is the layer of the Earth's atmosphere that lies just above the mesosphere and under the exosphere. Because of the absorption of highly intense solar radiation, the temperature of the atmosphere rises with height.
Exosphere	The exosphere is the topmost part of the Earth's atmosphere, which progressively vanishes into space. The thermosphere is the layer directly beneath the exosphere and the thermopause is the barrier between the two.

Human Impact on Environment

The impact of human on environment can be broadly divided into two categories :

Direct Impact

- Direct or intentional impacts are preplanned and premeditated because man is aware of the consequences, both positive and negative of any programme which can change or modify natural environment for the economic development of the region concerned.
- Such changes include land use changes, construction, nuclear programmes, etc.
- The direct impacts are noticeable within short period and may continue to affect the environment for long time. These effects are reversible.

Indirect Impact

- The indirect impacts of man ,on the environment are not premeditated and planned. e.g., activities which are directed to accelerate the pace of economic growth especially industrial development.
- The indirect impacts are experienced after long time.
- Majority of the indirect impacts of human activities on the environment are related to pollution and environmental degradation.

Impact of Environment on Human

- The direct impact of climatic factor on different races can be seen on the colour of skin, hair, nose, cheeks, shape of head, etc.
- Some of the human geographers established a close relationship with the weather conditions and crimes like suicide, rape and murder.
- Some scholars have also attempted to measure the suitability of an environment of human activity, and his comfort and discomfort.
- For example, the people of Central Asia region depend on livestock, the people of Kalahari and Congo basin depend on hunting and conventional agriculture, and the people of polar region depend on hunting and other activities for their subsistence.

28

Ecology, Ecosystem and Biome

[SOURCES]

New NCERT Class-VI Chap 5 (Major Domains of the Earth), New NCERT Class-VII Chap 1 (Environment), New NCERT Class-XI Geography Chap 15 (Life on Earth), New NCERT Class-X Science Chap 13 (Our Environment), New NCERT Class-XII Biology Chap 12 (Ecosystem), Tamil Nadu Board (Class XI), NIOS

Ecology

- The term 'Ecology' is derived from the Greek word '*Oikos*' meaning 'house', combined with the word '*Logy*' meaning the 'science of ' or 'the study of '.
- In 1866, the ecology was first used by the German Zoologist **Ernst Haeckel**, in his book *General Morphology* of *Organism*.
- **Ecology** is the study of the Earth as a '**household**', of plants, human beings, animals and micro-organisms. They all live together as interdependent components.
- It is a study of interactions between life forms (biotic) and the physical environment (abiotic).

Ecological Factors

The living organisms are influenced by a large number of environmental factors. These environmental factors are known as ecological factors or eco factors. These factors may be biotic (living) or abiotic (non-living).

The ecological factors are broadly divided into four parts:

- **Climatic Factors** These include light, temperature, rainfall, wind, humidity and pH. A variation in one or more of these factors affects the distribution and lifestyle of organisms.
- **Topographic Factors** These include altitude, slope and direction of mountain, exposure and valley.
- **Edaphic Factors** These include structure, formation and characteristics of different types of soils.
- **Biotic Factors** These are derived from the interactions between different species of living organisms (intra-specific as well as inter-specific).

Laws of Ecology

Barry Commoner has given some ecological laws which are followed by the environment and its functioning. These laws are as follows :

- **First Law of Ecology** 'Everything is connected (directly or indirectly) to everything else, we are all in it together.' It means that every component of ecological system is interrelated with each other.
- **Second Law of Ecology** 'Everything must go somewhere'. This law means that in nature, there is no such thing as waste. Everything can be used for various purposes. e.g., animals release carbon dioxide as a respiratory waste; this is an essential nutrient for green plants.
- **Third Law of Ecology** 'There is no such thing as a free lunch.' This law states that everything in the ecological system (ecosystem) has some cost and their payment cannot be avoided, it can only be delayed.
- **Fourth Law of Ecology** 'Nature knows best.' It means that any major man-made change in a natural system is likely to be detrimental to that system. The ecosystem do evolve with time and in this process, the ecosystem moulds itself to function in a best possible manner.

Levels of Organisation in Ecology

- The concept of levels of organisation are visualised as an ecological spectrum and as extended ecological hierarchy.
- **Hierarchy** means 'an arrangement into a graded series'. Interaction with the physical environment (energy and matter) at each level produces characteristic functional systems.
- The various levels of organisms are discussed below :

Organism or Individual

- It is a group of genetically linked individuals that can breed to generate fruitful offspring.
- Ecology tries to understand how different organisms are adapted to their environment in terms of survival and reproduction.
- Individuals are not considered members of the same species, if they are unable to generate offspring capable of having children.
- The distinct role and position of and Organism in its environment is called its Niche.
- By this, each organism tolerate various conditions, utilises various resources, etc.

Habitat

- A habitat is an ecological or environmental area that is inhabited by a particular species of animal, plant, or other organisms.There are four important habitats found on the Earth i.e., land, freshwater, estuary and ocean.
- The population in a habitat refers to the number of plants and animals living in that habitat. In present time, there is loss of biodiversity due to the loss of habitat of plants and animals, which is caused due to anthropogenic factors. Hence, in order to protect the biodiversity and ecosystem, the habitat must be protected.

Population

- Population consists of all organisms of plants and species inhabiting in a given area. For example, all individuals of tiger and lion in an area constitute their population.

Community

- Interdependence and interactions among populations of different species in a habitat lead to community organisation.
- This is a collection of plant, animal, bacterial and fungal populations that reside in a certain area and interact with one another.

Ecosystem

- It is a system formed by the interaction of all living organisms with the physical and chemical factors of the environment in which they live.
- All plants, animals and human beings are dependent on their immediate surroundings. Often, they are also interdependent on each other.
- This relation between the living organisms, as well as the relation between the organisms and their surroundings form an **ecosystem.**
- There is an ecosystem of large rain forest, grassland, desert, mountains, lake, river, ocean and even a small pond.

Components of Ecosystem

The components of ecosystems can be grouped into two categories: Biotic and Abiotic.

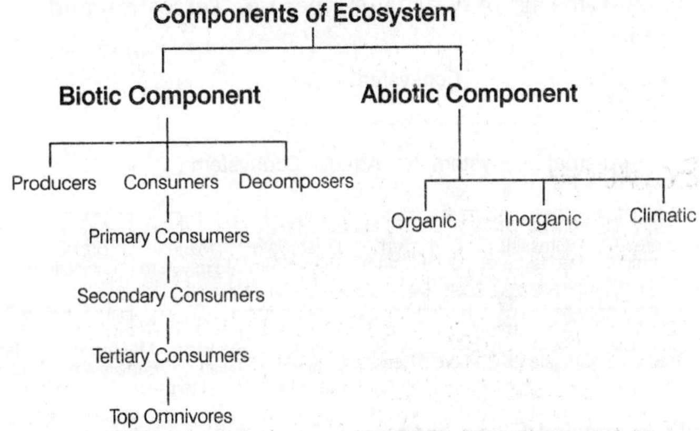

Biotic Component

- Biotic component can be further divided into **Producers, Consumers** and **Decomposers.**
  - The producers include all the green plants, which manufacture their own food through **photosynthesis.**
  - The **primary consumers** include herbivorous animals like deer, goats, mice and all plant-eating animals. The **carnivores** include all the flesh-eating animals like snakes, tigers and lions.
  - **Decomposers** are those that feed on dead organisms (for example, scavengers like vultures and crows) and further breaking down of the dead matter by other decomposing agents like bacteria and various microorganisms.
- The **producers** are consumed by the primary consumers whereas the primary consumers are, in turn, being eaten by the secondary **consumers.**

- The **secondary** consumers are consumed by the tertiary consumers.
- The decomposers feed on the dead at each and every level. They change them into various substances such as nutrients, organic and inorganic salts essential for soil fertility.

Abiotic Components

- These are the non-living components, e.g., air, water, soil, suspended particulate matter, etc.
- Abiotic components of an ecosystem include :
  - **Inorganic substances** Carbon dioxide, nitrogen, oxygen, water and elements involved in material cycles.
  - **Organic chemicals** Protein, carbohydrates, lipid etc.
  - **Climate factors** Light, temperature, pressure, humidity, etc.

Types of Ecosystem

Ecosystems are of two major types i.e., Terrestrial and Aquatic.

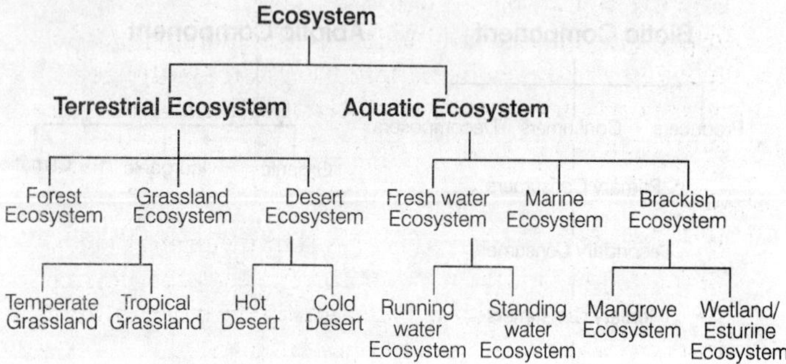

Terrestrial Ecosystem

- Terrestrial ecosystem can be found anywhere apart from heavily saturated places.
- These are broadly classified into forest ecosystem, grassland ecosystem and desert ecosystem.

Forest Ecosystem

- Forests represent the largest and most ecologically complex ecosystem. These are home to a large variety of trees, plants, mammals, reptiles, amphibians, invertebrates, insects and microorganisms which vary depending on the zone's climate.
- The density of living organism in forest ecosystem is very high. Forest ecosystems are further divided into the following categories:
  - **Tropical Rainforest** They are one of the most ecologically rich of the world's forests. These forests are vertically layered with dense vegetation growth. Each layer is shelter to different types of animals.
  - Broadleaf evergreen trees are dominant. Animal diversity is also higher than in any other terrestrial biome.
  - **Tropical Deciduous Forests** These are normally found in the regions of monsoon climate. The diversity of *flora* is far less in tropical deciduous forest than the tropical evergreen rainforest. Sal and teak are very common trees. These forests represent the largest number of domesticated mammals.
  - **Temperate Deciduous Forest** share close resemblance with Taiga forests and are found in areas with a milder, shorter winter season. In addition to evergreens, trees in the temperate forest include maple, elm, oak, cedar and other trees, which shed their leaves in the fall.
  - **Boreal or Taiga Forests** Cold regions with high rainfall, strong seasonal climate with long winters and short summers are home to boreal coniferous forest. These forests are dominated by cone-bearing trees such as pine, spruce, fir and hemlock.

Grassland Ecosystem

- Grasslands are unaltered areas of land, where grass is the dominant plant life, as opposed to other terrestrial ecosystems, where trees are predominant vegetation.
- Grasslands are located in both tropical and temperate regions of the world. Grasslands are classified into two main categories:
  - **Temperate Grassland** Major temperate grasslands include Velds of Africa, Pampas of South America, Steppes of Eurasia and Prairies of North America. Prairies are generally humid and are densely covered with tall grasses. Steppe grasses are generally shorter than prairie grassland.
  - **Tropical Grassland** These grasslands are located near the Equator, between the tropics. They cover much of Africa as well as large areas of Australia, South America and India. Tropical grasslands are dominated by grasses, often 3 to 6 feet tall at maturity. Tropical Savanna are most ecologically diverse grassland. Savanna plant life is highly adapted to the hot and dry climate.

Desert Ecosystem

- This ecosystem covers around one-fifth of the Earth's surface and are found in areas of water deficit, *Flora* and *Fauna* are scarce and poorly developed due to high temperature, low water availability and intense sunlight.
- The vegetation is mainly shrubs, bushes, grasses and rare trees. Plants have modified stems and leaves to conserve water. This ecosystem is divided into two types:

- **Hot Desert** These are caused by dry air and low precipitation due to presence in sub-tropical high pressure cell. A few of the sub-tropical deserts like Atacama, Arizona, Great Victoria are along the sea coast and are influenced by desiccating effect of the cold offshore ocean currents.
- **Cold Desert** Cold deserts have hot summers but extremely cold winters. These deserts are found in high, flat areas called Plateaus, mountainous areas in temperate region of the world. The combined effect of interior location and rain-shadow positioning produces the cold deserts of the Great Basin of Western-North America, Patagonia, Ladakh, Central Asia, Gobi and North-Western China.

Aquatic Ecosystem

Ecosystem consisting of water as the main habitat are known as aquatic ecosystems. Aquatic ecosystem is broadly divided into following types:

Marine Ecosystem

- Marine ecosystems are the biggest ecosystems covering around 71% of the Earth's surface.
- This ecosystem consists of oceanic, inter-tidal zones and also estuaries, coral reefs and salt marshes.

Lakes Ecosystem

- Lakes are bodies of non-marine standing water connected by water flow and aerial inputs to their surrounding landscapes. While it can exist for centuries, other inland bodies of water such as ponds tend to dry up fairly quicker.
- Lakes and ponds like the oceans, are divided into separate zones, which are defined by their distance from the shore. The lake sediment plays an important role as habitat for rooted plants and animals.

Wetland Ecosystem

- Other areas of still waters or wetlands, such as glades and marshes support a large variety of aquatic *flora* and *fauna*.
- Aside from plants such as sedges and pond lilies, the wetlands also support a few types of trees, such as cypress, which are highly adapted to the high humidity of these regions. The wetlands are rich in life forms, from reptiles to mammals, to amphibians and birds, to hundreds of insects.

Factors Affecting Ecosystem

The various factors affecting ecosystem are temperature, water, sunlight, soil, etc.

Temperature

- It is the most important ecologically relevant environmental factor.
- The average temperature on land varies seasonally, decreases progressively from the Equator towards the poles and from plains to the mountain tops.
- It ranges from sub-zero levels in polar areas and high altitudes to >50° C in tropical deserts in summer.

Water

- It is another the most important factor influencing the life of organisms.
- The productivity and distribution of plants is also heavily dependent on water. For aquatic organisms the quality (chemical composition, pH) of water becomes important.
- The salt concentration is less than 5 in inland waters, 30-35 in the sea and > 100 in some hypersaline lagoons.

Sunlight

- Since, plants produce food through photosynthesis, a process which is only possible when sunlight is available as a source of energy.
- Many species of small plants (herbs and shrubs) growing in forests are adapted to photosynthesise optimally under very low light conditions as they are overshadowed by tall trees.

Soil

- The nature and properties of soil in different places vary; it is dependent on the climate, the weathering process, whether soil is transported or sedimentary and how soil development occurred.
- Various characteristics of the soil such as soil composition, grain size and aggregation determine the percolation and water holding capacity of the soils.
- These characteristics along with parameters such as pH, Mineral composition and topography determine a large extent the vegetation in any area.
- This in turn dictates the type of animals that can be supported.

Functioning of Ecosystem

The components of the ecosystem are seen to function as a unit when considering the following aspects:

Productivity

- A constant input of solar energy is the basic requirement for any ecosystem to function and sustain. **Primary production** is defined as the amount of biomass or organic matter produced per unit area over a time period by plants during photosynthesis.
- It is expressed in terms of weight (gm^{-2}) or energy (kcal m^{-2}). The rate of biomass production is called Productivity.

- **Gross primary productivity** of an ecosystem is the rate of production of organic matter during photosynthesis.
- Gross primary productivity minus respiration losses (R), is the **Net Primary Productivity** (NPP).
- Secondary productivity is defined as the rate of formation of new organic matter by consumers.
- The annual net primary productivity of the whole biosphere is approximately 170 billion tonns (dry weight) of organic matter.
- Of this, despite occupying about 70 percent of the surface, the productivity of the oceans are only 55 billion tonns.

Decomposition

- Decomposers break down complex organic matter into inorganic substances like carbon dioxide, water and nutrients and the process is called Decomposition.
- Dead plant remains such as leaves, bark, flowers and dead remain of animals, including faecal matter, constitute detritus, which is the raw material for decomposition.
- The important steps in the process of decomposition are fragmentation, leaching, catabolism, humification and mineralisation.
- Decomposition is largely an oxygen-requiring process. The rate of decomposition is controlled by chemical composition of detritus and climatic factors.
- Decomposition rate is slower if detritus is rich in lignin and chitin, and quicker, if detritus is rich in nitrogen and water-soluble substances like sugars.
- Warm and moist environment favour decomposition whereas low temperature and anaerobiosis inhibit decomposition resulting in build up of organic materials.

Energy Flow

- The Sun is the source of all our energy.
- It is a continuously exploding hydrogen bomb, where hydrogen is converted to helium with the release of energy.
- There are laws of thermodynamics governing the relationships between different forms of energy. These are as follows:
  - **First Law of Thermodynamics** Energy can be changed from one form to another, but it can't be destroyed or created. The total amount of energy and matter in the universe remains constant, energy is always conserved.

    The energy of an isolated system (environment) is constant. This is also known an the **Law of Conservation of Energy**.
  - **Second Law of Thermodynamics** It states that 'in all energy exchange, if no energy enters or leaves the system, the potential energy of the state will always be less than that of the initial state.' It is also referred to as **entropy**.

Energy Flow in an Ecosystem

- The flow of energy from one trophic level to another within an ecosystem is called **Energy flow**.
- It flows from producers to subsequent tropic level and is unidirectional in nature. Energy decreases from the first trophic level upwards due to loss of energy in the form of heat at each trophic level.

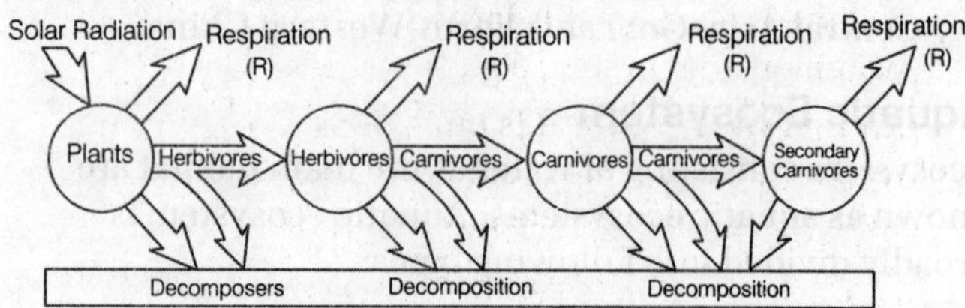

Energy Flow in an Ecosystem

Nutrient Cycle

- The nutrients are never lost from the ecosystems, rather they are recycled time and again indefinitely.
- The movement of nutrient elements through the various components of an ecosystem is called Nutrient cycle.
- Another name of nutrient cycling is **biogeochemical cycles** (*Bio*: living organism, *Geo*: rocks, air, water). Nutrient cycles are of two types i.e., gaseous and sedimentary.
- The reservoir for gaseous type of nutrient cycle (e.g., nitrogen, carbon cycle) exists in the atmosphere and for the sedimentary cycle (e.g., sulphur and phosphorus cycle), the reservoir is located in Earth's crust.
- Environmental factors, e.g., soil, moisture, pH, temperature, etc. regulate the rate of release of nutrients into the atmosphere.
- The function of the reservoir is to meet with the deficit which occurs due to imbalance in the rate of influx and efflux.

Ecological Pyramids

- Ecological Pyramid refers to relationship between organisms at different trophic levels.
- This, relationship is expressed in terms of number, biomass or energy.
- The base of each pyramid represents the producers or the first trophic level while the apex represents tertiary or top level consumer.

The three types of ecological pyramids that are usually studied as follows :

Pyramid of Biomass

- Biomass is renewable organic (living) material. A pyramid of biomass is a representation of the amount of energy contained in biomass, at different trophic levels for a particular time.
- It is measured in grams per square metre or calories per square metre. This demonstrates that the amount of matter lost between trophic levels. There are two types of biomass pyramids i.e., tupright and inverted.
  - An **upright pyramid** is one where the combined weight of producers is larger than the combined weight of consumers, e.g., forest ecosystem.
  - An **inverted pyramid** is one where the combined weight of producers is smaller than the combined weight of consumers, e.g., an aquatic ecosystem.

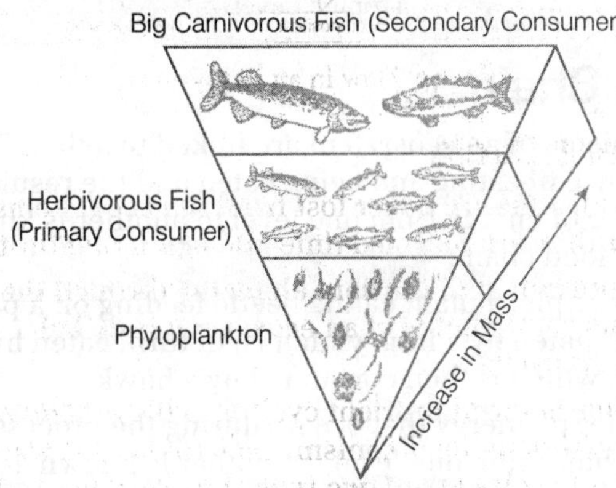

Inverted Pyramid of Biomass

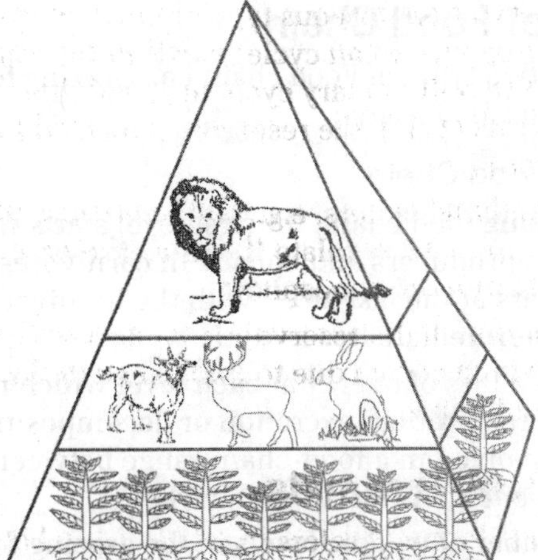
Upright Pyramid of Biomass

Pyramid of Numbers

- The pyramid of numbers represents the number of organisms at each trophic level. This pyramid deals with the relationships between the number of primary consumers, secondary consumers, tertiary consumers and so forth.
- Upright, partly upright and inverted are the three types of pyramids of numbers.
  - An aquatic ecosystem and grassland ecosystem are an example of **upright pyramid** where the number of organisms becomes fewer and fewer higher up in the pyramid.
  - A forest ecosystem is an example of a partially **upright pyramid**, as fewer producers support more primary consumers, but there are less secondary and tertiary consumers.
  - An **inverted pyramid** of numbers is one where the number of organisms depending on the lower levels grows going towards the apex, e.g., a parasitic food chain.

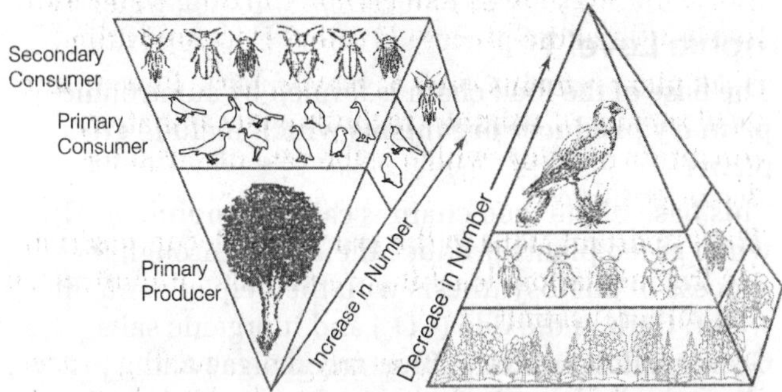

Inverted Pyramid of Number Upright Pyramid of Number

Pyramid of Energy

- The pyramid of energy represents the total amount of energy consumed at each trophic level.
- An energy pyramid is always upright as the energy available for utilisation in the above levels is less than the energy available in the lower levels.
- This happens because during energy transfer from lower to higher levels, some energy is always lost. Energy is also lost at every level in the form of heat, respiration, etc.

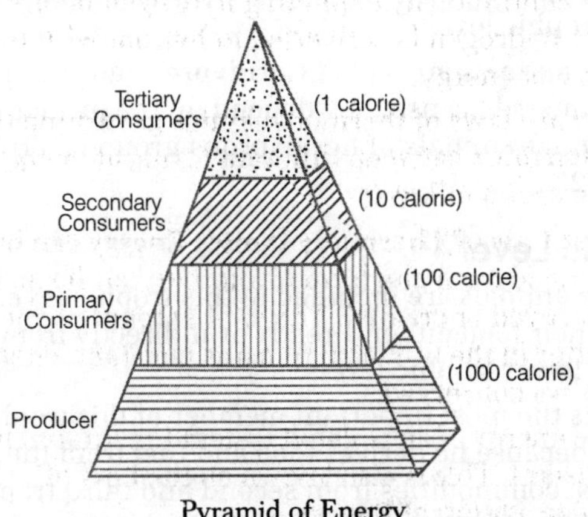

Pyramid of Energy

Limitations of Ecological Pyramids

- It does not take into account the same species belonging to two or more trophic levels. It assumes a simple food chain, something that almost never exists in nature.
- It does not accommodate a food web. Moreover, saprophytes are not given any place in ecological pyramids even though they play a vital role in the ecosystem.

Trophic Level

The trophic level of an organism is the position it occupies in a food chain. It is a point where food energy is transferred from one group of organisms to the other group. The chain of transfer of food energy from one group of organisms to other group is called **Food chain**.

Trophic Level 1

- The base of the food chain is formed by autotrophic **primary producer organisms** which include green plants.
- This base of the food chain is called **Trophic level** 1 when green plants produce their food through the process of photosynthesis with the help of sunlight, water, Carbon dioxide (CO_2) and inorganic salts. Green-yellow bacteria, Blue-green algae and phytoplankton are included under this.

Trophic Level 2

- The organisms, who do not produce their food themselves but depend on primary producers for their food, are included in **Trophic level 2.**
- These organisms are animals and are called **primary consumers.** They are basically grazers like sheep, cows, rabbits, goats, deer, etc.

Trophic Level 3

- The animals, who depend on animals, mainly herbivorous animals, for their food, are included in this trophic level 3.
- These animals are called **Carnivores** and secondary consumers because they depend on the primary consumer animals of herbivorous group of Trophic level 2.

Trophic Level 4

- Those animals are included in this trophic level which take their food either directly or indirectly from all the three lower trophic levels.
- Man is the most important member of this trophic level because he derives food and fuel from the given plants, commodities from second and third trophic levels. Such animals are called **Omnivores.**

Decomposers also derive their energy from all the trophic levels.

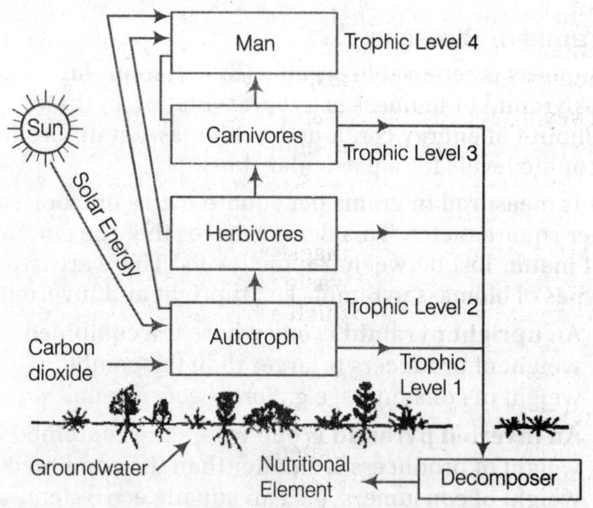

Trophic Level

Food Chain

- Organisms of an ecosystem are linked together. The sequence of eating and being eaten and the resultant transfer of energy from one level to another is known as the food chain.
- For example, a plant eating beetle feeding on a paddy stalk is eaten by a frog, which is, in turn, eaten by a snake, which is then consumed by a hawk.
- Transfer of energy that occurs during the process of a food chain from one level to another is known as **Flow of energy.**

Types of Food Chain

There are two types of Food chain i.e., Grazing food chain and Detritus food chain :

Grazing Food Chain

- In a grazing food chain, the first level starts with plants as producers and ends with carnivores as consumers at the last level, with the herbivores being at the intermediate level.
- There is a loss of energy at each level which may be through respiration, excretion or decomposition. The levels involved in a food-chain range between three to five and energy is lost at each level.
- The number of trophic levels in the grazing food chain is restricted as the transfer of energy follows 10% law – only 10% of the energy is transferred to each trophic level from the lower trophic level.

Grass ---------> Goat ---------> Man --------->
(Producer) (Primary Consumer) (Secondary Consumer)

Grasing Food Chain

Detritus Food Chain

- The Detritus Food Chain (DFC) begins with dead organic matter. It is made up of decomposers which are heterotrophic organisms, mainly fungi and bacteria.
- They meet their energy and nutrient requirements by degrading dead organic matter or detritus.
- These are also known as **Saprotrophs** (sapro means: to decompose).
- Decomposers secrete digestive enzymes that breakdown dead and waste materials into simple, inorganic materials, which are subsequently absorbed by them.

Food Web

- Food chains are not isolated from one another, rather they get interlocked with one another. This interconnecting network of species is known as **Food web.**
- Food web provides more chances of survival to species as compared to food chain because more food alternatives are available. A food web represents a more holistic view of energy transfer in the ecosystem compared to food chain.

Ecological Niche

- The term 'Niche' is used in ecology to define the role that an organism plays in a group. The physical and environmental characteristics of a species and its interactions (like predation or competition) with other species make up a species niche.
- Ecological niche is a very basic and fundamental ecological term that encompasses all interactions between a species and its biotic and abiotic environment.

Biogeochemical Cycles

- The transfer of nutrients and other elements between biotic and abiotic forces is referred to as biogeochemical cycles. Bio refers to living organisms and geo to rocks, soil, air and water of the Earth.
- There are two types of biogeochemical cycles i.e., the gaseous and the sedimentary cycle.

Gaseous Cycles

It is classified into four types. These are as follows:

Nitrogen Cycle

- Nitrogen is a major constituent of the atmosphere comprising about 78% of the atmospheric gases. It is also an essential constituent of different organic compounds such as the amino acids, nucleic acids, proteins, vitamins and pigments.
- Generally, nitrogen is usable only after it is fixed. 90% of fixed nitrogen is biological.
- Nitrogen can also be fixed in the atmosphere by lightning and cosmic radiation. In the oceans, some marine animals can fix it.
- After atmospheric nitrogen has been fixed into an available form, green plants can assimilate it.
- Herbivorous animals feeding on plants, in turn, consume some of it.
- Dead plants and animals, excretion of nitrogenous wastes is converted into nitrites by the action of bacteria present in the soil.
- Some bacteria can even convert nitrites into nitrates that can be used again by green plants.
- There are still other types of bacteria capable of converting nitrates into free nitrogen, a process known as **Denitrification.**

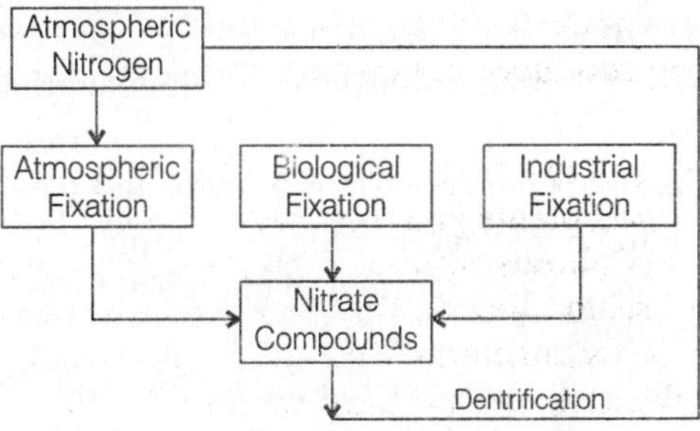

Nitrogen Cycle

Carbon Cycle

- Carbon is one of the basic elements of all living organisms. It forms the basic constituent of all the organic compounds.
- The carbon cycle is mainly the conversion of carbon dioxide. This conversion is initiated by the fixation of carbon dioxide from the atmosphere through **photosynthesis.**
- Such conversion results in the production of carbohydrate, glucose that may be converted to other organic compounds such as sucrose, starch, cellulose, etc.
- During this process, more carbon dioxide is generated and is released through its leaves or roots during the day.
- The remaining carbohydrates not being utilised by the plant become part of the plant tissue.
- Plant tissues are either being eaten by the herbivorous animals or get decomposed by the micro organisms.
- The herbivores convert some of the consumed carbohydrates into carbon dioxide for release into the air through respiration.

- The microorganisms decompose the remaining carbohydrates after the animal dies.
- The carbohydrates that are decomposed by the microorganisms then get oxidised into carbon dioxide and are returned to the atmosphere.

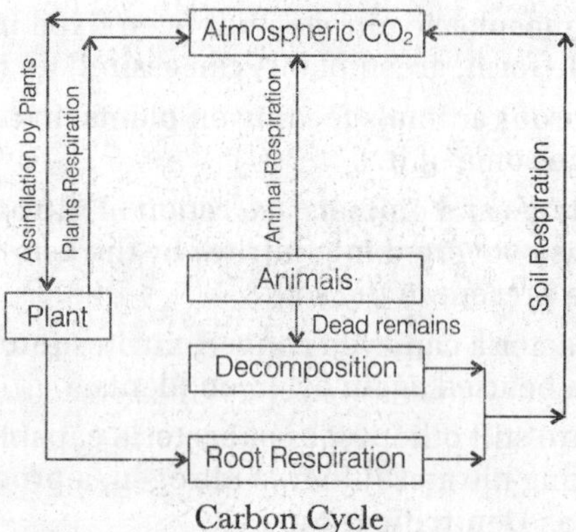

Carbon Cycle

Oxygen Cycle

- Oxygen is the main by-product of photosynthesis.
- It is involved in the oxidation of carbohydrates with the release of energy, carbon dioxide and water.
- The cycling of oxygen is a highly complex process. Oxygen occurs in a number of chemical forms and combinations.
- It combines with nitrogen to form nitrates and with many other minerals and elements to form various oxides such as the iron oxide, aluminium oxide and others.
- Much of oxygen is produced from the decomposition of water molecules by sunlight during photosynthesis and is released in the atmosphere through transpiration and respiration processes of plants.

Water Cycle

- All living organisms, the atmosphere and the lithosphere maintain between them circulation of water in solid, liquid or gaseous form referred to as the water or hydrologic cycle.
- It also refers to the continuous exchange of water between the oceans, atmosphere, land surface and subsurface and the organisms.

Sedimentary Cycles

- Sedimentary cycle refers to circulation of minerals like phosphorus, calcium and magnesium.
- These elements normally do not cycle through the atmosphere, but follow a basic pattern of flow through erosion, sedimentation, mountain building, volcanic activity and biological transport through the excreta of marine birds.
- Phosphorus and sulphur cycles are discussed below :

Phosphorus Cycle

- Phosphorus is a major constituent of biological membranes, nucleic acids and cellular energy transfer systems. Many animals also need large quantities of this element to make shells, bones and teeth.
- The natural reservoir of phosphorus is rock, which contains phosphorus in the form of phosphates. When rocks are weathered, minute amounts of these phosphates dissolve in soil solution and are absorbed by the roots of the plants.
- Herbivores and other animals obtain this element from plants. The waste products and the dead organisms are decomposed by phosphate-soluble bacteria that release phosphorus.

Sulphur Cycle

- Sulphur is locked in organic (coal, oil and peat) and inorganic (pyrite rock and sulphur rock) deposits in the form of sulphates, sulphides and organic sulphur in the soil and sediments.
- It is delivered to terrestrial and aquatic habitats in salt solution by weathering of rocks, erosional runoff and decomposition of organic materials.
- Sulphur enters the atmosphere from a variety of sources, including volcanic eruptions, fossil fuel combustion, ocean surface emissions and decomposition gases.
- Except for two of its constituents, hydrogen sulphide (H_2S) and sulphur dioxide (SO_2), which add a gaseous component to the sulphur cycle's usual sedimentary cycle, the sulphur cycle is primarily sedimentary.

Bioindicators

- Bioindicators are biological processes, species or groups that are used to monitor environmental quality and how it changes over time.
- Because of their moderate tolerance to environmental variability, bioindicator species effectively indicate the state of the ecosystem.

Ecological Succession

- All communities have one thing in common: their makeup and structure are always changing in response to changing environmental conditions. This change is orderly and sequential, parallel with the changes in the physical environment.
- These changes lead finally to a community that is in near equilibrium with the environment and that is called a **Climax community**.
- The gradual and fairly predictable change in the species composition of a given area is called **Ecological succession**.
- The entire sequence of communities that successively change in a given area are called **Sere(s)**.

- The individual transitional communities are termed **seral stages** or **seral communities.**
- In the successive seral stages, there is a change in the diversity of species of organisms, increase in the number of species and organisms as well as an increase in the total biomass.

Types of Ecological Succession

- Succession is a process that starts in an area where no living organisms are there – these could be areas where no living organisms ever existed or in areas that somehow, lost all the living organisms that existed there.
- The former is called **Primary succession**, while the latter is termed **secondary succession**.

Primary Succession

- Primary succession occurs on newly cooled lava, bare rock, newly created pond or reservoir.
- The establishment of a new biotic community is generally slow. Before a biotic community of diverse organisms can become established, there must be soil.
- In primary succession in water, the pioneers are the small phytoplankton's, which are replaced with time by rooted-submerged plants, rooted-floating angiosperms followed by free-floating plants, then reed-swamp, marsh-meadow, scrub and finally the trees.

Secondary Succession

- Secondary succession begins in areas where natural biotic communities have been destroyed such as in abandoned farm lands, burned or cut forests, lands that have been flooded.
- In secondary succession, the species that invade depend on the condition of the soil, availability of water, the environment, etc. Since, soil is already there, the rate of succession is much faster and hence, climax is also reached more quickly.

Succession of Plants

- Based on the nature of the habitat – whether it is water (or very wet areas) or it is on very dry areas- succession of plants is called **Hydrarch** or **xerarch**, respectively.
  - **Hydrarch succession** takes place in wet areas and the successional series progress from hydric to the mesic conditions.
  - As against this, **xerarch succession** takes place in dry areas and the series progress from xeric to mesic conditions.
- Both hydrarch and xerarch successions lead to medium water conditions (mesic) – neither too dry (**xeric**) nor too wet (**hydric**).
- The species that invade a bare area are called **Pioneer species.**
- In primary succession on rocks these are usually lichens which are able to secrete acids to dissolve rock, helping in weathering and soil formation.

Factors of Ecological Succession

The factors responsible for ecological succession are as follows :

- **Climatic Factors** Both macro and micro-climate are responsible for ecological succession.
- **Biotic Factors** Plants and animals are included in this factor.
- **Physical Factors** Factors like slope and structure are also important determinants of succession.
- **Soil Factor** It includes soil composition and soil structure.

Stages of Succession

- **Nudation** This is the development of a bare area without any form of life. The cause of nudation may be :
  - Topographic (gravity, water, mine),
  - Climatic (glaciers, hailstorm, frost, fire),
  - Biotic (man, fungi, viruses).
- **Invasion** This is the successful establishment of a species in a bare area. This whole process is completed in following stages:
  - **Migration dispersal** Seeds, spores, propagules of a species reach the bar area due to migration.
  - **Ecesis** Ecesis is the process of successful establishment of a speices in the bare area.
  - **Aggregation** After ecesis the individuals of a species increase their number and they stay close to each other. This process is called Aggregation.
- **Competition and Coactions** Different species in a limited area compete for space, light, nutrition, etc. Individuals of a species affect each other's life in various ways which is termed as coactions.
- **Reaction** It is the modification of the environment through the influences of living organisms. It creates the favourable environment for a new species.
- **Stabilisation** (Climax) Finally, there occurs a stage in process, when the final terminal community becomes more or less stabilised for a longer period of time. It can maintain itself in equilibrium with the climate of the area and it is known as **Climax community**. This community can maintain its equilibrium with the climate of the area.

Ecological Adaptation

- **Charles Darwin** first used adaptation in 1859 to describe how an organism adapts and changes to become better suited to living in its habitat and environment. An adaptation is a mutation or genetic change that helps an organism, such as a plant or animal to survive in its environment.
- Due to the helpful nature of the mutation, it is passed down from one generation to the next. As more and more organisms inherit the mutation, the mutation becomes a typical part of the species.
- The mutation has become an adaptation in environment. Mutation is the ability of a species to survive in a particular ecological niche, especially because of alterations of form or behaviour brought about through natural selection.

Biomes

- A biome can be defined as the total assemblage of plant and animal species interacting within specific conditions. These include rainfall, temperature, humidity and soil conditions. A biome is a plant and animal community that covers a large geographical area. The boundaries of different biomes on land are determined mainly by climate.
- Some of the major biomes of the world are: forest, grassland, desert and tundra biomes.

Types of Biomes

Biomes	Subtypes	Regions	Climatic Characteristics	Soil	Flora and Fauna
Forest	A Tropical				
	1. Equatorial	A1 10° N.S	A1. Temperature 20-25°C, evenly distributed	A1. Acidic, poor in nutrients	A1. Multi-layered canopy tall and large trees
	2. Deciduous	A2 10°-25° N-S	A2. Temperature 25-30°C, rainfall, ave. ann. 1,000mm, seasonal	A2. Rich in nutrients	A2. Less dense, trees of medium height; many varieties coexist. Insects, bats, birds and mammals are common species in both.
	B. Temperate	B. Eastern-North America. North- East Asia. Western and Central Europe	B. Temperature 20-30° C, rainfall evenly distributed 750- 1,500mm, Well-defined seasons and distinct winter.	B. Fertile, enriched with decaying litter	B. Moderately dense broad leaved trees with less diversity of plant species. Oak, Beach, Maple, etc. are some common species. Squirrels, rabbits, skunks, birds, black bears, mountain lions, etc.
	C. Boreal	C. Broad belt of Eurasia and North America (parts of Siberia, Alaska, Canada and Scandinavia)	C. Short moist moderately warm summers and long cold dry winter; very low temperatures. Precipitation mostly snowfall 400 -1,000mm	C. Acidic and poor in nutrients, thin soil cover	C. Evergreen conifers like pine, fur and spruce, etc. Wood peckers, hawks, bears, wolves, deer, hares and bats are common animals.
Desert	A. Hot and Dry desert	A. Sahara, Kalahari, Marusthali, Rub-el-Khali	A. Temperature 20 - 45°C.	Rich in nutrients with little or no organic matter	A-C. Scanty vegetation; few large mammals, insects, reptiles and birds.
	B. Semi arid desert	B. Marginal areas of hot deserts	B. 21 - 38°C.		
	C. Coastal desert	C. Atacama	C. 15 - 35°C.		–
	D. Cold desert	D. Tundra climatic regions	D. 2 - 25°C, A-D rainfall is less than 50 mm	–	D. Rabbits, rats, antelopes and ground squirrels.
Grassland	A. Tropical Savannah	A. Large areas of Africa, Australia, South America and India	A. Warm hot climates, Rainfall 500-1,250mm	A. Porous with thin layer of humus	A. Grasses; trees and large shrubs absent; giraffes zebras, buffalos, leopards, hyenas, elephants, mice, moles, snakes and worms etc. are common animals.
	B. Temperate Steppe	B. Parts of Eurasia and North America	B. Hot summers and cold winter Rainfall 500-900 mm	B. Thin flocculated soil, rich in bases	B. Grasses; occasional trees such as cottonwoods, oaks and willows; gazelles, zebras, rhinoceros, wild horses, lions, varieties of birds, worms, snakes etc are common animals.
Aquatic	A. Freshwater	A. Lakes, streams, rivers and wetlands	A-B Temperatures vary widely with cooler air temperatures and high humidity	A. Water, swamps and marshes	Algae and other aquatic and marine plant communities with varieties of water dwelling animals.
	B. Marine	B. Oceans, coral reefs, lagoons and estuaries	–	B.Water, tidal swamps and marshes	–
Altitudinal	—	Slopes of high mountain ranges like the Himalayas, the Andes and the Rockies	Temperature and precipitation vary depending upon latitudinal zone	Regolith over slopes	Deciduous to tundra vegetation varying according to altitude.

Inter-Species Interactions

- Interspecific interactions arise from the interaction of populations of two different species. They could be beneficial, detrimental or neutral (neither harm nor benefit) to one of the species or both.
- '+' sign for beneficial interaction, '-' sign for detrimental and 0 for neutral interaction.

Species A	Species B	Name of Interaction	Explanation
+	+	Mutualism	This interaction confers benefits on both the interacting species. For example, Lichens represent an intimate mutualistic relationship between a fungus and photosynthesising algae or cyanobacteria.
–	–	Competition	Competition occurs when closely related species as well as totally unrelated species compete for the same resources that are limiting. For example, plants which are in compete for nitrogen in roots.
+	–	Predation	It occurs when an individual from one species kills another individual of another species at once to feed on it. For example, carnivores' interaction.
+	–	Parasitism	It takes place when a species obtains the benefit from another species provoking a gradual damage that does not cause the immediate cause of the victim. For example, pig around worm.
+	0	Commensalism	This is the interaction in which one species benefits and the other is neither harmed nor benefited. For example, an orchid growing as an epiphyte on a mango branch and barnacles growing on the back of a whale benefit while neither the mango tree nor the whale derives any apparent benefit.
–	0	Amensalism	In Amensalism one species is harmed whereas the other is unaffected. For example, grazing cattle and insects. When cattle graze in grass, the insects are consumed by birds while cattle remain unaffected.

Extra Facts From Tamil Nadu Board and NIOS

- The term **Biosphere** was coined by **Eduard Suess** in 1875. Later contributions to the study of biosphere were made from, Charles Darwin and many other scientists.
- The term **Ecosystem** was first proposed by **Arthur George Tansley** in 1935. Tansley defined ecosystem as, 'the system resulting from the integration of all living and non-living factors of the environment'.
- **Detritivores** are consumers that feed on detritus. Detritus includes fallen leaves, parts of dead trees and faecal wastes of animals. Ants, termites, earthworms, milipedes, dung beetle, fiddler crabs and sea cucumbers are detritivores.
- An ecosystem becomes a biome when it extends over a large area. According to **I.G. Simmons** (1982), the most extensive ecosystem unit which is convenient to designate is called a 'Biome'.
- Corals are marine invertebrates which live in compact colonies. They inhabit tropical oceans and seas. Corals grow optimally in temperatures between 23°C and 29°C but corals cannot survive in waters below 18°C.
- The evergreen rainforest biome is found in the equatorial zone extending 10° North and South latitudes from the Equator. These evergreen forests are found in the equatorial belt including areas of Amazon lowland of South America, Congo basin of Africa and islands of South-East Asia.
- **Tundra biome** is located in the Northern parts of North America including Alaska, Northernmost areas of Canada, Greenland and the Arctic regions of Russia. This is a cold desert area where summers are very short and cool.

29

Biodiversity

[SOURCES]

Class-VIII New NCERT Chap 1 (Resources), Class-VIII New NCERT Chap 2 (Land, Soil, Water, Natural Vegetation and Wildlife Resources), Class-X New NCERT Chap 1 (Resources and Development), Class-XI New NCERT Chap 5 (Forest and Wildlife Resources), Class-XI (I) New NCERT Chap 14 (Biodiveirsity and Conservation), Class-XI (II) New NCERT Chap 5 (Natural Vegetation), Class-XII New NCERT Chap 13 (Biodiversity and Conservation (Biology)), Class-XII New NCERT Chap 6 (Planning and Sustainable Development in Indian Context), Tamil Nadu Board (Class XI), NIOS

Meaning of Biodiversity

- Biodiversity is a combination of two words, '*Bio*' (life) and '*diversity*' (variety). Biodiversity is the number and variety of organisms found within a specified geographic region.
- It refers to the varieties of plants, animals and micro-organisms, the genes they contain and the ecosystems they form.
- It relates to the variability among living organisms on the Earth, including the variability within and between the species and that within and between the ecosystems. The term biodiversity was first used by **Edward O Wilson** in 1985.
- Biodiversity on the Earth is not same everywhere. In tropical regions, a large number of species biodiversity are found.

Types of Biodiversity

Biodiversity can be classified at three levels :

Genetic Biodiversity

- Genetic biodiversity refers to the variation of genes within species. Genes are the basic building blocks of various life forms.
- Groups of individual organisms having certain similarities in their physical characteristics are called **species**.
- Human beings genetically belong to the *Homo sapiens* group and also differ in their characteristics such as height, colour and physical appearance.
- This is due to genetic diversity. This genetic diversity is essential for a healthy breeding of population of species.

Species Biodiversity

- Species biodiversity refers to the variety of species. It relates to the number of species in a defined area.
- The diversity of species can be measured through its richness, abundance and types.
- Some areas are richer in species than others. Areas rich in species diversity are called **hotspots of diversity**. For example, the Western ghats have a greater amphibian species diversity than the Eastern ghats.

Ecosystem Biodiversity

- The biodiversity of ecosystem refers to the variety of ecosystems, both in terms of nature and number, in which living organisms interact with their environment and with one another.
- At the ecosystem level, India, with its deserts, rain forests, mangroves, coral reefs, wetlands, estuaries and alpine meadows has a greater ecosystem diversity than a Scandinavian country like Norway.

Measurement of Biodiversity

Biodiversity can be measured by alpha, beta and gamma biodiversity.

- **Alpha Diversity** (α-diversity) It is defined as the mean diversity of species in different sites or habitats within a local scale.

- **Beta Diversity** (β-diversity) It is a comparison of diversity ecosystems, usually measured as the change in number of species in the ecosystem.
- **Gamma Diversity** (γ-diversity) It is a measure of total species diversity in a landscape.

Importance of Biodiversity

- Biodiversity has aided the development of human culture in numerous ways and human communities.
- Biodiversity plays the following roles: ecological, economic and scientific.

Ecological Role of Biodiversity

- Many different species contribute to the functioning of an ecosystem in one way or another. Nothing in an ecosystem evolves or persists for no reason.
- In addition to extracting its own needs, each organism gives something beneficial to other organisms.
- Species capture and store energy, produce and decompose organic materials, aid in the circulation of water and nutrients throughout the ecosystem, fix atmospheric gases and help to regulate the climate.
- The more diverse an ecosystem, better are the chances for the species to survive through **adversities** and attacks and consequently, is more productive.
- Just like a species with a high genetic diversity, an ecosystem with high biodiversity may have a greater chance of adapting to environmental change.

Economic Role of Biodiversity

- Crop diversity **Agro-biodiversity**, is an important component of biodiversity.
- Biodiversity is viewed as a resource reservoir from which food, pharmaceutical and cosmetic products can be derived.
- The concept of biological resources is to blame for the decline in biodiversity. At the same time, it is the source of new conflicts concerning natural resource division and appropriation rules.
- Food crops, animals, woods, fish, medicinal resources and so on are some of the essential economic commodities that biodiversity provides to humanity.

Scientific Role of Biodiversity

- Biodiversity is important because each species can give us some clue as to how life evolved and will continue to evolve.
- Biodiversity also helps in understanding how life functions and the role of each species in sustaining ecosystems of which we are also a species.
- It is immorally to cause the extinction of any species. The level of biodiversity is a good indicator of the state of our relationships with other living species.

Attributes of Biodiversity

There are three attributes of biodiversity for assessing the characteristics of any region:

- **Composition** It is the diversity and uniqueness of an ecological system. Composition descriptors are often lists of species residents in an area or ecosystem and composition metrics include species richness and diversity.
- **Structure** Ecosystem structure is a network of interactions between biotic and abiotic components of the system. It is a physical pattern of system, from habitat complexity as measured within communities to the pattern of habitats and other elements at a landscape level.
- **Functions** The quantity of various organisms and their relative frequencies in an ecosystem are all part of biodiversity. It also reflects the organisational structure of organisms at various levels. Biodiversity is important for both ecological and economic reasons. It provides us food, shelter, fuel, clothing, etc.

Depletion of Biodiversity

The current rate of loss of biodiversity is said to be 10,000 to 25,000 times faster than the natural rate of extinction.

The reasons of biodiversity depletion are as follows :

Habitat Fragmentation

- It is the process whereby a large continuous area of habitat is both reduced in area and divided into two or more fragments. They are divided into smaller pieces by roads, fields, towns and a wide range of other human activities.
- It leaves a patchwork of habitat fragments, which are isolated from one another by a degraded landscape.

  Fragmentation need not always involve a reduction in the overall area, but the setting up of barriers.

Overexploitation and Hunting

- Increased human population, increased demand and the methods of harvesting also became more efficient.
- More rapid harvesting over a wider area became possible with new technology, such as the introduction of motorboats and trawlers for fishing.
- The development of a commercial market for a particular product or item can also cause overexploitation and poaching. e.g. the demand for fur and fur-products led to the reduction of many species.
- Elephants, rhinos, tigers, leopards, Asiatic bear and pandas are all facing threats to their survival due to a flourishing trade in wildlife and wildlife products around the world.

- Hunting for pleasure used to be a major historical cause for the reduction of many species of game animals. However, game hunting is now an illegal activity in most of the countries and its actual contribution to biodiversity loss is on the decline.

Disaster and Pollution

- Even without destroying or fragmenting the habitats, human activities can make them unsuitable for other species.
- This can accelerate their rate of extinction. External factors like pollution and climate change can affect the quality of air, water and soil.
- Pesticide pollution, water and soil pollution, air pollution such as acid rain and contamination by hundreds of chemicals can force intolerant and poorly adaptable species to disappear.

Shifting Cultivation

- In shifting cultivation, a plot of land is cleared and cultivated for a short period of time.
- Once the land becomes inadequate for crop production, it is left to be reclaimed by natural vegetation or sometimes converted to different long term cyclical farming practice.

Invasion of Exotic Species

- Environmental and climatic barriers such as mountains, rivers, temperature zones and oceans have restricted the geographical ranges of species and have allowed the development of endemic species. Endemicity depends on the level of isolation.
- However, as the human population grew, people spread out to the every corner of the world. In the process, they have introduced many new species into new areas they settled.
- **Co-extinctions** When a species becomes extinct, the plant and animal species associated with it in an obligatory way also becomes extinct. When a host fish species becomes extinct, its unique assemblage of parasites also meets the same fate.
- Another example is the case of a coevolved plant-pollinator mutualism where extinction of one invariably leads to the extinction of the other.

Climate Change

- Climate change is the recent potent factor of depletion of biodiversity in different biomes.
- The impacts of rising temperature on vegetation communities mainly forests are now perceptible in Taiga forests which have shown shrinking in their areas whereas increased rainfall due to temperature rise in the tropical regions has positive impact on forest growth.

Classification of Species According to their Extinction

- The **International Union of Conservation of Nature and Natural Resources** (IUCN) has classified the threatened species of plants and animals into three categories for the purpose of their conservation :
  - **Endangered Species** It includes those species which are in danger of extinction. The IUCN publishes information about endangered species world-wide as the Red List of threatened species.
  - **Vulnerable Species** This includes the species which are likely to be in danger of extinction in near future if the factors threatening to their extinction continue. Survival of these species is not assured as their population has reduced greatly.
  - **Rare Species** Population of these species is very small in the world; they are confined to limited areas or thinly scattered over a wider area.

Geographical Biodiversity

- The biological variety and variability of life on Earth is referred to as biodiversity. Biodiversity is a measure of genetic, species and ecosystem variation.
- There are some countries which are situated in the tropical region; they possess a large number of the world's species diversity. They are called mega diversity centres.
- There are 12 such countries, namely Mexico, Columbia, Ecuador, Peru, Brazil, Democratic Republic of Congo, Madagascar, China, India, Malaysia, Indonesia and Australia in which these centres are located.

Regions of Excess Biodiversity

The growth of plants and animals in this region is greater than other parts of the world due to favourable climatic conditions.

Tropical Rainforest

- These forests are found in the Western slope of the Western Ghats, hills of the North-Eastern region and the Andaman and Nicobar Islands. They are found in warm and humid areas with an annual precipitation of over 200 cm and mean annual temperature above 22°C.
- Tropical evergreen forests are well stratified, with layers closer to the ground and are covered with shrubs and creepers, with short structured trees followed by tall variety of trees.
- In these forests, trees reach great heights up to 60 m or above. There is no definite time for trees to shed their leaves, flowering and fruition.

Coral Reef

- Coral reefs are large underwater structures composed of the skeletons of colonial marine invertebrates called coral.
- Corals are formed mostly of the calcium carbonate skeletons of corals.
- The Great Barrier Reef of Australia is blessed with the beauty of the world's largest coral reef.
- The four major coral reef areas identified for intensive conservation and management in India are :
  - Gulf of Mannar (Tamil Nadu)
  - Gulf of Kutch (Gujarat)
  - Lakshadweep
  - Andaman and Nicobar Islands

Tropical Oceanic Region

- The high temperature and high precipitation in tropical region is boon for excess biodiversity in this region.
- But the biodiversity of this region is lower than that of the temperate region.

Wetland

- A wetland is a place where the land is covered by water, either salty or fresh water.
- Marshes and ponds, the edge of a lake or ocean, the delta at the mouth of a river, low lying areas that frequently flood are the examples of wetlands.
- Wetlands often support high concentrations of animals including mammals, birds, fish and invertebrates and serve as nurseries for many of these species.
- There are two types of wetlands :

Inland

- Inland wetlands account for 69.22% of the total wetlands. The majority of the inland wetlands are directly or indirectly dependent on the major rivers like Ganga, Brahmaputra, Narmada, Godavari, Krishna, Kaveri and Tapti.
- They occur in the hot and arid regions of Gujarat and Rajasthan, the deltaic regions of the East and West coasts, highlands of Central India, wet humid zones of South Peninsular India and Andaman and Nicobar and Lakshadweep islands.

Coastal

- Marine and coastal wetlands encompass the enormous variety of marine and coastal species.
- They provide open sea habitats and ecosystems for species and the wealth of ecological province that support all of these species.

Regions of High Biodiversity

- Some regions of the world have high biodiversity because of the geomorphological structure and climate of that region. It includes Western Europe, monsoonic regions, grasslands, etc.
- Western Europe has temperate type of climate, which signifies high rainfall. Due to high moisture content in the soil, there is favourable condition for the growth of vegetation in these regions.

Regions of Normal Biodiversity

A large area of the world is very low in biodiversity because of the lack of favourable condition for the growth of plants and animals. Examples of these regions are desert and sub-polar regions.

Regions of Least Biodiversity

- Polar ice and arctic Tundra have least diversity. Tundra is a region where is permanently frozen.
- So, roots of plants cannot penetrate those areas. Without large vegetation, a whole segment that's present in other biomes is missing from the polar regions.

Indian Biodiversity

- India is a megadiverse country which is rich in biodiversity. With just 2.4% of the world's land area, India holds about 7-8% of the global biodiversity.
- The wide diversity in physical features and climatic situations have resulted in a variety of ecosystems such as forests, grasslands, wetlands, coastal and marine deserts.
- Forests ecosystems in particular exhibit tremendous variability ranging from temperate alpine to tropical wet evergreen forests.
- There is dense forest in Malabar coast and Andaman and Nicobar region of India. It includes trees like Saal, Sheesham, Mango tree, Palash, Peepal, etc.
- There are 16 major forest types in India. India is also one of the eight primary centres of the origin of cultivated plants and is rich agricultural biodiversity. Over 4,5000 species of plants and 91,000 species of animals have been recorded so far.
- India maintains this biodiversity while supporting 20% of the world's human and cattle population.
- India also has two of the 34 identified hotspots of the world, which are characterised by high degree of endemism and are therefore areas of global conservation concern.
- Eastern Himalayas is recognised as the **Cradle of Speciation** due to rich diversity of primitive flowering plants.

Biodiversity Hotspots

- A biodiversity hotspot is a biogeographic region with a significant reservoir of biodiversity that is under threat from humans.
- The concept of biodiversity hotspots was originated by Norman Myers in two articles in 'The Environmentalist' (1988 and 1990), revised after thorough analysis by Myers and others in 'Hotspots: Earth's Biologically Richest and Most Endangered Terrestrial Eco-regions'.
- To qualify as a biodiversity hotspot on Myers 2000 edition of the hotspot-map, a region must meet two strict criteria
  - (i) It must contain atleast 0.5% or 1500 species of vascular plants as endemics.
  - (ii) It must have 30% or less of its original natural vegetation. In other words, it must be threatened.
- Around the world, atleast 25% areas qualify under this definition. These sites support nearly 60% of the world's plant, bird, mammal, reptile and amphibian species, with a very high share of endemic species. Currently, there are **35 biodiversity hotspots** according to Conservation International, most of which occur in tropical forests.
- Each of them holds atleast 1500 endemic plant species and have lost atleast 70% of its original habitat extent. India has two biodiversity hotspots :

Eastern Himalaya Biodiversity Hotspot

- Eastern Himalaya forms a distinct floral region and comprises Nepal, Bhutan, states of East and North-East India and a contiguous sector of Yunnan Province in South-Western China.
- In the whole of Eastern Himalaya, there are an estimated 9000 plant species, out of which 3500 (i.e. 39%) are endemic.

Western Ghats Biodiversity Hotspot

- The Western Ghats region, which is spread into 6 states of India, is considered to be one of the most important biodiversity hotspots of India, as it is one of the richest centres of endemism.
- Due to varied topography and micro-climatic regimes some areas within the region are considered to be active zones of speciation. This hotspot account for around 25% of India's biodiversity.

Indo-Burma Hotspot

- This hotspot region spans various countries such as the North-Eastern region of India, Myanmar, the Southern part of the Brahmaputra river, Southern China's Yunnan province, along with Cambodia, Vietnam, Thailand and other areas.
- The region exhibits significant diversity in climate and habitat patterns. Despite being surrounded by extensive forest areas, environment imbalance is causing contraction with approximately 13,500 plant species found here.

Sundaland

- This hotspot region extends to the Western part of the Indo-Malayan archipelago in South-East Asia, including Thailand, Malaysia, Singapore and Indonesia.
- It also includes India's Andaman and Nicobar Islands within this region.

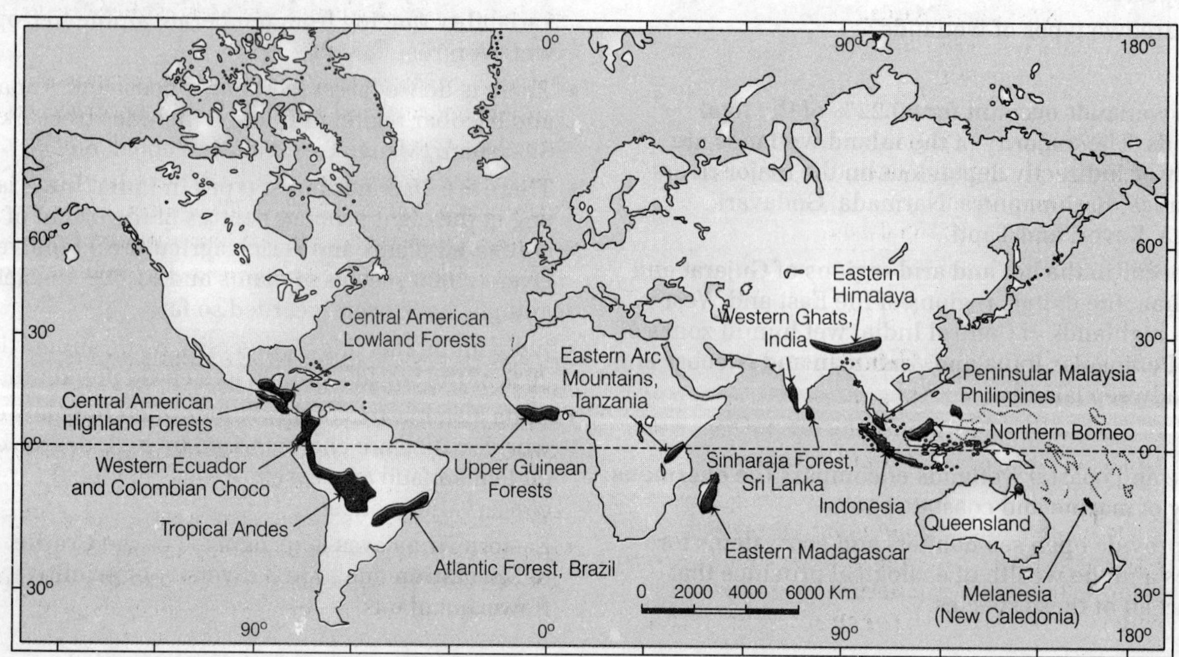

World Biodiversity Hotspots

At present, there are 36 biodiversity hotspots on our planet. Some major hotspots are following

Major Hotspots of World

Africa	• Eastern Afro-Montane • The Guinean Forests of Western Africa • Horn of Africa • Madagascar and the Indian Ocean Islands • Maputaland, Pondoland, Albany Hotspot • Succulent Karoo • South Africa's Cape Floristic Hotspot • Coastal Forests of Eastern Africa
Asia and Asia-Pacific	• Himalayan Hotspot • The Eastern Himalayas (Nepal/India) • Mountains of South-West China New Caledonia • New Zealand Biodiversity Hotspot • Philippine Biodiversity Hotspot • Polynesia and Micronesian Islands Complex including Hawaii • East Melanesian Islands
South-Western Australia	• Western Sunda • Wallacea (Eastern Indonesia) • The Western Ghats of India and Islands of Sri Lanka • Indo-Burma • Japan Biodiversity Hotspot
North Central America	• California Floristic Province • Caribbean Islands Hotspot • North American Coastal Plain
South America	• Brazil's Cerrado • Chilean Winter Rainfall (Valdivian) Forests • Tumbes Choco Magdalena • Tropical Andes • Atlantic Forest
Europe and Central Asia	• Caucasus Region • Iran-Anatolia Region • The Mediterranean Basin and its Eastern Coastal Region • Mountains of Central Asia

Biodiversity Conservation

Why should we Conserve Biodiversity

There are many reasons, some obvious and others not so obvious, but all equally important. They can be grouped into three categories: narrowly utilitarian, broadly utilitarian, and ethical.

- The narrowly utilitarian arguments for conserving biodiversity are obvious: humans derive countless direct economic benefits form nature food (cereals, pulses, fruits), firewood, fiber, construction material, industrial products (tannins, lubricants, dyes, resins, perfumes) and products of medicinal importance.
- With increasing resources put into **bioprospecting** (exploring molecular, genetic and species-level diversity for products of economic importance), nations endowed with rich biodiversity can expect of reap enormous benefits. The broadly utilitarian argument says the biodiversity plays a major role in many ecosystem services that nature provides. The fast-dwindling Amazon forest is estimated to produce, through photosynthesis, 20% of the total oxygen in the Earth's atmosphere.
- The ethical argument of conserving biodiversity relates to what we owe to millions of plant, animal and microbe species with whom we share this planet. Philosophically or spiritually, we need to realise that every species has an intrinsic value, even if it may not be of current or any economic value to us. We have a moral duty to care for their well-being and pass on our biological legacy in good order to future generations.

How do we conserve Biodiversity

The method of conservation of biodiversity can be classified into two groups :

In-Situ

- *In-situ* conservation means the conservation of ecosystems and natural habitats and the maintenance and recovery of viable populations of species in their natural surroundings.
- Examples; National parks, sanctuaries, natural reserves, reserves of the biosphere, sacred groves, etc.
- In India, ecologically unique and biodiversity-rich regions are legally protected as biosphere reserves, national parks and sanctuaries.
- In many cultures, tracts of forest were set aside and all the trees and wildlife inside it were given total protection.
- Sacred groves are found in Khasi and Jaintia hills in Meghalaya, Aravalli hills of Rajasthan, Western Ghat regions of Karnataka and Maharashtra and the Sarguja, Chanda and Bastar areas of Madhya Pradesh.

Ex-Situ

- In this approach, threatened animals and plants are taken out from their natural habitat and placed in special setting where they can be protected and given special care. For example, zoological parks, botanical gardens and wildlife safari parks.
- Many animals have become extinct in the wild but they are kept alive in zoological parks. *Ex-situ* conservation has gone beyond the confinement of threatened species in cages in recent years.

Action Plan associated with Biodiversity Conservation

Some important action plan associated with biodiversity conservation are as follows :

Wildlife Protection Act, 1972

- Wildlife Protection Act was enacted on 9th September, 1972. India is the first country in the world to have made provisions for the protection and conservation of environment in its Constitution.
- It was enacted to provide the main legal framework for conservation and protection of wildlife in India
- The two main objectives of the Act are, to provide protection to the endangered species listed in the schedule of the Act and to provide legal support to the conservation areas of the country classified as national parks, sanctuaries and closed areas.
- The Act was amended subsequently in 1982, 1986, 1991 and 1993 to accommodate provision for its effective implementation.
- The Wildlife Protection Act of 1972 established Wildlife Sanctuaries and National Parks. It also prohibits hunting of endangered animals and grants licences for the sale, transfer and possession of wildlife.

Environment Protection Act, 1986

- It was enacted on 9th January, 1986 in the wake of the Bhopal gas Tragedy by the Government of India under Article-253 of the Constitution.
- The Act empowers the Central Government to safeguard and improve environmental quality, control and decrease pollution from all sources. It also prohibits or restricts the establishment and/or operation of any industrial facility based on environmental considerations.

Biological Diversity Act, 2002

Biological Diversity Act cause into force on 5th February, 2003. It was designed to provide the protection of biological diversity and the sustainable use of its components. It also aims the fair and equal sharing of the advantages emerging from the use of biological resources, knowledge and matters related to or incidental to these.

Biodiversity Loss

- Since the last few decades, growth in human population has increased the rate of consumption of natural resources. It has accelerated the loss of species and habitation in different parts of the world.
- Biodiversity loss occurs when a specific species is extinct or the habitat necessary for its life is degraded. The latter is more common because habitat destruction is unavoidable by-product of development.
- Species which are not the natural inhabitants of the local habitat but are introduced into the system, are called **exotic species**. Some animals like tigers, elephants, rhinoceros, crocodiles, minks and birds were hunted mercilessly by poachers for their horn, tusks, hides, etc.

International Efforts towards Biodiversity Conservation

Some international efforts towards biodiversity conservation are as follows :

Rio Summit

It was held in Rio De Janeiro (Brazil) in 1992. In this historical Biodiversity Summit, the nations (155, including India) were asked to adopt correct and long term measures to conserve biodiversity.

Ramsar Convention

- It was signed in Ramsar city of Iran for conservation and wire use of weltands.
- About 1831 weltands of international importance have been listed as Ramsar sites.

Extra Facts From
Tamil Nadu Board and NIOS

- **Norman Myers** (1934-2019) was British environmentalist specialising in biodiversity hotspots. He was the first to alert global community to tropical deforestation, the mass extinction underway and environmental security.
- The IUCN's Red List of Threatened species, identified in 1964, is the world's most important inventory of the global conservation status of biological species.
- Conservation International (CI) is a American non-profit environmental organisation founded in 1987 in Virginia. Its goal is to protect nature as a source for food, fresh water, livelihood and a stable climate.
- In the Red List of 2012 that was released on 19th July, 2012 at Rio+20 Earth Summit 19,817 species were threatened with extinction.
- The **Pygmy Hog** is the smallest and rarest wild pig on Earth and it is a critically endangered species previously spread across Bangladesh, Bhutan, India and Nepal, but now only found in Assam, India.
- The **National Board for Wildlife** (NBWL) chaired by the Prime Minister of India, provides for policy framework for wildlife conservation in the country.
- The Black Buck (Chinkara) the Great Indian Bustard and the Snow Leopard have been given full or partial legal protection against hunting and trade throughout India.
- Reef-building corals cannot tolerate water temperatures below 18° C. Many grow optimally in water temperature between 23°-29° C, but some can tolerate temperature as high as 40° C.

30

Biosphere Reserves, National Parks and Wildlife Sanctuaries

(SOURCES)

Class-XI (II) New NCERT Chap 5 (Natural Vegetation), Class-XI (I) New NCERT Chap 14 (Biodiversity and Conservation), Class-XII New NCERT Chap 13 Biology (Biodiversity and Conservation) Class-VIII (Science) New NCERT Chap 5 (Conservation of Plants and Animals), Tamil Nadu Board (Class XI), NIOS

National Park

- A National park is an area designated by a National Government to preserve the natural environment. A national park may be established for the goal of public recreation and enjoyment, or for historical or scientific relevance.
- National Parks are declared in areas that are considered to be of adequate ecological, geomorphological and natural significance.
- According to National Wildlife Database, March 2024 there are 106 existing national parks in India, that covers an area of 43716 sq. km., which is 1.33% of the geographical area of the country.
- The first national park in India was established in 1936 by the name of **Hailey National Park**. In 1956, it was renamed as **Corbett National Park**.

Wildlife Sanctuary

- A Wildlife Sanctuary is a place where animals and their habitats are protected. Animal capture, slaughter and poaching are all severely prohibited in certain areas.
- According to **National Wildlife Database**, March 2024 there are 570 existing wildlife sanctuaries in India. It covers an area of 1255564.86 sq. km., which is 3.72% of the geographical area of the country.

Biosphere Reserves

- A biosphere reserve is a unique and representative ecosystem of terrestrial and coastal areas which are internationally recognised within the frame work of UNESCO's Man and Biosphere (MAB) Programme.
- The Man and Biosphere (MAB) Programme is an Intergovernmental Scientific Programme aiming to set a scientific basis for the improvement of the relationships between people and their environment globally.
- There are 18 Biosphere Reserves in India. 12 Biosphere Reserves have been recognised by the UNESCO on World Network of Biosphere Reserves.

Objectives of Biosphere Reserves

The Biosphere Reserve aims at achieving the three objectives.

- **Conservation** Conservation of biodiversity and ecosystem.
- **Development** Association of environment with development.
- **Objectives** International network for research and monitoring.

Important National Parks/Wildlife Sanctuaries of India

Location	National Park/Wildlife Sanctuary
Arunachal Pradesh	Namdapha National Park, Dihang Wildlife Sanctuary, Mehao Wildlife Sanctuary, Itanagar Wildlife Sanctuary
Assam	Kaziranga National Park, Sonai Rupai Sanctuary, Manas Wildlife Sanctuary, Pobitora Wildlife Sanctuary
Andhra Pradesh	Nagarjunasagar Srisailam Sanctuary, Rollapadu Wildlife Sanctuary, Papikonda
Bihar	Gautam Buddha Sanctuary, Valmiki National Park, Bhimbandh Wildlife Sanctuary, Kaimur Wildlife Sanctuary, Nagi Dam Wildlife Sanctuary
Chhattisgarh	Achanakmar Sanctuary, Indravati National Park
Gujarat	Valvadore National Park, Wild Ass Sanctuary, Gir Forest, Shoolpaneshwar Wildlife Sanctuary
Goa	Bondla Wildlife Sanctuary, Balaram Ambaji Wildlife Sanctuary, Bhagwan Mahavir National Park
Himachal Pradesh	Manali Sanctuary, Rupi Bhabha Sanctuary, Tundah Wildlife Sanctuary, Pong Dam Sanctuary, Great Himalayan National Park
Karnataka	Nagarhole National Park, (lies in Cauvery Basin) Dandeli Sanctuary, Bhadra Sanctuary, Bannerghatta National Park, Bandipur Sanctuary
Kashmir	Salim Ali National Park, Kishtwar National Park, Dachigam Sanctuary
Kerala	Neyyar Wildlife Sanctuary, Periyar National Park, Silent Valley National Park
Jharkhand	Hazaribagh Wildlife Sanctuary, Dalma Wildlife Sanctuary, Koderma Wildlife Sanctuary, Lawalong Wildlife Sanctuary
Madhya Pradesh	Pachmarhi Sanctuary, Gandhi Sagar Sanctuary, Bandhavgarh National Park, Madhav National Park, Bori Wildlife Sanctuary, Bagdara Wildlife Sanctuary, Pench Sanctuary, Karera Wildlife Sanctuary, Kamla National Park, Panna National Park
Maharashtra	Great Indian Bustard Sanctuary, Chandoli National Park, Gautala Autramghat Sanctuary, Phansad Wildlife Sanctuary, Painganga, Aner Dam
Manipur	Yangoupokpi Lok Chao, Keibul Lamjao National Park
Meghalaya	Nokrek National Park, Balpakram National Park, Bhagmara Wildlife Sanctuary
Odisha	Simlipal Sanctuary, Chilika Bird Sanctuary
West Bengal	Sundarban Tiger Reserve, Jaldapara Sanctuary
Rajasthan	Keoladeo Ghana Bird Sanctuary, Sariska Wildlife Sanctuary, Ranthambore Wildlife Sanctuary
Sikkim	Kanchenjunga National Park
Tamil Nadu	Vedanthangal Bird Sanctuary, Sathyamangalam Wildlife Sanctuary
Uttar Pradesh	Dudhwa National Park, Kishanpur Wildlife Sanctuary, Chandraprabha Sanctuary
Uttarakhand	Jim Corbett National Park (named in the memory of Jim Corbett), Askot Wildlife Sanctuary (Musk Deer), Rajaji National Park, Nanda Devi National Park
Haryana	Bhindawas Wildlife Sanctuary (WS), Sultanpur Bird Sanctuary
Tripura	GUMIT Sanctuary, Trisna Sanctuary
Punjab	Abhor National Park, Bir Moti (WS), Bir Bhadson WS, Harike WS
West Bengal	Sundarban National Park, Neora Valley National Park, Buxa tiger reserve

Biosphere Reserves in India

Biosphere Reserve and Area (sq. km.)	Year	Location in the States/UT
Nilgiri (5520)	1986	Part of Wayanad, Nagarhole, Bandipur and Mudumalai, Nilambur, Silent Valley and Siuvani Hills Tamil Nadu, Kerala and Karnataka
Nanda Devi (5860.691)	1988	Part of Chamoli, Pithoragarh and Almora districts in Uttarakhand
Nokrek (820)	1988	Part of East, West and South Garo Hill districts in Meghalaya.
Manas (2837)	1989	Part of Kokrajhar, Bongaigaon, Barpeta, Nalbari, Kamrup and Darang districts in Assam
Sunderban (9630)	1989	Part of delta of Ganges and Brahmaputra river system in West Bengal
Gulf of Mannar (10500)	1989	Indian part of Gulf of Mannar extending from Rameswaram Island in the North to Kanyakumari in the South of Tamil Nadu
Great Nicobar (8851	1989	Southernmost island of Andaman and Nicobar Islands
Similipal (4374)	1994	Part of Mayurbhanj district in Odisha
Dibru-Saikhowa (765)	1997	Part of Dibrugarh and Tinsuika districts in Assam
Dehang Dibang (5111)	1998	Part of Upper Siang, West Siang and Diang Valley districts in Arunachal Pradesh
Pachmarhi (4926)	1999	Part of Betul, Hoshangabad and Chhindwara districts in Madhya Pradesh
Khangchendzonga (2619.92)	2000	Part of North and West districts in Sikkim
Agasthyamalai (1828)	2001	Part of Tirunelveli and Kanyakumari districts in Tamil Nadu and Thiruvananthapuram, Kollam and Pathanamthitta districts in Kerala
Achanakmar-Amarkantak (3835.51)	2005	Part of Anuppur and Dindori Districts of Madhya Pradesh and Bilaspur district of Chhattisgarh

Biosphere Reserve and Area (sq. km.)	Year	Location in the States/UT
Kutch (12454)	2008	Part of Kutch, Rajkot, Surendranagar and Patan districts in Gujarat
Cold Desert (7770)	2009	Pin Valley National Park and surroundings: Chandratal and Sarchu and Kibber Wildlife Sanctuary in Himachal Pradesh
Seshachalam (4755.997)	2010	Seshachalam hill ranges in Eastern Ghats encompassing part of Chittoor and Kadapa Districts in Andhra Pradesh
Panna (2998.98)	2011	Parts of Panna and Chhatarpur districts in Madhya Pradesh

Wildlife Conservation Projects

Various conservation projects have been proposed by Government to conserve wildlife.

Some of these are as follows :

Project Tiger

- It was launched in 1973. Tigers are globally listed as 'Endangered' on the International Union for the Conservation of Nature (IUCN) Red List of Threatened Species. The main objective of the scheme is to ensure maintenance of viable population of tigers in India for scientific, aesthetic, cultural and ecological values.
- It also aimed to preserve areas of biological importance as natural heritage for the benefit, education and enjoyment of the people. India has 2967 tigers, according to the population estimation which was carried out in 2018.

List of Tiger Reserves in India

State	• Tiger Reserve	Year
Andhra Pradesh	• Nagarjunasagar-Srisailam Tiger Reserve (Largest Critical Tiger Habitat)	1982-83
Arunachal Pradesh	• Pakhui Tiger Reserve	1999-2000
	• Namdapha Tiger Reserve	1982-83
	• Kamlang Tiger Reserve	2016-17
Assam	• Nameri Tiger Reserve	1999-2000
	• Manas Tiger Reserve	1973-74
	• Kaziranga Tiger Reserve	2008-09
	• Orang Tiger Reserve	2016
Bihar	• Valmiki Tiger Reserve	1989-90
Chhattisgarh	• Indravati Tiger Reserve	1982-83
	• Udanti and Sitanadi Tiger Reserve	2008-09
	• Achanakmar Tiger Reserve	2008-09
Jharkhand	• Palamau Tiger Reserve	1973-74
Karnataka	• Bandipur Tiger Reserve	1973-74
	• Nagarhole Tiger Reserve	2008-09
	• Dandeli-Anshi Tiger Reserve	2008-09
	• Bhadra Tiger Reserve	1998-99
	• Biligiri Ranganatha Temple Tiger Reserve	2010-11
Kerala	• Periyar Tiger Reserve	1978-79
	• Parambikulam Tiger Reserve	2008-09
Madhya Pradesh	• Bandhavgarh Tiger Reserve	1993-94
	• Bori-Satpura Tiger Reserve	1999-2000
	• Kanha Tiger Reserve	1973-74
	• Panna Tiger Reserve	1994-95
	• Pench Tiger Reserve	1992-93
	• Sanjay Dubri Tiger Reserve	2008-09
	• Veerangana Durgavati Tiger Reserve	2023
Maharashtra	• Melghat Tiger Reserve	1973-74
	• Pench Tiger Reserve	1998-99
	• Tadoba-Andhari Tiger Reserve	1993-94
	• Sahyadri Tiger Reserve	2009-10
	• Bor Tiger Reserve	2014
	• Nawegaon-Nagzira Tiger Reserve	2013-14
Mizoram	• Dampa Tiger Reserve	1994-95
Odisha	• Simlipal Tiger Reserve	1973-74
	• Satkosia Tiger Reserve	2008-09
West Bengal	• Buxa Tiger Reserve	1982-83
	• Sunderbans Tiger Reserve	1973-74
Rajasthan	• Ranthambore Tiger Reserve	1973-74
	• Sariska Tiger Reserve	1978-79
	• Mukundara Hills Tiger Reserve	2013
	• Ramgarh Vishdhari Tiger Reserve	2022
Tamil Nadu	• Kalakad-Mundathurai Tiger Reserve	1988-89
	• Anamalai Tiger Reserve	2007
	• Mudumalai National Park	2008-09
	• Sathyamangalam	2013
	• Srivilliputhura Megamalai Tiger Reserve	2021
Telangana	• Amrabad Tiger Reserve	2014
	• Kawal Tiger Reserve	2012
Uttar Pradesh	• Dudhwa Tiger Reserve	1987-88
	• Pilibhit Tiger Reserve	2014
	• Ranipur Tiger Reserve	2022
Uttarakhand	• Corbett Tiger Reserve	1973-74
	• Rajaji National Park	2015

Project Snow Leopard

- The project was started on the lines of Project Elephant, Project Tiger and Project Rhino by the Ministry of Environment and Forests in 2006.
- India is believed to have between 200 and 600 snow leopards in the five Himalayan states i.e. Jammu and Kashmir, Himachal Pradesh, Uttarakhand, Sikkim and Arunachal Pradesh.

- The project aims to conserve and protect the highly endangered species in its natural habitat.

Project Elephant

- Project Elephant was launched in 7th December, 1992 to assist states having free ranging population of wild elephants.
- The African Forest Elephant is Critically Endangered and the African Savannah Elephant is Endangered on the IUCN Red List of Threatened Species. It was aimed at ensuring long-term survival of identified viable population of elephants in their natural habitat.
- The Project is being mainly implemented in 16 States / UTs , viz. Andhra Pradesh, Arunachal Pradesh, Assam, Chhattisgarh, Jharkhand, Karnataka, Kerala, Maharashtra, Meghalaya, Nagaland, Odisha, Tamil Nadu, Tripura, Uttarakhand, Uttar Pradesh, West Bengal.

Project Rhino

- The greater one-horned rhinoceros (or Indian Rhinoceros) is the largest of the rhino species. It is native to Indian subcontinent.
- The population of rhinos is highly threatened by illegal poaching for its horn, which is highly valued as an aphrodisiac in grey markets.
- The **Project Rhino** was initiated in 1987. Kaziranga and Manas in **Assam** and Jaldapara, West Bengal are the main habitats of Rhinos.

Project Manipur Thamin

- South-East part of lake Loktak in Manipur is home to Thamin deer. It is enlisted among the rarest species of mammals.
- Its population slipped to mere 18 in 1977. To conserve and increase the population, Project Thamin was launched in 1977 in **Manipur**.
- In order to fulfil the above objectives, the biosphere reserves are classified into zones like the core area, buffer area and transition area or area of cooperation.
- The Indian Government has established 18 biosphere reserves of India among which 9 are included in the list of the world network of biosphere reserves.

Project Olive Ridley Turtles

- The dwindling population of Olive Ridley Turtles made the Government of Odisha start the project in 1975.
- The project was launched at **Bhitarkanika in Cuttack** district. Bhitarkanika is the second largest mangrove forest. The project even extends to the **Rushikulya** and mouth of river Devi.

Crocodile Breeding Project

- Crocodile Breeding Project was launched in 1975. Crocodile is listed as a Critically Endangered by IUCN.
- The Gharial and Saltwater Crocodile Conservation Programme was launched in Odisha in early 1975, followed by the Mugger Conservation Programme.

Asiatic Lion Reintroduction Project

- The **Asiatic Lion Reintroduction Project** is an initiative of the Indian Government to provide safeguards to the Asiatic lion (*Panthera leo persica)* from extinction in the wild by means of reintroduction.
- The single population faces the threats of epidemics, natural disasters and other anthropogenic factors.
- The project aims to establish a second independent population of Asiatic lions at the Kuno Wildlife Sanctuary in the Indian state of Madhya Pradesh.

Project Hangul

- Hangul is known as Kashmiri stag, the only surviving species of red deer family in Kashmir.
- The **Project Hangul** had started in **1970** by the Kashmir Government with the help of WWF. Hangul is listed as a Critically Endangered specie by IUCN.

Project Red Panda

- Red Panda is found in the Eastern Himalayan region of India at a height between 1500 m and 4000 m. In Arunachal Pradesh, it is known as **Cat Bear**.
- The project was started in 1966 at Padmaja Naidu Himalayan Wildlife Park with the help of WWF.
- Red Panda is found in Arunachal Pradesh, Sikkim and Darjeeling region in Paschim Banga.

Institutes Associated with Biodiversity Conservation in India

Important institutes associated with biodiversity conservation in India are :

Botanical Survey of India

- It was established on 13th February, 1890 it is an apex research organisation under the ministry of environment and forest.
- The headquarters of **Botanical Survey of India** is located in **Kolkata**, West Bengal.
- The basic objective of this survey is to explore the plant resources of the country and to identify the plant species with economic virtues.

Zoological Survey of India

- Zoological Survey of India (ZSI) was established on 1st July, 1916. The headquarters of **Zoological Survey of India** is located in **Kolkata**, West Bengal.
- It aims to promote the survey, exploration, research and documentation leading to the advancement in our knowledge on various aspects of animal taxonomy of the Indian subcontinent.

Forest Survey of India

- Forest Survey of India was established on 1st June, 1981. The headquarters of Forest Survey of India is located in Dehradun, Uttarakhand.
- Its goal is to conduct forest surveys, studies and research on a regular basis to monitor the changing situation of land and forest resources. It presents the data for national planning, conservation and sustainable environmental management, as well as the implementation of social forestry projects.

Ramsar Convention for Wetland Conservation

- The Ramsar Convention is an International treaty for the conservation and wise use of wetlands.
- It is named after the Iranian city of Ramsar, on the Caspian Sea, where the treaty was signed on 2nd February, 1971.
- Two sites—Chilika Lake (Odisha) and Keoladeo National Park (Bharatpur) are protected as waterfowl habitats under the Convention of Wetlands of International Importance (Ramsar Convention).
- In 2021, Sultanpur National Park (Haryana), Thol Lake Wildlife Sanctuary (Gujarat), Wadhvana Wetland (Gujarat), Khijadia Wildlife Sanctury (Gujarat) and Haiderpur Wetland (Uttar Pradesh) were added to the Ramsar list.
- In 2022, Bakhira Wildlife Sanctury (Uttar Pradesh), Karikili Bird Santuary (Tamil Nadu), Pallikaranai Marsh Reserve Forest (Tamil Nadu), Pichavaram Mangrove Forest (Tamil Nadu), Pala Wetland (Mizoram) and Sakhya Sagar Lake (Madhya Pradesh) were added to the Ramsar list. In 2024, India has increased its Ramsar sites to 80.

Ramsar Sites (Wetlands) in India

Name of Site	State/UTs	Designated Year
Kolleru Lake	Andhra Pradesh	2002
Deepor Beel	Assam	2002
Kanwar (Kabar) Taal	Bihar	2020
Nanda Lake	Goa	2022
Khijadia Wildlife Sanctuary	Gujarat	2021
Nalsarovar Bird Sanctuary	Gujarat	2012
Thol Lake	Gujarat	2021
Wadhvana Wetland	Gujarat	2021
Bhindawas Wildlife Sanctuary	Haryana	2021
Sultanpur National Park	Haryana	2021
Chandra Taal	Himachal Pradesh	2005
Pong Dam Lake	Himachal Pradesh	2002
Renuka Lake	Himachal Pradesh	2005
Ranganathitu Bird Sanctuary	Karnataka	2022
Ankasamudra Bird Conservation	Karnataka	2024
Aghanashini Estuary	Karnataka	2024
Magadi Kere Conservation Reserve	Karnataka	2024
Ashtamudi Wetland	Kerala	2022
Sasthamkotta Lake Vembanad	Kerala	2002
Kol Wetland (Longest lake in India)	Kerala	1905
Bhoj Wetland	Madhya Pradesh	2002
Sakhya Sagar	Madhya Pradesh	2022
Sirpur Wetland	Madhya Pradesh	2022
Yashwant Sagar	Madhya Pradesh	2022
Lonar Lake (Impact Crater Lake)	Maharashtra	2020
Nandur Madhameshwar	Maharashtra	2019
Thane Creek	Maharashtra	2022
Loktak Lake	Manipur	1990
Pala Wetland	Mizoram	2021
Ansupa Lake	Odisha	2021
Bhitarkanika Mangroves	Odisha	2002
Chilika Lake (Oldest Ramsar Site in India)	Odisha	1981
Hirakud Reservoir	Odisha	2021
Satkosia Gorge	Odisha	2021
Tampara Lake	Odisha	2021
Beas Conservation Reserve	Punjab	2019
Harike Wetland	Punjab	1990
Kanjli Wetland	Punjab	2002
Keshopur-Miani Community Reserve	Punjab	2019
Nangal Wildlife Sanctuary	Punjab	2019

Name of Site	State/UTs	Designated Year
Ropar Wetland	Punjab	2002
Keoladeo National Park	Rajasthan	1981
Sambhar Lake	Rajasthan	1990
Chitrangudi Bird Sanctuary	Tamil Nadu	2021
Gulf of Mannar Marine Bird Sanctuary	Tamil Nadu	2022
Kanjirankulam Bird Sanctuary	Tamil Nadu	2022
Karikili Bird Sanctuary	Tamil Nadu	2022
Koonthankulam Bird Sanctuary	Tamil Nadu	2021
Pallikaranai Marsh Reserve Forest	Tamil Nadu	2022
Pichavaram Mangrove	Tamil Nadu	2022
Point Calimere Wildlife Sanctuary and Bird Sanctuary	Tamil Nadu	2002
Suchindram Theroor Wetland Complex	Tamil Nadu	2022
Udhayamarthandapuram Bird Sanctuary	Tamil Nadu	2022
Vaduvur Bird Sanctuary	Tamil Nadu	2022
Vedanthangal Bird Sanctuary	Tamil Nadu	2022
Vellode Bird Sanctuary	Tamil Nadu	2022
Vembannur Wetland Complex	Tamil Nadu	2022
Karaivetti Bird Sanctuary	Tamil Nadu	2024
Longwood Shola Reserve Forest	Tamil Nadu	2024
Rudrasagar Lake	Tripura	2005
Hokera Wetland	Jammu and Kashmir	2005
Hygam Wetland Conservation Reserve	Jammu and Kashmir	2022
Shallbugh Wetland Conservation Reserve	Jammu and Kashmir	2022
Surinsar-Mansar Lakes	Jammu and Kashmir	2005
Wular Lake	Jammu and Kashmir	1990

Name of Site	State/UTs	Designated Year
Tso Kar (High Altitude Ramsar Site)	Ladakh	2020
Tsomoriri (High Altitude Ramsar Site)	Ladakh	2002
Bakhira Wildlife Sanctuary	Uttar Pradesh	2021
Haiderpur Wetland	Uttar Pradesh	2021
Nawabganj Bird Sanctuary	Uttar Pradesh	2019
Parvati Arga Bird Sanctuary	Uttar Pradesh	2019
Saman Bird Sanctuary	Uttar Pradesh	2019
Samaspur Bird Sanctuary	Uttar Pradesh	2019
Sandi Bird Sanctuary	Uttar Pradesh	2019
Sarsai Nawar Jheel	Uttar Pradesh	2019
Sur Sarovar (Keetham Lake)	Uttar Pradesh	2020
Upper Ganga River (Brijghat to Narora)	Uttar Pradesh	2005
Asan Barrage	Uttarakhand	2020
East Kilkata Wetlands	West Bengal	2002
Sunderban Wetland (largest Ramsar Site in India)	West Bengal	2019

Extra Facts From Tamil Nadu Board and NIOS

- Activities like grazing, hunting, forestry or cultivation, etc., are strictly prohibited in National Park. No human activity is permitted inside the national park. There are 103 National Parks in India (National Wildlife Database, April, 2015).
- The difference between a Sanctuary and a national park lies mainly in the rights of people living inside. In a Sanctuary, certain rights are allowed but in a national park, no rights are allowed for grazing of any livestock. There are a total of 537 Wildlife Sanctuaries in India.
- Biosphere reserves may cover multiple national parks, sanctuaries and reserves which are contiguous example, the Nilgiri Biosphere covers; Bandipur National Park, Mudumalai Tiger Reserve, Silent Valley National Park, Nagarhole National Park and Mukurthi Natonal Park.
- Biosphere reserves are traditionally organised into 3 interrelated zones, known as, Core area, Buffer zone and Transition zone.

Climate Change, Greenhouse Effect and Ozone Depletion

[SOURCES]

Class-XI New NCERT Chap 11 (Geography) (World Climate and Climate Change), Class-XII New NCERT Chap 16 (Biology) (Environmental Issues), Class-XII New NCERT Chap 14 (Chemistry) (Environmental Chemistry)

Climate Change

- The planet Earth has witnessed many variations in climate since, the beginning. Geological records show alteration of glacial and inter-glacial periods.
- The geomorphological characteristics, particularly at high altitudes and latitudes, show evidence of glacier advances and retreats.
- Warm and cold area are also revealed by sediment deposits in glacial lakes.
- India has also experienced wet and dry spells. According to archaeological evidence, the Rajasthan desert experienced a moist and cool environment approximately 8,000 BC.
- Higher rainfall occurred between 3,000 and 1,700 BC. This region was the centre of the Harappan Civilisation from around 2,000 to 1,700 BC.
- Since then, dry conditions have become more pronounced.
- Around 500-300 million years ago, during the **Cambrian**, **Ordovician** and **Silurian periods**, the World was heated.
- Glacial and inter-glacial periods occurred during the **Pleistocene epoch**, with the last significant peak glacial period occurring around 18,000 years ago. The current interglacial epoch began 10,000 years ago.
- From roughly 1550 to 1850, Europe experienced a **Little Ice Age.** From around 1885 until 1940, the global temperature increased. After 1940, the rate of temperature rise slowed.

Historical Records of Climate Change

- The 19 decade of the last century witnessed extreme weather events. The 1990s recorded the warmest temperature of the century and some of the worst floods around the world.
- One example is the worst destructive drought in the Sahel region, South of the Sahara desert, from 1967 to 1977. The dust bowl was a catastrophic drought that occurred in the Southern Great Plains of the United States during the 1930s.

Causes of Climate Change

The causes of climate change can be grouped into astronomical and terrestrial causes.

Natural Causes of Climate Change

The natural causes of climate change are as follows :

- **Sunspot Activity** Sunspots are dark spots on surface of the Sun which have reduced surface temperature compared to the surrounding photosphere. Decrease in number of sunspots causes global temperature increase.
- **Continental Drift** The continents of the world are constantly drifting. This drift in past had an impact on climate due to change in physical features of the landmass, their position and position of water bodies.
- **Milankovitch Cycles** Earth's eccentricity, changes in axial tilt and precession of equinoxes taken together constitute **Milankovitch cycles.** This has large impact on climate change and are notable for their correlation with glacial and interglacial periods.

- **Volcanic Activity** Eruption of volcanoes causes outburst of gases and dust particles. These partially block the incoming rays of the Sun which lead to cooling of the weather.

Anthropogenic or Man-made Causes of Climate Change

The anthropogenic or man-made causes of climate change are as follows :

- **Deforestation** Forests act as carbon sink and play an important role in fight against global warming. When forest is disturbed or cleared, carbon stored is released as carbon dioxide causing global warming.
- **Burning of Fossil Fuel** Burning of carbon-based fossil fuels causes release of carbon dioxide in the atmosphere. This has led to increase in concentration of carbon dioxide (CO_2) in the atmosphere.
- **Modern Agricultural Practices** Agricultural practices adopted in recent years contribute to a large extent towards global warming. Flooded field used for rice cultivation is a major contributor of methane gas, a potent greenhouse gas.
- **Industrialisation and Urbanisation** The excessive exploitation of resources for industrial activities has large impact on climate change.
- Cutting down forests to create industrial complexes and settlements had led to changes in the amount of sunlight reflected from the ground back into space.

Global Warming

- The increased amount of CO_2 in the air is mainly responsible for global warming. About 75 % of the solar energy reaching the Earth is absorbed by the Earth's surface, which increases its temperature. The rest of the heat radiates back to the atmosphere.
- Some of the heat is trapped by gases such as carbon dioxide, methane, ozone, **Chlorofluorocarbon** (CFC) compounds and water vapour in the atmosphere. Thus, they add to the heating of the atmosphere. This causes Global warming.

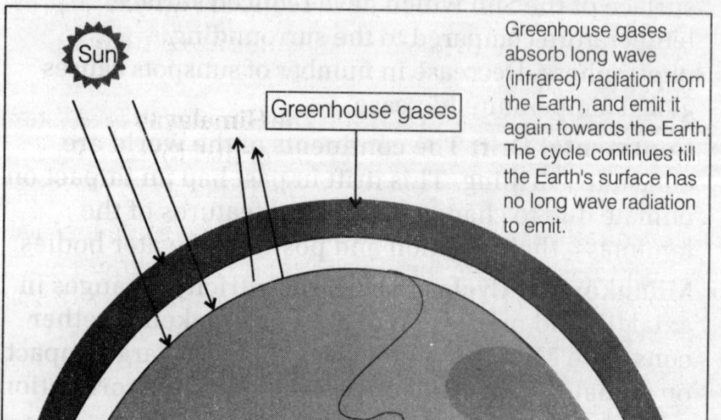

Impacts of Global Warming

The impacts of Global warming are as follows :

- **Melting of Ice** Since 1995, the ice shelf's area has shrunk by 40%. According to NASA, the polar ice cap is now melting at the alarming rate of 9% per decade. Arctic ice thickness has decreased 40% since the 1960s.
- **Rise in Sea Level** Human activities, such as burning coal and oil, cutting down tropical forests, have increased atmospheric concentration of heat-trapping gases.

  It caused the planet to warm by 1.4° Fahrenheit since, 1880. Rising temperatures are warming ocean waters, which expand as the temperature increases.
- **Change in Ocean Current** Far beneath the surface of the ocean, deep currents act as conveyer belts, channeling heat, carbon, oxygen and nutrients around the globe. A new study has found the recent climate change may be acting to slow down one of these conveyer belts, with potentially serious consequences for the future of the planet.
- **Impact on Biodiversity** Global warming does not only make vegetation 'gasp for air' but also leads to animal habitat loss. This is an especially big problem for sensitive species. The loss of these habitats leads to extinction of the amphibians dependent on these forests for their survival.

  Many species may be seriously affected by the spread of viruses and bacteria which normally thrive in warmer conditions. This, among many other things, may push these animals even closer to the brink of extinction.
- **Impact on Human Health** Warming oceans and a changing climate are resulting in extreme weather patterns which have brought about an increase of infectious diseases both new and re-emerging. An increase in temperature signifies an increase in mosquito populations, escalating the risk of malaria, dengue and other insect borne infections.

  These extreme weather patterns are creating extended rainy seasons in some areas and extended periods of drought in others as well as introducing new climates to different regions.
- **Impact on Climate** There is clear evidence of changes in the composition of the greenhouse gases in the lower atmosphere, with CO_2 in particular steadily increasing to its present level of about 400 ppm. It has increased by one-third in the last 200 years, and half of that in the last 30 years.
- **Impact on Food Production** Moderate warming and more carbon dioxide in the atmosphere may help plants to grow faster. More severe warming, however may reduce yield due to drought and floods.

Global Warming Potential

- The Global Warming Potential (GWP) for a gas is a measure of the total energy that a gas absorbs over a particular period of time (usually 100 years), compared to carbon dioxide.
- Gases with a higher GWP absorb more energy, than gases with a lower GWP and thus contribute more to warming Earth.

Climate Change Mitigation Methods

Climate change mitigation consists of actions to limit the magnitude and/or rate of long-term climate change. Climate change mitigation generally involves reduction in anthropogenic emissions of **Greenhouse gases.**

Mitigation may also be achieved by increasing the capacity of carbon sinks, through reforestation.

Mitigation policies can substantially reduce the risks associated with human induced global warming.

Few of the climate change mitigation methods are as follows:

- **Carbon Dioxide Capture and Sequestration** Carbon Sequestration is the process of capturing and string atmospheric carbon dioxide. It is a set of technologies that can greatly reduce CO_2 emission from new as well as existing coal and gas fired power plants and large industrial sources.
- **Carbon Offsetting** Mitigation of carbon footprints through the development of alternative projects is known as Carbon offsetting. The alternative projects may be the solar, wind, tidal energy or reforestation.
- **Carbon Tax** It is a tax levied on the carbon content of fuels. It is a form of carbon pricing. Carbon is present in every hydrocarbon fuel (coal, petroleum and natural gas) and is released as carbon dioxide when they are burnt. In contrast, non-combustion energy sources— wind, sunlight, hydropower and nuclear do not convert hydrocarbons to CO_2.
- **Carbon Footprint** It is the mark that we have on our planet as a result of our daily activities and usage or emission of carbon dioxide. In other words, it is the measures of impact that human activities have on the environment. This is calculated in proportion to the greenhouse gases produced and measured in units of carbon dioxide.
- **Carbon Credit** It is a permit that allows the holder to emit one tonne of carbon dioxide. Credits are credited to countries or groups that have reduced their greenhouse gases below their emission quota. Carbon credits can be traded in the International market at their current market price.

  The carbon credit system was ratified in conjunction with the **Kyoto Protocol**. Its goal is to stop the increase of carbon dioxide emissions.
- **Carbon Trading** Carbon trading is an exchange of credits between nations designed to reduce emissions of carbon dioxide. The carbon trade allows countries that have higher carbon emission to purchase the right to release more carbon dioxide into the atmosphere from countries that have lower carbon emissions.

  The concept of carbon trade was the outcome of Kyoto Protocol, signed in Kyoto, Japan by 180 countries in 1997. The Kyoto Protocol calls for 38 industrialised countries to reduce their greenhouse gas emission between 2008 to 2012 levels that are 5.2% lower than those of 1990.

Mission/Schemes Related to Climate Change

Important mission/schemes related to climate change are as follows :

National Action Plan on Climate Change (NAPCC)

- Government of India has launched eight missions as part of the National Action Plan on Climate Change (NAPCC) in specific areas.
- These areas are solar energy, enhanced energy efficiency, sustainable habitat, water, sustaining the Himalayan eco-system, green India, sustainable agriculture etc.
- It also includes strategic knowledge for climate change, which include assessment of the impact of climate change and actions needed to address climate change.
  - **National Solar Mission** The NAPCC aims to promote the development and use of solar energy for power generation and other uses through this mission. Its ultimate objective is to make solar competitive with fossil-based energy options.
  - **National Mission for Enhanced Energy Efficiency** It includes initiatives based on increasing the energy use efficiency were expected to yield savings of 10000 MW by 2012.
  - **National Mission on Sustainable Habitat** It aims to promote energy efficiency as a core component of urban planning.
  - **National Water Mission** With water scarcity projected to worsen as a result of climate change, the plan sets a goal of a 20% improvement in water use efficiency through pricing and other measures.
  - **National Mission for Sustaining the Himalayan Ecosystem** The plan aims to conserve biodiversity, forest cover and other ecological values in the Himalayan region.
  - **National Mission for a 'Green India'** Its goals include the afforestation of 6 million hectares of degraded forest lands, expanding forest cover from 23% to 33% and enhance annual CO_2 sequestration by 50-60 million tonnes in the year 2020.

- **National Mission for Sustainable Agriculture** The plan aims to support climate adaptation in agriculture through the development of climate-resilient crops, expansion of weather insurance mechanisms and agricultural practices.
- **National Mission on Strategic Knowledge for Climate Change** It aims to gain a better understanding of climate science, impacts and challenges. The plan envisions a new Climate Science Research Fund, improved climate modelling and increased international collaboration. It also encourages private sector initiatives to develop adaptation and mitigation technologies through venture capital funds.

National Clean Energy Fund (NCEF)

- The Finance Bill 2010-11 provided for creation of a corpus called National Clean Energy Fund to invest in entrepreneurial ventures and research in the field of clean energy technologies.
- **An Inter-Ministerial Group** (IMG) has been constituted to approve the projects/schemes eligible for financing under the National Clean Energy Fund. The National Clean Energy Fund will be used for funding research and innovative projects in clean energy technologies.

Conferences Related to Climate Change

Important conferences related to climate change are as follows :

- **Stockholm Conference, 1972** Stockholm was the first world conference to make the environment a major issue. It was adopted on 22 May, 2001 in Stockholm, Sweden and entered into force on 17th May, 2004. The objective of the Stockholm Convention is to protect human health and the environment from persistent organic pollutants.
- **Montreal Protocol, 1987** To stop depletion of Ozone layer, this conference was organised in Canada on 16th September, 1987. In this conference, an agreement was signed about the production of Chlorofluoro carbon gases in next ten years.
- **Helsinki Conference, 1989** This conference was organised to stop a mission of Chlorofluoro carbon (CFCs) gases in order to reduce Ozone depletion.
- **First Earth Summit, 1992** (Rio Summit) It is also known as The United Nations Conference on Environment and Development (UNCED) or Rio Summit. It was held in Rio de Janeiro from 3rd June to 14th June, 1992.
- It was attended by 172 countries. The theme of this conference was the state of the Global environment and the political relationship between economics, science and the environment. The Rio Summit produced conventions dealing with climate change, biodiversity, forestry and recommended a list of development practices called **'Agenda 21'**.
- **United Nations Framework Convention on Climate Change** (UNFCCC) The UNFCCC was signed in 1992, at the United Nations Conference on Environment and Development. The UNFCCC entered into force on 21st March, 1994, and has been ratified by 197 countries.
- The goal of UNFCCC is to stabilise greenhouse gas concentrations in the atmosphere at a level that prevents hazardous human involvement with the climate system while allowing ecosystems to adapt naturally and allowing for sustainable development.

Conference of Parties (COP) Summit

Place	Year	Important Facts
Berlin (Germany) (COP 1)	1995	The first UNFCCC Conference of the Parties took place from 28th March to 7th April, 1995 in Berlin, Germany. It voiced concerns about the adequacy of countries abilities to meet commitments under the subsidiary Body for Scientific and Technological Advice (SBSTA) and the Subsidiary Body for Implementation (SBI). CoP 1 agreed on "Activities Implemented Jointly", first joint measures in international climate action.
Geneva (Switzerland) (COP 2)	1996	Its ministerial declaration was noted (but not adopted) on 18th July, 1996 and reflected a United States position statement presented by Timothy Wirth, former under Secretary for Global Affairs for the United States Department of States. It accepted the scientific findings on climate change proffered by the Intergovernmental Panel on Climate Change (IPCC) in its second assessment (1995).
Kyoto (Japan) (COP 3)	1997	CoP 3 took place in December 1997 in Kyoto, Japan. The outcome was the famous Kyoto Protocol. The Kyoto Protocol was the legally binding protocol, which outlined the greenhouse gas emissions reduction obligation for Annex I countries. It also came out with some mechanisms collectively known as Kyoto mechanisms. These mechanisms include the emissions trading, Clean Development Mechanism (CDM) and joint implementation. The Government of India had decided to ratify the Kyoto Protocol in 2002 after various countries had ratified the protocol.
Buenos Aires (Argentina) (COP 4)	1998	In this conference, Plan of Action was incorporated to implement Kyoto Protocol.
Bonn (Germany) (COP 5)	1999	This conference was organised to discuss on technical subject of climate change.
The Hague (Netherlands) (COP 6)	2000	A major issue was discussed in this CoP was the proposal of the United States, in which it said that credit for carbon 'sinks' should be allowed in forests and agricultural lands.

Place	Year	Important Facts
Marrakesh (Morocco) (COP 7)	2001	The outcome of the session was a Bundle of decision known as **Marrakesh Accords**. In this session, US took part as an observer. By this time, the Kyoto Protocol was not put in force, as 55 countries had not ratified it. An Adaptation Fund was established, primarily in supporting developing countries better adapt to climate change.
New Delhi (India) (COP 8)	2002	Outcome of this session of UNFCCC was the Delhi Ministerial Declaration, which called the developed countries to transfer technology and minimise the impact of climate change on developing countries.
Milan (Itlay) (COP 9)	2003	In this conference, a fund was created for developing nations to control climate change.
Buenos Aires (Argentina) (COP 10)	2004	In this conference, Buenos Aires Action Plan was incorporated which aimed to promote issues of climate change.
Montreal (Canada) (COP 11)	2005	Important outcome of CoP 11 was the **Montreal Action Plan** (MAP). The MAP called for an extension to the life of the Kyoto Protocol beyond its 2012 expiration date and negotiate deeper cuts in greenhouse gas emissions. Thus, it became the basis of the negotiations for extending the Kyoto Protocol beyond 2012.
Nairobi (Kenya) (COP 12)	2006	A Five Year Plan of work to support climate change adaptation by developing countries was adopted and agreed on the procedures and modalities for the Adaptation Fund.
Bali (Indonesia) (COP 13)	2007	In this meeting, an Adhoc Working Group on Long-term Cooperative Action (AWGLCA) under the convention was established as a new subsidiary body to conduct the negotiations aimed at urgently enhancing the implementation of the convention upto and beyond 2012.
Poznan (Poland) (COP 14)	2008	—
Copenhagen (Denmark) (COP 15)	2009	In this conference, Green Climate Fund was established.
Cancun (Mexico) (COP 16)	2010	The agenda for Cancun was an agreement on a **Green Fund** to disburse the aid that the developed countries promised at Copenhagen i.e. $ 100 billion a year by 2020 for the developing countries to adapt the climate change by building the seawalls and shifting farming patterns and also to install clean energy sources.
Durban (South Africa) (COP 17)	2011	More than 190 countries met in Durban, South Africa, to agree on a global deal to succeed the Kyoto Protocol, which was to expire in 2012 and cut emissions of planet-warming greenhouse gases.
Doha (Qatar) (COP 18)	2012	The conference produced a package of documents collectively titled the **Doha Climate Gateway**. The documents collectively contained an amendment of the Kyoto Protocol featuring second commitment period running from 2012 until 2020, limited in scope to 15% of the global carbon dioxide emissions due to the lack of commitments of Japan.
Warsaw (Poland) (COP 19)	2013	In the conference, the rule book for **Reducing Emissions from Deforestation and Forest Degradation** (REDD) was agreed, together with measures to bolster forest preservation and a results based payment system to promote forest protection. The **Climate Technology Centre and Network** (CTCN) was established with an aim to stimulating technology cooperation and transfer to developing countries.
Lima (Peru) (COP 20)	2014	In the conference, 194 Nations pledged to reduce world carbon emission.
Paris (France) (COP 21)	2015	The 21st Conference of Parties under the UNFCCC agreed on adoption of the Paris Agreement on post-2020 actions on climate change. This universal agreement is to succeed the Kyoto Protocol. This agreement is different from the Kyoto Protocol in that, it provides a framework for all countries to take steps to curb climate change.
Marrakesh (Morocco) (COP 22)	2016	The Marrakesh Partnership for Global Climate Action was adopted at this conference.
Bonn (Germany) (COP 23)	2017	The purpose of this summit was to make plan for reaching the targets set under the Paris Agreement of 2015. Its key agenda was to bring out a so called 'Rule Book' or 'Paris Work Programme' which countries need to abide by in post 2020 world.
Katowice (Poland) (COP 24)	2018	It set up Overall Mitigation in Global Emissions (OMGE) under the Paris Agreement.
Madrid (Spain) (COP 25)	2019	The prime objective of the conference was to complete the rule-book to the 2015 Paris Agreement that will become effective in 2020 to replace the 1997 Kyoto Protocol (comes to an end in 2020).
Scotland (United Kingdom) (COP 26)	2021	Delayed for a year due to the COVID-19 pandemic, it was the 26th Conference of the Parties (CoP) to the United Nations Framework Convention on Climate Change (UNFCCC), the third meeting of the parties to the 2015 Paris Agreement and the 16th meeting of the parties to the Kyoto Protocol.
Sharm El-Sheikh (Egypt) (COP 27)	2022	It brought Governments together to accelerate global efforts to comfort the climate crisis.
United Arab Emirates (COP 28)	2023	COP28 countries agreed to launch the Loss and Damage (L and D) fund, hosted by the World Bank COP28 released the fifth iteration of the Global Stocktake (GST), adopting eight steps to limit global temperature rise to 1.5 degrees C. 66 Nantional signatories committed to a 68% reduction in cooling-related emissions by 2050. UNCTAD estimates that developed nations owe developing countries $500 billion in 2025 under the New Collective Quantified Goal (NCQG)
Baku, Azerbaijan (COP 29)	2024	—

Greenhouse Effect

- A Greenhouse/glasshouse is a building made of glass chambers in which plants are grown in cold countries or in cold climate areas.
- There is a continued increase in temperature in greenhouse when outside temperature remained low. It protects plants from frost.
- The greenhouse effect is a naturally occurring phenomenon that blankets the Earth lower atmosphere and warm it, maintaining the temperature suitable for living things to survive.
- Just as greenhouses, that keep the air warm inside their chamber, water vapour and greenhouse gases warm the Earth.

Greenhouse Gases

- Greenhouse gases play an important role in the balance of Earth's cooling and warming. The effect was first recognised by French scientist, **Jean-Baptiste Fourier.**
- Due to the presence of greenhouse gases, the atmosphere is behaving like a greenhouse. The atmosphere also transmits the incoming solar radiation but absorbs the vast majority of long-wave radiation emitted upwards by the Earth's surface.
- The primary GHGs of concern today are **carbon dioxide** (CO_2), **Chlorofluorocarbons** (CFCs), **methane** (CH_4), **nitrous oxide** (N_2O) and **ozone** (O_3). Some other gases such as **nitric oxide** (NO) and **carbon monoxide** (CO) easily react with GHGs and affect their concentration in the atmosphere.
- The effectiveness of any given GHG molecule will depend on the magnitude of the increase in its concentration, its life time in the atmosphere and the wavelength of radiation that it absorbs.
- The largest concentration of GHGs in the atmosphere is **Carbon dioxide**. The emission of CO_2 comes mainly from fossil fuel combustion (oil, gas and coal). Forests and oceans are the sinks for the carbon dioxide. Forests use CO_2 in their growth.

Major Greenhouse Gases

Greenhouse Gas	Sources	Sinks	Importance for Climate
Carbon Dioxide (CO_2)	• Burning of fossil fuel • Land-use change (deforestation)	• Ocean uptake • Plants photosynthesis	• Absorbs infrared radiation; affects stratospheric O_3
Methane (CH_4)	• Biomass burning • Enteric fermentation • Rice paddy	• Reactions with OH • Microorganisms uptake by soils	• Absorbs infrared radiation; affects tropospheric O_3, affects stratospheric O_3 and H_2O; produces CO_2
Nitrous Oxide (N_2O)	• Biomass burning • Fossil-fuel combustion • Fertilisers	• Removal by soils • Stratospheric photolysis and reaction with O	• Absorbs infrared radiation; affects stratospheric O_3
Ozone (O_3) (ground layer)	• Photochemical reactions involving O_2	• Catalytic chemical reactions involving NO_x, ClO_x and HO_x species	• Absorbs ultraviolet and infrared radiations
Carbon Monoxide (CO)	• Plant emissions • Man-made release (transport, industrial)	• Soil uptake • Reactions with OH	• Affects stratospheric O_3 and OH cycles; produces CO_2
Chlorofluorocarbons (CFCs)	• Industrial production	• Insignificant in troposphere, dissociated in stratosphere (photolysis and reaction with O)	• Absorbs ultraviolet and infrared radiation
Sulphur Dioxide (SO_2)	• Volcanoes • Coal and biomass burning	• Dry and wet deposition • Reactions with OH	• Forms aerosols, which scatter solar radiation
Water Vapour (H_2O)	• Evaporation of ocean	• Rain, snowfall	• Forms hydrological cycle

Ozone Layer Depletion

- Ozone (O_3) is a highly reactive gas that is made up of three oxygen atoms.
- It is both a natural and man-made product that occurs in the stratosphere and troposphere.
- Ozone influences life on Earth in either a positive or negative way depending on where it resides in the atmosphere.
- Ozone which absorbs ultra violet radiation in the stratosphere is very effective in absorbing terrestrial radiation when it is present in the lower troposphere.
- Ozone occurs in the stratosphere where ultra-violet rays convert oxygen into ozone.
- Thus, ultra violet rays do not reach the Earth's surface. The CFCs which drift into the stratosphere destroy the ozone. Large depletion of ozone occurs over Antarctica.

- The depletion of ozone concentration in the stratosphere is called the Ozone hole. The ozone hole over Antarctica develops every year between late August and early October. This allows the ultra violet rays to pass through the troposphere.
- The thickness of the ozone in a column of air from the ground to the top of the atmosphere is measured in terms of Dobson Units (DU).

Causes of Ozone Layer Depletion

- CFCs are used in refrigerants. Ozone gas is continuously generated in the stratosphere by the action of UV radiation on molecular oxygen and it is also degraded into molecular oxygen.
- Halogens are also responsible for depletion of ozone layer. Halogens are components of Fire Extinguisher.

Ozone Hole

- The ozone layer above the Antarctic has been particularly impacted by pollution since the mid of 1980s. This region's low temperature speeds up the conversion of CFCs to chlorine.
- The vast hole in the ozone layer above Antarctica appears to be healing. The study was published by researchers from the World Meteorological Organisation (WMO) and the UN Environment Programme (UNEP) states that, the size of the ozone hole has strunk on average by around 4 sq km since 2000.
- The Montreal Protocol, a 1987 international treaty ratified by all UN members, successfully spurred nations to eradicate the use of CFCs in products.

Consequences of Ozone Layer Depletion

- With the depletion of ozone layer, more UV radiation filters into troposphere. UV-B damages DNA and mutation may occur. It causes aging of skin, damage to skin cells and various types of skin cancers.
- In human eye, cornea absorbs UV-B radiation and a high dose of UV-B causes inflammation of cornea, called **Snow-blindness, Cataract**, etc. Such exposure may permanently damage the cornea.
- Plant proteins get easily affected by UV radiations which leads to the harmful mutation of cells.
- It also increases evaporation of surface water through the stomata of the leaves and decreases the moisture content of the soil. Increase in UV radiations damage paints and fibres, causing them to fade faster.

Acid Rain

- Acid rain refers to the ways in which acid from the atmosphere is deposited on the Earth's surface.
- Oxides of nitrogen and sulphur which are acidic in nature can be blown by wind along with solid particles in the atmosphere.
- Finally, they settle down either on the ground as dry deposition or in water, fog and snow as wet deposition.

Causes of Acid Rain

- Acid rain is a by-product of a variety of human activities that emit the oxides of sulphur and nitrogen in the atmosphere.
- Burning of fossil fuels (which contain sulphur and nitrogenous matter) such as coal and oil in power stations and furnaces or petrol and diesel in motor engines produce sulphur dioxide and nitrogen oxides.
- SO_2 and NO_2 after oxidation and reaction with water are major contributors to acid rain, because polluted air usually contains particulate matter that catalyse the oxidation.
- Aerosol particles of oxides or ammonium salts in rain drops result in wet deposition. SO_2 is also absorbed directly on both solid and liquid ground surfaces and is thus deposited as dry-deposition.

Impacts of Acid Rain

- Acid rain is harmful for agriculture, trees and plants as it dissolves and washes away nutrients needed for their growth.
- It causes respiratory ailments in human beings and animals. When acid rain falls and flows as ground water to reach rivers, lakes, etc. It affects plants and Animals life in Aquatic ecosystem.
- It corrodes water pipes resulting in the leaching of heavy metals such as iron, lead and copper into the drinking water.
- Acid rain damages buildings and other structures made of stone or metal. The Taj Mahal in India has been affected by acid rain.

Extra Facts From Tamil Nadu Board and NIOS

- Since the advent of industrialisation, the global annual temperature has risen to more than 1%. From **1680** to **1980**, it has increased on an average by 0.07% every decade. Since 1981, the rate of growth in the global temperature has doubled. For the last four decades, it has risen by 0.18% every 10 years. If the trend continues then the global temperature would reach around **1.5%** in **2040**.
- The Intergovernmental Panel on Climate Change was created by the United Nations Environment Programme and World Meteorological Organisation in **1988.** It is an organisaton of governments that are members of the UN or WMO. Presently, there are **195** members. The main objective of the panel was to provide scientific and rational information to all the governments of the world so that they can develop climate policies.

32

Environmental Issues

(SOURCES)

Class-IX Old NCERT Chap 11 (Geography) (Human Impact on Environment), Class-XII New NCERT Chap 16 (Biology) (Environmental Issues), Class-XII New NCERT Chap 9 (Geography) (Geographical Perspective on Selected Issues and Problems), Tamil Nadu Board (Class XI), NIOS

Environmental Pollution

- Environmental pollution is the effect of undesirable changes in our surroundings that have harmful effects on plants, animals and human beings.
- A substance, which causes pollution, is known as **pollutant**.
- Pollutants are solid, liquid, or gaseous chemicals that are present in greater concentration than in natural abundance and are formed as a result of human actions or natural occurrences.
- Pollutants can be biodegradable, such as discarded vegetables, which degrade quickly through natural processes.
- Pollutants that degrade slowly, on the other hand, can persist in the environment for many decades.
- Substances such as dichloro diphenyl trichloroethane (DDT), plastic polymers, heavy metals, numerous chemicals, nuclear wastes and others are difficult to remove once discharged into the environment.
- In the process of environmental pollution, pollutants originate from a source and get transported by air or water or are dumped into the soil by human beings.

Types of Pollution

- Mainly, there are following types of pollution :

—Air Pollution —Water Pollution
—Land Pollution —Noise Pollution

Air Pollution

- Air pollution occurs due to undesirable solid or gaseous particles, particulate matter in the air, in quantities that are harmful to human health and the environment.
- Air pollution is taken as addition of contaminants, like dust, fumes, gas, fog, odour, smoke or vapour to the air in substantial proportion and duration that may be harmful to *flora* and *fauna* and property.
- With increasing use of varieties of fuels as the source of energy, there is a marked increase in emission of toxic gases into the atmosphere resulting in the pollution of air.
- Combustion of fossil fuels, mining and industries are the main sources of air pollution. These processes release oxides of sulphur and nitrogen, hydrocarbons, carbon dioxide, carbon monoxide, lead and asbestos.

Air Pollutants

The following are the major gaseous and particulate pollutants present in the troposphere:

- **Gaseous air pollutants** These are oxides of sulphur, nitrogen and carbon, hydrogen sulphide, hydrocarbons, ozone and other oxidants.
- **Particulate pollutants** These are dust, mist, fumes, smoke, smog, etc.

Effects of Air Pollution

Effects of air pollution on human health are as follows:

- **Sulphur** (S) It causes irritation of eyes, nose, throat, damage to lungs when inhaled. It also causes diseases acute and chronic asthma, bronchitis, emphysema and lung cancer.

- **Ammonia** (NH_3) It plays a critical role in the transportation and enhanced deposition of acidic pollutant. Its high concentration also harms vegetation, animals and humans. Main source of ammonia in the environment are cattle. Dairy production systems are hot-spots of ammonia emission.
- **Suspended Particulate Matter** Airborne particles are tiny fragments of solid or liquid nature suspended in the air (which are called **aerosols**).
- **Acid Deposition** The process by which acidic air pollutants, generally sulphur dioxide and nitrogen oxides, are deposited on the Earth. Much of this deposition occurs when the pollutants condense in water and fall to the Earth as precipitation, generally known as **Acid rain.**

  Acid deposition causes changes in the pH of water and soil, leading to a host of environmental problems. Acid deposition may be reduced by switching to low-sulphur coal or by removing the sulphur either before or after combustion, often by adding scrubbers to smokestacks.
- **Wet Deposition** It refers to acid rain, fog and snow. If the acid chemicals in the air are blown into areas where the weather is wet, the acids can fall to the ground in the form of rain, snow, fog or mist.
- **Dry Deposition** In areas where the weather is dry, the acid chemicals may become incorporated into dust or smoke and fall to the ground through dry deposition, sticking to the ground, buildings, homes, cars and trees.

  Dry deposited gases and particles can be washed from these surfaces by rainstorms, leading to increased runoff. This runoff water makes the resulting mixture more acidic. About half of the acidity in the atmosphere falls back to the Earth through dry deposition.

Measures to Control Air Pollution

- Electrostatic precipitator, which can remove over 99% particulate matter present in the exhaust from a thermal power plant.
- A scrubber can remove gases like sulphur dioxide. In a scrubber, the exhaust is passed through a spray of water or lime. Proper maintenance of automobiles along with use of lead-free petrol or diesel can reduce the pollutants they emit.
- Catalytic converters, having expensive metals namely platinum-palladium and rhodium as the catalysts, are fitted into automobiles for reducing emission of poisonous gases.
- As the exhaust passes through the catalytic converter, unburnt hydrocarbons are converted into carbon dioxide and water and carbon monoxide and nitric oxide are changed to carbon dioxide and nitrogen gas, respectively.

Government Initiatives to Prevent Air Pollution

The initiatives taken by government to prevent air pollution are as follows :

- **The Air** (Prevention and Control of Pollution) Act. It was a law passed by India's Parliament to prevent and manage the detrimental impacts of air pollution in the country. This act is regarded as the government of India's first concrete effort toward combating air pollution.
- **The Government of India** Through a new auto fuel policy has laid out a roadmap to cut down vehicular pollution in Indian cities. More stringent norms for fuels means steadily reducing the sulphur and aromatic content in petrol and diesel fuels.
- **National Air Quality Monitoring Programme** The Central Pollution Control Board (CPCB) has been executing a nationwide programme of ambient air quality monitoring known as National Air Quality Monitoring Programme (NAMP).
- **National Ambient Air Quality Standards** National Ambient Air Quality Standards (NAAQS) were notified in the year 1982. It is based on health criteria and land uses.
- **Air Quality Index** (AQI) It was launched in 2015. The AQI has six categories of air quality viz, good, satisfactory, moderately polluted, poor, very poor and severe with distinct colour scheme. AQI considers eight pollutants i.e. PM10, PM 2.5, NO_2, SO_2, CO, O_3, NH_3 and Pb.

SAFAR

- SAFAR-Air (System of Air Quality and Weather Forecasting and Research) is the first mobile application service in India to provide a current and advanced forecast for air quality. The application was developed by scientists at **Indian Institute of Tropical Meteorology** (IITM), Pune.
- It will enable citizens to check their city's air quality in real time. The app will provide current data and a forecast for air quality in the user's current location through a colour-coded system- green is good, yellow is moderately polluted, orange is poor, red is very poor and maroon is critical.

Water Pollution

- Pollution of water originates from human activities. Through different paths, pollution reaches surface or ground water. Point sources of pollution are easily identified source or place of pollution. e.g., municipal and industrial discharge pipes where pollutants enter the water-source.
- **Non point sources of pollution** are those where a source of pollution cannot be easily identified, e.g., agricultural runoff (from farm, animals and crop-lands), acid rain, storm-water drainage (from streets, parking lots and lawns), etc.

Water Pollutants and their Sources

Pollutant	Source
Micro-organisms	Domestic sewage
Organic wastes	Domestic sewage, animal excreta and waste, decaying animals and plants, discharge from food processing factories.
Plant nutrients	Chemical fertilisers
Toxic heavy metals	Industries and chemical factories
Sediments	Erosion of soil by agriculture and strip mining
Pesticides	Chemicals used for killing insects, fungi and weeds
Radioactive substances	Mining of uranium containing minerals
Heat	Water used for cooling in industries

Causes of Water Pollution

- **Pathogens** The most serious water pollutants are the disease-causing agents called Pathogens. Pathogens include bacteria and other organisms that enter water from domestic sewage and animal excreta.
- **Organic wastes** The other major water pollutant is organic matter such as leaves, grass, trash etc. They pollute water as a consequence of run off. Excessive phytoplanktons growth within water is also a cause of water pollution. These wastes are biodegradable.
- **Chemical Pollutants** Water soluble inorganic chemicals that include heavy metals such as cadmium, mercury, nickel, etc constitute an important class of pollutants.

Measures to Control Water Pollution

The controlling measures of water pollution are as follows :

- **Clean Water Act** or other such acts are to regulate how industries and water treatment plants processed their water before releasing it.
- **Communities and industries** have come up with solutions for reducing the amount of sediment in water by preventing soil erosion through building dams and planting trees.Utility companies have improved the controls in their treatment plants and fixed broken pipes to reduce the amount of sewage & chemical detergents released into water supplies.
- The **method of Bioremediation** is used to treat contaminated water. Under this method, microorganisms (like Bacteria and Fungi) are used to degrade the environmental contaminants into less toxic forms.
- **The Water** (Prevention and Control of Pollution) **Act, 1974** was enacted in 1974 to provide for the prevention and control of water pollution and for the maintaining or restoring of wholesomeness of water in the country. The Act was amended in 1988.

Namami Gange Mission

An Integrated Ganga Conservation Mission called Namami Gange was set up in 2014 with as a budget of ₹ 20,000 crore. The amount has been allocated for developments of ghats and beautification of river fronts at Kedarnath, Haridwar, Kanpur, Varanasi, Allahabad, Patna and Delhi. Following are objectives of this projects :

- **Nirmal Dhara**
  - ensuring sustainable municipal sewage management.
  - managing sewage from rural areas.
  - managing industrial discharge.
- **Aviral Dhara**
  - Promotion of tourism and shipping in a rational and sustainable manner.
  - Knowledge management on Ganga through Ganga Knowledge Centre.

Sources of Pollution in the Ganga and the Yamuna Rivers

River and State	Polluted Stretches	nature of Pollution	Main Polluters
Ganga (Uttar Pradesh) Bihar and West Bengal	(a) Downstream of Kanpur (b) Downstream of Varanasi (c) Farrakka Barrage	1. Industrial Pollution from towns like Kanpur 2. Domestic wastes from urban centres 3. Dumping of carcasses in the river	Cities of Kanpur, Allahabad, Varanasi, Patna and Kolkata release domestic waste into the river
Yamuna (Delhi) and (Uttar Pradesh)	(a) Delhi to Confluence with Chambal (b) Mathura and Agra	1. Extraction of water by Haryana and Uttar Pradesh for irrigation 2. Agricultural run off resulting in high levels of micro-pollutants in the Yamuna 3. Domestic and industrial waste of Delhi flowing into the river	Delhi dumping its domestic waste

Methods of Measuring Water Quality

The various methods to measure water quality are as follows :

- **Biological Oxygen Demand** The amount of oxygen required by bacteria to break down the organic matter present in a certain volume of a sample of water, is called Biochemical Oxygen Demand (BOD).

  The amount of BOD in the water is a measure of the amount of organic material in the water, in terms of how much oxygen will be required to break it down biologically. Clean water would have BOD value of less than 5 (ppm) whereas highly polluted water could have a BOD value of 17 (ppm) or more.

- **Eutrophication** The process in which nutrient enriched water bodies support a dense plant population, which kills animal life by depriving it of oxygen and results in subsequent loss of biodiversity is known as Eutrophication.
- **Chemical Oxygen Demand** (COD) It is a test that determines the quantity of oxygen necessary to chemically oxidise organic and inorganic substances found in water, such as Ammonia and Nitrate.

Noise Pollution

- Noise pollution refers to the state of unbearable and uncomfortable to human beings which is caused by noise from different sources.
- The main sources of noise pollution are various factories, mechanised construction and demolition works, automobiles and aircraft, etc.
- There may be added periodical but polluting noise from sirens, loudspeakers used in various festivals, programmes associated with community activities.
- The level of steady noise is measured by sound level expressed in terms of **decibels** (dB).
- Sound upto 50 dB is considered as normal. Sound more than 80 dB is called as **Noise**.
- Noise pollution is location-specific and its intensity decreases with increasing distance from the source of pollution, such as industrial districts, transportation corridors, airports and so on.

Measures to Prevent Noise Pollution

- Turn off appliances at home and offices.
- When not in use, we can turn off home and office appliances such as TVs, games, computers and so on, which can cause unnecessary stress on the ears. We can also save electricity by turning them off.
- Close the door when using noisy machines. For rooms where dishwashers or washing machines are housed, we can close the door after turning them on.
- Obey the noise level limits.
- Community law should prohibit the use of loudspeakers, outdoor parties and political public announcements.
- Control noise levels near sensitive areas.

Soil Pollution

- Soil is a thin layer of organic and inorganic materials that covers the Earth's rocky surface.
- Soil pollution is defined as the "addition of substances to the soil, which adversely affect physical, chemical and biological properties of soil and reduces its productivity."
- Soil pollution primarily results from agricultural chemicals (e.g., pesticides) and leachates from solid wastes deposited over it.
- Measures to prevent soil pollution are :
  - Reducing chemical fertiliser and pesticide use
  - Use of bio pesticides, bio fertilisers
  - Organic farming
  - Four R's: Refuse, Reduce, Reuse and Recycle
  - Afforestation and Reforestation
  - Solid waste treatment
  - Reduction of waste from construction areas

Other Types of Pollution

Other important types of pollution are discussed as follows :

Radioactive Pollution

- Radioactive (or nuclear) waste is generated as a by product of nuclear reactors, fuel processing plants, hospitals and research institutes. Decommissioning and dismantling nuclear reactors and other nuclear facilities also generates radioactive waste.
- Radiation, given off by nuclear waste is extremely damaging to organisms, because it causes mutations at a very high rate.
- At high doses, nuclear radiation is lethal but at lower doses, it creates various disorders, the most frequent of all being cancer. Therefore, nuclear waste is an extremely potent pollutant and has to be deal with utmost caution.
- It has been recommended that storage of nuclear waste, after sufficient pre-treatment, should be done in suitably shielded containers buried within the rocks, about 500 m deep below the earth's surface. However, this method of disposal is meeting stiff opposition from the public.

Measures to Prevent Radioactive Pollution

- Safe disposal of radioactive waste.
- Regular monitoring through frequent sampling and quantitative analysis.
- Safety measures against nuclear accidents.
- Nuclear explosions and use of nuclear weapons should be completely banned.

Solid Waste Pollution

- Solid wastes refer to everything that goes out in trash. Municipal solid wastes are wastes from homes, offices, stores, schools, hospitals, etc., that are collected and disposed by the municipality.
- All waste that we generate can be categorised into the following three types :
  - **Bio-degradable waste** It is any product that can be easily broken down naturally by water, oxygen, the Sun's rays, radiation, or micro-organisms. e.g., Food waste, Human Waste, Manure, Sewage, etc.

- **Recyclable waste** Recycling is the process of converting waste materials into new materials and objects and those materials which can be recycled are called Recyclable waste. e.g., Glass, Paper, Metal, Plastic etc.
- **Non-Bio-degradable waste** Those which cannot be decomposed or dissolved by natural agents are called Non-Bio-degradable waste. e.g., Plastic Bottle, Medical waste, Carbon paper etc.

Measures to Prevent Solid Waste Pollution

- **Open Dumps** They dumps refer to uncovered areas that are used to dump solid waste of all kinds. The rainwater run-off from these dumps contaminates nearby land and water thereby spreading disease. Treatment by open dumps is to be phased out.
- **Landfills** They are generally located in urban areas. It is a pit that is dug in the ground. Sanitary landfills were adopted as the substitute for open-burning dumps. In a sanitary landfill, wastes are dumped in a depression or trench after compaction and covered with dirt every day.
- **Incineration plants** The process of burning waste in large furnaces at high temperature is known as **Incineration**. In these plants the recyclable material is segregated and the rest of the material is burnt and ash is produced.
- **Pyrolysis** It is a process of combustion in absence of oxygen or the material burnt under controlled atmosphere of oxygen. It can be seen an alternative to incineration.
- **Composting** It is a biological process in which microorganisms, mainly fungi and bacteria, decompose degradable organic waste into humus like substance in the presence of oxygen.
- **Vermiculture** It is also known as **Earthworm farming**. In this method, Earth worms are added to the compost. These worms break the waste and the added excreta of the worms makes the compost very rich in nutrients.

E-Waste Pollution

- Irreparable computers and other electronic goods are known as **Electronic wastes (e-wastes)**. E-wastes are buried in landfills or incinerated.
- More than half of the e-waste generated in the developed world is exported to developing countries, primarily China, India and Pakistan, where metals such as copper, iron, silicon, nickel and gold are recovered during the recycling process.
- In contrast to developed countries, which have specifically built facilities for E-waste recycling, recycling in developing countries frequently involves manual participation, exposing workers to toxic substances present in E-waste.
- Recycling is the sole method for the treatment of E-waste, provided it is done at an E-waste facility.

Impacts of E-Waste on Human Health

- **Lead** It is found in a wide variety of cell phone components including the circuit boards, batteries and as a stabiliser in PVC products. Lead exposure can cause damage to blood and nervous systems.
- **Cadmium** It is used in the battery of a cell phone. It is associated with deficits in cognition, learning, behaviour and neuromotor skills in children. It has also been linked to kidney damage.
- **Mercury** It is used in the cell phone's battery, crystal displays and circuit boards. A single cell phone contains upto 2 grams of mercury. Mercury exposure contributes to brain and kidney damage.
- **Barium** It is used in computers in the front panel of a CRT to protect users from radiation. Short term exposure to barium causes brain swelling, muscles weakness, damage to heart, etc.
- **Cobalt** Hazardous in case of inhalation and ingestion and is an irritant of the skin.

E-Waste Management Rules, 2016

The E-Waste Management Rules, 2016 has replaced the E-waste (Management and Handling) Rules, 2011 which introduced concept of 'extended producer responsibility'. Main provisions of E-Waste Management Rules 2016 are :

- State Government to prepare integrated plan.
- The transportation of E-Waste shall be carried out as per the manifest emphasis.
- Dealer or retailer or E-retailer shall refund the amount as per take back system. The manufacturer is also now responsible to collect E-waste.

Measures to Prevent E-Waste Pollution

- Proper education, awareness and alternative cost-effective technology must be supplied so that those who rely on this for a living can be provided with a better standard of living.
- To address India's E-waste management concerns, a comprehensive solution is required.
- A suitable system must be developed to incorporate small units from the unorganised sector and large units from the organised sector into a single value chain.

Soil Erosion and Desertification

- The degradation of natural resources can occur, not just by the action of pollutants but also by improper resource utilisation practices.
- The development of the fertile top-soil takes centuries. But it can be removed very easily due to human activities like over-cultivation, unrestricted grazing, deforestation and poor irrigation practices, resulting in arid patches of land.

- When large barren patches extend and meet over time, a desert is created. Desertification has become a major problem because of urbanisation.
- The pressure on agricultural land increases not only due to the limited availability but also by deterioration of quality of agricultural land. Soil erosion, waterlogging, salinisation and alkalinisation of land lead to land degradation.

Deforestation

- Deforestation is the conversion of forested areas to Non-forested ones.
- Factors which led to deforestation are :
  - A number of human activities altogether have contributed to deforestation.
  - One of the major reasons is the conversion of forest to agricultural land so as to feed the growing human population.
  - Trees are axed for timber, firewood, cattle ranching and for several other purposes.
  - Slash and burn agriculture, commonly called as **Jhum cultivation** in the North-Eastern states of India, has also contributed to deforestation.

Causes of Deforestation

- One of the major effects of deforestation is enhanced carbon dioxide concentration in the atmosphere because trees that could hold a lot of carbon in their biomass are lost with deforestation.
- Deforestation also causes loss of biodiversity due to habitat destruction, disturbs hydrologic cycle, causes soil erosion and may lead to desertification in extreme cases. Reforestation is the process of restoring a forest that once existed but was removed at some point of time in the past. Reforestation may occur naturally in a deforested area.

Strategies to Control Environmental Pollution

The strategies adopted to control environmental pollution are as follows :

'Swachh Bharat Abhiyan' or 'Clean India Mission'

- It was launched by Union Government in 2014. Two programmes are being implemented under the broad umbrella of the Swachh Bharat Abhiyan.
- These are **Swachh Bharat Mission–Urban** (SBM–U) and **Swachh Bharat Mission-Gramin** (SBM–G).
- The SBM–U primarily aims at making Urban India free from open defecation and achieving 100% scientific management of solid waste in the country. The SBM–G targets to bring about an improvement in the general quality of life in rural areas by promoting cleanliness and hygiene and eliminating open defecation.

Green Chemistry

- Green chemistry is a production process that would bring about minimum pollution or deterioration to the environment.
- Utilisation of existing knowledge base for reducing the chemical hazards along with the developmental activities is the foundation of green chemistry.
- Green chemistry, is a cost-effective approach which involves reduction in material, energy consumption and waste generation.

International Efforts to Control Environment Pollution

- **Basel Convention** Basel convention was established on 5th May, 1992. It is an international convention aimed at reducing the flow of hazardous waste between Nations and in particular, preventing the transfer of hazardous waste from developed to Less Developed Countries (LDCs).
- **The Rotterdam Convention** The Rotterdam convention was established on 10th September, 1998. It aims to promote shared responsibility and cooperative efforts among Parties in the international trade of certain hazardous chemicals in order to protect human health and the environment from potential harm.
- **Stockholm Convention** Stockholm was the first world conference to make the environment a major issue. It was adopted on 22nd May, 2001 in Stockholm, Sweden and entered into force on 17th May, 2004. The objective of the Stockholm Convention is to protect human health and the environment from persistent organic pollutants.

Extra Facts From Tamil Nadu Board and NIOS

- **Biomagnification** Entry of harmful, non-biodegradable chemicals in small concentration and their accumulation in greater concentration in the various levels of a food chain is called Biomagnification.
- **DDT** (dichloro-diphenyl-trichloro-ethane) used in small quantities to kill mosquitoes can enter the food chain and may get concentrated due to its non-biodegradable nature in the body of birds (top consumer). This causes adverse effects, such as weak egg shells, resulting in decreased population. The lowest intensity of sound that human ear can hear is 10 dB.
- Photochemical smog (smoke + fog) formed by the action of ultraviolet light from the Sun on particulate matter or formed due to burning of coal and petrol in an atmosphere containing SO_2. It prevents dissipation of pollutants and causes breathing disorders.
- Water forms lather with soap which is used for cleaning purposes. It is called Soft water. Sometimes water from some sources like rivers or hand pumps does not produce any lather with soap. It is called **Hard water**.

33

Sustainable Development

(SOURCES)

Class-XI New NCERT Chap 7 (Economics) (Environment and Sustainable Development) Class-XII New NCERT Chap 6 (Geography) (Planning and Sustainable Development in Indian Context), Tamil Nadu Board (Class XII), NIOS

Meaning of Sustainable Development

- The term development is generally used to describe the state of particular societies and the process of changes experienced by them.
- The concept of sustainable development was emphasised by the **United Nations Conference on Environment and Development** (UNCED).
- It defined sustainable development as 'Development that meets the need of the present generation without compromising the ability of the future generation to meet their own needs'.
- The use of the concept 'needs' in the definition is linked to distribution of resources.
- **Edward Barbier** defined sustainable development as "one which is directly concerned with increasing the material standard of living of the poor at the grass root level– this can be quantitatively measured in terms of increased income, real income, educational services, health care, sanitation, water supply etc".

Concept of Sustainable Development

- Sustainable development is a multi-dimensional concept and signifies the positive, irreversible transformation of the economy, society and environment.
- The notion of sustainable development emerged in the wake of general rise in the awareness of environmental issues in the late 1960s in Western world.
- It reflected the concern of people about undesirable effects of industrial development on the environment.
- The publication of **'The Population Bomb'** by **Ehrlich** in 1968 and **'The Limits to Growth'** by **Meadows** in 1972 further raised the level of fear among environmentalists and people.

Objectives of Sustainable Development

- Sustainable development aims at decreasing the absolute poverty of the poor by providing lasting and secure livelihoods that minimise resource depletion, environmental degradation, cultural disruption and social instability.
- The United Nations established a **World Commission** on **Environment** and **Development** (WCED) headed by the Norwegian Prime Minister Gro Harlem Brundtland. The commission was named as Brundtland Report. Brundtland Commission gave a report entitled as 'Our Common Future' in 1987.
- The report defines sustainable development as a **'development that meets the needs of the present without compromising the ability of future generations to meet their own needs.'**
- Sustainable development takes care of ecological, social and economical aspects of development during the present times.
- It urges for conservation of resources to enable the future generations to use these resources.
- It also takes into account the development of whole human kind which have common future.

Fundamental Ideas of Sustainable Development

- **Renewability** The rate of utilisation of renewable resource should be lower than or equal to the rate of regeneration of the resource. The resources that have already depleted due to 'over use' should be given a complete protection.
- **Adaptability** A sustainable developing society has ability to adapt in changing environment. It is also capable of creating opportunities for survival and recreation through innovation, manifested in Research and Development (R&D) activities.
- **Interdependence** A sustainable society neither imports resources from outside through deprivation of other communities, nor it exports its own wastes to create pollution in other societies.
- **Substitution** Sustainable development ensures substitution of use of non-renewable natural resources by the use of renewable natural resources.
- **Institutional Commitment** It includes political support, constitutional provisions, legal framework, coordination between legal institutions and above all the ability to understand the need of sustainable development in a society.

Parameters of Sustainable Development

Parameters of sustainable development refers to the guiding principles that help in understanding the concept of sustainable development.

The parameters include inter and intra-generational equity, carrying capacity and gender inequality.

Inter-generational Equity

It refers to the use of Earth's resources between generations in a manner that the present generation does not consume it completely to its exhaustion.

Three principles form the basis of inter-generational equity are as follows

- Conservation of Option
- Conservation of Quality
- Conservation of Access

Intra-generational Equity

- It refers to fair in utilisation of resources among human members of present generations, both domestically and globally.

Carrying Capacity

- It refers to the number of individuals who can be supported in a given area within natural resource limits, without degrading the natural social, cultural and economic environment for present and future generations.

Gender Inequality

- Due to the gender division of labour in society, women and men have different needs and uses of natural resources.
- The different responsibilities imposed by societies on males and females have implications for how they interact with their local environment.

Process of Sustainable Development

Sustainable development should be the basis for the employment. For this, it is required to collect informations which may be of two types

- **Environment Related Information** It includes information related to biodiversity, physical visual and changed visual land.
- **Human Related Information** It includes information related to the population increase rate, population size, food productivity, etc.
- These informations are collected, evaluated and lastly implemented. Social forestry in India is an important example of human related information.

Strategies for Achieving Sustainable Development

Following efforts are being made to achieve sustainable development

- **Lifestyle** It includes everything in our life; from the food we eat and how we interact with others to the way we get around.
- **Population** It is very closely related with sustainable development, population growth, population ageing and decline, as well as migration and urbanisation affect virtually all development objectives that are on the top of national and global development agendas.
- **Conservation** It concern for maintenance and sustainability is a rational response to the nature of living resources and also an ethical imperative, expressed in the belief that 'we have not inherited the Earth from our parents, we have borrowed it from our children'.

Measures for Promotion of Sustainable Development

Attaining sustainable development in the command area requires major thrust upon the measures to achieve ecological sustainability. The measures for promotion of Sustainable Development are as follows

- **Revamped Cropping Patterns** In general, the cropping pattern shall not include water intensive crops. It shall be adhered to and people shall be encouraged to grow plantation crops such as citrus fruits.

- **Measures to Reduce Water Loss** The CAD programmes such as lining of water courses, land development and levelling and Warabandi system (equal distribution of canal water in the command area of outlet) shall be effectively implemented to reduce the conveyance loss of water.
- **Achieving Social Sustainability** The social sustainability in the region can be achieved only if the land allottees having poor economic background are provided adequate financial and institutional support for cultivation of land.
- **Achieving Economic Sustainability** The agricultural and allied activities have to develop along with other sectors of economy.
- This shall lead to diversification of economic base and establishment of functional linkages between basic villages, agro-service centres and market centres.
- **Solar Power through Photovoltaic Cells** India is naturally endowed with a large quantity of solar energy in the form of Sunlight. With the help of photovoltaic cells, solar energy can be converted into electricity.
- **CNG in Urban Areas** In Delhi, the use of Compressed Natural Gas (CNG) as fuel in public transport system has significantly lowered air pollution and the air has become cleaner in the last few years.
- **Wind Power** In areas where speed of wind is usually high, wind mills can provide electricity without any adverse impact on the environment.
- **Traditional Knowledge and Practices** Traditionally, Indian people have been close to their environment. Use of more organic and environmental friendly products will be essential for environment.
- **Mini-hydel Plants** In mountainous regions, streams can be found almost everywhere. A large percentage of such streams are perennial. Mini-hydel plants use the energy of such streams to move small turbines. The turbines generate electricity which can be used locally.
- **Biocomposting** Farmers, in large numbers all over the country, have again started using compost made from organic wastes of different types. In certain parts of the country, cattle are maintained only because they produce dung which is an important fertiliser and soil conditioner. Earthworms can convert organic matter into compost faster than the normal compositioning process. This process is now being widely used.
- **Use of Non-conventional Sources of Energy** India, is hugely dependent on thermal and hydro power plants to meet its power needs. Both of these have adverse environmental impacts.

Thermal power plants emit large quantities of carbon dioxide which is a green house gas. It also produces fly ash which, if not used properly, can cause pollution of water bodies, land and other components of the environment. Hydroelectric projects inundate forests and interfere with the natural flow of water in catchment areas and the river basins.

New Sustainable Development Agenda

- On 25th September, 2015, United Nations adopted an agreement on the outcome document 'New Sustainable Development Agenda' for the next 15 years (till 2030). The document was adopted in 70th session of UN General Assembly at UN Headquarters, New York.
- The agreement has 169 target issues that comprise different socio-economic issues. The title of the agenda document is 'Transforming Our World, the 2030 Agenda for Sustainable Development'.
- Sustainable Development goals outline broader sustainability agenda dealing with five Ps-**People, Planet, Prosperity, Peace and Partnership**. It seeks to address the universal need for development that works for all people and root causes of poverty. It also includes specific goals on economic indicators for first time.

Sustainable Development Goals

- The United Nations approved the **Sustainable Development Goals** (SDGs), also **known as the Global Goals**, in 2015 as a universal call (to action to end poverty), safeguard the environment and ensure that by 2030, all people enjoy peace and prosperity.
- According to the latest SDG India Index from **NITI Aayog**, India has achieved steady progress toward meeting the United Nations' Sustainable Development Goals (SDGs) in the areas of health, energy and infrastructure. India's overall SDG score increased by 6 points, from 60 in 2019 to 66 in 2020-2021.

The 17 proposed SDGs are as follows

1. End poverty in all its forms everywhere.
2. End hunger, achieve food security and improved nutrition and promote sustainable agriculture.
3. Ensure healthy lives and promote well-beings for all ages.
4. Ensure inclusive and equitable quality education and promote lifelong learning opportunities for all.
5. Achieve gender equality and empower all women and girls.
6. Ensure availability and sustainable management of water and sanitation for all.
7. Ensure access to affordable, reliable, sustainable and modern energy for all.

8. Promote sustained, inclusive and sustainable economic growth, full and productive employment and decent work for all.
9. Build resilient infrastructure, promote inclusive and sustainable industrialisation and foster innovation.
10. Reduce inequality within and among countries.
11. Make cities and human settlements inclusive, safe, resilient and sustainable.
12. Ensure sustainable consumption and production patterns.
13. Take urgent action to combat climate change and its impacts.
14. Conserve and sustainably use the oceans, seas and marine resources for sustainable development.
15. Protect, restore and promote sustainable use of terrestrial ecosystems, sustainably manage forests, combat desertification and halt and reverse land degradation and halt biodiversity loss.
16. Promote peaceful and inclusive societies for sustainable development, provide access to justice for all and build effective, accountable and inclusive institutions at all levels.
17. Strengthen the means of implementation and revitalise the global partnership for sustainable development.

Extra Facts From
Tamil Nadu Board and NIOS

- Sustainability was first featured in the principles adopted by the United Nations Conference on the Human Environment held at Stockholm on 16th June, 1972.
- The United Nations Conference on Sustainable Development (UNCSD), also known as **Rio 2012, Rio+20** or Earth Summit 2012 was the third International Conference on Sustainable Development.
- It was hosted by Brazil in **Rio-de-Janeiro** from 13th to 22nd June, **2012**.
- Paris Agreement To address climate change, countries entered into force shortly thereafter, on 4th November, 2016.
- In the agreement, all countries agree to work of limit global temperature rise to well below 2°C and given the grave risks, to strive for 1.5°C.
- India ranks 116 out of 157 nations on a global index that assesses the performance of countries towards achieving the ambitious Sustainable Development Goals (SDGs).

34

Disaster Management

[SOURCES]

Class-VIII New NCERT Chap 12 (Some Natural Phenomone)
Class-XI New NCERT Chap 7 (India and the World, Natural Hazards and Disasters) Class-XI New NCERT, Class-XI, Chap 3 (Interinor of Earth)
Class-XI New NCERT Chap 10 (Atmostphenc circulations and weather system)

Disaster

- A disaster is a result of natural or man-made causes that leads to sudden disruption of normal life, causing severe damage to life and property to an extent that available social and economic protection mechanisms are inadequate to cope.
- As per origin, disasters can be classified as follows :
  —**Natural disasters** Earthquake, Flood, Drought, Tsunami, landslide, etc.
  —**Man-made disasters** Bhopal Gas Tragedy, Chernobyl Nuclear Disaster and Fukushima Nuclear Disaster, etc.

Natural Disasters in India

Some of the major natural disasters in India are as follows :

Earthquakes

- Earthquakes are by far the most unpredictable and highly destructive of all the natural disasters.
- **Tectonic earthquakes** result from a series of Earth movements brought about by a sudden release of energy during the tectonic activities in the Earth's crust and they are most devastating.
- **Volcanic earthquakes** associated with rock fall, landslides, subsidence, particularly in the mining areas, impounding of dams and reservoirs, etc., have limited area of influence and the scale of damage.
- It is due to movement of the Indian plate at a speed of one centimeter per year towards the North and North-Eastern direction.
- This movement of plates is being constantly obstructed by the Eurasian plate from the North.
- As a result of this, both the plates are said to be locked with each other resulting in accumulation of energy at different points of time.
- Excessive accumulation of energy results in building up of stress, which ultimately leads to the breaking up of the lock and the sudden release of energy causes earthquakes along the Himalayan arch.
- Some of the most vulnerable states are Jammu and Kashmir, Himachal Pradesh, Uttarakhand, Sikkim and the Darjeeling and subdivision of West Bengal and all the seven states of the North-East.

Earthquake Zones

- National Geophysical Laboratory, Geological Survey of India, Department of Meteorology, Government of India, along with the **National Institute of Disaster Management** divided India into the following five earthquake zones :
  —**Zone I** Very high damage risk zone
  —**Zone II** High damage risk zone
  —**Zone III** Moderate damage risk zone
  —**Zone IV** Low damage risk zone
  —**Zone V** Very low damage risk zone
- **Zone I** and **Zone II** had experienced some of the most devastating earthquakes in India. Areas vulnerable to these earthquakes are the North-East states, areas along the Indo-Nepal border in Bihar, Uttarakhand, Western Himachal Pradesh and Kashmir valley and the Kutch (Gujarat).

- **Zone III** covers Southern and South-Eastern parts of Rajasthan, larger parts of Madhya Pradesh, Maharashtra, Karnataka, Jharkhand and Northern and North-Western part of Odisha.
- **Zone IV** is least seismic activity zone. Most of the areas that can be considered safe are from the stable landmass covered under the Deccan Plateau.
- **Zone V** are considered as the weak zones for earthquakes in India-The western Himalaya region, North-Eastern part of India related to this zone.

Effects of Earthquakes

- Earthquakes have all encompassing disastres effects on the area of their occurrence.
- Surface seismic waves produce fissures on the upper layers of the Earth's Crust through which water and other volatile materials gush out, inundating the neighbouring areas.
- Earthquakes are also responsible for landslides and often these cause obstructions in the flow of rivers and channels resulting in the formation of reservoirs.

Effects of Earthquakes

On Ground	On Man-made Structures	On Water
Fissures	Cracking	Waves
Settlements	Slidings	Hydro-Dynamic Pressure
Landslides Liquefaction Earth Pressure Possible	Overturning Buckling Collapse	Tsunami
Chain-effects	Possible Chain-effects	Possible Chain-effects

Earthquake Hazard Mitigation

Some of the measures on disaster preparedness and mitigation are as follows:

- Establishing **Earthquake monitoring centres** (seismological centres) for regular monitoring and fast dissemination of information among the people in the vulnerable areas.
- Use of **Global Positioning System** (GPS) can be of great help in monitoring the movement of tectonic plates.
- Preparing a vulnerability map of the country and dissemination of vulnerability risk information among the people and educating them about the ways and means minimising the adverse impacts of disasters.
- Modifying the house types and building designs in the vulnerable areas and discouraging construction of high-rise buildings, large industrial establishments and big urban centres in such areas.
- Finally, making it mandatory to adopt earthquake-resistant designs and use light materials in major construction activities in the vulnerable areas.

Tsunami

- Earthquakes and Volcanic Eruptions that cause the sea-floor to move abruptly resulting in sudden displacement of ocean water in the form of high vertical waves are called '*tsunamis*'.
- Tsunamis are also known as **harbour** waves or **seismic sea waves.** The seismic waves cause only one instantaneous vertical wave.
- After the initial disturbance, a series of after waves are created in the water that oscilliate between high crest and low trough in order to restore the water level.
- The speed of wave in the ocean depends upon the depth of water. It is more in the shallow water than in the ocean deep.
- As a result of this, the impact of tsunami is less over the ocean and more near the coast where they cause large-scale devastations.
- A ship at sea is not much affected by tsunami. It is difficult to detect a tsunami in the deeper parts of sea because over deep water the tsunami has very long wave-length and limited wave-height.
- Wave length of Tsunami gets reduced and wave height increases when it enters a shallow water.
- Tsunamis are frequently observed along the **Pacific Ring of Fire**, particularly along the coast of Alaska, Japan, Philippines and other Islands of South-East Asia, Indonesia, Malaysia, Myanmar, Sri Lanka, & India etc.

Causes of Tsunami

- Most tsunamis are caused by earthquakes generated in subduction zone, an area where an oceanic plate is forced down into the mantle.
- In general, tsunami is caused by sudden motion on the ocean floor. This sudden motion could be an earthquake, volcanic eruption, or an underwater landslide. The impact of a large meteorite could also cause a tsunami.

Impacts of Tsunami

- After reaching the coast, the tsunami waves release enormous energy stored in them and water flows turbulently onto the land destroying port-cities and towns, structures, buildings and other settlements.
- The loss of life and property is likely to be much higher by a Tsunami as compared to other natural hazards in the coastal areas due to high population density and centre of economic activities. The whole coastline of mainland India alongwith islands in both oceans are prone to Tsunami disaster.

Tsunami Warning System in India

- The 26th December, 2004 Earthquake and the subsequent Tsunami exposed the vulnerability of the Indian coastline to Oceanic hazards.

- Following the event, India started its own interim tsunami warning centre in the first quarter of 2005 to issue tsunami bulletins generated from seismic information.
- The interim services were succeeded by setting up of a state-of-the-art **Indian Tsunami Early Warning System** (ITEWS) at the **Indian National Centre for Ocean Information Services** (INCOIS), Hyderabad, under the **Earth System Sciences Organisation** (ESSO).
- The system implemented in phases became full-fledged 24 × 7 operational early warning system in October 2007.
- The Indian Tsunami Early Warning System has the responsibility to provide tsunami advisories to Indian mainland and the Island regions.
- Acting as one of the **Regional Tsunami Advisory Service Providers** (RTSPs) for the Indian Ocean Region, ITEWS also provides tsunami advisories to the Indian Ocean rim countries alongwith Australia and Indonesia.

Tsunami Warning System (TWS)

- A Tsunami Warning System (TWS) is used to detect tsunamis in advance and issue warnings to prevent loss of life and damage.
- The Tsunami Warning System (TWS) in the Pacific, comprised of 26 participating international member states, has the functions of monitoring seismological and tidal stations throughout the Pacific Basin to evaluated potentially tsunamigenic earthquakes and disseminating tsunami warning information.
- The **Pacific Tsunami Warning Centre** (PTWC) is the operational centre of the Pacific TWS. Located near Honolulu, Hawaii, PTWC provides tsunami warning information to national authorities in the Pacific Basin.

Tropical Cyclone

- Tropical cyclones are intense low-pressure areas confined to the area lying between 30° N and 30° S latitudes, in the atmosphere around which high velocity winds blow.
- Horizontally, it extends up to 500-1000 km and vertically from surface to 12-14 km.
- A tropical cyclone also known as **hurricane** is like a heat engine that is energised by the release of latent heat on account of the condensation of moisture that the wind gathers after moving over the oceans and seas.

Conditions for Emergence of Tropical Cyclone

- Large and continuous supply of warm and moist air that can release enormous latent heat.
- Strong Coriolis force that can prevent filling of low pressure at the centre (absence of Coriolis force near the equator prohibits the formation of tropical cyclone between 0° -5° latitude).
- Unstable condition through the troposphere that creates local disturbances around which a cyclone develops. Absence of strong vertical wind wedge, which disturbs the vertical transport of latent heat.

Structure of Tropical Cyclone

- Tropical cyclones are characterised by large pressure gradients. The centre of the cyclone is mostly a warm and low-pressure, cloudless core known as **eye of the storm**.
- The isobars are closely placed to each other showing high-pressure gradients, which varies between 14-17mb/100 km, but sometimes it can be as high as 60 mb/100 km.

Consequences of Tropical Cyclones

- With the increase in distance from the sea, the force of the cyclone decreases.
- In India, the force of the cyclone decreases with increase in distance from the Bay of Bengal and the Arabian Sea.
- The coastal areas are often struck by severe cyclonic storms with an average velocity of 180 km/h.
- Often, this results in abnormal rise in the sea level known as **Storm Surge**. A surge is generated due to interaction of air, sea and land.
- They cyclone provides the driving of force in the form of very high horizontal pressure-gradient and very strong surface winds.
- The Sea water flows across the coast along with strong winds and heavy downpour.
- Tropical Cyclones results in inundation of human settlements, agricultural fields, damaging crops and destruction of structures created by human beings.

Tropical Cyclones in India

Indian subcontinent is one of the worst cyclone affected areas of the world. Around 8% of the total geographical area, particularly along the Eastern coast and coast of Gujarat is vulnerable to tropical cyclones. Some divastating cyclones that occurred in India are :

- **Cyclone Thane** This cyclone hit the Southern state of Tamil Nadu, killing dozens of people in 2001.
- **Odisha Super Cyclone** This super cyclone that hit Odisha coast in 1999 killed more than 10,000 people.
- **Phailin** It was the most intense tropical cyclone to hit Eastern coast of India since Odisha super cyclone. It swept through Odisha and Andhra coast in 2013.
- **Hudhud Cyclone** Hudhud (2014) pounded India's Eastern coast, killing more than 40 people.
- **Nilofar** This cyclone hit the Gujarat coast in 2014. It was categorised as severe storm.

Thunderstorms and Tornadoes

- Severe local storms are thunderstorms and tornadoes. They are of short duration, occurring over a small area but are violent.
- Thunderstorms are caused by intense convection on moist hot days. A thunderstorm is a well-grown cumulonimbus cloud producting thunder and lightening. When the clouds extend to heights where sub-zero temperature prevails, hails are formed and they come down as hailstorm.
- If there is insufficient moisture, a thunderstorm can generate dust- storms. A thunderstorm is characterised by intense updraft of rising warm air, which casuses the clouds to grow bigger and rise to greater height.
- This causes precipitation. Later, downdraft brings down to Earth the cool air and the rain.
- Form severe thunderstorms sometimes spiralling wind descends like a trunk of an elephant with great force, with very low pressure at the centre, causing massive destruction on its way. Such a phenomenon is called Water Spouts.
- These violent storms are the manifestation of the atmosphere's adjustments to varying energy distribution. They potential and heat energies are converted into kinetic energy in these storms and the restless atmosphere again returns to its stable state.

Lightning

- During the development of a thunderstorm, the air currents move upward while the water droplets move downward. These vigorous movements cause separation of charges. By a Process not yet completely understood, the positive charges accumulate near the lower edges.
- There is accumulation of positive charges near the ground also. When the magnitude of the accumulated charges becomes very large, the air which is normally a poor conductor of electricity, is no longer able to resist their flow.
- Negative and positive charges meet, producing streaks of bright light and sound called an Electric discharge.
- The process of electric discharge can occur between two or more Clouds, or between Clouds and the Earth
- Lightning strike could destroy life and property. It is, therefore, necessary to take measures to protect ourselves.

Lightning Safety

During lightning and thunderstorm no open place is safe.

- Hearing thunder is a alert to rush to a safer place.
- After hearing the last thunder, wait for some time before coming out of the safe place.

Do's and Don'ts During a Thunderstorm

Outside

- Open vehicles, like motorbikes, tractors, construction machinery, open cars are not safe. Open fields, tall trees, shelters in parks, eleveated places do not protect us form lightning strokes.
- In no shelter is available and you are in an open field, stay far away from all trees. Stay away from poles or other metal object. Do not lie on the ground. Instead squat low on the ground.

Inside the House

- Lightning can strike telephone cords, electrical wires and metal pipes.
- During a thunderstorm contact with these should be avoided. Bathing should be avoided during thunderstorms to avoid contact with running water.
- Electrical appliances like computers, TVs, etc., should be unplugged. Electrical lights can remain on. They do not cause any harm.

Flood

- Flooding is defined as the inundation of land and human settlements caused by the rise of water in the channels and its spill-over.
- Floods occur commonly when water in the form of surface run-off exceeds the carrying capacity of the river channels and streams and flows into the neighbouring low-lying flood plains.
- Floods are also caused due to a storm surge in the coastal areas, high intensity rainfall for a considerably longer time period, melting of ice and snow, etc.
- **Assam**, **West Bengal** and **Bihar** are among the high flood-prone states of India. **Tamil Nadu** experiences flooding during November and January due to the retreating monsoon.

Causes of Flood

- **Heavy Rainfall** Heavy rain in the catchment area of a river causes water to overflow its banks, which results in the flooding of nearby areas.
- **Sediment Deposition** River beds become shallow due to sedimentation. The water carrying capacity of such river is reduced. As a result, the rainwater overflows the river banks.
- **Deforestation** Vegetation hampers the flow of water and forces it to percolate in the ground. As a result of deforestation, the land becomes obstruction free and water flows with greater speed into the rivers and causes flood.
- **Cyclone** Cyclone generated sea waves of abnormal height spread the water in the adjoining coastal areas.

In October 1999, Odisha cyclone generated severe floods and caused unprecedent loss of life and property.

- **Interference in Drainage System** Drainage congestion caused by badly planned construction of bridges, roads, railway tracks, canals, etc hampers the flow of water and the result is flood.
- **Change in the Course of River** Meanders and change in the course of river cause floods.
- **Tsunami** Large coastal areas are flooded by rising sea water, when a tsunami strikes the coast.

Consequence of Floods

Floods are also responsible for spread of diseases like cholera, gastro-enteritis, hepatitis and other water-borne diseases spread in the flood-affected areas.

Flood Prone Zones in India

- In India, around 40 million hectare area is flood-prone, which is one-eighth of the total area. The most flood prone areas are the Brahmaputra, Ganga and Indus basins.
- Uttar Pradesh, Bihar, West Bengal and Odisha are the most flood affected states followed by Haryana, Punjab and Andhra Pradesh.
- Now-a-days, Rajasthan and Gujarat also feel the fury of floods. Karnataka and Maharashtra are no longer immune to floods.
- In September 2014, the Kashmir region witnessed disastrous floods across majority of its districts caused by torrential rainfall.

Impact of Floods

- Frequent inundation of agricultural land and human settlement has serious consequences on the national economy and society.
- Floods do not only destroy valuable crops every year but also damage physical infrastructure such as roads, rails, bridges and human settlements.
- Millions of people are rendered homeless and are also washed down alongwith their cattle in the floods.
- Spread of diseases like cholera, gastro-enteritis, hepatitis and other water-borne diseases spread in the flood-affected areas.
- Floods also make a few positive contributions. Every year, floods deposit fertile silt over agricultural fields, which is good for the crops.

Flood Mitigation and Control Measures

- **Warning** With the advancement of technology such as satellite and remote-sensing equipments, flood can be tracked as the water level rises. Evacuation is possible with suitable monitoring and warning. Warning is issued by the **Central Water Commission** (CWC), **Irrigation and Flood Control Department** and **Water Resources Department**.
- **Mapping of the Flood Prone Areas** Flood hazard mapping will give the proper indication of water flow during floods.
- **Land Use Control** It will reduce danger of life and property, when waters inundate the floodplains and the coastal areas. No major development should be permitted in the areas which are subjected to high flooding.
- **Flood Control** It aims to reduce flood damage. This can be done by decreasing the amount of run-off with the help of reforestation. Flood diversion includes levees, embankments, dams and channel improvement. Dams can store water and can release water at a manageable rate. But failure of dams in Earthquakes and operation of releasing the water can cause floods in the lower areas.
- **Flood Proofing** It reduces the risk of damage. Measures include use of sand bags to keep flood water away, blocking or sealing of doors and windows of houses, etc.
- **Restoration of Original Drainage System** Drainage system is generally choked by the construction of roads, canals, railway tracks, etc. Floods could be checked if the original form of drainage system is restored.

Drought

- The term 'drought' refers to a prolonged time in which there is a scarcity of water due to insufficient precipitation, an excessive rate of evaporation and over-utilisation of water from reservoirs and other storages, including ground water.

Types of Drought

- **Meteorological Drought** It is a situation when there is a prolonged period of inadequate rainfall marked with mal-distribution of the same over time and space.
- **Agricultural Drought** It is also known as soil moisture drought, characterised by low soil moisture that is necessary to support the crops, thereby resulting in crop failures.
- **Hydrological Drought** It results when the availability of water in different storages and reservoirs like aquifers, lakes, reservoirs, etc. Falls below what the precipitation can replenish.
- **Ecological Drought** When the productivity of a natural Ecosystem fails due to shortage of water and as a consequence of ecological distress, damages are induced in the ecosystem.

Consequences of Drought

- Droughts have cascading effects on various other aspects of Environment and society.
- Crop failure leading to scarcity of food grains (**Akal**), fodder (**Trinkal**), inadequate rainfall, resulting in shortage of water (**Jalkal**) and often shortage in all the three (*Trikal*).
- Large-scale death of cattle and other animals, migration of humans and livestock. Scarcity of water compels people to consume contaminated water resulting in spread of many waterborne diseases like gastro-enteritis, cholera, hepatitis, etc.

Drought Prone Areas in India

On the basis of severity of droughts, India can be divided into three regions :

- **Extreme Drought Affected Areas** Most parts of Rajasthan, particularly areas to the West of the Aravalli hills i.e., Marusthali and Kutch region of Gujarat fall in this category. The districts like Jaisalmer and Barmer from the Indian desert receive less than 90 mm average annual rainfall.
- **Severe Drought Prone Areas** Parts of Eastern Rajasthan, most parts of Madhya Pradesh, Eastern parts of Maharashtra (including Marathawada), interior parts of Andhra Pradesh and Karnataka plateau, Northern parts of interior Tamil Nadu and Southern parts of Jharkhand and interior Odisha.
- **Moderate Drought Affected Areas** Northern parts of Rajasthan, Haryana, Southern districts of Uttar Pradesh, the remaining parts of Gujarat, Maharashtra, (including Marathawada) except Konkan, Jharkhand and Coimbatore plateau of Tamil Nadu and interior Karnataka.

Drought Mitigation Measures

- **Drought Monitoring** It is continuous observation of the rainfall situation, availability of water in the reservoirs, lakes, rivers, etc and comparing with the existing water needs in various sectors of the society.
- **Sowing Drought Resistant Crops** By sowing drought resistant crops of cotton, split green gram, pearl millet, wheat, etc, the impact of drought could be mitigated to a certain extent.
- **Rain Water Harvesting** Collection of each and every drop of rain could help in coping with the drought. Small quantity of water can irrigate comparatively larger area by using drip irrigation and sprinkler methods.
- **Drought Planning** The basic goal of drought planning is to improve the effectiveness of preparedness and response efforts by enhancing monitoring, mitigation and response measures.

Planning for Drought

- Provision for the distribution of safe drinking water, medicines for the victims and availability of fodder and water for the cattle and shifting of the people and their livestock to safer places.
- Identification of ground water potential in the form of aquifers, transfer of river water from the surplus to the deficit areas and particularly planning for inter-linking of rivers and construction of reservoirs and dams, etc.
- Remote sensing and satellite imageries can be useful in identifying the possible river-basins that can be inter- linked and in identifying the ground water potential. Rainwater harvesting can also be an effective method in minimising the effects of drought.

Landslides

Landslide is the rapid sliding of large mass of bedrocks. Unlike other disasters that are sudden, unpredictable and are largely controlled by macro, regional and highly localised factors.

Consequences of Landslides

- Landslides have relatively small and localised area of direct influence, but roadblock, destruction of railway lines and channel blocking due to rock-falls have far-reaching consequences.
- Diversion of river courses due to landslides can also lead to flood and loss of life and property.
- It also makes spatial interaction difficult, risky as well as a costly affair, which, in turn, adversely affects the developmental activities in these areas.

Mitigation

- **Restriction on the construction** and other developmental activities such as roads and dams. Limiting agriculture to valleys and areas with moderate slopes and control on the development of large settlements in the high vulnerability zones, should be enforced.
- **Construction of bunds** to reduce the flow of water. Terrace farming should be encouraged in the North-Eastern hill states where Jhumming (Slash and Burn/Shifting Cultivation) is still prevalent.

Landslide Vulnerability Zones

- **Very High Vulnerability Zone** Highly unstable, relatively young mountainous areas in the Himalayas and Andaman and Nicobar, high rainfall regions with steep slopes in the Western Ghats and Nilgiris, the North-Eastern regions, along with areas that experience frequent ground shaking due to earthquakes, etc. The areas of intense human activities particularly those related to construction of roads, dams, etc., are also included in this zone.

- **High Vulnerability Zone** Areas that have almost similar conditions to these included in the very high vulnerability zone are also included in this category. The only difference between these two is the combination, intensity and frequency of the controlling factors.

  All the Himalayan states and the states from the North-Eastern regions except the plains of Assam are included in the high vulnerability zones.
- **Moderate to Law Vulnerability Zone** Areas that receive less precipitation such as Trans-Himalayan areas of Ladakh and Spiti (Himachal Pradesh), undulated yet stable relief and low precipitation areas in the Aravalli, rain shadow areas in the Western and Eastern Ghats and Deccan Plateau also experience occasional landslides.

  Landslides due to mining and subsidence are most common in states like Jharkhand, Odisha, Chhattisgarh, Madhya Pradesh, Maharashtra, Andhra Pradesh, Karnataka, Tamil Nadu, Goa and Kerala.
- **Other Areas** The remaining parts of India, particularly states like Rajasthan, Haryana, Uttar Pradesh, Bihar, West Bengal (except district Darjeeling), Assam (except district Karbi Anglong) and Coastal regions of the Southern states are safe as far as landslides are concerned.

Man-Made Disasters

- Man-made disasters refer to non-natural disastrous occurrences that can be sudden for longer term.
- Sudden man-made disasters include structural collapses, such as building and mine collapse, when this occurs independently without any outside force.
- Man-made disaster includes communal riots, civil strife, international war, nuclear blast, fire, accidents, etc.

Important man-made disasters are as follows :

Bhopal Gas Tragedy (1984), India

- Bhopal Gas Tragedy was a gas leak incident in India. It is considered one of the world's worst industrial disasters.
- It occurred on the mid night 2nd-3rd December, 1984 at the **Union Carbide India Limited** (UCIL) pesticide plant in Bhopal, Madhya Pradesh. Over 5,00,000 people were exposed to **Methyl Isocyanate** (MIC) gas and other chemicals.

Chernobyl Nuclear Disaster (1986)

- A dangerous large-scale release of nuclear radiation occurred during the nuclear accident in nuclear power plant at Chernobyl in Ukraine on 25th April, 1986.
- The radiation leaks and fallout of radioactivity was quite widespread covering almost most of **Belarus**, large part of **Russia** and **Ukraine** and even **European territories**.

Fukushima Nuclear Disaster (2011), Japan

- Fukushima Daiichi incident was a nuclear disaster, resulting in a meltdown of the plant's six nuclear reactors. The failure occurred when the plant was hit by a tsunami triggered by the magnitude 9.0 Tohoku earthquake.
- The plant began releasing substantial amounts of radioactive material on 12th March, becoming the largest nuclear incident since the Chernobyl disaster in April 1986 and the second after Chernobyl to measure level 7 on the **International Nuclear Event Scale** (INES).

Disaster Management in India

- Disaster management is the process of planning for and responding to natural disasters.
- It entails carefully coordinating resources to mitigate the damage caused by calamities. It also entails a systematic strategy to handling catastrophe prevention, readiness, response, and recovery duties.
- There are three stages involved in disaster mitigation and management :
  - (i) **Pre-disaster management** involves generating data and information about the disasters, preparing vulnerability zoning maps and spreading awareness among the people about these. Apart from these, disaster planning, preparedness and preventive measures are other steps that need to be taken in the vulnerable areas.
  - (ii) **During disasters**, rescue and relief operations such as evacuation, construction of shelters and relief camps, supplying of water, food, clothing and medical aids etc. should be done on an emergency basis.
  - (iii) **Post-disaster operations** should involve rehabilitation and recovery of victims. It should also concentrate on capacity building in order to cope up with future disasters.

Government Initiatives for Disaster Management

Important initiatives of Government of India regarding disaster management are as follows :

National Disaster Management Act (NDMA), 2005

- The NDM Act provides for disaster management institutions at the National, State and District levels, and represents a shift in emphasis from relief to preparedness, prevention and mitigation.

- The NDM Act provides for the establishment of a National Disaster Management Authority (NDMA) headed by the Prime Minister, **State Disaster Management Authorities** (SDMAs) headed by Chief Ministers and **District Disaster Management Authorities** (DDMAs) headed by District Collectors/ Magistrates.
- The NDM Act has constituted funds related to disaster management such as **National Disaster Response Fund** (NDRF), **State Disaster Response Fund** (SDRF) and **National Disaster Mitigation Fund** (NDMF).

National Disaster Response Force (NDRF)

- The National Disaster Response Force (NDRF) is the specialised force for disaster response which works under the overall supervision and control of the NDMA.
- Vision of NDRF is to emerge as the most visible and vibrant multi-disciplinary, multi-skilled, high-tech force capable to deal with all types of natural as well as man-made disasters and to mitigate the effects of disasters.

National Policy on Disaster Management, 2009

- India's National Policy on Disaster Management was approved by the Union Cabinet on 22nd October, 2009.
- It aims to minimise the losses to lives, livelihoods and property, caused by natural or man-made disasters with a vision to build a safe and disaster resilient India by developing a holistic, proactive, integrated and technology driven strategy.
- The themes underpinning the policy include community based disaster management, capacity development in all spheres, consolidation of past initiatives and best practices.
- The policy aims cooperation with agencies at National and International levels with multi-sectoral synergy.

Objectives of National Policy of Disaster Management

The objectives of the National Policy of Disaster Management are :

- Promoting a culture of prevention, preparedness and resilience at all levels through knowledge innovation and education.
- Encouraging mitigation measures based on technology, traditional wisdom and environmental sustainability.
- Mainstreaming disaster management into the development planning process.
- Establishing institutional and techno-legal frameworks to create an enabling regulatory environment and a compliance regime.

National Disaster Management Plan (NDMP), 2016

- It covers all phases of disaster management– prevention, mitigation, response and recovery.
- It provides for horizontal and vertical integration among all the agencies and departments of the government.
- The plan also spells out the roles and responsibilities of all levels of government right up to **Panchayat** and **Urban Local Body level** in a matrix format.
- The plan has a regional approach, which will be beneficial not only for disaster management but also for development planning.
- It identifies major activities such as early warning, information dissemination, medical care, fuel, transportation, search and rescue, evacuation, etc to serve as a checklist for agencies responding to a disaster.
- The vision of NDMP is to make India disaster resilient, achieve substantial disaster risk reduction, and significantly decrease the losses of life, livelihoods, and assets– economic, physical, social, cultural and environmental– by maximising the ability to cope with disasters at all levels of administration as well as among communities.

Extra Facts From Tamil Nadu Board and NIOS

- **Nepal-India Earthquake** The April 2015 Nepal Earthquake (also known as the Gorkha Earthquake) killed nearly 9,000 people and injured nearly 22,000. It occurred on 25 April, with a magnitude of 8.1 Richter scale. Its epicentre was East of Gorkha district at Barpak. It was the worst natural disaster to strike Nepal since 1934 Nepal-Bihar Earthquake.
- Tropical Cyclone **Vardha** hit Chennai on 12th December, 2016. National Disaster Management Authority (NDMA) reports that at least 10 people have died in Tamil Nadu. Maximum sustained wind speeds of over 130 km/h was recorded, and the storm has caused severe damage to parts of the city of Chennai. Over 4,000 trees have been uprooted, power lines downed and buildings damaged.
- Lightning bolts travel at the speed of up to 80,000 km/second. The average length of a single lightning bolt is 3-4 km.
- Out of 28 States and 8 Union territories, 27 of them are disaster prone. Almost 68% of cultivable area is prone to droughts; 58.6% of land is prone to Earthquakes of severe intensity; 12% vulnerable to floods 76% of the total coastal length is prone to Cyclones and Tsunamis; around 8% of greater Himalayas and middle Himalayas is vulnerable to avalanches during winter months around 15% forest areas experience forest fires during dry season.

Appendix

Imaginary Lines on the Surface of the Earth

Equator	It is an imaginary line on globe between the North and South Pole at 0° latitude.
Tropic of Cancer	It is a line of Latitude circling the Earth at approximately 23.5° North of the Equator. It is the Northernmost point on Earth where the Sun's rays can appear directly overhead at local noon.
Tropic of Capricorn	It occurs at the Latitude approximately 23°27' North of the Terrestrial Equator, corresponds to the Northernmost declination of the Sun's ecliptic to the celestial Equator.
Tropic of Arctic	The Arctic circle is a circle of Latitude encompassing the Northernmost pole of the Earth and is located at approximately 66°33'45.6 North of the Equator. The Arctic circle is about 7,700,000 square miles. This line of Latitude separates the Arctic Zone in the North from the Northern Temperate Zone in the South.
Tropic of Antarctica	The Antarctic circle is an imaginary line located at 66.5° South Latitude or 23.5° Northward of the South Pole.

Countries on Equator

Sao Tome and Principe	Maldives
Gabon	Indonesia
Republic of the Congo	Kiribati
Uganda	Ecuador
Kenya	Colombia
Somalia	Brazil
Democratic Republic of the Congo	

Countries on Tropic of Cancer (18)

Hawaii-Island	Chad	Mexico	Oman
Bahamas	Saudi Arabia	Mali	United Arab Emirates
Mauritania	Egypt	Niger	Bangladesh
Algeria	India	China	Taiwan
Libya	Myanmar		

Countries on Tropic of Capricorn (12)

Brazil	Artelia	Chile	South Africa
Paraguay	Madagascar	French Polynesia	Tonga
Argentina	Mozambique	Botswana	Namibia

Difference Between Latitude and Longitude

Latitude	Longitude
The Latitude of place is the angular distance of a place North or South of the Equator, as measured in degrees from the Center of the Earth.	The Longitude alludes to the Geographic coordinate, which identifies the distance of a point, East-West of the prime Meridian.
The line of Latitude is drawn parallel to the Equator in circles, so called parallels and grow smaller towards the poles. Thus, Latitude of the great circle or Equator is the largest and nearly a point at the Poles.	It is measured from 0° to 180° East or West of Greenwich. All lines of Longitude parallel to the Earth are perpendicular to the Equator.
The average Latitudinal Distance of 1° is about 69 miles or 111 km. As the Earth is slightly flattened at the poles, the linear distance of a degree of Latitude at the pole is little longer than that at the Equator.	All the Longitudes of a parallel circle appear like a circle, passing through the poles. Approximately the distance between Longitude is maximum (0° km) at the Poles, it is 79 km at 45° latitude in the middle.
There are 180 latitude lines.	There are 360 Longitude lines.
The length of the Latitudes are different.	The length of the Longitudes are the same.

Important Land Borders

Boundary Lines	Related Countries
Radcliffe Line	India-Pakistan(Imposed Border) India-Bangladesh
McMahon Line	India-China
Durand Line	India-Afghanistan (This line is currently located in Pakistan occupied Kashmir (POK)

Important Channels and Straits

Major Channel/Strait	Divided Area
8° Channel	Maldives-Minicoy (India)
6° Channel	Great Nicobar and Sumatra (Indonesia)
9° Channel	Minicoy-Lakshadweep Island
10° Channel	Andaman (Little Andaman) and Nicobar
Great Channel	Indira Point-Indonesia
Palk Strait	India-Sri Lanka
Coco Strait	Andaman-Cocoa Island (Myanmar)

Indian States and Uniton Territories

Arunachal Pradesh

Latitude	26°30′N to 29°30′N
Longitude	91°30′E to 97°30′E
Area	83,743 sq km
Population	13,83,727
Density	17
Sex Ratio	938
Literacy Rate	65.38%
Capital	Itanagar
Districts	25
Major Tribes	Monpa, Miji, Aka, Sherdukpen, Apatani, Adi, Hill Miri, Tangsa, Wancho, etc
Languages	English, Nyishi, Bengali
Establishment	Arunachal Pradesh became a full-fledged state on 20th February, 1987. Till 1972, it was known as the North-East Frontier Agency (NEFA). It gained the Union Territory status on 20th January, 1972 and renamed as Arunachal Pradesh.
Geography	The topography here is characterised by an undulating hilly terrain nestled amid the foothills of the Shiwalik ranges. It makes boundary with Bhutan, China and Myanmar.

Assam

Latitude	24°3′N to 27°58′N
Longitude	89°42′E to 96°30′E
Area	78,438 sq km
Population	3,12,05,576
District	33
Density	398
Sex Ratio	958
Literacy Rate	72.2%
Capital	Dispur
Languages	Assamese, Bengali, Bodo, Nepali, Mising, Karbi and Dimasa
Establishment	Assam became a British protectorate in 1825 when the Burmese ceded Assam to the British under the provision of the Treaty of Yandabo. It became an independent state on 15th August, 1947. Assam is the sentinels of North-East India and gateway to the North-Eastern states. The state is close to India's international borders with Bangladesh and Bhutan.
Geography	Assam is geographically almost separated from Central India by Bangladesh. From North-Eastern corners to West and further towards South, the Brahmaputra river spreads its rich Alluvial Plain.

Bihar

Latitude	24°20′N to 27°13′N
Longitude	83°19′E to 88°17′E
Area	94,163 sq km
Population	10,40,99,452
Density	1,106
Sex Ratio	918
Literacy Rate	61.80%
Capital	Patna
Districts	38
Language	Hindi
State Bird	Sparrow
State Animal	Gaur/Ox
State Tree	Peepal
State Flower	Marigold
Establishment	Bihar remained a part of the Bengal Presidency of British India until 1912, when the province of Bihar and Odisha was carved out as a separate province. Since 2010, Bihar has been celebrating its foundation day as Bihar Diwas on 22nd March.
Geography	Bihar is rich alluvial plain lying on the North consisting chiefly of the Gangetic valley. The three major types of soil in Bihar are Piedmont Swamp soil, Terai soil and the Gangetic Alluvium soil. The soil covering most of the state is thick alluvium which shrouds the Shiwalik and older tertiary rocks.

Chhattisgarh

Latitude	17°46′N to 24° N
Longitude	80°60′E to 84°25′E
Area	1,37,898 sq km
Population	2,55,45,198
Density	189
Sex Ratio	991
Literacy Rate	70.3%
Capital	Raipur
Districts	28
Language	Hindi
Establishment	Chhattisgarh has been carved out of the state of Madhya Pradesh and came into being on 1st November, 2000 as the 26th state of the Union. Chhattisgarh takes its name from the 36 pillars of Chhattisgarhi Devi Temple (Chhattis means 36 and Garh means pillar).
Geography	The Northern and Southern parts are hilly while the central part is the fertile plain. The highest point in the state is the Bailadila range. Amrit Dhara waterfall in Koriya is among the most famous waterfalls in Koriya.

Goa

Latitude	15°29′N to 15°40′N
Longitude	73°40′E to 74°20′E
Area	3,702 sq km
Population	14,58,545
Density	394
Sex Ratio	973
Literacy Rate	88.7%
Capital	Panaji
Districts	2
Languages	Konkani, Marathi, English and Hindi
Establishment	On 19th December, 1961, Goa was liberated and made a composite Union Territory with Daman and Diu. On 30th May, 1987, the Union Territory was split and Goa was made India's 25th state with Daman and Diu remaining a Union Territory.
Geography	Located on the Konkan coastal belt, Goa has a natural border made of the Terekhol river that separates from Maharashtra in the North. The Western ghats stand to the East of the state and Arabian sea lies to the West.

Gujarat

Latitude	20°10′to 23°21′N
Longitude	73°40′to 74°20′E
Area	1,96,024 sq km
Population	6,04,39,692
Density	308
Sex Ratio	919
Literacy Rate	78.03%
Capital	Gandhinagar
Districts	33
Language	Gujarati
Establishment	Gujarat is derived from Gujjar-ratra. The state of Gujarat came into being on 1st May, 1960. The first capital of Gujarat was Ahmedabad, the capital was moved to Gandhinagar in 1970.
Geography	The state comprises of three geographical regions, *viz.* the peninsula (traditionally known as Saurashtra), hilly tract sprinkled with two mountains and the famous Rann of Kutch (desert).

Haryana

Latitude	27°37′to 30°35′N
Longitude	74°60′to 77°36′E
Area	44,212 sq km
Population	27,761,063
Density	573
Sex Ratio	879
Literacy Rate	75.60%
Capital	Chandigarh
Districts	22
Language	Hindi
Establishment	The present day Haryana was established as a state on 1st November, 1966.
Geography	It just covers 1.37% of the total geographical area of the country. The geographical area of Haryana can be divided into three parts, Hilly area, Plain area and Sandy area. Red soil is found in Sirsa district.

Himachal Pradesh

Latitude	30°22′N to 33°12′N
Longitude	75°45′E to 79°42′E
Area	55,673 sq km
Population	68,64,602
Density	123
Sex Ratio	972
Literacy Rate	82.80%
Capital	Shimla
Districts	12
Languages	Hindi and Pahari
Establishment	It came into being as a Union Territory in April, 1948 and on 26th January, 1950, it became a part of state. On 25th January, 1971, Himachal Pradesh became the 18th state of Indian Union. Himachal means **Abode of Snow,** situated in the heart of the Western Himalaya, identified as 'Dev Bhoomi' and is believed to be the abode of Gods and Goddesses.
Geography	The entire region of Himachal Pradesh is hilly with altitude ranging from 350 m to 7000 m above sea level. Some important peaks here are Shilla, Shipki, Kinner, Kailash, Shigrila, Pir Panjal, Bara Kanda, etc. Some important hot springs are Manikaran, Kheerganga, Kasol, Vashist (district Kullu), Tattapani (district Mandi).

Jharkhand

Latitude	21°28′N to 25°18′N
Longitude	83°26′E to 87°51′E
Area	79,714 sq km
Population	3,29,88,134
Growth Rate	22.4%
Density	414
Sex Ratio	949
Literacy Rate	66.4%
Capital	Ranchi
Districts	24
Language	Hindi

Establishment	It became a full-fledged state on 15th November, 2000.
Geography	Most of the Jharkhand region is part of Chotanagpur plateau. Parasnath is the highest peak here. Different kinds of soil are found here, *viz* red soil (Rajmahal area, Damodar valley), Sandy soil (Hazaribagh, Dhanbad), Black soil (Rajmahal) and Laterite soil (Western Ranchi, Singhbhum, Santhal Parganas).

Karnataka

Latitude	11°31′ to 18°14′N
Longitude	74°12′ to 78°10′E
Area	1,91,791 sq km
Population	6,10,95,297
Density	320
Sex Ratio	973
Literacy Rate	75.4%
Capital	Bengaluru
Districts	30
Language	Kannada
Establishment	Karnataka has a recorded history of more than 2000 years. After Independence, the Mysore state was created in 1953. In 1956, all the Kannada dominated areas were unified after which the enlarged Mysore state was carved in 1956 and was renamed as Karnataka in 1973.
Geography	The state can be divided into four regions i.e., Northern Region, Coastal Region, Central Region and Southern Region. The Red soil constitutes major soil type, followed by Black soil.

Kerala

Latitude	8°17′N to 12°47′N
Longitude	74°27′E to 77°37′E
Area	38,863 sq km
Population	3,34,06,061
Density	860
Sex Ratio	1,084
Literacy Rate	94.01%
Capital	Thiruvananthapuram
Districts	14
Language	Malayalam
Establishment	Under the State's Re-organisation Act, 1956, Travancore- Cochin state and Malabar were united to from Kerala state on 1st November, 1956.
Geography	Kerala can be divided into three geographical regions—1. High lands, 2. Mid lands 3. Low lands. Anaimudi is the highest peak (2695 m).

Madhya Pradesh

Latitude	21°2′N to 26°87′N
Longitude	74°E to 82°49′E
Area	3,08,000 sq km
Population	7,26,26,809
Density	236
Sex Ratio	931
Literacy Rate	69.3%
Capital	Bhopal
Districts	52
Language	Hindi
Establishment	Madhya Pradesh was given the status of full-fledged state w.e.f. 1st November, 1956. The area covered by the present day Madhya Pradesh includes the area of the ancient Avanh Mahajanapada, whole capital was Ujjain (also known as Avanti).
Geography	The Madhya Pradesh, centrally located in India and frequently called as the Heart of India, comprises of big plateau (Malwa plateau), amazing range, round about rivers.

Maharashtra

Latitude	15°5′N to 22° N
Longitude	72°5′E to 80°09′E
Area	3,07,713 sq km
Population	11,23,74,333
Density	365
Sex Ratio	929
Literacy Rate	69.3%
Capital	Mumbai
Districts	36
Language	Marathi
Establishment	The administrative evolution of the state of Maharashtra is the outcome of the linguistic reorganisation of the states of India, which came into effect on 1st May, 1960.
Geography	The most important physical feature of Maharashtra is the Deccan plateau, which is separated from the Konkan coastline by Ghats. The Satpura hills alongwith Bhamragad-Chiroli-Gaikhuri from North to East serve as its natural borders. The soils of the state are residual, derived from underlying basalts. In the semi dry plateau (Deccan plateau), the regur (black-cotton soil) is pre-dominant.

Manipur

Latitude	23°80′N to 25°68′N
Longitude	93°03′E to 94°78′E
Area	22,327 sq km
Population	28,55,794
Density	128
Sex Ratio	985
Literacy Rate	79.21%
Capital	Imphal
Districts	16
Languages	Manipuri, Meitei
Establishment	The state of Manipur was established on 21st January, 1972.
Geography	This state is virtually the meeting point between India and South-East Asia. The blue hill ranges surrounding the valley are higher on the North and gradually diminish in height towards the South.

Meghalaya

Latitude	23°83′N to 25°68′N
Longitude	93°03′E to 94°78′E
Area	22,429 sq km
Population	3,211,000
Density	140
Sex Ratio	989
Literacy Rate	74.43%
Capital	Shillong
Districts	11
Languages	Khasi, Garo and English
Establishment	Meghalaya was inaugurated as an autonomous state on 2nd April, 1970. It was declared a state of Indian Union on 21st January, 1972.
Geography	The Khasi hills and Jaintia hills, which form the Central and Eastern part of Meghalaya form an imposing plateau with rolling grassland, hills and river valleys. A narrow strip of plain runs along the international border with Bangladesh.

Mizoram

Latitude	21°58′N to 24°35′N
Longitude	92°15′E to 93°29′E
Area	21,081 sq km
Population	10,97,206
Density	52
Sex Ratio	976
Literacy Rate	91.33%
Capital	Aizawl
Districts	11
Languages	Mizo and English
Establishment	Mizoram became full-fledged 23rd state on 20th February, 1987.
Geography	The terrain of Mizoram is hilly with a number of valleys, rivers and lakes. There are 21 hill ranges in the state which run as ridges from North to South. The Palak lake is the biggest lake here, formed as a result of an earthquake. Phawngpui is the highest peak of the state.

Nagaland

Latitude	25°6′N to 27°4′N
Longitude	93°20′to 95°15′E
Area	16,579 sq km
Population	19,78,502
Density	119
Sex Ratio	931
Literacy Rate	79.6%
Capital	Kohima
Districts	12
Languages	Angami, Ao, Chang Konyak, Lotha, English
Establishment	Nagaland became 16th state of India on 1st December, 1963.
Geography	The state is mostly mountainous except areas bordering Assam valley. Mount Saramati (highest peak in Nagaland) and its ranges form a natural barrier between Nagaland and Myanmar.

Odisha

Latitude	17°4′N to 22°3′N
Longitude	81°2′E to 87°2′E
Area	1,55,707 sq km
Population	4,19,74,218
Density	270
Sex Ratio	979
Literacy Rate	72.87%
Capital	Bhubaneshwar
Districts	30
Language	Odia
Establishment	It became Indian state on 15th August, 1947.
Geography	Its diverse landscape comprises coastal plains, mountainous terrain, plateaus, Verdant river valleys and spots dotted with watersheds, springs and lakes.

Punjab

Latitude	29°30′N to 32°32′N
Longitude	73°55′E to 76°50′E
Area	50,362 sq km
Population	2,77,43,338
Density	551
Sex Ratio	895
Literacy Rate	75.84%
Capital	Chandigarh
Districts	22
Language	Punjabi
Establishment	It became full-fledged state on 1st November, 1966.
Geography	Due to the presence of a large number of rivers, most of the state is a fertile plain. The South-East region of the state is semi-arid and gradually presents a desert landscape.

Rajasthan

Latitude	23°3′N to 30°12′N
Longitude	69°3′E to 78°17′E
Area	3,42,239 sq km
Population	6,85,48,437
Density	200
Growth Rate	21.31%
Sex Ratio	928
Literacy Rate	66.11%
Capital	Jaipur
Districts	33
Languages	Hindi and Rajasthani
Establishment	It became full-fledged state on 1st November, 1956.
Geography	The oldest chain of fold mountain, the Aravalli range, splits the state into two geographical zones– desert in leeward side and forest belt in the other. Guru Shikhar Peak is the highest peak of the Aravalli.

Sikkim

Latitude	27°05′N to 28°07′N
Longitude	87°59′E to 88°56′E
Area	7,096 sq km
Population	6,10,577
Density	86
Sex Ratio	890
Literacy Rate	81.42%
Capital	Gangtok
Districts	4
Languages	Lepcha, Bhutia, Nepali and English
Establishment	It became Indian state on 16th May, 1975.
Geography	Sikkim is well-known for its scenic beauty and has wide altitudinal variation from about 300m to 8500m (above mean sea level). Mount Khangchendzonga, the third highest peak in the world and adjacent Singalila range strongly govern the relief features on the Western part of the state.

Tamil Nadu

Latitude	20°25′to 20°45′
Longitude	85°35′to 86°5′E
Area	1,30,058 sq km
Population	7,21,47,030
Density	555
Sex Ratio	996
Literacy Rate	80.01%
Capital	Chennai
Districts	38
Language	Tamil
Establishment	Tamil Nadu was one of the first of British settlements in India. The state is the successor to the old Madras Presidency. It became full-fledged state on 26th January, 1950.
Geography	It has a long coastline and the Eastern ghats (mountain range) run parallel to the same. The coastal plains run North to South. There are only two major gaps (Palakkad gap and Shencottah gap) into the long chain of hills that border Western Tamil Nadu. Doddabetta Peak is the highest peak in the state (2,639 m).

Tripura

Latitude	22°56′N to 24°32′N
Longitude	90°09′E to 90°10′E
Area	10,491.69 sq km
Population	36,73,917
Density	350
Sex Ratio	960
Literacy Rate	87.22%
Capital	Agartala
Districts	8
Languages	Bengali, Kokborok and Manipuri
Establishment	Tripuri dynasty ruled Tripura for several centuries till 15th October, 1949 and merged with the Indian Union as Part 'C' state. On 21st January, 1972, Tripura attained the full-fledged status of a state.
Geography	The state has three distinct physiographic zones (1) Hill range (2) Undulating plateau land (3) Low-lying alluvial land. The highest peak lies at Betalongchhip.

Andhra Pradesh

Latitude	12°41′N to 22° N
Longitude	77° E to 84°40′E
Area	1,60,205 sq km
Population	4,93,78,776
Density	308
Sex Ratio	993
Literacy Rate	67.66%
Capital	Amaravati
Districts	13
Languages	Telugu, Urdu and English
Establishment	Andhra Pradesh came into being on 1st November, 1956. On 1st March, 2014 , Andhra Pradesh Reorganisation Act, 2014 got President's assent, which bifurcated the erstwhile Andhra Pradesh into Andhra Pradesh and Telangana.
Geography	Eastern Andhra includes Eastern part of Deccan plateau and considerable part of the Eastern ghats. Northern part of Andhra Pradesh is marked as the Telangana region and the Southern part is known as the Rayalaseema region. Lambasingi in Andhra Pradesh is the only place in South India, which has snowfall and is also nicknamed as Kashmir of Andhra Pradesh.

Telangana

Latitude	15°8′N to 19°8′N
Longitude	77°7′E to 81°8′E
Area	1,14,840 sq km
Population	3,51,94,000
Density	310
Sex Ratio	988
Literacy Rate	66.50%
Capital	Hyderabad
Districts	33
Languages	Telugu, Urdu
Establishment	After prolonged movement for separate Telangana state in February 2014, Andhra Pradesh Reorganisation Act, 2014 Bill was passed by the Parliament of India for the formation of Telangana state. The Bill received the assent of the President and published in the Gazette on 1st March, 2014. The state of Telangana was officially formed on 2nd June, 2014.
Geography	Telangana is situated on the Deccan plateau, in the central stretch of the Eastern seaboard of the Indian Peninsula and most of the land is arid.

Uttar Pradesh

Latitude	23°5′N to 31°2′N
Longitude	77°3′E to 84°3′E
Area	2,40,928 sq km
Population	19,98,12,341
Density	829
Sex Ratio	912
Literacy Rate	67.7%
Capital	Lucknow
Districts	75
Languages	Hindi and Urdu
Establishment	The British combined Agra and Oudh into one province and called it United Provinces of Agra and Oudh. The name was shortened to the United Provinces in 1935. In January 1950, the United Provinces was renamed as Uttar Pradesh.
Geography	This state can be divided into 3 distinct geographical regions i.e., the Himalayan region in the North, the Gangetic plain in the centre and the Vindhya hills and plateau in the South.

Uttarakhand

Latitude	28°43′N to 31°27′N
Longitude	77°34′E to 81°02′E
Area	53,483 sq km
Population	1,00,86,292
Density	189
Sex Ratio	963
Literacy Rate	78.82%
Capital	Dehradun
Districts	13
Languages	Hindi, English, Garhwali, Kumaoni
Establishment	In January 1950, the United Province was renamed as Uttar Pradesh and Uttaranchal remained a part of Uttar Pradesh, before it was carved out of Uttar Pradesh on 9th November, 2000. It is incepted as the 27th state of India and the Uttaranchal was renamed as Uttarakhand on 1st January, 2007.
Geography	Physiographically, the state can be divided into three zones, *viz* the Kumaon, the Garhwal and the Tarai region.

West Bengal

Latitude	22°56′N to 27°3′N
Longitude	85° 8′to 89°9′E
Area	88,752 sq km
Population	9,12,76,115
Density	1028
Sex Ratio	950
Literacy Rate	76.3%
Capital	Kolkata
Districts	23
Language	Bengali

Establishment	In 1947, when India became independent, Bengal was partitioned between India and Pakistan. Later, the state of Cooch Behar, French enclave of Chandannagar and some parts of Bihar added to West Bengal and the state got its present political boundary according to the State Reorganisation Act, 1956.
Geography	The land forms have features like Darjeeling Himalayan hill region, Terai region, North Bengal plains, Rarh region, coastal plain, Sunderban, Western plateau and high lands and Ganges delta.

Union Territories

Andaman and Nicobar Islands

Latitude	6° to 14° N
Longitude	92° to 94° E
Area	8,249 sq km
Population	3,80,581
Density	46
Sex Ratio	876
Literacy Rate	86.63%
Capital	Port Blair
Districts	3
Languages	Hindi, Nicobarese, Bengali, Tamil, Malayalam, Telugu
Establishment	It became Indian Union Territory on 1st November, 1956.
Geography	The islands located North of 10° North latitude are known as Andaman Group of Islands, while islands located South of 10° North latitude are called Nicobar Group of Islands. The climate of the islands can be defined as humid, tropical, coastal climate. The islands receive rainfall from both the South-West and North-East monsoons and maximum precipitation is between May and December.

Chandigarh

Latitude	30°75′N
Longitude	76°78′E
Area	114 sq km
Population	10,55,450
Density	9258
Sex Ratio	818
Literacy Rate	86%
Capital	Chandigarh
District	1
Languages	Hindi, Punjabi, English
Establishment	Chandigarh and the area surrounding it, were constituted as a Union Territory on 1st November, 1966. It serves as the joint capital of both Punjab and Haryana states.
Geography	The subsurface formation comprises of beds of boulders, pebbles, gravel, sand, silt, clays and some kankar. The area is drained by two seasonal rivulets *viz* Sukhna Choe in the East and Patiala-Ki-Rao Choe in the West. 15.14% of area is recorded as forest coverage.

Dadra and Nagar Haveli and Daman and Diu

Latitude	20°42′N
Longitude	73°83° E
Area	603
Population	585,674
Density	970 sq. km
Sex Ratio	Dadar and Nagar Haveli (774) and Daman and Diu (618)
Literacy Rate	Dadar and Nagar Haveli (76.2%) and Daman and Diu (87.1%)
Capital	Daman
Districts	3
Languages	Gujarati, Hindi, Marathi, English.
Establishment	The Portuguese ruled over Dadra and Nagar Haveli and Daman and Diu until 1954 and 1961, respectively. Both were merged with Indian Union in 1961. Until 2019 both were governed as different Union Territories. In December 2019, Parliament passed an Act which merged both the Union Territories. The merger Act came into effect on 26th January, 2020.
Geography	While 'Nagar Haveli' is located between Maharashtra and Gujarat, 'Dadra' is an enclave which is a few kilometres North of 'Nagar Haveli' in Gujarat. Daman is bound on the East by Gujarat, on the West by the Arabian sea, on the North by the Kolak river and on the South by Kalai river. Diu is an island connected by two bridges. The neighbouring district of Diu is Junagadh in Gujarat.

Lakshadweep

Latitude	8° to 12°3′N
Longitude	71° to 74′E
Area	32 sq km
Population	64,473
Density	2013
Sex Ratio	946
Literacy Rate	91.8%
Capital	Kavaratti
Districts	1

Language	Jeseri, Mahal
Establishment	In 1956, the islands were constituted into a single territory and since then, have been directly administered by the Union Government through an administrator. The Laccadives, Minicoy and Aminidivi group of islands were renamed as Lakshadweep in 1973.
Geography	Lakshadweep, a group of coral islands, consists of 12 atolls, three reefs and submerged sand banks. Of the 27 islands, only 11 are inhabited. These lie scattered in the Arabian Sea about 280 km to 480 km off Kerala coast.

Delhi (National Capital Territory)

Latitude	28°38′N
Longitude	77°13′E
Area	1,483 sq km
Population	1,67,87,941
Density	11,297
Sex Ratio	868
Literacy Rate	86.2%
Capital	Delhi
Districts	11
Languages	Hindi, Punjabi, Urdu and English
Establishment	In 1911, Delhi became the centre of all activities after the capital was shifted from Kolkata. It was made a Union Territory in 1956. It got a Legislative Assembly with the enactment of the National Capital Territory Act, 1991.
Geography	There are three major geographical regions-the Yamuna flood plain, the ridge and the Gangetic plains.

Puducherry

Latitude	11°93′N
Longitude	79°83′E
Area	490 sq km
Population	12,47,953
Density	2,598
Sex Ratio	1,037
Literacy Rate	85.8%
Capital	Puducherry
Districts	4
Languages	Tamil, Telugu, Malayalam, English and French
Establishment	Puducherry, the capital of the territory, was once the original headquarters of the French in India. It was under the French rule for 138 years and merged with the Indian Union on 1st November, 1954.
Geography	Puducherry more or less is a flat land with no hills and forests. The soil of Puducherry is mainly red fertile, black clay and alluvial with sandy elements.

Jammu and Kashmir

Latitude	32°44′N to 35°20′ N
Longitude	73°30′ to 76°80′E
Area	53,258
Population	12,267,013 (Including Ladakh)
Density	889 (Including Ladakh)
Literacy Rate	67.16% (Including Ladakh)
Capital	Srinagar (Summer) and Jammu (Winter)
Districts	20
Languages	Kashmiri, Dogri, Urdu
Establishment	On 26th October, 1947, Jammu and Kashmir became state of India by signing Instrument of Accession by Raja Hari Singh. On 31st October, 2019, it was made Union Teritory by Jammu and Kashmir Reorganisation Bill, 2019.
Geography	There are many valleys such as the Kashmir valley, Tawi valley, Chenab valley, Poonch valley, Sind valley and Lidder valley.

Ladakh

Latitude	32°44′N
Longitude	80°05″ E
Area	1,69,421
Population	2,74,289
Density	4.6
Sex Ratio	889 (Census 2011)
Literacy Rate	67.16% (Census 2011)
Capital	Leh
Districts	2
Languages	Ladakhi, Urdu
Establishment	Until 2019, Ladakh was a part of state of Jammu and Kashmir. In August 2019, the Parliament of India enacted Reorganisation Act, 2019 which created the Union Territory of Ladakh on 31st October, 2019. It consist of two district i.e. Leh and Kargil. It has huge strategic importance due to its strategic location.
Geography	It is highest plateau in India with the height of 98,00 ft. It is divided into different valleys, prominent one includes Baltistan, Indus and Nubra valley. Most of the area of the Union territory is designated as cold desert as Himalayas create a rain shadow.

Glossary

- **Abiotic** It refers to a non-living thing. Usually, they are physical and chemical components of an organism's environment.
- **Adiabatic Lapse Rate** It is the rate of change of temperature by an ascending or descending airmass.
- **Aphelion** It is the point in the Earth's orbit when it is farthest from the Sun 152.5 million km). Aphelion occurs on the 3rd or 4th of July.
- **Archipelago** It is a group of islands that lie in fairly close proximity.
- **Agro-climatic** It is the climatic and land resource conditions in totality which are crucial for the development of agriculture and allied economic conditions of a region.
- **Aquifer** It is a saturated geological unit (e.g. sands, gravels, fractured rocks) which can yield water to wells at a sufficient rate to support a well.
- **Air Mass** A body of air whose temperature and humidity characteristics, acquired in source region, remain relatively constant over a horizontal distance of hundreds to thousands of km. Air masses develop their climatic characteristics by remaining stationary over a source region for a number of days. Air masses are classified according to their temperature and humidity characteristics.
- **Anticline** A fold in sedimentary strata that resembles an arch.
- **Aphelion** It is the point in the Earth's orbit when it is farthest from the Sun (152.5 million km). Aphelion occurs on the 3rd or 4th of July.
- **Asthenosphere** Zone in the Earth's mantle that exhibits plastic properties. Located below the lithosphere at between 100 and 200 km.
- **Atmospheric Pressure** Weight of the atmosphere on a surface. At sea-level, the average atmospheric pressure is 1013.25 mb. Pressure is measured by a device called a barometer.
- **Aurora** Multicoloured lights that appear in the upper atmosphere (ionosphere) over the Polar regions and visible from locations in the middle and high latitudes. Caused by the interaction of solar wind with oxygen and nitrogen gas in the atmosphere. Aurora in the Northern Hemisphere are called aurora borealis and aurora australis in the Southern Hemisphere.
- **Batholith** It is a large mass of subsurface intrusive igneous rock that has its origins from mantle magma.
- **Backwater** It is a stretch of water that has become bypassed by the main flow of a stream, although still joined to it. It has a very low rate of flow.
- **Bedrock** It is the solid rock lying beneath soil and weathered material.
- **Bunding** It is the practice of constructing embankments of Earth or stone for conserving water and soil to increase crop production.
- **Base Population** It is the total population of an area at the beginning of a given time period.
- **Balance of Trade** The difference between the total value of a country's exports and imports. An excess of export over import makes a favourable balance of trade, and the converse an unfavourable balance.
- **Barte** A direct exchange of excess produce between two parties to the mutual advantages of both, without the use of tokens, credit or money in the transaction.
- **Birth Rate** It is the number of live births for every 1000 persons in a year.
- **Big Bang** Theory about the origin of universe. It suggests that about 15 billion years ago all of the matter and energy in the universe wasz concentrated into an area smaller than an atom. At this instant, matter, energy, space and time were not existent. Then suddenly with a bang, the universe began to expand at an incredible rate and matter, energy, space and time came into being. As the universe expanded, matter began to coalesce into gas clouds and then stars and planets.
- Biodiversity is all the different kinds of all of life find in one area the variety of animals, plant, fungi, even micro-organisms like bacteria that makeup our natural world.
- **Biodiversity** The diversity of different species (species diversity), genetic variability among individuals within each species (genetic diversity) and variety of ecosystems (ecosystem diversity).
- **Biomass** The weight of living tissues usually measured per unit area over a particular time interval. It include the dead parts of organisms like bark, hair and nails.
- **Biome** Largest recognisable assemblage of animals and plants on the Earth. The distribution of the biomes is controlled mainly by climate.
- **Calcification** It is a dry environment soil-forming process that results in the accumulation of calcium carbonate in surface soil layers.
- **Cold Front** It is a transition zone in the atmosphere where an advancing cold air mass displaces a warm air mass.
- **Coriolis Force** It is an apparent force due to the Earth's rotation.
- **Calcareous** It is composed of or containing a high proportion of calcium carbonate.
- **Catchment Area** It is the area drained by a major river and its tributaries.
- **Coastal Plain** It is a flat low lying land between the coast and higher ground inland.
- **Coral** It is a small calcium secreting marine polyp that occurs in colonies, mainly in warm shallow sea water. It forms the coral reefs.
- **Command Area** It is the area served by a canal system through supply of water for irrigation and other purposes.
- **Culturable Command Area** It refers to the culturable land irrigated by a canal system. It is different from gross command area. The later includes all the area served by a canal system including unculturable.
- **Caldera Volcano** Explosive type of volcano that leaves a large circular depression. Some of these depressions can be as large as 40 km in diameter. These volcanoes form when wet granitic magma quickly rises to the surface of the Earth.
- **Census** A census is an official enumeration of population done periodically. In India the first census was held in the year 1872.
- **Chemical Fertilisers** Substance of natural or artificial origin containing chemical elements such as phosphorus, potassium and nitrogem that are necessary to plan life. They are added to the soil for increasing its productivity.
- **Chlorofluorocarbons** (CFCs) It is an artificially created gas that has become concentrated in the Earth's atmosphere. This is very strong greenhouse gas is released from aerosol sprays, refrigerants and the production of fumes.

- **Contour Ploughing** Tilling or ploughing hillsides or sloping lands along the contour lines, that is, around rather than up and down a slope mainly with a view to conserving soil and water
- **Cirrocumulus Clouds** Patchy white high altitude cloud composed of ice crystals. (Found in an altitude range from 5,000 - 18,000 m.)
- **Cirrostratus Clouds** High altitude sheet like clouds composed of ice crystals. These thin clouds often cover the entire sky. (Found in an altitude range from 5,000-18,000 m.)
- **Continental Crust** Granitic portion of the Earth's crust that makes up the continents. Thickness of the continental crust varies between 20 to 75 km.
- **Crop Rotation** Growing of different crops in succession on the same field from season to season to maintain soil fertility.
- **Desert Pavement** It is a veneer of coarse particles left on the ground after the erosion of finer particles by wind.
- **Depression** In meteorology, it denotes an area of relatively low atmospheric pressure, which is found mainly in temperate regions. It is also used as synonym for temperate cyclones.
- **Dependency Ratio** It is the ratio of people of dependent age (below 15 and above 60 years) to people of economically active ages (15-59 years).
- **Ebb Tide** It is the flow of tide during the tidal period when the water level in the sea is falling.
- **El Nino** It is the name given to the occasional development of warm ocean surface waters along the coast of Ecuador and Peru. The El Nino normally occurs around Christmas and lasts usually for a few weeks to a few months.
- **Epicentre** It is a place on the surface of the Earth located at the shortest distance from the focus of the earthquake, the point at which the seismic energy gets released.
- **Estuary** It is the tidal mouth of a river where fresh and saline water get mixed.
- **Eco-development** It is the process of development of a region by means of conservation and regeneration of degraded ecosystem and ecological sustainability.
- **Emigration** It is a movement of people from one place to another usually from one country to another with a purpose of earning, living, residing and settling.
- **Earthquake** A sudden motion or shaking in the Earth. The motion is caused by the quick release of slowly accumulated energy in the form of seismic waves.
- **Earthquake Focus** Point of stress release in an earthquake (also known as hypocenter).
- **Economic Geography** The aspect or branch of geography which deals with the influences of the environment, both physical and cultural, on the economic activity of man, bringing out similarities and differences from place to place in the ways people make a living.
- **Extensive Agriculture** Farming in which the amount of capital and labour applied to a given area is relatively small.
- **Flow System or Channel** It is a channel of canal where water flows under the influence of gravity.
- **Fault** It is a linear break in rocks of the Earth's crust along which there has been displacement in a horizontal, vertical or oblique direction.
- **Fold** It is a bend in the rock strata resulting from compression of an area of the Earth's crust.
- **Fazenda** A coffee plantation in Brazil.
- **Foreign Exchange** The mechanism or process by which payments between any two places operating under different national currency systems are effected without passing of actual money or gold, etc.
- **Freeways** The wide highways on which cross-roads are avoided by providing overhead links where one turns in only one direction to ensure smooth and speedy traffic.
- **Geomagnetism** It is a property of magnetically susceptible minerals to get aligned to the Earth's magnetic field during the period of rock formation.
- **Geostrophic Wind** It is a Horizontal wind in the upper atmosphere that moves parallel to isobars. Results from a balance between Pressure Gradient force and Coriolis force.
- **Geosyncline** It is a narrow, shallow, elongated basin with a sinking bottom in which a considerable thickness of sediments was deposited by the rivers coming from Angara and Gondwanaland.
- **Gorge** It is a deep valley with steep and rocky side walls.
- **Groundwater Table** It is the top of the zone in which all pore spaces or fissures are totally filled with water.
- **Gross Domestic Product** (GDP) It is a monetary measure of the value of goods and services produced within a natural for economy at a given period of time. Normally, it is one year
- **Gross Value Added** The GVA is estimated from GDP by adding subsidies on production & substracting indirect taxes.
- **Geologist** A scientist who studies the composition, structure and history of the Earth.
- **Geothermal Gradient** The gradual increase in temperature with depth in the crust. The average is 30°C per kilometer in the upper crust.
- **Greenhouse Effect** The greenhouse effect causes the atmosphere to trap more heat energy at the Earth's surface and within the atmosphere by absorbing and re-emitting longwave energy.
- **Greenhouse Gases** Gases responsible for the greenhouse effect. These gases include: carbon dioxides (CO_2), methane (CH_4), nitrous oxide (N_2O), chlorofluorocarbons (CFC) and tropospheric ozone (O_3).
- **Hail** It is a type of precipitation received in the form of ice pellets or hail stones. The size of hailstones can be between 5 and 190 mm in diameter.
- **Halocline** It is the distinct zone in the ocean below which the salinity increases sharply.
- **Hydration** It is a form of chemical weathering that involves the rigid attachment of H^+ and OH^- ions to the atoms and molecules of a mineral.
- **Hydrolysis** It is chemical weathering process that involves the reaction between mineral ions and the ions of water (OH^- and H^+) and results in the decomposition of the rock surface by forming new compounds.
- **Habitat** Location where a plant or animal lives.
- **Harbour** An extensive stretch of deep water where vessels can anchor securely to obtain protection from sea and swell either through natural features or artificial works.
- **Highway** Public road connecting distant places. Such a road of national importance is called the national highway.
- **Horticulture** Cultivation of vegetables and fruits, often on small plots, involving higher intensiveness than in field cultivation.

- **Infiltration** It is a portion of the precipitation which reaches the Earth surface seeps into the ground in the permeable strata. This process is known as infiltration.
- **Insolation** It is an incoming solar radiation in short wave form.
- **Inter Tropical Convergence Zone** (ITCZ) It is a zone of low atmospheric pressure and ascending air located at near the equator. Rising air currents are due to global wind convergence and convection from thermal heating.
- **Immigration** It is the movement of a person as a permanent resident into another area, usually into a foreign country.
- **Intrusive Irrigation** It is a strategy of irrigation development where per unit application of water is high.
- **Indian Standard Time** It is the local time along the Standard Meridian of India (82°30′E).
- **Inland drainage** It is a drainage system in which the waters of the rivers do not reach the oceans but fall into an Inland sea or lake.
- **Industrial Revolution** The change in manufacturing from hand operated tools to power-driven machinery began in England during the middle of the 18th century.
- **Intensive Agriculture** Farming in which large amounts of capital and labour are applied per unit area of land, in order to obtain high yield.
- **Inter Cropping** It is a practice of growing two or more crops together on the same field in the same season.
- **International Trade** Trade carried on between nations primarily to exchange their surpluses and make up their deficits.
- **Jet Stream** It is a very strong and steady westerly wind blowing just below the tropopause.
- **Katabatic Wind** It is any wind blowing down the slope of a mountain.
- **La Nina** It is the condition opposite of an El Nino. In a La Nina, the tropical Pacific trade winds become very strong and an abnormal accumulation of cold water occurs in the central and Eastern Pacific ocean.
- **Latent Heat** It is the energy required to change a substance to a higher state of matter (solid > liquid > gas). This same energy is released from the substance when the change of state is reversed (gas > liquid > solid).
- **Lift System or Channel** It is a channel of canal where water is forced to flow against the slope of land by upliftment.
- **Lagoon** It is a Salt-water lake separated from the sea by the sandbars and spits.
- **Lithospheric Plates** It is a large segments of the Earth's crust composed of continental and oceanic lithospheric parts, floating above the asthenosphere.
- **Life Expectancy** It is the average number of years one is expected to live.
- **Local Time** It is the time of a place determined by the midday Sun is called the local time.
- **Meander** It is a pronounced curve or loop in the course of a river channel.
- **Migration Stream** It refers to a group of migrants with the common origin and destination.
- **Million Plus Cities** They are cities with a population of more than one million or 10 lakh.
- **Metropolis** A very large city or agglomeration of population in a district or a country and is often the chief centre or seat of some form of activity- administrative, commercial or industrial. It generally serves a large hinterland.
- **Mineral** A substance that is found in the Earth's crust, and which generally has a definite chemical composition unlike most rocks.
- **Mineral Fuel** Non-metallic minerals such as coal and petroleum which are used as fuel.
- **Mineral Oil** A mixture of hydrocarbons in solid, gaseous or liquid form found in the Earth. It is commonly known as petroleum. It became a commercial product only in 1859.
- **Mineral Ore** Metals in their raw state is extracted from the Earth.
- **Mining** An economic activity concerned with the extraction of commercially valuable minerals from the bowels of the Earth.
- **Mixed Farming** A type of farming in which cultivation of crops and raising of livestock go hand in hand. Both these activities play an important part in the economy.
- **Natural Resources** Resources that are drown from nature and used without much modification are called natural resources.
- **Neap Tide** Tide that occurs every 14 - 15 days and coincides with the first and last quarter of the Moon. This tide has a small tidal range because the gravitational forces of the Moon and Sun are perpendicular to each other.
- **Nimbostratus Clouds** Dark, grey low altitude cloud that produces continuous precipitation in the form of rain or snow. Found in an altitude range from the surface to 3,000 m.
- **Nomadism** A way of life of the people who are required to shift their dwellings frequently from place to place in search of pastures for their animals and the mainstay of their economy.
- **Occluded Front** It is a transition zone in the atmosphere where an advancing cold air mass sandwiches a warm air mass between another cold air mass pushing the warm air into the upper atmosphere.
- **Ozone Hole** It is a sharp seasonal decrease in stratospheric ozone concentration that occurs over Antarctica in the spring. First detected in the late 1970s, the ozone hole continuous to appear as a result of complex chemical reaction in the atmosphere that involves CFCs.
- **Open-cast Mine** A place where soil and its outward cover are first removed and a mineral or ore is extracted by quarrying. In a way, it is a quarry on a large scale. This method of mining is known as open-cast mining.
- **Palaeomagnetism** It is the alignment in terms of inclination from horizon acquired by magnetically susceptible minerals in the rock during the period of their formation.
- **Plate Tectonics** It is a theory suggesting that the Earth's surface is composed of a number of oceanic and continental plates. Driven by convection currents in the mantle, these plates have the ability to slowly move across the Earth's plastic asthenosphere.
- **Precipitation** It is a showering of the raindrops, snow or hailstones from the clouds onto the surface of the Earth. Rainfall, snowfall, cloud burst and hailstones are forms of precipitation.

- **Pass** It is a route through a mountain range which follows the line of a col or a gap.
- **Peninsula** It is a piece of land jutting out into the sea.
- **Playa** The low flat central area of a basin of inland drainage. Playas occurs in areas of low rainfall.
- **Protected Forest** It is an area notified under the provisions of Indian Forest Act or the State Forest Acts having limited degree of protection. In Protected Forests, all activities are permitted unless prohibited.
- **Pastoralism** An economy that solely depends upon animals. Whereas nomadic pastoralism is practiced mainly for subsistence, the modern ranches present an example of commercial pastoralism.
- **Plantation Agriculture** A large-scale one-crop farming resembling factory production. It is usually characterised by large estate, huge capital investment, and modern and scientific techniques of cultivation and trade.
- **Port** The commercial part of a harbour containing facilities for embarking and disembarking passengers, loading and unloading, and some facilities for the storage of cargo.
- **Photosynthesis** It is the chemical process where plants and some bacteria can capture and organically fix the energy of the Sun.
- **Primary Activity** Activities concerned with collecting or making available materials, provided by nature, for example, agriculture, fishing, forestry, hunting or mining.
- **Quarry** An open-air excavation from which stone is obtained by cutting, blasting, etc.
- **Runoff** It is the flow of water over land through different channels.
- **Rapids** It is a stretch of swift flowing water where a river bed suddenly becomes steeper due to the presence of hard rocks.
- **Rainwater Harvesting** It is the technique of collection and storage of rain water at surface or in sub-surface aquifer.
- **Relief** It is the differences in elevation or the physical outline of the land surface or ocean floor.
- **Remittance** It refers to the all cash or kinds sent by the migrants to their place of origin. Money order is one form of remittance.
- **Ranches** Large stock farms, usually fenced in, where animals are bred and reared on a commercial scale. They are found especially in the United States.
- **Rotation of Crops** A systematic succession of different crops on a given piece of land carried out in order to avoid exhaustion of the soil.
- **Solar Wind** It is a mass of ionised gas emitted to space by the Sun. Plays a role in the formation of auroras.
- **Subsurface flow** It is the movement of water below the surface of the Earth. After infiltration, the subsurface water returns to the surface through seepage into the streams or eventually goes into the ocean.
- **Sanctuary** It is an area, which is reserved for the conservation of animals only and operations such as harvesting of timber, collection of minor forest products are allowed so long as they do not affect the animals adversely.
- **Soil Profile** It is the vertical section of soil from the ground surface to the parent rock.
- **Sub-continent** It is a big geographical unit which stands out distinctly from the rest of the continent.
- **Subsidence** In meteorology, it is the downward movement of the air. In geology, it refers to the sinking of a portion of the Earth's surface.
- **Secondary Activity** Activities which transform the material provided by primary activities into commodities more directly useful to man.
- **Sedentary Agriculture** Farming practiced more or less permanently on the same piece of land, the same as settled agriculture.
- **Shaft Mine** An underground excavation made deep into the Earth for digging minerals like coal, precious stones and iron. Such mines contain vertical and inclined shafts and horizontal tunnels at various levels.
- **Shifting Agriculture** A method of farming in which a patch of ground is cultivated for a period of few years until the soil is partly exhausted or overrun by weeds, and after which the land is left to natural vegetation while cultivation is carried on elsewhere.
- **Subsistence Agriculture** Farming in which its produce is mainly consumed in the farmer's household unlike commercial agriculture whose products enter into trade on a very large scale.
- **Thermocline** It is a boundary in a body of water where the greatest vertical change in temperature occurs. This boundary is usually the transition zone between the layer of warm water near the surface that is mixed and the cold deep water layer.
- **Terai** It is a belt of marshy ground and vegetation on the lower parts of the alluvial fans.
- **Tectonic Forces** They originate within the Earth and responsible for bringing widespread changes in the landform features.
- **Transhumance** It is the practice of seasonal migration where the pastoral communities migrate to the pastures along with their herds during summer season. These communities return to their permanent residence in winter.
- **Transport** The action of carrying persons and goods from one place to another.
- **Truck Farming** Growing of vegetables around the urban centres to meet the daily demand of the people is known as truck farming. It is governed by the distance a truck can cover overnight between the farm and the market.
- **Unclassed Forest** It is an area recorded as forest but not included in reserved or protected forest category. Ownership status of such forests varies from state to state.
- **Urbanisation** It refers to the population shift from rural to urban areas, the corresponding decrease in the proportion of pepole living in area and the ways in which societies adapt to this change.
- **Warabandi System** It is a system of equitable distribution of water in the command area of a canal outlet.
- **Watershed** It is a natural geo-hydrological unit of land, which collects water and drains it through a common point by a system of streams. Such a unit can be a small area of a few hectares or it could be an area of hundreds of square kilometres like the Ganga river basin.
- **Young Mountain** These are the fold mountains formed during the most recent major phase of folding in the Earth's crust.